Population Gazetteer Of England And Wales And The Islands In The British Seas, Showing The Number Of Inhabitants Of Every Parish And Place According To The Census Of 1861

Charles Anthony Coke

POPULATION GAZETTEER

OF

ENGLAND AND WALES

AND THE

ISLANDS IN THE BRITISH SEAS.

Showing the Number of **Inhabitants** of every **Parish** and **Place** according to the **Census of 1861**, namely, of each :—

Borough.
Chapelry.
City.
Consolidated Chapelry, or New Parish.
County.
Diocese.
Division.
Ecclesiastical District.
Hamlet.
Hundred.
Incorporation.

Island.
Lathe.
Liberty.
Lordship.
Metropolitan Ward.
Municipal City, or Borough.
Parish.
Parliamentary Borough.
Parliamentary Division of County.
Parochial Chapelry.
Poor Law Union.
Precinct.

Province.
Rape.
Registrar's Sub-district.
Sub-division of Lieutenancy.
Superintendent Registrar's District.
Tithing.
Town.
Township.
Wapentake.
Ward, etc., etc.

DERIVED FROM THE OFFICIAL RETURNS OF THE CENSUS.

By CHARLES ANTHONY COKE,

GENERAL REGISTER OFFICE, SOMERSET HOUSE, LONDON;

Compiler of " Statistical Charts of the Population," and " A Compendium of the Registration Statutes," etc.

London:

HARRISON, 59, PALL MALL,

BOOKSELLER TO HER MAJESTY AND H.R.H. THE PRINCE OF WALES.

1864.

PREFACE.

A **Census** is an Enumeration of the " Inhabitants of a Country " taken by order of the Legislature. In the first three chapters of the " Book of Numbers " is given the Mosaic Census in the Wilderness of " Sinai,"—the earliest on record, and numbered " *every male from twenty years old and upward, all that were able to go forth to war.*"

All the 12 Tribes numbered 603,550 males, from 20 years old and upwards, showing in relative proportion the " Israelites " in the Wilderness to have been about 3,621,300 Men, Women, and Children,—a number by far exceeding the present population of " London," to be supplied with daily food and raiment.

" Great cities represent the civilization of their age, and offer great facilities for the study of masses of mankind under singular circumstances. But the materials for this study have been only recently collected. Little more than the stony monuments of the cities of antiquity remain. *Babylon* had vast walls and palaces ; *Thebes* had a hundred gates, out of which, *Homer* tells us, twenty thousand chariots issued. But what was the condition of their People ? The numbers are unknown."

" At *Rome* itself, in later days, the citizen gave in his name and age, with the name and age of his wife and children, to the Censors* in the curule chairs ;† but the slaves of the City figured only among the property ; so that while the Census has supplied history with the numbers of Roman citizens, it has left no records of the Population."

In those Empires Monarchies, and States that have a settled form of Government, and advance n civilisation, a Census of the People is considered to be indispensable, and is taken at intervals of *ten, seven, five,* and even at *two* years apart, although it is comparatively only in recent times that the *Legislature* of the " British Empire " has sanctioned the Enumeration of its Inhabitants.

The first Census of " England and Scotland " was taken A.D. 1801, and the first Census of " Ireland " A.D. 1821.

In **GREAT BRITAIN** and **IRELAND**, by an Act of the " Legislature," the Enumeration of its Peoples taken decennially, or once in every *ten* years.

The *Local Machinery* employed in " **ENGLAND** and **WALES** " for taking the last Decennial Census on the 8th of April, 1861, and also on two former occasions, was the 634 " Superintendent Registrars " of Districts generally co-extensive with the " Poor Law Unions," or with single " Parishes " which were divided into 2,194 " Registrar's " sub-districts, each having a local *Registrar* of Births and Deaths *Pursuant to the Act 6 and 7 Will. IV., c. 86.*

---

* *Censor.*—magistrate of great power and authority in Ancient Rome, whose business was to take an account of the number and classes of the citizens.

† *Curule chr.*—A state chair among the Ancient Romans in which the chief magistrates had a right to sit and be carried. This chair was richly adorned and fitted to a kind of chariot, from whence it received its name ; it was also used by successful generals in a public triumph.

Under the supervision of the *Superintendent Registrars*, it was the duty of the *Registrars* to divide their sub-districts into *Enumeration Districts*, in accordance with directions furnished by the Census Commissioners, *Major George Graham*, Registrar-General for England and Wales, *Dr. Farr, M.D., D.C.L., F.R.S.*, and *James T. Hammick, Esquire, F.S.S.* Accordingly we find in the Census Report the sub-division of the Registrar's Districts to consist of 30,329 *Enumerator's Districts*, for "England and Wales," and 300 for the "Islands in the British Seas," to each of which an intelligent Enumerator was appointed; and there were also in addition 533 Public Institutions, with a separate Enumerator to each—forming in the aggregate the large number of 33,990 persons employed in the Enumeration of the People on one day, the 8th April, 1861, exclusive of the Official staff, exceeding 100 persons at the Central Office in London under the indefatigable supervision of *George Wyatt, Esquire*, Chief Clerk, and Messrs. *Bacon, Williams,* and *Keith*, officially belonging to the "General Register Office," but who were especially appointed to superintend this most important and responsible duty, and further aided by the experienced services of a large staff of official *employés*, in the office of the Registrar-General, who were engaged in classifying and tabulating the Census Returns, under the able superintendence of *William Clode, Esquire*.

The POPULATION GAZETTEER is literally a complete *Census* of every Place in "*England and Wales*" and the "*Islands in the British Seas*;"—which has been obtained from the united exertions of this large number of intelligent persons, presided over by the Commissioners appointed by the Legislature, and some idea may be formed of the magnitude of the work,—in completing a Census of every Place;—when it is stated that nearly 100 persons were employed fully a year and a half in perfecting with official accuracy a revision of the Enumerators' Returns, and in the collating and arranging *Alphabetically* every Place that had recognised boundaries wherein a resident Population was enumerated, at the last Census,—from the "Hamlet" to the "City," —and from the "Parish," "Town," "Borough," "District," etc., to the "County," "Diocese," and "Province."

All alike are placed in their *Alphabetical* position,—forming a complete **Population Gazetteer,** of every **Parish,** *Town, and Place, in "England and Wales,"*—exceeding 16,000 Names; and, remarkable as it may appear, it is ascertained from official sources, that for every Place that is given in this Alphabetical nomenclature and separately returned to the Census Commissioners, that the cost for collecting the information was the small amount of about £6 on an average for each, —with a wide range, where there were 100,000 or more people located,—and where there were but 100 or less domiciled,—and we find the average cost for enumerating each person, Man, Woman, and Child in England and Wales at the last Census of 1861 to be only 1½d. per head; at the former Census of 1851, 1¼d. per head, and at the prior Census of 1841, 1½d. per head;—or *per thousand* of the population the cost was £5 9s. in 1841;—£5 4s. in 1851;—and £4 15s. 5d. in 1861, when the inquiry was greatly extended.

In extracting the numerical results of the last Census, so admirably arranged in the "Official Returns" of 1861, published by authority of the Registrar-General

(Major George Graham), and presented to Parliament,—extreme care has been bestowed on this most important portion of the Publication,—collated and authenticated by the Official Returns of the Census of 1861, and the valuable assistance rendered by *Mr. J. W. Maunders*, in revising the numerals and letter-press, is here duly acknowledged,—in the earnest hope that the *Population Gazetteer of the Census of 1861* may be found to be complete in every respect—comprehensive,—authentic, and minute in its details, and alike valuable in combining a vast amount of reliable information—derived from official sources,—which is here arranged with every facility for reference.

CHARLES ANTHONY COKE.

Somerset House, London, 1864.

₄ For the convenience of many persons, it has been decided to publish the CENSUS OF THE BRITISH EMPIRE in Sections—the First Section, or Part I, to include the Census of ENGLAND AND WALES, with LONDON.

(*Fifth thousand*).   Price 1s. 6d. plain, or 2s. bound.

PART I.—ENGLAND and WALES.—The "Anglo-Saxon" race.—The progress of Population during the last Seven Censuses, with the *increase*, and rate of increase in each decennium.
Population of each City, Borough, and Town of 2,000 inhabitants and upwards, in Alphabetical Order, showing the *increase* or *decrease* of Inhabitants between the Census of 1851 and 1861.
Increasing Towns, Declining Towns, and Towns with Stationary Populations.
Cities and Towns in the present Century that have *doubled, trebled,* and *quadrupled* their Population.
Ancient Cities.—The magnitude and progress of "London" during the present Century.
The London commissariat, for supplying,—its increasing Population,—its *daily* requirements.
Population and *Occupation*, showing the number of People that support a Trade, a Profession, *etc.*
The progress of "ENGLAND" compared with the progress of "FRANCE," *etc., etc.*

Price 1s. 6d. plain, or 2s. bound.

PART II.—Census of SCOTLAND and IRELAND,— the Emigration to our "Colonies," Population Area, and Climate, Natives of Foreign Countries, British Subjects in Foreign Countries, "British Colonies" and "Foreign Possessions," *etc., etc.*

Will be Published shortly.   Price 2s. plain. or 2s. 6d. bound.

PART III.—Census of the UNITED KINGDOM of GREAT BRITAIN AND IRELAND;—to include Empires, Monarchies, and States, with their Foreign Possessions, dispersed over the four ancient divisions of the World, including Australasia and Oceanica ; with a short Treatise on the "Human Race," the duration of "Human Life," or the expectation of future lifetime of males and females, at each age of life,—as computed by DR. FARR.   The computed Antediluvian Population ; the natural period of human life as determined by DR. FARR and M. FLOURENS ; and a few remarks on Surnames, on the diversity of Languages;—the Area and Population in the World; and the Population according to Creed,—or "Religion" in the World, *etc. etc.*

Price 2s. 6d. plain, or 3s. bound.

PART IV.—A POPULATION GAZETTEER for 1861, or "Parochial" and "Town" Population in "England and Wales," and the "Islands in the British Seas,"—to comprise more than 16,000 *Names of Places,* wherein the Population was separately returned in Parishes, Towns, Registration Districts, Boroughs, Cities, Counties, Dioceses, Ecclesiastical Districts, Townships, Tithings, Hamlets, *etc., etc.*   Arranged in Alphabetical Order (nearly 300 pages).

₄ Derived from the Official Census of England and Wales.   Published by Authority of the Registrar-General, Vol. I, pp. 753-909.

The Four Parts will form a complete "Census of the British Empire," with an Index, handsomely bound in one Volume of nearly 700 pages.

A Population Gazetteer of the Census.
1861.
THE TERRITORIAL DIVISIONS
OF
England and Wales
AND THE ISLANDS IN THE BRITISH SEAS:

INTRODUCTION.

The name of **ENGLAND** is derived from *Engle, the Angles*, and *land;* meaning the land of the "Angles," a very important tribe of the Saxons, who conquered the Country. They called the British whom they conquered *Wealas*, which means Foreigners; and from that term has arisen the name of that part of the country in which the "British" most resided, viz., Wales, which thus means the *foreign country.* The Welsh call themselves *Cymry;* their country *Cymru or Cambria;* and the name of the language, *Cymraeg*, from which they are supposed to be from the *Cimbri* of Jutland.

The invading chieftains established seven co-temporary Kingdoms in Britain, called the *Saxon Heptarchy.*

" While undecided yet which part should fall,
Which Nation rise, the glorious lord of all."—*Creech.*

After a series of wars, the whole of the **Heptarchy** became subject to the power of *Egbert*, King of Wessex, who caused himself to be Crowned at Winchester, at that time considered the capital of "England," by the title of *King of England,* about A.D. **827,** or nearly **400** years after the "first arrival of the Saxons,"—and thus was laid the foundation of the "**English Monarchy.**"

Population of 1,899 Cities and Towns in "England and Wales." Census 1861.

Cities or Towns with a Population above	Number of Cities or Towns.
2 800 000	1
400 000	2
300 000	3
200 000	5
100 000	12
50 000	29
20 000	75
10 000	153
5 000	305
2 000	533
1 000	781

Area and Population.

England and Wales contains 58,320 square miles of surface, or 37,324,883 statute acres, and is sub-divided into 2 Provinces, 28 Dioceses, 52 Counties, 634 Unions and Superintendent Registrar's Districts, 2,194 Registrar's Sub-districts, 16,160 Parishes or Places, 30,862 Enumeration Districts, with a population of 20,066,224 persons, enumerated at the Census of 1861, inhabiting 3,739,505 Houses. The average at that time was about 5 persons to a House, 1 House to 10 Acres, and nearly 2 Acres to each Person.

The Population of **Great Britain** and **Ireland**, enumerated at the Census of 1861, was 29,321,288 persons.

Area, 121,115 square miles.

Territorial Divisions.

Derived from the Official Returns of the Census of England and Wales for 1851 and 1861.
Presented to Parliament.

Islands.—"The greater part of the islands, and of points on the coast terminating in *ey, ay, a* (island), *ness* (promontory), *holm,* as well as others, bear names which the Northmen gave them;* and were seized, partly for the purposes of commerce, but more commonly as naval stations, from which they could harry and tax the coasts and inland country."

"An 'island' was a market, a warehouse, and a castle to these Northmen, who, bred round the sinuosities of the Danish peninsula, the recesses of the Baltic, and the Fiords of Norway, practised their arts as udal farmers, fishermen, and merchants —forged anchors, built ships—that lived in the Atlantic, fought incessantly along their own coast, from the Elbe to the Naze, to Drontheim, Lofoden Islands, Cape North; and in the *eighth* century and the centuries following, sailed in fleets, at one time down the east and west coasts of Great Britain; at another either round France, Portugal, and Spain into the Mediterranean, or to Iceland and the coasts of North America. Men of the Atlantic in their ships, their sea-horses, their ocean-skates—as they called their craft—braved the dangers of the rocks and the waves at sea —where their foes never met them (*the arms of* **Celts, Gaels,** *and* **Saxons,** *on land*) and succeeded in effecting permanent settlements in France and England."

The Northmen in the Islands.—"As the Jutes and Saxons settled on the south coast, so the Danes held and have left the most permanent traces in Suffolk, Norfolk, Lincolnshire, Yorkshire, and the lowlands of Scotland. The Norwegians for some time made the Orkneys the great centre of their expeditions. *Rollo*, from whom *William I.* was the fifth in descent, was some time in the Orkneys before he conquered Normandy; and the Northmen from these islands extended their power over the Hebrides, Ireland, and the coast of France, and in 1066 conquered England, and added the **Channel Islands** '*Jersey,*' '*Guernsey,*' '*Alderney,*' '*Sark,*' '*Herm,*' and '*Jethou,*' to the newly conquered Country."

Descendants of the Scandinavians.—"The Scandinavian race survives in its descendants round the coasts of the British Isles; and the soul of the old viking still burns in the seamen of the British fleet, in the Deal boatmen, in the fishermen of the Orkneys, and in that adventurous, bold, direct, skilful, Mercantile class, that has encircled the World by its peaceful conquests. What the Greeks were in the Mediterranean Sea, the *Scandinavians* have been in the Atlantic Ocean."

Counties.—"The division of **England** into Counties, each having an Ealdorman, discharging civil and military functions under the King and his council, was evidently based on the old divisions of the Country.

Two small Kingdoms became the Counties of "Kent" and "Sussex"; the Kingdom of the East Saxons became "Essex" and "Middlesex;" of the East Angles "Norfolk" and "Suffolk." The lands of the Wilsætan, Dornsætan, Sumorsætan (from Sætan, settlers), became "Wilts," "Dorset," "Somerset," —to which **shire** was perhaps unnecessarily added. *Damnonia* and *Cernaw*, wrung

---

* See "*Histoire des Expéditions Maritimes des Normands,*" *par* G. B. Depping; *Danes and Norwegians in England, Scotland, and Ireland, by J. J. A. Worsaae,* 1852; *Heimskringla Sagas.— Preliminary Dissertation and Translation by S. Laing.*

successively from the Welsh, as they retreated first beyond the Exe and then over the Tamar, were named "Devonshire" and "Cornwall." The district of "Berkshire," whose men, under their *Ealdorman*, fought and put the "army" of Northmen to flight in A.D. 860 and 871,* was, it is said, so named from the character of the country.

Another class of Counties was evidently constructed on different principles: thus the County containing Winchester, the capital of Wessex, was called Hámtúnscír, from Hámtún, now Southampton."

" All the Counties into which Mercia was divided were named from their large central towns, which became the County Towns :—thus it was with Hert*ford*shire, Buckin*gham*shire, Ox*ford*shire, Northamp*ton*shire, Hunting*don*shire, Bed*ford*shire, Cam*bridge*shire, Glou*cester*shire, Here*ford*shire, Shropshire [Scrobbes*byrig*scir, also Scrob*setan*], Worcestershire, Staf*ford*shire, War*wick*shire, Lei*cester*shire, Nottin*gham*-shire, Der*by*shire, *Chester*shire, Lan*caster*shire."

The termination in *bridge, ford,* and *chester, cester,* or *caster,* in *wick, ton, ham, bury, by,* clearly indicate town names, which, by extension, served to designate a *shire,* share, division of the kingdom. Lincolnshire, Yorkshire, Durham, are also named from the county towns; Rutland, Northumberland, Cumberland, and Westmorland are not named from towns, but like the counties in the south, from the people, and the locality—after the analogy of Eng*land,* Scot*land,* Ire*land*."

County Boundaries.

—" All the estuaries, and the large, as well as some of the small rivers on the east coast, serve to mark the bounds of extensive Counties; the Tweed, Tyne, Tees, Humber, Wash, Yare, Stour, Thames, separate Northumberland, Durham, Yorkshire, Lincolnshire, Norfolk, Suffolk, Essex, and Kent, which were at one time or other of the **Saxon** period, separately or conjointly, small kingdoms.

> " Rivers arise! whether thou be the son
> Of utmost *Tweed,* or *Ouse,* or gulfy *Don* ;
> Or *Trent,* who like some earth-born giant spreads
> His thirsty arms along th' indented meads ;
> Or sullen *Mole,* that runneth underneath,
> Or *Severn* swift, guilty of maiden's death,
> Or rocky *Avon,* or of sedgy *Lea,*
> Or coaly *Tyne,* or ancient hallowed *Dee,*
> Or *Humber* loud, that keeps the Scythian's name,
> Or *Medway* smooth, or royal tower'd *Thame.*"—*Milton.*

" On the south coast, the smaller rivers appear to have been disregarded in fixing the bounds of Kent, Sussex, Hampshire, Dorset, and Devon; but the 'Tamar' divides Devon from Cornwall."

"The 'Bristol Channel' and the estuary of the 'Severn' separate Somerset and Devon from Glamorganshire and Monmouthshire; the indentations of the coast by estuaries, mark, on the west coast, the divisions of the Welsh counties; the 'Dee' divides Flint from Cheshire, the 'Mersey,' Cheshire from Lancashire; which now extends over the Ribble and Morecambe Bay, to the Dudden and Windermere, where it touches Cumberland and Westmoreland."

"The 'Thames' is a boundary from its mouth almost to its source; it separates Essex, Middlesex, Buckinghamshire, and Oxfordshire, on its north bank—from Berkshire, Surrey, and Kent on the south bank. The arrangement on the 'Severn' is different; the county towns of Gloucester, Worcester, and Shrewsbury, are on its banks, and the Counties extend to the hills on both sides. Herefordshire, in like manner, extends over the middle portion of the basin of the 'Wye.'"

---

* Saxon Chronicle. Asser, Life of Alfred.

Sub-division of Lieutenancy. — "The laws relating to the **Militia** may be said to affect, directly or indirectly, every man in the country. At the present time the Militia force for England and Wales is fixed at 80,000 men, who could be called out and embodied upon a short notice. But in order to meet the contingency of a falling off in voluntary enlistment, a machinery is provided for procuring a sufficient number of men by means of the ballot.

"The several Sub-divisions of Lieutenancy in many Counties are identical with the Petty Sessional Divisions. Assuming the exempted classes to be pretty equally distributed, the total male population will afford a basis for computing the proportionate number of Militiamen to be raised in each Sub-division of Lieutenancy.

"The persons liable to serve in the Militia are those between the ages of 18 and 35 ; but the following, amongst others, are exempt :—Army, Navy, Marines, and members of any corps of Yeomanry or Volunteers ; resident members of the Universities, Clergymen, Ministers of registered places of worship, Attorneys, Constables, and other Peace Officers, Articled Clerks, Apprentices, Seamen, or seafaring men, Artificers in H.M. dockyards, Ordnance Artificers, and '**any poor man who has more than one child born in wedlock.**' " *See* 43d sect. of 42 Geo. 3. c. 90.

Hundreds, Tithings, Hides. — "Sub-divisions of the **shires** have existed since the age of *Alfred ;* and 'hundreds,' 'tythings,' and 'hides,' are named in the early Saxon laws, charters, and other records.

The simplest view may be thus stated : England was divided into hides—about **274,950** in number ;* and a **hide** of land, containing **100** or **120** acres, supported a free family ; *ten* such free families constituted a **tything** ; *ten* or *twelve tythings* a **hundred** ; an indefinite number of hundreds, a **shire.** The hundred is used in the Domesday return (**1086**), as a well-defined territorial division of the county."†

"*Sir Henry Ellis cites passages from ancient records, in which the Hide is said to contain* 120 *acres*—sexies viginti acras terræ. *He adds,* "*The circumstance that six score went to the hundred, is countenanced by an entry relating to the* mansiones *in Lincoln.* '*Ex prædictis mansionibus quæ* T.R.E. *fuerunt* hospitatæ, *sunt modo* waste ꝏ Anglico numero—ꝏcXL.' *Domesd. tom. i. fol.* 336. *So before, in the same folio,* 'In civitate Lincolia erant tempore regis Edwardi novies centum et LXX mansiones hospitatæ. Hic numerus Anglice computatur* I centum pro cxx.' *Hence, probably, the old saw*—

'*Five score* of men, money, and pins,
Six score of all other things.'
Introduction to Domesday, vol. 1, pp. 147–9."

Wapentake. — The name had its origin in a custom of touching of lances or spears when the *hundreder,* or chief, entered upon his office ; the custom originated with the Danes. "In naming the districts corresponding to hundreds in Yorkshire, Lincolnshire, and Nottinghamshire, the term 'hundred' was abandoned, and wapentake was used.

"The Danes, like the ancient inhabitants of the North in general, elected their chiefs, and signified their assent to any proposition at the *Things,* by *Vaabentag,* or Vaabentarm (sound, or clang of arms). *Vaabentag* (wapentake) might thus have become the name of a small district, having its own chief and

---

* Brady, History of England, vol. i, p. 270.

† *Palgrave, English Commonwealth, vol. i. p.* 97. *He quotes Hickes' Gram. Isl. p.* 43, *to show that in the North a hundred was six score ; and that the decad in their numeration contained* 10 *or* 12 *units.* "Hundrade— *usurpatur pro numero* cxx. . . . . . . *Causa istius computationi hæc est, quod istas gentes duplex est decas, nempe minor, cæteris nationibus communis decem continens unitates ; et major, continens* duodecim, *id est,* tolf *unitates.*"

own *Thing.* A law of King Ethelred's 'ordains' that there shall be in every Wapentake a *Gemot*, *Thing.*

"In Scandinavia, and particularly in the south of Norway, provinces or *Fylker* (petty kingdoms) re not only divided into halves (hálfur), and fourths (*fjórthungar*), but also into thirds or *trenger* (thridjungar), which completely answer to the north English 'thrithing' [riding]. It was, oreover, to the *Tredings-things* that all disputed cases were referred from the smaller district ings.—*The Danes and Northmen in England*, by Worsaae, pp 158-9."

Rapes. — The *Rapes* of Sussex were military governments at the time when omesday Book was compiled, the Conqueror having stationed his principal captains ere in such manner as to secure a ready passage to and from the coast, and thereby is communication with Normandy.

Lathes. — The *Lathes* of Kent seem to have been civil jurisdictions and of rlier date, connected perhaps with the Cinque Ports, and for defence of the coast gainst invasion.

Sessional Divisions. — "The divisions existing in all the Counties of England nd Wales for the purposes of special and petty sessions, are in general based on the undreds and other ancient County Sub-divisions.*

Municipal Cities and Boroughs.—"When the 'Anglo-Saxons' first invaded ngland, 'the woods' were no longer 'the towns' of the natives. The Britons ad been collected in cities, polished but subjugated by the Roman legionaries, who ved in villas, and towns on taxes which their publicans collected. Unlike the dventurous Colonists and "Pilgrim Fathers," who planted the British race in merica, they did not find nations less civilized than themselves.

"The 'Saxon' borough was a modification of the 'Hundred,' the burgesses were freemen bound each other as neighbours, responsible for each other to surrounding communities, sharing common urthens; classified further in Guilds of Trades, or Companies, which sprang up with the divisions of bour; and banded firmly together for the defence of their walls, and dwellings."

"It must be clearly understood," observes one of the ablest of our constitutional historians, that a Saxon Burgh was nothing more than a *Hundred*, or an assemblage of Hundreds, surrounded y a moat, a stockade, or a wall; and the name of the Hundred was actually given to some of the most considerable cities, burghs, and towns of England [as Norwich, Thetford, Chelmsford, Maldon, Colchester, Winchelsea, Canterbury, Faversham, Fordwich, Exeter, several of them on Roman oundations]."†

Boroughs in Domesday, An. 1086. — "*London, Winchester, Abingdon,* and ome other boroughs of importance are not entered in 'Domesday;' and were probably ot surveyed by the commissioners of *William I.* The customs of **41** cities and urghs are noticed with some detail.

"The eleven cities of London, Bristol, Canterbury, Chester, Exeter, Gloucester, Lichfield, Lincoln, Norwich, Worcester, York; and the five towns of Kingston-on-Hull, Newcastle-on-Tyne, Nottingham, Poole, Southampton, in England: and two, Carmarthen and Haverfordwest, in Wales, are 'Counties of themselves,' as was also the city of Coventry until lately.

New Municipal Boroughs.—" Eleven Towns have received Charters of

---

* *Such entries as the following occur in Domesday :—"In the Hundred and City of Canterbury,"* "*in the Hundred of Rochester," "Sandwich lies in its own proper Hundred."* f 3ª, 5ª, 5ᵇ, 9ᵇ.

† See Palgrave: English Commonwealth, vol. i. pp. 102-3. *See* also the chapter on Towns, in Kemble's Saxons in England; Merewether and Stephens on Boroughs; and the Reports of Commissioners of Inquiry into Municipal Corporations.

Incorporation since 1851, namely, Aberavon, Brighton, Burnley, Dewsbury, Hanley, Margate, Middlesborough, Rochdale, Stalybridge, Wrexham, and Yeovil.

"The Municipal boundaries of the Borough of Salford have been extended, and made coextensive with those of the Parliamentary Borough; those of Stockton have also been enlarged by the Stockton Extension and Improvement Act, 1852.

Townships, Parishes, Manors.—Re-distribution of England after the Conquest.

"In 1066, the Conqueror seized, besides the Crown lands, the lands of the Anglo-Saxon or Danish proprietors, who fell in the battle of Hastings; and, in the course of his reign, acquired the estates of many rebellious Thanes. He distributed a large portion of these lands as the pay of past and of future services, among the chieftains in his army, who retained large domains for themselves, and distributed the rest on similar terms among the officers and men under their command.

"The Estates of the Church, and of the chief Monasteries also, passed into the hands of the Norman clergy.

"The tenants who held immediately of the King, including ecclesiastical corporations, amounted to 1,400 the under-tenants to 7,871, at the time of the great survey (A. D. 1086),* which exhibits an apparently new division of the country into manors."

"In the **Domesday Record** the Kingdom is divided into Counties; the Counties into the *lands* (*terras*) of the King, Bishop, and tenants-in-chief (*tenentes terras*); and these again into **manors**, under the respective Hundreds; which generally included the whole or parts of several Manors."

"The ancient demesne of the Crown consisted of 1,422 manors; *Earl Moretaine*, the Conqueror's half-brother, held 793 manors; *Alan Earl of Bretagne*, 442; *Odo Bishop of Baieux*, 439; the *Bishop of Coutance*, 280; *Roger de Busli*, 174; six other tenants, 174, 164, 162, 150, 116, 100 Manors;† thus 4,416 Manors were held; 1,422 by the King, and 2,994 by eleven of his followers.

"Villa was another term for manor (manerium) or Lordship; and in the Exeter Domesday, *mansio* is almost constantly used for *manerium*. The Manor was what Bede had called the '*place*' (locus), in the midst of which the churches were built,‡ or the old temples had stood; the village and surrounding neighbourhood, where the people lived for the sake of society and of defence, with their headman or Thane, dwelling in his capacious *hall*, built of wood by the bondmen from his demesne, covered with reeds and straw, or a roof of wooden shingles, through which the smoke from the hearth ascended.§ This hall often became a stone mansion, and the home of the chief tenant a castle, in the period immediately following the Norman Conquest."

"The Kingdom was held securely; there was a Military chief and a strong post in every Parish

---

* *See vol. ii. of Sir Henry Ellis's valuable introduction to Domesday, p. 511, et passim.*

† *Enumerated by Lord Lyttelton, Brady, Hutchins, Kelham, and collected in Introduction to Domesday, vol. i, pp. 225-6. Ed. 8vo. The tenants in chief and the under tenants have been enumerated by the diligence of Sir Henry Ellis.*

‡ *The Scotch missionaries, about* A.D. *635, came to Britain.* "*Construebantur ergo ecclesiae per loca, confluebant ad audiendum verbum populi gaudentes, donabantur numere regis possessiones, et rritoria ad instituenda monasteria.*" *Hist. Ec. iii. 3.*

§ *Domestic Architecture in England. T. H. Turner, pp. ix.-x.*

f the Country; surrounded by **60,215** knights, in the possession of as many fees or portions of erritory. Of *forty-nine* castles which are mentioned in 'Domesday,' only that of Arundel existed n the time of Edward the Confessor: *eight* it is known were built by the Conqueror, *ten* by great arons, *one* by an under-tenant: and the numbers increased so rapidly that **1,115** 'adulterine' astles were counted at the close of Stephen's reign (An. **1153**)."

" The lord, resident, either in a Castle with its keep and mount—in a hall, or in a fortified house *domus defensabilis*),—and his court encroaching on the hundred court,—for a time gave a new haracter and name to the Township, the priest*shire*, or the **parish**; but it is much more probable hat the old sub-divisions, which had existed for centuries, and are sometimes named *vils* in the reign f Edward the Confessor, were chosen as the limit of the manor, than that the country was wholly ecast and divided into the same number of new districts in the reign of *William I.*

" **Manors** underwent changes, and new manors were frequently created, until the Statute *Quia em-ores* put an end to their increase in the reign of *Edward I.* (A.D. 1290): the lords of new manors robably erected churches and appointed clergymen—according to the common theory; but the parish oundaries, surrounding the old township—guarded by the spiritual supervision of the priest, and by he tithe-owner—were not originally derived from the manor; and only assumed their legitimate mportance in the reign of Queen Elizabeth, when they were made the area of the district which by ates maintained its own poor."

Dioceses.—" The division of the Country ecclesiastically into **Dioceses, Arch-deaconries,** and **Deaneries,** took place in very early times. Most of the present Bishoprics were founded in the Saxon period. Originally there were three Arch-bishoprics—of 'Canterbury,' 'York,' and 'Caerleon,' in Wales; the latter was sup-pressed by *Henry I.*, and the Territory annexed to the See of Canterbury. Most of the Dioceses, on their first formation, had their limits coextensive with the boundaries of the Kingdoms of the sovereigns who formed them; sub-divisions soon, however, were discovered to be necessary, and the Council of Hertford, convened by *Archbishop Theodore*, decreed that, as the faithful grew to be more numerous, the number of the Sees should also be increased."

" **Archdeacons** anciently were only members of Chapters without territorial jurisdiction. The assignment of specific limits for 'Archdeaconries' took place soon after the Conquest.*

" The Act of 6 & 7 Wm. IV., cap. 77, gives power to the Ecclesiastical Commissioners to re-arrange the boundaries of the ancient, and to form certain new, Archdeaconries. The new ones formed in exercise of this authority, are Bristol, Maidstone, Monmouth, Westmoreland, Manchester, Lancaster, and Craven."

Deaneries.—" *Deans* are principally of two kinds: (1) those attached to Cathedrals, who are the heads of the different Chapters; and (2) Rural Deans, who perform certain functions as assistants to the Bishops, in particular definite portions of the several Dioceses.

" These *Rural Deaneries* were recognized Ecclesiastical Divisions of a Diocese in Saxon times. They seem to have been designed to correspond with *Hundreds* in the political division of the country, as Archdeaconries were possibly intended to correspond with Counties."

" The etymology of the word (Decanus) favours this idea; and it is not improbable that all such Deaneries originally embraced Districts with **ten** churches, and no more; their boundaries, once settled, never having been disturbed, although increase of population caused an increase in the number of religious edifices. Some of them still contain ten churches only. These Deaneries gradually fell into disuse from the period of the Conquest; but recent Legislation tends to their revival." (*See 6 & 7 Wm. IV., cap.* 77.)

---

* The first assignment was by Archbishop Lanfranc, A.D. 1165.

" Parishes.—The Parish, although an Ecclesiastical Division, was early adopted by the State as a circumscription for civil purposes both in Great Britain and Ireland; and unless in the centres of population, the Parish, more or less accurately defined; is the object of primary interest to its inhabitants, especially in Religious and Educational matters, that the interest of almost every man is attached to the concerns, civil and spiritual, of his own 'parish,' before it diverges to those of the Country at large."

The population of every Parish is returned in the present publication; and in the northern counties, where the parishes are of vast extent, and are sub-divided into well-defined townships, the population of each township is separately returned, and also each Ecclesiastical District.

Dioceses, Ecclesiastical Districts, and New Parishes.—" By the Census Act it was required that the account to be taken should include not only, as at former Censuses, the population of Parishes and Townships, but also the population of '*Ecclesiastical Districts*' in **England and Wales.**

" The ancient primary division of the land, for 'spiritual purposes,' was exclusively into **Parishes**; but, in the course of time, as Population increased and additional Churches were erected, certain *portions* of particular Parishes came to be assigned by custom to the newly Established Places of Worship; and these at length, under the name of **Chapelries**, acquired boundaries as definite and generally recognized as those of the parent parish."

" This is especially the case in the more Northern Counties, where, the Parishes being of very large extent, while the Population has increased with great rapidity, the need for such a further sub-division soon became apparent. The number of such Chapelries throughout England and Wales is not exactly ascertainable, but it must be very considerable."

Ecclesiastical Districts.—" The term 'Ecclesiastical District,' as employed in the Census Act, was not intended to apply either to these merely *conventional* districts or to the ancient Chapelries, but to that considerable number of districts which have in late years been 'formed under the authority of the various Acts of Parliament providing for extensions of the Establishment.

" By these Acts, which commence in 1818, power is given to the Commissioners for building new Churches (established by 58 Geo. III., cap. 45) to the Ecclesiastical Commissioners (established by 6 & 7 Wm. IV., cap. 77), and to the Bishops of the various Dioceses (authorized by 1 & 2 Wm. IV., cap. 38), to assign appropriate districts to any New Churches for which an adequate endowment is secured, either by the Sub-division of single Parishes, or by the consolidation of parts of several Parishes.

" The Acts contain various provisions defining the precise Ecclesiastical character of these new Districts: some of them being merely subordinate portions of the original Parish, while others are, under certain circumstances, to become 'New Parishes,' being, for all Ecclesiastical objects, entirely independent of the mother Parish."

" In 1856 the *Act of* 19 & 20 *Vict.* c. 104 (commonly known as Lord Blandford's Act) was passed, for the creation from time to time of new Parishes for all Ecclesiastical purposes, with the same status as those created under Sir R. Peel's Act of 1843. The Act comes into operation on the avoidance of the living of the mother-parish, or sooner; and it is expected that the removal of many anomalies will be effected through its operation."

Districts (Unions), and Registrar's Districts.—" The Act for '*the*

Amendment and Better Administration of the Laws relating to the Poor,' empowered the Poor Law Commissioners ' to declare so many Parishes as they may think fit to be united for the Administration of the Laws for the Relief of the Poor.' * The united Parishes were designated **Unions,** which generally are co-extensive with Superintendent Registrar's Districts.

" The Act also provided for the Election of a Representative *Board of Guardians,* and for the appointment of Officers in every Union, by whom the Local rates for the relief of the poor, and for many other purposes, are collected and expended.

"The ' *Unions,*' under the Act for Registering *Births, Deaths,* and *Marriages* in England (6 and 7 Will. IV., c. 86, 1836), were sub-divided into as many smaller Districts as the Commissioners, subject to the approval of the Registrar-General, thought fit.

" The whole of England and Wales under the **Registration Act** is divided at the present time into **634** Superintendent Registrar's Districts. A district comprises on an average three or four *sub-districts* (in all **2,194,** to each of which there is a Registrar of Births and Deaths.

New Poor Law Unions and Superintendent Registrar's Districts.—

'During the last ten years eleven ' New Poor Law Unions ' and ' Superintendent Registrars' Districts,' have been formed, either from the severance of Parishes from large Unions (as in the case of Birkenhead taken from the Wirral Union), or by bringing into Unions parishes previously in Gilberts' Incorporations, or under the Act of Elizabeth. The new Unions, or Superintendent Registrars' districts, are Bedwelty, Birkenhead, Dulverton, Gower, Great Ouseburn, Hartlepool, Kirkdeighton, Mile-End Old Town, Wetherby, Wharfedale, and Whitchurch."

Wards.—"Under the *Metropolitan Local Management Act,* 19 *Vict., c.* 120. The **Population** is given according to the Census of **1861** in the several **Wards** formed for the *Election of Vestrymen* in metropolitan parishes."

The boundaries are given in the Supplement to the " London Gazette." No. 21,802, Oct. 20th, 1855.)

** As a guide to the Official Alphabetical Name of Places, the following is an extract from the Census of England and Wales, 1861—Vol. I. p. 752 :—

" *Owing to the still unsettled orthography of the Names of Places, and to the number of ' compound names,' it is not easy to supply a ready and unfailing reference. The difficulty is increased in the case of Places having additional names for the sake of distinction; as Great, or Little, East, West, North, or South, and the like. In some instances these prefixes become entirely incorporated in the Name; as in* Easthampstead, Northallerton, Littlehampton; *while in others the distinctive and the principal names are arbitrarily written separately or not, thus:* New Church *or* Newchurch, Old Swinford *or* Old-winford, *and so on.*

" *In the present arrangement the principle has been adopted of inserting every 'name' in the order indicated by its ordinary pronunciation in the locality; thus,* East Ham, West Ham, Little Bampton, Nether Witton, *&c., will be severally found under the letters E, W, L, and N; but as in some cases the distinctive name might not be known, and as in others the search would perhaps be given up when the place was not found where it was sought*

---

* 4 & 5 Will., cap. 74, s. 26 (An. 1834).

for, the **second name** *has also been inserted in its alphabetical order, as* Molton, South ; Shields, North, &c."

"*Superintendent Registrar's District, Union &c.*—The Districts are generally co-extensive with the Poor Law Unions of the same name, but in some instances two or more Unions are combined to form one Registration District. In cases where the Union differs from the District, the name of the former is also inserted."

"For **Parishes** (in cities and boroughs) known only by the name of a *Saint*, search should be made under the letter S, where the abbreviation *St.* is classed as though written *Saint* in full.

"The **Ecclesiastical Districts** are usually inserted under the name of the Parish or Place out of which they have been formed, unless they have a clearly defined name. It is further to be observed that I and J, U and V., are deemed distinct letters.

"Should any place not be found on a first reference, it should be searched for under some probable variation of spelling. In some cases the words in the column headed 'Name of Place' have been abbreviated to reserve space."

"When the same word occurs as the principal name of places in different *Counties*, the *alphabetical order of the county* settles the priority of insertion, and in all such cases a departure from a strictly alphabetical arrangement has been deemed allowable.

"Before quitting the subject of our "Territorial Divisions," it may be useful to point out how necessary it is, when citing the Population of a Place, to state explicitly what limits are referred to. For example, the term 'Manchester' may mean the Parish, the Township, the Parliamentary Borough, the Municipal Borough, the Registration or Poor Law District, or the City in a popular sense, including suburban places. A want of precision in speaking of places which give name to several local sub-divisions not unfrequently leads to mistakes, and when such Places are compared with others, without proper care being taken to apply the comparison to corresponding boundaries, *erroneous inferences are drawn.*"

ABBREVIATIONS USED IN THE COLUMN HEADED "DESCRIPTION."

Boro.—Borough with Municipal and Parliamentary limits co-extensive.

Chap.—Chapelry.

District.—Superintendent Registrar's District, generally co-extensive with "Poor Law Unions," and when not otherwise distinguished it applies to the "Union" of the same name.

Divsn.—Petty Sessional Division.

Ecl. Dis.—Ecclesiastical District, Consolidated Chapelry, or New Parish.

Hund.—Hundred.

Incor.—Incorporation.

L. Sub.—Lieutenancy Sub-division, in many Counties identified with the "Petty Sessional Divisions."

M. Boro.—Municipal Borough.

P. Boro.—Parliamentary Borough, that Returns Members to Parliament, and also those Boroughs in Wales; that *share* with other similar Boroughs, in the Return of Members to the House of Commons.

P. Chap.—Parochial Chapelry.

Sub-Dist. — Registrar's District, to which a local Registrar of Births and Deaths is appointed.

Union.—The "**District**" of the same name shows the population of the "Union," when not otherwise expressed.

Wapen.—Wapentake.

Those places not distinguished in the Column headed "Description," are generally not separately assessed to the poor, and are without any assigned description but that which locally is attached to the place;—and Parcel, Manor, Stoke, Watch, Quarter, &c., are purely local terms.

ENGLAND AND WALES,
AND THE
ISLANDS IN THE BRITISH SEAS.

THE **POPULATION** of 1861 as separately returned in the following **TER-TORIAL DIVISIONS** in **ALPHABETICAL ORDER**, for each :—

...ough.	Lathe.	Province.
...pelry.	Liberty.	Rape.
...y.	Lordship.	Registrar's Sub-district.
...solidated Chapelry, or New Parish.	Metropolitan Ward.	Sub-division of Lieutenancy.
...unty.	Municipal City, or Borough.	Superintendent Registrar's District.
...cese.	Parish.	
...ision.	Parliamentary Borough.	Tithing.
...lesiastical District.	Parliamentary Division of County.	Town.
...mlet.	Parochial Chapelry.	Township.
...ndred.	Poor Law Union.	Wapentake.
...orporation.	Precinct.	Ward, etc., etc.
...and.		

This **ALPHABETICAL** *arrangement includes the Names of all Places in " England and Wales," and the " Islands in the British Seas," having recognized boundaries, rein a resident population was enumerated, on the 8th April, 1861.*

* Derived from the Official Census, 1861, of England and Wales,—Published by Authority of the Registrar-General. Vol. 1, pp. 753—909.

Name of Place.	County.	Description.	Population.	Name of Place.	County.	Description.	Population.
...bas Combe ..	Somerset ..	Parish	487	Abbots Bromley.	Stafford ..	Parish	1 538
...erley	Worcester ..	Parish	692	Abbotsbury ..	Dorset ..	Sub-dis.	2 034
...erton	Essex ..	Parish	269	Abbotsbury ..	,, ..	Parish	1 089
...erton	Worcester ..	Parish	82	Abbotsham ..	Devon ..	Parish	365
...erwick ..	Northumberland	Tnship.	133	Abbotside, High.	York ..	Tnship.	552
...ey ..	Carnarvon ..	Parish	18	Abbotside, Low .	,, ..	Tnship.	163
...ey ..	Somerset ..	Sub-dis.	11 086	Abbots-Kerswell.	Devon ..	Parish	437
...ey ..	Wilts ..	Parish	143	Abbots Langley..	Herts ..	Sub-dis.	2 400
...eycwmhir ..	Radnor ..	Parish	537	Abbots Langley..	,, ..	Parish	2 400
...ey Dore ..	Hereford ..	Parish	551	Abbots-Leigh ..	Somerset ..	Parish	366
...ey Holme ..	Cumberland.	Sub-dis.	8 024	Abbots Lench ..	Worcester ..	Hamlet	66
...ey Holme ..	,,	Tnship.	982	Abbotsley ..	Hunts ..	Parish	486
...ey Hulton ..	Stafford ..	Ldship.	726	Abbots Roothing	Essex ..	Parish	220
...ey Lands	Northumberland	Tnship.	288	Abbotts Morton .	Worcester ..	Parish	245
...ots Ann ..	Hants ..	Parish	640	Abbotts Ripton..	Hunts ..	Parish	381
...ots, Astley ..	Salop ..	Parish	668	Abdick & Bulstone .	Somerset .	Hund.	12 047
...ots Bickington .	Devon ..	Parish	71	Abdon ..	Salop ..	Parish	170
...ots Bromley.	Stafford ..	Sub-dis.	2 976	Abenburyfawr ..	Denbigh ..	Tnship.	167

B

Name of Place.	County.	Description.	Population.	Name of Place.	County.	Description.	Population.
Abenburyfechan.	*Flint*	Tnship.	145	Abney ..	*Derby*	Hamlet	87
Aber ..	*Carnarvon*..	Parish	582	Above Derwent .	*Cumberland*.	Tnship.	951
Aberavon	*Glamorgan*	Parish	2 916	Above Sawthe ..	*Carmarthen*.	Hamlet	746
Aberavon ..	„ {	M. Bor.	2 916	Abram ..	*Lancaster* ..	Tnship.	911
		P. Boro.	7 754	Abram St. John .	„	Ecl. Dis.	1 544
Aberayron ..	*Cardigan* ..	District.	13 540	Abson & Wick ..	*Gloucester* ..	Parish	833
Aberdare ..	*Glamorgan* .	Sub-dis.	37 487	Abthorpe ..	*Northampton*	Sub-dis.	5 473
Aberdare ..	„	Parish	32 299	Abthorpe ..	„	Parish	541
Aberdare St.Fagan	„	Ecl. Dis.	1 740	Aby ..	*Lincoln* ..	Parish	407
Aberdaron ..	*Carnarvon*..	Sub-dis.	3 800	Acaster Malbis ..	*York* ..	Parish	359
Aberdaron ..	„ ..	Parish	1 266	Acaster Selby ..	„ ..	Tnship.	154
Aberdovey ..	*Merioneth* ..	Ecl. Dis.	1 186	Acaster Selby ..	„ ..	Ecl. Dis.	154
Aberedw ..	*Radnor* ..	Parish	281	Accrington ..	*Lancaster* ..	Sub-dis.	17 688
Abererch ..	*Carnarvon*..	Parish	1 652	**Accrington** ..	„ ..	Town	13 872
Aberffraw ..	*Anglesey* ..	Parish	1 238	Accrington, New.	„	Tnship.	11 853
Aberford ..	*York* ..	Sub-dis.	5 973	„ Christchurch	„	Ecl. Dis.	5 322
Aberford ..	„ ..	Parish	1 009	Accrington, Old .	„	Tnship.	5 835
Aberford ..	„ ..	Tnship.	759	Acklam ..	*York* ..	Parish	774
Abergavenny ..	*Monmouth*..	Hund.	54 742	Acklam, West ..	„	Parish	108
Abergavenny ..	„ ..	L. Sub.	13 710	Acklam w. Barthorpe	„	Tnship.	366
Abergavenny.	*Mon. & Hereford*	District	19 527	Acklington ..	*Northumberland*	Ecl. Dis.	635
Abergavenny ..	*Monmouth* ..	Sub-dis.	8 669	Acklington ..	„	Tnship.	255
Abergavenny ..	„ ..	Parish	6 086	Acklington Park.	„	Tnship.	163
Abergavenny ..	„ ..	Town	4 621	Ackton ..	*York* ..	Tnship.	67
Abergele ..	*Denbigh* ..	Sub-dis.	6 543	Ackworth ..	„ ..	Parish	1 813
Abergele ..	„ ..	Parish	3 308	Acle ..	*Norfolk* ..	Parish	926
Abergwessin ..	*Brecon* ..	Sub-dis.	2 897	Acol ..	*Kent* ..	Parish	260
Abergwilly ..	*Carmarthen*.	Parish	2 197	Acomb, East..	*Northumberland*	Tnship.	62
Aberhafesp ..	*Montgomery*.	Parish	486	Acomb, West ..	„	Tnship.	800
Aberllunvey ..	*Brecon* ..	Parish	132	Acomb ..	*York* ..	Parish	1 034
Abernant ..	*Carmarthen*.	Parish	793	Acomb ..	„ ..	Tnship.	897
Aberporth ..	*Cardigan* ..	Parish	454	Aconbury ..	*Hereford* ..	Parish	183
Abersychan ..	*Monmouth* ..	Ecl. Dis.	7 979	Acre, South ..	*Norfolk* ..	Parish	92
Aberwheeler ..	*Denbigh* ..	Tnship.	430	Acre, West ..	„	Parish	415
Aberyscir ..	*Brecon* ..	Parish	125	Acrise ..	*Kent* ..	Parish	173
Aberystruth ..	*Monmouth* ..	Sub-dis.	16 055	Acton ..	*Cheshire*	Parish	3 125
Aberystruth ..	„ ..	Parish	16 055	Acton (Acton P.)	„	Tnship.	297
Aberystwith ..	*Cardigan* ..	District	25 464	Acton (Weaverham P.)	„	Tnship.	484
Aberystwith ..	„ ..	Sub-dis.	8 772	Acton Grange ..	„	Tnship.	180
Aberystwith ..	„ ..	Chap.	5 561	Acton ..	*Denbigh* ..	Tnship.	220
Aberystwith ..	„ ..	Boro.	5 641	Acton Turville ..	*Gloucester*..	Parish	310
Abingdon ..	*Berks* ..	L. Sub.	18 776	Acton ..	*Middlesex* ..	Sub-dis.	6 443
Abingdon ..	*Berks & Oxon*	District	20 861	Acton ..	„	Parish	3 151
Abingdon ..	*Berks* ..	Sub-dis.	8 672	Acton & Old Felton ..	*Northmb.*	Tnship.	93
Abingdon ..	„ ..	Boro.	5 680	Acton Burnell ..	*Salop* ..	Parish	361
Abinger ..	*Surrey* ..	Parish	906	Acton Round ..	„	Parish	173
Abinghall ..	*Gloucester* ..	Parish	228	Acton Scott ..	„ ..	Parish	207
Abington in Clay	*Cambs* ..	Parish	228	Acton Trussell &c.	*Stafford* ..	Tnship.	617
Abington, Great.	„ ..	Parish	330	Acton ..	*Suffolk* ..	Parish	558
Abington, Little.	„ ..	Parish	316	Acton Beauchamp	*Worcester* ..	Parish	205
Abington ..	*Northampton*	Parish	164	Adbaston ..	*Stafford* ..	Parish	593
Abkettleby ..	*Leicester* ..	Parish	371	Adbaston w. Knighton	„	Tnship.	210
Abkettleby ..	„ ..	Tnship.	224	Adderbury ..	*Oxon* ..	Parish	2 146
Ablington ..	*Gloucester* ..	Tithing	118	Adderbury, East.	„ ..	Tnship.	895

Name of Place.	County.	Description.	Population.	Name of Place.	County.	Description.	Population.
dderbury, West	Oxon	Tnship.	346	Ainsty	York.	Wapen.	9 896
dderley	Salop	Parish	428	Ainsty & City of York	„	L. Sub.	50 329
dderstone	Northumberland	Tnship.	321	Ainsworth	Lancaster	Tnship.	1 803
ddingham	Cumberland.	Parish	754	Aintree	„	Tnship.	300
ddingham	York	Sub-dis.	3 157	Airton	„ York.	Tnship.	236
ddingham	„	Parish	1 938	Airyholme & Howthorpe	„	Tnship.	35
ddingham	„	Tnship.	1 859	Aisholt	Somerset	Parish	181
ddington	Bucks	Parish	111	Aiskew	York	Tnship.	759
ddington	Kent	Parish	262	Aislaby	Durham	Tnship.	152
ddington, Great	Northpton.	Parish	307	Aislaby (Middleton P.)	York.	Tnship.	180
ddington, Little	„	Parish	337	Aislaby (Whitby P.)	„	Tnship.	330
ddington	Surrey	Parish	639	Aismunderby w. Bondgate.	„	Tnship.	620
ddle	York	Parish	1 145	Aisthorpe	Lincoln	Parish	100
ddle w. Eccup	„	Tnship.	801	Akebar	York	Tnship.	37
ddlestone	Surrey	Ecl. Dis.	2 896	Akeld	Northumberland	Tnship.	162
ddlestrop	Gloucester	Parish	184	Akeley w. Stockholt	Bucks	Parish	366
ddlethorpe	Lincoln	Parish	302	Akenham	Suffolk	Parish	94
dforton, &c.	Hereford	Tnship.	250	Alberbury	Salop & Mont.	Sub-dis.	2 235
disham	Kent	Parish	492	Alberbury	„ „	Parish	1 918
dlingfleet	York	Parish	480	Alberbury Lo. Quar.	Salop	Tnship.	632
dlingfleet	„	Tnship.	225	Albourne	Sussex	Parish	34?
dlington	Cheshire	Tnship.	987	Albrighton	Salop	L. Sub.	2 595
dlington	Lancaster	Ecl. Dis.	3 331	Albrighton	Salop & Stafford	Sub-dis.	4 145
dlington	„	Tnship.	1 975	Albrighton	Salop	Parish	1 156
dmington	Gloucester	Hamlet	161	Albrighton	„	Chap.	78
dmiston	Dorset	Parish	95	Albrighton St. John	„	Ecl. Dis.	78
Adpar	Card. & Carm.	P. Boro.	1 473	Alburgh	Norfolk	Parish	587
Adstock	Bucks	Parish	385	Albury	Herts	Parish	700
Adstone	Northampton	Hamlet	165	Albury	Oxon	Parish	183
Advent	Cornwall	Parish	208	Albury	„	—	42
Adwell	Oxon	Parish	68	Albury	Surrey	Sub-dis.	4 453
Adwick-le-street	York	Parish	440	Albury	„	Parish	1 041
Adwick-le-street	„	Tnship.	280	Alby	Norfolk	Parish	231
Adwick-upon-Dearne	„	Parish	226	Alcester	Dorset	Liberty	342
Affpuddle	Dorset	Parish	455	Alcester	Warw. & Worcester	District	16 878
Agbrigg & Morley	York	Wapen.	475 985	Alcester	Warwick	Sub-dis.	4 787
Agbrigg, Lower	„	L. Sub.	130 136	Alcester	„	Parish	2 128
Agbrigg, Upper	„	L. Sub.	147 553	Alciston	Sussex	Parish	220
Agden (Malpas P.)	Cheshire	Tnship.	110	Alconbury	Hunts	Parish	909
Agden (Rostherne, &c. P.)	„	Tnship.	98	Alconbury Weston	„	Parish	561
Aglionby	Cumberland	Tnship.	119	Aldborough	Norfolk	Parish	305
Agmondesham	Bucks	Parish	3 550	Aldborough	York	Parish	2 279
Aigburgh St. Anne	Lancaster	Ecl. Dis.	1 994	Aldborough	„	Tnship.	522
Aighton	„	Hamlet	1 109	Aldbourn	Wilts	Parish	1 539
Aikbar	York	Tnship.	37	Aldbrough	York E.	Sub-dis.	1 735
Aike	„	Tnship.	103	Aldbrough	„	Parish	1 095
Aikton	Cumberland	Parish	806	Aldbrough	„	Tnship.	831
Aikton	„	Tnship.	284	Aldbrough	York N.	Sub-dis.	1 706
Ailesworth	Northampton	Hamlet	366	Aldbrough	„	Tnship.	420
Ainderby-Myers, &c.	York.	Tnship.	97	Aldbury	Herts	Parish	848
Ainderby Quernhow	„	Tnship.	99	Aldcliffe	Lancaster	Tnship.	74
Ainderby Steeple	„	Parish	848	Aldeburgh	Suffolk	Sub-dis.	4 049
Ainderby Steeple	„	Tnship.	319	Aldeburgh	„	Parish	1 721
Ainstable	Cumberland	Parish	542	Aldeby	Norfolk	Sub-dis.	4 954

Name of Place.	County.	Description.	Population.	Name of Place.	County.	Description.	Population
Aldeby	Norfolk ..	Parish	557	Alford	Somerset ..	Parish	109
Aldenham ..	Herts ..	Parish	1 769	Alfreton ..	Derby ..	Sub-dis.	11 549
Alderbury ..	Wilts ..	Hund.	4 887	Alfreton	,, ..	Parish	11 549
Alderbury	,, ..	District	14 770	**Alfreton**	,, ..	Town	4 090
Alderbury	,, ..	Sub-dis.	4 357	Alfrick	Worcester ..	Tnship.	474
Alderbury	,, ..	Parish	1 334	Alfriston ..	Sussex ..	Parish	522
Alderbury	,, ..	—	697	Algarkirk ..	Lincoln ..	Parish	772
Alderford ..	Norfolk ..	Parish	29	Alkborough ..	,, ..	Parish	497
Alderholt, St. James ..	Dorset .	Ecl. Dis.	708	Alkerton ..	Gloucester ..	Tithing	1 005
Alderley ..	Cheshire ..	Sub-dis.	4 526	Alkerton ..	Oxon ..	Parish	194
Alderley	,, ..	Parish	1 418	Alkham	Kent ..	Parish	520
Alderley, Nether.	,,	Tnship.	617	Alkington ..	Gloucester ..	Tithing	1 010
Alderley, Over ..	,, ..	Tnship.	421	Alkmonton ..	Derby ..	Tnship.	82
Alderley ..	Gloucester ..	Parish	98	Alkmonton, St. Jno. ,, ..		Ecl. Dis.	164
Aldermaston ..	Berks ..	Parish	585	Alkrington ..	Lancaster ..	Tnship.	423
Alderminster ..	Worcester ..	Parish	520	All Cannings ..	Wilts ..	Parish	1 013
Alderney ..	Chan. Island	Island	4 932	All Cannings	..	—	602
Aldersey ..	Cheshire ..	Tnship.	119	Allendale	Northumberland	Sub-dis.	8 622
Aldershott ..	Hants ..	Parish	16 720	Allendale	,,	Parish	6 401
Alderton ..	Gloucester ..	Parish	487	Allensmore ..	Hereford ..	Parish	612
Alderton ..	Northampton	Parish	131	Allenton	Northumberland	Parish	899
Alderton ..	Suffolk ..	Parish	634	Aller	Somerset ..	Parish	518
Alderton ..	Wilts ..	Parish	192	Allerdale above Derwent.	Cumb.	Ward	65 046
Alderwasley ..	Derby ..	Tnship.	372	Allerdale above Derwent .	,,	L. Sub.	47 694
Aldfield ..	York ..	Tnship.	128	Allerdale below Derwent.	,,	Ward	34 841
Aldford ..	Cheshire ..	Parish	731	Allerdale below Derwent .	,,	L. Sub.	21 455
Aldford	,, ..	Tnship.	438	Allerston	York ..	Sub-dis.	2 526
Aldgate	Middlesex ..	Sub-dis.	9 971	Allerston	,, ..	Parish	413
Aldham	Essex ..	Parish	406	Allerthorpe	,, ..	Parish	205
Aldham	Suffolk ..	Parish	267	Allerthorpe	,, ..	Tnship.	147
Aldingbourn ..	Sussex ..	Parish	772	Allerton ..	Lancaster ..	Tnship.	559
Aldingham ..	Lancaster ..	Parish	1 011	Allerton ..	York	Tnship.	2 014
Aldington ..	Kent ..	Sub-dis.	2 487	Allerton-Bywater	,,	Tnship.	704
Aldington	,, ..	Parish	658	Allerton-Mauleverer ..	,,	Parish	283
Aldington ..	Worcester ..	Hamlet	141	Allerton-Mauleverer, &c.	,,	Tnship.	261
Aldmondbury ..	York ..	Parish	42 889	Allertonshire	,,	Wapen.	9 603
Aldridge ..	Stafford ..	Sub-dis.	7 026	Allertonshire	,,	L. Sub.	10 304
Aldridge	,, ..	Parish	2 254	Allesley	Warwick ..	Parish	974
Aldridge	,, ..	Tnship.	1 179	Allestree ..	Derby ..	Parish	529
Aldringham ..	Suffolk ..	Parish	471	Allhallows ..	Berks ..	Parish	139
Aldrington ..	Sussex ..	Parish	7	Allhallows	,, ..	—	86
Aldsworth ..	Gloucester ..	Parish	430	Allhallows ..	Cumberland .	Parish	256
Aldwark ..	Derby ..	Tnship.	65	Allhallows, Goldsmth-st.	Devon	Parish	371
Aldwark ..	York ..	Tnship.	155	Allhallows on Walls ..	,,	Parish	1 002
Aldwinkle All Saints .	Nrthptn.	Parish	364	Allhallows ..	Kent ..	Parish	236
Aldwinkle St. Peter .	,,	Parish	222	Allhallows, Barking ..	Mddlx.	Parish	1 679
Aldworth ..	Berks ..	Parish	275	Allhallows, Bread-st. ..	,,	Parish	95
Alethorpe ..	Norfolk ..	Parish	6	Allhallows the Gt. ..	,,	Parish	603
Alexton ..	Leicester ..	Parish	67	Allhallows, Honey-lane	,,	Parish	65
Alfold ..	Surrey & Sussex	Parish	535	Allhallows the Less ..	,,	Parish	79
Alford ..	Lincoln ..	L. Sub.	45 877	Allhallows, Lombard-st.	,,	Parish	415
Alford	,, ..	Sub-dis.	7 804	Allhallows, London-wall	,,	Parish	1 999
Alford	,, ..	Parish	2 658	Allhallows, Staining ..	,,	Parish	358
Alford	,, ..	Town	2 658	Allington ..	Denbigh ..	Tnship.	889

4

Name of Place.	County.	Description.	Population.	Name of Place.	County.	Description.	Population.
Allington, East..	Devon	Parish	521	Almondbury	York	Tnship.	10 361
Allington, West..	„	Parish	925	Almondsbury	Gloucester	Sub-dis.	5 233
Allington	Dorset	Parish	1 915	Almondsbury	„	Parish	1 864
Allington	Hants	Tithing	475	Almondsbury	„	Tithing	686
Allington	Kent	Parish	66	Almsford	Somerset	Parish	306
Allington, East..	Lincoln	Parish	275	Alne, Great	Warwick	Parish	347
Allington, West..	„	Parish	135	Alne	York	Parish	1 542
Allington	Wilts	Parish	93	Alne	„	Tnship.	453
Allington	„	Tithing	159	Alnesbourne Priory	Suffolk	Parish	54
Allithwaite, Lower..	Lancaster	Tnship.	933	Alnham	Northumberland	Parish	295
Allithwaite, Upper..	„	Tnship.	729	Alnham	„	Tnship.	119
Allostock	Cheshire	Tnship.	536	Alnmouth	„	Tnship.	452
All Saints	Cambs	Parish	1 496	Alnwick	„	District	21 053
All Saints	Derby	Parish	4 049	Alnwick	„	Sub-dis.	7 359
All Saints	Dorset	Parish	946	Alnwick	„	Parish	7 850
All Saints	Essex	Sub-dis.	4 714	Alnwick	„	Tnship.	5 958
All Saints, Maldon	„	Parish	957	**Alnwick**	„	Town	5 670
All Saints, Colchester	„	Parish	680	Alnwick St. Paul	„	Ecl. Dis.	3 277
All Saints	Gloucester	Parish	121	Alnwick, South Side	„	Tnship.	268
All Saints	Hants	Parish	10 245	Alphamstone	Essex	Parish	317
All Saints	Hereford	Parish	4 525	Alpheton	Suffolk	Parish	298
All Saints	Herts	Parish	2 516	Alphington	Devon	Sub-dis.	4 097
All Saints	„	—	1 175	Alphington	„	Parish	1 250
All Saints	Hunts	Parish	430	Alpington	Norfolk	Parish	208
All Saints	Kent	Parish	457	Alpraham	Cheshire	Tnship.	530
All Saints	Leicester	Parish	5 945	Alresford	Essex	Parish	248
All Saints	Lincoln	Parish	2 070	Alresford	Hants	District	7 182
All Saints, Conisford	Norfolk	Parish	667	Alresford	„	Sub-dis.	3 674
All Saints, King's Lynn	„	Parish	4 534	Alresford, Old	„	Parish	526
All Saints	Northampton	Sub-dis.	14 028	Alresford, New..	„	Parish	1 546
All Saints	„	Parish	9 058	Alrewas..	Stafford	Parish	1 633
All Saints	Northumberland	Sub-dis.	26 765	Alrewas..	„	Tnship.	1 125
All Saints	„	Parish	37 529	Alrewas-Hays	„	Parish	48
All Saints	„	—	29 490	Alsager	Cheshire	Tnship.	703
All Saints	Oxon	Parish	478	Alsager, Christchurch	„	Ecl. Dis.	703
All Saints	Suffolk	Parish	1 350	Alsop le Dale and Eaton	Derby	Chap.	76
All Saints	Sussex	Sub-dis.	7 559	Alstoe	Rutland	Hund.	4 296
All Saints, Hastings	„	Parish	3 486	Alston	Cumberland	District	6 404
All Saints, Chichester	„	Parish	265	Alston	„	Parish	6 404
All Saints, Lewes	„	Parish	2 092	Alston	„	Tnship.	2 918
All Saints	Warwick	Sub-dis.	19 820	Alston	Lancaster	Sub-dis.	4 414
All Saints, Evesham	Worcester	Parish	1 722	Alston	„	Tnship.	1 098
All Saints, Worcester	„	Parish	2 421	Alstone..	Gloucester	Hamlet	96
All Saints, North St.	York	Parish	1 417	Alstonefield	Stafford	Parish	4 117
All Saints, Pavement	„	Parish	387	Alstonefield	„	Tnship.	651
All Saints, Peasholm	„	Parish	384	Alstonefield	„	Incor.	1 799
All Souls	Middlesex	Sub-dis.	29 952	Altcar	Lancaster	Parish	540
Alltmawr	Brecon	Parish	45	Alternon	Cornwall	Sub-dis.	2 496
Almeley..	Hereford	Parish	637	Alternon	„	Parish	1 389
Almer	Dorset	Parish	155	Altham..	Lancaster	Tnship.	410
Almington, &c...	Stafford	Tnship.	814	Althorne	Essex	Parish	389
Almington, &c...	Warwick	Tnship.	449	Althorp..	Northampton	Parish	78
Almondbury	York	Sub-dis.	11 063	Althorpe	Lincoln	Parish	1 316
Almondbury	„	Parish	42 889	Althorpe	„	Tnship.	391

Name of Place.	County.	Description.	Population.	Name of Place.	County.	Description.	Population.
Altofts ..	York ..	Tnship.	1 210	Amble ..	Northumberland	Tnship.	1 275
Alton Pancras ..	Dorset ..	Parish	270	Amblecote ..	Stafford ..	Hamlet	2 613
Alton ..	Hants ..	L. Sub.	14 0 \8	Amblecote, Trinity	,, ..	Ecl. Dis.	2 613
Alton	,, ..	Division	14 048	Ambleside ..	Westmoreland	L. Sub.	3 583
Alton	,, ..	District	12 063	Ambleside ..	,,	Sub-dis.	8 404
Alton	,, ..	Sub-dis.	7 197	Ambleside ..	,,	Tnship.	1 603
Alton	,, ..	Parish	3 769	Ambleston ..	Pembroke ..	Parish	524
Alton	,, ..	Town	3 286	Ambrosden ..	Oxon ..	Parish	871
Alton	Stafford ..	Sub-dis.	2 693	Ambrosden ..	,, ..	—	161
Alton ..	,,	Parish	2 250	Amcotts ..	Lincoln ..	Tnship.	374
Alton	,, ..	Tnship.	1 173	Amersham ..	Bucks ..	District	18 240
Alton Barnes ..	Wilts ..	Parish	177	Amersham ..	,, ..	Sub-dis.	3 550
Alton Priors ..	,, ..	Chap.	207	Amersham	,, ..	Parish	3 550
Altrincham ..	Cheshire ..	District	40 517	Amersham	,, ..	—	3 019
Altrincham ..	,,	Sub-dis.	18 214	Amesbury ..	Wilts ..	Hund.	5 242
Altrincham ..	,,	Tnship.	6 628	Amesbury ..	,, ..	District	8 127
Altrincham ..	,,	Town	6 628	Amesbury ..	,, ..	Sub-dis.	3 756
Altrincham, St. Geo.	,, ..	Ecl. Dis.	2 800	Amesbury ..	,, ..	Parish	1 138
Alumn Green ..	Hants ..	—	22	Amington, &c. ..	Warwick ..	Tnship.	449
Alvanley ..	Cheshire ..	Tnship.	330	Amlwch ..	Anglesey ..	Sub-dis.	7 777
Alvanley, St. John	,, ..	Ecl. Dis.	330	Amlwch ..	,, ..	Parish	5 949
Alvaston ..	,,	Tnship.	28	**Amlwch**	,, ..	P. Boro.	3 207
Alvaston ..	Derby ..	Tnship.	558	Amotherby ..	York ..	Tnship.	256
Alvechurch ..	Worcester ..	Parish	1 713	Amounderness ..	Lancaster ..	Hund.	47 716
Alveley	Salop ..	Parish	1 018	Amounderness ..	,,	L. Sub.	130 728
Alveley	,, ..	Tnship.	882	Ampfield ..	Hants ..	Ecl. Dis.	464
Alverdiscott ..	Devon ..	Parish	336	Ampleforth ..	.. York.	Parish	450
Alverstoke ..	Hants ..	District	22 653	Ampleforth Birdforth ..	,,	Tnship.	205
Alverstoke ..	,, ..	Sub-dis.	22 653	Ampleforth Oswaldkirk ..	,,	Tnship.	305
Alverstoke ..	,, ..	Parish	22 653	Ampleforth St. Peter ..	,,	Tnship.	245
Alverstoke ..	,, ..	Liberty	11 384	Ampney Crucis ..	Gloucester ..	Parish	648
Alverthorpe ..	York	Sub-dis.	6 645	Ampney St. Mary	,, ..	Parish	125
Alverthorpe w. Thornes	,,	Tnship.	6 645	Ampney St. Peter	,, ..	Parish	188
Alverthorpe	,,	Ecl. Dis.	4 590	Amport ..	Hants ..	Parish	706
Alverton ..	Notts ..	Hamlet	40	Ampthill ..	Beds ..	L. Sub.	16 970
Alvescot ..	Oxon ..	Parish	407	Ampthill ..	,, ..	District	16 970
Alvesdiston ..	Wilts ..	Parish	267	Ampthill ..	,, ..	Sub-dis.	9 076
Alveston ..	Gloucester ..	Parish	841	Ampthill ..	,, ..	Parish	2 144
Alveston ..	Warwick ..	Parish	844	**Ampthill** ..	,, ..	Town	2 011
Alveton ..	Stafford ..	Parish	2 250	Ampton ..	Suffolk ..	Parish	131
Alvingham ..	Lincoln ..	Parish	350	Amroth ..	Pemb. & Carm.	Sub-dis.	3 265
Alvington, West.	Devon ..	Parish	925	Amroth ..	Pembroke ..	Parish	889
Alvington ..	Gloucester ..	Parish	369	Amwell, Great ..	Herts ..	Parish	1 660
Alwalton ..	Hunts ..	Parish	342	Amwell, Little ..	,, ..	Liberty	500
Alwington ..	Devon ..	Parish	359	Amwell ..	Middlesex ..	Sub-dis.	17 250
Alwinton	Northumberland	Parish	899	Ancaster ..	Lincoln ..	Parish	682
Alwinton ..	,,	Tnship.	87	Ancoats ..	Lancaster ..	Sub-dis.	55 983
Alwoodley ..	York ..	Tnship.	140	Ancoats, All Souls	,, ..	Ecl. Dis.	11 263
Amberley ..	Gloucester ..	Ecl. Dis.	1 438 '	Ancoats, St. Andrew	,, ..	Ecl. Dis.	16 070
Amberley ..	Hereford ..	Tnship.	30	Ancroft ..	Northumberland	Parish	2 113
Amberley ..	Sussex ..	Parish	650	Anderby ..	Lincoln ..	Parish	276
Amberley	,, ..	—	456	Andersfield ..	Somerset ..	Hund.	2 807
Ambersham, North	,, ..	Tithing	111	Anderson ..	Dorset ..	Parish	62
Ambersham, South	,, ..	Tithing	143	Anderton ..	Cheshire ..	Tnship.	334

6

Name of Place.	County.	Description.	Population.	Name of Place.	County.	Description.	Population.
Anderton	.. *Lancaster* ..	Tnship.	243	Appleby	.. *Lincoln* ..	Parish	579
Andover	.. *Hants* ..	L. Sub.	19 979	Appleby	.. ,, ..	Tnship.	553
Andover	.. ,, ..	Division	14 758	Appleby	.. *Westmoreland*	Sub-dis.	5 529
Andover	.. *Hants & Wilts*	District	17 132	Appleby	.. ,,	Tnship.	960
Andover	.. *Hants* ..	Sub-dis.	6 435	Appleby St. Lawrence	,,	Parish	1 569
Andover	.. ,, ..	Parish	5 221	Appleby St. Michael	,,	Parish	1 255
Andover	.. ,, {	M. Bor.	5 221	Appledore	.. *Devon* ..	Ecl. Dis.	2 210
		P. Boro.	5 430	Appledore	.. *Kent* ..	Parish	640
Andreas..	.. *Isle of Man* .	Parish	1 955	Appledram	.. *Sussex* ..	Parish	129
Andwell	.. *Hants* ..	Parish	26	Appleford	.. *Berks* ..	Chap.	288
Angell Town, St. John .	*Surrey*	Ecl. Dis.	4 967	Appleshaw	.. *Hants* ..	Parish	284
Angersleigh	.. *Somerset* ..	Parish	30	Applethwaite	.. *Westmoreland*	Tnship.	1 285
Angerton	.. *Lancaster* ..	Parish	31	Applethwaite, St. Mary	,,	Ecl. Dis.	1 235
Angerton, High .	*Northmb.* ..	Tnship.	105	Appleton	.. *Berks* ..	Parish	549
Angerton, Low..	,, ..	Tnship.	80	Appleton	.. ,, ..	—	443
Angle ..	.. *Pembroke* ..	Parish	512	Appleton, &c.	.. *Cheshire* ..	Tnship.	1 828
Anglesey	.. *County* ..	Island	54 609	Appleton, E. & West	.. *York.*	Tnship.	115
Anglesey First ..	*Anglesey* ..	L. Sub.	22 858	Appleton-le-Moors	.. ,,	Tnship.	265
Anglesey Second.	,, ..	L. Sub.	31 751	Appleton Roebuck	.. ,,	Sub-dis.	1 272
Anglesey	.. ,, ..	District	38 157	Appleton Roebuck	.. ,,	Tnship.	622
Anglesey	.. ,, ..	Union	17 840	Appleton-le-Street	.. ,,	Parish	987
Anglezarke	.. *Lancaster* ..	Tnship.	134	Appleton-le-Street	.. ,,	Tnship.	185
Angmering	.. *Sussex* ..	Parish	953	Appleton-upon-Wiske..	,,	Sub-dis.	2 952
Angram..	.. *York* ..	Tnship.	59	Appleton-upon-Wiske..	,,	Chap.	466
Angram-Grange.	,, ..	Tnship.	31	Appletree	.. *Derby* ..	Hund.	34 702
Anick ..	*Northumberland*	Tnship.	137	Appletree	.. ,, ..	L. Sub.	34 702
Anick-Grange ..	,, ..	Tnship.	48	Appletree	.. *Northampton*	Hamlet	88
Anlaby ..	.. *York* ..	Tnship.	493	Appletrewick	.. *York* ..	Tnship.	354
Anmer ..	.. *Norfolk* ..	Parish	142	Arborfield	.. *Berks* ..	Parish	286
Annesley	.. *Notts* ..	Parish	288	Arbory ..	.. *Isle of Man* .	Parish	1 410
Ansford..	.. *Somerset* ..	Parish	306	Arbour Sq. St. Thos.	. *Mddlx.*	Ecl.Dis.	16 433
Ansley ..	.. *Warwick* ..	Parish	685	Archbishop's Palace	. *Kent* ..	Precinct	160
Anslow ..	.. *Stafford* ..	Tnship.	348	Archdeacon Newton	. *Durh.* ..	Tnship.	61
Anstey, East	.. *Devon* ..	Parish	227	Arclid ..	.. *Cheshire* ..	Tnship.	265
Anstey, West ..	,, ..	Parish	299	Arddynwent	.. *Flint* ..	Tnship.	463
Anstey ..	.. *Herts* ..	Parish	473	Ardeley..	.. *Herts* ..	Parish	574
Anstey ..	.. *Leicester* ..	Chap.	734	Arden w. Ardenside	.. *York.*	Tnship.	129
Anstey Pastures.	,, ..	Parish	34	Ardingly	.. *Sussex* ..	Parish	626
Anstey ..	.. *Warwick* ..	Parish	171	Ardington	.. *Berks* ..	Parish	354
Anstey ..	.. *Wilts* ..	Parish	298	Ardleigh	.. *Essex* ..	Sub-dis.	4 964
Anston ..	.. *York* ..	Sub-dis.	3 222	Ardleigh	.. ,, ..	Parish	1 582
Anston ..	.. ,, ..	Tnship.	1 126	Ardley ..	.. *Oxon* ..	Parish	169
Anston-cum-Membris	,, ..	Parish	1 290	Ardsley..	.. .. *York.*	Tnship.	1 772
Anthorn	.. *Cumberland* .	Tnship.	197	Ardsley, Christchurch..	,,	Ecl. Dis.	1 712
Antingham	.. *Norfolk* ..	Parish	227	Ardsley..	.. .. ,,	Sub-dis.	2 786
Antony ..	.. *Cornwall* ..	Sub-dis.	7 878	Ardsley, East ..	.. .. ,,	Parish	1 069
Antony ..	.. ,, {	Parish	3 887	Ardsley, West ..	.. .. ,,	Parish	1 646
Antrobus	.. *Cheshire* ..	Tnship.	514	Ardudwyisantro.	*Merioneth* ..	Hund.	13 324
Antrobus, St. Mark	,, ..	Ecl. Dis.	673	Ardudwyuwchartro	,, ..	Hund.	11 750
Anwick ..	.. *Lincoln* ..	Parish	277	Ardwick	.. *Lancaster* ..	Sub-dis.	47 752
Apethorpe	.. *Northampton*	Parish	248	Ardwick	.. ,, ..	Tnship.	21 757
Apley ..	.. *Lincoln* ..	Parish	221	Ardwick, St. Silas	,, ..	Ecl. Dis.	10 375
Apperley	*Northumberland*	Parish	20	Ardwick, St. Thomas	,, ..	Ecl. Dis.	10 147
Appleby ..	*Leicester & Derby*	Parish	1 070	Areley Kings	.. *Worcester* ..	Parish	564

Name of Place.	County.	Description.	Population.	Name of Place.	County.	Description.	Population.
Argam	York	Parish	27	Ascot	Oxon.	Hamlet	20
Argoed & Ystrad	Cardigan	Tnship.	882	Ascot un. Wychwood	„	Parish	458
Argoed	Flint	Tnship.	874	Asfordby	Leicester	Parish	485
Arkendale	York	Tnship.	242	Asgarby	Lincoln	Parish	83
Arkengarth Dale	„	Parish	1 147	Asgarby	„	Parish	80
Arkesden	Essex	Parish	506	Ash	Derby	Hamlet	46
Arkholme	Lancashire	Sub-dis.	910	Ash	Durham	Tnship.	942
Arkholme w. Cawood	„	Tnship.	331	Ash	Kent	Parish	587
Arlecdon	Cumberland.	Parish	1 550	Ash-next-Sandwich „		Parish	2 039
Arleston & Sinfin	Derby	Liberty	54	Ash	Salop	Ecl. Dis.	545
Arley, Upper	Stafford	Parish	886	Ash, Holy Trinity	Somerset	Ecl. Dis.	543
Arlsey	Warwick	Parish	230	Ash-Bocking	Suffolk	Parish	324
Arlingham	Gloucester	Parish	693	Ash	Surrey	Incor.	2 853
Arlington	Devon	Parish	219	Ash	„	Parish	4 164
Arlington	Gloucester	Tithing	415	Ash	„	—	1 072
Arlington	Sussex	Parish	623	Ashampstead	Berks	Parish	385
Arlington Sq. St. Phil	Mdlx.	Ecl. Dis.	9 015	Ashborne	Derby & Stafford	Union	19 997
Arlsey	Beds	Parish	1 401	Ashborne	„	District	20 648
Armin	York	Tnship.	557	Ashborne	Derby	Sub-dis.	4 876
Armingford	Cambs	Hund.	9 256	Ashborne	„	Parish	5 078
Arminghall	Norfolk	Parish	75	Ashborne	„	Tnship.	2 120
Armitage	Stafford	Parish	937	**Ashborne**	„	Town	3 501
Armitage Bridge	York	Ecl. Dis.	2 455	Ashbrittle	Somerset	Parish	525
Armley		Tnship.	6 734	Ashburnham	Sussex	Parish	844
Armston	Northampton	Hamlet	23	Ashburton	Devon	Sub-dis.	6 362
Armthorpe	York	Parish	424	Ashburton	„	Parish	3 062
Arncliffe	„	Parish	326	**Ashburton**	„	P. Boro.	3 062
Arncliffe	„	Sub-dis.	405	Ashbury	Berks	Parish	742
Arncliffe	„	Parish	740	Ashbury	„	—	422
Arncliffe	„	Tnship.	174	Ashbury	Devon	Parish	80
Arncot	Oxon	Hamlet	334	Ashby-de-la-Zouch	Leicester	L. Sub.	22 807
Arne	Dorset	Parish	139	Ashby-de-la-Z.	Leic. & Derby	District	28 480
Arnesby	Leicester	Parish	573	Ashby-de-la-Z.	„	Sub-dis.	8 290
Arnold	Notts	Sub-dis.	8 378	Ashby-de-la-Zouch	Leicester	Parish	6 958
Arnold	„	Parish	4 642	Ashby-de-la-Zouch	„	Tnship.	6 337
Arrathorne	York	Tnship.	76	**Ashby-de-la-Zouch**	„	Town	3 772
Arreton	Hants	Parish	1 880	Holy-Trinity	„	Ecl. Dis.	2 270
Arrington and Melborn	Cambs	L. Sub.	14 759	Ashby-Folville	„	Parish	450
Arrington	„	Parish	302	Ashby-Folville	„	Tnship	160
Arrow	Cheshire	Tnship.	109	Ashby Magna	„	Parish	315
Arrow	Warwick	Parish	590	Ashby Parva	„	Parish	160
Arrow	„	Tnship.	295	Ashby	Lincoln	Tnship	503
Arthington	York	Tnship.	344	Ashby-de-la-Laund	„	Parish	176
Arthingworth	Northampton	Parish	275	Ashby-by-Partney	„	Parish	148
Arthuret	Cumberland.	Parish	3 714	Ashby Puerorum	„	Parish	149
Artillery	Middlesex	Sub-dis.	6 557	Ashby, West	„	Parish	526
Artington	Surrey	Tithing	944	Ashby w. Fenby	„	Parish	274
Arundel	Sussex	Rape	29 975	Ashby, Loddon	Norfolk	Parish	257
Arundel	„	L. Sub.	13 154	Ashby, Flegg	„	Parish	16
Arundel	„	Sub-dis.	3 797	Ashby St. Ledgers	Nrthptn.	Parish	300
Arundel	„	Parish	2 498	Ashby	Suffolk	Parish	70
Arundel	„	Boro.	2 498	Ashchurch	Gloucester	Parish	771
Aryholme & Howthorpe	York	Tnship.	35	Ashcombe	Devon	Parish	212
Asby	Westmoreland	Parish	440	Ashcott	Somerset	Parish	817

Name of Place.	County.	Description.	Population.	Name of Place.	County.	Description.	Population.
Ashdon	Essex	Parish	1 235	Ashton, Cold	Gloucester	Parish	503
Ashdon	"	—	1 011	Ashton under Hill	"	Parish	411
Ashe	Hants	Parish	145	Ashton-in-Maker field	Lanc.	Sub-dis.	6 566
Asheldham	Essex	Parish	212	Ashton-in-Maker field	"	Parish	10 181
Ashen	"	Parish	344	Ashton-in-Maker field	"	Tnship.	6 566
Ashendon	Bucks	Hund.	13 389	Ashton, St. Thomas	"	Ecl. Dis.	6 863
Ashendon	"	L. Sub.	12 587	Ashton under Lyne	"	L. Sub.	82 305
Ashendon	"	Parish	325	Ashton under Lyne	Lan. & Ch.	District	134 753
Ashfield, Great	Suffolk	Parish	408	Ashton Town	Lancashire	Sub-dis.	33 917
Ashfield w. Thorpe	"	Parish	306	Ashton under Lyne	"	Parish	66 801
Ashford	Derby	Tnship.	829	Ashton under Lyne	"	M. Bor.	34 886
Ashford	Devon	Parish	157			P. Bor.	33 917
Ashford	Kent	L. Sub.	33 032	Christchurch	"	Ecl. Dis.	7 478
Ashford	"	Sub-dis.	9 826	St. Peter	"	Ecl. Dis.	11 694
Ashford	"	Parish	6 950	Ashton w. Stodday	"	Tnship.	184
Ashford	"	Town	5 522	Ashton	Northampton	Parish	374
Ashford	Middlesex	Parish	784	Ashton, Oudle	"	Hamlet	177
Ashford-Bowdler	Salop	Parish	106	Ashton, Barnack	"	Hamlet	115
Ashford-Carbonell	"	Parish	282	Ashton, Long	Somerset	Parish	2 000
Ashfordby	Leicester	Parish	485	Ashton Keynes	Wilts	Parish	1 382
Ashill	Norfolk	Parish	696	Ashton Keynes	"	Hamlet	1 070
Ashill	Somerset	Parish	445	Ashton, West	"	Tithing	314
Ashingdon	Essex	Parish	99	Ashton, W., St. John	"	Ecl. Dis.	314
Ashington, &c.	Northmb.	Tnship.	76	Ashurst	Kent	Parish	247
Ashington	Somerset	Parish	57	Ashurst	Sussex	Parish	374
Ashington	Sussex	Parish	234	Ashwater	Devon	Parish	803
Ashleworth	Gloucester	Parish	547	Ashwell	Herts	Parish	1 507
Ashley & Silverley	Cambs	Parish	509	Ashwell	Rutland	Parish	206
Ashley	Cheshire	Tnship.	875	Ashwellthorpe	Norfolk	Parish	409
Ashley	Gloucester	Sub-dis.	11 690	Ashwick	Somerset	Parish	778
Ashley	Hants	Parish	104	Ashwicken	Norfolk	Parish	108
Ashley	Northampton	Parish	348	Ashworth	Lancashire	Tnship.	233
Ashley	Stafford	Parish	870	Aske	York	Tnship.	140
Ashley	Wilts	Parish	90	Askern	"	Tnship.	379
Ashleyhay	Derby	Tnship.	232	Askern, St. Peter	"	Ecl. Dis.	379
Ashmanhaugh	Norfolk	Parish	136	Askerswell	Dorset	Parish	223
Ashmansworth	Hants	Parish	201	Askerton	Cumberland	Tnship.	380
Ashmore	Dorset	Parish	254	Askew	York	Tnship.	759
Asholt	Somerset	Parish	181	Askham	Notts	Parish	287
Ashover	Derby	Sub-dis.	10 757	Askham	Westmoreland	Parish	503
Ashover	"	Parish	3 286	Askham	"	Tnship.	323
Ashover	"	Tnship.	2 351	Askham Bryan	York	Parish	362
Ashow	Warwick	Parish	149	Askham Richard	"	Parish	235
Ashperton	Hereford	Parish	534	Askrigg	"	District	5 649
Ashprington	Devon	Parish	537	Askrigg	"	Sub-dis.	3 207
Ash-Priors	Somerset	Parish	207	Askrigg	"	Tnship.	668
Ashreigney	Devon	Parish	842	Askwith & Snowdon	"	Tnship.	338
Ashtead	Surrey	Parish	729	Aslackby	Lincoln	Sub-dis.	4 730
Ashted, St. James	Warwick	Ecl. Dis.	13 392	Aslackby	"	Parish	534
Ashton	Cheshire	Tnship.	411	Aslackby	"	Tnship.	428
Ashton Hayes, St. John	"	Ecl. Dis.	626	Aslacoe	"	Wapen.	5 925
Ashton upon Mersey	"	Parish	4 507	Aslacton	Norfolk	Parish	356
Ashton upon Mersey	"	Tnship.	1 476	Aslockton	Notts	Tnship.	410
Ashton	Devon	Parish	347	Aspall	Suffolk	Parish	156

Name of Place.	County.	Description.	Population.	Name of Place.	County.	Description.	Population.
Aspatria	Cumberland.	Parish	2 305	Aston St. Saviour	Stafford	Ecl. Dis.	625
Aspatria & Brayton	,,	Tnship.	1 210	Aston	Warwick	District	100 522
Aspeden	Herts	Parish	577	Aston	,,	Parish	94 995
Aspley-Guise	Beds	Parish	1 437	Aston	,,	Manor	16 337
Aspley	Stafford	Tnship.	30	Aston Cantlow	,,	Parish	1 055
Aspull	Lancashire	Sub-dis.	8 372	Aston Magna	Worcester	Ecl. Dis.	259
Aspull	,,	Tnship.	4 290	Aston w. Aughton	York.	Parish	1 032
Asselby	York	Tnship.	276	Aston w. Aughton	,,	Tnship.	995
Assington	Suffolk	Parish	747	Astwell	Northampton	Hamlet	37
Astbury	Cheshire	Parish	19 351	Astwick	Beds	Parish	64
Asterby	Lincoln	Parish	304	Astwood	Bucks	Parish	247
Asthall	Oxon	Parish	424	Aswarby	Lincoln	Sub-dis.	3 059
Astley	Lancashire	Tnship.	2 109	Aswarby	,,	Parish	128
Astley	,,	Ecl. Dis.	2 109	Aswardby	,,	Parish	68
Astley Bridge, St. Paul ,,		Ecl. Dis.	3 210	Aswardhurn	,,	Wapen.	7 685
Astley	Salop	Chap.	239	Atcham	Salop & Mont.	District	19 455
Astley, St. Mary.	,,	Ecl. Dis.	239	Atcham	Salop	Sub-dis.	1 699
Astley-Abbots	,,	Parish	668	Atcham	,,	Parish	406
Astley	Warwick	Parish	332	Athelhampstone	Dorset	Parish	95
Astley	Worcester	Parish	864	Athelington	Suffolk	Parish	115
Aston Tirrold	Berks	Parish	395	Atherington	Devon	Parish	598
Aston Upthorpe	,,	Liberty	169	Atherington	Sussex	Parish	7
Aston-Abbotts	Bucks	Parish	311	Atherstone	Warwick & Leic.	District	12 118
Aston Clinton	,,	Sub-dis.	5 246	Atherstone	,,	Sub-dis.	12 118
Aston Clinton	,,	Parish	1 297	Atherstone	Warwick	Tnship.	3 877
Aston Clinton	,,	Tnship.	1 108	Atherstone St. Mary	,,	Ecl. Dis.	3 877
St. Leonard	,,	Ecl. Dis.	189	**Atherstone**	,,	Town	3 857
Aston Sandford	,,	Parish	59	Atherstone on Stour	,,	Parish	90
Aston	Cheshire	Ecl. Dis.	616	Atherton	Lancashire	Sub-dis.	11 936
Aston by Budworth	,,	Tnship.	459	Atherton	,,	Tnship.	5 907
Aston by Sutton	,,	Tnship.	207	**Atherton**	,,	Town	2 692
Aston Grange	,,	Tnship.	42	Atherton St. John	,,	Ecl. Dis.	5 641
Aston nr. Mondrum	,,	Tnship.	146	Atlow	Derby	Chap.	129
Aston	Derby	Tnship.	103	Attenborough	Notts	Parish	1 110
Aston upon Trent	,,	Parish	551	Attenborough	,,	Tnship.	95
Aston	Flint	Tnship.	333	Atterby	Lincoln	Tnship.	95
Aston Blank	Gloucester	Parish	325	Attercliffe	York.	Sub-dis.	7 464
Aston Somerville	,,	Parish	105	Attercliffe w. Darnall	,,	Tnship.	7 464
Aston-sub-Edge	,,	Parish	128	Attercliffe Christchurch	,,	Ecl. Dis.	5 061
Aston	Hereford	Parish	34	Atterton	Leicester	Hamlet	78
Aston Ingham	,,	Parish	568	Attington	Oxon	Parish	15
Aston	Herts	Parish	639	Attleborough	Norfolk	Sub-dis.	5 506
Aston Flamville	Leicester	Parish	1 946	Attleborough	,,	Parish	2 221
Aston Flamville	,,	Tnship.	81	Attleborough	Warwick	Ecl. Dis.	1 392
Aston	Montgomery	Tnship.	62	Attlebridge	Norfolk	Parish	93
Aston-le-Walls	Northampton	Parish	221	Atwick	York	Parish	319
Aston-le-Walls	,,	—	133	Atworth & S. Wraxhall	Wilts	Ecl. Dis.	949
Aston and Coate	Oxon	Hamlet	811	Aubourn	Lincoln	Parish	376
Aston, North	,,	Parish	296	Aubourn	,,	Tnship.	308
Aston Rowant	,,	Parish	884	Auburn	York	Tnship.	16
Aston Steeple	,,	Parish	736	Auckland	Durham	District	50 491
Aston Botterell	Salop	Parish	171	Auckland, St. Andrew	,,	Parish	32 111
Aston Eyre	,,	Tnship.	85	Auckland, St. Andrew	,,	Tnship.	1 401
Aston	Stafford	Tnship.	237	Auckland, St. Helen	,,	Tnship.	842

Name of Place.	County.	Description.	Population.	Name of Place.	County.	Description.	Population
ckland, St. Helen	Durham	Chap.	4 792	Axminster, All Sts.	Devon & Dor.	Ecl. Dis.	453
ckland, West	,,	Tnship.	2 581	Axmouth	Devon	Parish	662
denshaw	Lancashire	Sub-dis.	15 125	Aycliffe	Durham	Sub-dis.	4 955
denshaw	,,	Div.	6 327	Aycliffe	,,	Parish	1 458
denshaw, St. Stephen	,,	Ecl. Dis.	5 185	Aycliffe, Great	,,	Tnship.	840
dlem	Cheshire	Parish	2 287	Aydon	Northumberland	Tnship.	78
dlem	,,	Tnship.	1 510	Aydon Castle	,,	Tnship.	30
dley	Stafford	Sub-dis.	7 625	Aylburton	Gloucester	Tithing	604
dley	,,	Parish	6 494	Aylesbeare	Devon	Parish	1 079
dley	,,	Tnship.	1 556	Aylesbeare	,,	—	418
ghton	Lancashire	Sub-dis.	3 862	Aylesbury	Bucks	Hund.	27 090
ghton	,,	Parish	1 870	Aylesbury	,,	L. Sub.	26 120
ghton	York	Parish	633	Aylesbury	,,	District	23 600
ghton	,,	Tnship.	202	Aylesbury	,,	Sub-dis.	8 272
gustine Friars	Leicester	Parish	119	Aylesbury	,,	Parish	6 168
gustine, St.	Kent	Lathe	66 143	**Aylesbury**	,,	P. Boro.	27 090
lt-Hucknall	Derby	Parish	686	Aylesby	Lincoln	Parish	130
nby	Lincoln	Hamlet	58	Aylesford	Kent	Lathe	138 752
nsby	,,	Parish	140	Aylesford	,,	Sub-dis.	8 036
st	Gloucester	Tithing	187	Aylesford	,,	Parish	2 057
sterfield	York	Tnship.	389	Aylestone	Leicester	Parish	575
sterson	Cheshire	Tnship.	57	Aylestone	,,	Tnship.	392
sthorpe	York	Tnship.	231	Aylmerton	Norfolk	Parish	250
stin	,,	Ward	2 406	Aylsham	,,	District	19 052
stonley	,,	Tnship.	1 901	Aylsham	,,	Parish	2 623
strey	Warwick	Parish	557	**Aylsham**	,,	Town	2 388
stwick	York	Tnship.	561	Aylton	Hereford	Parish	89
thorpe	Lincoln	Parish	134	Aymestrey	,,	Parish	855
ebury	Wilts	Parish	725	Aynho	Northampton	Parish	595
eland	Lincoln	Wapen.	11 868	Ayott, St. Lawrence	Herts	Parish	122
eley	Essex	Parish	930	Ayott, St. Peter	,,	Parish	234
enbury	Hereford	Parish	371	Aysgarth	York	Parish	5 649
ening	Gloucester	Parish	2 070	Aysgarth	,,	Tnship.	283
erham	Notts	Parish	237	Ayston	Rutland	Parish	97
erham	,,	Tnship.	175	Aythorp Roothing	Essex	Parish	269
eton-Gifford	Devon	Parish	839	Ayton	York	Parish	1 688
rington	Berks	Parish	104	Ayton, East	,,	Tnship.	406
vington	Hants	Parish	162	Ayton, Great	,,	Tnship.	1 450
von Dassett	Warwick	Parish	280	Ayton, Little	,,	Tnship.	78
von	Wilts	—	20	Ayton, West	,,	Tnship.	385
von, Nether	,,	Parish	546	Azenby	,,	Tnship.	202
wkley	Notts & York	Tnship.	309	Azerley	,,	Tnship.	606
wliscombe	Devon	Parish	579				
wre	Gloucester	Parish	1 526	**Babcary**	Somerset	Parish	426
xbridge	Somerset	L. Sub.	36 106	Babergh	Suffolk	Hund	24 198
xbridge	,,	District	36 106	Babingley	Norfolk	Parish	67
xbridge	,,	Sub-dis.	5 856	Babington	Somerset	Parish	129
xbridge	,,	Parish	799	Babraham	Cambs	Parish	304
xford	Wilts	Tithing	362	Babworth	Notts	Parish	701
xminster	Devon	Hund.	10 823	Bache	Cheshire	Tnship	34
xminster	,,	L. Sub.	13 077	Backford	,,	Parish	525
xminster	Devon & Dorset	District	19 758	Backford	,,	Tnship	150
xminster	,,	,,	Sub-dis.	5 537	Backwell	Somerset	Parish	926
xminster	,,	,,	Parish	2 918	Backworth	Northumberland	Tnship	954

Name of Place.	County.	Description.	Population.	Name of Place.	County.	Description.	Population.
Baconsthorpe	Norfolk	Parish	328	Bainton Beacon..	York	L. Sub.	13 436
Bacton	Hereford	Parish	154	Bainton..	,,	Sub-dis.	4 009
Bacton	Norfolk	Sub-dis.	2 574	Bainton..	,,	Parish	465
Bacton	,,	Parish	490	Bainton..	,,	Tnship.	399
Bacton	Suffolk	Parish	733	Bakewell	Derby	District	31 378
Bacup	Lancashire..	Town	10 935	Bakewell	,,	Sub-dis.	12 547
Bacup, Christch..	,,	Ecl. Dis.	5 730	Bakewell	,,	Parish	11 254
Bacup, St. John..	,,	Ecl. Dis.	8 981	Bakewell	,,	Tnship.	2 704
Badby	Northampton	Parish	618	Bakewell	,,	Town	2 704
Baddesley, North.	Hants	Parish	258	Bala	Merioneth	District	6 352
Baddesley, South.	,,	Ecl. Dis.	561	Bala	,,	Sub-dis.	6 352
Baddesley Clinton	Warwick	Parish	143	Balby w. Hexthorpe	York.	Tnship.	1 058
Baddesley Ensor.	,,	Parish	872	Balby w. Hexthorpe	,,	Ecl. Dis.	1 707
Baddiley	Cheshire	Parish	272	Balcombe	Sussex	Parish	880
Baddington	,,	Tnship.	135	Baldersby	York.	Tnship.	333
Baddow, Great..	Essex	Parish	2 061	Baldersby, St. James	,,	Ecl. Dis.	713
Baddow, Little..	,,	Parish	605	Balderstone	Lancashire .	Tnship.	532
Badger	Salop	Parish	178	Balderstone	,,	Ecl. Dis.	532
Badgeworth	Gloucester	Parish	1 048	Balderton	Notts	Parish	987
Badgington	,,	Parish	175	Baldhu	Cornwall	Ecl. Dis.	2 070
Badgworth	Somerset	Parish	279	Baldock	Herts	Sub-dis.	8 738
Badingham	Suffolk	Parish	749	Baldock..	,,	Parish	1 974
Badlesmere	Kent	Parish	133	Baldon-Marsh	Oxon	Parish	342
Badley	Suffolk	Parish	70	Baldon-Toot	,,	Parish	260
Badminton, Great	Gloucester	Parish	524	Bale	Norfolk	Parish	227
Badminton, Little	,,	Tithing	113	Balk	York	Tnship.	86
Badsey	Worcester	Parish	546	Balkholme	,,	Tnship.	184
Badsey	,,	Tnship.	405	Balking	. Berks.	Chap.	181
Badsworth	York	Parish	744	Balking w. Woolstone	,,	Ecl. Dis.	437
Badsworth	,,	Tnship.	219	Ballaugh	Isle of Man.	Parish	1 228
Badwell-Ash	Suffolk	Parish	527	Ballidon	Derby	Tnship.	110
Bagborough, West	Somerset	Parish	495	Ballingdon w. Brundon	Essex.	Parish	861
Bagby w. Islebeck	York	Tnship.	302	Ballingham	Hereford	Parish	168
Bag Enderby	Lincoln	Parish	81	Balls Pond, St. Paul	Middlesex.	Ecl. Dis.	11 789
Baggrave	Leicester	Liberty	26	Balne	York	Tnship.	367
Bagillt, St. Mary.	Flint	Ecl. Dis.	2 935	Balne, St. John..	,,	Ecl. Dis.	863
Baginton	Warwick	Parish	213	Balsall	Warwick	Hamlet	1 140
Baglan	Glamorgan	Parish	715	Balsall Heath	Worcester	Ecl. Dis.	7 651
Baglan, Higher..	,,	Hamlet	259	Balscott..	Oxon	Chap.	211
Baglan, Lower ..	,,	Hamlet	456	Balsham	Cambs	Sub-dis.	3 925
Bagley Wood	Berks	Parish	8	Balsham	,,	Parish	1 162
Bagnall	Stafford	Tnship.	424	Balterley	Stafford	Tnship.	281
Bagthorpe	Norfolk	Parish	69	Baltonsborough	Somerset	Parish	763
Baguley	Cheshire	Tnship.	611	Bamber Bridge..	Lancashire .	Ecl. Dis.	2 182
Bagworth	Leicester	Chap.	534	Bambrough	Northumberland	Ward	11 244
Baildon	York	Tnship.	3 895	Bambrough Ward	,,	L. Sub.	19 814
Bailey	Cumberland.	Tnship.	363	Bambrough	,,	Parish	4 105
Bailey, North	Durham	Parish	300	Bambrough	,,	Tnship.	403
Bailey, South	,,	Parish	106	Bambrough Castle	,,	Tnship.	38
Bailey	Lancashire..	Hamlet	200	Bamburgh	Lincoln	Parish	393
Bainbridge	York	Incor.	4 949	Bamford	Derby	Tnship.	377
Bainbridge	,,	Tnship.	807	Bampton, Kirk..	Cumberland.	Parish	497
Bainton..	Northampton	Parish	217	Bampton, Kirk..	,,	Tnship.	205
Bainton..	Oxon	Hamlet	40	Bampton, Little .	,,	Tnship.	172

Name of Place.	County.	Description.	Population.	Name of Place.	County.	Description.	Population.
Bampton	Devon	Hund.	6 628	Bardsey w. Rigton	York	Tnship.	295
Bampton	„	Sub-dis.	3 296	Bardsley, Trinity.	Lancashire	Ecl. Dis.	2 721
Bampton	„	Parish	1 971	Bardwell	Suffolk	Parish	882
Bampton	Oxon	Hund.	16 123	Barford	Beds	Hund.	6 988
Bampton	„	Sub-dis.	5 629	Barford	„	Sub-dis.	3 100
Bampton	„	Parish	2 863	Barford, Great	„	Parish	907
Bampton	„	Tnship.	865	Barford, Little	„	Parish	91
Bampton Aston	„	Ecl. Dis.	968	Barford	Norfolk	Parish	419
Bampton Lew	„	Ecl. Dis.	182	Barford St. John	Oxon	Chap.	107
Bampton Proper	„	Ecl. Dis.	1 713	Barford St. Michael	„	Parish	332
Bampton	Westmoreland	Parish	541	Barford	Warwick	Parish	754
Banbury	Oxon	Hund.	10 393	Barford St. Martin	Wilts	Parish	519
Banbury	„	L. Sub.	21 251	Barforth	York	Tnship.	167
Banbury	Oxon, &c.	District	30 171	Barfreston	Kent	Parish	144
Banbury	Oxon & Northtn	Sub-dis.	13 293	Barham	Hunts	Parish	115
Banbury	Oxon	Parish	9 140	Barham	Kent	Sub-dis.	6 296
Banbury	„	—	4 059	Barham	„	Parish	1 090
Banbury	„	M. Bor.	4 059	Barham	Suffolk	Parish	568
Banbury {	Oxon & Nrthptn	P. Bor.	10 216	Barholm	Lincoln	Parish	192
Banbury, South	Oxon	Ecl. Dis.	4 043	Barkby	Leicester	Parish	791
Bangley	Stafford	Liberty	12	Barkby	„	Tnship.	504
Bangor	—	Diocese	195 390	Barkby Thorpe	„	Hamlet	78
Bangor	Cardiganshire	Parish	204	Barkestone	„	Parish	411
Bangor	„	Ecl. Dis.	1 919	Barkham	Berks	Parish	280
Bangor	Carnv. & Anglesey	District	36 309	Barking Town	Essex	Sub-dis.	5 591
Bangor	Carnarvon	Sub-dis.	14 043	Barking	„	Parish	10 996
Bangor	„	Parish	10 662	Barking	„	Town	5 076
Bangor	„	P. Bor.	6 738	Barking Side	„	Ecl. Dis.	1 712
Bangor	Flint & Denbigh	Parish	1 240	Barking	Suffolk	Parish	1 850
Bangor	Flint	Tnship.	585	Barking	„	—	409
Banham	Norfolk	Sub-dis.	5 516	Barkisland	York	Tnship.	2 003
Banham	„	Parish	1 163	Barkisland, Christch.	„	Ecl. Dis.	1 374
Bankfoot, St. Matthew	York	Ecl. Dis.	2 641	Barkston	Lincoln	Parish	540
Bank-Newton	„	Tnship.	106	Barkston Ash	York	Wapen.	27 866
Bannel	Flint	Tnship.	124	Barkston Ash	„	L. Sub.	27 866
Banningham	Norfolk	Parish	302	Barkston Ash	„	Tnship.	319
Banstead	Surrey	Parish	1 461	Barkway	Herts	Parish	1 221
Banwell	Somerset	Sub-dis.	12 649	Barkway	„	—	940
Banwell	„	Parish	1 853	Barkwith, East	Lincoln	Parish	387
Bapchild	Kent	Parish	389	Barkwith, West	„	Parish	150
Barbon	Westmoreland	Tnship.	364	Barlaston	Stafford	Parish	637
Barby	Northampton	Parish	645	Barlavington	Sussex	Parish	136
Barcheston	Warwick	Parish	190	Barlborough	Derby	Parish	1 170
Barcombe	Sussex	Parish	1 090	Barlby	York	Chap.	471
Barden	York N.	Tnship.	76	Barlestone	Leicester	Chap.	544
Barden	York W.	Tnship.	371	Barley	Herts	Parish	809
Bardfield, Great	Essex	Parish	1 065	Barley, &c.	Lancashire	Tnship.	485
Bardfield, Little	„	Parish	429	Barleythorpe	Rutland	Manor	168
Bardfield, Saling	„	Parish	356	Barlichway	Warwick	Hund.	25 604
Bardney	Lincoln	Parish	1 425	Barling	Essex	Parish	354
Bardon	Leicester	Parish	63	Barlings	Lincoln	Parish	475
Bardsea, Holy Trinity	Lanc.	Ecl. Dis.	272	Barlow, Great	Derby	Chap.	682
Bardsey	Carnarvon	Island	81	Barlow, Little	„	Tnship.	54
Bardsey	York	Parish	318	Barlow Moor	Lancashire	Ecl. Dis.	1 013

Name of Place.	County.	Description.	Population.	Name of Place.	County.	Description.	Population.
Barlow	York.	Tnship.	239	Barnsley, St. Geo.	York	Ecl. Dis.	5 94?
Barmbrough	„	Sub-dis.	5 860	Barnsley, St. John	„	Ecl. Dis.	4 23?
Barmbrough	„	Parish	462	Barnstaple	Devon	District	36 29?
Barmby on the Marsh	„	Tnship.	456	Barnstaple	„	Sub-dis.	10 65?
Barmby on the Moor	„	Parish	537	Barnstaple	„	Parish	8 12?
Barmer	Norfolk	Parish	62	Barnstaple	„	Borough	10 743
Barming	Kent	Parish	589	Barnstaple, St. Mary	„	Ecl. Dis.	2 53?
Barming, West	„	Parish	24	Barnstaple, Trinity	„	Ecl. Dis.	1 855
Barmingham	Suffolk	Parish	489	Barnston	Cheshire	Tnship.	252
Barmouth	Merioneth	Sub-dis.	7 643	Barnston	Essex	Parish	192
Barmston	Durham	Tnship.	475	Barnton	Cheshire	Tnship.	1 219
Barmston	York	Parish	206	Barnton, Christchurch	„	Ecl. Dis.	1 431
Barnack	Northampton, &c.	Sub-dis.	5 692	Barnwell, All Saints	Nrthptn.	Parish	115
Barnack	Northampton	Parish	948	Barnwell, St. Andrew	„	Parish	240
Barnack	„	Tnship.	569	Barnwood	Gloucester	Parish	507
Barnacre w. Bonds	Lancashire	Tnship.	907	Barony	Durham	Tnship.	2 674
Barnard Castle	Durh. & York	Sub-dis.	8 555	Barrasford	Northumberland	Tnship.	215
Barnard Castle	Durham	Tnship.	4 477	Barr, Great	Stafford	Tnship.	1 075
Barnard Castle	„	Town	4 178	Barrington	Cambs	Parish	563
Barnardiston	Suffolk	Parish	280	Barrington, Great	Gloucester	Parish	496
Barnard's Inn	Middlesex	Parish	69	Barrington, Little	„	Parish	151
Barnby in Willows	Notts.	Parish	302	Barrington	Somerset	Parish	501
Barnby Moor	„	Tnship.	245	Barrons Park	Leicester	Hamlet	11
Barnby	Suffolk	Parish	270	Barrow	Cheshire	Parish	623
Barnby	York	Tnship.	247	Barrow upon Trent	Derby.	Parish	526
Barnby upon Don	„	Parish	644	Barrow upon Trent	„	Tnship.	260
Barnby upon Don	„	Tnship.	537	Barrow on Soar	Leicester	District	19 778
Barnes	Surrey	Parish	2 359	Barrow on Soar	„	Sub-dis.	5 144
Barnet	Herts	L. Sub.	7 107	Barrow on Soar	„	Parish	5 621
Barnet	Herts & Middlesex	District	19 128	Barrow on Soar	„	Tnship.	1 800
Barnet	„ „	Sub-dis.	5 466	Barrow on Humber	Lincoln	Parish	2 443
Barnet, Chipping	Herts	Parish	2 989	Barrow	Northumberland	Tnship.	14?
Barnet, East	„	Parish	851	Barrow	Rutland	Hamlet	146
Barnet, Fryern	Middlesex	Parish	3 344	Barrow	Salop	Parish	365
Barnetby-le-Wold	Lincoln	Parish	828	Barrow Gurney	Somerset	Parish	321
Barney	Norfolk	Parish	283	Barrow, North	„	Parish	114
Barnham Broom	„	Parish	481	Barrow, South	„	Parish	140
Barnham	Suffolk	Parish	475	Barrow	Suffolk	Parish	1 030
Barnham	Sussex	Parish	125	Barrowby	Lincoln	Parish	862
Barningham, Little	Norfolk	Parish	273	Barrowden	Rutland & Nhptn.	Sub-dis.	3 887
Barningham Norwood	„	Parish	30	Barrowden	Rutland	Parish	653
Barningham Winter	„	Parish	125	Barrowford	Lancashire	Tnship.	2 880
Barningham	Suffolk	Parish	489	Barrowford, St. Thos.	„	Ecl. Dis.	2 796
Barningham	York	Parish	526	Barry	Glamorgan	Parish	87
Barningham	„	Tnship.	307	Barry	„	Island	21
Barnoldby-le-Beck	Lincoln	Parish	242	Barsby	Leicester	Chap.	290
Barnoldswick	York	Sub-dis.	5 986	Barsham, East	Norfolk	Parish	221
Barnoldswick	„	Parish	3 478	Barsham, North	„	Parish	57
Barnoldswick	„	Tnship.	2 810	Barsham, West	„	Parish	92
Barnsley	Gloucester	Parish	327	Barsham	Suffolk	Parish	239
Barnsley	York	District	45 797	Barstable	Essex	Hund.	15 280
Barnsley	„	Sub-dis.	25 468	Barston	Warwick	Parish	336
Barnsley	„	Tnship.	17 890	Bartestree	Hereford	Chap.	61
Barnsley	„	Town	17 890	Barthomley	Chesh. & Stafford	Parish	3 002

Name of Place.	County.	Description.	Population.	Name of Place.	County.	Description.	Population
rthomley	Cheshire	Tnship.	416	Baschurch	Salop	Sub-dis.	3 435
rtington	,,	Tnship.	63	Baschurch	,,	Parish	1 559
rtlow-End	Essex	Hamlet	224	Baschurch	,,	Tnship.	1 321
rtlow, Great	Cambs	Parish	120	Basford	Cheshire	Tnship.	60
rton in the Clay	Beds	Parish	956	Basford	Notts & Derby	District	73 285
rton Hartshorn	Bucks	Parish	126	Basford	Notts	Sub-dis.	15 935
rton	Cambs	Parish	324	Basford	,,	Parish	12 185
rton	Cheshire	Tnship.	131	Basford, New	,,	Ecl. Dis.	3 241
rton Blount	Derby	Parish	73	Basford	Stafford	Tnship.	428
rton Hill, St.Luke	Gloucester	Ecl. Dis.	2 989	Bashall Eaves	York	Tnship.	251
rton Regis	,,	Hund.	19 853	Basildon	Berks	Parish	712
rton St. Mary	,,	Hamlet	4 335	Basildon	Essex	Chap.	180
rton St. Michael	,,	Hamlet	2 315	Basing	Hants	Parish	1 193
rton & Eastley	Hants	Tithing	253	Basingstoke	,,	Div.	12 790
rton St. Paul	,,	Ecl. Dis.	1 314	Basingstoke	,,	L. Sub.	17 444
rton Stacey	,,	Parish	516	Basingstoke	Hants & Berks	District	17 429
rton, &c.	Hereford	Tnship.	389	Basingstoke	Hants	Sub-dis.	7 784
rton on Irwell	Lancashire	District	39 038	Basingstoke	,,	Parish	4 654
rton	,,	Sub-dis.	14 216	Basingstoke	,,	M. Bor.	4 654
rton on Irwell	,,	Tnship.	14 216	Baslow	Derby	Chap.	785
rton	,,	Ecl. Dis.	886	Bassaleg	Monmouth	Parish	2 169
rton	,,	Tnship.	343	Bassenthwaite	Cumberland	Parish	570
rton in the Beans	Leicester	Tnship.	159	Bassetlaw	Notts	Wapen.	44 348
rton	Lincoln	Sub-dis.	12 599	Bassingbourn	Cambs	Parish	2 213
rton St. Mary	,,	Parish	2 125	Bassingbourn	,,	—	1 933
rton St. Peter	,,	Parish	1 672	Bassingham	Lincoln & Notts	Sub-dis.	3 852
rton upon Humber	,,	Town	3 797	Bassingham	Lincoln	Parish	928
rton Bendish	Norfolk	Parish	484	Bassingthorpe	,,	Parish	154
rton Turf	,,	Parish	379	Bassington	Northumberland	Tnship.	9
rton Earls	Northampton	Parish	1 557	Baston	Lincoln	Parish	787
rton Seagrave	,,	Parish	199	Baswich	Stafford	Parish	1 555
rton in Fabis	Notts	Parish	295	Baswich, &c.	,,	Tnship.	660
rton Westcott	Oxon	Parish	302	Batcombe	Dorset	Parish	184
rton St.David	Somerset	Parish	404	Batcombe	Somerset	Parish	713
rton un. Needwood	Stafford	Tnship.	1 589	Bath and Wells	—	Diocese	422 527
rton, Great	Suffolk	Parish	848	Bath	Somerset	L. Sub.	68 920
rton Mills	,,	Parish	531	Bath	,,	District	68 336
rton on the Heath	Warwick	Parish	184	Bath, Holy Trinity	,,	Ecl. Dis.	7 555
rton	Westmoreland	Parish	1 808	Bath, St. Saviour	,,	Ecl. Dis.	4 107
rton, High	,,	Tnship.	303	Bath	,,	City	52 528
rton	York	Parish	584	Bathampton	,,	Parish	382
rton	,,	Tnship.	507	Bathealton	,,	Parish	135
rton-le-Street	,,	Parish	454	Batheaston	,,	Sub-dis.	6 989
rton-le-Street	,,	Tnship.	184	Batheaston	,,	Parish	1 698
rton-le-Willows	,,	Tnship.	225	Batherton	Cheshire	Tnship.	24
rugh	,,	Tnship.	1 771	Bathford	Somerset	Parish	892
rughs Ambo	,,	Tnship.	318	Bath Forum	,,	Hund.	9 213
rwell	Leicester	Parish	1 613	Bathley	Norfolk	Parish	227
rwell	,,	Tnship.	1 358	Bathley	Notts	Tnship.	234
rwick	Norfolk	Parish	26	Bathwick	Somerset	Sub-dis.	7 132
rwick	Somerset	Parish	458	Bathwick	,,	Parish	5 266
rwick in Elmet	York	Incor.	18 641	Batley	York	Sub-dis.	14 173
rwick in Elmet	,,	Parish	2 374	Batley	,,	Parish	25 278
rwick in Elmet	,,	Tnship.	1 804	Batley	,,	Tnship.	14 173

15

Name of Place.	County.	Description.	Population.	Name of Place.	County.	Description.	Population.
Batley	York ..	Town	7 206	Beaghall ..	York ..	Tnship.	488
Batley Carr, Trinity „ ..		Ecl. Dis.	3 859	Beaksbourne ..	Kent ..	Parish	475
Batsford ..	Gloucester ..	Parish	130	Bealings, Great..	Suffolk ..	Parish	338
Battersby ..	York ..	Tnship.	119	Bealings, Little..	„ ..	Parish	278
Battersea ..	Surrey ..	Sub-dis.	19 600	Beaminster	Dorset & Somerset	District	13 587
Battersea	„ ..	Parish	24 615	Beaminster ..	Dorset ..	Sub-dis.	4 112
Battersea	„ ..	—	19 600	Beaminster ..	„ ..	Parish	2 614
Battersea, St. George „ ..		Ecl. Dis.	3 697	Beamsley ..	York ..	Tnship.	264
Battisford ..	Suffolk ..	Parish	504	Beanley ..	Northumberland	Tnship.	116
Battle	Brecon ..	Parish	118	Beard, Thorpsett, &c.	Derby ..	Tnship.	4 822
Battle	Sussex ..	L. Sub.	11 679	Beard, St. George	„ ..	Ecl. Dis.	4 822
Battle	„ ..	District	12 680	Bearl ..	Northumberland	Tnship.	58
Battle	„ ..	Sub-dis.	5 494	Bearley	Warwick ..	Parish	238
Battle	„ ..	Parish	3 293	Bearsted ..	Kent ..	L. Sub.	43 382
Battle Bridge ..	Middlesex ..	Ecl. Dis.	17 489	Bearsted	„ ..	Parish	638
Battleburn ..	York ..	Hamlet	29	Bearwardcote ..	Derby ..	Tnship.	32
Battlefield ..	Salop ..	Sub-dis.	1 881	Bearwood, St. Kath. ..	Berks	Ecl. Dis.	814
Battlefield ..	„ ..	Parish	81	Beats, Great ..	Lincoln ..	Parish	4
Battlesden ..	Beds ..	Parish	143	Beats, Little	„ ..	Parish	10
Battyeford, Christch. ..	York.	Ecl. Dis.	3 115	Beauchamp-Roothing ..	Essex	Parish	226
Baughurst ..	Hants ..	Parish	563	Beauchief Abbey	Derby ..	Parish	122
Baumber ..	Lincoln ..	Parish	393	Beaudesert ..	Warwick ..	Parish	172
Baunton ..	Gloucester ..	Parish	122	Beaufort	Brecon & Monmouth	Ecl. Dis.	5 880
Bauseley ..	Montgomery.	Tnship.	404	Beaulieu ..	Hants ..	Parish	1 176
Baverstock ..	Wilts ..	Parish	168	Beaumanor ..	Leicester ..	Lib.	137
Bavington, Great	Northmb. ..	Tnship.	61	Beaumaris ..	Anglesey..	Sub-dis.	13 139
Bavington, Little	„ ..	Tnship.	67	Beaumaris ..	„ ..	Parish	2 210
Bawburgh ..	Norfolk ..	Parish	433	Beaumaris	„ ..	Boro.	2 558
Bawdeswell ..	„ ..	Sub-dis.	3 333	Beaumaris, Parl. Dist. of „ ..		Boros.	13 275
Bawdeswell ..	„ ..	Parish	515	Beaumont ..	Cumberland.	Parish	287
Bawdrip ..	Somerset ..	Parish	472	Beaumont w. Moze	Essex ..	Parish	490
Bawdsey ..	Suffolk ..	Parish	426	Beaumont Leys .	Leicester ..	Parish	31
Bawsey ..	Norfolk ..	Parish	32	Beaumont Chase.	Rutland ..	Parish	31
Bawtry ..	York & Notts	Sub-dis.	5 623	Beausall ..	Warwick ..	Hamlet	273
Bawtry ..	York ..	Tnship.	1 011	Beauworth ..	Hants ..	Parish	127
Baxterley ..	Warwick ..	Parish	273	Beaworthy ..	Devon ..	Parish	298
Bayards Leap ..	Lincoln ..	Parish	18	Bebington ..	Cheshire ..	Parish	15 105
Baydon	Wilts ..	Parish	380	Bebington, Higher	„ ..	Tnship.	2 086
Bayfield.. ..	Norfolk ..	Parish	30	Bebington, Lower	„ ..	Tnship.	2 485
Bayford.. ..	Herts ..	Parish	297	Bebside ..	Northumberland	Tnship.	53
Bay Hall, St. John	York	Ecl. Dis.	4 466	Beccles	Suffolk ..	L. Sub.	37 669
Baylham ..	Suffolk ..	Parish	327	Beccles	„ ..	Sub-dis.	7 221
Bayston Hill, Christch.	Salop..	Ecl. Dis.	605	Beccles	„ ..	Parish	4 266
Bayswater, St. Mat.	Middlesex .	Ecl. Dis.	5 513	Beccles	„ ..	M. Bor.	4 266
Bayton	Worcester ..	Parish	447	Beckbury ..	Salop ..	Parish	297
Bayvil	Pembroke ..	Parish	118	Beckenham ..	Kent ..	Parish	2 124
Beachampton ..	Bucks ..	Parish	272	Beckering, Holton	Lincoln ..	Parish	179
Beachley, St. John	Gloucester..	Ecl. Dis.	188	Beckett.. ..	Berks ..	Tithing	23
Beaconsfield ..	Bucks ..	Sub-dis.	3 092	Beckford ..	Gloucester ..	Parish	473
Beaconsfield ..	„ ..	Parish	1 662	Beckham, East..	Norfolk ..	Parish	73
Beadlam ..	York ..	Tnship.	145	Beckham, West..	„ ..	Parish	329
Beadnell	Northumberland	Tnship.	311	Beckingham ..	Lincoln ..	Parish	431
Beadnell .. „ ..		Ecl. Dis.	577	Beckingham ..	Notts ..	Parish	450
Beaford ..	Devon ..	Parish	639	Beckington ..	Somerset ..	Parish	1 036

Name of Place.	County.	Description.	Population.	Name of Place.	County.	Description.	Population.
Beckley	Oxon ..	Parish	749	Beechamwell ..	Norfolk ..	Parish	356
Beckley	,, ..	—	329	Beech Hill ..	Berks ..	Tithing	260
Beckley	Sussex ..	Sub-dis.	5 574	Beeching Stoke..	Wilts ..	Parish	180
Beckley	,, ..	Parish	1 252	Beeding, Lower .	Sussex ..	Parish	1 149
Beck Row ..	Suffolk ..	Watch	684	Beeding, Upper .	,, ..	Parish	553
Becontree ..	Essex ..	Hund.	73 023	Becdon	Berks ..	Parish	317
Bedale	York ..	District	8 650	Beeford	York ..	Parish	1 006
Bedale	,, ..	Sub-dis.	6 000	Beeford	,, ..	Tnship.	808
Bedale	,, ..	Parish	2 860	Beeley	Derby ..	Tnship.	420
Bedale	,, ..	Tnship.	1 157	Beelsby	Lincoln ..	Parish	181
Bedburn, North .	Durham ..	Tnship.	1 771	Beenham-Vallence	Berks ..	Parish	505
Bedburn, South .	,, ..	Tnship.	332	Beer	Devon ..	Tithing	1 157
Beddgelert ..	Carn. & Mer.	Parish	1 375	Beer-Croeombe..	Somerset ..	Parish	175
Beddgelert ..	Carnarvon..	Hamlet	1 066	Beerferris ..	Devon ..	Parish	2 847
Beddingham ..	Sussex ..	Parish	334	Beer-Hackett ..	Dorset ..	Parish	96
Beddington ..	Surrey ..	Parish	1 556	Beerhall	,, ..	Tithing	22
Beddington ..	,, ..	—	573	Becsby-in-Marsh	Lincoln ..	Parish	174
Bedfield.. ..	Suffolk ..	Parish	415	Beeston ..	Cheshire ..	Tnship.	355
Bedfont, East ..	Middlesex ..	Parish	1 150	Beeston All Saints	Norfolk ..	Parish	615
Bedfordshire ..	.. ..	County	135 287	Beeston Regis ..	,, ..	Parish	196
Bedford.. ..	Beds.	L. Sub.	18 079	Beeston, St. Andrew	,, ..	Parish	37
Bedford.. ..	,,	District	38 072	Beeston, St. Lawrence	,, ..	Parish	50
Bedford & Cardington ..	,,	Sub-dis.	11 734	Beeston ..	Notts ..	Parish	3 195
Bedford & Kempston ..	,,	Sub-dis.	11 921	Beeston ..	York ..	Tnship.	2 547
Bedford	,,	Borough	13 413	Beetham ..	Westmoreland	Parish	1 510
Bedford, Holy Trinity ..	,,	Ecl. Dis.	3 044	Beetham	,, ..	Tnship.	776
Bedford Circus ..	Devon ..	Precinct	145	Beetley	Norfolk ..	Parish	363
Bedford.. ..	Lancaster ..	Tnship.	6 558	Begbroke ..	Oxon ..	Parish	104
Bedford.. ..	,, ..	Ecl. Dis.	6 558	Begelly	Pembroke ..	Sub-dis.	4 313
Bedford New Town	Middlesex .	Ecl. Dis.	7 768	Begelly	,, ..	Parish	1 311
Bedhampton ..	Hants ..	Parish	576	Begelly	,, ..	Hamlet	776
Bedingfield ..	Suffolk ..	Parish	321	Beighton ..	Derby & York	Sub-dis.	3 279
Bedingham ..	Norfolk ..	Parish	288	Beighton ..	Derby ..	Parish	1 284
Bedlington	Northumberland	Sub-dis.	15 577	Beighton ..	Norfolk ..	Parish	365
Bedlington ..	,,	Parish	8 328	Belaugh ..	,, ..	Parish	154
Bedlingtonshire .	,,	Ward	8 328	Belbroughton ..	Worcester ..	Sub-dis.	4 867
Bedminster ..	Somerset ..	L. Sub.	41 257	Belbroughton ..	,, ..	Parish	1 995
Bedminster ..	,, ..	District	41 257	Belby	York ..	Tnship.	44
Bedminster ..	,, ..	Sub-dis.	22 346	Belchamp-Otton	Essex ..	Parish	375
Bedminster ..	,, ..	Parish	22 346	Belchamp, St. Paul	,, ..	Parish	832
St. Luke ..	Som. & Glouc.	Ecl. Dis.	6 425	Belchamp Walter	,, ..	Parish	708
St. Paul ..	Somerset ..	Ecl. Dis.	4 416	Belchford ..	Lincoln ..	Parish	638
Bedstone ..	Salop ..	Parish	164	Belford ..	Northumberland	District	6 260
Bedwas ..	Monm. & Glam.	Parish	1 081	Belford	,, ..	Sub-dis.	6 260
Bedwas, Lower ..	Monmouth ..	Hamlet	422	Belford	,, ..	Parish	1 724
Bedwas, Upper..	,, ..	Hamlet	597	Belford	,, ..	Tnship.	1 067
Bedwelty ..	,, ..	L. Sub.	55 461	Belgrave ..	Leicester ..	Parish	2 808
Bedwelty ..	,, ..	District	47 565	Belgrave ..	,, ..	Tnship.	1 510
Bedwelty ..	,, ..	Parish	31 510	Belgrave ..	Middlesex ..	Sub-dis.	55 113
Bedwin, Great ..	Wilts ..	Parish	2 263	Bellasize ..	York ..	Tnship.	281
Bedwin, Little ..	,, ..	Parish	496	Bellbank (Bewcasl. P.)	Cumbd.	Tnship.	415
Bedworth ..	Warwick ..	Parish	5 656	Bellbank (Stapleton P.)	,,	Tnship.	111
Bedworth	,, ..	Town	3 968	Bellchalwell ..	Dorset ..	Parish	158
Beeby	Leicester ..	Parish	119	Belleau	Lincoln ..	Parish	214

Name of Place.	County.	Description.	Population.	Name of Place.	County.	Description.	Population.
Belleau	Lincoln	Tnship.	114	Bentham	York	Sub-dis.	5 436
Bellerby	York	Tnship.	391	Bentham	,,	Parish	3 589
Bellerby	,,	Ecl. Dis.	391	Bentham	,,	Tnship.	2 342
Bellingham	Northumberland	District	7 080	Bentley, Great	Essex	Parish	1 033
Bellingham	,,	Sub-dis.	4 247	Bentley, Little	,,	Parish	458
Bellingham	,,	Parish	1 662	Bentley	Hants	Parish	721
Bellingham	,,	Tnship.	866	Bentley	Stafford	Tnship.	346
Bellister	,,	Tnship.	117	Bentley	Suffolk	Parish	453
Belmont	Durham	Ecl. Dis.	3 337	Bentley	Warwick	Hamlet	233
Belmont, St. Peter	Lancaster	Ecl. Dis.	1 033	Bentley Pauncefoot	Worcester.	Tnship.	238
Belper	Derby	District	51 711	Bentley	York	Hamlet	57
Belper	,,	Sub-dis.	9 509	Bentley w. Arksey	,,	Parish	1 099
Belper	,,	Tnship.	9 509	Bentworth	Hants	Parish	647
Belper	,,	Ecl. Dis.	6 106	Benwell	Northumberland	Tnship.	1 771
Belper	,,	Town.	9 509	Benwell, St. James	,,	Ecl. Dis.	4 323
Belsay	Northumberland	Tnship.	384	Benwick	Cambs.	Hamlet	773
Belstead	Suffolk	Parish	292	Beoley	Worcester	Parish	682
Belstone	Devon	Parish	181	Bepton	Sussex	Parish	211
Beltisloe	Lincoln	Wap.	8 289	Berden	Essex	Parish	414
Belton	Leicester	Parish	781	Berechurch	,,	Parish	112
Belton, Grantham	Lincoln	Parish	142	Bere Regis	Dorset	Sub-dis.	4 749
Belton, Epworth	,,	Parish	1 871	Bere Regis	,,	Parish	1 624
Belton	Rutland	Parish	441	Bere Regis	,,	—	1 189
Belton	Suffolk	Parish	516	Bergholt, West	Essex	Parish	906
Belvoir	Leicester	L. Sub.	4 553	Bergholt, East	Suffolk	Parish	1 397
Belvoir	,,	Parish	171	Berkeley	Gloucester	Hund.	24 453
Bembridge	Hants	Ecl. Dis.	783	Berkeley	,,	Sub-dis.	5 396
Bemersley	Stafford	Tnship.	258	Berkeley	,,	Parish	4 316
Bempstone	Somerset	Hund.	8 383	Berkeley	,,	Old Bor.	1 011
Bempton	York	Parish	346	Berkeswell	Warwick	Parish	1 624
Benacre	Suffolk	Parish	212	Berkhampstead	Herts, &c.	District	13 204
Benefield	Northampton	Parish	527	Berkhampstead	Herts & Bucks	Sub-dis.	5 733
Benenden	Kent	Parish	1 662	**Berkhampstead**	Herts.	Town	3 631
Benfieldside	Durham	Tnship.	4 026	Berkhampstead, Great	,,	Parish	3 585
Benfieldside	,,	Ecl. Dis.	9 223	Berkhampstead, Little	,,	Parish	450
Benfleet, North	Essex	Parish	285	Berkhampstead, St. Mary	,,	Parish	1 638
Benfleet, South	,,	Parish	573	Berkley	Somerset	Parish	386
Bengeo	Herts	Parish	1 791	Berkshire		County	176 256
Bengeworth	Worcester	Parish	1 259	Bermondsey	Surrey	District	58 355
Benhall	Suffolk	Parish	678	Bermondsey	,,	Parish	58 355
Benningbrough	York.	Tnship.	88	Ward No. 1	,,	Ward	15 408
Benningholme & Grange	,,	Tnship.	106	Ward No. 2	,,	Ward	16 011
Bennington	Herts	Parish	637	Ward No. 3	,,	Ward	12 482
Bennington	Lincoln	Sub-dis.	6 572	Ward No. 4	,,	Ward	14 454
Bennington	,,	Parish	588	Christchurch	,,	Ecl. Dis.	5 672
Bennington	Lincoln & Notts	Sub-dis.	4 666	St. James	,,	Ecl. Dis.	19 339
Bennington, Grange	Lincoln	Parish	13	St. Paul	,,	Ecl. Dis.	9 770
Bennington, Long	,,	Parish	1 066	Berners Roothing	Essex	Parish	94
Benniworth	,,	Parish	431	Berrick Salome	Oxon	Parish	141
Benridge	Northumberland	Tnship.	49	Berrier & Murrah	Cumberland.	Tnship.	109
Benson	Oxon	Parish	1 169	Berriew	Montgomery.	Parish	2 155
Benson	,,	—	1 157	Berrington	Salop	Parish	772
Bentfield	Essex	Hamlet	529	Berrington	Worcester	Hamlet	234
Benthall	Salop	Parish	499	Berrow	Somerset	Parish	489

Name of Place.	County.	Description.	Population.	Name of Place.	County.	Description.	Population.
Berrow	Worcester ..	Parish	453	Betton Strange ..	Salop ..	Ecl. Dis.	70
Berrynarbor ..	Devon ..	Parish	775	Bettws	Carmarthen.	Parish	1 547
Berry Pomeroy..	,, ..	Parish	1 065	Bettws	Glamorgan .	Parish	371
Bersham ..	Denbigh ..	Tnship.	3 073	Bettws	Monmouth..	Parish	84
Bersted, South ..	Sussex ..	Parish	3 128	Bettws	Montgomery.	Parish	730
Bersted, South ..	,, ..	—	605	Bettws	Salop ..	Parish	520
Berwick ..	Carmarthen.	Hamlet	1 809	Bettwsabergele ..	Denbigh ..	Parish	838
Berwick Street..	Middlesex ..	Sub-dis.	10 607	Bettwsbleddrws .	Cardigan ..	Parish	222
Berwick	Northumberland	District	21 862	Bettwsclyro ..	Radnor ..	Chap.	188
Berwick on Tweed.	,,	Sub-dis.	14 027	Bettwsdisserth ..	,, ..	Parish	130
Berwick on Tweed.	,,	L. Sub.	13 265	Bettwsevan ..	Cardigan ..	Parish	419
Berwick on Tweed	,,	Parish	8 613	Bettwsgarmon ..	Carnarvon ..	Parish	94
Berwick St. Mary	,,	Ecl. Dis.	2 062	Bettwsgwerfilgoch	Merth., &c. .	Parish	258
Berwick on Tweed	,,	Borough	13 265	Bettwsleiki ..	Cardigan ..	Parish	349
Berwick Hill ..	,,	Tnship.	98	Bettwsnewydd ..	Monmouth..	Parish	129
Berwick, Little..	Salop ..	Ecl. Dis.	186	Bettwsycoed ..	Carnarvon..	Sub-dis.	2 735
Berwick.. ..	Sussex ..	Parish	169	Bettwsycoed ..	,, ..	Parish	509
Berwick Bassett .	Wilts ..	Parish	171	Bettwsynrhös ..	Denbigh ..	Parish	838
Berwick, St. James	,, ..	Parish	252	Bevercoates ..	Notts ..	Parish	48
Berwick, St. John	,, ..	Parish	499	Beverley ..	York ..	District	21 029
Berwick, St. Leonard	,, ..	Parish	40	Beverley ..	,, ..	Sub-dis.	13 007
Bescaby ..	Leicester ..	Parish	26	Beverley .. .. {	,,	M. Bor.	9 654
Besford.. ..	Worcester ..	Chap.	164			P. Bor.	10 868
Besselsleigh ..	Berks ..	Parish	92	Beverley Park ..	,, ..	Hamlet	259
Bessingby ..	York ..	Parish	70	Beverstone ..	Gloucester ..	Parish	170
Bessingham ..	Norfolk ..	Parish	153	Bevington ..	Lancaster ..	Ecl. Dis.	14 381
Besthorpe ..	,, ..	Parish	554	Bewaldeth, &c...	Cumberland .	Tnship.	95
Besthorpe ..	Notts ..	Tnship.	338	Bewcastle ..	,,	Parish	1 091
Beswick.. ..	Lancaster ..	Parish	881	Bewcastle ..	,,	Tnship.	152
Beswick.. ..	York ..	Tnship.	252	Bewdley ..	Worcester, &c.	Sub-dis.	4 142
Betchton ..	Cheshire ..	Tnship.	798	Bewdley .. {	Worcester	M. Bor.	2 905
Betchworth ..	Surrey ..	Parish	1 389			P. Bor.	7 084
Bethersden ..	Kent ..	Parish	1 124	Far Forest	Worc. & Salop.	Ecl. Dis.	655
Bethnal Green ..	Middlesex ..	District	105 101	St. Anne	Worcester ..	Ecl. Dis.	1 143
Bethnal Green ..	,, ..	Parish	105 101	Bewerley ..	York ..	Tnship.	1 297
1. East Ward.	,, ..	Ward	21 802	Bewick, New	Northumberland	Tnship.	78
2. North Ward	,, ..	Ward	19 874	Bewick, Old ..	,,	Tnship.	204
3. West Ward	,, ..	Ward	30 836	Bexhill ..	Sussex ..	Sub-dis.	4 512
4. South Ward	,, ..	Ward	32 589	Bexhill ..	,, ..	Parish	2 084
St. Andrew ..	,, ..	Ecl. Dis.	9 913	Bexhill	,,	—	2 011
St. Bartholomew	,, ..	Ecl. Dis.	9 922	Bexhill, St. Mark	,,	Ecl. Dis.	682
St. James the Great,	,, ..	Ecl. Dis.	4 269	Bexley ..	Kent ..	Sub-dis.	13 026
St. James the Less	,, ..	Ecl. Dis.	5 291	Bexley	,, ..	Parish	4 944
St. John ..	,, ..	Ecl. Dis.	10 275	Bexton ..	Cheshire ..	Tnship.	66
St. Jude ..	,, ..	Ecl. Dis.	14 039	Bexwell ..	Norfolk ..	Parish	94
St. Matthias ..	,, ..	Ecl. Dis.	9 369	Beynhurst ..	Berks ..	Hund.	3 407
St. Peter ..	,, ..	Ecl. Dis.	6 735	Beyton ..	Suffolk ..	Parish	360
St. Philip ..	,, ..	Ecl. Dis.	11 397	Bibury ..	Gloucester ..	Sub-dis.	5 642
St. Simon Zelotes	,, ..	Ecl. Dis.	6 216	Bibury	,, ..	Parish	1 080
St. Thomas ..	,, ..	Ecl. Dis.	8 315	Bibury	,,	Tnship.	371
Betley ..	Stafford ..	Parish	850	Bicester ..	Oxon ..	L. Sub.	15 903
Betshanger ..	Kent ..	Parish	43	Bicester ..	Oxon & Bucks	District	15 555
Bettiscombe ..	Dorset ..	Parish	76	Bicester ..	,, ,,	Sub-dis.	8 115
Bettisfield ..	Flint ..	Tnship.	361	Bicester ..	Oxon ..	Parish	3 049

Name of Place.	County.	Description.	Population.	Name of Place.	County.	Description.	Population.
Bicester	Oxon	Town	2 978	Biggin	York	Tnship.	14?
Bicester Kings End	„	Tnship.	338	Biggleswade	Beds	Hund.	12 37?
Bicester MarketEnd	„	Tnship.	2 711	Biggleswade	„	L. Sub.	25 58?
Bickenhall	Somerset	Parish	229	Biggleswade	„	District	25 39?
Bickenhall	Warwick	Parish	744	Biggleswade	„	Sub-dis.	16 11?
Bicker	Lincoln	Parish	832	Biggleswade	„	Parish	4 63?
Bickerstaffe	Lancaster	Sub-dis.	2 826	**Biggleswade**	„	Town	4 02?
Bickerstaffe	„	Tnship.	1 637	Bighton	Hants	Parish	29?
Bickerstaffe	„	Ecl. Dis.	1 637	Biglands & Gamblesby	Cumbd.	Tnship.	20?
Bickerton	Cheshire	Tnship.	379	Bignall End	Stafford	Tnship.	737
Bickerton, Trinity	„	Ecl. Dis.	1 357	Bignor	Sussex	Parish	167
Bickerton	Northumberland	Tnship.	22	Bilborough	Notts	Parish	232
Bickerton	York	Tnship.	149	Bilbrough	York	Parish	216
Bickington	Devon	Parish	294	Bildeston	Suffolk	Parish	788
Bickington, High	„	Parish	738	Bilham	York	Tnship.	68
Bickleigh, Plympton	„	Parish	402	Billericay	Essex	District	15 031
Bickleigh, Silverton	„	Parish	254	Billericay	„	Hamlet	1 390
Bickley	Cheshire	Tnship.	397	Billericay	„	Ecl. Dis.	1 390
Bickmarsh, &c.	Warwick	Hamlet	50	Billesdon	Leicester	District	7 272
Bicknoller	Somerset	Parish	345	Billesdon	„	Sub-dis.	7 272
Bicknor, English	Gloucester	Parish	592	Billesdon	„	Parish	1 085
Bicknor, Welsh	Hereford	Parish	80	Billesdon	„	Tnship.	909
Bicknor	Kent	Parish	53	Billesley	Warwick	Parish	35
Bicton	Devon	Parish	166	Billing, Great	Northampton	Parish	425
Bicton, Trinity	Salop	Ecl. Dis.	569	Billing, Little	„	Parish	76
Bidborough	Kent	Parish	210	Billingborough	Lincoln	Parish	1 149
Biddenden	„	Parish	1 412	Billinge Chapel End	Lancaster	Tnship.	2 015
Biddenham	Beds	Parish	350	Billinge Higher End	„	Tnship.	1 051
Biddestone, St. Nich.	Wilts	Parish	407	Billingford, Bawdeswell	Norfk.	Parish	354
Biddestone, St. Peter	„	Parish	34	Billingford, Diss	„	Parish	199
Biddick, South	Durham	Tnship.	48	Billingham	Durham	Parish	2 166
Biddisham	Somerset	Parish	147	Billingham	„	Tnship.	931
Biddlesden	Bucks	Parish	169	Billinghay	Lincoln	Sub-dis.	5 423
Biddlestone	Northumberland	Tnship.	198	Billinghay	„	Parish	2 247
Biddulph	Stafford	Parish	3 468	Billinghay	„	Tnship.	1 403
Bideford	Devon	L. Sub.	17 871	Billingley	York	Tnship.	192
Bideford	„	District	17 790	Billingshurst	Sussex	Sub-dis.	4 245
Bideford	„	Sub-dis.	5 851	Billingshurst	„	Parish	1 495
Bideford	„	Parish	5 742	Billingside	Durham	Tnship.	10
Bideford	„	M. Bor.	5 742	Billingsley	Salop	Parish	144
Bidford	Warwick	Sub-dis.	2 749	Billington	Beds	Hamlet	484
Bidford	„	Parish	1 565	Billington	Lancaster	Sub-dis.	1 717
Bidstone	Cheshire	Parish	2 154	Billington	„	Tnship.	1 038
Bidstone w. Ford	„	Tnship.	282	Billockby	Norfolk	Parish	46
Bielby	York	Tnship.	268	Bilney, East	„	Parish	198
Bierley, North	„	Union	85 775	Bilney, West	„	Parish	253
Bierley, North	„	Tnship.	12 500	Bilsborrow	Lancaster	Tnship.	176
Bierton w. Broughton	Bucks	Parish	691	Bilsby	Lincoln	Parish	572
Bieston	Denbigh	Tnship.	104	Bilsdale Midcable	York	Chap.	738
Bigbury	Devon	Parish	497	Bilsdale West Side	„	Tnship.	162
Bigby	Lincoln	Parish	249	Bilsington	Kent	Parish	360
Bigges Quarter	Northumberland	Tnship.	259	Bilsthorpe	Notts	Parish	197
Biggin	Derby	Tnship.	133	Bilston	Stafford	Sub-dis.	24 364
Biggin, St. Thomas	„	Ecl. Dis.	399	Bilston	„	Tnship.	24 364

Name of Place.	County.	Description.	Population.	Name of Place.	County.	Description.	Population.
Bilston St. Leonard	Stafford	Ecl. Dis.	7 457	Birdforth	York	Wapen.	14 072
Bilston St. Luke	,,	Ecl. Dis.	4 902	Birdforth	,,	Tnship	40
Bilston St. Mary	,,	Ecl. Dis.	9 040	Birdforth	,,	L. Sub.	14 540
Bilstone	Leicester	Tnship.	116	Birdham	Sussex	Parish	436
Bilton	Warwick	Parish	1 096	Birdingbury	Warwick	Parish	184
Bilton w. Harrogate	York	Tnship.	4 563	Birdsall	York	Parish	355
Bilton	,,	Ecl. Dis.	407	Birkby	Cumberland.	Tnship.	157
Bilton, Skirlaugh	,,	Tnship.	102	Birkby	York	Parish	298
Bilton	,,	Sub-dis.	1 493	Birkby	,,	Tnship.	87
Bilton	,,	Parish	926	Birkdale	Lancaster	Tnship.	1 286
Bilton, Tadcaster	,,	Tnship.	242	Birkenhead	Cheshire	District	61 420
Binbrooke	Lincoln	Sub-dis.	4 468	Birkenhead	,,	Sub-dis.	36 212
Binbrooke	,,	Parish	1 334	Birkenhead	,,	P.Chap.	36 212
Binchester	Durham	Tnship.	33	Birkenhead	,,	P. Bor.	51 649
Bincombe	Dorset	Parish	194	Holy Trinity	,,	Ecl. Dis.	15 319
Binderton	Sussex	Parish	109	St. Anne	,,	Ecl. Dis.	2 590
Binegar	Somerset	Parish	302	St. John	,,	Ecl. Dis.	5 573
Binfield	Berks	Parish	1 371	St. Paul	,,	Ecl. Dis.	3 936
Binfield	Oxon	Hund.	9 598	Birkenshaw	York	Ecl. Dis.	3 633
Bingfield	Northumberland	Tnship.	93	Birker & Austhwaite	Cumberld.	Tnship.	114
Bingham	Notts	Wapen.	13 553	Birkin	York	Parish	821
Bingham	,,	L. Sub.	13 553	Birkin	,,	Tnship.	168
Bingham	Notts & Leicester	District	15 670	Birley	Hereford	Parish	190
Bingham	,, ,,	Sub-dis.	7 879	Birling	Kent	Parish	662
Bingham	Notts	Parish	1 918	Birling	Northumberland	Tnship.	83
Bingley	York	Parish	15 367	Birlingham	Worcester	Parish	353
Bingley	,,	Sub-dis.	15 367	Birmingham	Warwick	L. Sub.	334 418
Bingley	,,	Town	5 238	Birmingham	,,	District	212 621
Bingley w. M'klethwaite	,,	Tnship.	13 254	Birmingham	,,	Parish	212 621
Binham	Norfolk	Parish	512	**Birmingham** *(1868)* 362 296	,,	Borough	296 076
Binley	Warwick	Parish	196	All Saints	,,	Ecl. Dis.	11 469
Binnington	York	Tnship.	90	St. Barnabas	,,	Ecl. Dis.	6 982
Binsey	Oxon	Parish	67	St. Bartholomew	,,	Ecl. Dis.	10 281
Binstead	Hants	Parish	486	St. George	,,	Ecl. Dis.	17 138
Binsted	,,	Sub-dis.	4 866	St. John, Ladywood	,,	Ecl. Dis.	9 389
Binsted	,,	Parish	1 195	St. Jude	,,	Ecl. Dis.	4 810
Binsted	Sussex	Parish	110	St. Luke	,,	Ecl. Dis.	19 623
Binton	Warwick	Parish	230	St. Mark	,,	Ecl. Dis.	10 899
Bintree	Norfolk	Parish	406	St. Mary	,,	Ecl. Dis.	7 023
Birch	Essex	Parish	940	St. Matthias	,,	Ecl. Dis.	10 934
Birch, Little	Hereford	Parish	336	St. Paul	,,	Ecl. Dis.	16 817
Birch, Much	,,	Parish	496	St. Peter	,,	Ecl. Dis.	4 356
Birch in Rusholme	Lancaster	Ecl. Dis.	2 043	St. Stephen	,,	Ecl. Dis.	16 333
Birch, St. Mary	,,	Ecl. Dis.	3 773	St. Thomas	,,	Ecl. Dis.	27 417
Bircham, Great	Norfolk	Parish	489	Birstal	York	Parish	43 505
Bircham Newton	,,	Parish	118	Birstall	Leicester	Chap.	405
Bircham Tofts	,,	Parish	169	Birstwith	York	Tnship.	655
Birchanger	Essex	Parish	358	Birstwith	,,	Ecl. Dis.	640
Birches	Cheshire	Tnship.	9	Birthorpe	Lincoln	Hamlet	65
Birchington	Kent	Parish	813	Birtle	Lancaster	Sub-dis.	4 758
Bircholt	,,	Parish	30	Birtle	,,	Ecl. Dis.	2 135
Birchover	Derby	Tnship.	51	Birtle w. Bamford	,,	Tnship.	2 350
Birdall, &c.	York	Tnship.	87	Birtles	Cheshire	Tnship.	73
Birdbrook	Essex	Parish	643	Birtley	Durham	Tnship.	2 246

21

Name of Place.	County.	Description.	Population.	Name of Place.	County.	Description.	Population.
Birtley ..	.. Durham ..	Ecl. Dis.	3 888	Bishopstone	.. Wilts ..	Sub-dis.	4 904
Birtley ..	Northumberland	Parish	404	Bishopstone ..	„ ..	Parish	716
Birts Morton ..	Worcester ..	Parish	289	Bishopstone ..	„ ..	Parish	685
Bisbrooke ..	Rutland ..	Parish	266	Bishop Stortford	Herts ..	L. Sub.	8 479
Biscathorpe ..	Lincoln ..	Parish	90	Bishop Stortford	„ ..	District	20 212
Bisham..	.. Berks ..	Parish	665	Bishop Stortford	„ ..	Sub-dis.	7 982
Bishampton ..	Worcester ..	Parish	469	Bishop Stortford	„ ..	Parish	5 390
Bishop Auckland	Durham ..	Sub-dis.	34 878	**Bishop Stortford**	„ ..	Town	4 673
Bishop Auckland	„ ..	Tnship.	7 279	Bishopstrow ..	Wilts ..	Parish	268
Bishop Auckland	„ ..	Town	6 480	Bishops Waltham	Hants ..	Sub-dis.	3 267
Bishop Burton..	York ..	Parish	499	Bishops Waltham	„ ..	Parish	2 267
Bishopdale ..	„ ..	Tnship.	87	Bishops Wood, All Saints	Hereford & Gloucester.	Ecl. Dis.	403
Bishop-Middleham	Durham ..	Parish	2 272				
Bishop-Middleham	„ ..	Tnship.	432	Bishops Wood, St. John	Staff.	Ecl. Dis.	588
Bishop Monkton.	York ..	Tnship.	444	Bishopsworth, St. Peter	Som. ..	Ecl. Dis.	1 606
Bishop Morley's Col.	Hants ..	Parish	25	Bishop Thornton	York ..	Tnship.	541
Bishop Norton ..	Lincoln ..	Parish	459	Bishopthorpe ..	„ ..	Parish	452
Bishop Norton ..	„ ..	Tnship.	364	Bishopton ..	Durham ..	Parish	448
Bishop Ryder's Ch.	Warwick..	Ecl. Dis.	9 346	Bishopton ..	„ ..	Tnship.	342
Bishopsbourne ..	Kent ..	Parish	416	Bishopton ..	York ..	Tnship.	81
Bishops Cannings	Wilts ..	Sub-Dis.	3 812	Bp. Wearmouth North	Durham	Sub-dis.	23 749
Bishops Cannings	„ ..	Parish	4 062	Bp. Wearmouth South	„	Sub-dis.	25 083
Bishops Cannings	„ ..	—	1 109	Bishop Wearmouth	„	Parish	50 541
Bishops Castle ..	Salop ..	L. Sub.	1 778	Bishop Wearmouth	„	Tnship.	45 673
Bishops Castle ..	Salop & Mont.	Sub-dis.	2 924	Bp. Wearmouth Pans	„	Tnship.	272
Bishops Castle ..	Salop ..	Parish	2 083	Bp. Wearmouth, St. Thos.	„	Ecl. Dis.	7 413
Bishops Cleeve..	Gloucester ..	Parish	1 970	Bishop Wilton ..	York ..	Parish	910
Bishops Cleeve..	„ ..	Tnship.	703	Bishop Wilton, &c.	„ ..	Tnship.	658
Bishops Fonthill	Wilts ..	Parish	187	Bishton ..	.. Monmouth ..	Parish	188
Bishops Frome	Heref. & Worc.	Sub-dis.	4 439	Bisley ..	.. Gloucester ..	Hund.	18 483
Bishops Frome..	Hereford ..	Parish	1 014	Bisley ..	.. „ ..	Sub-dis.	4 692
Bishops Frome..	„ ..	Tnship.	850	Bisley ..	.. „ ..	Parish	4 692
Bishops Hatfield.	Herts ..	Parish	3 871	Bisley ..	.. Surrey ..	Parish	313
Bishops Hull ..	Somerset ..	Parish	1 614	Bispham ..	.. Lancaster ..	Parish	4 344
Bishopside ..	York ..	Tnship.	2 052	Bispham w. Norbreck	„ ..	Tnship.	437
Bishops Itchington	Warwick ..	Parish	598	Bispham ..	.. „ ..	Tnship.	277
Bishops Lavington	Wilts ..	Parish	1 589	Bistree ..	.. Flint ..	Tnship.	1 733
Bishops Lavington	„ ..	—	974	Bistree ..	.. „ ..	Ecl. Dis.	2 347
Bishops Lydeard.	Somerset ..	Sub-dis.	4 030	Bitchfield	.. Lincoln ..	Parish	159
Bishops Lydeard.	„ ..	Parish	1 459	Bitchfield	Northumberld.	Tnship.	26
Bishops Nympton	Devon ..	Parish	1 198	Bittadon ..	.. Devon ..	Parish	65
Bishops Offlow ..	Stafford ..	Tnship.	200	Bittering, Little .	Norfolk ..	Parish	30
Bishops Palace ..	Lincoln ..	Parish	7	Bitterley ..	.. Salop ..	Parish	972
Bishops Sutton..	Hants ..	Parish	537	Bitterne & Pollack	Hants ..	Tithings	1 733
Bishops Tachbrook	Warwick..	Parish	603	Bitterne, Holy Saviour	„ ..	Ecl. Dis.	1 603
Bishops Tachbrook	„ ..	Tnship.	540	Bitterscote ..	Stafford ..	Liberty	62
Bishops Tawton	Devon ..	Sub-dis.	6 307	Bittesby ..	.. Leicester ..	Liberty	12
Bishops Tawton	„ ..	Parish	1 857	Bitteswell	.. „ ..	Parish	438
Bishopsteignton	„ ..	Parish	974	Bitton ..	Glouc. & Som.	Sub-dis.	5 071
Bishops Stoke ..	Hants ..	Parish	1 390	Bitton ..	.. Gloucester ..	Parish	9 630
Bishopston ..	Glamorgan .	Parish	418	Bitton ..	.. „ ..	—	2 537
Bishopstone ..	Hereford ..	Parish	288	Bix ..	.. Oxon ..	Parish	392
Bishopstone ..	Monmouth ..	Parish	188	Bixley ..	.. Norfolk ..	Parish	161
..hopstone ..	Sussex ..	Parish	322	Blaby ..	.. Leicester ..	District	14 171

Name of Place.	County.	Description.	Population.	Name of Place.	County.	Description.	Population.
Blaby	Leicester	Parish	1 998	Blackwell	Derby	Tnship.	37
Blaby	"	Tnship.	1 023	Blackwell	Durham	Tnship.	336
Blackawton	Devon	Sub-dis.	2 571	Blackwell	Worcester	Hamlet	203
Blackawton	"	Parish	1 229	Blackwood, &c.	Stafford	Tnship.	590
Blackborough	"	Parish	76	Blacon w. Crabhall	Cheshire	Tnship.	69
Blackbourn	Suffolk	Hund.	15 703	Bladon	Oxon	Parish	666
Blackbourton	Oxon	Parish	269	Bladon	"	—	395
Blackburn	Lancashire	Hund.	188 129	Blaenaeron	Cardigan	Tnship.	276
Blackburn	"	L. Sub.	286 955	Blaenavon	Monmouth	Sub-dis.	7 114
Blackburn	"	District	119 942	Blaenavon	"	Ecl. Dis.	5 876
Blackburn	"	Sub-dis.	63 126	Blaencaron	Cardigan	Tnship.	99
Blackburn	"	Parish	110 349	Blaengwrach	Glamorgan	Chap.	280
Blackburn	"	Tnship.	63 126	Blaenhonddan	"	Hamlet	1 661
Blackburn	"	Borough	63 126	Blaenpenal	Cardigan	Chap.	522
Christchurch	"	Ecl. Dis.	6 642	Blaenporth	"	Parish	732
Holy Trinity	"	Ecl. Dis.	4 560	Blagdon	Somerset	Sub-dis.	5 629
St. John	"	Ecl. Dis.	8 261	Blagdon	"	Parish	1 083
St. Michl.& All Angels	"	Ecl. Dis.	6 269	Blagrave	Berks	Tithing	196
St. Paul	"	Ecl. Dis.	9 718	Blainey w. Duffryn	Brecon	Parcel	3 045
St. Peter	"	Ecl. Dis.	8 244	Blaisdon	Gloucester	Parish	282
Black Callerton	Northumberland	Tnship.	172	Blakemere	Hereford	Parish	175
Blackcarts w. Ryehill	"	Parish	19	Blakeney, All Saints	Gloucester	Ecl. Dis.	1 079
Blackden	Cheshire	Tnship.	157	Blakeney	Norfolk	Parish	961
Blackenhurst	Worcester	Hund.	3 643	Blakenhall	Cheshire	Tnship.	236
Blackford	Somerset	Parish	164	Blakenham, Great	Suffolk	Parish	291
Blackford	"	Ecl. Dis.	677	Blakenham, Little	"	Parish	146
Blackfordby	Leicester	Chap.	645	Blakesley	Northampton	Parish	777
Blackfriars	"	Parish	1 173	Blakesley	"	—	523
Blackheath, All Saints	Kent	Ecl. Dis.	1 827	Blanchland	Northumberland	Tnship.	474
Blackheath	"	L. Sub.	187 696	Blandford	Dorset	L. Sub.	13 414
Blackheath	Surrey	Hund.	10 473	Blandford	"	Division	12 211
Blackheddon	Northumberland	Tnship.	68	Blandford	"	District	14 827
Blackland	Wilts	Parish	54	Blandford	"	Sub-dis.	8 542
Blackley	Lancashire	Sub-dis.	4 939	Blandford	"	M. Bor.	1 521
Blackley	"	Tnship.	4 112	Blandford	"	Town	3 857
Blackley, St. Peter	"	Ecl. Dis.	4 112	Blandford Forum	"	Parish	3 900
Blackmanstone	Kent	Parish	8	Blandford, St. Mary	"	Parish	409
Blackmore	Essex	Parish	644	Blankney	Lincoln	Parish	560
Black-Notley	"	Parish	489	Blaston	Leicester	Parish	93
Blackpool	Lancashire	Town	3 506	Blaston, St. Giles	"	—	25
Blackpool, St. John	"	Ecl. Dis.	1 957	Blaston, St. Michael	"	—	68
Black Princes Chantry	Kent	Parish	3	Blatchington, East	Sussex	Parish	128
Blackrod	Lancashire	Tnship.	2 911	Blatchington, West	"	Parish	59
Blackrod, St. Catherine	"	Ecl. Dis.	2 911	Blatchinworth	Lancashire	Sub-dis.	4 860
Blackthorn	Oxon	Hamlet	376	Blatchinworth, &c.	"	Tnship.	4 860
Blacktoft	York	Parish	534	Blatherwick	Northampton	Parish	189
Blacktoft	"	Tnship	420	Blawith	Lancashire	Tnship.	193
Black Torrington	Devon	Hund.	18 295	Blaxhall	Suffolk	Parish	589
Black Torrington	"	Sub-dis.	1 970	Blaxton	York	Tnship.	153
Black Torrington	"	Parish	1 020	Blayney	Brecon	Parcel	141
Blackwell, High	Cumberland	Tnship.	341	Bleadon	Somerset	Parish	623
Blackwell, Low	"	Tnship.	183	Blean	Kent	District	16 161
Blackwell	Derby	Sub-dis.	4 552	Blean	"	Parish	626
Blackwell	"	Parish	517	Bleasby	Notts	Parish	332

Name of Place.	County.	Description.	Population.	Name of Place.	County.	Description.	Population.
Bleasdale	Lancashire	Chap.	372	Blunsdon St. Andw.	Wilts	Parish	84
Bledington	Gloucester	Parish	396	Bluntisham	Hunts	Parish	1 351
Bledisloe	,,	Hund.	4 784	Bluntisham	,,	Tnship.	720
Bledlow	Bucks	Parish	1 189	Blurton	Stafford	Ecl. Dis.	2 730
Blencogo	Cumberland	Tnship.	218	Blurton, &c.	,,	Tnship.	2 857
Blencow, Great	,,	Tnship.	99	Blyborough	Lincoln	Parish	209
Blencow, Little	,,	Tnship.	68	Blyford	Suffolk	Parish	193
Blendworth	Hants	Parish	219	Blymhill	Stafford	Parish	591
Blenheim	Oxon	Parish	118	Blyth	Northumberland	Sub-dis.	12 989
Blenkinsopp	Northumberland	Tnship.	444	Blyth, South	,,	Tnship.	1 953
Blennerhasset, &c.	Cumberland	Tnship.	234	Blyth	Notts & York	Parish	3 486
Bletchingly	Surrey	Parish	1 691	Blyth	Notts	Tnship.	698
Bletchington	Oxon	Sub-dis.	7 440	Blythburgh	Suffolk	Parish	832
Bletchington	,,	Parish	659	Blything	,,	L. Sub.	25 648
Bletchley	Bucks	Parish	1 658	Blything	,,	Hund.	23 343
Bletchley	,,	Tnship.	426	Blything	,,	District	26 848
Bletherston	Pembroke	Parish	255	Blyton	Lincoln	Parish	746
Blethvaugh	Radnor	Parish	250	Boarhunt	Hants	Parish	267
Bletsoe	Beds	L. Sub.	12 496	Boarstall	Bucks	Parish	255
Bletsoe	,,	Parish	412	Bobbing	Kent	Parish	449
Blewbury	Berks	Parish	1 114	Bobbington	Stafford & Salop	Parish	431
Blewbury	,,	—	639	Bobbingworth	Essex	Sub-dis.	5 465
Blickling	Norfolk	Parish	392	Bobbingworth	,,	Parish	334
Blidworth	Notts	Sub-dis.	1 188	Bockenfield	Northumberland	Tnship.	127
Blidworth	,,	Parish	1 166	Bocking	Essex	Sub-dis.	5 281
Blindbothel	Cumberland	Tnship.	116	Bocking	,,	Parish	3 555
Blindcrake, &c.	,,	Tnship.	335	Bockleton	Worcester & Heref.	Sub-dis.	3 046
Blisland	Cornwall	Parish	553	Bockleton	,, ,,	Parish	346
Blisworth	Northampton	Parish	1 022	Bockleton	Worcester	Tnship.	259
Blithfield	Stafford	Parish	338	Boconnoc	Cornwall	Parish	323
Blithfield	,,	Tnship.	199	Boddicot	Oxon	Chap.	626
Blockhouse	Worcester	Parish	1 671	Boddington	Gloucester	Parish	392
Blockley	,,	L. Sub.	6 591	Boddington, Lower	Nrthpton.	Parish	315
Blockley	,,	Parish	2 596	Boddington, Upper	,,	Parish	409
Blofield & Walsham	Norfolk	L. Sub.	11 521	Bodedern	Anglesey	Parish	1 084
Blofield	,,	Hund.	6 280	Bodelwyddan	Flint	Ecl. Dis.	630
Blofield	,,	District	11 521	Bodenham	Hereford	Sub-dis.	4 021
Blofield	,,	Sub-dis.	5 787	Bodenham	,,	Parish	1 096
Blofield	,,	Parish	1 155	Bodewryd	Anglesey	Parish	26
Blo'-Norton	,,	Parish	370	Bodfary	Flint & Denbigh	Parish	813
Blore	Stafford	Parish	320	Bodfary	Flint	Tnship.	383
Blore w. Swinscoe	,,	Tnship.	248	Bodferin	Carnarvon	Parish	50
Bloxham	Oxon	Hund.	8 855	Bodham	Norfolk	Parish	316
Bloxham	,,	Sub-dis.	6 216	Bodicote	Oxon	Ecl. Dis.	626
Bloxham	,,	Parish	1 607	Bodiham	Sussex	Parish	303
Bloxham	,,	—	1 366	Bodmin	Cornwall	District	19 691
Bloxholme	Lincoln	Parish	115	Bodmin	,,	Sub-dis.	6 524
Bloxwich	Stafford	Sub-dis.	9 237	Bodmin	,,	Parish	4 809
Bloxwich	,,	Ecl. Dis.	7 345	Bodmin	,,	—	343
Bloxworth	Dorset	Parish	264	Bodmin	,,	M. Bor.	4 466
Blubberhouses	York	Tnship.	87	Bodmin	,,	P. Bor.	6 381
Blundeston	Suffolk	Parish	664	Bodney	Norfolk	Parish	117
Blunham	Beds	Parish	1 150	Bodvean	Carnarvon	Parish	382
Blunham	,,	—	647	Bodwrog	Anglesey	Parish	319

Name of Place.	County.	Description.	Population.	Name of Place.	County.	Description.	Population.
Bognor..	.. *Sussex* ..	Town	2 523	Bolton Abbey	.. *York* ..	Tnship.	112
Bolam ..	.. *Durham* ..	Tnship.	113	Bolton by Bowland	„ ..	Parish	739
Bolam ..	*Northumberland*	Parish	685	Bolton on Dearne	„ ..	Parish	479
Bolam ..	.. „	Tnship.	102	Bolton Percy ..	„	Parish	1 118
Bolam Vicarage .	„	Tnship.	16	Bolton Percy ..	„	Tnship.	292
Bolas Magna ..	*Salop* ..	Parish	278	Bolton on Swale	„ ..	Tnship.	105
Bold ..	.. *Lancaster* ..	Tnship.	798	Bolventor	.. *Cornwall* ..	Ecl. Dis.	344
Boldmere St. Michael	*Warwick*	Ecl. Dis.	848	Bonby ..	.. *Lincoln* ..	Parish	471
Boldon ..	.. *Durham* ..	Parish	1 024	Bonchurch	.. *Hants* ..	Parish	564
Boldre ..	.. *Hants* ..	Parish	2 842	Bondary	.. *Derby* ..	Parish	52
Boldre, East ..	„ ..	Ecl. Dis.	690	Bondleigh	.. *Devon* ..	Parish	279
Boldron..	.. *York* ..	Tnship.	178	Bonehill	.. *Stafford* ..	Liberty	299
Bole ..	.. *Notts* ..	Parish	238	Bongate	.. *Westmoreland*	Parish	1 255
Bolehall & Glascote	*Warwick* .	Tnship.	1 191	Bongate..	.. „	Tnship.	654
Bolingbroke ..	*Lincoln* ..	Parish	12 376	Boningale or ⎫ Boninghall ⎭	.. *Salop* ..	Parish	187
Bolingbroke ..	„ ..	Soke	1 018				
Bolingbroke, New	„ ..	Ecl. Dis.	947	Bonnington	.. *Kent* ..	Parish	187
Bollin Fee ..	.. *Chesh.*	Tnship.	2 143	Bonsall ..	.. *Derby* ..	Parish	1 290
Bollington ..	.. „	Sub-dis.	10 357	Bonvilston	.. *Glamorgan* .	Parish	291
Bollington (Prestbury P.)	„	Tnship.	5 439	Bonwick	.. *York* ..	Tnship.	31
Bollington, St. John ..	„	Ecl. Dis.	5 439	Bookham, Great	*Surrey* ..	Parish	1 106
Bollington	„	Town	3 845	Bookham, Little	„ ..	Parish	219
Bollington (Rostherne,&c.,P)	„	Tnship.	277	Boongate, St. Mary	*Northpton*..	Ecl. Dis.	4 034
Bolney ..	.. *Sussex* ..	Parish	789	Bootham ..	.. *York* ..	Sub-dis.	14 425
Bolnhurst	.. *Beds* ..	Parish	348	Boothby	.. *Lincoln* ..	Parish	218
Bolsover ..	.. *Derby* ..	Sub-dis.	2 402	Boothby-Graffoe	„ ..	Wapen.	11 797
Bolsover ..	.. „ ..	Parish	1 629	Boothby-Pagnell	„ ..	Parish	112
Bolsover ..	.. „ ..	Tnship	1 526	Boothen	.. *Stafford* ..	Tnship.	253
Boltby ..	.. *York* ..	Tnship.	316	Booths, Higher..	*Lancaster* ..	Tnship.	5 131
Bolton ..	.. *Cumberland* .	Parish	1 048	Booths, Lower ..	.. „ ..	Tnship.	4 655
Bolton, High ..	„	Tnship.	330	Bootle ..	.. *Cumberland*.	L. Sub.	4 885
Bolton, Low, &c..	„	Tnship.	718	Bootle ..	.. „	District	5 880
Bolton Wood, &c.	„	Tnship.	718	Bootle ..	.. „	Sub-dis.	3 598
Bolton ..	.. *Lancaster* ..	L. Sub.	141 699	Bootle	„	Parish	901
Bolton ..	.. „ ..	District	130 269	Bootle w. Linacre	*Lancaster* ..	Tnship.	6 414
Bolton Eastern..	„ ..	Sub-dis.	24 996	Booton ..	.. *Norfolk* ..	Parish	246
Bolton Little ..	„ ..	Sub-dis.	24 942	Boraston	.. *Salop* ..	Tnship.	176
Bolton Western .	„ ..	Sub-dis.	18 439	Borden ..	.. *Kent* ..	Parish	1 023
Bolton, Great ..	„ ..	Tnship.	43 435	Bordesley	.. *Warwick* ..	Hamlet	21 339
Bolton-le-Moors .	„ ..	Parish	97 215	Bordesley, St. Andw.	„ ..	Ecl. Dis.	7 017
Bolton	„ ..	Borough	70 395	Bordley..	.. *York* ..	Tnship.	31
All Saints ..	„ ..	Ecl. Dis.	3 294	Boreham ..	.. *Essex* ..	Parish	989
Christchurch..	„ ..	Ecl. Dis.	5 635	Boresford, &c. ..	*Hereford* ..	Tnship.	110
Emmanuel ..	„ ..	Ecl. Dis.	9 329	Borley ..	.. *Essex* ..	Parish	190
Holy Trinity..	„ ..	Ecl. Dis.	16 256	Boroughbridge..	*York* ..	Sub-dis.	5 061
St. George ..	„ ..	Ecl. Dis.	14 288	Boroughbridge..	„ ..	Tnship.	909
Bolton, Little ..	„ ..	Tnship.	25 891	Borough Fen ..	*Northampton*	Parish	202
Bolton, Little, St.John	„ ..	Ecl. Dis.	5 233	Borough Road ..	*Surrey* ..	Sub-dis.	16 668
Bolton-le-Sands .	„ ..	Parish	1 713	Borrashovah	.. *Denbigh* ..	Tnship.	49
Bolton-le-Sands .	„ ..	Tnship.	692	Borrasriffre	.. „ ..	Tnship.	20
Bolton ..	*Northumberld.*	Tnship.	151	Borrowby (Leake P.)	*York* ..	Tnship.	345
Bolton ..	.. *Westmoreland*	Chap.	390	Borrowby (Lythe P.)	„ ..	Tnship.	98
Bolton ..	.. *York* ..	Tnship.	127	Borrowdale	.. *Cumberland*.	Tnship.	422
Bolton ..	.. „ ..	Tnship.	937	Borwick..	.. *Lancaster* ..	Tnship.	194

Name of Place	County	Description	Population
Bosbury ..	Hereford ..	Parish	1 090
Boscastle ..	Cornwall ..	Sub-dis.	2 429
Boscobel ..	Salop ..	Parish	22
Boscombe ..	Wilts ..	Parish	143
Bosden ..	Cheshire ..	Hamlet	1 779
Bosham..	Sussex ..	Parish	1 158
Bosherston ..	Pembroke ..	Parish	200
Bosley ..	Cheshire ..	Tnship.	461
Bosmere ..	Suffolk ..	District	16 174
Bosmere & Claydon ,, ..		Hund.	13 128
Bossall ..	York ..	Parish	1 075
Bossall ..	,, ..	Tnship.	62
Bossington ..	Hants ..	Parish	45
Bostock..	Cheshire ..	Tnship.	154
Boston ..	Lincoln ..	L. Sub.	40 977
Boston ..	,, ..	District	37 969
Boston ..	,, ..	Sub-dis.	17 527
Boston ..	,, ..	Parish	15 078
Boston.. ,, {		M. Bor.	14 712
		P. Bor.	17 893
Boston ..	York ..	Hamlet	1 123
Boston Spa, St. Mary ,, ..		Ecl. Dis.	1 123
Botcherby ..	Cumberland.	Tnship.	176
Botchergate ..	,,	Tnship.	9 122
Botcheston, &c..	Leicester ..	Hamlets	113
Botesdale ..	Suffolk ..	Sub-dis.	5 288
Botesdale ..	,, ..	Hamlet	580
Bothal ..	Northumberland	Parish	1 233
Bothal Demesne .	,,	Tnship.	642
Bothamsall ..	Notts ..	Parish	296
Bothel & Threapland	Cumberld.	Tnship.	430
Bothenhampton.	Dorset ..	Parish	546
Both Hergests ..	Hereford ..	Tnship.	163
Botley ..	Hants ..	Parish	860
Botleys & Lyne..	Surrey ..	Ecl. Dis.	494
Botloe ..	Gloucester ..	Hund.	7 204
Bottesford ..	Leicester ..	Parish	1 415
Bottesford ..	Lincoln ..	Parish	1 616
Bottesford ..	,, ..	Tnship.	157
Botteslow ..	Stafford ..	Tnship.	167
Bottisham ..	Cambs ..	L. Sub.	8 523
Bottisham ..	,, ..	Sub-dis.	3 373
Bottisham ..	,, ..	Parish	1 508
Bottwnog ..	Carnarvon ..	Parish	138
Botusfleming ..	Cornwall ..	Parish	237
Boughrood ..	Radnor ..	Parish	292
Boughton, Great	Chest. & Flint	District	58 501
Boughton, Great	Chester ..	Tnship.	1 387
Boughton, Aluph ..	Kent.	Parish	475
Boughton ..	,,	Sub-dis.	5 333
Boughton under Blean..	,,	Parish	1 624
Boughton Malherbe ..	,,	Parish	408
Boughton Monchelsea..	,,	Parish	1 190
Boughton ..	Norfolk ..	Parish	238

Name of Place	County	Description	Population
Boughton ..	Northampton	Parish	37
Boughton ..	Notts ..	Parish	39
Bouldon ..	Salop ..	Tnship.	6
Boulge ..	Suffolk ..	Parish	3
Boulmer, &c.	Northumberland	Tnship.	15
Boulston ..	Pembroke ..	Parish	25
Boulstone ..	Hereford ..	Parish	6
Boultham ..	Lincoln ..	Parish	9
Boulton..	Derby ..	Tnship.	22
Boundary ..	,, ..	Parish	5
Bourn ..	Cambs. ..	Parish	88
Bourn-Moor ..	Durham ..	Tnship.	97
Bourn & Stamford	Lincoln ..	L. Sub.	32 16
Bourn ..	,,	District	21 29
Bourn ..	,,	Union	20 11
Bourn ..	,,	Sub-dis.	7 35
Bourn ..	,,	Parish	3 73
Bourn ..	,,	—	3 37
Bourn ..	,,	Town	3 06
Bournemouth St. Peter	Hants .	Ecl. Dis.	1 94
Bourton..	Berks ..	Tithing	32
Bourton..	Bucks ..	Hamlet	4
Bourtonhold ..	,,	Hamlet	56
Bourton..	Dorset ..	Chap.	92
Bourton St. George	,,	Ecl. Dis.	92
Bourton on the Hill	Gloucester	Parish	50
Bourton on the Water	,,	Sub-dis.	462
Bourton on the Water	,,	Parish	1 01
Bourton..	Oxon ..	Hamlet	56
Bourton on Dunsmore	Warwk.	Parish	38
Boustead-Hill ..	Cumberland.	Tnship.	7
Boveney ..	Bucks ..	Liberty	15
Bovey, North ..	Devon ..	Parish	51
Bovey-Tracey ..	,,	Parish	2 08
Bovingdon ..	Herts ..	Parish	1 15
Bow Brickhill ..	Bucks ..	Parish	54
Bow ..	Devon ..	Sub-dis.	3 51
Bow ..	,,	Parish	90
Bow ..	Middlesex ..	Sub-dis.	35 66
Bow ..	,,	Parish	11 59
Bow, St. Stephen	,,	Ecl. Dis.	7 15
Bow Common, St. Paul	,,	Ecl. Dis.	2 07
Bowden..	Cheshire ..	Parish	14 82
Bowden..	,,	Tnship.	1 82
Bowden Edge ..	Derby ..	Tnship.	1 29
Bowden, Great..	Leicester ..	Parish	3 69
Bowden, Great..	,,	Tnship.	1 39
Bowden, Little..	Northampton	Parish	48
Bower-Chalk ..	Wilts ..	Parish	49
Bowers-Gifford..	Essex ..	Parish	25
Bowes ..	York ..	Parish	84
Bowes ..	,,	Tnship.	70
Bowland ..	Lancaster ..	Tnship.	12
Bowland Forest High	York ..	Tnship.	16

Name of Place.	County.	Description.	Population.	Name of Place.	County.	Description.	Population.
owland Forest Low	York ..	Tnship.	319	Bradbury ..	Durham ..	Tnship.	174
owling Green..	Surrey ..	Parish	47	Braddan ..	Isle of Man.	Parish	2 794
owling.. ..	York ..	Sub-dis.	14 494	Bradden ..	Northampton	Parish	140
owling.. ..	,, ..	Tnship.	14 494	Bradenham ..	Bucks ..	Parish	185
owling St. John	,, ..	Ecl. Dis.	3 488	Bradenham, East	Norfolk ..	Parish	399
owling St. Stephen	,, ..	Ecl. Dis.	1 297	Bradenham, West	,, ..	Parish	387
owness ..	Cumberland.	Parish	1 321	Bradeston ..	,, ..	Parish	133
owness ..	,,	Tnship.	484	Bradfield ..	Berks & Oxon	District	15 771
owood.. ..	Wilts ..	Liberty	106	Bradfield ..	Berks ..	Parish	1 167
owscale ..	Cumberland.	Tnship.	32	Bradfield ..	Essex ..	Parish	914
owthorpe ..	Norfolk ..	Parish	21	Bradfield ..	Norfolk ..	Parish	226
ox	Wilts ..	Parish	2 051	Bradfield Combust	Suffolk ..	Parish	173
oxford.. ..	Berks ..	Parish	636	Bradfield, St. Clare	,, ..	Parish	233
oxford.. ..	Suffolk ..	Parish	986	Bradfield, St. George	,, ..	Parish	427
oxford.. ..	,, ..	—	806	Bradfield ..	York ..	Sub-dis.	9 089
oxgrove ..	Sussex ..	Sub-dis.	3 632	Bradfield ..	,, ..	Tnship.	9 089
oxgrove ..	,, ..	Parish	666	Bradford ..	Devon ..	Parish	444
oxley	Kent ..	Parish	1 470	Bradford Abbas .	Dorset & Som.	Sub-dis.	3 872
oxmoor ..	Herts ..	Ecl. Dis.	3 813	Bradford Abbas .	Dorset	Parish	585
oxted	Essex ..	Parish	935	Bradford Peverell	,, ..	Parish	361
oxted	Suffolk ..	Parish	192	Bradford ..	Lancaster ..	Tnship.	3 523
oxwell.. ..	Gloucester ..	Parish	255	Bradford-rd., St. Philip ,,	..	Ecl. Dis.	10 540
oxworth ..	Cambs ..	Parish	347	Bradford	Northumberld.	Tnship.	18
oycott.. ..	Bucks ..	Hamlet	20	Bradford ..	,,	Tnship.	49
oylstone ..	Derby ..	Parish	268	Bradford Drayton	Salop ..	L. Sub.	10 939
oyne Hill, All Saints Berks	..	Ecl. Dis.	1 071	Bradford Newport	,, ..	L. Sub.	11 192
oynton ..	York ..	Parish	128	Bradford, North	,, ..	Hund.	27 279
oyton ..	Cornw. & Dev.	Parish	476	Bradford, South	,, ..	Hund.	48 820
oyton	Cornwall ..	—	379	Bradford Wellington	,, ..	L. Sub.	37 924
oyton	Suffolk ..	Parish	254	Bradford Wem..	,, ..	L. Sub.	7 094
oyton	Wilts ..	Parish	410	Bradford Whitchwich ,,	..	L. Sub.	9 427
ozeat	Northampton	Parish	955	Bradford ..	Somerset ..	Parish	552
Brabourne ..	Kent ..	Sub-dis.	4 032	Bradford ..	Wilts ..	Hund.	9 422
Brabourne ..	,, ..	Parish	743	Bradford, &c. ..	,, ..	L. Sub.	38 875
Braceborough ..	Lincoln ..	Parish	220	Bradford on Avon	Wilts & Som.	District	10 475
Bracebridge ..	,, ..	Parish	836	Bradford, N.Wn.	Wilts ..	Sub-dis.	3 796
Braceby.. ..	,, ..	Parish	168	Bradford, S.E...	Wilts & Som.	Sub-dis.	6 679
Brace Meole ..	Salop .	Parish	1 215	Bradford on Avon	Wilts ..	Parish	8 032
Bracewell ..	York ..	Parish	140	Christchurch..	,, ..	Ecl. Dis.	2 028
Bracken.. ..	,, ..	Tnship.	34	**Bradford on Avon**	,, ..	Town	4 291
Brackenborough.	Lincoln ..	Parish	59	Bradford ..	York ..	District	196 475
Brackenfield ..	Derby ..	Tnship.	317	Bradford ..	,, ..	Union	106 218
Brackenfield ..	,, ..	Ecl. Dis.	317	Bradford ..	,, ..	Tnship.	48 646
Brackenholme, &c. York	..	Tnship.	102	Bradford	,, ..	Parish	156 053
Brackenthwaite .	Cumberland.	Tnship.	115	Bradford *(1662) 108, C19* ..		Borough	106 218
Brackley ..	Northampton	L. Sub.	16 255	Bradford East End ,,	..	Sub-dis.	28 579
Brackley	Northampton, &c.	District	13 471	Bradford, St. Andw. ,,	..	Ecl. Dis.	3 781
Brackley ..	,, ,,	Sub-dis.	7 656	Bradford, St. John ,,	..	Ecl. Dis.	10 248
Brackley ..	Northampton	Town	2 239	Bradford West End ,,	..	Sub-dis.	20 067
Bracknell ..	Berks ..	Sub-dis.	6 165	Bradford, West . ,,	..	Tnship.	289
Bracknell, Holy Trinity ,,	..	Ecl. Dis	1 007	Brading ..	Hants ..	Parish	3 709
Bracon Ash ..	Norfolk ..	Parish	271	Bradley ..	Cheshire ..	Tnship.	110
Bradbourne ..	Derby ..	Parish	1 187	Bradley ..	Derby ..	Parish	253
Bradbourne ..	,, ..	Tnship.	144	Bradley , ..	Gloucester ..	Hund.	5 943

Name of Place.	County.	Description.	Population.	Name of Place.	County.	Description.	Population.
Bradley	Hants	Parish	106	Bramble Hill Walk, &c. Hants		—	4
Bradley	Lincoln	Parish	⁊98	Bramcote	Notts	Parish	691
Bradley Haverstoe	„	Wapen	10 771	Bramdean	Hants	Parish	282
Bradley, West	Somerset	Parish	136	Bramerton	Norfolk	Parish	300
Bradley	Stafford	Parish	597	Bramfield	Suffolk	Parish	649
Bradley in Moors	„	Parish	43	Bramford	„	Parish	1 019
Bradley, Great	Suffolk	Parish	460	Bramhall	Cheshire	Tnship.	1 615
Bradley, Little	„	Parish	28	Bramham	York	Sub-dis.	4 990
Bradley	Wilts	Sub-dis.	2 510	Bramham	„	Parish	3 484
Bradley, North	„	Parish	2 196	Bramham w. Oglethorpe	„	Tnship.	1 331
Bradley, North	„	Tithing	955	Bramhope	„	Tnship.	312
Bradleys Both	York	Tnship.	442	Bramley	Hants & Berks	Sub-dis.	5 006
Bradmore	Notts	Parish	296	Bramley	Hants	Parish	467
Bradninch	Devon	Precinct	91	Bramley	Surrey	Parish	1 129
Bradninch	„	Parish	1 796	Bramley, Maltby York		Tnship.	335
Bradnop	Stafford	Tnship.	454	Bramley, Kirkstall „		Tnship.	8 690
Bradon, South	Somerset	Parish	38	Brampford-Speke Devon		Parish	494
Bradpole	Dorset	Parish	1 449	Brampton	Cumberland	District	10 866
Bradshaw Edge	Derby	Tnship.	2 518	Brampton	„	Sub-dis.	5 501
Bradshaw	Lancaster	Tnship.	792	Brampton	„	Parish	3 585
Bradshaw	„	Ecl. Dis.	1 968	Brampton	„	Tnship.	2 933
Bradshaw, St. John York		Ecl. Dis.	2 171	**Brampton**	„	Town	2 379
Bradstone	Devon	Parish	142	Brampton	Derby	Parish	4 927
Bradwall	Cheshire	Tnship.	437	Brampton, St. Thos. „		Ecl. Dis.	5 259
Bradwell	Bucks	Parish	1 658	Brampton	Durham	Tnship.	127
Bradwell Abbey	„	Parish	14	Brampton-Abbotts Hereford		Parish	257
Bradwell	Derby	Tnship.	1 304	Brampton Bryan Heref. & Rad.		Parish	430
Bradwell	Essex	Sub-dis.	2 828	Brampton Bryan Hereford		Tnship.	158
Bradwell by Sea	„	Parish	1 094	Brampton	Hunts	Parish	1 270
Bradwell by Cog'shall	„	Parish	273	Brampton	Lincoln	Tnship.	92
Bradwell	Suffolk	Parish	387	Brampton	Norfolk	Parish	195
Bradworthy	Devon	Sub-dis.	911	Brampton Ash	Northampton	Parish	107
Bradworthy	„	Parish	981	Brampton	Suffolk	Parish	310
Brafferton	Durham	Tnship.	254	Brampton Bierlow York		Tnship.	1 938
Brafferton	York	Parish	904	Rrampton Bierlow	„	Ecl. Dis.	1 733
Brafferton	„	Tnship.	199	Brampton en le Morthen	„	Tnship.	116
Brafield	Northampton	Sub-dis.	3 414	Bramshall	Stafford	Parish	199
Brafield on the Green	„	Parish	494	Bramshaw	Hants & Wilts	Parish	746
Brailes	Warwick	Parish	1 347	Bramshill, Great Hants		Tithing	141
Brailsford	Derby	Sub-dis.	3 168	Bramshill, Little	„	Tithing	13
Brailsford	„	Parish	773	Bramshott	„	Parish	1 367
Braintfield	Herts	Parish	191	Brancaster	Norfolk	Parish	1 002
Braintree	Essex	District	17 170	Brancepeth	Durham	Parish	15 712
Braintree	„	Sub-dis.	6 600	Brancepeth	„	Tnship.	1 496
Braintree	„	Parish	4 620	Branch and Dole Wilts		Hund.	7 748
Braintree	„	Town	4 305	Brandeston	Suffolk	Parish	469
Braiseworth	Suffolk	Parish	164	Brandistone	Norfolk	Parish	181
Braishfield, All Sts. Hants		Ecl. Dis.	452	Brandon & Byshottles Durham		Tnship.	1 486
Braithwaite	Cumberland	Tnship.	326	Brandon Hill	Gloucester	Ecl. Dis.	5 284
Braithwell	York	Parish	757	Brandon Parva	Norfolk	Parish	208
Braithwell	„	Tnship.	422	Brandon	Northumberld.	Tnship.	134
Brakes	Hereford	Tnship.	179	Brandon	Suffolk & Norfolk	Parish	2 218
Bramber	Sussex	Rape	35 497	**Brandon**	„ „	Town	2 203
Bramber	„	Parish	119	Brandon & Bretford Warwick		Tnship.	449

Name of Place.	County.	Description.	Population.	Name of Place.	County.	Description.	Population.
Brandsburton	York	Sub-dis.	1 616	Brayton..	York	Parish	1 794
Brandsburton	„	Parish	811	Brayton..	„	Tnship.	367
Brandsburton	„	Tnship.	784	Breadsall	Derby	Parish	592
Brandsby w. Stearsby,		Parish	284	Breadstone	Gloucester	Tithing	129
Branksea, St. Mary	Dorset	Ecl. Dis.	123	Breage ..	Cornwall	Sub-dis.	6 188
Bransby..	Lincoln	Hamlet	78	Breage ..	„	Parish	5 173
Branscombe	Devon	Parish	936	Bream ..	Gloucester	Tithing	824
Bransdale West Side	York	Tnship.	73	Bream, St. James	„	Ecl. Dis.	2 083
Bransford	Worcester	Chap.	270	Breamore	Hants	Parish	565
Branston	Leicester	Parish	297	Brean ..	Somerset	Parish	145
Branston	Lincoln	Parish	1 469	Brearton	York	Tnship.	235
Branstone	Stafford	Tnship.	542	Breaston	Derby	Chap.	709
Brant Broughton	Lincoln	Parish	755	Brechfa..	Carmarthen	Parish	122
Brantham	Suffolk	Parish	445	Breckenbrough, &c.	York	Tnship.	184
Branthwaite	Cumberland.	Tnship.	281	Breckles	Norfolk	Parish	130
Brantingham	York	Parish	572	Brecknockshire..	..	County	61 627
Brantingham	„	Tnship.	152	**Brecknock** .. Brecon {		M. Bor.	5 235
Branton..	Northumberland	Tnship.	106			P. Bor.	5 639
Branxton..	„	Parish	255	Brecknock	„	District.	17 279
Brascote	Leicester	Hamlet	40	Brecknock	„	Sub-dis.	7 054
Brassington	Derby	Sub-dis.	4 470	Brecon ..	„	L. Sub.	5 235
Brassington	„	Tnship.	718	Breconhill	Cumberland.	Tnship.	340
Brasted..	Kent	Parish	1 182	Bredbury	Cheshire	Tnship.	3 408
Brathay, Trinity	Lancaster	Ecl. Dis.	212	Bredbury, St. Mark	„	Ecl. Dis.	3 408
Bratoft ..	Lincoln	Parish	280	Brede ..	Sussex	Parish	1 083
Brattleby	„	Parish	153	Bredenbury	Hereford	Parish	52
Bratton Clovelly	Devon	Sub-dis.	2 339	Bredfield	Suffolk	Parish	454
Bratton Clovelly	„	Parish	706	Bredgar..	Kent	Parish	547
Bratton Fleming	„	Parish	686	Bredhurst	„	Parish	117
Bratton Seymour	Somerset	Parish	80	Bredicot	Worcester	Parish	53
Bratton..	Wilts	Chap.	744	Bredon ..	„	Parish	1 555
Bratton, St. James	„	Ecl. Dis.	744	Bredon ..	„	Tnship.	1 150
Braughing	Herts	Hund.	20 481	Bredwardine	Hereford	Parish	420
Braughing	„	Sub-dis.	2 912	Bredy, Little	Dorset	Parish	199
Braughing	„	Parish	1 180	Bredy, Long	„	Parish	250
Brauncewell	Lincoln	Parish	112	Breedon	Leicester	Tnship.	893
Braunston	Northampton	Parish	1 228	Breedon on Hill.	„	Parish	2 417
Braunston	Rutland	Parish	398	Brightmet	Lancaster	Tnship.	1 562
Braunstone	Leicester	Chap.	197	Breighton w. Gunby	York	Tnship.	207
Braunstone Frith	„	Parish	7	Breinton	Hereford	Parish	398
Braunton	Devon	Hund.	14 786	Bremhill	Wilts	Parish	1 357
Braunton	„	Sub-dis.	6 957	Bremilham	„	Parish	29
Braunton	„	L. Sub.	35 802	Brenchley	Kent	Sub-dis.	5 486
Braunton	„	Parish	2 168	Brenchley	„	Parish	2 844
Brawby..	York	Tnship.	215	Brendon	Devon	Parish	291
Brawdy..	Pembroke	Parish	644	Brenkley	Northumberland	Tnship.	51
Braxted, Great..	Essex	Parish	384	Brent, South	Devon	Parish	1 205
Braxted, Little..	„	Parish	111	Brent w. Wrington	Somerset	Hund.	4 781
Bray ..	Berks	Hund.	2 936	Brent, East	„	Parish	797
Bray ..	„	Sub-dis.	6 714	Brent, South	„	Parish	905
Bray ..	„	Parish	4 801	Brent Eleigh	Suffolk	Parish	228
Bray ..	„	—	2 936	Brentford	Middlesex	L. Sub.	45 362
Braybrooke	Northampton	Parish	458	Brentford	„	District	50 516
Braydon	Wilts	Hamlet	49	Brentford	„	Sub-dis.	13 958

Name of Place.	County.	Description.	Population.	Name of Place.	County.	Description.	Population.
Brentford, New	*Middlesex*	Tp. or P.	1 995	Bridgford, East	*Notts*	Parish	1 078
Brentford, Old	"	Chap.	6 748	Bridgford, West	"	Parish	390
Brentford	"	Town	9 521	Bridgford, West	"	Tnship.	280
Brentford, Old	"	Ecl. Dis.	6 720	Bridgham	*Norfolk*	Parish	328
Brentor	*Devon*	Parish	128	Bridghampton	*Somerset*	Tithing	112
Brent Pelham	*Herts*	Parish	286	Bridgnorth	*Salop*	L. Sub.	6 240
Brentwood	*Essex*	L. Sub.	19 420	Bridgnorth	"	District	15 920
Brentwood	"	Sub-dis.	8 167	Bridgnorth	"	Sub-dis.	6 240
Brentwood	"	Hamlet	3 093			M. Bor.	6 240
Brentwood	"	Town	2 811	**Bridgnorth**	" {	P. Bor.	7 699
Brentwood, St. Thos.,		Ecl. Dis.	3 093	Bridgwater	*Somerset*	L. Sub.	34 420
Brenzett	*Kent*	Parish	270	Bridgwater	"	District	34 420
Brereton	*Cheshire*	Parish	592	Bridgwater	"	Sub-dis.	13 694
Brereton	*Stafford*	Ecl. Dis.	1 359	Bridgwater	"	Parish	12 120
Bressingham	*Norfolk*	Parish	596	Bridgwater, Trinity	"	Ecl. Dis.	3 201
Bretby	*Derby*	Chap.	324	**Bridgwater**	"	Borough	11 320
Bretforton	*Worcester*	Parish	565	Bridlington	*York*	District	14 371
Bretherton	*Lancaster*	Tnship.	775	Bridlington	"	Sub-dis.	8 518
Bretherton	"	Ecl. Dis.	775	Bridlington	"	Parish	6 833
Brettenham	*Norfolk*	Parish	72	Bridlington & Quay	"	Tnship.	5 775
Brettenham	*Suffolk*	Parish	426	**Bridlington**	"	Town	5 775
Bretton	*Flint*	Tnship.	258	Bridlington Quay	"	Ecl. Dis.	2 677
Bretton	*York*	Sub-dis.	5 057	Bridport	*Dorset*	L. Sub.	34 051
Bretton, West	"	Tnship.	504	Bridport	"	Division	23 848
Brewery Fld., St. Barnab. "		Ecl. Dis.	6 869	Bridport	"	District	16 828
Brewham, North	*Somerset*	Parish	321	Bridport	"	Sub Dis.	8 009
Brewham, South	"	Parish	519	Bridport	"	Parish	4 645
Brewhouse Yard	*Notts*	Parish	108	**Bridport**	"	Borough	7 719
Brewood	*Stafford*	Sub-dis.	5 629	Bridstow	*Hereford*	Parish	717
Brewood	"	Parish	3 399	Briercliffe w. Extwisle	*Lanc*	Tnship.	1 332
Brices Lodge	*Oxon*	Parish	3	Briercliffe, St. James	"	Ecl. Dis.	2 024
Bricett, Great	*Suffolk*	Parish	207	Brierly	*York*	Tnship.	491
Brickendon	*Herts*	Liberty	841	Brierly Hill	*Stafford*	Ecl. Dis.	10 755
Brickhill, Bow	*Bucks*	Parish	546	Brierton	*Durham*	Tnship.	30
Brickhill, Great	"	Parish	590	Briery Cottages	*Cumberland*	Parish	62
Brickhill, Little	"	Parish	423	Brieryhurst	*Stafford*	Tnship.	4 072
Bricklehampton	*Worcester*	Chap.	187	Brigg	*Lincoln*	L. Sub.	55 674
Bride	*Isle of Man*	Parish	919	Brigg	"	Sub-dis.	12 326
Bridekirk	*Cumberland*	Parish	2 876	Brigg, Glanford	"	Tnship.	1 704
Bridekirk	"	Tnship.	125	**Brigg**	"	Town	3 138
Bridell	*Pembroke*	Parish	326	Brigham	*Cumberland*	Parish	7 874
Bridestow	*Devon*	Parish	832	Brigham	"	Tnship.	504
Bridewell	*Middlesex*	Precinct	410	Brigham	*York*	Tnship.	114
Bridford	*Devon*	Parish	576	Brighouse	"	Sub-dis.	9 992
Bridge	*Kent*	District	11 316	Brighouse, St. Martin	"	Ecl. Dis.	4 562
Bridge	"	Parish	893	Brighthampton	*Oxon*	Hamlet	89
Bridge Hewick	*York*	Tnship.	89	Brightling	*Sussex*	Parish	661
Bridge Hill	*Derby*	Ecl. Dis.	2 839	Brightlingsea	*Essex*	Parish	2 585
Bridgmere	*Cheshire*	Tnship.	187	Brighton, New, St. Jas.	*Chesh.*	Ecl. Dis.	2 404
Bridgend	*Glamorgan*	District	26 465	Brighton	*Sussex*	L. Sub.	90 407
Bridgend	"	Sub-dis.	11 417	Brighton	"	District	77 693
Bridgerule	*Devon*	Parish	410	Brighton	"	Parish	77 693
Bridge Sollars	*Hereford*	Parish	62			M. Bor.	77 693
Bridge Trafford	*Cheshire*	Tnship.	50	**Brighton**	" {	P. Bor.	87 317

Name of Place.	County.	Description.	Population.	Name of Place.	County.	Description.	Population.
rightside	York	Sub-dis.	29 818	Bristol, St. Barnabas	Gloucester	Ecl. Dis.	3 735
rightside	„	Ecl. Dis.	10 101	Bristol, St. Barthol.	„	Ecl. Dis.	1 826
rightside Bierlow	„	Tnship.	29 818	Bristol, St. Clement	„	Ecl. Dis.	5 301
rightwaltham	Berks	Parish	450	Bristol, St. Jude	„	Ecl. Dis.	4 039
rightwell	„	Parish	703	Bristol, St. Simon	„	Ecl. Dis.	1 932
rightwell Baldwin	Oxon	Parish	277	Bristol, Trinity	„	Ecl. Dis.	12 735
rightwell Prior	„	Chap.	43	Bristol, Weir	„	Ecl. Dis.	4 011
rightwell Salome	„	Parish	217	Briston	Norfolk	Parish	931
rightwell	Suffolk	Parish	81	Britford	Wilts	Sub-dis.	5 623
rightwells Barrow	Gloucester	Hund.	8 020	Britford	„	Parish	872
rignall	York	Parish	193	Brithdir	Glamorgan	Hamlet	3 879
rigsley	Lincoln	Parish	152	Briton Ferry	„	Parish	3 781
rigstock	Northampton	Parish	1 159	Britwell Prior	Oxon	Chap.	43
rill	Bucks & Oxon	Sub-dis.	5 646	Britwell Salome	„	Parish	217
rill	Bucks	Parish	432	Brixham	Devon	Sub-dis.	6 750
rilley	Hereford & Radn.	Sub-dis.	2 067	Brixham	„	Parish	5 984
rilley	Hereford	Parish	517	**Brixham**	„	Town	4 390
rimfield	„	Parish	665	Brixham, Lower.	„	Ecl. Dis.	4 586
rimington	Derby	Chap.	1 808	Brixton	„	Parish	691
rimpstield	Gloucester	Parish	392	Brixton	Hants	Parish	630
rimpton	Berks	Parish	462	Brixton	Surrey	Hund.	409 504
rimpton	Somerset	Parish	135	Brixton	„	Sub-dis.	20 067
rimscombe	Gloucester	Ecl. Dis.	1 430	Brixton, Christch.	„	Ecl. Dis.	3 776
rimstage	Cheshire	Tnship.	185	Brixton, St. John	„	Ecl. Dis.	4 967
rimstree	Salop	Hund.	13 125	Brixton, St. Matthew	„	Ecl. Dis.	10 305
rimstree Bridgnorth	„	L. Sub.	3 649	Brixton-Deverill.	Wilts	Parish	225
rimstree Shiffnal	„	L. Sub.	10 118	Brixworth	Northampton	District	15 359
rindle	Lancashire	Sub-dis.	6 021	Brixworth	„	Sub-dis.	4 555
rindle	„	Parish	1 501	Brixworth	„	Parish	1 253
rindley	Cheshire	Tnship.	227	Brize-Norton	Oxon	Parish	716
ringhurst	Leicester	Parish	825	Broad Blunsdon	Wilts	Tithing	806
ringhurst	„	Tnship.	109	Broad Chalk	„	Parish	796
rington	Hunts	Parish	191	Broad Clist	Devon	Sub-dis.	3 537
rington	Northampton	Parish	806	Broad Clist	„	Parish	2 318
riningham	Norfolk	Parish	206	Broadfield	Herts	Parish	19
rinkburn	Northumberld.	P. Chap.	220	Broadgate	Leicester	Parish	9
rinkburn, H. Ward	„	Tnship.	134	Broad Green, Ch. ch.	Surrey	Ecl. Dis.	4 203
rinkburn, L. Ward	„	Tnship.	47	Broadhembury	Devon	Parish	817
rinkburn, S. Side	„	Tnship.	39	Broadhempston	„	Parish	661
rinkhill	Lincoln	Parish	175	Broad Hinton	Berks	Liberty	531
rinkley	Cambs	Parish	317	Broad Hinton	Wilts	Parish	657
rinklow	Warwick	Parish	736	Broadholme	Notts	Tnship.	115
rinkworth	Wilts	Parish	1 273	Broad Lane	Flint	Tnship.	57
rinkworth	„	—	1 081	Broad Marston	Gloucester	Hamlet	230
rinnington	Cheshire	Tnship.	5 346	Broadmayne	Dorset	Parish	506
rinsop	Hereford	Parish	145	Broadoak	Cornwall	Parish	274
rinsworth	York	Tnship.	777	Broadstairs	Kent	Ecl. Dis.	1 378
rinton	Norfolk	Incor.	295	Broad Town, Ch. ch.	Wilts	Ecl. Dis.	473
rinton	„	Parish	177	Broadwas	Worcester	Parish	311
risco	Cumberland	Tnship.	323	Broadwater	Herts	Hund.	18 800
risley	Norfolk	Parish	362	Broadwater	Sussex	Sub-dis.	8 387
rislington	Somerset	Parish	1 489	Broadwater	„	Parish	6 466
ristol	Gloucester	District	66 027	Broadwater	„	—	661
Bristol	Glouc. & Som.	City	154 093	Broadway	Dorset	Parish	614

Name of Place.	County.	Description.	Population.	Name of Place.	County.	Description.	Population.
Broadway	Somerset	Parish	431	West, St. Mary	Middlesex	Ecl. Dis.	4 236
Broadway	Worcester	Sub-dis.	6 870	Brompton & Rhiston	Salop	Tnship.	176
Broadway	,,	Parish	1 566	Brompton Ralph	Somerset	Parish	436
Broadwell	Gloucester	Parish	398	Brompton Regis	,,	Parish	929
Broadwell	Oxon	Parish	1 103	Brompton	York	Chap.	1 398
Broadwell	,,	—	211	Brompton	,,	Parish	1 484
Broadwinsor	Dorset	Parish	1 538	Brompton	,,	Tnship.	538
Broadwood Kelly	Devon	Parish	342	Brompton on Swale	,,	Tnship.	406
Broadwoodwidger	,,	Sub-dis.	803	Bromsberrow	Gloucester	Parish	305
Broadwoodwidger	,,	Parish	845	Bromsgrove	Worcester	L. Sub.	19 844
Brobury	Hereford	Parish	76	Bromsgrove	,,	District	26 207
Brockdish	Norfolk	Parish	544	Bromsgrove	,,	Sub-dis.	12 444
Brockenhurst	Hants	Parish	1 083	Bromsgrove	,,	Parish	10 822
Brockhall	Northampton	Parish	54	**Bromsgrove**	,,	Town	5 262
Brockham Green, Ch. ch.	Surrey	Ecl. Dis.	761	Bromwich, West	Stafford	Parish	41 795
Brockhampton	Heref. & Worc.	Sub-dis.	3 716	Christchurch	,,	Ecl. Dis.	22 246
Brockhampton	Hereford	Parish	140	St. James	,,	Ecl. Dis.	8 521
Brockholes	Lancaster	Hamlet	54	Trinity	,,	Ecl. Dis.	4 593
Brocklebank	Cumberland.	Tnship.	148	Bromwich, Little	Warwick	Hamlet	405
Brocklesby	Lincoln	Parish	232	Bromyard	Hereford	L. Sub.	11 510
Brockley	Somerset	Parish	93	Bromyard	Heref. & Wor.	District	11 811
Brockley	Suffolk	Parish	340	Bromyard	Hereford	Sub-dis.	3 656
Brockmoor	Stafford	Ecl. Dis.	3 844	Bromyard	,,	Parish	2 995
Brockton	,,	Tnship.	278	Bromyard	,,	Tnship.	1 385
Brockworth	Gloucester	Parish	475	Broncastellan	Cardigan	Tnship.	195
Brodsworth	York	Parish	412	Broncoed	Flint	Tnship.	458
Brogden	,,	Tnship.	122	Brongwyn	Cardigan	Parish	339
Brokenborough	Wilts	Parish	503	Bronington	Flint	Tnship.	675
Bromborough	Cheshire	Parish	1 279	Bronygarth	Salop	Tnship.	295
Bromborough	,,	Tnship.	1 094	Brook	Hants	Parish	156
Bromby	Lincoln	Tnship.	204	Brook	Kent	Parish	120
Brome	Suffolk	Parish	291	Brook	Somerset	Hamlet	295
Bromeswell	,,	Parish	210	Brooke	Norfolk	Parish	746
Bromfield	Cumberland.	Parish	2 269	Brooke	Rutland	Parish	112
Bromfield	,,	Tnship.	411	Brookfield, St. Ann	Middlesex	Ecl. Dis.	491
Bromfield	Denbigh	Hund.	33 484	Brooksby	Leicester	Parish	44
Bromfield	Salop	Parish	762	Brookhampton	Salop	Tnship.	86
Bromfield	,,	Tnship.	621	Brookland	Kent	Parish	459
Bromham	Beds	Parish	361	Brookthorpe	Gloucester	Parish	180
Bromham	Wilts	Sub-dis.	4 884	Broom	Beds	Hamlet	387
Bromham	,,	Parish	1 402	Broom	Durham	Tnship.	136
Bromley, Great	Essex	Parish	758	Broom	Worcester	Parish	118
Bromley, Little	,,	Parish	371	Broome	Norfolk	Parish	505
Bromley	Kent	L. Sub.	25 312	Broomfield	Essex	Parish	849
Bromley	,,	District	20 368	Broomfield	Kent	Parish	150
Bromley	,,	Sub-dis.	11 755	Broomfield	Somerset	Parish	525
Bromley	,,	Parish	5 505	Broomfleet	York	Tnship.	193
Bromley Common	,,	Ecl. Dis.	1 163	Broomhall	Cheshire	Tnship.	120
Bromley	Middlesex	Parish	24 077	Broomhaugh	Northumberland	Tnship.	151
Bromley	Stafford	Tnship.	41	Broomhill	Kent & Sussex	Parish	102
Bromley Regis	,,	Parish	638	Broomley	Northumberland	Tnship.	478
Brompton	Kent	Ecl. Dis.	8 119	Broom Park	,,	Tnship.	77
Brompton	Middlesex	Sub-dis.	18 198	Broomsthorpe	Norfolk	Hamlet	16
Holy Trinity	,,	Ecl. Dis.	10 650	Broomy Walk	Hants	—	117

Name of Place.	County.	Description.	Population.	Name of Place.	County.	Description.	Population.
Broseley	Salop	Sub-dis.	5 853	Broxbourne	Herts	Parish	2 663
Broseley	,,	Parish	4 724	Broxbourne	,,	—	765
Brothercross	Norfolk	Hund.	4 614	Broxfield	Northumberland	Tnship.	27
Brothertoft	Lincoln	Tnship.	124	Broxholme	Lincoln	Parish	125
Brotherton	York	Parish	1 449	Broxted..	Essex	Parish	782
Brotherton	,,	Tnship.	1 339	Broxton..	Cheshire	Hund.	18 499
Brotherwick	Northumberland	Tnship.	7	Broxton..	,,	L. Sub.	18 499
Brotton ..	York	Parish	509	Broxton..	,,	Tnship.	546
Brotton ..	,,	Tnship.	330	Broxtow	Notts	Wapen.	88 886
Brough, &c.	Derby	Tnship.	102	Broynllis	Brecon	Parish	305
Brough ..	Westmoreland	Parish	1 728	Bruen Stapleford	Cheshire	Tnship.	153*
Brough ..	,,	Tnship.	840	Bruera ..	,,	Chap.	44
Brough Sowerby.	,,	Tnship.	140	Bruern ..	Oxon	Ville	51
Brough (Catterick P.)	York	Tnship.	128	Bruisyard	Suffolk	Parish	222
Brougham	Westmoreland	Parish	239	Brumstead	Norfolk	Parish	99
Broughton	Bucks	Parish	155	Brundall	,,	Parish	104
Broughton, Great	Cumberland.	Tnship.	836	Brundish	Suffolk	Parish	451
Broughton, Little	,,	Tnship.	641	Brunstock	Cumberland.	Tnship.	84
Broughton	Denbigh	Tnship.	3 165	Bruntingthorpe	Leicester	Parish	413
Broughton	Flint	Tnship.	388	Brunton	Northumberland	Tnship.	86
Broughton	Hants & Wilts	Sub-dis.	3 709	Brunton, East ..	,,	Tnship.	134
Broughton	Hants	Parish	1 001	Brunton, West..	,,	Tnship.	128
Broughton	,,	—	955	Brushfield	Derby	Tnship.	39
Broughton	Hunts	Parish	376	Brushford	Devon	Parish	132
Broughton	Lancaster	Sub-dis.	7 850	Brushford	Somerset	Parish	328
Broughton	,,	Tnship.	709	Bruton ..	,,	Hund.	4 209
Broughton	,,	Sub-dis.	9 885	Bruton ..	,,	Sub-dis.	3 969
Broughton	,,	Tnship.	9 885	Bruton ..	,,	Parish	2 232
Broughton, St. John	,,	Ecl. Dis.	7 138	Bruton ..	,,	—	2 023
Broughton, East	,,	Tnship.	534	Bryan, Askham..	York	Parish	362
Broughton, West	,,	Tnship.	1 183	Bryanstone	Dorset	Parish	206
Broughton Astley	Leicester	Parish	785	Bryher ..	Isle of Scilly	Island	115
Broughton Astley	,,	Tnship.	354	Brymbo..	Denbigh	Tnship.	2 432
Broughton Nether	,,	Parish	519	Brymbo..	,,	Ecl. Dis.	5 475
Broughton	Lincoln	Parish	1 280	Bryncoedifor, St. Paul	Merion.	Ecl. Dis.	186
Broughton Brant	,,	Parish	755	Bryncroes	Carnarvon..	Parish	889
Broughton	Northampton	Parish	738	Bryneglwys	Denbigh	Parish	444
Broughton Sulney	Notts	Parish	406	Brynford	Flint	Ecl. Dis.	910
Broughton	Oxon	Parish	641	Bryngwran	Anglesey	Sub-dis.	5 746
Broughton	,,	—	213	Bryngwyn	Monmouth..	Parish	313
Broughton Poggs	Oxon & Glouc.	Parish	135	Bryngwyn	Radnor	Parish	334
Broughton	Salop	Parish	223	Bryning, &c.	Lancaster	Tnship.	116
Broughton & Croxton	Stafford	Tnship.	821	Brynmawr	Brecon	L. Sub.	8 804
Broughton Gifford	Wilts	Parish	621	Brynuchel Tafalog	Montgomy.	Tnship.	327
Broughton Hackett	Worcester .	Parish	164	Bubbenhall	Warwick	Parish	346
Broughton, Stokesley	York	Tnship.	577	Bubnell..	Derby	Tnship.	118
Broughton, Malton	,,	Tnship.	123	Bubwith	York	Sub-dis.	2 108
Broughton	,,	Parish	274	Bubwith	,,	Parish	1 453
Broughton, Skipton	,,	Tnship.	162	Bubwith	,,	Tnship.	554
Brown Candover	Hants	Parish	322	Buckabank	Cumberland.	Tnship.	617
Brown Edge, St. Anne	Stafford	Ecl. Dis.	670	Buckby, Long	Northampton	Parish	2 500
Brownsover	Warwick	Tnship.	71	Buckden	Hunts	Parish	1 099
Broxa ..	York	Tnship.	51	Buckden	York	Tnship.	335
Broxash..	Hereford	Hund.	11 878	Buckenham	Norfolk	Parish	49

Name of Place.	County.	Description.	Population.	Name of Place.	County.	Description.	Population.
Buckenham nr. Tofts	Norfolk	Parish	60	Buckton & Coxall	Hereford ..	Tnship.	168
Buckenham, New	,, ..	Parish	656	Buckton ..	York ..	Tnship.	181
Buckenham, Old	,, ..	Parish	1 214	Buckworth ..	Hunts ..	Parish	201
Buckerell ..	Devon ..	Parish	318	Budbrooke ..	Warwick ..	Sub-dis.	4 446
Buckfastleigh ..	,, ..	Sub-dis.	4 263	Budbrooke .	,, ..	Parish	492
Buckfastleigh ..	,, ..	Parish	2 544	Budby ..	Notts ..	Tnship.	113
Buckholt ..	Hants ..	Parish	118	Budehaven, St. Mich.	Cornwall	Ecl. Dis.	766
Buckhorn Weston	Dorset ..	Parish	509	Budle ..	Northumberland	Tnship.	106
Buckhurst Hill, St. John	Essex	Ecl. Dis.	902	Budleigh, East..	Devon ..	Hund.	22 797
Buckinghamshire	..	County	167 993	Budleigh, West..	,, ..	Hund.	2 981
Buckingham ..	Bucks ..	Hund.	10 644	Budleigh, East..	,, ..	Parish	2 496
Buckingham	Bucks & Nrptn.	District	13 756	Budock ..	Cornwall ..	Parish	2 251
Buckingham ..	Bucks ..	Sub-dis.	5 987	Budworth ..	Chester ..	Sub-dis.	4 311
Buckingham ..	,, ..	Parish	3 849	Budworth, Great	,, ..	Parish	18 852
Buckingham ..	,, ..	—	1 729	Budworth, Great	,, ..	Tnship.	613
Buckingham ..	,,	M. Bor.	3 849	Budworth, Little	,, ..	Parish	582
Buckingham ..	,,	P. Bor.	7 626	Buerton (Aldford P.)	,, ..	Tnship.	68
Buckland ..	Berks ..	Sub-dis.	4 945	Buerton (Audlem P.)	,, ..	Tnship.	464
Buckland ..	,, ..	Parish	912	Bugbrooke ..	Northampton	Sub-dis.	3 450
Buckland ..	Bucks ..	Parish	732	Bugbrooke ..	,, ..	Parish	935
Buckland Brewer	Devon..	Parish	922	Buglawton ..	Cheshire ..	Tnship.	2 014
Buckland, East	,, ..	Parish	151	Buglawton, St. John	,, ..	Ecl. Dis.	2 014
Buckland Filleigh	,, ..	Parish	258	Bugthorpe ..	York ..	Parish	245
Buckland in Moor	,, ..	Parish	113	Buildwas ..	Salop ..	Parish	276
Buckland Monachorum	,, ..	Sub-dis.	8 698	Builth ..	Brecon ..	Hund.	6 492
Buckland Monachorum	,, ..	Parish	1 489	Builth ..	,, ..	L. Sub.	7 020
Buckland, Tout Saints	,, ..	Parish	31	Builth ..	Brecon & Radnor	District	8 305
Buckland, West..	,, ..	Parish	321	Builth ..	,, ,,	Sub-dis.	8 444
Buckland Newton	Dorset ..	Parish	972	Builth ..	Brecon ..	Parish	1 110
Buckland Ripers	,, ..	Parish	113	Bulby ..	Lincoln ..	Hamlet	71
Buckland ..	Gloucester..	Parish	355	Bulcote ..	Notts ..	Chap.	136
Buckland ..	Herts ..	Parish	385	Bulford..	Wilts ..	Parish	383
Buckland, Faversham	Kent ..	Parish	18	Bulk ..	Lancaster ..	Tnship.	109
Buckland, Dover	,, ..	Parish	2 162	Bulkeley ..	Cheshire ..	Tnship.	196
Buckland Dinham	Somerset ..	Parish	459	Bulkington ..	Warwick ..	Parish	1 858
Buckland, St. Mary	,, ..	Parish	715	Bulkington ..	Wilts ..	Tithing	240
Buckland, West..	,, ..	Parish	901	Bulkworthy ..	Devon ..	Parish	128
Buckland ..	Surrey ..	Parish	869	Bullers Green	Northumberland	Tnship.	269
Bucklebury ..	Berks & Oxon	Sub-dis.	5 532	Bulley ..	Gloucester..	Parish	226
Bucklebury ..	Berks ..	Parish	1 178	Bullingdon ..	Oxon ..	Hund	12 185
Bucklesham ..	Suffolk ..	Parish	362	Bullingham, Lower	Hereford..	Parish	255
Bucklow ..	Cheshire ..	Hund.	60 039	Bullingham, Upper	,, ..	Parish	83
Bucklow Daresbury	,, ..	L. Sub.	36 045	Bullington ..	Hants ..	Parish	171
Bucklow, East ..	,, ..	L. Sub.	26 717	Bullington ..	Lincoln ..	Chap.	44
Buckminster ..	Leicester ..	Parish	655	Bullocks Hall	Northumberland	Tnship.	14
Buckminster ..	,, ..	Tnship.	348	Bulmer ..	Essex ..	Sub-dis.	4 853
Bucknall ..	Lincoln ..	Parish	406	Bulmer ..	,, ..	Parish	758
Bucknall ..	Stafford ..	Tnship.	1 498	Bulmer ..	York ..	Wapen.	24 257
Bucknall Eaves..	,, ..	Tnship.	248	Bulmer, East ..	,, ..	L. Sub.	11 010
Bucknell ..	Oxon ..	Parish	326	Bulmer, West ..	,, ..	L. Sub.	10 501
Bucknell	Salop & Hereford	Parish	790	Bulmer ..	,, ..	Sub-dis.	4 074
Bucknell ..	Salop ..	Tnship.	622	Bulmer ..	,, ..	Parish	1 077
Buckrose ..	York ..	Wapen.	15 333	Bulmer ..	,, ..	Tnship.	345
Buckrose ..	,, ..	L. Sub.	15 333	Bulphan .	Essex ..	Parish	268

Name of Place.	County.	Description.	Population.	Name of Place.	County.	Description.	Population.
Bulwell ..	.. Notts ..	Sub-dis.	7 823	Burham..	.. Kent ..	Parish	775
Bulwell ..	.. ,, ..	Parish	3 660	Buriton ..	.. Hants ..	Parish	1 050
Bulwick..	.. Northampton	Parish	393	Burland..	.. Cheshire ..	Tnship.	672
Bulwick Short Leys	,,	Parish	69	Burlescombe	.. Devon ..	Parish	856
Bunbury..	.. Cheshire ..	Sub-dis.	7 959	Burlestone	.. Dorset ..	Parish	45
Bunbury .	.. ,, ..	Parish	4 727	Burley ..	.. Hants ..	Ville	515
Bunbury .	.. ,, ..	Tnship.	990	Burley Ville, St. John ,, ..		Ecl. Dis.	672
Bungay ..	.. Suffolk ..	Sub-dis.	6 398	Burley Walk	.. ,, ..	—	62
Bungay .	.. ,, ..	Town	3 805	Burley ..	.. Rutland ..	Parish	237
Bungay, Holy Trinity	,, ..	Parish	1 809	Burley ..	.. York ..	Ecl. Dis.	3 530
Bungay, St. Mary	,, ..	Parish	1 996	Burley in Wharfedale	,, ..	Tnship.	2 136
Bunhill Row, St. Paul	Middlx.	Ecl. Dis.	5 896	Burley, St. Mary	,, ..	Ecl. Dis.	2 454
Bunny ..	.. Notts ..	Parish	273	Burlingham :—			
Buntingford	.. Herts ..	L. Sub.	4 864	St. Andrew	.. Norfolk ..	Parish	186
Buntingford	.. ,, ..	Union	6 389	St. Edmund ..	,, ..	Parish	85
Buntingford	.. ,, ..	Sub-dis.	6 389	St. Peter	.. ,, ..	Parish	80
Bunwell..	.. Norfolk ..	Parish	907	Burmantofts, St. Stephen	York	Ecl. Dis.	5 062
Burbage	.. Leic. & Warw.	Sub-dis.	5 137	Burmarsh	.. Kent ..	Parish	170
Burbage	.. Leicester ..	Chap.	1 801	Burmington	.. Warwick ..	Parish	212
Burbage	.. Wilts ..	Parish	1 603	Burn ..	.. York ..	Tnship.	320
Burcombe	.. ..	Parish	374	Burnage	.. Lancaster ..	Tnship.	624
Burcott..	.. Oxon ..	Hamlet	172	Burnaston	.. Derby ..	Tnship.	188
Burdon ..	.. Durham ..	Tnship.	95	Burnby ..	.. York ..	Parish	126
Burdon, Great ..	,, ..	Tnship.	104	Burneston	.. ,, ..	Parish	1 554
Bures ..	Suffolk & Essex	Sub-dis.	5 642	Burneston	.. ,, ..	Tnship.	290
Bures ..	.. Essex ..	Hamlet	623	Burnett..	.. Somerset ..	Parish	98
Bures, St. Mary	Suffolk & Essex	Parish	1 659	Burnham	.. Bucks ..	Hund.	20 534
Bures, St. Mary	Suffolk ..	—	1 036	Burnham	.. ,, ..	Sub-dis.	6 134
Burford..	.. Oxon & Glouc.	Sub-dis.	4 816	Burnham	.. ,, ..	Parish	2 233
Burford..	.. Oxon ..	Parish	1 649	Burnham	.. ,, ..	—	2 081
Burford..	.. ,, ..	Tnship.	1 435	Burnham	.. Essex ..	Parish	1 870
Burford..	.. Salop ..	Parish	1 121	Burnham	.. Norfolk ..	Sub-dis.	6 497
Burford..	.. ,, ..	Tnship.	314	Burnham Deepdale	,, ..	Parish	81
Burgate..	.. Suffolk ..	Parish	359	Burnham Norton	,, ..	Parish	172
Burgh ..	.. Cumberland	Sub-dis.	1 493	Burnham Overy .	,, ..	Parish	650
Burgh by Sands	,,	Parish	986	Burnham Sutton, &c.	,, ..	Parish	380
Burgh by Sands	,,	Tnship.	460	Burnham Thorpe	,, ..	Parish	427
Burgh ..	.. Lincoln ..	Sub-dis.	4 941	Burnham Westgate	,, ..	Parish	1 094
Burgh in Marsh	,, ..	Parish	1 223	Burnham ..	Somerset ..	Sub-dis.	5 707
Burgh upon Bain	,, ..	Parish	203	Burnham	.. ,, ..	Parish	2 252
Burgh ..	.. Norfolk ..	Parish	227	Burniston	.. York ..	Tnship.	350
Burgh Apton ..	,, ..	Parish	544	Burnley..	.. Lancaster ..	District	75 595
Burgh or Flegg Burgh	,, ..	Parish	554	Burnley..	.. ,, ..	Sub-dis.	42 702
Burgh, St. Peter	,, ..	Parish	298	Burnley..	.. ,, ..	Tnship.	19 971
Burgh, South ..	,, ..	Parish	317	Burnley ..	.. ,, ..	M. Bor.	28 700
Burgh ..	.. Suffolk ..	Parish	271	Burnley, St. James	,, ..	Ecl. Dis.	4 420
Burgh Castle ..	,, ..	Parish	458	Burnop ..	.. Durham ..	Tnship.	155
Burgh Wallis ..	York ..	Parish	237	Burnsall	.. York ..	Parish	1 275
Burgh Wallis ..	,, ..	Tnship.	226	Burnsall	.. ,, ..	Tnship.	200
Burghclere	.. Hants ..	Parish	819	Burntwood	.. Stafford ..	Tnship.	1 634
Burghfield	.. Berks ..	Parish	1 130	Burntwood, Christch. ,, ..		Ecl. Dis.	1 634
Burghill	.. Hereford ..	Sub-dis.	5 737	Burpham	.. Sussex ..	Parish	256
Burghill	.. ,, ..	Parish	934	Burradon (Earsdon P.)	Nrthmb.	Tnship.	50
Burghill	.. ,, ..	Tnship.	411	Burradon (Alwinton P.)	,,	Tnship.	1

Name of Place.	County.	Description.	Population.	Name of Place.	County.	Description.	Population.
Burrell w. Cowling	York	Tnship.	111	Burton on Trent, Chrstch.	Staff.	Ecl. Dis.	6 896
Burrels	Westmoreland	Tnship.	66	Burton on Trent, Trinity	„	Ecl. Dis.	5 465
Burringham	Lincoln	Tnship.	632	**Burton on Trent**	„	Town	13 671
Burrington	Devon	Parish	939	Burton	Sussex	Parish	45
Burrington	Hereford	Parish	231	Burton Dassett	Warwick	Parish	655
Burrington	Somerset	Parish	477	Burton Hastings	„	Parish	199
Burrough Green	Cambs	Parish	427	Burton in Kendal	Westm. &c.	Parish	2 118
Burrough	Leicester	Parish	138	Burton in Kendal	Westmoreld.	Tnship	751
Burrow w. Burrow	Lancaster	Tnship.	225	Burton Hill	Wilts	Tithing	290
Burrow Bridge	Somerset	Ecl. Dis.	692	Burton Agnes	York	Parish	723
Burscough	Lancaster	Tnship.	2 461	Burton Agnes	„	Tnship.	344
Burscough Bridge, St. Jno.	„	Ecl. Dis.	3 175	Burton Constable	„	Tnship.	224
Bursledon	Hants	Parish	659	Burton w. Walden	„	Tnship.	478
Burslem	Stafford	Sub-dis.	22 327	Burton Fleming	„	Parish	525
Burslem	„	Parish	22 327	Burton in Lonsdale	„	Tnship.	597
Burslem	„	Tnship.	17 821	Burton Leonard	„	Parish	507
Burslem, St. Paul	„	Ecl. Dis.	7 801	Burton, North	„	Parish	525
Burstall	Suffolk	Parish	222	Burton Pidsea	„	Parish	408
Burstead, Great	Essex	Parish	2 095	Burton Salmon	„	Tnship.	247
Burstead, Great	„	—	705	Burton upon Ure	„	Tnship.	120
Burstead, Little	„	Parish	186	Burtonwood	Lancaster	Tnship.	990
Burstock	Dorset	Parish	220	Burwardsley	Cheshire	Tnship.	500
Burston	Norfolk	Parish	419	Burwarton	Salop	Parish	156
Burstow	Surrey	Parish	927	Burwash	Sussex	L. Sub.	8 082
Burstwick	York	Parish	728	Burwash	„	Parish	2 143
Burstwick w. Skeckling	„	Tnship.	485	Burwell	Cambs	Parish	1 987
Burtholme	Cumberland	Tnship.	338	Burwell	Lincoln	Parish	159
Burtle	Somerset	Ecl. Dis.	248	Bury	Hunts	Parish	362
Burton	Cheshire	Parish	425	Bury	Lancaster	L. Sub.	101 135
Burton	„	Tnship.	265	Bury	„	District	101 135
Burton by Tarvin	„	Tnship.	77	Bury, North	„	Sub-dis.	15 375
Burton	Denbigh	Tnship.	570	Bury, South	„	Sub-dis.	15 726
Burton Bradstock	Dorset	Sub-dis.	6 724	Bury	„	Parish	80 558
Burton Bradstock	„	Parish	1 010	Bury	„	Tnship.	30 397
Burton Lazars	Leicester	Chap.	233	Bury, St. John	„	Ecl. Dis.	4 512
Burton on Wolds	„	Tnship.	441	Bury, St. Paul	„	Ecl. Dis.	10 803
Burton Overy	„	Parish	465	Bury	„	P. Boro.	37 563
Burton	Lincoln	Parish	171	Bury	Suffolk	L. Sub.	41 146
Burton-Coggles	„	Parish	288	Bury St. Edmunds	„	District	13 318
Burton Gate	„	Parish	115	Bury St. Edmunds	„	Sub-dis.	13 318
Burton Pedwardine	„	Parish	135	Bury, St. John	„	Ecl. Dis.	3 492
Burton on Stather	„	Parish	983	**Bury St. Edmunds**	„	Boro.	13 318
Burton Latimer	Northampton	Parish	1 158	Bury	Sussex	Parish	500
Burton	Northmb.	Tnship.	103	Burythorpe	York	Parish	265
Burton Joyce	Notts	Parish	834	Busby, Great	„	Tnship.	117
Burton Joyce	„	Tnship.	698	Busby, Little	„	Tnship.	38
Burton, West	„	Parish	67	Buscot	Berks	Parish	467
Burton	Pembroke	Parish	1 029	Bushbury	Stafford	Parish	2 051
Burton Extra	Stafford	Tnship.	2 849	Bushby	Leicester	Hamlet	60
Burton on Trent	„	L. Sub.	21 363	Bush End, St. John	Essex	Ecl. Dis.	410
Burton on Trent	Staf. & Derby	District	41 065	Bushey	Herts	Sub-dis.	4 928
Burton on Trent	„ „	Sub-dis.	18 745	Bushey	„	Parish	3 159
Burton on Trent	„ „	Parish	16 824	Bushley	Worcester	Parish	282
Burton on Trent	Stafford	Tnship	9 534	Bushwood	Warwick	Hamlet	35

Name of Place.	County.	Description.	Population.	Name of Place.	County.	Description.	Population.
Buslingthorpe	Lincoln	Parish	55	Byley, St. John	Cheshire	Ecl. Dis.	460
Buslingthorpe, St. Mich.	York	Ecl. Dis.	4 548	Byley w. Yatehouse	„	Tnship.	124
Bussage, St. Michael	Gloucester	Ecl. Dis.	312	Byram w. Pool	York	Tnship.	65
Bustabeck Bound	Cumberland	Tnship.	221	Byron	Notts	Sub-dis.	14 673
Buston, High	Northumbld.	Tnship.	120	Bytham, Castle	Lincoln	Parish	1 024
Buston, Low	„	Tnship.	129	Bytham, Castle	„	—	813
Butcombe	Somerset	Parish	223	Bytham, Little	„	Parish	362
Butleigh	„	Parish	1 038	Bythorn	Hunts	Parish	292
Butlers Marston	Warwick	Parish	271	Byton	Hereford	Parish	214
Butley	Cheshire	Tnship.	674	Bywell	Northumberland	Sub-dis.	8 128
Butley	Suffolk	Parish	385	Bywell, St. Andrew	„	Parish	508
Butsfield	Durham	Tnship.	319	Bywell, St. Andrew	„	Tnship.	19
Butter Crambe	York	Tnship.	126	Bywell, St. Peter	„	Parish	1 574
Butterlaw	Northumberland	Tnship.	10	Bywell, St. Peter	„	Tnship.	94
Butterleigh	Devon	Parish	153				
Buttermere	Cumberland	Chap.	101	**Cabourn**	Lincoln	Parish	171
Buttermere	Wilts	Parish	128	Cabus	Lancaster	Tnship.	209
Buttershaw	York	Ecl. Dis.	2 247	Cacca Dutton	Denbigh	Tnship.	93
Butterton (Mayfield P.)	Staff.	Tnship.	325	Cadbury	Devon	Parish	241
Butterton, St. Thomas	„	Ecl. Dis.	379	Cadbury, North	Somerset	Parish	997
Butterton (Trentham P.)	„	Tnship.	57	Cadbury, South	„	Parish	287
Butterwick	Durham	Tnship.	48	Caddington	Herts & Beds	Parish	1 851
Butterwick	Lincoln	Parish	605	Cadeby	Leicester	Parish	422
Butterwick, East	„	Tnship.	420	Cadeby	„	Tnship.	194
Butterwick, West, &c.	„	Tnship.	907	Cadeby	York	Tnship.	165
Butterwick, West	„	Ecl. Dis.	907	Cadeleigh	Devon	Parish	358
Butterwick	York E.	Tnship.	109	Cadmore End	Bucks & Oxon	Ecl. Dis.	332
Butterwick	„ N.	Tnship.	79	Cadney	Lincoln	Parish	570
Butterworth Freehold	Lanc.	Sub-dis.	2 909	Cadoxton	Glamorgan	Sub-dis.	7 522
Butterworth Lordship	„	Sub-dis.	3 795	Cadoxton	„	Parish	8 209
Butterworth	„	Tnship.	6 704	Cadoxton by Barry	„	Parish	279
Buttington	Montgomery	Parish	935	Cadworth w. Cawden	Wilts	Hund.	4 624
Buttolphs	Sussex	Parish	54	Caenby	Lincoln	Parish	125
Buttsbury	Essex	Parish	531	Caereinionfechan	Montgomery	Tnship.	111
Buxhall	Suffolk	Parish	536	Caerfallwch	Flint	Tnship.	925
Buxted	Sussex	Parish	1 624	Caergwyle	„	P. Bor.	844
Buxton	Derby	Sub-dis.	4 142	Caerhun	Carnarvon	Parish	1 314
Buxton	„	Tnship.	1 877	Caerleon	Monmouth	L. Sub.	6 908
Buxton	Norfolk	Sub-dis.	10 092	Caerleon	„	Sub-dis.	7 615
Buxton	„	Parish	640	Caerleon	„	Tnship.	1 268
Bwlch Trewyn	Monmouth	Hamlet	95	Caerphilly	Glamorgan	Hund.	67 612
Byers Green	Durham	Tnship.	1 634	Caerphilly, Higher	„	L. Sub.	53 673
Byers Green	„	Ecl. Dis.	2 691	Caerphilly, Lower	„	L. Sub.	11 665
Byfield	Northampton	Parish	901	Caerphilly	„	Sub-dis.	10 012
Byfleet	Surrey	Parish	770	Caerphilly, St. Martin	„	Ecl. Dis.	1 193
Byford	Hereford	Parish	201	Caerseddfan	Montgomery	Tnship.	547
Bygrave	Herts	Parish	195	Caerwent	Monmouth	Parish	445
Byker	Northumberland	Sub-dis.	12 994	Caerwent	„	—	307
Byker	„	Tnship.	7 663	Caerwys	Flint	Parish	853
Byker	„	Ecl. Dis.	10 388	Caerwys	„	P. Bor.	637
Byland Abbey	York	Tnship.	104	Cainham	Salop	Sub-dis.	2 227
Byland, Old	„	Parish	157	Cainham	„	Parish	755
Bylaugh	Norfolk	Parish	82	Cainscross	Gloucester	Ecl. Dis.	1 916
Bylchau	Denbigh	Ecl. Dis.	537	Caira or Cairau	Glamorgan	Parish	131

Name of Place.	County.	Description.	Population.	Name of Place.	County.	Description.	Population.
Caistor	Lincoln	L. Sub.	31 972	Calshot	Hants	—	23
Caistor	,,	District	37 517	Calstock	Cornwall	Parish	7 090
Caistor	,,	Sub.-dis.	9 005	Calstone Wellington	Wilts	Parish	36
Caistor	,,	Parish	2 348	Calthorpe	Norfolk	Parish	187
Caistor	,,	Tnship.	2 141	Calthwaite	Cumberland	Tnship.	269
Caistor by Norwich	Norfolk	Parish	162	Calton	Staff. & Derb	Sub.-dis.	3 036
Caistor by Yarmouth	,,	Parish	1 203	Calton (Blore P.)	Stafford	Tnship.	72
Caistron	Northumberland	Tnship.	41	Calton (Mayfield P.)	,,	Tnship.	70
Cakemore	Worcester	Tnship.	448	Calton (Waterfall P.)	,,	Tnship.	65
Calbourn	York	Tnship.	142	Calton	York	Tnship.	56
Calbourne	Hants, I. W.	Sub.-dis.	5 417	Calveley	Cheshire	Tnship.	285
Calbourne	,, ,,	Parish	728	Calver	Derby	Tnship.	617
Calbourne	,, ,,	—	629	Calverhall	Salop	Ecl. Dis.	279
Calceby	Lincoln	Parish	66	Calverleigh	Devon	Parish	86
Calcethorpe	,,	Parish	84	Calverley	York	Sub.-dis.	5 559
Calceworth	,,	Hund.	13 972	Calverley	,,	Parish	28 563
Caldbeck	Cumberland	Sub.-dis.	5 197	Calverley w. Farsley	,,	Tnship.	5 559
Caldbeck	,,	Parish	1 560	Calverton	Bucks	Parish	595
Caldbeck Haltcliff	,,	Tnship.	521	Calverton	Notts	Parish	1 372
Caldbeck, High	,,	Tnship.	313	Calwich	Stafford	Tnship.	85
Caldbeck, Low	,,	Tnship.	675	Cam	Gloucester	Parish	1 500
Caldbridge	York	Tnship.	97	Camberwell	Surrey	District	71 488
Caldecot	Norfolk	Parish	39	Camberwell	,,	Sub.-dis.	21 297
Caldecote	Cambs.	Parish	93	Camberwell	,,	Parish	71 488
Caldecote	Hunts	Parish	70	1 St. George's W. Ward	,,	Ward	10 368
Caldecote	Warwick	Parish	130	2 St. George's E. Ward	,,	Ward	9 965
Caldecott	Beds	Hamlet	591	3 Camden Ward	,,	Ward	14 321
Caldecott	Cheshire	Tnship.	66	4 North Peckham Ward	,,	Ward	14 377
Caldecott	Herts	Parish	44	5 South Peckham Ward	,,	Ward	13 758
Caldecott	Rutland	Parish	346	6 Camberwell & Dulwich Wd.		Ward	8 699
Caldewgate	Cumberland	Tnship.	9 732	Christchurch	,,	Ecl. Dis.	8 176
Caldicott	Monmouth	Hund.	13 624	Emmanuel	,,	Ecl. Dis.	8 923
Caldicott	,,	Parish	579	St. George	,,	Ecl. Dis.	20 324
Caldwell	York	Tnship.	162	Camblesforth	York	Tnship.	322
Caldy	Cheshire	Tnship.	147	Cambo	Northumberland	Tnship.	111
Caldy Island, &c.	Pembroke	Parish	73	Cambo, Holy Trinity	,,	Ecl. Dis.	780
Calchill	Kent	Sub.-dis.	5 311	Camborne	Cornwall	Sub.-dis.	14 056
Calf of Man		Island	25	Camborne	,,	Parish	14 056
Calke	Derby	Parish	78	Camborne	,,	Town	7 208
Callaley & Yetlingtn.	Nthmb.	Tnship.	261	Cambridgeshire		County	176 016
Callerton, High	,,	Tnship.	97	Cambridge	Cambs	District	26 361
Callerton, Little	,,	Tnship.	20	Cambridge	,,	Borough	26 361
Callington	Cornwall	Sub.-dis.	8 899	Cambridge, St. Paul	,,	Ecl. Dis.	3 229
Callington	,,	Parish	2 202	Camden Town	Middlesex	Sub.-dis.	23 266
Callow	Derby	Tnship.	91	Camden Town	,,	Ecl. Dis.	15 832
Callow	Hereford	Parish	137	Camden N. T., St. Paul	,,	Ecl. Dis.	5 145
Calne	Wilts	Hund.	4 297	Camden Chapel	Surrey	Ecl. Dis.	11 291
Calne & Chippenham	,,	L. Sub.	31 271	Cameley	Somerset	Parish	526
Calne	,,	District	8 885	Camelford	Cornwall	District	7 784
Calne	,,	Sub.-dis.	8 885	Camelford	,,	Sub.-dis.	5 355
Calne	,,	Parish	5 098	Camel Queen	Somerset	Parish	734
Calne	,,	M. Bor.	2 494	Camel, West	,,	Parish	338
Calne	,,	P. Bor.	5 179	Camerton	,,	Parish	1 368
Calow	Derby	Tnship.	575	Camerton	York	Hamlet	29

Name of Place.	County.	Description.	Population.	Name of Place.	County.	Description.	Population.
Cammeringham	Lincoln	Parish	137	Canterbury	Kent	L. Sub.	21 688
Cammerton	Cumberland	Parish	1 326	Canterbury	"	District	16 643
Cammerton	"	Tnship.	224	Canterbury	"	Sub-dis.	16 643
Campden	Gloucester	L. Sub.	10 268	Canterbury	"	City	21 324
Campden	Glouc. & Warwick	Sub-dis.	4 845	Cantley	Norfolk	Parish	235
Campsall	York	Sub-dis.	4 549	Cantley	York	Parish	663
Campsall	"	Parish	1 948	Canton, St. John	Glamorgan	Ecl. Dis.	3 920
Campsall	"	Tnship.	349	Cantreff	Brecon	Parish	221
Campsey Ash	Suffolk	Parish	379	Cantreff	"	—	126
Campton	Beds	Parish	1 544	Cantsfield	Lancaster	Tnshp.	116
Campton	"	—	529	Canvey	Essex	Island	241
Camrose	Pembroke	Parish	1 126	Canwell	Stafford	Parish	43
Candlesby	Lincoln	Parish	240	Canwick	Lincoln	Parish	228
Candleshoe	"	Wapen.	10 662	Capel	Kent	Parish	611
Canewdon	Essex	Parish	661	Capel	Surrey	Sub-dis.	4 094
Canfield, Great	"	Parish	468	Capel	"	Parish	1 074
Canfield, Little	"	Parish	314	Capel Cynon	Cardigan	Ecl. Dis.	413
Canford	Dorset	Sub-dis.	2 326	Capel-le-Ferne	Kent	Parish	193
Canford Magna	"	Parish	4 877	Capel, St Andrew	Suffolk	Parish	231
Canford Magna	"	—	1 125	Capel, St. Mary	"	Sub-dis.	6 592
Cann	"	Parish	547	Capel, St. Mary	"	Parish	669
Cannington	Somerset	Hund.	5 700	Capenhurst	Cheshire	Tnshp.	131
Cannington	"	Parish	1 419	Capenhurst, Trinity	"	Ecl. Dis.	224
Cannington	"	—	1 398	Capesthorne	"	Tnshp.	114
Cannock	Stafford	Sub-dis.	8 773	Capheaton	Northumberland	Tnshp.	195
Cannock	"	Parish	3 964	Carbrooke	Norfolk	Parish	751
Cannock	"	Tnship.	2 913	Carburton	Notts & Derby	Sub-dis.	5 523
Canon Frome	Hereford	Parish	115	Carburton	Notts	Chap.	177
Canongate	Northumberland	Tnship.	536	Car-Colston	"	Parish	299
Canon Pyon	Hereford	Parish	768	Carden	Cheshire	Tnship.	208
Canons Ashby	Northampton	Parish	220	Cardeston	Salop	Parish	294
Canons Ashby	"	—	55	Cardiff Town	Glamorgan	L. Sub.	32 954
Canterbury		Province	14071164	Cardiff	Glam. & Mon.	District	74 575
Diocese of Bangor		Diocese	195 390	Cardiff	" "	Sub-dis.	46 954
" Bath and Wells		Diocese	422 527	Cardiff, St. John	Glamorgan	Parish	8 666
" Canterbury		Diocese	474 603	Cardiff, St. Mary	"	Parish	24 288
" Chichester		Diocese	363 735	Cardiff	"	Boro.	32 954
" Ely		Diocese	480 716	Cardiff Parl. Dist. of	"	Boros.	35 541
" Exeter		Diocese	953 763	Cardiganshire		County	72 245
" Gloucester & Bristol		Diocese	568 574	Cardigan	Card. & Pemb.	District	18 585
" Hereford		Diocese	232 401	Cardigan	" "	Sub-dis.	8 886
" Lichfield		Diocese	1 221 404	Cardigan, St. Mary	Cardigan	Parish	2 706
" Lincoln		Diocese	706 026	Cardigan	Card. & Pemb.	Boro.	3 543
" Llandaff		Diocese	418 113	Cardigan, Par. Dis. of	Card. &c.	Boros.	11 646
" London		Diocese	2 570 079	Cardington	Beds	Parish	1 419
" Norwich		Diocese	667 704	Cardington	"	—	572
" Oxford		Diocese	515 083	Cardington	Salop	Parish	768
" Peterborough		Diocese	486 977	Cardinham	Cornwall	Parish	717
" Rochester		Diocese	608 914	Careby	Lincoln	Parish	107
" St. Asaph		Diocese	246 337	Carew	Pembroke	Parish	993
" St. David		Diocese	435 912	Cargo	Cumberland	Tnship.	262
" Salisbury		Diocese	377 337	Carham	Northumberland	Parish	1 274
" Winchester		Diocese	1 267 794	Carhampton	Somerset	Hund.	8 502
" Worcester		Diocese	857 775	Carhampton	"	Parish	706

Name of Place.	County.	Description.	Population.	Name of Place.	County.	Description.	Population.
Carisbrooke	Hants, I. W.	Parish	7 502	Carmarthen	Carmarthen.	L. Sub.	20 026
Carisbrooke, St. John	„ „	Ecl. Dis.	3 264	Carmarthen Boro.	„ ..	L. Sub.	9 993
Carkin	York ..	Hamlet	55	Carmarthen	„ ..	District	36 675
Carlatton	Cumberland .	Parish	71	Carmarthen	„ ..	Sub.-dis.	12 583
Carlby	Lincoln ..	Parish	183	Carmarthen		Boro.	9 993
Carleton	Cumberland .	Tnship.	181	Carmarthen, St. David „		Ecl. Dis.	4 332
Carleton, Gt. & Lt.	Lancaster .	Tnship.	363	Carmarthen Par. Dis. of „		Boros.	21 439
Carleton-Forehoe	Norfolk ..	Parish	124	Carmenellis	Cornwall ..	Ecl. Dis.	3 094
Carleton-Rode	„ ..	Parish	905	Carnaby	York ..	Parish	152
Carleton, St. Peter	„ ..	Parish	79	Carnarvonshire..	..	County	95 694
Carleton	York ..	Tnship.	191	Carnarvon	Carnarvon..	L. Sub.	39 774
Carlford	Suffolk ..	Hund.	6 227	Carnarvon	Carnv. & Ang.	District	32 425
Carlford	„ ..	Sub.-dis.	5 358	Carnarvon	Carnarvon..	Sub.-dis.	10 190
Carlisle	.. ..	Diocese	266 591	Carnarvon	„ ..	Boro.	8 512
Carlisle	Cumberland .	District	44 820	Carnarvon Par. Dis. of „		Boros.	22 907
Carlisle	„	City	29 417	Carnforth	Lancaster ..	Tnship.	393
Carlisle, Christchurch „		Ecl. Dis.	8 925	Carngiwich	Carnarvon..	Parish	130
Carlisle, Trinity..	„	Ecl. Dis.	10 555	Carno	Montgomery	Parish	969
Carlton	Beds ..	Parish	470	Carnwallon	Carmarthen .	Commt.	20 944
Carlton w. Willngm.	Cambs ..	Parish	402	Caron	„	Parish	2 608
Carlton	Durham ..	Tnship.	176	Caron-Uwch-Clawdd	Cardigan.	Tnship.	868
Carlton	Leicester ..	Chap.	277	Carperby w. Thoresby	York ..	Tnship.	345
Carlton-Curliew	„ ..	Parish	308	Carreghofa	Montgomery	Tnship.	400
Carlton-Curliew	„ ..	Tnship.	73	Carr House Lib., &c.	York ..	Parish	24
Carlton, Castle ..	Lincoln ..	Parish	45	Carrington	Cheshire ..	Tnship.	521
Carlton, Great ..	„ ..	Parish	338	Carrington	Lincoln ..	Parish	197
Carlton-le-Moorland „		Parish	384	Carrington	Notts ..	Ecl. Dis.	2 426
Carlton, Little ..	„	Parish	181	Carshalton	Surrey ..	Sub.-dis.	8 341
Carlton, North..	„	Parish	163	Carshalton	„ ..	Parish	2 538
Carlton-Scroop ..	„	Parish	266	Carsington	Derby ..	Parish	269
Carlton, South ..	„	Parish	181	Carthorpe	York ..	Tnship.	347
Carlton, East ..	Norfolk ..	Parish	244	Cartington	Northumberland	Tnship.	84
Carlton, East ..	Northampton	Parish	70	Cartmel..	Lancaster ..	Sub.-dis.	5 108
Carlton	Notts ..	Sub.-dis.	4 328	Cartmel..	„ ..	Parish	5 108
Carlton	Notts & York	Sub.-dis.	3 586	Cartmel Fell	„ ..	Tnship.	308
Carlton	Notts ..	Hamlet	2 559	Cartworth	York ..	Tnship.	2 503
Carlton in Lindrick „		Parish	1 035	Carver Street	„ ..	Ecl. Dis.	4 592
Carlton, North ..	„	Tnship.	699	Cary-Coats	Northumberland	Tnship.	41
Carlton, South ..	„	Tnship.	336	Cascob	Radnor ..	Parish	153
Carlton on Trent	„	Chap.	290	Cascob	„ ..	—	117
Carlton	Suffolk ..	Parish	116	Cashio	Herts ..	Hund.	33 058
Carlton Colville..	„ ..	Parish	946	Cashio & Leavesden „		Hams.	2 338
Carlton	York ..	Parish	243	Cassington	Oxon ..	Parish	433
Carlton (Coverham P.) „		Tnship.	276	Cassington	„ ..	—	390
Carlton (Guiseley P.) „		Tnship.	192	Cassop	Durham ..	Tnship.	1 661
Carlton (Roystone P.) „		Tnship.	351	Castellan	Pembroke ..	Chap.	165
Carlton	„	Sub.-dis.	2 423	Casterton, Great	Rutland ..	Parish	323
Carlton (Snaith P.)	„	Tnship.	752	Casterton, Little	„ ..	Parish	118
Carlton	„	Incor.	69 558	Casterton	Westmoreland	Tnship.	587
Carlton	„	Parish	1 506	Castle	Northumberland	Ward	58 132
Carlton Highdale	„	Tnship.	363	Castle	Notts ..	Sub.-dis.	6 723
Carlton-Husthwaite	„	Tnship.	170	Castle Acre	Norfolk ..	Parish	1 405
Carlton-Miniott	„	Tnship.	314	Castle-Ashby	Northampton	Parish	183
Carmarthenshire	..	County	111 796	Castle Bolton	York ..	Tnship.	259

Name of Place.	County.	Description.	Population.	Name of Place.	County.	Description.	Population.
astle Bromwich	Warwick ..	Hamlet	613	Castle View ..	Leicester ..	Liberty	139
astle Bytham ..	Lincoln ..	Parish	1 024	Castle Ward	Northumberland	L. Sub.	91 928
astle Bytham ..	,, ..	—	813	Castle Ward ..	,,	District	14 943
astlebythe ..	Pembroke ..	Parish	227	Castlewright ..	Montgomery	Tnship.	145
astle Cacreinion	Montgomery	Parish	682	Castle Yard ..	Devon ..	—	4
astle-Camps ..	Cambs ..	Parish	901	Castley ..	York ..	Tnship.	73
astle Carlton ..	Lincoln ..	Parish	45	Caston ..	Norfolk ..	Parish	510
astle Carrock ..	Cumberland.	Parish	337	Castor ..	Northampton	Parish	1 323
astle Cary ..	Somerset ..	Sub-dis.	6 129	Castor ..	,,	—	745
astle Cary ..	,, ..	Parish	2 060	Catcherside	Northumberland	Tnship.	19
astle Church ..	Stafford ..	Sub-dis.	5 413	Catcliffe..	York ..	Tnship.	279
astle Church ..	,, ..	Parish	3 362	Catcott ..	Somerset ..	Chap.	740
astle Combe ..	Wilts ..	Sub-dis.	3 286	Catel ..	Is. Guernsey	Parish	2 071
astle Combe ..	,, ..	Parish	534	Caterham ..	Surrey ..	Parish	815
astle Donington	Leic. & Notts	Sub-dis.	5 775	Catesby Abbey..	Northampton	Parish	107
astle Donington	Leicester ..	Parish	2 445	Catfield ..	Norfolk ..	Parish	660
astle Donington	,, ..	Town	2 291	Catfoss ..	York ..	Tnship.	68
astle Dykings ..	Lincoln ..	Parish	188	Cathedine ..	Brecon ..	Parish	191
astle Dyrran ..	Carmarthen.	Hamlet	92	Cathedral Division	Cheshire ..	Sub-dis.	19 762
astle Eaton ..	Wilts ..	Parish	286	Cathedral Ch. Prec.	,, ..	—	376
astle Eden ..	Durham ..	Parish	535	Cathedral Ch. Prec.	Kent ..	—	206
astleford ..	York ..	Parish	4 365	Cathedral Close .	Pembroke ..	Parish	37
astleford ..	,, ..	Tnship.	3 876	Cathedral Close Pr.	Sussex ..	—	156
astleford ..	,, ..	Town	3 876	Cathedral Close .	Wilts ..	Liberty	602
astle-Frome ..	Hereford ..	Parish	160	Catherington ..	Hants ..	District	2 497
astle Green ..	Carmarthen.	—	195	Catherington ..	,, ..	Parish	1 151
astle-Gresley ..	Derby ..	Tnship.	236	Catherston Lewston	Dorset ..	Parish	34
astle Hall ..	Cheshire ..	Ecl. Dis.	7 612	Cathinog ..	Carmarthen.	Hund.	10 161
astle Hedingham	Essex ..	Parish	1 203	Catmore ..	Berks ..	Parish	121
astle Inn ..	Brecon ..	Parish	34	Caton ..	Lancaster ..	Sub-dis.	1 817
astle Leavington	York ..	Tnship.	53	Caton ..	,, ..	Incorpo.	9 312
astlemartin ..	Pembroke ..	Hund.	5 856	Caton w. Littledale	,, ..	Tnship.	1 160
astlemartin ..	,, ..	L. Sub.	21 944	Catsash ..	Somerset ..	Hund.	7 912
astlemartin ..	,, ..	Parish	422	Catsfield ..	Sussex ..	Parish	584
astle Morton ..	Worcester ..	Parish	818	Catshill, Christch.	Worcester ..	Ecl. Dis.	2 393
astle Northwich	Cheshire ..	Tnship.	1 395	Cattal ..	York ..	Tnship.	189
astle, Old ..	Wilts ..	Parish	7	Catterall ..	Lancaster ..	Tnship.	867
astle Precincts, &c.	Durham ..	Parish	24	Catterick ..	York ..	Sub-dis.	3 164
astle Precincts..	Gloucester ..	Sub-dis.	10 194	Catterick ..	,, ..	Parish	2 914
astle Precincts..	,, ..	Parish	1 537	Catterick ..	,, ..	Tnship.	623
astle Precincts..	Sussex ..	Parish	32	Catterlin ..	Cumberland.	Tnship.	112
astlerigg, &c. ..	Cumberland.	Tnship.	605	Catterton ..	York ..	Tnship.	43
astle Rising ..	Norfolk ..	Sub-dis.	2 420	Catthorpe ..	Leicester ..	Parish	146
astle Rising ..	,, ..	Parish	377	Cattistock ..	Dorset ..	Parish	510
astle Sowerby..	Cumberland.	Parish	906	Catton ..	Derby ..	Tnship.	76
astle Thorpe ..	Bucks ..	Parish	338	Catton ..	Norfolk ..	Parish	646
astleton ..	Derby ..	Parish	1 157	Catton, New ..		Ecl. Dis.	2 991
astleton ..	,, ..	Tnship.	771	Catton ..	York ..	Parish	1 189
astleton ..	Dorset ..	Parish	59	Catton, High ..	,, ..	Tnship.	215
astleton Within	Lancaster ..	Sub-dis.	13 971	Catton, Low ..	,, ..	Tnship.	179
astleton Without	,, ..	Sub-dis.	9 800	Catton ..	,, ..	Tnship.	104
astleton ..	,, ..	Tnship.	23 771	Catwick ..	,, ..	Parish	248
astletown ..	Isle of Man.	Town	2 873	Catworth, Great .	Hunts ..	Parish	640
astle Town Qr.	Cumberland.	Tnship.	502	Catworth, Little .	,, ..	Hamlet	52

Name of Place.	County.	Description.	Population.	Name of Place.	County.	Description.	Population.
Caughall	Cheshire	Tnship.	19	Cenarth	Radnor	Tnship.	500
Cauldon	Stafford	Parish	400	Cenol	Brecon	Parcel	264
Cauldwell	Derby	Tnship.	132	Cerne	Dorset	L. Sub.	7 318
Caundle Bishop	Dorset	Parish	371	Cerne	,,	Divisn.	7 318
Caundle Marsh	,,	Parish	84	Cerne	,,	Union	7 318
Caundle Purse	,,	Parish	185	Cerne	,,	Sub-dis.	7 318
Caundle Stourton	,,	Parish	395	Cerne Abbas	,,	Parish	1 185
Caunton	Notts	Parish	596	Cerne, Nether	,,	Parish	95
Caurse	Montgomery	Hund.	2 548	Cerne, Up	,,	Parish	75
Caurse	,,	L. Sub.	6 367	Cerney, North	Gloucester	Parish	692
Causeway	Gloucester	—	28	Cerney, South	,,	Parish	1 006
Causey Park	Northumberland	Tnship.	101	Cerrigceinwen	Anglesey	Parish	465
Cautley & Dowbiggin	York	Ecl. Dis.	276	Cerrigydruidion	Denbigh	L. Sub.	3 753
Cave, North	,,	Parish	1 281	Cerrigydruidion	,,	Parish	1 243
Cave	,,	Sub-dis.	3 390	Ceulanymaesmawr	Cardigan	Tnship.	840
Cave, South	,,	Parish	1 377	Chaceley	Worcester	Parish	307
Cave, South	,,	Tnship.	894	Chacewater	Cornwall	Ecl. Dis.	4 629
Cavendish	Suffolk	Parish	1 301	Chacombe	Northampton	Parish	468
Cavendish Square	Middlesex	Sub-dis.	15 090	Chaddenwicke	Wilts	Tithing	21
Cavenham	Suffolk	Parish	229	Chadderton	Lancaster	Sub-dis.	12 092
Caversfield	Oxon	Parish	183	Chadderton	,,	Tnship.	7 486
Caversham	,,	Parish	1 783	Chadderton, St. John	,,	Ecl. Dis.	6 081
Caverswall	Stafford	Parish	3 046	Chadderton, St. Mathw.	,,	Ecl. Dis.	4 273
Cawden & Cadworth	Wilts	Hund.	4 624	Chaddesden	Derby	Parish	465
Cawkwell	Lincoln	Parish	36	Chaddesden	,,	Ecl. Dis.	465
Cawood	York	Parish	1 243	Chaddesley Corbett	Worcester	Sub-dis.	2 991
Cawston	Norfolk	Parish	1 019	Chaddesley Corbett	,,	Parish	1 457
Cawthorn	York	Tnship.	33	Chaddleworth	Berks	Parish	539
Cawthorne	,,	Sub-dis.	4 825	Chadlington	Oxon	Hund.	13 837
Cawthorne	,,	Parish	1 283	Chadlington, E & West	,,	Hams.	753
Cawthorpe	Lincoln	Hamlet	94	Chadshunt	Warwick	Parish	37
Cawthorpe, Little	,,	Parish	223	Chadwell	Essex	Ward	882
Cawton	York	Tnship.	79	Chadwell, St. Mary	,,	Parish	457
Caxton	Cambs	L. Sub.	7 237	Chaffcombe	Somerset	Parish	246
Caxton	Cambs & Hunts	District	10 966	Chafford	Essex	Hund.	16 001
Caxton	,, ,,	Sub-dis.	10 966	Chagford	Devon	Sub-dis.	2 907
Caxton	Cambs	Parish	545	Chagford	,,	Parish	1 379
Cayo	Carmarthen	Hund.	12 339	Chaigley	Lancaster	Hamlet	191
Caythorpe	Lincoln	Parish	822	Chailey	Sussex	Union	8 895
Caythorpe	Notts	Tnship.	304	Chailey	,,	Sub-dis.	4 947
Cayton	York N.	Parish	534	Chailey	,,	Parish	1 344
Cayton	,,	Tnship.	457	Chalbury	Dorset	Parish	194
Cefn	Glamorgan	Hamlet	659	Chalcombe	Northampton	Parish	468
Cefnllys	Radnor	Hund.	3 579	Chaldon Herring	Dorset	Parish	341
Cefnllys	,,	L. Sub.	3 037	Chaldon	Surrey	Parish	169
Cefnllys	,,	Parish	395	Chale	Hants	Parish	584
Cefnllys	,,	P. Bor.	39	Chalfield, Great	Wilts	Parish	12
Cefnpawl	,,	Tnship.	164	Chalfield, Lit. & Cottles	,,	Parish	43
Cefnpost	Merioneth	Tnship.	70	Chalfont	Bucks	Sub-dis.	3 029
Cefyn	Flint	Tnship.	220	Chalfont, St. Giles	,,	Parish	1 217
Ceidio	Carnarvon	Parish	153	Chalfont, St. Peter	,,	Parish	1 344
Ceirchiog	Anglesey	Parish	174	Chalford	Gloucester	Ecl. Dis.	2 008
Cellan	Cardigan	Parish	532	Chalgrave	Beds	Parish	961
Cemmes	Montgomery	Parish	872	Chalgrove	Oxon	Parish	549

Name of Place.	County.	Description.	Population.	Name of Place.	County.	Description.	Population.
Chalgrove	Oxon	—	531	Charlcoate	Warwick	Parish	245
Chalk	Kent	Parish	382	Charlcombe	Somerset	Parish	378
Chalk	Wilts	Hund.	3 493	Charles	Devon	Parish	356
Challacomb	Devon	Parish	282	Charles the Martyr	„	Sub-dis.	23 390
Challock	Kent	Parish	373	Charles the Martyr	„	Parish	24 270
Challow, East	Berks	Tnship.	391	Charlestown	Cornwall	Ecl. Dis.	3 367
Challow, West	„	Tnship.	192	Charlesworth	Derby	Tnship.	1 565
Challow, East & West	„	Ecl. Dis.	583	Charlesworth	„	Ecl. Dis.	2 564
Chalton	Hants	Parish	619	Charleton	Devon	Parish	568
Chalton	„		286	Charley	Leicester	Parish	34
Chalvington	Sussex	Parish	149	Charlinch	Somerset	Parish	241
Chandlings Farm	Berks	Parish	5	Charlton	Berks	Hund.	3 202
Channel Islands		Islands	90 978	Charlton	„	Hamlet	255
Alderney		Island	4 932	Charlton Marshall	Dorset	Parish	553
Guernsey		Island	29 804	Charlton	Gloucester	Tithing	425
Herm		Island	41	Charlton Abbots	„	Parish	109
Jersey		Island	55 613	Charlton Kings	„	Sub-dis.	10 099
Jethou		Island	5	Charlton Kings	„	Parish	3 443
Sark		Island	583	Charlton by Dover	Kent	Parish	4 093
Chantry, Holy Trinity	Somerset	Ecl. Dis.	264	Charlton nr. Woolwich	„	Parish	8 472
Chapel	Essex	Parish	370	Charlton E. Quarter	Northmb.	Tnship.	119
Chapel Allerton	Somerset	Parish	292	Charlton W. Quarter	„	Tnship.	184
Chapel Allerton	York	Tnship.	3 083	Charlton, North	„	Tnship.	184
Chapel Ascote	Warwick	Parish	6	Charlton, South	„	Tnship.	153
Chapel Brampton	Northampton	Parish	170	Charlton, South	„	Ecl. Dis.	261
Chapelcolman	Pembroke	Parish	157	Charlton on Otmoor	Oxon	Parish	687
Chapel-en-le-Frith	Derby	District	14 020	Charlton on Otmoor	„	—	374
Chapel-en-le-Frith	„	Sub-dis.	9 878	Charlton Adam	Somerset	Parish	530
Chapel-en-le-Frith	„	Parish	4 264	Charlton Horethorne	„	Parish	506
Chapelgate	Notts	Hamlet	149	Charlton Mackrell	„	Parish	387
Chapel Haddlesey	York	Tnship.	210	Charlton Musgrove	„	Parish	418
Chapel Hill	Monmouth	Parish	497	Charlton	Sussex	Hamlet	216
Chapel, Isle of	Lancaster	Island	5	Charlton	Wilts	Parish	222
Chapel, North	Sussex	Parish	785	Charlton	„	Parish	621
Chapel Sucken	Cumberland	Tnship.	291	Charlton, All Saints	„	Ecl. Dis.	393
Chapelthorpe, St. James	York	Ecl. Dis.	2 021	Charlton	Worcester	Hamlet	374
Chapeltown	„	Sub-dis.	5 930	Charlwood	Surrey	Parish	1 542
Chapeltown	„	Ecl. Dis.	4 063	Charminster	Dorset	Parish	1 020
Chard	Somerset	L. Sub.	25 817	Charmouth	„	Parish	678
Chard	Somerset, &c.	District	25 591	Charndon	Bucks	Hamlet	170
Chard	Somerset	Sub-dis.	6 661	Charnes	Stafford	Tnship.	107
Chard	„	Parish	5 316	Charney	Berks	Chap.	241
Chard	„	M. Bor.	2 276	Charnham-Street	Wilts	Tithing	450
Chardstock	Dorset & Devon	Sub-dis.	3 827	Charnock Heath	Lancaster	Tnship.	772
Chardstock	Dorset	Parish	1 461	Charnock Richard	„	Tnship.	899
Chardstock, All Saints	„	Ecl. Dis.	453	Charnock Richard Ch. ch.	„	Ecl. Dis.	1 047
Charfield	Gloucester	Parish	629	Charnwood Oaks Ch.	Leicester	Ecl. Dis.	702
Charford, North	Hants	Parish	70	Charsfield	Suffolk	Parish	484
Charford, South	„	Parish	70	Charter House	Middlesex	Parish	255
Charing	Kent	Parish	1 285	Charter House, St. Thos.	„	Ecl. Dis.	10 840
Charing Cross	Middlesex	Sub-dis.	11 071	Charter H. Hinton	Somerset	Parish	615
Charlbury	Oxon	Sub-dis.	8 915	Charter H. on Mendip	„	Ville	82
Charlbury	„	Parish	3 074	Chart, Great	Kent	Parish	806
Charlbury	„	—	1 380	Chart, Little	„ „	Parish	304

Name of Place.	County.	Description.	Population.	Name of Place.	County.	Description.	Population.
Chart by Sutton Valence	Kent	Parish	693	Checsehill, St. Peter	Hants ..	Parish	752
Chartham	.. .. ,,	Sub-dis.	5 020	Cheetham	.. Lancaster ..	Sub-dis.	21 731
Chartham	.. .. ,,	Parish	1 094	Cheetham	.. ,, ..	Tnship.	17 446
Chartley Holme	Stafford ..	Parish	36	Cheetham, St. Luke	,, ..	Ecl.Dis.	4 719
Charwelton	.. Northampton	Parish	214	Cheetham, St. Mark	,, ..	Ecl.Dis.	2 377
Chastleton	.. Oxon ..	Parish	218	Chelborough, East	Dorset ..	Parish	93
Chatburn	.. Lancaster..	Tnship.	521	Chelborough, West	,, ..	Parish	73
Chatburn, C. Ch.	,,	Ecl.Dis.	605	Cheldon..	.. Devon ..	Parish	97
Chatcull..	.. Stafford ..	Tnship.	68	Chelford	.. Cheshire ..	Tnship.	256
Chatham	.. Kent ..	Parish	25 183	Chellaston	.. Derby ..	Parish	484
Chatham	.. ,, ..	P. Boro.	36 177	Chell, Grt. & Lit.	Stafford ..	Tnship.	1 219
Chatham, St. John	,, ..	Ecl.Dis.	5 168	Chellington	.. Beds ..	Parish	136
Chatham, St. Paul	,, ..	Ecl.Dis.	6 302	Chelmarsh	.. Salop ..	Parish	564
Chathill..	Northumberland	Tnship.	55	Chelmondiston..	Suffolk ..	Parish	949
Chatley Hill	.. Somerset ..	—	4	Chelmorton	.. Derby ..	Tnship.	229
Chatsworth	.. Derby ..	Parish	53	Chelmsford	.. Essex ..	Hund.	32 608
Chatteris	.. Cambs ..	Sub-dis.	8 222	Chelmsford	.. ,, ..	L. Sub.	31 591
Chatteris	.. ,, ..	Parish	4 731	Chelmsford	.. ,, ..	District	32 765
Chatterley	.. Stafford ..	Tnship.	798	Chelmsford	.. ,, ..	Sub-dis.	8 664
Chattisham	.. Suffolk ..	Parish	192	Chelmsford	.. ,, ..	Parish	8 407
Chatton ..	Northumberland	Parish	1 651	**Chelmsford**	.. ,, ..	Town	5 513
Chawleigh	.. Devon ..	Parish	801	Chelsea ..	.. Middlesex ..	District	63 439
Chawton	.. Hants ..	Parish	464	Chelsea North-east	,,	Sub-dis.	21 886
Cheadle ..	.. Cheshire ..	Sub-dis.	4 941	Chelsea North-west	,,	Sub-dis.	19 899
Cheadle ..	.. ,, ..	Parish	10 852	Chelsea South ..	,,	Sub-dis.	21 654
Cheadle Bulkeley	,, ..	Tnship.	6 115	Chelsea ..	.. ,, ..	Parish	63 439
Cheadle Moseley	,, ..	Tnship.	2 329	1 Stanley Ward	.. ..	Ward	8 586
Cheadle ..	.. Stafford ..	L. Sub.	17 158	2 Church Ward	.. ..	Ward	24 526
Cheadle ..	.. ,, ..	District	20 988	3 Hans Town Ward	..	Ward	17 549
Cheadle ..	.. ,, ..	Sub-dis.	7 107	4 Royal Hospital Ward	..	Ward	12 778
Cheadle ..	.. ,, ..	Parish	4 803	Chelsea, Holy Trinity	,, ..	Ecl.Dis.	6 150
Cheadle	.. ,, ..	Town	3 191	Chelsea, Up. St. Jude	,, ..	Ecl.Dis.	4 561
Cheam ..	.. Surrey ..	Parish	1 156	Chelsea, Up. St. Sav.	,, ..	Ecl.Dis.	8 837
Cheapsides	.. York ..	Parish	36	Chelsea. Up. St. Simon	,, ..	Ecl.Dis.	3 959
Chearsley	.. Bucks ..	Parish	287	Chelsfield	.. Kent ..	Parish	784
Chebsey..	.. Stafford ..	Parish	514	Chelsham	.. Surrey ..	Parish	401
Chebsey..	.. ,, ..	Tnship.	472	Chelsworth	.. Suffolk ..	Parish	273
Checkendon	.. Oxon ..	Parish	357	Cheltenham	.. Gloucester ..	Hund.	45 886
Checkley w. Wrinehill	Cheshire	Tnship	202	Cheltenham	.. ,, ..	L. Sub.	55 576
Checkley	.. Stafford ..	Parish	2 428	Cheltenham	.. ,, ..	District	49 792
Checkley	.. ,, ..	—	2 304	Cheltenham	.. ,, ..	Sub-dis.	39 693
Chedburgh	.. Suffolk ..	Parish	325	Cheltenham	.. ,, ..	Parish	39 693
Cheddar..	.. Somerset ..	Parish	2 032	**Cheltenham**	.. ,, ..	P. Boro.	39 693
Cheddington	.. Bucks ..	Parish	628	Cheltenham, St. Luke	,, ..	Ecl.Dis.	2 961
Cheddington	.. Dorset ..	Parish	176	Cheltenham, St. Paul	,, ..	Ecl.Dis.	5 989
Cheddleton	.. Stafford ..	Parish	2 050	Cheltenham, St. Peter	,, ..	Ecl.Dis.	3 855
Cheddleton, &c.	,, ..	Tnship.	1 374	Chelveston	.. Northampton	Parish	454
Cheddon-Fitzpaine	Somerset ..	Parish	338	Chelvey..	.. Somerset ..	Parish	54
Chedgrave	.. Norfolk ..	Parish	387	Chelwood	.. ,, ..	Parish	180
Chediston	.. Suffolk ..	Parish	418	Chenies..	.. Bucks ..	Parish	468
Chedworth	.. Gloucester ..	Sub-dis.	5 253	Chepstow	.. Monmouth ..	L. Sub.	8 661
Chedworth	.. ,, ..	Parish	954	Chepstow	Monm. & Gloucester	District	17 941
Chedzoy	.. ,, ..	Parish	442	Chepstow	.. ,, ,,	Sub-dis.	7 141
Cheeseburn-Grange	Nrthmbld.	Tnship.	75	Chepstow	.. Monmouth ..	Parish	3 455

Name of Place.	County.	Description.	Population.
epstow ..	Monmouth ..	Town	3 364
equer.. ..	Norfolk ..	Ward	825
erhill.. ..	Wilts ..	Parish	364
erington ..	Warwick ..	Parish	311
eriton Bishop	Devon ..	Parish	696
eriton Fitzpaine	,, ..	Sub-dis.	5 656
eriton Fitzpaine	,, ..	Parish	1 111
eriton ..	Glamorgan .	Parish	230
eriton ..	Hants ..	Parish	621
eriton ..	Kent ..	Parish	7 534
eriton, North .	Somerset ..	Parish	302
errington ..	Gloucester ..	Parish	232
errington ..	Salop ..	Tnship.	151
erry Burton ..	York ..	Parish	502
erry Hinton..	Cambs ..	Parish	734
erry Willingham	Lincoln ..	Parish	173
ertsey ..	Surrey ..	L. Sub.	17 958
ertsey ..	,, ..	District	18 642
ertsey ..	,, ..	Sub-dis.	7 740
ertsey ..	,, ..	Parish	6 589
ertsey ..	,, ..	Town	2 910
esham ..	Bucks ..	L. Sub.	15 159
esham ..	,, ..	Sub-dis.	6 203
esham ..	,, ..	Parish	5 985
esham ..	,, ..	Town	2 208
esham Bois ..	,, ..	Parish	218
eshire ..	.. ..	County	505 428
Northern Division ..		N. Div.	262 188
Southern Division ..		S. Div.	243 240
eshunt ..	Herts ..	L. Sub.	9 920
eshunt ..	,, ..	Sub-dis.	6 592
eshunt ..	,, ..	Parish	6 592
esilborne ..	Dorset ..	Parish	432
eslyn Hay ..	Stafford ..	Parish	1 177
essington ..	Surrey ..	Parish	219
ester ..	.. ..	Diocese	1248416
ester ..	Cheshire ..	City	31 110
ester ..	,, ..	Incor.	29 408
ester Castle ..	,, ..	Sub-dis.	21 672
ester Castle ..	,, ..	—	128
ester, Christch.	,, ..	Ecl. Dis.	5 242
ester, St. Paul	,, ..	Ecl. Dis.	3 002
ester, Little ..	Derby ..	Tnship.	431
ester ..	Durham ..	Ward	99 872
ester Ward ..	,, ..	L. Sub.	192 017
esterfield ..	Derby ..	District	61 779
esterfield ..	,, ..	Sub-dis.	28 983
esterfield ..	,, ..	Parish	18 970
esterfield ..	,, ..	Tnship.	9 836
esterfield ..	,, ..	M. Bor.	9 836
esterfield, Trinity	,, ..	Ecl. Dis.	3 814
esterford, Great	Essex ..	Parish	1 027
esterford, Little	,, ..	Parish	276
ester-le-Street	Durham ..	District	27 660

Name of Place.	County.	Description.	Population.
Chester-le-Street	Durham ..	Sub-dis.	14 237
Chester-le-Street	,, ..	Parish	23 076
Chester-le-Street	,, ..	Tnship.	3 013
Chester-le-Street	,, ..	Town	2 550
Chesterton ..	Cambs ..	Hund.	6 970
Chesterton ..	,, ..	District	25 083
Chesterton ..	,, ..	Parish	2 986
Chesterton ..	Hunts ..	Parish	129
Chesterton ..	Oxon ..	Parish	384
Chesterton ..	Stafford ..	Tnship.	2 459
Chesterton ..	,, ..	Ecl. Dis.	4 067
Chesterton ..	Warwick ..	Parish	217
Cheswardine ..	Salop ..	Parish	1 159
Chetnole ..	Dorset ..	Chap.	269
Chettle	Dorset ..	Parish	177
Chetton.. ..	Salop ..	Sub-dis.	4 725
Chetton.. ..	,, ..	Parish	590
Chetton.. ..	,, ..	Tnship.	490
Chetwode ..	Bucks ..	Parish	177
Chetwynd ..	Salop ..	Parish	719
Chetwynd Aston	,, ..	Tnship.	392
Cheveley ..	Cambs ..	Hund.	4 570
Cheveley ..	,, ..	Sub-dis.	6 489
Cheveley ..	,, ..	Parish	607
Chevening ..	Kent ..	Parish	932
Cheverell, Great	Wilts ..	Parish	561
Cheverell, Little	,, ..	Parish	234
Chevet	York ..	Tnship.	58
Chevington ..	Suffolk ..	Parish	621
Chevington, East	Northumbld.	Tnship.	651
Chevington, West	,, ..	Tnship.	161
Chew	Somerset ..	Hund.	6 200
Chew Magna ..	,, ..	Sub-dis.	4 422
Chew Magna ..	,, ..	Parish	1 855
Chew Stoke ..	,, ..	Parish	758
Chewton ..	,, ..	Hund.	12 112
Chewton Mendip	,, ..	Parish	976
Chewton Mendip	,, ..	—	875
Chicheley ..	Bucks ..	Parish	265
Chichester ..	..	Diocese	363 735
Chichester ..	Sussex ..	Rape	33 327
Chichester ..	,, ..	L. Sub.	30 380
Chichester ..	,, ..	District	14 775
Chichester ..	,, ..	Sub-dis.	8 884
Chichester ..	,, ..	Incor.	8 687
Chichester ..	,, ..	City	8 059
Chichester ..	,, ..	Ecl. Dis.	3 232
Chichester, St. Paul	,, ..	Parish	660
Chickerell, West	Dorset ..	Parish	143
Chicklade ..	Wilts ..	Parish	76
Chickney ..	Essex ..	Parish	77
Chicksands Priory	Beds ..	Parish	1 167
Chiddingfold ..	Surrey ..	Parish	992
Chiddingly ..	Sussex ..	Parish	1 200
Chiddingstone ..	Kent ..	Parish	1 200

Name of Place.	County.	Description.	Population.	Name of Place.	County.	Description.	Popula
Chideock	*Dorset*	Parish	794	Chinley, &c.,	*Derby*	Tnship.	12
Chidham	*Sussex*	Parish	310	Chinnock, East..	*Somerset*	Parish	5
Chidlow..	*Cheshire*	Tnship.	18	Chinnock, Middle	,,	Parish	2
Chieveley	*Berks*	Parish	1 923	Chinnock, West	,,	Parish	5
Chieveley	,,	—	1 161	Chinnor..	*Oxon*	Parish	1 2
Chignal, St. Jas.	*Essex*	Parish	258	Chinnor..	,,	—	1 0
Chignal Smealy..	,,	Parish	70	Chippenham	*Cambs*	Parish	7
Chigwell	,,	Sub-dis.	5 987	Chippenham	*Wilts*	Hund.	20 2
Chigwell	,,	Parish	2 676	Chippenham	,,	District	22 0
Chigwell Row	,,	Ecl. Dis.	665	Chippenham	,,	Sub-dis.	8 5
Chilbolton	*Hants*	Parish	398	Chippenham	,,	Parish	5 3
Chilcomb	,,	Parish	278	Chippenham ..	,,	M. Bor.	1 6
Chilcombe	*Dorset*	Parish	24	Chippenham ..	,,	P. Bor	7 0
Chilcompton	*Somerset*	Parish	730	Chippenhurst	*Oxon*	Hamlet	
Chilcote..	*Derby*	Tnship.	129	Chipping	*Lancaster*	Sub-dis.	3 2
Childerditch	*Essex*	Parish	239	Chipping	,,	Parish	1 4
Childerley	*Cambs*	Parish	50	Chipping	,,	Tnship.	1 0
Childer Thornton	*Cheshire*	Tnship.	435	Chipping Barnet	*Herts*	Parish	2 9
Child Okeford	*Dorset*	Parish	783	Chipping Campden	*Gloucester*	Parish	1 9
Childrey	*Berks*	Parish	504	Chipping Lambourn	*Berks*	Tnship.	1 2
Childs Ercall	*Salop*	Parish	470	Chipping Norton	*Oxon*	L. Sub.	16 7
Childs Hill, All Saints	*Middlesex*	Ecl. Dis.	906	Chipping Norton	*Oxon & War.*	District	17 3
Childs Wickham	*Gloucester*	Parish	440	Chipping Norton	,, ,,	Sub-dis.	8 3
Childwall	*Lancaster*	Parish	17 917	Chipping Norton	*Oxon*	Parish	3 5
Childwall	,,	Tnship.	174	Chipping Norton	,,	M. Bor.	3 1
Chilford..	*Cambs*	Hund.	5 776	Chipping Norton		Tnship.	3 1
Chilfroome	*Dorset*	Parish	120	Chipping-Ongar	*Essex*	Sub-dis.	5 8
Chilham	*Kent*	Parish	1 319	Chipping-Ongar		Parish	8
Chillenden	,,	Parish	127	Chipping-Sodbury	*Gloucester*	District	18 7
Chillesford	*Suffolk*	Parish	214	Chipping-Sodbury		Sub-dis.	5 2
Chillingham	*Northumberld.*	Parish	328	Chipping-Sodbury	,,	Parish	1 1
Chillingham	,,	Tnship.	147	Chipping-Warden	*Northampton*	Hund.	4 4
Chillington	*Somerset*	Parish	298	Chipping-Warden		Parish	4
Chilmark	*Wilts*	Parish	642	Chipping Wycombe	*Bucks*	Parish	8 3
Chilmark	,,	—	466	Chipping Wycombe	,,	—	4 1
Chilthorne Domer	*Somerset*	Parish	242	Chipping Wycombe ..	,,	M. Bor.	4 2
Chiltington, East	*Sussex*	Hamlet	281	Chipping Wycombe		P. Boro.	8 3
Chiltington, West	,,	Parish	668	Chipstable	*Somerset*	Parish	3
Chilton ..	*Berks*	Parish	315	Chipstead	*Surrey*	Parish	5
Chilton ..	*Bucks*	Parish	364	Chirbury	*Salop & Montg*	Sub-dis.	5 7
Chilton ..	*Durham*	Tnship.	1 456	Chirbury	*Salop*	Hund.	4 9
Chilton Candover	*Hants*	Parish	142	Chirbury	,,	L. Sub.	4 9
Chilton Cantelo	*Somerset*	Parish	112	Chirbury	,,	Parish	1 5
Chilton on Polden	,,	Chap.	511	Chirdon..	*Northumberld.*	Tnship.	
Chilton Trinity ..	,,	Parish	53	Chirk ..	*Denbigh*	Hund.	12 4
Chilton ..	*Suffolk*	Parish	149	Chirk ..	,,	Parish	1 6
Chilton Foliatt..	*Wilts & Berks*	Parish	691	Chirton ..	*Northumberld.*	Tnship.	5 5
Chilvers Coton	*Warwick*	Parish	2 764	Chirton ..	*Wilts*	Parish	3
Chilwell..	*Notts*	Hamlet	815	Chirton ..	,,	—	2
Chilworth	*Hants*	Parish	176	Chiselborough	*Somerset*	Parish	4
Chilworth	*Oxon*	Hamlet	79	Chiselhampton	*Oxon*	Parish	1 3
Chimney	,,	Hamlet	27	Chishall, Great..	*Essex*	Parish	4 2
Chimney Mills..	*Suffolk*	Parish	10	Chishall, Little ..	,,	Parish	1
Chingford	*Essex*	Parish	1 174	Chisledon	*Wilts*	Parish	1 2 0

Chippenham .. ,, {

Chipping Norton ,,

Chipping Wycombe ,, {

Name of Place.	County.	Description.	Population.	Name of Place.	County.	Description.	Population.
Chislehurst	Kent	Sub-dis.	8 613	Christchurch	Hants	Parish	7 042
Chislehurst	,,	Parish	2 287	Christchurch	,,	P. Bor.	9 368
Chislett	,,	Parish	1 072	Christchurch	Kent	Precinct	224
Chiswick	Middlesex	Sub-dis.	6 505	Christchurch	Middlesex	Sub-dis.	34 913
Chiswick	,,	Parish	6 505	Christch., Newgate-st.	,,	Parish	1 975
Chisworth	Derby	Tnship.	434	Christch., Spitalfields	,,	Parish	20 593
Chithurst	Sussex	Parish	215	Christchurch	Monmouth	L. Sub.	6 311
Chitterne, All Saints	Wilts	Parish	509	Christchurch	,,	Parish	3 004
Chitterne, St. Mary	,,	Parish	201	Christch., Southwark	Surrey	Sub-dis.	17 069
Chittlehampton	Devon	Parish	1 660	Christch., Southwark	,,	Parish	17 069
Chittoe	Wilts	Tithing	180	Christ College	Brecon	Parish	87
Chittoe, St. Mary	,,	Ecl. Dis.	382	Christian Malford	Wilts	Sub-dis.	3 190
Chivelstone	Devon	Parish	523	Christian Malford	,,	Parish	898
Chobham	Surrey	Sub-dis.	5 289	Christleton	Cheshire	Parish	1 006
Chobham	,,	Parish	2 098	Christleton	,,	Tnship.	698
Cholderton, West	Wilts	Parish	191	Christon	Somerset	Parish	81
Chollerton	Northumberland	Sub-dis.	5 365	Christow	Devon	Sub-dis.	2 207
Chollerton	,,	Parish	1 156	Christow	,,	Parish	941
Chollerton	,,	Tnship.	151	Chudleigh	,,	Sub-dis.	6 747
Cholmondeley	Cheshire	Tnship.	306	Chudleigh	,,	Parish	2 108
Cholmondestone	,,	Tnship.	176	Chulmleigh	,,	Sub-dis.	5 062
Cholsall	Berks	Hamlet	27	Chulmleigh	,,	Parish	1 705
Cholsey	Berks & Oxon	Sub-dis.	6 232	Chunall	Derby	Tnship.	116
Cholsey	Berks	Parish	1 127	Church	Middlesex	Sub-dis.	25 528
Chopwell	Durham	Tnship.	563	Church	Lancaster	Town	3 000
Chorley (Wilmslow P.)	Cheshire	Tnship.	1 760	Churcham	Gloucester	Parish	1 002
Chorley (Wrenbury P.)	,,	Tnship.	166	Churcham	,,	—	606
Chorley	Lancaster	District	41 678	Church Aston	Salop	Tnship.	574
Chorley	,,	Sub-dis.	18 027	Church Aston, St. Andw.	,,	Ecl. Dis.	966
Chorley	,,	Parish	15 013	Church Brampton	Northptn.	Parish	158
Chorley	,,	Town	15 013	Church Broughton	Derby	Parish	651
Chorley, St. George	,,	Ecl. Dis.	9 619	Church Coniston	Lancaster	Tnship.	1 324
Chorley, St. Peter	,,	Ecl. Dis.	2 207	Church Coppenhall	Cheshire	Tnship.	822
Chorley Wood, Ch. ch.	Herts	Ecl. Dis.	939	Churchdown	Gloucester	Parish	1 119
Chorlton (Malpas P.)	Cheshire	Tnship.	113	Churchdown	,,	—	659
Chorlton (Wybunbury P.)	,,	Tnship.	113	Church Eaton	Stafford	Parish	643
Chorlton by Backford	,,	Tnship.	85	Church End (Shenley P.)	Bucks	Tnship.	203
Chorlton	Lancaster	District	169 579	Church Enstone	Oxon	Hamlet	287
Chorlton upon Medlock	,,	Sub-dis.	44 795	Church Gresley	Derby	Parish	4 416
Chorlton upon Medlock	,,	Tnship.	44 795	Church Gresley	,,	Tnship.	2 108
All Saints	,,	Ecl. Dis.	13 668	Church Honeybourne	Worcester	Parish	144
St. Luke	,,	Ecl. Dis.	7 380	Church Hulme	Cheshire	Sub-dis.	2 514
St. Saviour	,,	Ecl. Dis.	7 908	Church Hulme	,,	Tnship.	573
St. Stephen	,,	Ecl. Dis.	6 379	Church Iccomb	Gloucester	Tnship.	152
Chorlton w. Hardy	,,	Chap.	789	Churchill	Oxon	Parish	642
Chorlton w. Hardy	,,	Ecl. Dis.	739	Churchill	Somerset	Parish	810
Chorlton	Stafford	Tnship.	484	Churchill, Wolverley	Worcester	Parish	181
Choseley	Norfolk	Parish	7	Churchill, Pershore	,,	Parish	78
Choulesbury	Bucks	Parish	105	Church Kirk	Lancaster	Tnship.	4 753
Chowley	Cheshire	Tnship.	67	Church Knowle	Dorset	Parish	511
Chrishall	Essex	Parish	643	Church Langton	Leicester	Parish	842
Christchurch	Gloucester	Parish	1 073	Church Lawford	Warwick	Parish	311
Christchurch	Hants	District	10 438	Church Lawton	Cheshire	Parish	724
Christchurch	,,	Sub-dis.	10 438	Church Lench	Worcester	Parish	422

47

Name of Place.	County.	Description.	Population.	Name of Place.	County.	Description.	Population.
Church Minshull	Cheshire	Parish	392	Clapcot	Berks	Lib.	53
Church Oakley	Hants	Parish	287	Clapham	Beds	Parish	502
Church Over	Warwick	Parish	357	Clapham	Surrey	Sub-dis.	20 894
Church Preen	Salop	Parish	97	Clapham	,,	Parish	20 894
Church Pulverbatch	,,	Parish	534	1. North Ward	,,	Ward	13 359
Church, Shocklach	Cheshire	Tnship.	180	2. South Ward	,,	Ward	7 535
Churchstanton	Devon	Parish	961	Clapham Park	,,	Ecl. Dis.	3 474
Churchstoke	Mont. & Salop	Parish	1 545	Clapham, St. James	,,	Ecl. Dis.	4 127
Churchstoke	Montgomery	Tnship.	1 369	Clapham, St. John	,,	Ecl. Dis.	2 543
Churchstow	Devon	Parish	376	Clapham	Sussex	Parish	249
Church Stretton	Salop	District	6 289	Clapham	York	Parish	1 708
Church Stretton	,,	Sub-dis.	3 928	Clapham w. Newby	,,	Tnship.	809
Church Stretton	,,	Parish	1 695	Clapton	Gloucester	Parish	123
Church Town Qr.	Cumberland	Tnship.	447	Clapton	Northampton	Parish	153
Church Wilne	Derby	Liberty	140	Clapton	Somerset	Parish	173
Churston Ferrers	Devon	Parish	766	Clarach	Cardigan	Tnship.	240
Churton by Aldford	Cheshire	Tnship.	217	Clarbeston	Pembroke	Parish	191
Churton by Farndon	,,	Tnship.	128	Clarborough	Notts	Sub-dis.	6 076
Churton Heath	,,	Chap.	44	Clarborough	,,	Parish	2 412
Churwell	York	Tnship.	1 564	Clare Quarter	Devon	—	535
Chute	Wilts	Parish	538	Clare	Suff. & Essex	Sub-dis.	5 279
Chute Forest	,,	Parish	170	Clare	Suffolk	Parish	1 657
Cilcen	Flint	Parish	1 028	Clarendon Park	Wilts	Liberty	181
Cilcennin	Cardigan	Parish	603	Clareton	York	Tnship.	22
Cilie Aeron	,,	Parish	301	Clarewood	Northumberland	Tnship.	50
Cilwych	Brecon	Parcel	355	Claro	York	L. Sub.	55 648
Cilycwm	Carmarthen	Sub-dis.	1 380	Claro	,,	Wapen.	49 476
Cilycwm	,,	Parish	1 380	Clase	Radnor	Tnship.	261
Cilymaenllwyd	,,	Parish	640	Clase	Glamorgan	Hamlet	9 436
Cilymaenllwyd	,,	Hamlet	513	Clatford, Goodworth	Hants	Parish	427
Cinque Ports	Kent & Suss	Juris-diction.	104629	Clatford, Upper	,,	Parish	703
Cirencester	Gloucester	L. Sub.	14 361	Clatford Park	Wilts	Parish	9
Cirencester	,,	Hund.	6 336	Clattercot	Oxon	Parish	8
Cirencester	Glos. & Wilts	District	20 934	Clatworthy	Somerset	Parish	313
Cirencester	,, ,,	Sub-dis.	10 840	Claughton w. Grange	Cheshire	Tnship.	1 584
Cirencester	Gloucester	Parish	6 336	Claughton	Lancaster	Tnship.	608
Cirencester	,,	P. Bor.	6 336	Claughton	,,	Parish	94
City Road	Middlesex	Sub-dis.	17 860	Claverdon	Warwick	Parish	755
City Road, St. Matthew	,,	Ecl. Dis.	3 561	Claverdon	,,	Tnship.	561
Clackclose	Norfolk	Hund.	21 420	Clavering	Essex	Hund.	4 954
Clackclose	,,	L. Sub.	21 420	Clavering	,,	Parish	1 047
Clacton, Great	Essex	Parish	1 280	Clavering	Norfolk	Hund.	6 674
Clacton, Little	,,	Parish	584	Claverley	Salop	Parish	1 667
Claife	Lancaster	Tnship.	540	Claverton	Somerset	Parish	213
Claines	Worcester	Sub-dis.	7 465	Clawddmadog	Brecon	Hamlet	287
Claines	,,	Parish	8 106	Clawrplwyf	Monmouth	Hamlet	2 409
Claines	,,	Tnship.	4 915	Clawson	Leic. & Notts	Sub-dis.	5 537
Clanaborough	Devon	Parish	61	Clawson	Leicester	Parish	820
Clandon, East	Surrey	Parish	283	Clawton	Devon & Cornwall	Sub-dis.	1 805
Clandon, West	,,	Parish	329	Clawton	Devon	Parish	549
Clandown	Somerset	Ecl. Dis.	1 075	Claxby, Caistor	Lincoln	Parish	237
Clanfield	Hants	Parish	265	Claxby, Alford	,,	Parish	103
Clanfield	Oxon	Parish	547	Claxby Pluckacre	,,	Parish	39
				Claxton	Durham	Tnship.	55

Name of Place.	County.	Description.	Population.	Name of Place.	County.	Description.	Population.
Claxton	Norfolk ..	Parish	202	Cleley	Northampton	Hund.	8 310
Claxton	York ..	Tnship.	195	Clements Inn ..	Middlesex ..	—	85
Claybrooke ..	Leic. & War.	Parish	1 274	Clenchwarton ..	Norfolk ..	Parish	599
Claybrooke, Great	Leicester ..	Tnship.	424	Clennell..	Northumberland	Tnship.	27
Claybrooke, Little	,, ..	Tnship.	84	Clent	Worcester ..	Parish	966
Clay-Coton ..	Northampton	Parish	112	Cleobury Mort...	Salop & Wor.	District	8 304
Clay-Cross ..	Derby ..	Town	3 501	Cleobury Mortimer ,, ,,		Sub-dis.	5 514
Clay-Cross ..	,, ..	Ecl. Dis.	4 922	Cleobury Mortimer	Salop ..	Parish	1 619
Claydon, East ..	Bucks ..	Parish	385	Cleobury, North	,, ..	Parish	168
Claydon, Middle	,, ..	Parish	146	Clerkenwell ..	Middlesex ..	District	65 681
Claydon, Steeple	,, ..	Parish	946	Clerkenwell ..	,, ..	Parish	65 681
Claydon ..	Oxon ..	Chap.	317	Ward No. 1 ..	,, ..	Ward	11 607
Claydon ..	Suffolk ..	Parish	501	Ward No. 2 ..	,, ..	Ward	13 613
Claygate ..	Surrey ..	Manor	535	Ward No. 3 ..	,, ..	Ward	9 381
Claygate	,, ..	Ecl. Dis.	535	Ward No. 4 ..	,, ..	Ward	16 996
Clayhanger ..	Devon ..	Parish	274	Ward No. 5 ..	,, ..	Ward	14 084
Clayhidon	,, ..	Parish	705	Clerkenwell, St. John	,, ..	Ecl. Dis.	6 941
Claylane ..	Derby ..	Tnship.	4 096	Clerkenwell, St. Philip	,, ..	Ecl. Dis.	9 640
Claypole ..	Lincoln ..	Sub-dis.	4 487	Cletterwood ..	Montgomery	Tnship.	241
Claypole	,, ..	Parish	774	Clevedon ..	Somerset ..	Parish	2 941
Claythorpe ..	,, ..	Chap.	100	Cleveley.. ..	Lancaster ..	Tnship.	62
Clayton-le-Dale .	Lancaster ..	Tnship.	375	Cleveley.. ..	Oxon ..	Hamlet	178
Clayton-le-Moors	,, ..	Tnship.	4 682	Clewer	Berks ..	Parish	5 418
Clayton-le-Moors	,, ..	Ecl. Dis.	4 682	Cley next the Sea	Norfolk ..	Parish	791
Clayton-le-Woods	,, ..	Tnship.	705	Cliburn.. ..	Westmoreland	Parish	367
Clayton	Stafford ..	Tnship.	149	Cliddesden ..	Hants ..	Parish	320
Clayton Griffith .	,, ..	Tnship.	33	Cliff w. Lund ..	York ..	Tnship.	615
Clayton	Sussex ..	Parish	863	Cliff, North ..	,, ..	Tnship.	76
Clayton	York ..	Tnship.	5 655	Cliff, South ..	,, ..	Tnship.	119
Clayton, St. John	,, ..	Ecl. Dis.	3 228	Cliffe	,, ..	Tnship.	54
Clayton, West ..	,, ..	Tnship.	1 532	Cliffe at Hoo ..	Kent ..	Parish	980
Clayton w. Frickley	,, ..	Parish	312	Cliffe, East ..	,, ..	Parish	271
Clayworth ..	Notts ..	Parish	538	Cliffe, West ..	,, ..	Parish	122
Clayworth	,, ..	Tnship.	414	Cliffe-Pypard ..	Wilts ..	Parish	910
Clearwell ..	Gloucester ..	Tithing	816	Clifford	Hereford ..	Parish	895
Clearwell, St. Peter	,, ..	Ecl. Dis.	1 244	Clifford Chambers	Gloucester ..	Parish	344
Cleasby	York ..	Parish	189	Clifford w. Boston	York ..	Tnship.	2 153
Cleatham ..	Lincoln ..	Tnship.	109	Clifford, St. Luke	,, ..	Ecl. Dis.	1 030
Cleatlam ..	Durham ..	Tnship.	95	Clifton	Beds ..	Hund.	10 224
Cleator ..	Cumberland.	Parish	3 995	Clifton	,, ..	Parish	1 478
Cleckheaton ..	York ..	Sub-dis.	10 446	Clifton Reynes ..	Bucks ..	Parish	212
Cleckheaton ..	,, ..	Tnship.	6 231	Clifton	Cheshire ..	Tnship.	30
Cleckheaton ..	,, ..	Town	4 721	Clifton, Great ..	Cumberland.	Tnship.	609
Cleckheaton, St. Jno.	,, ..	Ecl. Dis.	4 721	Clifton, Little ..	,, ..	Tnship.	476
Clee	Lincoln ..	Parish	1 555	Clifton, &c. ..	Derby ..	Tnship.	894
Clee, &c.	,, ..	Tnship.	325	Clifton, Holy Trinity	,, ..	Ecl. Dis.	503
Clee, St. Margaret	Salop ..	Parish	281	Clifton Maybank	Dorset ..	Parish	73
Cleethorpe, &c...	Lincoln ..	Tnship.	1 230	Clifton	Gloucester	District	94 687
Cleeve	Gloucester ..	Hund.	1 970	Clifton	,,	Sub-dis.	21 375
Cleeve	,, ..	Sub-dis.	4 108	Clifton	,,	Parish	21 375
Cleeve, Holy Trinity	Leicester .	Ecl. Dis.	406	Clifton, Christchurch	,,	Ecl. Dis.	4 176
Cleeve, Old ..	Somerset ..	Parish	1 529	Clifton, St. John Evang.	,,	Ecl. Dis.	4 577
Cleeve, Prior ..	Worcester ..	Parish	340	Clifton, St. Paul	,,	Ecl. Dis.	1 444
Clehonger ..	Hereford ..	Parish	451	Clifton Wood, St. Peter	,,	Ecl. Dis.	2 519

Name of Place.	County.	Description.	Population.	Name of Place.	County.	Description.	Population.
Clifton	Lancaster ..	Tnship.	2 140	Close, The ..	Stafford ..	Parish	23?
Clifton w. Salwick	,, ..	Tnship.	447	Closworth ..	Somerset ..	Parish	18?
Clifton w. Glapton	Notts ..	Parish	382	Clothall.. ..	Herts ..	Parish	49?
Clifton, North ..	,, ..	Parish	1 110	Clotherholme ..	York ..	Tnship.	1?
Clifton, North ..	,, ..	Tnship.	269	Clotton Hoofield	Cheshire ..	Tnship.	398
Clifton, South ..	,, ..	Tnship.	319	Cloudesley Sq. Trin.	Middlesex	Ecl. Dis.	11 70?
Clifton	Oxon ..	Hamlet	244	Cloughton ..	York ..	Tnship.	44?
Clifton Hampden	,, ..	Parish	355	Clovelly.. ..	Devon ..	Parish	82?
Clif. Campville	Staff. & Derby	Parish	881	Clowance ..	,,	Sub-dis.	10 662
Clifton Campville	Stafford	Tnship.	328	Clown	Derby ..	Parish	704
Clifton on Dunsmore	Warwick	Parish	732	Clun	Salop ..	Hund.	3 869
Clifton on Dunsmore	,,	Tnship.	379	Clun	..	L. Sub.	3 689
Clifton	Westmoreland	Parish	342	Clun ..	Salop & Montg.	District	10 615
Clifton upon Teme	Worcester .	Parish	542	Clun	Salop ..	Sub-dis.	4 152
Clifton	York N...	Tnship.	2 659	Clun	,, ..	Parish	2 338
Clifton w. Norwood	,, W...	Tnship.	364	Clun	,, ..	Tnship.	1 105
Clifton (Dewsbury P.)	,, ,, ..	Hamlet	1 873	Clunbury ..	,,	Parish	1 029
Clifton upon Ure	York ..	Tnship.	43	Clungunford ..	,,	Parish	647
Climping ..	Sussex ..	Parish	331	Clutton	Cheshire ..	Tnship.	74
Clint	York ..	Tnship.	482	Clutton	Somerset ..	L. Sub.	23 721
Clippesby ..	Norfolk ..	Parish	97	Clutton	,,	District	23 721
Clipsham ..	Rutland ..	Parish	213	Clutton	,,	Sub-dis.	6 663
Clipston.. ..	Northampton	Parish	877	Clutton	,,	Parish	1 149
Clipston.. ..	Notts ..	Tnship.	73	Clydach.. ..	Glamorgan .	Hamlet	821
Clipstone ..	,, ..	Tnship.	266	Clydach.. ..	,, ..	Ecl. Dis.	2 942
Clist-Hydon ..	Devon ..	Parish	329	Clydey	Pembroke ..	Parish	1 074
Cliston	,, ..	Hund.	3 699	Clyne	Glamorgan .	Hamlet	103
Clist, Honiton ..	,, ..	Parish	416	Clynnog.. ..	Carnarvon ..	Parish	1 671
Clist, St. George	,, ..	Parish	300	Clyro ..	Radnor & Brecon	Sub-dis.	3 521
Clist, St. Lawrence	,, ..	Parish	154	Clyro	Radnor ..	Parish	888
Clist, St. Mary ..	,, ..	Parish	176	Clyro	,, ..	Hamlet	700
Clitheroe ..	Lanc. & York	District	20 476	Clytha	Monmouth ..	Hamlet	354
Clitheroe ..	,, ,,	Sub-dis.	9 804	Coal-Aston ..	Derby ..	Tnship.	547
Clitheroe ..	Lancaster ..	Tnship.	6 990	Coalbrookdale ..	Salop ..	Ecl. Dis.	1 805
Clitheroe ..	,, {	M. Bor.	7 000	Coaley	Gloucester ..	Parish	777
		P. Bor.	10 864	Coalpit, Heath ..	,, ..	Ecl. Dis.	1 828
Clitheroe, St. James	,, ..	Ecl.Dis.	2 895	Coalville, Christch.	Leicester..	Ecl. Dis.	1 540
Clitheroe Castle	,, ..	Parish	10	Coanwood	Northumberland	Tnship.	171
Clive	Cheshire ..	Tnship.	193	Coates, Holy Trinity	Cambs ..	Ecl. Dis.	1 394
Clive, All Saints	Salop ..	Ecl. Dis.	302	Coates	Gloucester ..	Parish	417
Clive	,, ..	Chap.	302	Coates	Lincoln ..	Parish	54
Cliviger.. ..	Lancaster ..	Tnship.	1 770	Coates, Great ..	,, ..	Parish	206
Clixby	Lincoln ..	Chap.	27	Coates, Little ..	,, ..	Parish	59
Cloatly	Wilts ..	Tithing	108	Coates, North ..	,, ..	Parish	290
Clocaenog ..	Denbigh ..	Parish	439	Coates	Sussex ..	Parish	78
Clodock.. ..	Hereford ..	Sub-dis.	2 864	Coates	.. York ..	Tnship.	122
Clodock.. ..	,, ..	Parish	1 794	Coatham, East, Christch	,,	Ecl. Dis.	727
Cloford	Somerset ..	Parish	218	Coatham, Mundeville	Durham	Tnship.	139
Clophill.. ..	Beds ..	Parish	1 169	Coatsaw Moor ..	,,	Tnship.	16
Clopton.. ..	Gloucester..	Hamlet	37	Coatyards	Northumberland	Tnship.	12
Clopton.. ..	Suffolk ..	Parish	407	Cobham.. ..	Kent ..	Parish	864
Close of St. Peter	Devon ..	Precinct	595	Cobham.. ..	Surrey ..	Parish	1 998
Close of Winchest.	Hants ..	Parish	138	Cobhouse Estate	Lancaster ..	—	25
Close of St. Peter	Middlesex ..	Parish	323	Cobridge, Christch.	Stafford ..	Ecl. Dis.	3 378

Clitheroe ..   ,,

Name of Place.	County.	Description.	Population.	Name of Place.	County.	Description.	Population.
Cockayne-Hatley	Beds	Parish	126	Colby	Norfolk	Parish	269
Cocken	Durham	Tnship.	77	Colby	Westmoreland	Tnship.	178
Cockerham	Lancaster	Parish	2 922	Colchester	Essex	L. Sub.	46 306
Cockerham	,,	Tnship.	778	Colchester	,,	District	23 815
Cockerington, North	Lincoln	Parish	265	Colchester, 1st Ward	,,	Sub-dis.	11 456
Cockerington, South	,,	Parish	300	Colchester, 2nd Ward	,,	Sub-dis.	5 870
Cockermouth	Cumberland	District	41 292	Colchester, 3rd Ward	,,	Sub-dis.	6 489
Cockermouth	,,	Sub-dis.	10 546	Colchester	,,	Borough	23 809
Cockermouth	,,	Tnship.	5 388	Cold-Ashby	Northampton	Parish	446
Cockermouth	,,	P. Bor.	7 057	Cold-Ashton	Gloucester	Parish	503
Cockersand Abbey	Lancaster	Parish	33	Cold Bath House	Lincoln	Parish	5
Cockerton	Durham	Tnship.	576	Cold Brayfield	Bucks	Parish	99
Cockfield	,,	Parish	1 256	Coldcoats	Northumberland	Tnship.	40
Cockfield	,,	Tnship.	1 004	Cold Coniston	York	Tnship.	238
Cockfield	Suffolk	Parish	992	Cold Coniston	,,	Ecl. Dis.	265
Cocking	Sussex	Parish	430	Cold-Dunghills	Suffolk	Parish	44
Cockington	Devon	Parish	210	Cold-Hanworth	Lincoln	Parish	91
Cocklaw	Northumberland	Tnship.	200	Cold Harbour	Surrey	Ecl. Dis.	531
Cockle Park	,,	Tnship.	42	Coldhesledon	Durham	Tnship.	89
Cockley Cley	Norfolk	Parish	263	Cold Higham	Northampton	Parish	349
Cockthorpe	,,	Parish	42	Coldhurst	Lancaster	Ecl. Dis.	3 046
Coddenham	Suffolk	Sub-dis.	8 480	Cold-Kirby	York	Parish	193
Coddenham	,,	Parish	903	Coldmeece	Stafford	Tnship.	47
Coddington	Cheshire	Parish	325	Cold-Newton	Leicester	Tnship.	138
Coddington	,,	Tnship.	139	Cold-Norton	Essex	Parish	207
Coddington	Hereford	Parish	168	Cold-Norton	Stafford	Tnship.	42
Coddington	Notts	Parish	510	Coldon, Trinity	Hants	Ecl. Dis.	652
Codford, St. Mary	Wilts	Parish	404	Cold Overton	Leicester	Parish	97
Codford, St. Peter	,,	Parish	859	Coldred	Kent	Parish	134
Codicote	Herts	Parish	1 227	Coldrey	Hants	Parish	15
Codnor	Derby	Hamlet	2 638	Coldsmouth, &c.	Nrthumberld.	Tnship.	30
Codnor Park	,,	Parish	795	Cold Waltham	Sussex	Parish	447
Codnor w. Loscoe	,,	Ecl. Dis.	3 829	Coldwell	Northumberland	Tnship.	4
Codsall	Stafford	Parish	1 204	Cold Weston	Salop	Parish	36
Codsall	,,	—	890	Colebrooke	Devon	Parish	802
Coedana	Anglesey	Parish	275	Coleby	Lincoln	Parish	458
Coedcanlass	Pembroke	Parish	155	Coledale	Cumberland	Tnship.	261
Coedfrank	Glamorgan	Hamlet	2 151	Coleford	Gloucester	L. Sub.	21 532
Coedkernew	Monmouth	Parish	163	Coleford	,,	Sub-dis.	13 964
Coedlasson	Radnor	Tnship.	255	Coleford	,,	Tithing	2 600
Coffinswell	Devon	Parish	194	Coleford	Somerset	Ecl. Dis.	1 387
Cogan	Glamorgan	Parish	283	Coleham, Trinity	Salop	Ecl. Dis.	2 773
Cogenhoe	Northampton	Parish	360	Colemore	Hants	Parish	151
Coggeshall	Essex	Sub-dis.	4 954	Cole-Orton	Leicester	Parish	626
Coggeshall, Great	,,	Parish	3 679	Cole Park	Wilts	Tithing	24
Coggeshall, Little	,,	Parish	429	Coleridge	Devon	Hund.	10 967
Coggeshall	,,	Town	3 166	Coleridge	,,	Parish	613
Coggs	Oxon	Parish	714	Colerne	Wilts	Parish	1 040
Cogshall	Cheshire	Tnship.	103	Colesborne	Gloucester	Parish	261
Coker	Somerset	Sub-dis.	6 321	Coleshill	Berks & Wilts	Parish	464
Coker, East	,,	Parish	1 186	Coleshill	Bucks	Hamlet	531
Coker, West	,,	Parish	1 012	Coleshill	Flint	Hund.	19 637
Colan	Cornwall	Parish	255	Coleshill	,,	L. Sub.	23 065
Colaton-Raleigh	Devon	Parish	830	Coleshill	Warwick	L. Sub.	38 228

Name of Place.	County.	Description.	Population.	Name of Place.	County.	Description.	Population.
Coleshill	Warwick	Sub-dis.	4 903	Colwick	Notts	Parish	110
Coleshill	„	Parish	2 053	Colwinstone	Glamorgan	Parish	274
Colkirk	Norfolk	Parish	473	Colworth Farm	Beds	—	3
College Mill	Hants	Parish	8	Colwyn	Brecon	Sub-dis.	1 964
College Precincts	Gloucester	Parish	217	Colwyn, St. Cath.	Carnarvon	Ecl. dis.	574
College Precincts	Worcester	Parish	89	Colwyn	Radnor	Hund.	2 411
College Wharf	Hants	Parish	1	Colwyn	„	L. Sub.	2 411
Collierley	Durham	Tnship.	1 322	Colton	Devon	Hund.	7 810
Collierley	„	Ecl. Dis.	3 223	Colyton	„	Sub-dis.	6 190
Collingbourne Ducis	Wilts	Parish	564	Colyton	„	Parish	2 446
Collingbourne Kingston	„	Parish	903	Combe	Hants	Parish	225
Collingham, North	Notts	Parish	1 010	Combe	Hereford	Tnship.	101
Collingham, South	„	Parish	863	Combe	Oxon	Parish	627
Collingham	York	Parish	309	Combe St. Nicholas	Som. & Dor.	Sub-dis.	3 398
Collington	Hereford	Parish	150	Combe St. Nicholas	Somerset	Parish	1 228
Collingtree	Northampton	Parish	237	Combe Fields	Warwick	Parish	177
Collyhurst, St. Oswald	Lanc.	Ecl. Dis.	2 247	Combe Florey	Somerset	Parish	383
Collyweston	Northampton	Parish	473	Combedown	„	Ecl. Dis.	940
Colman, Chapel	Pembroke	Parish	157	Combeinteignhead	Devon	Parish	417
Colmworth	Beds	Parish	527	Comberbach	Cheshire	Tnship.	266
Colnbrook	Bucks & Middlx.	Ecl. Dis.	1 196	Comberton	Cambs	Parish	562
Colne	Hunts	Parish	385	Comberton, Great	Worcester	Parish	247
Colne	Lancaster	Sub-dis.	21 203	Comberton, Little	„	Parish	257
Colne	„	Tnship.	7 906	Combhay	Somerset	Parish	245
Colne	„	Town	6 315	Combmartin	Devon	Sub-dis.	3 875
Colne-Barrowford	„	Ecl. Dis.	2 796	Combmartin	„	Parish	1 484
Colne, Christchurch	„	Ecl. Dis.	2 817	Combpyne	„	Parish	118
Colne Engaine	Essex	Parish	627	Combrawleigh	„	Parish	299
Colneis	Suffolk	Hund.	4 774	Combrook	Warwick	Tnship.	228
Colneis	„	Sub-dis.	5 883	Combrook	„	Ecl. Dis.	322
Colney St. Mark	Herts	Ecl. Dis.	854	Combs	Suffolk	Parish	1 243
Colney, St. Peter	„	Ecl. Dis.	792	Commitmaen	Carnarvon	Hund.	4 825
Colney	Norfolk	Parish	84	Commondale	York	Tnship.	130
Coln-Rogers	Gloucester	Parish	116	Compton	Berks	Hund.	2 711
Coln, St. Aldwins	„	Parish	516	Compton	„	Parish	590
Coln, St. Denis	„	Parish	206	Compton Beauchamp	„	Parish	128
Colstead	Lincoln	—	7	Compton Gifford	Devon	Tithing	880
Colsterworth	„	Sub-dis.	5 391	Compton Abbas or W.	Dorset	Parish	117
Colsterworth	„	Parish	1 163	Compton Abbas	„	Parish	456
Colsterworth, &c.	„	Tnship.	969	Compton, Nether	„	Parish	376
Colston Basset	Notts	Parish	297	Compton, Over	„	Parish	150
Coltishall	Norfolk	Parish	978	Compton Vallence	„	Parish	136
Colton	Lancaster	Sub-dis.	3 838	Compton	Gloucester	Tithing	113
Colton	„	Parish	1 794	Compton Abdale	„	Parish	258
Colton	Norfolk	Parish	228	Compton Greenfield	„	Parish	52
Colton	Stafford	Parish	629	Compton	Hants	Parish	279
Colton	York	Tnship.	129	Compton Bishop	Somerset	Parish	663
Colva	Radnor	Parish	185	Compton Dando	„	Parish	347
Colveston	Norfolk	Parish	59	Compton Dunden	„	Parish	662
Colwall	Hereford	Parish	1 628	Compton Martin	„	Parish	558
Colwell & Swinburn	Nrthmbld.	Tnship.	373	Compton Pauncefoot	„	Parish	253
Colwich	Stafford	Sub-dis.	4 322	Compton	Surrey	Parish	502
Colwich	„	Parish	1 828	Compton	Sussex	Parish	266
Colwich	„	Tnship.	1 608	Compton Little	Warwick	Parish	398

Name of Place.	County.	Description.	Population.	Name of Place.	County.	Description.	Population.
Compton Long	Warwick	Parish	703	Cookham	Berks	District	13 031
Compton Verney	”	Parish	94	Cookham	”	Sub-dis.	6 317
Compton Wyniates	”	Parish	37	Cookham	”	Parish	4 468
Compton Bassett	Wilts	Parish	369	Cookham	”	—	2 438
Compton Chamberlain	”	Parish	348	Cookham Dean, St. John	”	Ecl. Dis.	743
Conchan	Isle of Man	Parish	14 195	Cookley	Suffolk	Parish	252
Conderton	Worcester	Hamlet	186	Cookley	Worcester	Ecl. Dis.	1 454
Condicote	Gloucester	Parish	182	Cooling	Kent	Parish	121
Condover	Salop	Hund.	6 551	Cool Pilate	Cheshire	Tnship.	44
Condover	”	L. Sub.	8 016	Coombe Bissett	Wilts	Parish	337
Condover	, ”	Sub-dis.	6 063	Coombe Keynes	Dorset	Parish	163
Condover	”	Parish	1 871	Coombs	Sussex	Parish	77
Conduit, New	Norfolk	Ward	829	Coombs Edge	Derby	Tnship.	449
Coneysthorpe	York	Tnship.	191	Coopersale	Essex	Ecl. Dis.	539
Coneythorpe	”	Tnship.	115	Copdock	Suffolk	Parish	341
Coney Weston	Suffolk	Parish	254	Copford	Essex	Parish	775
Congerston	Leicester	Parish	250	Copgrove	York	Parish	68
Congham	Norfolk	Parish	315	Cople	Beds	Parish	565
Congleton	Chesh. & Staff.	District	34 328	Copmanthorpe	York	Chap.	350
Congleton	” ”	Sub-dis.	19 124	Copp	Lancaster	Ecl. Dis.	1 140
Congleton	Cheshire	Tnship.	12 344	Coppenhall	Cheshire	Parish	8 981
Congleton	”	M. Bor.	12 344	Coppenhall	Stafford	Tnship.	88
Congleton, St. James	”	Ecl. Dis.	4 250	Coppingford	Hunts	Parish	62
Congleton, St. Stephen	”	Ecl. Dis.	3 411	Copping Syke	Lincoln	Parish	7
Congresbury	Somerset	Parish	1 190	Coppull	Lancaster	Tnship.	1 230
Coningsby	Lincoln	Parish	1 938	Coppull	”	Ecl. Dis.	1 230
Conington	Cambs.	Parish	233	Copston Magna	Warwick	Hamlet	109
Conington	Hunts	Parish	301	Copt Hewick	York	Tnship.	194
Conisbrough	York	Parish	1 655	Copthorne	Surrey	Hund.	13 964
Coniscliffe	Durham	Parish	434	Copt Oak, St. Peter	Leicester	Ecl. Dis.	393
Coniscliffe, High	”	Tnship.	234	Coquet, Isle	Northumberland	Island	13
Coniscliffe, Low, &c.	”	Tnship.	200	Coquetdale	”	L. Sub.	21 526
Conisford	Norfolk	Sub-dis.	12 983	Coquetdale	”	Ward	21 333
Conisholme	Lincoln	Parish	167	Corbridge	”	Parish	2 170
Coniston	York	Tnship.	101	Corbridge	”	Tnship.	1 340
Coniston, Cold	”	Ecl. Dis.	265	Corby, Great	Cumberland	Tnship.	323
Conistone w. Kilnsey	”	Tnship.	160	Corby, Little	”	Tnship.	241
Connahs Quay	Flint	Ecl. Dis.	1 422	Corby	Lincoln	Sub-dis.	3 396
Conock	Wilts	Tithing	138	Corby	”	Parish	818
Cononley	York	Tnship.	905	Corby	Northampton	Hund.	10 959
Conside, &c.	Durham	Tnship.	4 953	Corby	”	Sub-dis.	4 210
Constantine	Cornwall	Sub-dis.	3 199	Corby	”	Parish	794
Constantine	”	Parish	2 014	Corely	Salop	Parish	515
Conway	Carnarvon	L. Sub.	28 473	Corfe Castle	Dorset	Sub-Dis.	2 411
Conway	Carn. & Denb.	District	13 896	Corfe Castle	”	Parish	1 900
Conway	Carnarvon	Sub-dis.	3 956	Corfe Mullen	”	Parish	724
Conway	”	Parish	1 855	Corfe	Somerset	Parish	381
Conway	”	P. Boro.	2 523	Corhampton	Hants	Parish	189
Conwil	Carmarthen	Sub-dis.	8 196	Corley	Warwick	Parish	327
Conwil Cayo	”	Sub-dis.	2 251	Cornard, Great	Suffolk	Parish	904
Conwil Cayo	”	Parish	2 251	Cornard, Little	”	Parish	404
Conwil in Elfet	”	Parish	1 703	Cornbrough	York	Hamlet	54
Cookbury	Devon	Parish	249	Cornbury Park	Oxon	Parish	39
Cookham	Berks	Hund.	3 809	Cornelly	Cornwall	Parish	99

Name of Place.	County.	Description.	Population.	Name of Place.	County.	Description.	Population.
Corney	Cumberland.	Parish	256	Cothelstone	Somerset	Parish	107
Cornforth	Durham	Tnship.	1 619	Cotheridge	Worcester	Parish	233
Cornhill	Northumberland	Chap.	853	Cotherston	York	Tnship.	561
Cornish Hall End	Essex	Ecl. Dis.	722	Cotleigh	Devon	Parish	188
Cornsay	Durham	Tnship.	367	Cotmanhay	Derby	Ecl. Dis.	2 615
Cornwall		County	369 390	Cotness	York	Tnship.	46
Eastern Division		E. Div.	155 104	Coton	Cambs	Parish	311
Western Division		W. Div.	214 286	Coton in the Elms	Derby	Tnship.	353
Cornwell	Oxon	Parish	97	Coton	Northampton	Hamlet	104
Cornwood	Devon	Parish	1 087	Coton	Stafford	Tnship.	446
Cornworthy	,,	Parish	479	Cotswold	Gloucester	Sub-dis.	3 946
Corpusty	Norfolk	Parish	425	Cottam	Notts	Chap.	86
Corridge	Northumberland	Tnship.	16	Cottam	York	Tnship.	95
Corringham	Essex	Parish	229	Cottenham	Cambs	Parish	2 415
Corringham	Lincoln	Wapen.	14 190	Cottered	Herts	Parish	470
Corringham	,,	Parish	717	Cotterstock	Northampton	Parish	211
Corscombe	Dorset	Parish	753	Cottesbach	Leicester	Parish	125
Corse	Gloucester	Parish	552	Cottesbrook	Northampton	Parish	201
Corsenside	Northumberland	Parish	505	Cottesloe	Bucks	Hund.	21 149
Corsham	Wilts	Sub-dis.	6 979	Cottesmore	Rutland	Parish	627
Corsham	,,	Parish	3 196	Cottesmore	,,	Tnship.	481
Corsley	,,	Parish	1 235	Cottingham	Northampton	Parish	1 139
Corston	Somerset	Parish	472	Cottingham	,,	—	718
Corston	Wilts	Tithing	315	Cottingham	York	Sub-dis.	3 391
Corton	Suffolk	Parish	530	Cottingham	,,	Parish	3 131
Corton-Denham	Somerset	Parish	413	Cottingwith, East	,,	Tnship.	316
Corwen	Mer. & Denb.	District	16 107	Cottisford	Oxon	Parish	269
Corwen	,,	Sub-dis.	10 628	Cotton	Cheshire	Tnship.	62
Corwen	Merioneth	Parish	2 042	Cotton Abbotts	,,	Tnship.	20
Coryton	Devon	Parish	238	Cotton Edmunds	,,	Tnship.	59
Cosby	Leicester	Parish	974	Cotton	Suffolk	Parish	542
Coseley, Christch.	Stafford	Ecl. Dis.	5 796	Cotts, East	Beds	Tnship.	847
Cosford	Suffolk	Hund.		Coughton	Warwick	Parish	883
Cosford	,,	District	17	Coughton	,,	Tnship.	248
Cosford	Warwick	Tnship.	46	Coulsdon	Surrey	Parish	993
Cosgrove	Northampton	Parish	776	Coulston, East	Wilts	Parish	119
Cosheston	Pembroke	Parish	602	Coulton	York	Tnship.	146
Coslany	Norfolk	Sub-dis.	13 260	Cound	Salop	Parish	908
Cossall	Notts	Parish	256	Cound	,,	Tnship.	552
Cossington	Leicester	Parish	408	Coundon	Durham	Tnship.	2 765
Cossington	Somerset	Parish	252	Coundon	,,	Ecl. Dis.	3 095
Costessey	Norfolk	Sub-dis.	4 116	Coundon-Grange	,,	Tnship.	552
Costessey	,,	Parish	1 047	Coundon	Warwick	Hamlet	225
Costock	Notts	Parish	440	Countess Wear	Devon	Ecl. Dis.	508
Coston	Leicester	Parish	179	Countesthorpe	Leicester	Chap.	975
Coston	Norfolk	Parish	58	Counthorpe	Lincoln	Hamlet	62
Coston Hackett	Worcester	Parish	173	Countisbury	Devon	Parish	176
Cotcliffe	York	Parish	13	County Lun. Asylum	Lincoln	Parish	106
Cotehill	Cumberland	Hamlet	300	Coupe Lench, &c.	Lancaster	Tnship.	2 851
Cotes	Leicester	Tnship.	55	Coupland	Northumberland	Tnship.	109
Cotes	Stafford	Tnship.	288	Courteenhall	Northampton	Parish	162
Cotes Heath	,,	Ecl. Dis.	479	Courtney, Sutton	Berks	Parish	1 581
Cotgrave	Notts	Parish	878	Courtney, Nuneham	Oxon	Parish	314
Cotham	,,	Parish	95	Cove	Hants	Tithing	671

Name of Place.	County.	Description.	Population.	Name of Place.	County.	Description.	Population.
ove, North	Suffolk	Parish	200	Coxley	Somerset	Ecl. Dis.	495
ove, South	,,	Parish	187	Coxlodge	Northumberland	Tnship.	1 092
ovehithe	,,	Parish	192	Coxwell, Great	Berks	Parish	371
oven, St. Paul	Stafford	Ecl. Dis.	766	Coxwell, Little	,,	Tnship.	302
oveney	Cambs	Parish	1 756	Coxwold	York	Sub-dis.	1 824
oveney	,,	—	550	Coxwold	,,	Parish	1 205
ovenham, St. Barth.	Lincoln	Parish	298	Coxwold	,,	Tnship.	374
ovenham, St. Mary	,,	Parish	196	Coychurch	Glamorgan	Parish	1 431
oventry	Warwick	L. Sub.	87 742	Coychurch, Higher	,,	Hamlet	316
oventry	,,	District	41 647	Coychurch, Lower	,,	Hamlet	295
oventry	,, {	M. City	40 936	Coyty	,,	Parish	2 685
		P. City	41 647	Coyty, Higher	,,	Hamlet	511
Holy Trinity	,,	Parish	19 815	Coyty, Lower	,,	Hamlet	2 174
Holy Trinity	,,	—	18 770	Crackenthorpe	Westmoreland	Tnship.	130
St. Michael w. St. Jno.	,,	Parish	22 733	Cracoe	York	Tnship.	139
St. Michael w. St. Jno.	,,	—	22 166	Cradley	Hereford	Parish	1 830
St. Peter	,,	Ecl. Dis.	9 809	Cradley	Worcester	Tnship.	4 075
St. Thomas	,,	Ecl. Dis.	5 496	Craike	York	Parish	585
overham	York	Parish	1 191	Crakehall	,,	Tnship.	583
overham w. Agglethorpe	,,	Tnship.	220	Crakehall	,,	Ecl. Dis.	817
ovington	Hunts	Parish	188	Crambe	,,	Parish	591
owarne, Little	Hereford	Parish	186	Crambe	,,	Tnship.	165
owarne, Much	,,	Parish	563	Cramlington	Northumberland	Chap.	3 301
owbit	Lincoln	Parish	649	Cranage	Cheshire	Tnship.	391
owbridge	Glamorgan	Hund.	6 084	Cranborne	Dorset	Sub-dis.	7 624
owbridge	,,	L. Sub.	6 084	Cranborne	,,	Parish	2 656
owbridge	,,	Sub-dis.	6 486	Cranbourne, St. Peter	Berks	Ecl. Dis.	1 514
owbridge	,,	Parish	1 094	Cranbrook	Kent	L. Sub.	22 472
owbridge	,,	P. Bor.	1 094	Cranbrook	,,	District	13 412
owden	Kent	Parish	772	Cranbrook	,,	Sub-dis.	6 688
owdens Ambo	York	Tnship.	154	Cranbrook	,,	Parish	4 128
owes	Hants, I.W.	Sub-dis.	10 449	Cranfield	Beds	Sub-dis.	3 706
owes, East, St. James	,, I.W.	Ecl. Dis.	1 954	Cranfield	,,	Parish	1 591
owes, West	,, I.W.	Ecl. Dis.	4 591	Cranford	Middlesex	Parish	530
owfold	Sussex	Parish	946	Cranford, St. Andw.	Nrthptn.	Parish	228
owgill	York	Ecl. Dis.	330	Cranford, St. John	,,	Parish	325
ow Honeybourne	Gloucester	Parish	360	Cranham	Essex	Parish	385
owick	York	Hamlet	849	Cranham	Gloucester	Parish	424
owick, East	,,	Ecl. Dis.	818	Cranley	Surrey & Sussex	Sub-dis.	7 553
owlam	,,	Parish	69	Cranley	Surrey	Parish	1 393
owley	Gloucester	Parish	311	Cranmore, East	Somerset	Parish	70
owley	Middlesex	Parish	371	Cranmore, West	,,	Parish	292
owley	Oxon	Parish	1 404	Cranoe	Leicester	Parish	107
owling	York	Tnship.	1 815	Cransford	Suffolk	Parish	284
owling	,,	Ecl. Dis.	1 729	Cransley	Northampton	Parish	350
owlinge	Suffolk	Parish	842	Crantock	Cornwall	Parish	381
owpen-Bewley	Durham	Tnship.	448	Cranwell	Lincoln	Parish	233
owpen	Northumberland	Tnship.	6 291	Cranwich	Norfolk	Parish	88
owsby	York	Parish	105	Cranworth	,,	Parish	264
owthorp	,,	Parish	141	Crasswell	Hereford	Tnship.	356
owton, East	,,	Parish	472	Craster	Northumberland	Tnship.	216
owton, North	,,	Tnship.	312	Cratfield	Suffolk	Parish	604
owton, South	,,	Chap.	167	Crathorne	York	Parish	256
oxhoe	Durham	Tnship.	4 171	Crawcrook	Durham	Tnship.	319

Name of Place.	County.	Description.	Population.	Name of Place.	County.	Description.	Population.
Crawley, North ..	*Bucks* ..	Parish	981	Criccieth	*Carnarvon* ..	Sub-dis.	5 591
Crawley ..	*Hants* ..	Parish	502	Criccieth	,, ..	Parish	769
Crawley ..	.. ..	—	397	**Criccieth**	,, ..	P. Bor.	498
Crawley ..	*Northumberland*	Tnship.	26	Crich	*Derby* ..	Parish	3 970
Crawley ..	*Oxon* ..	Hamlet	253	Crich	,, ..	Tnship	2 829
Crawley ..	*Susex* ..	Parish	473	Crick ..	*Monmouth* ..	Hamlet	138
Cray ..	*Brecon* ..	Hamlet	545	Crick ..	*Northampton, &c.*	Sub-dis.	4 962
Cray, Foots ..	*Kent* ..	Parish	286	Crick ..	*Northampton*	Parish	999
Cray, North ..	,, ..	Parish	578	Crickadarn ..	*Brecon* ..	Parish	448
Cray, St. Mary ..	,, ..	Parish	1 464	Cricket-Malherbie	*Somerset* ..	Parish	21
Cray, St. Paul ..	,, ..	Parish	532	Cricket, St. Thomas	,, ..	Parish	66
Crayford ..	,,	Parish	3 103	Crickhowell ..	*Brecon* ..	Hund.	22 351
Creacombe ..	*Devon* ..	Parish	63	Crickhowell ..	,, ..	L. Sub.	13 653
Creake, North ..	*Norfolk* ..	Parish	708	Crickhowell ..	,, ..	District	22 457
Creake, South ..	,, ..	Parish	1 058	Crickhowell ..	,, ..	Sub-dis.	2 445
Creaton, Great ..	*Northampton*	Parish	510	Crickhowell ..	,, ..	Parish	1 516
Creaton, Little ..	,,	Hamlet	73	Cricklade & Swindon	*Wilts* ..	L. Sub.	31 338
Credenhill ..	*Hereford* ..	Parish	199	Cricklade ..	,, ..	District	11 470
Crediton ..	*Devon* ..	L. Sub.	15 906	Cricklade ..	,, ..	Sub-dis.	5 795
Crediton ..	,, ..	Hund.	11 233	**Cricklade**	*Wilts & Glou.*	P. Bor.	36 893
Crediton ..	,, ..	District	20 274	Cricklade, St. Mary	*Wilts* ..	Parish	367
Crediton ..	,, ..	Sub-dis.	6 535	Cricklade, St. Sampson	,, ..	Parish	1 453
Crediton ..	,, ..	Parish	5 731	Cridling Stubbs .	*York* ..	Tnship.	154
Crediton ..	,, ..	Town	4 048	Criggion ..	*Montgomery*	Tnship.	187
Creech, St. Michael	*Somerset* ..	Parish	1 121	Crigglestone ..	*York* ..	Tnship.	2 021
Creed ..	*Cornwall* ..	Parish	743	Crimplesham ..	*Norfolk* ..	Parish	328
Creeksea ..	*Essex* ..	Parish	175	Cringleford ..	,, ..	Parish	205
Creeting, All Saints	*Suffolk* ..	Parish	333	Crinow ..	*Pembroke* ..	Parish	70
Creeting, St. Mary	,, ..	Parish	202	Cripplegate ..	*Middlesex* ..	Sub-dis.	19 697
Creeting, St. Olave	,, ..	Parish	41	Cripton ..	*Dorset* ..	Hamlet	9
Creeting, St. Peter	,, ..	Parish	248	Critchell, Long..	,, ..	Parish	145
Creeton ..	*Lincoln* ..	Parish	79	Crixea ..	*Essex* ..	Parish	175
Cregina ..	*Radnor* ..	Parish	124	Crockernhill ..	*Kent* ..	Ecl. Dis.	677
Crendon, Long ..	*Bucks* ..	Parish	1 570	Crockenwell ..	*Devon* ..	L. Sub.	10 226
Creslow ..	,, ..	Parish	9	Crockham Hill..	*Kent* ..	Ecl. Dis.	542
Cressage ..	*Salop* ..	Chap.	356	Croes & Berwyn .	*Cardigan* ..	Tnship.	208
Cressing ..	*Essex* ..	Parish	582	Croft ..	*Hereford* ..	Parish	155
Cressingham, Great	*Norfolk* ..	Parish	530	Croft ..	,, ..	Tnship.	55
Cressingham, Little	,, ..	Parish	243	Croft, &c. ..	*Lancaster* ..	Parish	1 094
Cresswell	*Northumberland*	Tnship.	244	Croft ..	*Leicester* ..	Parish	319
Cresswell ..	,,	Ecl. Dis.	508	Croft ..	*Lincoln* ..	Parish	784
Creswell ..	*Stafford* ..	Parish	12	Croft ..	*York* ..	Parish	761
Cretingham ..	*Suffolk* ..	Parish	343	Croft ..	,, ..	Tnship.	466
Creuddyn ..	*Carnarvon* ..	Hund.	5 025	Crofton ..	*Cumberland*.	Tnship.	105
Creuddyn ..	*Carn. & Denb.*	Sub-dis.	7 903	Crofton ..	*York* ..	Parish	402
Crewe ..	*Cheshire*	Tnship.	102	Crogdean	*Northumberland*	Tnship.	6
Crewe (Barthomley P.)	,,	Tnship.	387	Croghton ..	*Cheshire* ..	Tnship.	28
Crewe ..	,,	Town	8 159	Croglin ..	*Cumberland*.	Parish	254
Crewe, Christchurch	,,	Ecl. Dis.	5 961	Cromer ..	*Norfolk* ..	Sub-dis.	7 145
Crewe, St. Michael	,,	Ecl. Dis.	387	Cromer ..	,, ..	Parish	1 367
Crewkerne ..	*Somerset* ..	Hund.	7 781	Cromford ..	*Derby* ..	Tnship.	1 140
Crewkerne ..	,, ..	Sub-dis.	8 084	Cromhall ..	*Gloucester* ..	Parish	681
Crewkerne ..	,, ..	Parish	4 705	Crompton ..	*Lancaster* ..	Sub-dis.	7 032
Crewkerne ..	,, ..	Town	3 566	Crompton ..	,, ..	Tnship.	7 032

Name of Place.	County.	Description.	Population.	Name of Place.	County.	Description.	Population.
Crompton, East .	*Lancaster* ..	Ecl. Dis.	3 414	Crowan	*Cornwall* ..	Parish	4 131
Cromwell ..	*Notts* ..	Parish	162	Crowborough, &c.	*Stafford* ..	Tnship.	590
Crondall ..	*Hants* ..	Parish	2 764	Crowcombe ..	*Somerset* ..	Parish	573
Crondall, &c. ..	,, ..	Tithing	492	Crowell	*Oxon* ..	Parish	162
Cronton.. ..	*Lancaster* ..	Tnship.	412	Crowfield ..	*Suffolk* ..	Parish	353
Crook & Billy-row	*Durham* ..	Tnship.	5 134	Crowhurst ..	*Surrey* ..	Parish	211
Crook, St. Catherine	,, ..	Ecl. Dis.	8 603	Crowhurst ..	*Sussex* ..	Parish	430
Crook ..	*Westmoreland*	Tnship.	258	Crowland.	*Linc. & Nrthptn.*	Sub-dis.	8 004
Crookdean	*Northumberland*	Tnship.	6	Crowland ..	*Lincoln* ..	Parish	3 148
Crookham ..	*Hants* ..	Tithing	1 020	**Crowland** ..	,, ..	Town	2 413
Crookham w. Ewshott	,, ..	Ecl. Dis.	1 283	Crowle ..	*Linc. & York*	Sub-dis.	4 498
Crookes, St. Thomas	*York* ..	Ecl. Dis.	3 452	Crowle	,, ,,	Parish	3 182
Crookhouse	*Northumberland*	Tnship.	24	Crowle	,, ,,	Tnship.	2 648
Croome-D'Abitot	*Worcester* ..	Parish	163	**Crowle**.. ..	*Lincoln* ..	Town	2 304
Cropredy	*Oxon & Warw.*	Sub-dis.	4 443	Crowle ..	*Worcester* ..	Parish	576
Cropredy .. ,, ,,		Parish	2 478	Crowley.. ..	*Cheshire* ..	Tnship.	183
Cropredy ..	*Oxon* ..	Tnship.	497	Crowmarsh-Gifford	*Oxon* ..	Parish	360
Cropston ..	*Leicester* ..	Tnship.	113	Crown Farm ..	*Hants* ..	Parish	5
Cropthorne ..	*Worcester* ..	Parish	839	Crownthorpe ..	*Norfolk* ..	Parish	97
Cropthorne ..	,, ..	Tnship.	374	Crowthorne ..	*Gloucester* ..	Hund.	6 259
Cropton.. ..	*York* ..	Tnship.	360	Crowton.. ..	*Cheshire* ..	Tnship.	413
Cropwell Bishop	*Notts* ..	Parish	638	Croxall ..	*Derby & Staff.*	Parish	247
Cropwell Butler .	,, ..	Tnship.	604	Croxall	*Derby* ..	—	143
Crosby	*Cumberland* .	Tnship.	506	Croxby	*Lincoln* ..	Parish	147
Crosby upon Eden	,,	Parish	426	Croxdale, St. Marg.	*Durham* ..	Ecl. Dis.	468
Crosby, High ..	,,	Tnship.	177	Croxden.. ..	*Stafford* ..	Parish	224
Crosby, Low ..	,,	Tnship.	125	Croxden w. Gt. Yate	,, ..	—	205
Crosby	*Lancaster* ..	Sub-dis.	5 075	Croxteth Park ..	*Lancaster* ..	Parish	46
Crosby, Great ..	,, ..	Chap.	3 794	Croxton.. ..	*Cambs* ..	Parish	267
Crosby, Little ..	,, ..	Tnship.	418	Croxton.. ..	*Cheshire* ..	Tnship.	46
Crosby	*Lincoln* ..	Tnship.	247	Croxton Keyrial .	*Leicester* ..	Parish	594
Crosby Garrett	*Westmoreland*	Parish	306	Croxton, South ..	,, ..	Parish	311
Crosby Garrett..	,,	Tnship.	245	Croxton ..	*Lincoln* ..	Parish	122
Crosby Ravensworth	,,	Parish	927	Croxton.. ..	*Norfolk* ..	Parish	428
Crosby	*York* ..	Tnship.	38	Croxton.. ..	*Stafford* ..	Ecl. Dis.	1 075
Croscombe ..	*Somerset* ..	Parish	729	Croydon w. Clapton	*Cambs* ..	Parish	508
Crosland, South .	*York* ..	Tnship.	2 794	Croydon.. ..	*Surrey*..	L. Sub.	42 344
Crosland, South, Trinity	,, ..	Ecl. Dis.	2 259	Croydon.. ..	,, ..	District	46 474
Cross-Canonby ..	*Cumberland*.	Parish	6 900	Croydon.. ..	,, ..	Sub-dis.	37 093
Cross-Canonby ..	,,	Tnship.	87	Croydon.. ..	,, ..	Parish	30 240
Crossens, St.John	*Lancaster* ..	Ecl. Dis.	756	**Croydon** ..	,, ..	Town	20 325
Crossgate ..	*Durham* ..	Tnship.	2 591	Croydon, Christchurch	,, ..	Ecl. Dis.	4 203
Cross Town, St.Cross	*Cheshire* .	Ecl. Dis.	784	Croydon Common, St.Jas.	,, ..	Ecl. Dis.	7 590
Crosswayham, &c.	*Northampton*	Lodges	21	Crudwell ..	*Wilts* ..	Parish	799
Crosthwaite ..	*Cumberland*.	Parish	5 070	Crumpsall ..	*Lancaster* ..	Tnship.	4 285
Crosthwaite, &c..	*Westmoreland*	Tnship.	740	Crumpsall, St. Mary	,, ..	Ecl. Dis.	3 306
Croston	*Lancaster* ..	Sub-dis.	5 369	Crundale ..	*Kent* ..	Parish	279
Croston	,, ..	Parish	4 242	Crunwear ..	*Pembroke* ..	Parish	261
Croston	,, ..	Tnship.	1 790	Crutch	*Worcester* ..	Parish	11
Crostwick ..	*Norfolk* ..	Parish	144	Cruwys Morchard	*Devon* ..	Parish	685
Crostwight ..	,, ..	Parish	73	Crux Easton ..	*Hants* ..	Parish	76
Croughton ..	*Chester* ..	Tnship.	28	Cubberley ..	*Gloucester* ..	Parish	343
Croughton ..	*Northampton*	Parish	580	Cubbington ..	*Warwick* ..	Parish	964
Crowan	*Cornwall* ..	Sub-dis.	4 131	Cubert	*Cornwall* ..	Parish	420

Name of Place.	County.	Description.	Population.
Cubley ..	.. Derby ..	Parish	383
Cublington ..	.. Bucks ..	Parish	288
Cuby ..	.. Cornwall ..	Parish	139
Cuckfield ..	.. Sussex ..	L. Sub.	17 066
Cuckfield ..	.. ,, ..	District	17 163
Cuckfield ..	.. ,, ..	Sub-dis.	6 792
Cuckfield ..	.. ,, ..	Parish	3 539
Cucklington ..	.. Somerset ..	Parish	280
Cuckney ..	.. Notts ..	Tnship.	540
Cuddesdon ..	.. Oxon ..	Parish	1 591
Cuddesdon ..	.. ,, ..	—	384
Cuddington ..	.. Bucks ..	Parish	590
Cuddington ..	.. Cheshire ..	Tnship.	317
Cuddington ..	.. Salop ..	Tnship.	268
Cuddington ..	.. Surrey ..	Parish	148
Cudham ..	.. Kent ..	Parish	988
Cudworth ..	.. Somerset ..	Parish	151
Cudworth ..	.. York ..	Tnship.	521
Cuerdale ..	.. Lancaster ..	Tnship.	56
Cuerden.. ..	.. ,, ..	Tnship.	666
Cuerdley ..	.. ,, ..	Tnship.	192
Culbone.. ..	.. Somerset ..	Parish	41
Culcheth ..	.. Lancaster ..	Sub-dis.	10 881
Culcheth ..	.. ,, ..	Tnship.	2 214
Culford ..	.. Suffolk ..	Parish	346
Culgaith ..	.. Cumberland.	Tnship.	323
Culham ..	.. Oxon & Berks	Parish	474
Cullercoats	Northumberland	Tnship.	866
Cullercoats ..	.. ,,	Ecl. Dis.	1 566
Cullingworth ..	.. York ..	Ecl. Dis.	1 943
Cullompton ..	.. Devon ..	L. Sub	37 551
Cullompton ..	.. ,, ..	Sub-dis.	4 482
Cullompton ..	.. ,, ..	Parish	3 185
Cullompton ..	.. ,, ..	Town	2 205
Culmington ..	.. Salop ..	Parish	517
Culmstock ..	.. Devon ..	Sub-dis.	4 435
Culmstock ..	.. ,, ..	Parish	1 102
Culpho ..	.. Suffolk ..	Parish	56
Culverthorpe ..	.. Lincoln ..	Chap.	120
Culworth ..	.. Northampton	Parish	652
Cumberland ..	.. ..	County	205 276
Eastern Division ..	..	E. Div.	105 389
Western Division ..	..	W. Div.	99 887
Cumberland ..	.. Cumberland.	L. Sub.	46 638
Cumberland ..	.. ,,	Ward	21 692
Cumberworth ..	.. Lincoln ..	Parish	266
Cumberworth ..	.. York ..	Tnship.	2 414
Cumberworth Half	,, ..	Tnship.	1 974
Cumdivock ..	.. Cumberland.	Tnship.	334
Cummersdale ..	.. ,,	Tnship.	829
Cumnor..	.. Berks & Oxon	Sub-dis.	2 853
Cumnor..	.. Berks ..	Parish	1 021
Cumrew..	.. Cumberland.	Parish	136
Cumrew Inside..	,,	Tnship.	95
Cumrew Outside	Cumberland.	Tnship.	4
Cumwhinton ..	,,	Hamlet	33
Cumwhitton ..	,,	Parish	55
Cumwhitton ..	,,	Tnship.	22
Cundall..	.. York ..	Parish	39
Cundall w. Leckby	,, ..	Tnship.	21
Cunnahs Quay ..	Flint	Ecl. Dis.	1 42
Cunsall ..	.. Stafford ..	Tnship.	29
Curbar ..	.. Derby ..	Tnship.	35
Curborough w. Elmhurst	Staff.	Tnship.	22
Curbridge ..	.. Oxon ..	Hamlet	62
Curdridge, St. Peter	Hants ..	Ecl. Dis.	53
Curdworth ..	.. Warwick ..	Parish	64
Curdworth ..	.. ,, ..	—	33
Curland..	.. Somerset ..	Parish	24
Curry ..	.. Cornwall ..	Parish	51
Curry Mallett ..	Somerset ..	Parish	54
Curry, North ..	.. ,, ..	Hund.	4 27
Curry, North ..	.. ,, ..	Parish	1 83
Curry Rivell ..	.. ,, ..	Sub-dis.	5 18
Curry Rivell ..	.. ,, ..	Parish	1 70
Curtain Rd. St. Jas.	Middlesex.	Ecl. Dis.	11 24
Cusop ..	.. Hereford ..	Parish	21
Cutcombe ..	.. Somerset ..	Parish	79
Cutsdean ..	.. Worcester ..	Chap.	16
Cuttleston ..	.. Stafford ..	Hund.	29 15
Cuttridge ..	.. Devon ..	—	2
Cuxham..	.. Oxon ..	Parish	17
Cuxton ..	.. Kent ..	Parish	44
Cuxwold ..	.. Lincoln ..	Parish	8
Cwm ..	.. Flint ..	Parish	49
Cwmamman	Carm. & Glam.	Ecl. Dis.	4 35
Cwmcarvan ..	Monmouth ..	Parish	33
Cwmdû ..	.. Brecon ..	Sub-dis.	1 056
Cwmdû.. ..	,, ..	Parish	1 056
Cwmdû.. ..	Glamorgan .	Hamlet	4 15
Cwmrheidol ..	Cardigan ..	Tnship.	1 304
Cwmtoyddwr ..	Radnor ..	Parish	798
Cwmyoy	Monm. & Heref.	Parish	649
Cwmyoy Lower..	Monmouth ..	—	272
Cwmyoy Upper..	.. ,,	—	172
Cydplwyf ..	Cardigan ..	Parcel	239
Cyfartha ..	Glamorgan .	Ecl. Dis.	7 888
Cyflic ..	Carmarthen	Parish	468
Cyfocthybrenin..	Cardigan ..	Tnship.	1 089
Cyfronydd ..	Montgomery	Tnship.	64
Cylch-Bycham ..	Pembroke ..	Divsn.	278
Cylch-Gwylod-y-Wlad	,,	Divsn.	419
Cylch-Mawr ..	,, ..	Divsn.	460
Cylch-y-Dre ..	,,	Divsn.	1 027
Cynnillmawr ..	Cardigan ..	Tnship.	616
Dacorum ..	Herts ..	Hund.	38 081
Dacre ..	.. Cumberland.	Parish	967

Name of Place.	County.	Description.	Population.	Name of Place.	County.	Description.	Population.
Dacre	Cumberland	Tnship.	151	Dane Bridge, St. Paul	Cheshire	Ecl. Dis.	2 315
Dacre	York	Tnship.	739	Dane Hill, Trinity	Sussex	Ecl. Dis.	963
Dacre Banks	,,	Sub-dis.	3 071	Danthorpe	York	Tnship.	62
Dadlington	Leicester	Chap.	216	Darcy Lever	Lancaster	Tnship.	2 071
Dagenham	Essex	Parish	2 708	Darenth	Kent	Parish	626
Daglingworth	Gloucester	Parish	355	Daresbury	Cheshire	Sub-dis.	2 841
Dalbury w. Lees	Derby	Parish	263	Daresbury	,,	Tnship.	136
Dalby, Great	Leicester	Parish	484	Darfield	York	Sub-dis.	10 028
Dalby, Little	,,	Parish	183	Darfield	,,	Parish	12 231
Dalby on the Wolds	,,	Parish	359	Darfield	,,	Tnship.	746
Dalby w. Skewsby	Lincoln	Parish	115	Darlaston	Stafford	Sub-dis.	13 230
Dalby	York	Parish	149	Darlaston	,,	Parish	12 884
Dalderby	Lincoln	Parish	40	Darlaston, St. George	,,	Ecl. Dis.	3 972
Dale Abbey	Derby	Parish	366	Darley	Derby	Parish	2 156
Dale-street	Lancaster	Sub-dis.	29 078	Darley	,,	Tnship.	1 574
Dale	Pembroke	Parish	463	Darley Abbey	,,	Chap.	967
Dale Town	York	Tnship.	60	Darley Abbey, St. Matthew	,,	Ecl. Dis.	967
Dalham	Suffolk	Parish	539	Darley, South, St. Mary	,,	Ecl. Dis.	582
Dallaghill, St. Peter	York	Ecl. Dis.	320	Darlingscott	Worcester	Hamlet	160
Dallinghoe	Suffolk	Parish	370	Darlington	Durham	Ward	113 167
Dallington	Northampton	Parish	686	Darlington Ward	,,	L. Sub.	113 167
Dallington	Sussex	Parish	591	Darlington	,,	District.	26 122
Dalston	Cumberland	Sub-dis.	3 865	Darlington	,,	Sub-dis.	21 167
Dalston	,,	Parish	2 568	Darlington	,,	Parish	16 762
Dalston	,,	Tnship.	884	Darlington	,,	Tnship.	15 789
Dalston, St. Philip	Middlesex	Ecl. Dis.	10 247	Darlington	,,	Town	15 781
Dalton-le-Dale	Durham	Parish	8 432	Holy Trinity	,,	Ecl. Dis.	4 993
Dalton-le-Dale	,,	Tnship.	102	St. John	,,	Ecl. Dis.	5 573
Dalton Piercy	,,	Tnship.	98	Darlton	Notts	Parish	163
Dalton, Kirkby Lonsdale	Lancr.	Tnship.	129	Darmsden	Suffolk	Hamlet	64
Dalton	,,	Sub-dis.	11 243	Darnall	York	Ecl. Dis.	2 403
Dalton, Upholland	,,	Tnship.	453	Darnhall	Cheshire	Tnship.	176
Dalton	,,	Town	2 812	Darowen	Montgomery	Sub-dis.	4 160
Dalton in Furness	,,	Parish	9 152	Darowen	,,	Parish	1 227
Dalton	Northumberland	Tnship.	114	Darras Hall	Northumberland	Tnship.	14
Dalton (Topcliffe P.)	York	Tnship.	307	Darrington	York	Parish	744
Dalton (Kirby Hill P.)	,,	Tnship.	222	Darrington	,,	Tnship.	614
Dalton (K. Leatham P.)	,,	Tnship.	4 692	Darsham	Suffolk	Parish	409
Dalton, Trinity	,,	Ecl. Dis.	369	Dartford	Kent	L. Sub.	27 372
Dalton (Rotherham, &c. P.)	,,	Tnship.	336	Dartford	,,	District	32 316
Dalton-Holme	,,	Parish	506	Dartford	,,	Sub-dis.	13 180
Dalton, North	,,	Parish	486	Dartford	,,	Parish	6 597
Dalton, South	,,	Parish	338	Dartford	,,	Town	5 314
Dalton upon Tees	,,	Tnship.	211	Dartington	Devon	Parish	626
Dalwood	Devon	Parish	492	Dartmoor-Forest	,,	Quarter	2 599
Damerham North	Wilts	Hund.	2 958	Dartmouth	,,	Sub-dis.	5 429
Damerham South	,,	Hund.	3 008	Dartmouth	,,	Boro.	4 444
Damerham South	,,	Parish	697	Darton	York	Sub-dis.	4 450
Danbury	Essex	Parish	1 113	Darton	,,	Parish	4 592
Danby	York	Sub-dis.	2 046	Darton	,,	Tnship.	2 216
Danby	,,	Parish	2 711	Darwen	Lancaster	Sub-dis.	21 447
Danby	,,	Tnship.	1 637	Darwen, Lower	,,	Tnship.	3 301
Danby Wiske	,,	Parish	557	Darwen, Lower, St. Jas.	,,	Ecl. Dis.	2 081
Danby Wiske	,,	Tnship.	853	Darwen, Over	,,	Tnship.	16 492

Name of Place.	County.	Description.	Population.	Name of Place.	County.	Description.	Population.
Darwen, Over, Trinity	Lancaster	Ecl. Dis.	14 101	Deansgate	Lancaster ..	Sub-dis.	29 029
Darwen, Over, St. Jas.	,, ..	Ecl. Dis.	4 045	Dearham	.. Cumberland	Parish	2 595
Darwen, Over..	,, ..	Town	14 327	Dearham	.. ,,	Tnship.	1 509
Datchett	.. Bucks ..	Parish	982	Debach ..	.. Suffolk ..	Parish	144
Datchworth	.. Herts ..	Parish	635	Debden..	.. Essex ..	Parish	942
Dauntsey	.. Wilts ..	Parish	578	Debdon..	Northumberland	Tnship.	11
Davenham	.. Cheshire ..	Parish	6 855	Debenham	.. Suffolk ..	Parish	1 488
Davenham	.. ,, ..	Tnship.	518	Debtling	.. Kent ..	Parish	344
Davenport	.. ,, ..	Tnship.	117	Deddington	.. Oxon ..	L. Sub.	6 822
Daventry	.. Northampton	L. Sub.	22 782	Deddington	.. ,, ..	Sub-dis.	6 458
Daventry	.. ,,	District	20 600	Deddington	.. ,, ..	Parish	2 024
Daventry	.. ,,	Sub-dis.	8 917	Deddington	.. ,, ..	—	1 551
Daventry	.. ,,	Parish	4 124	Dedham	.. Essex ..	Sub-dis.	4 553
Daventry	.. ,,	M. Bor.	4 124	Dedham	.. ,, ..	Parish	1 734
Davidstow	.. Cornwall ..	Parish	394	Dedworth	.. Berks ..	Hamlet	195
Davington	.. Kent ..	Parish	149	Deene ..	.. Northampton	Parish	540
Davy Hall	.. York ..	Parish	22	Deene ..	.. ,,	—	281
Dawdon..	.. Durham ..	Tnship.	6 137	Deenthorpe	.. ,,	Hamlet	259
Dawley ..	.. Salop ..	Sub-dis.	11 323	Deeping..	.. Lincoln ..	Sub-dis.	5 813
Dawley Magna ..	,, ..	Parish	11 013	Deeping, Market	,, ..	Parish	1 337
Dawley Magna	,, ..	Town	6 365	Deeping, St. James	,, ..	Parish	1 763
Dawley Little ..	,, ..	Ecl. Dis.	2 327	Deeping, St. Nicholas	,, ..	Parish	1 180
Dawlish	.. Devon ..	Parish	4 014	Deeping, West ..	,, ..	Parish	349
Dawlish	.. ,, ..	Town	3 505	Deeping-Gate ..	Northampton	Hamlet	224
Daylesford	.. Worcester ..	Parish	108	Deerhurst	.. Gloucester ..	Hund.	4 994
Dayrell ..	.. Bucks ..	Parish	198	Deerhurst	.. ,, ..	Sub-dis.	4 229
Deal ..	.. Kent ..	Sub-dis.	12 105	Deerhurst	.. ,, ..	Parish	930
Deal ..	.. ,, ..	Parish	7 531	Defford ..	.. Worcester ..	Chap.	463
Deal ..	.. ,, ..	M. Bor.	7 531	Deighton (Escrick P.)	York ..	Tnship.	201
Deal, St. Andrew	,, ..	Ecl. Dis.	2 697	Deighton	.. ,, ..	Chap.	141
Deal, St. George	,, ..	Ecl. Dis.	2 731	Deighton, Kirk ..	,, ..	Parish	485
Dean ..	.. Beds ..	Parish	552	Deighton, Kirk ..	,, ..	Tnship.	364
Dean ..	.. Cumberland.	Parish	829	Deighton, North	,, ..	Tnship.	121
Dean ..	.. ,,	Tnship.	195	Delamere	.. Cheshire ..	Parish	1 146
Dean-Prior	.. Devon ..	Parish	422	Delamere	.. ,, ..	Tnship.	474
Dean, East	.. Gloucester ..	Tnship.	9 212	Delph ..	.. York ..	Sub-dis.	9 754
Dean Forest, Christch.	,, ..	Ecl. Dis.	1 777	Dembleby	.. Lincoln ..	Parish	51
St. John	,, ..	Ecl. Dis.	4 417	Denaby..	.. York ..	Tnship.	203
St. Paul	,, ..	Ecl. Dis.	4 909	Denardiston	.. Suffolk ..	Parish	277
Trinity	,, ..	Ecl. Dis.	3 218	Denbighshire ..	.. ..	County	100 778
Deanhill, Little..	,, ..	—	98	Denbigh	.. Denbigh ..	L. Sub.	14 028
Dean, Little ..	,, ..	Parish	887	Denbigh	.. ,, ..	Sub-dis.	9 053
Dean, West ..	,, ..	Tnship.	8 254	Denbigh	.. ,, ..	Parish	4 054
Deane ..	.. Hants ..	Parish	135	**Denbigh**	.. ,, ..	Boro.	5 946
Dean, East	.. ,, ..	Parish	223	Denbigh Parl. Dis. of	,, ..	Boros.	17 888
Dean, Priors	.. ,, ..	Parish	129	Denbury	.. Devon ..	Parish	410
Deane ..	.. Lancaster ..	Parish	35 746	Denby ..	.. Derby ..	Parish	1 338
Deanham	Northumberland	Tnship.	41	Denby ..	.. York ..	Tnship.	1 813
Dean, East, Eastbourne	Sussex	Parish	334	Denby, St. John.	,, ..	Ecl. Dis.	2 262
Dean, East, Singleton	,,	Parish	343	Denchworth	.. Berks ..	Parish	257
Dean, West, Westbourne	,,	Parish	681	Denford	.. ,, ..	Ecl. Dis.	77
Dean, West, Eastbourne	,,	Parish	153	Denford	.. Northampton	Parish	429
Dean, West	.. Wilts & Hants	Parish	446	Dengie ..	.. Essex ..	Hund.	11 224
Dean, West	... ,, ,,	—	310	Dengie ..	.. ,, ..	L. Sub.	17 678

Name of Place.	County.	Description.	Population.	Name of Place.	County.	Description.	Population.
engie	Essex	Parish	298	**Derby**	Derbyshire	Boro.	43 091
enham	Bucks	Parish	1 068	Derby, St. John	,,	Ecl. Dis.	6 228
enham, Stradbroke	Suffolk	Parish	282	Derby, St. Paul	,,	Ecl. Dis.	2 400
enham, Fornham	,,	Parish	200	Derby, Trinity	,,	Ecl. Dis.	6 989
enholme Gate	York	Ecl. Dis.	2 816	Derby-Hills	,,	Liberty	37
enio	Carnarvon	Parish	2 420	Derby, West	Lancaster	Sub Dis.	52 740
enmark Hill	Surrey	Ecl. Dis.	5 249	Derby, West	,,	Parish	52 694
ennington	Suffolk	Sub-dis.	7 002	Dereham, East	Norfolk	Sub-dis.	7 531
ennington	,,	Parish	895	Dereham, East	,,	Parish	4 368
enny Lodge Walk, &c.	Hants	—	195	Dereham, West	,,	Parish	679
enstone	Stafford	Tnship.	241	**Dereham**	,,	Town	3 070
enstone	,,	Ecl. Dis.	443	Deritend	Warwick	Sub-dis.	31 788
ent	York	Sub-dis.	1 427	Deritend	,,	Hamlet	10 449
ent	,,	Tnship.	1 427	Derllys	Carmarthen	Hund.	14 949
enton, Nether	Cumberland	Parish	302	Derry Hill, Christch.	Wilts	Ecl. Dis.	1 388
enton, Upper	,,	Parish	100	Dersingham	Norfolk	Parish	822
enton	Durham	Tnship.	111	Derwen	Denbigh	Parish	573
enton	Hunts	Parish	87	Derwent	Cumberland	L. Sub.	34 543
enton, Hougham	Kent	Parish	183	Derwent	Derby	Tnship.	165
enton, Northfleet	,,	Parish	101	Desborough	Bucks	Hund.	19 198
enton	Lancaster	Sub-dis.	6 706	Desborough, First	,,	L. Sub.	8 747
enton	,,	Tnship.	3 335	Desborough, Second	,,	L. Sub.	17 808
Christchurch	,,	Ecl. Dis.	3 579	Desborough	Northampton	Parish	1 428
St. Lawrence	,,	Ecl. Dis.	3 127	Desford	Leicester	Parish	981
enton	Lincoln	Sub-dis.	7 225	Desford	,,	—	970
enton	,,	Parish	637	Detchant	Northumberland	Tnship	145
enton	Norfolk	Parish	518	Dethick & Lea	Derby	Chap.	935
enton	Northampton	Parish	578	Deuxhill	Salop	Parish	43
enton, East	Northumberland	Tnship.	600	Devizes	Wilts	L. Sub.	22 669
enton, West	,,	Tnship.	466	Devizes	,,	District	21 680
enton	Oxon	Hamlet	157	Devizes	,,	Sub-dis.	7 364
enton	Sussex	Parish	206	**Devizes**	,,	Boro.	6 638
enton	York	Tnship.	170			M. Bor.	50 440
enver	Norfolk	Parish	932	**Devonport**	Devon {	P. Bor.	64 783
enwick	Northumberland	Tnship.	183	Devonport, St. James	,,	Ecl. Dis.	6 655
eopham	Norfolk	Parish	483	Devenport, St. Mary	,,	Ecl. Dis.	5 997
epden	Suffolk	Parish	265	Devonport, St. Paul	,,	Ecl. Dis.	8 750
eptford, St. Andrew	Durham	Ecl. Dis.	10 908	Devonport, St. Stephen	,,	Ecl. Dis.	3 306
eptford, St. Nicholas	Kent	Sub-dis.	8 139	Devonshire		County	584 373
eptford, St. Nicholas	,,	Parish	8 139	Northern Division		N. Div.	171 368
eptford, St. John	,,	Ecl. Dis.	7 626	Southern Division		S. Div.	413 005
eptford, St. Paul	Kent & Sur.	Sub-dis.	37 834	Devynnock	Brecon	Hund.	10 225
eptford, St. Paul	,, ,,	Parish	37 834	Devynnock	,,	L. Sub.	4 227
1. North Ward	,,	Ward	8 395	Devynnock	,,	Sub-dis.	4 075
2. South Ward	,,	Ward	10 162	Devynnock	,,	Parish	1 798
3. East Ward	,,	Ward	13 472	Dewchurch	Hereford	Sub-dis	4 352
4. West Ward	,,	Ward	5 805	Dewchurch, Little	,,	Parish	322
Depwade	Norfolk	Hund.	9 617	Dewchurch, Much	,,	Parish	608
Depwade	,,	L. Sub.	9 617	Dewlish	Dorset	Parish	458
Depwade	,,	District	25 248	Dewsall	Hereford	Parish	36
Derbyshire		County	339 327	Dewsbury	York	District	92 883
Northern Division		N. Div.	159 044	Dewsbury	,,	Sub-dis.	18 148
Southern Division		S. Div.	180 283	Dewsbury	,,	Parish	34 988
Derby	Derbyshire	District	51 049	Dewsbury	,,	Tnship.	18 148

Name of Place.	County.	Description.	Population.	Name of Place.	County.	Description.	Populati
Dewsbury	*York*	M. Bor.	18 148	Dinsdale, Low	*Durham*	Parish	20?
Dewsbury Moor	,,	Ecl. Dis.	3 256	Dinsdale, Over	*York*	Tnship.	8?
Dewsland	*Pembroke*	Hund.	10 452	Dinting	*Derby*	Tnship.	730
Dewsland	,,	L. Sub.	10 452	Dinton	*Bucks*	Parish	81?
Deythur	*Montgomery*	Hund.	2 933	Dinton	*Wilts*	Parish	50?
Deythur	,,	L. Sub.	2 529	Dippenhall	*Hants*	Tithing	52?
Dibden	*Hants*	Parish	513	Diptford	*Devon*	Parish	65?
Dicker Common, Trinity	*Sussex*	Ecl. Dis.	550	Durham w. Hinton	*Gloucester*	Parish	45?
Dickering	*York*	Wapen.	19 747	Discove	*Somerset*	Tithing	4?
Dickering	,,	L. Sub.	19 747	Discoyd	*Radnor*	Tnship.	11?
Dickleburgh	*Norfolk*	Parish	895	Diseworth	*Leicester*	Parish	56?
Didbrook	*Gloucester*	Parish	221	Dishforth	*York*	Sub-dis.	1 794
Didbrook	,,	—	182	Dishforth	,,	Tnship.	40?
Didcot	*Berks*	Parish	349	Dishley w Thorpacre	*Leicester*	Parish	19?
Diddington	*Hunts*	Parish	204	Disley Stanley	*Cheshire*	Chap.	2 26?
Diddlebury	*Salop*	Sub-dis.	2 086	Diss	*Norfolk*	Hund.	9 85?
Diddlebury	,,	Parish	829	Diss	,,	L. Sub.	9 85?
Didling	*Sussex*	Parish	85	Diss	,,	Sub-dis.	7 567
Didlington	*Norfolk*	Parish	80	Diss	,,	Parish	3 71?
Didmarton	*Gloucester*	Sub-dis.	1 470	**Diss**	,,	Town	3 16?
Didmarton	,,	Tnship.	92	Disserth	*Radnor*	Parish	52?
Didsbury	*Lancaster*	Sub-dis.	5 904	Disserth	,,	Hamlet	31?
Didsbury	,,	Tnship.	1 829	Dissington, North	*Northumbld.*	Tnship.	7?
Didsbury, St. James	,,	Ecl. Dis.	803	Dissington, South	,,	Tnship.	6?
Digby	*Lincoln*	Parish	330	Distington	*Cumberland.*	Parish	785
Digswell	*Herts*	Parish	243	Ditchburn	*Northumberland*	Tnship.	8?
Dihewid	*Cardigan*	Parish	454	Ditcheat	*Somerset*	Parish	1 21?
Dilham	*Norfolk*	Parish	425	Ditchingham	*Norfolk*	Parish	1 10?
Dilhorne	*Stafford*	Sub-dis.	5 070	Ditchling	*Sussex*	Sub-dis.	3 94?
Dilhorne	,,	Parish	1 573	Ditchling	,,	Parish	1 08?
Dilhorne	,,	—	849	Ditteridge	*Wilts*	Parish	11?
Dillicar	*Westmoreland*	Tnship.	205	Dittesham	*Devon*	Parish	76?
Dilston	*Northumberland*	Tnship.	241	Ditton	*Bucks*	Hamlet	9?
Dilton Marsh, Trinity	*Wilts*	Ecl. Dis.	1 561	Ditton	*Kent*	Parish	25?
Dilworth	*Lancaster*	Tnship.	959	Ditton	*Lancaster*	Tnship.	764
Dilwyn	*Hereford*	Sub-dis.	3 701	Ditton, Prior	*Salop*	Parish	61?
Dilwyn	,,	Parish	1 069	Ditton, Long	*Surrey*	Parish	1 44?
Dinas	*Pembroke*	Parish	820	Ditton, Long	,,	—	1 01?
Dinas Powis	*Glamorgan*	Hund.	7 661	Ditton, Thames	,,	Parish	2 25?
Dinas Powis	,,	L. Sub.	7 661	Dixton Newton	*Monmouth*	Parish	75?
Dinder	*Somerset*	Parish	244	Dobcross, Holy Trinity	*York*	Ecl. Dis.	1 972
Dinedor	*Hereford*	Parish	270	Dockenfield	*Hants*	Parish	224
Dingestow	*Monm. & Heref.*	Sub-dis.	5 459	Docker	*Westmoreland*	Tnship.	7?
Dingestow	*Monmouth*	Parish	231	Docking	*Norfolk*	District	17 59?
Dingley	*Northampton*	Parish	111	Docking	,,	Sub-dis.	5 39?
Dinham	*Monmouth*	Hamlet	37	Docking	,,	Parish	1 62?
Dinkley	*Lancaster*	Tnship.	120	Docklow	*Hereford*	P...	
Dinlaen	*Carnarvon*	Hund.	7 215	Dodbrooke	*Devon*	Parish	6?
Dinmore	*Hereford*	Parish	42	Dodcott w. Wilkesley	*Cheshire*	Tnship.	672
Dinmore	*Salop*	Parish	9	Doddenham	*Worcester*	Parish	27?
Dinnington	*Northumberland*	Parish	774	Dodderhill	,,	Parish	2 14?
Dinnington	,,	Tnship.	284	Dodderhill	,,	—	1 19?
Dinnington	*Somerset*	Parish	146	Dodderhill	,,	In Libs.	55?
Dinnington	*York*	Parish	272	Doddinghurst	*Essex*	Parish	39?

Name of Place.	County.	Description.	Population.	Name of Place	County.	Description.	Population.
dington	Cambs.	Parish	8 722	St. Matthew	Salop	Ecl. Dis.	1 351
dington	,,	—	1 380	Donnington	Sussex	Parish	188
dington	Cheshire	Tnship.	71	Donyatt..	Somerset	Parish	494
dington, St. John	,,	Ecl. Dis.	566	Donyland, East	Essex	Parish	1 052
dington	Kent	Parish	476	Dorchester	Dorset	L. Sub.	46 807
dington	Lincoln	Parish	264	Dorchester	,,	Div.	28 868
dington	,,	Tnship.	174	Dorchester	,,	District	24 773
dington, Dry	,,	Parish	283	Dorchester	,,	Union	17 492
dington, Great	Nrthamptn.	Parish	580	Dorchester	,,	Sub-dis.	7 709
dington	Northumberland	Parish	795	**Dorchester**	,,	Boro.	6 823
dington	,,	Tnship.	381	Dorchester	Oxon	Hund.	3 529
dington, St. John	Salop	Ecl. Dis.	356	Dorchester	,,	Parish	1 097
dingtree	Worcester	Hund.	14 038	Dorchester	,,	—	925
discombsleigh	Devon	Parish	343	Dore	Derby	Tnship.	610
dleston	Chesh. & Flint	Parish	814	Dore w. Totley	,,	Ecl. Dis.	1 006
dleston	Cheshire	Tnship.	304	Dore	Hereford	Union	9 509
lford	Northampton	Parish	238	Dore	,,	L. Sub.	8 772
lington	Gloucester	Parish	126	Dore Abbey	,,	Parish	551
lington	Somerset	Parish	98	Dorking	Surrey	L. Sub.	12 445
lworth	York	Tnship.	2 117	Dorking	,,	District	12 445
lworth, St. John	,,	Ecl. Dis.	2 117	Dorking	,,	Sub-dis.	8 351
zdyke	Lincoln	Tnship.	239	Dorking	,,	Parish	6 997
glane..	Stafford	Liberty	19	**Dorking**	,,	Town	4 061
gmersfield	Hants	Parish	251	Dorking, St, Paul	,,	Ecl. Dis.	1 355
gsthorpe	Northampton	Hamlet	425	Dormington	Hereford	Parish	138
benmaen	Carnarvon	Parish	387	Dormington	,,	—	77
garrog	,,	Tnship.	134	Dormston	Worcester	Parish	97
gelly	Merioneth	L. Sub.	12 371	Dorney ..	Bucks	Parish	367
gelly	Mer. & Montg.	District	12 482	Dorrington	Lincoln	Parish	467
gelly	Merioneth	Parish	3 457	Dorrington, St. Edward	Salop	Ecl. Dis.	382
gelly	,,	Town	2 217	Dorsetshire	..	County	188 789
lton ..	Devon	Sub-dis.	3 181	Dorsington	Gloucester	Parish	118
lton ..	,,	Parish	938	Dorstone	Hereford	Parish	547
lwyddelan	Carnarvon	Parish	811	Dorton ..	Bucks	Parish	137
ncaster	York & Notts	District	39 388	Dothie-Camddwr	Cardigan	Tnship.	136
ncaster	York	Sub-dis.	16 406	Dothie-Piscottwr	,,	Tnship.	121
ncaster	,,	Parish	17 632	Dotton ..	Devon	Parish	17
ncaster	,,	M. Bor.	16 406	**Douglas**	Isle of Man	Town	12 511
ncaster, Christch.	,,	Ecl. Dis.	9 106	Doulting	Somerset	Parish	667
ncaster	,,	Tnship.	16 406	Dovenby	Cumberland	Tnship.	272
nhead	Wilts	Sub-dis.	4 154	Dover ..	Kent	District	31 575
nhead, St. Andrew	,,	Parish	830	Dover ..	,,	Union	30 350
nhead, St. Mary	,,	Parish	1 482	Dover Castle	,,	Parish	954
nington Castle	Leicester	Parish	2 445	Dover, Trinity	,,	Ecl. Dis.	4 490
nington	Lincoln	Sub-dis.	2 691	**Dover** ..	,,	Borough	25 325
nington	,,	Parish	1 690	Dovercourt	Essex	Parish	1 231
nington	,,	Parish	552	Doverdale	Worcester	Parish	43
nham	Salop	Parish	456	Doveridge	Derby	Parish	737
nha	c. & Derby	Hamlet	544	Dowdeswell	Gloucester	Parish	350
nistho pe	,,	Ecl. Dis.	2 132	Dowlais ..	Glamorgan	Ecl. Dis.	15 590
nnington	Gloucester	Hamlet	141	Dowland	Devon	Parish	205
nnington	Hereford	Parish	105	Dowles ..	Salop	Parish	98
nnington Wood :—				Dowlish-Wake	Somerset	Parish	319
St. George	Salop	Ecl. Dis.	614	Dowlish-West	,,	Parish	52

Name of Place.	County.	Description.	Population.	Name of Place.	County.	Description.	Population
Down, East	Devon	Parish	418	Drayton..	Somerset	Parish	557
Down, St. Mary	„	Parish	426	Drayton Bassett	Stafford	Parish	441
Down, West	„	Parish	554	Drayton or Tyrley	„	Tnship.	814
Down-Ampney	Gloucester	Parish	429	Drewern	Radnor	Tnship.	217
Down	Kent	Parish	496	Drewsteignton	Devon	Parish	1 067
Downham	Cambs.	Parish	2 158	Drewton w. Everthorpe	York..	Tnship.	186
Downham	Essex	Parish	247	Driby	Lincoln	Parish	79
Downham	Lancaster	Tnship.	292	Driffield..	Gloucester	Parish	132
Downham	Norf.& Cambs.	District	20 264	Driffield..	York	District	19 226
Downham	„ „	Sub-dis.	8 878	Driffield..	„	Sub-dis.	7 787
Downham	Norfolk	Town	2 458	Driffield..	„	Parish	4 734
Downham Market	„	Parish	3 133	Driffield, Great	„	Tnship.	4 405
Downham, Santon	Suffolk	Parish	81	**Driffield, Great**	„	Town	4 244
Downhead	Somerset	Parish	249	Driffield, Little..	„	Tnship.	197
Down Holland	Lancaster	Tnship.	748	Drigg	Cumberland.	Parish	440
Downholme	York	Parish	241	Drighlington	York	Sub-dis.	7 309
Downholme	„	Tnship.	138	Drighlington	„	Tnship.	4 274
Downside	Somerset	Ecl. Dis.	697	Drighlington	„	Ecl. Dis.	4 274
Down Stonebeck	York	Tnship.	400	Dringhoe, &c.	„	Tnship.	157
Downton	Hereford	Parish	184	Dringhouses	„	Tnship.	379
Downton	Wilts	Hund.	6 612	Dringhouses	„	Ecl. Dis.	400
Downton	„	Sub-dis.	4 790	Drinkstone	Suffolk	Parish	496
Downton	„	Parish	3 566	Droitwich	Worcester	L. Sub.	12 754
Dowsby	Lincoln	Parish	195	Droitwich	„	District	19 289
Doxford	Northumberland	Tnship.	74	Droitwich	„	Sub-dis.	6 643
Doynton	Gloucester	Parish	448	**Droitwich**	„	M. Bor. { P. Bor.	3 124 7 086
Drainage Marsh	Lincoln	Parish	5				
Drakelow	Derby	Tnship.	85	Dronfield	Derby	Sub-dis.	5 689
Draughton	Northampton	Parish	190	Dronfield	„	Parish	6 013
Draughton	York	Tnship.	178	Dronfield	„	—	2 998
Drax	„	Parish	1 231	Drove End	Lincoln	Ecl. Dis.	778
Drax	„	Tnship.	446	Droxford	Hants	L. Sub.	10 605
Drax, Long	„	Tnship.	162	Droxford	„	Division	10 665
Draycot Moor	Berks	Hamlet	261	Droxford	„	District	10 665
Draycott	Derby	Liberty	1 016	Droxford	„	Parish	2 194
Draycott	Oxon	Hamlet	21	Droylsden	Lancaster	Tnship.	8 798
Draycott in Clay	Stafford	Tnship.	484	Droylsden, St. Mary	„	Ecl. Dis.	8 798
Draycott in Moors	„	Parish	451	**Droylsden**	„	Town	5 980
Draycot Foliatt	Wilts	Parish	27	Drumburgh	Cumberland	Tnship.	421
Draycot Cerne	„	Parish	158	Drybeck	Westmoreland	Tnship.	87
Drayton..	Berks	Parish	605	Dry Doddington	Lincoln	Parish	283
Drayton Beauchamp	Bucks	Parish	268	Dry Drayton	Cambs.	Parish	470
Drayton Parslow	„	Parish	468	Drypool..	York	Sub-dis.	6 617
Drayton, Fen	Cambs	Parish	445	Drypool..	„	Parish	6 241
Drayton..	Leicester	Tnship.	126	Drypool..	„	Tnship.	3 437
Drayton, West	Middlesex	Parish	951	Duchy of Lancaster	Gloucester	Hund.	2 717
Drayton..	Norfolk	Parish	451	Duckington	Cheshire	Tnship.	86
Drayton, East	Notts	Parish	263	Ducklington	Oxon	Parish	606
Drayton, West	„	Parish	96	Ducklington	„	—	472
Drayton, Swalcliffe	Oxon	Parish	186	Dudcott..	Berks	Parish	349
Drayton, Sutton Courtney	„	Parish	327	Duddeston	Warwick	Sub-dis.	38 760
Drayton in Hales	Salop & Staff.	Parish	5 242	Duddeston, St. Matthew	„	Ecl. Dis.	18 693
Drayton, Little	„ „	Ecl. Dis.	2 162	Duddeston w. Nechells	„	Hamlet	38 760
Drayton, Magna, &c.	Salop	Tnship.	4 428	Duddington	Northampton	Parish	422

Name of Place.	County.	Description.	Population.	Name of Place.	County.	Description.	Population.
Duddo ..	Northumberland	Tnship.	311	Dunkeswell, Trinity	Devon ..	Ecl. Dis.	224
Duddon..	.. Cheshire ..	Tnship	168	Dunkeswick ..	York ..	Tnship.	210
Dudley ..	.. Worcester ..	L. Sub.	46 158	Dunkirk..	.. Kent ..	Ville	721
Dudley ,.	.. Worc. & Staff.	District	130 267	Dunmow	.. Essex ..	L. Sub.	14 487
Dudley ..	.. Worcester ..	Sub-dis.	44 975	Dunmow	.. ,, ..	Hund.	13 649
Dudley..	.. ,, ..	P. Bor.	44 975	Dunmow	.. ,, ..	District	19 759
Dudley ..	.. ,, •.	Parish	44 951	Dunmow	.. ,, ..	Sub-dis.	5 686
Dugley Castle Hill	,, ..	—	24	Dunmow, Great .	,, ..	Parish	2 976
Dudley, St. Edmund	,, ..	Ecl. Dis.	3 213	Dunnow, Little .	,, ..	Parish	379
Dudstone & Kgs Barton	Glouc..	Hund.	20 442	Dunnerdale	.. Lancaster ..	Tnship.	118
Dueshill..	Northumberland	Tnship.	29	Dunnington	.. .. York	Sub-dis.	3 066
Duffield..	.. Derby ..	Sub-dis.	6 466	Dunnington	.. .. ,,	Parish	906
Duffield..	.. ,, ..	Parish	16 776	Dunnington	.. .. ,,	Tnship.	842
Duffield..	.. ,, ..	Tnship.	2 639	Dunnington (Beeford P.)	,,	Tnship.	86
Duffield, North..	York ..	Tnship.	470	Dunnockshaw ..	Lancaster ..	Tnship.	167
Duffield, South..	,, ..	Tnship.	236	Dunsby..	.. Lincoln ..	Parish	195
Duffryn..	.. Monmouth ..	Hamlet	275	Dunsfold	.. Surrey ..	Parish	716
Dufton ..	.. Westmoreland	Parish	495	Dunsford	.. Devon ..	Parish	921
Duggleby ..	York ..	Tnship.	272	Dunsforth, Lower	York ..	Tnship.	144
Dukers Hagg	Northumberland	Tnship.	5	Dunsforth, Upper, &c.	,,	Tnship.	151
Dukinfield ..	Cheshire ..	Sub-dis.	29 953	Dunstable ..	Beds ..	Sub-dis.	9 293
Dukinfield ..	,, ..	Tnship.	29 953	Dunstable ..	,, ..	Parish	4 470
Dukinfield, St. John	,, ..	Ecl. Dis.	14 214	**Dunstable** ..	,, ..	Town	4 470
Dukinfield, St. Mark	,, ..	Ecl. Dis.	8 127	Dunstall ..	Stafford ..	Liberty	6
Dukinfield, St. Mathw.	,, ..	Ecl. Dis.	5 535	Dunstall ..	.. ,, ..	Tnship.	240
Dukinfield ..	,, ..	Town	15 024	Dunstall, St. Mary	,, ..	Ecl. Dis.	240
Dulas ..	.. Hereford ..	Parish	76	Dunstan, St.	.. Kent ..	Parish	1 520
Dullingham ..	.. Cambs ..	Parish	800	Dunster..	.. Somerset ..	Sub-dis.	4 293
Duloe ..	.. Cornwall ..	Parish	1 096	Dunster..	.. ,, ..	Parish	1 112
Dulverton ..	Somerset ..	District	6 051	Dunstew ..	Oxon ..	Parish	407
Dulverton ..	,, ..	Parish	1 552	Dunston ..	Lincoln ..	Parish	575
Dulwich..	.. Surrey ..	Sub-dis.	1 723	Dunston ..	Norfolk ..	Parish	83
Dulwich..	.. ,, ..	Hamlet	1 723	Dunston	Northumberland	Tnship.	303
Dumbleton ..	Gloucester ..	Parish	465	Dunston ..	Stafford ..	Tnship.	275
Dummer ..	Hants ..	Sub-dis.	4 639	Dunterton ..	Devon ..	Parish	181
Dummer ..	,, ..	Parish	400	Duntisborne Abbotts	Gloucester	Parish	354
Dunchideock ..	Devon ..	Parish	155	Duntisborne Abbotts	,,	—	237
Dunchurch ..	Warwick ..	Sub-dis.	5 873	Duntisborne Leer	,,	Tithing	117
Dunchurch ..	,, ..	Parish	1 309	Duntisborne Rouse	,,	Parish	127
Dunchurch ..	,, ..	—	981	Dunton ..	.. Beds ..	Parish	518
Duncton ..	Sussex ..	Parish	258	Dunton ..	.. Bucks ..	Parish	106
Dundrew & Kelsick	Cumberland	Tnship.	314	Dunton ..	.. Essex ..	Parish	174
Dundry..	.. Somerset ..	Parish	556	Dunton Bassett .	Leicester ..	Parish	524
Dungleddy ..	Pembroke ..	Hund.	6 153	Dunton w. Doughton	Norfolk ·	Parish	126
Dungleddy ..	,, ..	L. Sub.	7 036	Dunwich ..	Suffolk ..	Parish	227
Dunham Massey	Cheshire ..	Tnship.	1 535	Dunwood ..	Hants ..	Parish	11
Dunham Massey	,, ..	Ecl. Dis.	4 569	Dunworth	.. Wilts ..	Hund.	6 842
Dunham on the Hill	,, ..	Tnship.	320	Durham ..	.. ..	Diocese	858 095
Dunham, Great .	Norfolk ..	Parish	493	Durham ..	.. ..	County	508 666
Dunham, Little .	,, ..	Parish	327	Northern Division	..	N. Div.	338 254
Dunham ..	Notts ..	Parish	327	Southern Division	..	S. Div.	170 412
Dunholm ..	Lincoln ..	Parish	453	Durham ..	Durham ..	District	70 274
Dunkerton ..	Somerset ..	Parish	1 060	Durham ..	.. ,, ..	Union	42 358
Dunkeswell ..	Devon ..	Parish	492	**Durham** ..	.. ,, ..	City	14 088

Name of Place.	County.	Description.	Population.	Name of Place.	County.	Description.	Population
Durham, St. Cuthbert	*Durham*	Ecl. Dis.	3 486	Eardley-End ..	*Stafford* ..	Tnship.	190
Durham College .	,, ..	Parish	62	Earith ..	*Hunts* ..	Hamlet	631
Durleigh ..	*Somerset* ..	Parish	158	Earl ..	*Northmb.* ..	Tnship.	67
Durley ..	*Hants* ..	Parish	411	Earldoms ..	*Wilts*	Parish	48
Durnford ..	*Wilts* ..	Parish	553	Earley ..	*Berks* ..	Liberty	566
Durrington ..	*Sussex* ..	Parish	171	Earley, St. Peter	,,	Ecl. Dis.	774
Durrington ..	*Wilts* ..	Parish	440	Earl-Framingham	*Norfolk*	Parish	136
Dursley ..	*Gloucester* ..	L. Sub.	18 538	Earlham ..	,, ..	Parish	195
Dursley ..	,, ..	District	13 331	Earls Barton ..	*Northampton*	Sub-dis.	6 239
Dursley ..	,, ..	Sub-dis.	5 106	Earls Barton ..	,,	Parish	1 557
Dursley ..	,, ..	Parish	2 477	Earls Colne ..	*Essex* ..	Parish	1 540
Dursley ..	,, ..	Town	2 477	Earls Court, St. Philip	*Middlesex*	Ecl. Dis.	5 264
Durston..	*Somerset* ..	Parish	223	Earls Croome ..	*Worcester* ..	Parish	189
Durweston ..	*Dorset* ..	Parish	364	Earls Heaton, S. Peter	*York* ..	Ecl. Dis.	4 019
Duston ..	*Northampton*	Parish	1 162	Earl Shilton ,,.	*Leicester* ..	Sub-dis.	3 579
Dutton ..	*Cheshire* ..	Tnship.	442	Earl Shilton ..	,, ..	Chap.	2 176
Dutton Cacca ..	*Denbigh* ..	Tnship.	93	Earl-Soham ..	*Suffolk* ..	Sub-dis.	2 629
Dutton Diffeth ..	,, ..	Tnship.	148	Earl-Soham ..	,, ..	Parish	745
Duttonybran ..	,, ..	Tnship.	43	Earl-Stoke ..	*Wilts* ..	Parish	378
Dutton ..	*Lancaster* ..	Tnship.	312	Earl Stonham ..	*Suffolk* ..	Parish	752
Duxbury ..	,, ..	Tnship.	341	Earnley..	*Sussex* ..	Parish	116
Duxford ..	*Cambs* ..	Sub-dis.	4 772	Earnshill ..	*Somerset* ..	Parish	17
Duxford ..	,, ..	Parish	841	Earsdon	*Northumberland*	Tnship.	83
Dwygyfylchi ..	*Carnarvon* ..	Parish	1 386	Earsdon Forest .	,,	Tnship.	24
Dyers Hill ..	*York W.* ..	Ecl. Dis.	7 717	Earsdon ..	,,	Sub-dis.	9 543
Dyffrin ..	*Brecon* ..	Hamlet	318	Earsdon ..	,,	Parish	12 444
Dyffrinhonddu, Low ,, ..		Hamlet	196	Earsdon ..	,,	Tnship.	577
Dyffrinhonddu, Up. ,, ..		Hamlet	187	Earsham ..	*Norfolk* ..	Hund.	8 484
Dyffruncidrich ..	*Carmarthen* .	Hamlet	689	Earsham ..	,, ..	L. Sub.	8 484
Dyffrynclydach .	*Glamorgan* .	Hamlet	1 022	Earsham ..	,, ..	Parish	697
Dyffrynelan ..	*Radnor* ..	Tnship.	338	Earswick ..	*York* ..	Tnship.	97
Dyffryngwy ..	,, ..	Tnship.	460	Eartham ..	*Sussex* ..	Parish	121
Dyke ..	*Lincoln* ..	Hamlet	266	Easby ..	*Cumberland* .	Tnship.	95
Dylais, Lower ..	*Glamorgan* ..	Hamlet	348	Easby ..	*York* ..	Parish	844
Dylais Upper ..	,, ..	Hamlet	622	Easby ..	,, ..	Tnship.	118
Dyliffe ..	*Montgomery*	Ecl. Dis.	858	Easby (Stokesley P.) ,, ..		Tnship.	124
Dymchurch ..	*Kent* ..	Parish	618	Easebourne ..	*Sussex* ..	Parish	859
Dymeirchion ..	*Flint* ..	Parish	707	Easenhall ..	*Warwick* ..	Tnship.	179
Dymock..	*Gloucester* ..	Parish	1 870	Easington ..	*Durham* ..	Ward	77 257
Dyserth..	*Flint* ..	Parish	1 098	Easington Ward .	,, ..	L. Sub.	146 237
				Easington ..	,, ..	District	27 293
Eachwick	*Northumberland*	Tnship.	87	Easington ..	,, ..	Sub-dis.	27 293
Eagle ..	*Lincoln* ..	Parish	533	Easington ..	,, ..	Parish	7 336
Eagle Hall ..	,, ..	Parish	81	Easington ..	,, ..	Tnship.	1 073
Eagle Woodhouse	,, ..	Parish	11	Easington	*Northumberland*	Tnship.	192
Eaglesfield ..	*Cumberland* .	Tnship.	304	Easington Grange	,,	Tnship.	71
Eaglesfield Abbey	,,	—	40	Easington ..	*Oxford* ..	Parish	26
Eakring..	*Notts* ..	Parish	650	Easington ..	*York E.* ..	Parish	666
Ealing ..	*Middlesex* ..	Parish	11 963	Easington ..	,, ..	Tnship.	600
Ealing ..	,, ..	—	5 215	Easington ..	*York N.* ..	Parish	752
Ealing, Christch.	,, ..	Ecl. Dis.	3 324	Easington ..	,, ..	Tnship.	566
Eardington ..	*Salop* ..	Tnship.	370	Easington ..	*York W.* ..	Tnship.	338
Eardisland ..	*Hereford* ..	Parish	894	Easingwold ..	*York* ..	District	10 148
Eardisley ..	,, ..	Parish	826	Easingwold ..	,, ..	Sub-dis.	5 478

Name of Place.	County.	Description.	Population.	Name of Place.	County.	Description.	Population.
Easingwold	York	Parish	2 724	Eastbury, &c.	Berks	Tithing	480
Easingwold	,,	Tnship.	2 147	East Butterwick.	Lincoln	Tnship.	420
East	Cornwall	Hund.	44 899	East Carlton	Norfolk	Parish	244
East	,,	L. Sub.	49 078	East Carlton	Northampton	Parish	70
East	Rutland	Hund	3 945	East Challow	Berks	Tnship.	391
East	Westmoreland	Ward	15 411	Eastcheap, St. Clem.	Middlesex	Parish	198
East Ward	,,	L. Sub.	15 411	Eastcheap, St. Leonard	,,	Parish	111
East Acomb	Northumberland	Tnship.	62	East Chelborough	Dorset	Parish	93
East Adderbury	Oxon	Tnship.	895	East Chevington	Nrthmbld.	Tnship.	651
East Allington	Devon	Parish	521	East Chiltington	Sussex	Hamlet	281
East Allington	Lincoln	Parish	275	East Chinnock	Somerset	Parish	552
E.&Mid. Herrington	Durham	Tnship.	242	Eastchurch	Kent	Sub-dis.	1 557
E. & W. Appleton	York	Tnship.	115	Eastchurch	,,	Parish	996
E. & W. Buckholt	Hants	Parish	118	East Clandon	Surrey	Parish	283
E. & W. Chadlington	Oxon	Hamlet	753	East Claydon	Bucks	Parish	385
E. & W. Challow	Berks	Ecl. Dis.	583	East Cliffe	Kent	Parish	271
E. & W. Hyde	Beds	Hamlet	869	E. Coatham, Christch.	York	Ecl. Dis.	727
E. & W. Kenton	Nrthmbld.	Tnship.	658	East Coker	Somerset	Parish	1 186
E. & W. Looe	Cornwall	Ecl. Dis.	1 860	Eastcott	Wilts	Tithing	146
E. & W. Lutton	York	Tnship.	432	East Cottingwith	York	Tnship.	316
E.&W. Newbiggin	Durham	Tnship.	33	East Cotts	Beds	Tnship.	847
E.&W. Thirston, &c.	Nrthmbld.	Tnship.	294	East Coulston	Wilts	Parish	119
E. & W. Whorlton	,,	Tnship.	62	E. Cowes, St. James	Hants, I. W.	Ecl. Dis.	1 954
East Anstey	Devon	Parish	227	E. Cowick, Trinity	York	Ecl. Dis.	818
East Ardsley	York	Parish	1 069	East Cowton	,,	Parish	472
East Ashford	Kent	District	12 286	East Cranmore	Somerset	Parish	70
East Ayton	York	Tnship.	406	East Crompton	Lancaster	Ecl. Dis.	3 414
East Barkwith	Lincoln	Parish	387	East Dean	Gloucester	Tnship.	9 212
East Barnet	Herts	Parish	851	E. Dean, St. John Evan	,,	Ecl. Dis.	4 417
East Barsham	Norfolk	Parish	221	East Dean Trinity	,,	Ecl. Dis.	3 218
East Beckham	,,	Parish	73	East Dean	Hants	Parish	223
East Bedfont	Middlesex	Parish	1 150	Eastdean	Sussex	Parish	334
East Bergholt	Suffolk	Parish	1 397	East Dean	,,	Parish	343
East Bilney	Norfolk	Parish	198	East Denton	Northumberland	Tnship.	600
East Blatchington	Sussex	Parish	128	East Dereham	Norfolk	Sub-dis.	7 531
East Boldre	Hants	Ecl. Dis.	690	East Dereham	,,	Parish	4 368
Eastbourne	Sussex	District	10 721	East Donyland	Essex	Parish	1 052
Eastbourne	,,	Sub-dis.	8 127	East Down	Devon	Parish	418
Eastbourne	,,	Parish	5 795	East Drayton	Notts	Parish	263
Eastbourne	,,	Town	5 795	Eastergate	Sussex	Parish	162
Eastbourne Trinity	,,	Ecl. Dis.	3 796	Easter, Good	Essex	Parish	539
East Bradenham	Norfolk	Parish	399	Easter, High	,,	Parish	947
East Brent	Somerset	Parish	797	Eastern St. Andrew	Middlesex	Sub-dis.	12 947
Eastbridge	Kent	Parish	45	Easterton	Wilts	Tithing	461
East Bridge Hospital	,,	Parish	32	East Farlam	Cumberland	Tnship.	813
East Bridgford	Notts	Parish	1 078	East Farleigh	Kent	Parish	1 559
East Broughton	Lancaster	Tnship.	534	East Farndon	Northampton	Parish	242
East Brunton	Northumberland	Tnship.	134	East Ferry	Lincoln	Tnship.	190
East Buckland	Devon	Parish	151	Eastfield	Northampton	Hamlet	150
East Budleigh	,,	Hund.	22 797	East Firsby	Lincoln	Parish	108
East Budleigh	,,	Sub-dis.	4 649	East Firsby	,,	Tnship.	47
East Budleigh	,,	Parish	2 496	East Flegg	Norfolk	Sub-dis.	4 060
East Bulmer	York	L. Sub.	11 010	East Garston	Berks	Parish	589
Eastburn	,,	Tnship.	24	East Gilling	York	Wapen.	7 736

Name of Place.	County.	Description.	Population.	Name of Place.	County.	Description.	Population.
East Gilling	York	L. Sub.	5 769	East Kirkby	Lincoln	Parish	432
East Goscote	Leicester	Hund.	16 239	East Knottingley	York	Ecl. Dis.	2 181
East Grafton, St. Nich.	Wilts	Ecl. Dis.	1 011	East Knoyle	Wilts	Parish	1 034
East Greenwich	Kent	Sub-dis.	18 306	East Langbaurgh	York	Liberty	28 343
East Grimstead	Wilts	Chap.	136	East Langbaurgh	„	L. Sub.	15 862
East Grinstead	Sussex	L. Sub.	11 422	East Langdon	Kent	Parish	362
East Grinstead	Suss. & Sur.	District	14 097	East Langton	Leicester	Tnship.	303
East Grinstead	„ „	Sub-dis.	6 468	East Lavant	Sussex	Parish	421
East Grinstead	Sussex	Parish	4 266	East Lavington	Wilts	Parish	1 583
East Guildford	„	Parish	152	East Lavington	„	—	1 122
East Haddon	Northampton	Parish	727	East Layton	York	Tnship.	133
East Hagbourne	Berks	Liberty	631	East-Leach-Martin	Gloucester	Parish	216
East Haggerstone	Middlesex	Sub-dis.	17 310	East-Leach-Turville	„	Parish	506
East Halton	Lincoln	Parish	727	East Leake	Notts	Parish	1 059
East Halton	York	Tnship.	94	East Leicester	Leicester	Sub-dis.	41 194
Eastham	Cheshire	Sub-dis.	9 167	East Leicester Forest	„	Parish	82
Eastham	„	Parish	2 641	East Lexham	Norfolk	Parish	226
Eastham	„	Tnship.	522	East Lilburn	Northumberland	Tnship.	85
East Ham	Essex	Parish	2 264	Eastling	Kent	Parish	399
Eastham	Worcester	Parish	645	East Lockinge	Berks	Parish	318
Eastham	„	—	347	East London	Middlesex	District	40 687
Easthampstead	Berks	District	7 436	East Looe	Cornwall	Tnship.	1 154
Easthampstead	„	Parish	789	East Lulworth	Dorset	Parish	453
East Hang	York	Wapen.	10 378	East Lydford	Somerset	Parish	178
East Hang	„	L. Sub.	10 025	East Macclesfield	Cheshire	Sub-dis.	10 901
East Hanney	Berks	Tnship.	563	East Maidstone	Kent	Sub-dis.	12 109
East Hanningfield	Essex	Parish	453	East Malling	„	Parish	1 974
East Hardwick	York	Tnship.	213	East Marden	Sussex	Parish	63
East Harling	Norfolk	Parish	1 109	East Markham	Notts	Parish	807
East Harlsey	York	Parish	430	East Matfen	Northumberland	Tnship.	147
East Harnham	Wilts	Ecl. Dis.	461	East Meon	Hants	Sub-dis.	2 681
East Harptree	Somerset	Parish	657	East Meon	„	Parish	1 486
East Hartburn	Durham	Tnship.	163	East Mersea	Essex	Parish	305
East Hartford	Northumberland	Tnship.	13	East Morton	Durham	Tnship.	2 104
East Hatley	Cambs	Parish	139	East Moulsey	Surrey	Parish	1 568
East Haukswell	York	Tnship.	98	East Ness	York	Tnship.	49
East Heddon	Northumberland	Tnship.	43	East Newton	„	Tnship.	31
East Hendred	Berks	Parish	889	E. Newton & Laysthorp	„	Tnship.	84
East Heslerton	York	Tnship.	262	Eastnor	Hereford	Parish	478
East Hoathly	Sussex	Parish	615	East Norton	Leicester	L. Sub.	5 337
East Holme	Dorset	Parish	50	East Norton	„	P Chap.	139
Easthope	Salop	Parish	109	Eastoft	Lincoln	Tnship.	534
East Horndon	Essex	Parish	475	Eastoft, St. Barth.	Linc. & York	Ecl. Dis.	624
Easthorpe	„	Parish	144	Eastoft	York	Tnship.	90
East Horsley	Surrey	Parish	228	East Ogwell	Devon	Parish	275
East Hyde	Beds	Ecl. Dis.	419	Easton, Great	Essex	Parish	891
East Ilsley	Berks	Parish	746	Easton, Little	„	Parish	357
Eastington	Gloucester	Parish	1 717	Easton, St. Mark	Gloucester	Ecl. Dis.	2 939
Eastington	„	Tithing	712	Easton	Hants	Parish	455
Eastington (N'Leach P.)	„	Tithing	442	Easton	Hunts	Parish	155
East Islington	Middlesex	Sub-dis.	79 899	Easton, Great	Leicester, &c.	Sub-dis.	3 135
East Keal	Lincoln	Parish	393	Easton Magna	Leicester	Tnship.	590
East Kennet	Wilts	Parish	78	Easton	Lincoln	Tnship.	150
East Keswick	York	Tnship.	468	Easton	Norfolk	Parish	233

Name of Place.	County.	Description.	Population.	Name of Place.	County.	Description.	Population.
...ston on Hill ..	Northampton	Parish	984	E. Stamford Bridge	York ..	Sub-dis	4 502
...ston Maudit ..	,,	Parish	207	E. Stamford Bridge	,,	Tnship.	417
...ston Neston ..	,,	Parish	160	East Stockwith ..	Lincoln ..	Tnship.	313
...ston	Somerset ..	Ecl. Dis.	259	E. Stockwith, St.Peter	,, ..	Ecl. Dis.	378
...ston in Gordano	,, ..	Parish	2 028	East Stoke ..	Dorset ..	Parish	594
...ston	Suffolk ..	Parish	400	East Stoke ..	Notts ..	Parish	490
...ston Bavents .	,, ..	Parish	7	East Stoke ..	,, ..	—	280
...ston	Wilts ..	Parish	463	East Stonehouse .	Devon ..	District.	14 343
...ston Grey ..	,, ..	Parish	177	East Stonehouse.	,, ..	Sub-dis.	14 343
...ston Piercy ..	,, ..	Tithing	10	East Stonehouse.	,, ..	Parish	14 343
...ston	York ..	Hamlet	27	East Stower ..	Dorset ..	Parish	426
...st Orchard ..	Dorset ..	Parish	227	East Stratton ..	Hants ..	Parish	365
...stover, St.John	Somerset ..	Ecl.Dis.	4 792	East Sunderland.	Durham ..	Sub-dis.	9 915
...st Peckham ..	Kent ..	Sub-dis.	7 554	East Sutton ..	Kent ..	Parish	385
...st Peckham ..	,, ..	Parish	2 341	East Tadcaster..	York ..	Tnship.	920
...st Peckham, Trinity	,, ..	Ecl. Dis.	1 918	East Tanfield ..	,, ..	Tnship.	38
...st Pennard ..	Somerset ..	Parish	631	East Teignmouth	Devon ..	Parish	2 059
...st Pickering Lythe	York ..	L. Sub.	26 030	East Thickly ..	Durham ..	Tnship.	1 142
...st Poringland .	Norfolk ..	Parish	464	East Thornton	Northumberland	Tnship.	65
...st Portlemouth	Devon ..	Parish	403	East Tilbury ..	Essex ..	Parish	403
...st Preston ..	Sussex ..	Incor.	15 384	East Tisbury ..	Wilts ..	Parish	940
...st Preston ..	,, ..	Parish	320	East Tisted ..	Hants ..	Parish	221
...st Putford ..	Devon ..	Parish	190	East Torrington .	Lincoln ..	Parish	120
...st Quantoxhead	Somerset ..	Parish	339	East Tuddenham	Norfolk ..	Parish	512
...st Rainham ..	Norfolk ..	Parish	139	East Tytherley ..	Hants ..	Parish	352
...st Rainton ..	Durham ..	Tnship.	1 505	Eastville ..	Lincoln ..	P. Tp.	246
...st Ravendale .	Lincoln ..	Parish	144	East Walton ..	Norfolk ..	Parish	175
...st Ravendale .	,, ..	Tnship.	94	East Walton ..	Pembroke ..	Parish	223
...st Retford ..	Notts ..	Wapen.	2 982	East Ward ..	Westmoreland	L. Sub.	15 411
...st Retford ..	,, ..	District	22 677	East Ward ..	,,	District	15 411
...st Retford ..	,, ..	Sub-dis.	8 157	East Waver Holme	Cumberld.	Tnship.	526
...st Retford ..	,, ..	Parish	2 982	Eastwell ..	Kent ..	Parish	126
...ast Retford ..	,, {	M. Bor.	2 982	Eastwell ..	Leicester ..	Parish	160
		P. Bor.	47 330	East Wellow ..	Hants ..	Parish	332
...astridge ..	Wilts ..	Tithing	183	East Wells, St. Thos	Somerset	Ecl. Dis.	973
...astrington ..	York ..	Parish	1 906	Eastwick ..	Herts ..	Parish	116
...astrington ..	,, ..	Tnship.	432	East Wickham ..	Kent ..	Parish	836
...astrip	Somerset ..	Parish	15	East Winch ..	Norfolk ..	Parish	434
...astrop	Hants ..	Parish	130	East Wittering..	Sussex ..	Parish	223
...astrop	Wilts ..	Tithing	876	East Witton ..	York ..	Parish	621
...st Rounton ..	York ..	Tnshp.	114	East Witton Within	,, ..	Tnship.	326
...st Rudham ..	Norfolk ..	Parish	956	East Witton Without	,, ..	Tnship.	295
...st Rudham ..	,, ..	—	940	Eastwood ..	Essex ..	Parish	573
...st Ruston ..	,, ..	Parish	757	Eastwood ..	Notts ..	Parish	1 860
...astry	Kent ..	District	25 900	Eastwood ..	York ..	Ecl. Dis.	3 442
...astry	,, ..	Parish	1 505	East Woodhay..	Hants ..	Parish	1 533
...st Scaleby ..	Cumberland.	Tnship.	206	East Worldham .	,, ..	Parish	235
...st Sculcoates .	York ..	Sub-dis.	12 160	East Worlington	Devon ..	Parish	284
...st Shaftoe	Northumberland	Tnship.	32	East Wretham ..	Norfolk ..	Parish	257
...st Shefford ..	Berks ..	Parish	79	East Wykeham .	Lincoln ..	Parish	35
...st Shutford ..	Oxon ..	Tnship.	26	East Wymer ..	Norfolk ..	Sub-dis.	13 641
...st Smithfield .	Middlesex ..	Liberty	4 000	Eathorpe ..	Warwick ..	Tnship.	153
...st Somerton ..	Norfolk ..	Parish	62	Eatington ..	,, ..	Parish	713
...t. Staincliffe & Ewecross	York	L. Sub.	52 565	Eaton Bray ..	Beds ..	Parish	1 440

Name of Place.	County.	Description.	Population.	Name of Place.	County.	Description.	Population.
Eaton Socon	Beds	Parish	2 766	Eckington	Worcester	Sub-dis.	4 228
Eaton	Berks	Tnship.	106	Eckington	,,	Parish	748
Eaton Hastings	,,	Parish	185	Ecton	Northampton	Parish	640
Eaton (Astbury P.)	Cheshire	Tnship.	485	Edale	Derby	Tnship.	386
Eaton, Christchurch	,,	Ecl. Dis.	485	Edale	,,	Ecl. Dis.	386
Eaton (Davenham P.)	,,	Tnship.	11	Edburton	Sussex	Parish	300
Eaton (Eccleston P.)	,,	Tnship.	82	Edburton	,,	—	112
Eaton (Tarporley P.)	,,	Tnship.	465	Eddisbury	Cheshire	Hund.	30 339
Eaton	Derby	Hamlet	—	Eddisbury	,,	L. Sub.	30 339
Eaton, Long	,,	Tnship.	1 551	Eddisbury	,,	Tnship.	228
Eaton, Little	,,	Chap.	775	Eddlethorpe	York	Tnship.	51
Eaton Bishop	Hereford	Parish	465	Edenbridge	Kent	Parish	1 736
Eaton	Leicester	Parish	421	Edenfield	Lancaster	Sub-dis.	4 723
Eaton, St. Andrew	Norfolk	Parish	930	Edenhall	Cumberland	Parish	287
Eaton	Notts	Parish	184	Edenham	Lincoln	Parish	644
Eaton	Salop	Parish	544	Edensor	Derby	Parish	592
Eaton	,,	Tnship.	152	Edensor	,,	Tnship.	272
Eaton Constantine	,,	Parish	242	Edensor	Stafford	Ecl. Dis.	4 943
Eaves, Bucknall	Stafford	Tnship.	248	Edernion	Merioneth	Hund.	5 043
Eavestone	York	Tnship.	64	Edernion	,,	L. Sub.	5 043
Ebberston	,,	Parish	572	Edeyrn	Carnarvon	Parish	613
Ebbesborne Wake	Wilts	Parish	326	Edgbaston	Warwk. & Worces.	Sub-dis.	16 037
Ebchester	Durham	Tnship.	697	Edgbaston	Warwick	Parish	12 907
Ebony	Kent	Parish	184	Edgbaston, St. George	,,	Ecl. Dis.	3 178
Ebrington	Gloucester	Parish	570	Edgbaston, St. James	,,	Ecl. Dis.	4 694
Ecchinswell	Hants	Parish	452	Edgcott	Bucks	Parish	182
Eccles	Lancaster	Parish	52 679	Edgcott	Northampton	Parish	103
Eccles, Kenninghall	Norfolk	Parish	194	Edge	Cheshire	Tnship.	270
Eccles, Stalham	,,	Parish	28	Edge	Gloucester	Tithing	1 176
Ecclesall Bierlow	York & Dur.	District	63 618	Edgefield	Norfolk	Parish	624
Ecclesall Bierlow	York	Sub-dis.	41 224	Edge, High	Derby	Ecl. Dis.	2 286
Ecclesall Bierlow	,,	Tnship.	38 771	Edge Hill, St. Steph.	Lancaster	Ecl. Dis.	8 003
Ecclesall	,,	Ecl. Dis.	2 869	Edgerley	Cheshire	Tnship.	8
Ecclesfield	,,	Sub-dis.	12 479	Edgeworth	Gloucester	Parish	139
Ecclesfield	,,	Parish	21 568	Edgeworth	Lancaster	Sub-dis.	2 025
Ecclesfield	,,	Tnship.	12 479	Edgeworth	,,	Tnship.	1 350
Eccleshall	Stafford	L. Sub.	9 878	Edgmond	Salop	Parish	2 598
Eccleshall	,,	Sub-dis.	6 139	Edgmond	,,	—	1 129
Eccleshall	,,	Parish	4 882	Edgton	,,	Parish	186
Eccleshall	,,	Town	1 491	Edgware	Middlesex	Sub-dis.	3 423
Eccleshill	Lancaster	Tnship.	543	Edgware	,,	Parish	705
Eccleshill	York	Tnship.	4 482	Ediclift	Salop	Pa. Div.	519
Eccleshill, St. Luke	,,	Ecl. Dis.	4 482	Edingale	Stafford	Parish	208
Eccleston	Cheshire	Parish	349	Edingley	Notts	Parish	390
Eccleston	,,	Tnship.	267	Edington	Berks	Tithing	552
Eccleston	Lancaster	Tnship.	965	Edington	Northumberland	Tnship.	32
Eccleston	,,	Parish	3 496	Edington	Somerset	Chap.	432
Eccleston (Prescot P.)	,,	Tnship.	11 640	Edington	Wilts	Sub-dis.	3 490
Eccleston, Christch.	,,	Ecl. Dis.	2 328	Edington	,,	Parish	994
Eccleston, St. Thos.	,,	Ecl. Dis.	8 206	Edingthorpe	Norfolk	Parish	181
Eccleston, Great	,,	Tnship.	641	Edithweston	Rutland	Parish	387
Eccleston, Little	,,	Tnship.	209	Edlaston & Wyaston	Derby	Parish	207
Eckington	Derby	Sub-dis.	13 948	Edlesborough	Bucks & Beds	Sub-dis.	8 436
Eckington	,,	Parish	6 064	Edlesborough	Bucks	Parish	1 671

Name of Place.	County.	Description.	Population.	Name of Place.	County.	Description.	Population.
...leston	Cheshire	Tnship.	89	Eglwysbrewis	Glamorgan	Parish	21
...lingham	Northumberland	Parish	676	Eglwyseymmin	Carmarthen	Parish	260
...lingham	,,	Tnship.	133	Eglwysfach	Denbigh & Carnv.	Parish	1 530
...llington	Lincoln	Parish	212	Eglwysfach	Denbigh	—	1 157
...llington	York	Parish	149	Eglwysfairachyrig	Carmarthen	Chap.	268
...mondbyers	Durham	Parish	455	Eglwysilan	Glamorgan	Parish	6 383
...mondsham	Dorset	Parish	279	Eglwysrhôs	Carnarvon	Parish	832
...mondsley	Durham	Tnship.	434	Eglwyswrw	Pembroke	Parish	490
...mondthorpe	Leicester	Parish	233	Egmanton	Notts	Parish	386
...monton	Middlesex	L. Sub.	43 202	Egmere	Norfolk	Parish	56
...monton	,,	Hund.	40 885	Egremont	Carmarthen	Parish	124
...monton	Middlesex, &c.	District	59 312	Egremont	Cumberland	Sub-dis.	10 440
...monton	Middlesex	Sub-dis.	10 930	Egremont	,,	Parish	3 481
...monton	,,	Parish	10 930	Egremont	,,	Town	2 511
...monton, Up. St. Jas.	,,	Ecl. Dis.	2 945	Egton	York	Sub-dis.	4 226
...dnol	Radnor	Tnship.	34	Egton	,,	Tnship.	1 115
...dstaston	Salop	Ecl. Dis.	799	Egton w. Newland	Lancaster	Tnship.	1 231
...dstock & Beer	Somerset	Hamlet	21	Eidda	Carnarvon	Tnship.	396
...dstone, Great	York	Parish	152	Eirias	,,	Tnship.	295
...dstone, Great	,,	Tnship.	135	Eisey	Wilts	Parish	198
...dstone, Little	,,	Tnship.	21	Elberton	Gloucester	Parish	180
...dvin-Loach	Worcester	Parish	53	Elden	Suffolk	Parish	193
...dvin-Ralph	Hereford	Parish	165	Eldersfield	Worcester	Parish	782
...dwalton	Notts	Parish	115	Eldon	Durham	Tnship.	311
...dwardstone	Suffolk	Parish	462	Eldon, Upper	Hants	Parish	13
...dwinstowe	Notts	Parish	2 651	Eldon	York	Ecl. Dis.	6 030
...dwinstowe	,,	Tnship.	1 065	Elerch	Cardigan	Tnship.	238
...dwinstree	Herts	Hund.	9 471	Elford	Northumberland	Tnship.	103
...dworth	Beds	Parish	99	Elford	Stafford	L. Sub.	9 003
...fenechtyd	Denbigh	Parish	211	Elford	,,	Parish	461
...ffingham	Surrey	Hund.	1 958	Elham	Kent	L. Sub.	17 103
...ffingham	,,	Parish	633	Elham	,,	District	26 925
...gdean	Sussex	Parish	85	Elham	,,	Sub-dis.	3 841
...gerton	Cheshire	Tnship.	115	Elham	,,	Parish	1 159
...gerton	Kent	Parish	816	Eling	Hants	Sub-dis.	5 952
...ggbrough	York	Tnship.	299	Eling	,,	Parish	5 947
...gg Buckland	Devon	Parish	1 348	Eling, North, St. Mary	,,	Ecl. Dis.	1 239
...ggesford	,,	Parish	126	Elkington, North	Lincoln	Parish	108
...gginton	Beds	Hamlet	439	Elkington, South	,,	Parish	333
...gginton	Derby	Parish	355	Elkington	Northampton	Parish	60
...gglescliffe	Durham	Parish	698	Elksley	Notts	Parish	362
...gglescliffe	,,	Tnship.	496	Elkstone	Gloucester	Parish	320
...gglestone	,,	Tnship.	788	Elkstone & Warslow	Stafford	Tnship.	689
...gglestone	,,	Ecl. Dis.	788	Ella, Kirk	York	Parish	1 148
...gglestone Abbey	York	Tnship.	59	Ella, West	,,	Tnship.	154
...ggleton	Hereford	Tnship.	164	Elland	,,	Sub-dis.	13 373
...gham	Surrey & Berks	Sub-dis.	7 680	Elland w. Greetland	,,	Tnship.	8 716
...gham	Surrey	Parish	4 864	Elland	,,	Town	3 643
...gleton	Rutland	Parish	131	Ellastone	Stafford	Parish	1 230
...glingham	Northumberland	Parish	1 845	Ellastone	,,	Tnship.	384
...glingham	,,	Tnship.	363	Ellel	Lancaster	Sub-dis.	4 020
...gloshayle	Cornwall	Sub-dis.	4 964	Ellel	,,	Tnship.	1 968
...gloshayle	,,	Parish	1 479	Ellel, St. John	,,	Ecl. Dis.	1 877
...gloskerry	,,	Parish	510	Ellenboro' & Ewanrigg	Cumbld.	Tnship.	1 086

Name of Place.	County.	Description.	Population.	Name of Place.	County.	Description.	Population.
Ellenhall	Stafford	Parish	300	Elmstead	Essex	Parish	953
Ellenthorpe	York	Tnship.	45	Elmsted..	Kent	Parish	492
Ellerbeck	,,	Tnship.	84	Elmsthorpe	Leicester	Parish	45
Ellerburn	,,	Parish	648	Elmstone	Kent	Parish	75
Ellerby ..	York E.	Tnship.	304	Elmstone Hardwicke	Gloucester	Parish	440
Ellerby ..	York N.	Tnship.	103	Elmswell	Suffolk	Parish	759
Ellerker..	York	Tnship.	341	Elmton ..	Derby	Parish	469
Ellerton Abbey..	,,	Tnship.	50	Elsdon ..	Northumberland	Sub-dis.	1 837
Ellerton Priory..	,,	Parish	338	Elsdon ..	,,	Parish	1 521
Ellerton on Swale	,,	Tnship.	153	Elsdon Ward ..	,,	Tnship.	266
Ellesborough	Bucks	Parish	724	Elsecar ..	York	Ecl. Dis.	1 912
Ellesmere	Salop & Flint	District	14 611	Elsenham	Essex	Parish	480
Ellesmere	Salop	Sub-dis.	6 878	Elsfield ..	Oxon	Parish	179
Ellesmere	Salop & Flint	Parish	6 453	Elsham ..	Lincoln	Parish	409
Ellesmere	Salop	Town	2 114	Elsing ..	Norfolk	Parish	392
Ellingham	Hants	Parish	306	Elslack ..	York	Hamlet	112
Ellingham	Norfolk	Parish	386	Elson, St. Thomas	Hants	Ecl. Dis.	1 530
Ellingham, Great	,,	Parish	717	Elstead ..	Surrey	Parish	818
Ellingham, Little	,,	Parish	382	Elsted ..	Sussex	Parish	174
Ellingham	Northumberland	Parish	813	Elstob ..	Durham	Tnship.	30
Ellingham	,,	Tnship.	280	Elston ..	Lancaster	Tnship.	53
Ellingstring	York	Tnship.	164	Elston ..	Notts	Parish	262
Ellington	Hunts	Parish	413	Elston ..	,,	Chap.	210
Ellington	Northumberland	Tnship.	264	Elstow ..	Beds	Parish	618
Ellingtons	York	Tnship.	114	Elstree ..	Herts	Parish	402
Ellisfield	Hants	Parish	255	Elstronwick	York	Tnship.	130
Elloe ..	Lincoln	Wapen.	37 928	Elstub and Everley	Wilts	Hund.	6 328
Ellough..	Suffolk	Parish	126	Elswick ..	Lancaster	Tnship.	290
Elloughton	York	Parish	688	Elswick..	Northumberland	Tnship.	14 345
Elloughton w. Brough	,,	Tnship.	641	Elswick, High, St. Paul	,,	Ecl. Dis.	22 275
Elm ..	Cambs	Parish	1 729	Elsworth	Cambs	Parish	787
Elm ..	Somerset	Parish	377	Eltham ..	Kent	Sub-dis.	3 009
Elmbridge	Surrey	Hund.	13 184	Eltham ..	,,	Parish	3 009
Elmbridge	Worcester	Chap.	391	Eltham ..	,,	—	2 867
Elmdon..	Essex	Parish	731	Elthorne	Middlesex	Hund.	31 516
Elmdon..	Warwick	Parish	206	Eltisley..	Cambs	Parish	478
Elmham, North .	Norfolk	Sub-dis.	4 626	Elton ..	Cheshire	Tnship.	507
Elmham, North .	,,	Parish	1 251	Elton (Thornton P.)	,,	Tnship.	190
Elmham, South :				Elton ..	Derby	Tnship.	491
All Saints	,,	Parish	197	Elton ..	Durham	Parish	108
St. Cross	,,	Parish	238	Elton ..	Hereford	Parish	108
St. James	,,	Parish	294	Elton ..	Hunts	Parish	947
St. Margaret .	,,	Parish	152	Elton ..	Lancaster	Sub-dis.	9 584
St. Michael ..	,,	Parish	156	Elton ..	,,	Tnship.	8 172
St. Nicholas ..	,,	Parish	103	Elton, All Saints	,,	Ecl. Dis.	7 716
St. Peter	,,	Parish	88	Elton ..	Notts	Parish	94
Elmire w. Crakehill	York	Tnship.	49	Eltringham	Northumberland	Tnship.	159
Elmley ..	Kent	Parish	140	Elvaston	Derby	Parish	499
Elmley Castle ..	Worcester	Parish	373	Elveden	Suffolk	Parish	193
Elmley Lovett ..	,,	Parish	353	Elvet ..	Carmarthen	Hund.	13 745
Elmore ..	Gloucester	Parish	374	Elvet ..	Durham	Tnship.	4 140
Elmsall, North..	York	Tnship.	236	Elvetham	Hants	Parish	475
Elmsall, South..	,,	Tnship.	468	Elvington	York	Parish	472
Elmsett..	Suffolk	Parish	459	Elwick ..	Durham	Tnship.	240

Name of Place.	County.	Description.	Population.	Name of Place.	County.	Description.	Population
Elwick Hall	Durham	Parish	206	Ensham	Oxon	Parish	2 096
Elwick	Northumberland	Tnship.	73	Enstone	"	Parish	1 198
Elworth, St. Peter	Cheshire	Ecl. Dis.	1 153	Enstone, Church	"	Hamlet	287
Elworthy	Somerset	Parish	197	Enstone, Neat	"	Hamlet	414
Ely		Diocese	480 716	Entwistle	Lancaster	Tnship.	422
Ely	Cambs	Isle	64 595	Enville	Stafford	Parish	850
Ely	"	Union	21 790	Epperstone	Notts	Parish	518
Ely	"	Hund.	13 868	Epping	Essex	L. Sub.	24 683
Ely	"	L. Sub.	21 910	Epping	"	District	16 549
Ely	"	District	21 910	Epping	"	Sub-dis.	5 018
Ely	"	Sub-dis.	7 919	Epping	"	Parish	2 105
Ely	"	City	6 179	Eppleby	York	Tnship.	245
Ely College	"	—	101	Eppleton, Great	Durham	Tnship.	71
Ely, Holy Trinity	"	Parish	5 185	Eppleton Little	"	Tnship.	26
Ely, St. Mary	"	Parish	2 696	Epsom	Surrey	L. Sub.	18 302
Ely, Westmore Fen.	"	—	40	Epsom	"	District	22 409
Elyhaugh	Northumberland	Tnship.	21	Epsom	"	Sub-dis.	7 908
Ember & Weston	Surrey	Hamlet	1 718	Epsom	"	Parish	4 890
Emberton	Bucks	Parish	624	Epsom	"	Town	4 890
Embleton	Cumberland	Tnship.	363	Epwell	Oxon	Tnship.	358
Embleton	Durham	Tnship.	136	Epworth	Lincoln	Sub-dis.	4 360
Embleton	Northumberland	Sub-dis.	6 063	Epworth	"	Parish	2 097
Embleton	"	Parish	2 302	Erbistock	Denbigh & Flint	Parish	337
Embleton	"	Tnship.	727	Ercall Magna	Salop	Sub-dis.	3 230
Emborough or Emborrow	Som.	Parish	178	Ercall Magna	"	Parish	1 969
Embsay w. Eastby	York	Tnship.	1 028	Erdington	Warwick	Sub-dis.	24 447
Embsay w. Eastby	"	Ecl. Dis.	1 083	Erdington	"	Hamlet	3 906
Emley	"	Parish	2 771	Erdington, St. Barnabas	"	Ecl. Dis.	3 906
Emley	"	Tnship.	1 441	Eridge Green	Sussex	Ecl. Dis.	575
Emmington	Oxon	Parish	88	Eriswell	Suffolk	Parish	473
Emneth	Norfolk	Parish	1 023	Erith	Kent	Parish	4 143
Empingham	Rutland	Parish	921	Erlas	Denbigh	Tnship.	61
Empshott	Hants	Parish	167	Ermington	Devon	Hund.	9 826
Emswell w. Kelleythorpe	York	Tnship.	132	Ermington & Plympton	"	L. Sub.	19 541
Emsworth, St. James	Hants	Ecl. Dis.	1 655	Ermington	"	Parish	1 785
Enborne	Berks	Parish	412	Erpingham, North	Norfolk	Hund.	11 191
Endellion	Cornwall	Parish	1 192	Erpingham, North	"	L. Sub.	10 534
Enderby	Leicester	Sub-dis.	6 857	Erpingham, South	"	Hund.	14 322
Enderby	"	Parish	1 333	Erpingham, South	"	L. Sub.	14 979
Endon, &c.	Stafford	Tnship.	1 241	Erpingham	"	District	20 874
Energlyn	Glamorgan	Hamlet	1 047	Erpingham	"	Union	20 579
Enfield	Middlesex	Sub-dis.	12 424	Erpingham	"	Parish	423
Enfield	"	Parish	12 424	Erringden	York	Tnship.	1 764
Enfield, Jesus Chapel	"	Ecl. Dis.	927	Erthig	Denbigh	Tnship.	117
Enfield, St. James	"	Ecl. Dis.	4 954	Erwarton	Suffolk	Parish	243
Enford	Wilts	Parish	893	Eryholme	York	Tnship.	176
Enford	"	—	810	Esclusham Above	Denbigh	Tnship.	493
Englefield	Berks	Parish	392	Esclusham Below	"	Tnship.	745
English Bicknor	Gloucester	Parish	592	Escomb	Durham	Parish	3 743
Englishcombe	Somerset	Parish	559	Escot	Devon	Ecl. Dis.	534
English Street	Cumberland	Tnship.	2 967	Escrick	York	Sub-dis.	2 786
Enmore	Somerset	Parish	314	Escrick	"	Parish	1 237
Ennerdale	Cumberland	Tnship.	254	Escrick	"	Tnship.	654
Ensham	Oxon	Sub-dis.	5 237	Esh	Durham	Tnship.	942

Name of Place.	County.	Description.	Population.	Name of Place.	County.	Description.	Population.
Esher	Surrey	Sub-dis	7 185	Evershot	Dorset	Sub-dis.	2 874
Esher	"	Parish	1 460	Evershot	"	Parish	595
Esholt	York	Tnship.	369	Eversley	Hants	Parish	829
Esholt, St. Paul	"	Ecl. Dis.	369	Eversley	"	—	675
Eshott	Northumberland	Tnship.	177	Everton	Beds	Parish	248
Eshton	York	Tnship.	81	Everton	Lancaster	Sub-dis.	70 983
Eskat	Cumberland.	Hamlet	—	Everton	"	Tnship.	54 848
Eskdale	"	Ward	25 605	Everton, Christch.	"	Ecl. Dis.	9 334
Eskdale	"	L. Sub.	21 335	Everton, St. Augustine	"	Ecl. Dis.	12 922
Eskdale	"	Chap.	346	Everton, St. Chrysostom	"	Ecl. Dis.	9 453
Eskdaleside	York	Tnship.	814	Everton, St. Peter	"	Ecl. Dis.	14 589
Eske	"	Tnship.	33	Everton	Notts	Parish	849
Espershields	Northumberland	Tnship.	182	Everton	"	Tnship.	605
Essendine	Rutland	Parish	193	Evesbatch	Hereford	Parish	87
Essendon	Herts	Parish	672	Evesham	Worcester	L. Sub.	11 532
Essex		County	404 851	Evesham	Wor. & Glouc	District	14 767
Northern Division		N. Div.	191 320	Evesham	"	Sub-dis.	7 897
Southern Division		S. Div.	213 531	Evesham	Worcester	Borough	4 680
Essington	Stafford	Tnship.	976	Evesham All Saints	"	Parish	1 722
Estimaner	Merioneth	Hund.	5 099	Evesham, St. Lawrence	"	Parish	1 699
Estimaner	"	L. Sub.	3 447	Evesham St. Peter	"	Parish	1 259
Eston	York	Tnship	2 835	Evington	Leicester	Parish	275
Etchells (Northen P.)	Cheshire	Tnship.	721	Evionydd	Carnarvon	Hund.	9 612
Etchells (Stockport P.)	"	Tnship.	860	Ewart	Northumberland	Tnship	133
Etchilhampton	Wilts	Tithing	252	Ewecross & Staincliffe	York	Wapen.	75 879
Etchingham	Sussex	Parish	864	Ewell	Kent	Parish	429
Etherley	Durham	Ecl. Dis.	1 712	Ewell	Surrey	Parish	2 195
Eton	Bucks	District.	22 353	Ewell	"	—	1 922
Eton	"	Sub-dis.	10 432	Ewelme	Oxon	Hund.	6 418
Eton	"	Parish	3 122	Ewelme	"	Parish	684
Eton	"	Town	2 840	Ewenny	Glamorgan	Parish	273
Etruria	Stafford	Ecl.Dis.	2 922	Ewerby	Lincoln	Parish	473
Etterby	Cumberland.	Tnship.	319	Ewesley	Northumberland	Tnship.	19
Ettingshall, Trinity	Stafford	Ecl. Dis.	3 210	Ewhurst	Hants	Parish	12
Etton	Northampton	Parish	160	Ewhurst	Surrey	Parish	881
Etton	York	Parish	502	Ewhurst	Sussex	Sub-dis..	2 674
Etwall	Derby	Parish	846	Ewhurst	"	Parish	1 043
Etwall	"	Tnship.	626	Ewloe Town	Flint	Tnship.	1 252
Euston	Suffolk	Parish	225	Ewloe Wood	"	Tnship.	513
Euxton	Lancaster	Tnship.	1 491	Ewshott	Hants	Tithing	730
Evedon	Lincoln	Parish	62	Ewyas-Harold	Hereford	Parish	407
Eve Hill, St. James	Worcester	Ecl.Dis.	6 745	Ewyas-Lacy	"	Hund.	3 305
Evenjobb, &c.	Radnor	Tnship.	334	Exbourne	Devon	Parish	459
Evenlode	Worcester	Parish	276	Exbury	Hants	Parish	373
Evenly	Northampton	Parish	525	Exchange	Notts	Sub-dis.	8 964
Evercreech	Somerset	Sub-dis.	5 141	Exelby, Leeming, &c.	York	Tnship.	780
Evercreech	"	Parish	1 321	Exe, Nether	Devon	Parish	78
Everdon	Northampton	Parish	740	Exe, Up	"	Tithing	97
Everingham	York	Parish	321	Exe, West, St. Paul	"	Ecl. Dis.	2 622
Everley & Pewsey	Wilts	L. Sub.	13 068	Exeter		Diocese	953 763
Everley	"	Parish	294	Exeter City	Devon	L. Sub.	33 738
Eversden, Great	Cambs	Parish	314	Exeter	"	District	33 742
Eversden, Little	"	Parish	239	Exeter	"	M. City	33 738
Eversholt	Beds	Parish	885	Exeter	"	P. City	41 749

Name of Place.	County.	Description.	Population.	Name of Place.	County.	Description.	Population.
Exeter, St. James	Devon	Ecl.Dis.	4 200	Fairford	Glouc. & Wilts	Sub-dis.	6 148
Exford	Somerset	Parish	546	Fairford	Gloucester	Parish	1 654
Exhall, Foleshill	Warwick	Parish	964	Fairhaugh	Northumberland	Tnship.	8
Exhall, Bidford	,,	Parish	203	Fairlight	Sussex	Parish	501
Exminster	Devon	Hund.	20 389	Fairnley	Northumberland	Tnship.	10
Exminster	,,	Parish	1 781	Fair Park	Devon	Parish	67
Exmoor	Som. & Devon	Parish	323	Fairsted	Essex	Parish	351
Exmoor	,, ,,	Ecl. Dis.	323	Fakenham	Norfolk	Sub-dis.	7 325
Exmouth	Devon	Sub-dis.	7 171	**Fakenham**	,,	Town	2 182
Exmouth	,,	Town	5 228	Fakenham	,,	Parish	2 456
Exning	Suffolk	Parish	1 348	Fakenham Magna	Suffolk	Parish	196
Exton	Hants	Parish	257	Falcutt	Northampton	Hamlet	46
Exton	Rutland	Parish	805	Faldingworth	Lincoln	Parish	365
Exton	Somerset	Parish	410	Falfield & Moorton	Gloucester	Tithing	884
Eyam	Derby	Parish	1 673	Falkenham	Suffolk	Parish	270
Eyam	,,	Tnship.	1 172	Falkingham	Lincoln	Parish	650
Eydon	Northampton	Parish	576	Falloden	Northumberland	Tnship.	104
Eye	Hereford	Parish	733	Fallowfield	,,	Tnship.	43
Eye, Moreton, &c.	,,	Tnship.	302	Fallowlees	,,	Tnship.	5
Eye	Northampton	Parish	1 375	Fallybroom	Cheshire	Tnship.	35
Eye and Dunsden	Oxon	Liberty	799	Falmer	Sussex	Parish	512
Eye	Suffolk	Sub-dis.	6 547	Falmouth	Cornwall	District	23 332
Eye	,,	Parish	2 430	Falmouth	,,	Sub-dis.	11 643
	,,	M. Bor.	2 430	Falmouth	,,	Parish	9 392
Eye	,,	P. Bor.	7 038	Falmouth	,,	—	3 683
Eyeworth Lodge	Hants	—	4	**Falmouth**	,,	M. Bor.	5 709
Eyford	Gloucester	Parish	44	**Falmouth & Penryn**	,,	P. Bor.	14 485
Eyke	Suffolk	Parish	486	Falsgrave	York	Tnship.	1 173
Eynesbury	Hunts	Parish	1 314	Falstone	Northumberland	Parish	1 016
Eynesford	Kent	Parish	1 738	Fambridge, North	Essex	Parish	191
Eynsford	Norfolk	Hund.	10 748	Fambridge, South	,,	Parish	104
Eynsford	,,	L. Sub.	10 748	Fangfoss	York	Parish	170
Eynsford	,,	Sub-dis.	8 960	Farcett	Hunts	Chap.	778
Eythorn	Kent	Sub-dis.	2 158	Fareham	Hants	Divisn.	45 001
Eythorn	,,	Parish	461	Fareham	,,	L. Sub.	45 001
Eyton	Denbigh	Tnship.	261	Fareham	,,	District	14 864
Eyton	Hereford	Parish	155	Fareham	,,	Sub-dis.	9 640
Eyton on Wild Moors	Salop	Parish	451	Fareham	,,	Parish	6 197
Eyworth	Beds	Parish	149	**Fareham**	,,	Town	4 011
				Fareham, Holy Trinity	,,	Ecl. Dis.	2 308
Faccombe	Hants	Parish	243	Farewell	Stafford	Parish	209
Faceby	York	Tnship.	164	Farforth	Lincoln	Parish	103
Faddiley	Cheshire	Tnship.	285	Faringdon	Berks	Hund.	4 073
Fadmore	York	Tnship.	156	Faringdon	,,	L. Sub.	16 218
Failinge & Healey	Lancaster	Hams.	9 867	Faringdon	Berks, &c.	District	15 688
Failsworth	,,	Sub-dis.	6 312	Faringdon	,,	Sub-dis.	6 222
Failsworth	,,	Tnship.	5 113	**Faringdon**	Berks	Town	2 943
Failsworth	,,	Ecl.Dis.	5 113	Faringdon, Great	,,	Parish	3 702
Fairburn	York	Tnship.	458	Faringdon, Great	,,	—	3 400
Faircross	Berks	Hund.	15 899	Faringdon, Little	Oxon	Tithing	136
Fairfield	Derby	Tnship.	1 075	Farington	Lancaster	Tnship.	1 791
Fairfield	Kent	Parish	69	Farington, St. Paul	,,	Ecl. Dis.	2 292
Fairfield St. John	Lancaster	Ecl.Dis.	4 289	Farlam	Cumberland	Parish	1 311
Fairford	Gloucester	L. Sub.	8 498	Farlam, East	,,	Tnship.	813

Name of Place.	County.	Description.	Population.	Name of Place.	County.	Description.	Population.
Farlam, West	Cumberland.	Tnship.	498	Farnley (Leeds P.)	York	Tnship.	3 064
Farleigh Wallop	Hants	Parish	118	Farnley	,,	Ecl. Dis.	3 064
Farleigh, East	Kent	Parish	1 559	Farnley-Tyas	,,	Tnship.	702
Farleigh, West	,,	Parish	399	Farnsfield	Notts	Parish	1 071
Farleigh-Hungerford	Somerset	Parish	127	Farnworth	Lancaster	Sub-dis.	8 879
Farleton	Lancaster	Tnship.	75	Farnworth, St. Luke	,,	Ecl. Dis.	6 447
Farleton	Westmoreland	Tnship.	92	Farnworth	,,	Sub-dis.	13 723
Farley	Stafford	Tnship.	390	Farnworth & Kearsley	,,	Ecl. Dis.	13 723
Farley	Surrey	Parish	105	Farnworth	,,	Tnship.	8 720
Farley	Wilts	Chap.	241	Farnworth	,,	Town	8 720
Farley-Chamberlayne	Hants	Parish	179	Farringdon	Devon	Parish	331
Farlington	,,	Parish	931	Farringdon	Hants	Parish	535
Farlington	York	Chap.	174	Farrington Gurney	Somerset	Parish	482
Farlow	Salop	Tnship.	304	Farsley, St. John	York	Ecl. Dis.	3 117
Farlow	,,	Ecl. Dis.	593	Farthinghoe	Northampton	Parish	392
Farlsthorpe	Lincoln	Parish	135	Farthingstone	,,	Parish	316
Farmanby	York	Tnship.	467	Farway	Devon	Parish	373
Farmborough	Somerset	Parish	965	Faugh and Fenton	Cumberland.	Tnship.	412
Farmington	Gloucester	Parish	284	Faulkbourn	Essex	Parish	143
Farnborough	Berks	Parish	232	Fauls	Salop	Ecl. Dis.	504
Farnborough	Hants & Surrey	District	14 318	Faversham	Kent	L. Sub.	45 753
Farnborough	,, ,,	Sub-dis.	11 190	Faversham	,,	District	18 867
Farnborough	Hants	Incor.	8 337	Faversham	,,	Sub-dis.	9 473
Farnborough	,,	Parish	5 529	Faversham	,,	Parish	6 383
Farnborough	Kent	Parish	955	In Liberty	,,	—	5 708
Farnborough	Warwick	Parish	401	Out Liberty	,,	—	675
Farncomb	Surrey	Ecl. Dis.	2 084	Faversham	,,	M. Bor.	5 858
Farndale East Side	York	Tnship.	390	Fawcet Forest	Westmoreland	Tnship.	51
Farndale H. Quarter	,,	Tnship.	338	Fawdington	York	Tnship.	35
Farndale L. Quarter	,,	Tnship.	154	Fawdon (Gosfort P.)	Nrthmbld.	Tnship.	486
Farndish	Beds	Parish	67	Fawdon, &c.	,,	Tnship.	62
Farndon	Cheshire	Parish	992	Fawfieldhead	Stafford	Tnship.	817
Farndon	,,	Tnship.	557	Fawkham	Kent	Parish	233
Farndon, East	Northampton	Parish	242	Fawler	Berks	Hamlet	134
Farndon	Notts	Parish	692	Fawler	Oxon	Hamlet	143
Farnham-Royal	Bucks	Parish	1 378	Fawley	Berks	Parish	243
Farnham-Royal	,,	—	817	Fawley	Bucks	Parish	272
Farnham	Dorset	Parish	121	Fawley	Hants	Sub-dis.	4 202
Farnham Tollard	,,	Tithing	217	Fawley	,,	Parish	1 849
Farnham	Essex	Parish	556	Fawns	Northumberland	Tnship.	6
Farnham	Northumberland	Tnship.	59	Fawsley	Northampton	Hund.	10 841
Farnham	Suffolk	Parish	184	Fawsley	,,	Parish	64
Farnham	Surrey	Hund.	12 567	Faxfleet	York	Tnship.	290
Farnham	,,	L. Sub.	15 250	Faxton	Northampton	Parish	79
Farnham	Surrey & Hants	District	30 707	Fazakerley	Lancaster	Tnship.	407
Farnham	,, ,,	Sub-dis.	11 304	Fazeley	Staff. & War.	Sub-dis.	6 857
Farnham	Surrey	Parish	9 278	Fazeley	Stafford	Tnship.	1 341
Farnham	,,	Town	3 926	Fazeley	,,	Ecl. Dis.	1 652
Farnham	York	Parish	609	Fearby	York	Tnship.	242
Farnham	,,	Tnship.	165	Featherstone	Northumberland	Tnship.	307
Farnhill	,,	Tnship.	464	Featherstone	Stafford	Tnship.	54
Farningham	Kent	Sub-dis.	6 110	Featherstone	York	Parish	2 406
Farningham	,,	Parish	944	Featherstone	,,	Tnship.	853
Farnley	York	Tnship.	186	Feckenham	Worc. & War.	Sub-dis.	5 068

Name of Place.	County.	Description.	Population.	Name of Place.	County.	Description.	Population.
Feckenham	Worcester	Parish	3 217	Fernham	Berks	Tnship.	246
Feering	Essex	Parish	804	Fernhurst	Sussex	Sub-dis.	2 786
Felaws Houses	Suffolk	Parish	25	Fernhurst	,,	Parish	769
Felbrigg	Norfolk	Parish	136	Fernilee	Derby	Tnship.	767
Feliskirk	York	Parish	878	Ferrensby	York	Tnship.	86
Feliskirk	,,	Tnship.	111	Ferriby	,,	Sub-dis.	1 858
Felixstow	Suffolk	Parish	673	Ferriby, North	,,	Parish	948
Felkington	Northumberland	Tnship.	122	Ferriby, North	,,	Tnship.	434
Felkirk	York	Parish	1 106	Ferriby, South	Lincoln	Parish	573
Felley	Notts	Parish	33	Ferring	Sussex	Parish	253
Felliscliffe	York	Tnship.	347	Ferry Corner	Lincoln	Parish	50
Fellside	Durham	Tnship.	1 602	Ferry, East	,,	Tnship.	190
Felmersham	Beds	Parish	483	Ferry Frystone	York	Parish	904
Felmersham	,,	—	281	Ferry Hill	Durham	Tnship.	1 423
Felmingham	Norfolk	Parish	434	Ferry Hill, St. Luke	,,	Ecl. Dis.	2 879
Felpham	Sussex	Parish	592	Fersfield	Norfolk	Parish	295
Felsham	Suffolk	Parish	394	Festiniog	Merioneth	L. Sub.	11 750
Felstead	Essex	Parish	1 804	Festiniog	Mer. & Carn.	District	18 289
Feltham	Middlesex	Parish	1 837	Festiniog	Merioneth	Sub-dis.	7 783
Felthorpe	Norfolk	Parish	514	Festiniog	,,	Parish	4 553
Felton	Hereford	Parish	149	Fetcham	Surrey	Parish	390
Felton	Northumberland	Parish	1 591	Fewcott	Oxon	Hamlet	160
Felton	,,	Tnship.	693	Fewston	York	Sub-dis.	2 526
Felton Path Foot	,,	—	5	Fewston	,,	Parish	1 485
Felton, West	Salop	Parish	1 067	Fewston	,,	Tnship.	496
Felton	Somerset	Parish	394	Fforest	Carmarthen	Hamlet	310
Feltwell	Norfolk	Parish	1 553	Fiddington	Somerset	Parish	213
Feltwell Anchor	,,	—	62	Field	Stafford	Tnship.	84
Feltwell Fen Farms	,,	—	8	Field-Dalling	Norfolk	Parish	342
Fence in Pendle	Lancaster	Ecl. Dis.	1 331	Fifehead-Magdalen	Dorset	Parish	200
Fencot	Oxon	Hamlet	313	Fifehead-Neville	,,	Parish	87
Fen Ditton	Cambs	Parish	581	Fifield	Oxon	Hamlet	12
Fen Drayton	,,	Parish	445	Fifield	,,	Parish	234
Fenham	Northumberland	Tnship.	89	Fifield	Wilts	Tithing	83
Feniscowles, Immanl.	Lancaster	Ecl. Dis.	3 501	Fifield-Bavant	,,	Parish	33
Feniton	Devon	Parish	361	Figheldean	,,	Parish	472
Fenny Bentley	Derby	Parish	305	Filby	Norfolk	Parish	517
Fenny Compton	Warwick	Parish	639	Filey	York	Sub-dis.	3 728
Fenny Drayton	Leicester	Parish	134	Filey	,,	Parish	2 244
Fenny Stratford	Bucks	Sub-dis.	10 453	Filey	,,	Tnship.	1 881
Fenny Stratford	,,	Tnship.	1 199	Filkins	Oxon	Hamlet	641
Fenrother	Northumberland	Tnship.	78	Filleigh	Devon	Parish	311
Fen Stanton	Hunts	Parish	1 120	Filley	Cornwall	Parish	363
Fenton	Lincoln	Tnship.	277	Fillingham	Lincoln	Parish	316
Fenton	,,	Parish	103	Fillongley	Warwick	Parish	1 105
Fenton	Stafford	Sub-dis.	7 882	Filton	Gloucester	Parish	317
Fenton	,,	Ecl. Dis.	5 348	Fimber	York	Tnship.	204
Fenton Culvert & Fenton Vivian	,,	Tnship.	7 882	Finborough, Great	Suffolk	Parish	419
				Finborough, Little	,,	Parish	62
Fenton Little	York	Tnship.	100	Fincham	Norfolk	Sub-dis.	5 215
Fenwick	Northumberland	Tnship.	103	Fincham	,,	Parish	886
Fenwick	York	Tnship.	244	Finchampstead	Berks	Parish	637
Fenwick, St. John	,,	Ecl. Dis.	486	Finchingfield	Essex	Sub-dis.	5 289
Fern or Staples	Nrthumberld.	Isles	23	Finchingfield	,,	Parish	2 441

Name of Place.	County.	Description.	Population.	Name of Place.	County.	Description.	Population
Finchley	Middlesex	Sub-dis.	8 281	Flagg	Derby	Tnship.	238
Finchley	,,	Parish	4 937	Flamborough	York	Parish	1 287
Finchley, Holy Trinity	,,	Ecl. Dis.	1 944	Flamstead	Herts	Sub-dis.	3 066
Findern	Derby	Tnship.	399	Flamstead	,,	Parish	1 919
Findon	Sussex	Parish	655	Flasby w. Winterburn	York	Tnship.	113
Finedon	Northampton	Parish	1 840	Flashbrook	Stafford	Tnship.	111
Fineshade	,,	Parish	73	Flaunden	Herts	Parish	244
Fingest	Bucks	Parish	352	Flawborough	Notts	Chap.	64
Finghall	York	Parish	406	Flawith	York	Tnship.	84
Finghall	,,	Tnship.	111	Flax-Bourton	Somerset	Parish	215
Fingland	Cumberland	Tnship.	219	Flaxby	York	Tnship.	76
Fingringhoe	Essex	Parish	670	Flaxley	Gloucester	Parish	272
Finmere	Oxon	Parish	338	Flaxton	York	Sub-dis.	1 677
Finningham	Suffolk	Parish	542	Flaxton on the Moor	,,	Tnship.	367
Finningley	Notts & York	Parish	896	Flaxwell	Lincoln	Wapen.	7 835
Finningley	Notts	Tnship.	434	Fleckney	Leicester	Parish	581
Finsbury	Middlesex	L. Sub.	303 777	Fledborough	Notts	Parish	115
Finsbury	,,	Sub-dis.	12 931	Fleet	Dorset	Parish	160
Finsbury	,,	P. Bor.	387 278	Fleet	Lincoln	Parish	1 312
Finstock	Oxon	Hamlet	533	Fleetham	Northumberland	Tnship.	67
Finstock & Fawler	,,	Ecl. Dis.	676	Fleet-Marston	Bucks	Parish	23
Firbank	Westmoreland	Tnship.	345	**Fleetwood**	Lancaster	Town	3 834
Firbeck	York	Parish	195	Fleetwood, St. Peter	,,	Ecl. Dis.	4 258
Firby, Westow	,,	Tnship.	51	Flegg	Norfolk	District	8 631
Firby, Bedale	,,	Tnship.	82	Flegg, Burgh	,,	Parish	554
Firle, West	Sussex	Parish	631	Flegg, East	,,	Hund.	4 060
Firsby	Lincoln	Parish	237	Flegg, West	,,	Hund.	4 571
Firsby, East	,,	Parish	108	Flegg, East and West	,,	L. Sub.	8 631
Firsby, East	,,	Tnship.	47	Flemingston	Glamorgan	Parish	63
Firsby, West	,,	Tnship.	61	Flempton	Suffolk	Parish	190
Fishbourne, New	Sussex	Parish	341	Flendish	Cambs	Hund.	3 496
Fishburn	Durham	Tnship.	255	Fletching	Sussex	Parish	2 028
Fisherton Anger	Wilts	Parish	2 424	Fletton	Hunts	Parish	1 449
Fisherton-de-la-Mere	,,	Parish	333	Flimby	Cumberland	Parish	1 178
Fisherwick	Stafford	Tnship.	101	Flimwell	Sussex & Kent	Ecl. Dis.	811
Fishguard	Pembroke	Sub-dis.	7 895	Flintshire		County	69 737
Fishguard	,,	Parish	2 084	Flint	Flint	Sub-dis.	8 079
Fishguard	,,	P. Bor.	1 593	Flint	,,	Parish	3 088
Fishlake	York	Parish	1 208	**Flint**	,,	Borough	3 428
Fishlake	,,	Tnship	585	Flint, Parl. Dist. of	,,	Boros.	18 845
Fishley	Norfolk	Parish	10	Flintham	Notts	Parish	524
Fishtoft	Lincoln	Parish	586	Flinton	York	Tnship.	125
Fishwick	Lancaster	Tnship.	1 884	Flitcham	Norfolk	Parish	533
Fiskerton	Lincoln	Parish	524	Flitt	Beds	Hund.	24 793
Fiskerton	Notts	Tnship.	319	Flitton	,,	Parish	1 310
Fitling	York	Tnship.	139	Flitton	,,	Tnship.	597
Fittleton	Wilts	Parish	393	Flitwick	,,	Parish	773
Fittleworth	Sussex	Parish	683	Flixborough	Lincoln	Parish	236
Fitz	Salop	Parish	323	Flixborough	,,	Tnship.	214
Fitzhead	Somerset	Parish	309	Flixton	Lancaster	Parish	2 050
Fivehead	,,	Parish	489	Flixton	,,	Tnship.	1 302
Fixby	York	Tnship.	388	Flixton	Suffolk	Parish	165
Fladbury	Worcester	Parish	1 514	Flixton nr. Lowestoft	,,	Parish	37
Fladbury	,,	—	411	Flixton	York	Tnship.	362

Name of Place.	County.	Description.	Population.	Name of Place.	County.	Description.	Population.
Flockton	.. York ..	Chap.	1 090	Forebridge, St. Paul	Stafford ..	Ecl. Dis.	2 531
Flockton, St. James	,, ..	Ecl. Dis.	2 057	Forehoe..	.. Norfolk ..	Hund.	13 146
Floore ..	.. Northampton	Parish	1 138	Forehoe..	.. ,, ..	L. Sub.	13 146
Flordon..	.. Norfolk ..	Parish	163	Forehoe..	.. ,, ..	District	12 818
Flotterton	Northumberland	Tnship.	79	Foremark	.. Derby ..	Parish	233
Flowton..	.. Suffolk ..	Parish	151	Foremark	.. ,, ..	—	93
Flushing, St. Peter	Cornwall ..	Ecl. Dis.	1 006	Forest ..	.. Brecon ..	Hamlet	172
Flyford-Flavel	.. Worcester ..	Parish	173	Forest ..	.. Carmarthen	Hamlet	195
Fobbing	.. Essex ..	Parish	393	Forest ..	.. Is. Guernsey	Parish	612
Fockerby	.. York ..	Tnship.	108	Forest and Frith	Durham ..	Tnship.	862
Foggathorpe	.. ,, ..	Tnship.	128	Forest Quarter ..	.. ,, ..	Tnship.	4 600
Foleshill	.. Warwick ..	District	19 997	Forest Gate, Emanl.	Essex ..	Ecl. Dis.	3 792
Foleshill	.. ,, ..	Sub-dis.	15 327	Forest-Hill	.. Oxon ..	Parish	191
Foleshill	.. ,, ..	Parish	8 140	Forest-Hill, Christch.	Kent ..	Ecl. Dis.	4 640
Foleshill, St. Paul	,, ..	Ecl. Dis.	3 231	Forest-Row, Trinity	Sussex ..	Ecl. Dis.	1 411
Folke ..	.. Dorset ..	Parish	332	Formby..	.. Lancaster ..	Sub-dis.	3 606
Folkestone	.. Kent ..	Sub-dis.	17 341	Formby..	.. ,, ..	Tnship.	1 780
Folkestone	.. ,, ..	Parish	9 674	Forncett	.. Norfolk ..	Sub-dis.	5 694
Folkestone	.. ,, ..	M. Bor.	8 507	Forncett, St. Mary	,, ..	Parish	299
Folkestone Christch.	,, ..	Ecl. Dis.	2 744	Forncett, St. Peter	,, ..	Parish	665
Folkington	.. Sussex ..	Parish	154	Fornham	.. Suffolk ..	Sub-dis.	5 789
Folksworth	.. Hunts ..	Parish	207	Fornham, All Saints	,, ..	Parish	381
Folkton..	.. York ..	Parish	559	Fornham, St. Geneveve	,, ..	Parish	64
Folkton..	.. ,, ..	Tnship.	197	Fornham, St. Martin	,, ..	Parish	350
Follifoot	.. ,, ..	Tnship.	419	Forrabury	.. Cornwall ..	Parish	366
Fonthill-Gifford	.. Wilts ..	Parish	430	Forsbrook	.. Stafford ..	Tnship.	724
Fontmell	.. Dorset ..	Sub-dis.	3 353	Forsbrook St. Peter	,, ..	Ecl. Dis.	765
Fontmell Magna	,, ..	Parish	875	Forscote	.. Somerset ..	Parish	46
Fontmell Magna	,, ..	—	690	Forthampton	.. Gloucester ..	Parish	442
Foolow ..	.. Derby ..	Hamlet	243	Fortherley, High	Nrthumbld. ..	Tnship.	104
Foots Cray	.. Kent ..	Parish	286	Forton St. John	. Hants ..	Ecl. Dis.	6 425
Forcett ..	.. York ..	Parish	776	Forton ..	.. Lancaster ..	Tnship.	574
Forcett ..	.. ,, ..	Hamlet	167	Forton ..	.. Stafford ..	Parish	729
Ford ..	.. Durham ..	Tnship.	2 036	Forty-foot Bank, Nrth.	Lincoln	Parish	300
Ford ..	.. Hereford ..	Parish	29	Fosbury..	.. Berks & Wilts	Ecl. Dis.	336
Ford ..	Northumberland	Sub-dis.	6 833	Fosdyke..	.. Lincoln ..	Parish	549
Ford ..	.. ,, ..	Parish	2 072	Foston ..	.. Derby ..	Tnship.	239
Ford ..	.. Salop ..	Hund.	7 767	Foston ..	.. Leicester ..	Parish	27
Ford ..	.. ,, ..	L. Sub.	8 055	Foston ..	.. Lincoln ..	Parish	479
Ford ..	.. ,, ..	Parish	351	Foston ..	.. York ..	Sub-dis.	3 171
Ford ..	.. Sussex ..	Parish	82	Foston ..	.. ,, ..	Parish	355
Forden ..	.. Montgomery	Parish	926	Foston ..	.. ,, ..	Tnship.	85
Fordham	.. Cambs ..	Parish	1 406	Foston on Wolds	,, ..	Parish	759
Fordham	.. Essex ..	Sub-dis.	4 621	Foston on Wolds	,, ..	Tnship.	311
Fordham	.. ,, ..	Parish	782	Fotherby	.. Lincoln ..	Parish	267
Fordham	.. Norfolk ..	Parish	211	Fotheringhay	Nrthptn. & Hunts	Sub-dis.	6 251
Fordingbridge	.. Hants, &c. ..	District	6 377	Fotheringhay	.. Northampton	Parish	246
Fordingbridge	.. Hants & Wilts	Sub-dis.	6 377	Foulby, &c.	.. York ..	Parish	145
Fordingbridge	.. Hants ..	Parish	2 925	Foulden..	.. Norfolk ..	Parish	517
Fordington	.. Dorset..	Parish	3 258	Foulk Stapleford	Cheshire ..	Tnship.	245
Fordington, W., Chrstch.	,, ..	Ecl. Dis.	1 059	Foulmire	.. Cambs ..	Parish	560
Fordon ..	.. York ..	Chap.	38	Foulness	.. Essex ..	Parish	681
Fordsbridge	.. Hereford ..	Parish	29	Foulridge	.. Lancaster ..	Tnship.	988
Fordwich	.. Kent ..	Parish	202	Foulsham	.. Norfolk ..	Parish	1 022

Name of Place.	County.	Description.	Population.	Name of Place.	County.	Description.	Population.
Fountains Earth	York	Tnship.	415	Freebridge Lynn	Norfolk	L. Sub.	14 450
Four Towers	Somerset	Parish	6	Freebridge Lynn	"	District	13 486
Fovant	Wilts	Parish	600	Freebridge Marshland	"	Hund.	14 435
Fowey	Cornwall	Sub-dis.	9 343	Freebridge Marshland	"	L. Sub.	14 435
Fowey	"	Parish	1 429	Freeby	Leicester	Chap.	126
Fownhope	Hereford	Sub-dis.	5 614	Freefolk Manor	Hants	Parish	66
Fownhope	"	Parish	1 112	Freeford	Stafford	Hamlet	20
Foxcott	Bucks	Parish	96	Freeford	"	Parish	9
Foxcott	Hants	Parish	50	Freehay, St. Chad	"	Ecl. Dis.	643
Foxearth	Essex	Parish	400	Freeholders Quatr.	Nrthmbld.	Tnship.	160
Foxhall	Suffolk	Parish	190	Freethorpe	Norfolk	Parish	425
Foxholes	York	Parish	428	Fremington	Devon	Hund.	5 861
Foxholes & Boythorpe	"	Tnship.	319	Fremington	"	Parish	1 245
Foxley	Norfolk	Parish	278	Frenchay & Hambrook	Glouc.	Tithing	1 621
Foxley	Wilts	Parish	65	Frenchay, St. Jno., Bpt.	"	Ecl. dis.	1 531
Foxt	Stafford	Tnship.	124	Frenchmoor	Hants	Hamlet	46
Foxton	Cambs	Parish	405	Frensham	Surrey	Parish	1 750
Foxton & Shotton	Durham	Tnship.	56	Frenze	Norfolk	Parish	49
Foxton	Leicester	Parish	388	Fresden	Wilts	Tithing	21
Foy	Hereford	Parish	318	Freshford	Somerset	Parish	584
Fradley	Stafford	Tnship.	333	Freshwater	Hants	Parish	1 678
Fradswell	"	Tnship.	220	Freshwell	Essex	Hund.	7 568
Fraisthorpe	York	Parish	101	Freshwell	"	L. Sub.	7 317
Fraisthorpe	"	Tnship.	85	Fressingfield	Suffolk	Parish	1 325
Framfield	Sussex	Sub-dis.	3 102	Freston	"	Parish	256
Framfield	"	Parish	1 355	Fretherne	Gloucester	Parish	237
Framilode, St. Peter	Gloucester	Ecl. Dis.	635	Frettenham	Norfolk	Parish	221
Framingham, Earl	Norfolk	Parish	136	Freystrop	Pembroke	Parish	576
Framingham, Pigot	"	Parish	312	Friar Mere, St. Thomas	York	Ecl. Dis.	2 979
Framland	Leicester	Hund.	23 455	Friary	Stafford	Parish	8
Framlingham	Suffolk	Sub-dis.	3 330	Friary	Surrey	Parish	373
Framlingham	"	Parish	2 252	Friday Bridge	Cambs	Ecl. Dis.	869
Framlington, Long	Nrthmbld.	Parish	447	Fridaythorpe	York	Parish	332
Frampton	Dorset	Parish	435	Friesthorpe	Lincoln	Parish	46
Frampton	Gloucester	Sub-dis.	4 499	Frieston	"	Parish	1 239
Frampton	"	Tithing	237	Friezland	York & Chesh.	Ecl. Dis.	2 191
Frampton Cotterel	"	Parish	1 931	Frilford	Berks	Tnship.	160
Frampton on Severn	"	Parish	983	Frilsham	"	Parish	183
Frampton	Lincoln	Parish	843	Frimley	Surrey & Hants	Sub-dis.	19 403
Framsden	Suffolk	Parish	811	Frimley	Surrey	Hamlet	2 683
Framwellgate	Durham	Tnship.	4 326	Frindsbury	Kent	Parish	2 219
Frankby	Cheshire	Tnship.	137	Fring	Norfolk	Parish	173
Frankley	Worcester	Parish	122	Fringford	Oxon	Parish	401
Frankton	Warwick	Parish	239	Frinsted	Kent	Parish	219
Fransham, Great	Norfolk	Parish	295	Frinton	Essex	Parish	29
Fransham, Little	"	Parish	256	Frisby	Leicester	Tnship.	19
Frant	Sussex	L. Sub.	11 784	Frisby on Wreak	"	Parish	424
Frant	Sussex & Kent	Sub-dis.	2 469	Friskney	Lincoln	Parish	1 604
Frant	" "	Parish	2 469	Friston	Suffolk	Parish	432
Frating	Essex	Parish	235	Friston	Sussex	Parish	89
Freaks Ground	Leicester	Parish	7	Frithelstock	Devon	Parish	635
Freckenham	Suffolk	Parish	476	Frithville	Lincoln	Parish	317
Freckleton	Lancaster	Tnship.	879	Frittenden	Kent	Parish	898
Freebridge Lynn	Norfolk	Hund.	14 450	Fritton	Norfolk	Parish	235

Name of Place.	County.	Description.	Population.	Name of Place.	County.	Description.	Population.
ton ..	Suffolk	Parish	209	Fulnetby	Lincoln	Chap.	73
well..	Oxon	Parish	542	Fulshaw..	Cheshire	Tnship.	532
ester	Gloucester	Parish	262	Fulstone	York	Tnship.	2 414
desley	Salop	Parish	256	Fulstow	Lincoln	Parish	577
dingham	Lincoln	Parish	910	Fulwell ..	Durham	Tnship.	208
dingham	,,	Tnship.	113	Fulwood	Lancaster	Tnship.	2 313
dingham, North	York	Parish	837	Fulwood	Notts	Parish	7
dingham, South	,,	Tnship.	59	Fulwood	York	Ecl. Dis.	1 801
lsham	Cheshire	Sub-dis.	6 050	Fundenhall	Norfolk	Parish	334
lsham	,,	Parish	5 890	Funtington	Sussex	Sub-dis.	3 231
lsham	,,	Tnship.	1 869	Funtington	,,	Parish	1 099
lsham	,,	Lordsp.	968	Furneux-Pelham	Herts	Parish	620
ggatt	Derby	Tnship.	129	Furnivals Inn ..	Middlesex	Parish	202
gmore, Trinity	Herts	Ecl. Dis.	975	Furtho ..	Northampton	Parish	16
ne, St. Quinton	Dorset	Parish	129	Furzy Park & Portfield	Pemb..	Parish	202
ne Vauchurch	,,	Parish	171	Fwthog ..	Hereford	Hamlet	110
ne ..	Somerset	Hund.	17 674	Fyfield ..	Berks	Sub-dis.	1 861
ne ..	,,	L. Sub.	23 704	Fyfield ..	,,	Parish	439
ne ..	,,	District	23 704	Fyfield ..	Essex	Parish	629
ne ..	,,	Sub-dis.	11 543	Fyfield ..	Hants	Parish	222
ne ..	,,	Parish	11 200	Fyfield ..	Wilts	Parish	200
me ..	,,	P. Boro.	9 522	Fylde ..	Lancaster	District	25 682
ne, Christchurch	,,	Ecl. Dis.	2 885	Fylingdales	York	Parish	1 721
ne, Holy Trinity	,,	Ecl. Dis.	3 819				
n Goch, St. Mark	Merioneth	Ecl. Dis.	650	**Gaddesby**	Leicester	Parish	341
stenden	Suffolk	Parish	409	Gaddesden, Great	Herts	Parish	1 147
sterley Quarter	Durham	Tnship.	486	Gaddesden, Little	,,	Parish	386
wlesworth	Leicester	Parish	291	Gafllogian	Carnarvon	Hund.	2 241
xfield	Hants	Parish	657	Gagingwell	Oxon	Hamlet	57
xfield	Wilts	Parish	530	Gainford	Durham	Parish	7 264
yle ..	Hants	Parish	766	Gainford	,,	Tnship.	735
stfield	Wilts	Hund.	1 551	Gainsborough	Lincoln	L. Sub.	14 218
ern Barnet	Middlesex	Parish	3 344	Gainsborough	Linc. & Notts	District	25 973
erning	Essex	Parish	707	Gainsborough	Lincoln	Sub-dis.	7 339
ton ..	York	Tnship.	109	Gainsborough ..	,,	Parish	7 339
glestone	Wilts	Parish	609	Gainsborough ..	,,	Tnship.	6 320
beck..	Lincoln	Parish	728	**Gainsborough** .	,,	Town	6 320
bourn	Cambs	Sub-dis.	8 293	Gainsborough, Trinity,	,,	Ecl. Dis.	2 436
bourn	,,	Parish	1 548	Galby ..	Leicester	Parish	93
brook	Oxon	Parish	392	Galby ..	,,	Tnship.	74
brook	Warwick	Parish	76	Gallow ..	Norfolk	Hund.	10 024
fen ..	Stafford	Parish	10	Gallow ..	,,	L. Sub.	10 024
fords Ambo..	York	Parish	2 478	Gallow Hill	Northumberland	Tnship.	52
ford Gate ..	,,	Tnship.	2 443	Gamblesby	Cumberland	Tnship.	262
ford Water..	,,	Tnship.	35	Gamlingay	Cambs	Parish	2 004
ham..	Middlesex	Sub-dis.	15 539	Gamston	Notts	Parish	282
ham..	,,	Parish	15 539	Gamston	,,	Tnship.	110
ham..	,,	Union	40 058	Ganarew	Hereford	Parish	116
king ..	Sussex	Hamlet	188	Ganfield	Berks	Hund.	3 750
llaway	Wilts	Tithing	20	Ganstead	York	Tnship.	80
lletby	Lincoln	Parish	303	Ganthorpe	,,	Tnship.	109
ll Sutton ·	York	Parish	174	Ganton ..	,,	Parish	352
lmer ..	Bucks	Parish	351	Garboldisham	Norfolk	Parish	701
lmodeston, &c.	Norfolk	Parish	400	Garendon	Leicester	Parish	38

Name of Place.	County.	Description.	Population.	Name of Place.	County.	Description.	Population.
Garford	Berks	Chap.	173	Gaydon	Warwick	Parish	292
Garforth	York	Parish	1 504	Gayhurst	Bucks	Parish	129
Gargrave	,,	Sub-dis.	1 852	Gayles	York	Tnship.	197
Gargrave	,,	Parish	1 641	Gayton	Cheshire	Tnship.	193
Gargrave	,,	Tnship.	1 103	Gayton-le-Marsh	Lincoln	Parish	331
Garmondsway-Moor	Durham	Tnship.	125	Gayton-le-Wold	,,	Parish	118
Garrigill	Cumberland	Chap.	1 447	Gayton	Norfolk	Sub-dis.	4 284
Garrison Side	York	Parish	376	Gayton	,,	Parish	920
Garriston	,,	Tnship.	41	Gayton Thorpe	,,	Parish	169
Garsdale	,,	Sub-dis.	618	Gayton	Northampton	Parish	459
Garsdale	,,	Tnship.	618	Gayton	Stafford	Parish	249
Garsdon	Wilts	Parish	206	Gaywood	Norfolk	Parish	1 368
Garsington	Oxon	Parish	643	Gazeley	Suff. & Cambs	Sub-dis.	3 446
Garstang	Lancaster	District	12 425	Gazeley	Suffolk	Parish	884
Garstang	,,	Sub-dis.	6 029	Gazeley	,,	—	477
Garstang	,,	Parish	7 221	Gedding	,,	Parish	150
Garstang	,,	Tnship.	714	Geddington	Northampton	Parish	888
Garston, East	Berks	Parish	589	Gedgrave	Suffolk	Parish	60
Garston	Lancaster	Tnship.	4 720	Gedling	Notts	Parish	3 130
Garston, St. Michael	,,	Ecl. Dis.	2 016	Gedling	,,	Tnship.	397
Garth & Ystrad	Cardigan	Tnship.	89	Gedney Hill	Lincoln	Sub-dis.	2 994
Garthbeibio	Montgomery	Parish	326	Gedney	,,	Parish	2 459
Garthbrengy	Brecon	Parish	162	Gedney	,,	,,	1 993
Garthely	Cardigan	Chap.	296	Gedney Hill	,,	Hamlet	466
Garthgynyd	Glamorgan	Hamlet	125	Geldeston	Norfolk	Parish	345
Garthorpe	Leicester	Parish	113	Gelligaer	Glamorgan	Sub-dis.	16 840
Garthorpe	Lincoln	Tnship.	580	Gelligaer	,,	Parish	5 778
Garton	York	Parish	195	Geltsdale Forest	Cumberland	Parish	13
Garton w. Grimston	,,	Tnship.	154	Gembling	York	Tnship.	123
Garton on Wolds	,,	Parish	572	Geneurglynn	Cardigan	Hund.	11 276
Gartree	Leicester	Hund.	18 762	Geneurglynn, Lower	,,	L. Sub.	5 657
Gartree	Lincoln	Wapen.	8 479	Geneurglynn, Upper	,,	L. Sub.	5 619
Garvestone	Norfolk	Parish	383	Geneurglynn	,,	Sub-dis.	4 638
Garway	Hereford	Parish	585	Gentleshawe	Stafford	Ecl. Dis.	625
Gasper	Somerset	Hamlet	295	Georgeham	Devon	Parish	873
Gasthorpe	Norfolk	Parish	87	George Nympton	,,	Parish	258
Gatcombe	Hants	Parish	201	George Street	Suffolk	Parish	9
Gateforth	York	Tnship.	174	German	Isle of Man	Parish	4 772
Gate Fulford	,,	Tnship.	2 443	Germansweek	Devon	Parish	325
Gate Helmsley	,,	Parish	200	Germoe	Cornwall	Parish	1 015
Gately	Norfolk	Parish	134	Gerrans	,,	Parish	935
Gatenby	York	Tnship.	80	Gestingthorpe	Essex	Parish	769
Gateshead	Durham	District	59 409	Gibbet Hills, &c.	Lincoln	Parish	49
Gateshead	,,	Sub-dis.	32 749	Gidding, Great	Hunts	Parish	543
Gateshead	,,	Parish	32 749	Gidding, Little	,,	Parish	45
Gateshead	,,	Borough	33 587	Gidley	Devon	Parish	134
Gateshead Fell	,,	Ecl. Dis.	4 613	Giggleswick	York	Parish	3 187
Gatton	Surrey	Parish	191	Giggleswick	,,	Tnship.	727
Gaunts Earthcote	Gloucester	Tithing	41	Gilberdike	,,	Tnship.	725
Gautby	Lincoln	Parish	113	Gilcrux	Cumberland	Parish	653
Gawber, St. Thomas	York	Ecl. Dis.	1 421	Gildersome	York	Tnship.	2 701
Gawcott	Bucks	Chap.	571	Gildersome	,,	Ecl. Dis.	2 701
Gawsworth	Cheshire	Sub-dis.	3 118	Gildingwells	,,	Tnship.	83
Gawsworth	,,	Parish	713	Gileston	Glamorgan	Parish	70

Name of Place.	County.	Description.	Population.	Name of Place.	County.	Description.	Population.
moor ..	York ..	Tnship.	160	Glasson Christch.	Lancaster ..	Ecl. Dis.	857
gate ..	Durham ..	Parish	6 135	Glassonby ..	Cumberland	Tnship.	147
ng, East ..	York ..	Wapen.	7 736	Glaston	Rutland ..	Parish	238
ng, West ..	" ..	Wapen.	16 115	Glastonbury ..	Somerset ..	Sub-dis.	10 635
ng, East ..	" ..	L. Sub.	5 769	Glastonbury ..	" ..	Parish	3 593
ng, West ..	" ..	L. Sub.	21 078	**Glastonbury** ..	" ..	M. Bor.	3 496
ng, Oswaldkirk " ..		Parish	401	Glaston Twelve Hides " ..		Hund.	3 834
ng " " :		Tnship.	244	Glatton	Hunts ..	Parish	937
ng, Richmond " ..		Parish	1 554	Glatton	" ..	Tnship.	293
ng " " ..		Tnship.	899	Glazeley.. ..	Salop ..	Parish	67
ngham " ..	Dorset ..	Sub-dis.	4 688	Glemham, Great.	Suffolk ..	Parish	354
ngham ..	" ..	Parish	3 957	Glemham, Little.	" ..	Parish	325
ngham ..	" ..	—	3 036	Glemsford ..	" ..	Parish	1 932
ngham ..	Kent ..	Sub-dis.	34 255	Glendale	Northumberland	Ward	11 521
ngham ..	" ..	Parish	14 608	Glendale Ward..	"	L. Sub.	11 521
ngham ..	Norfolk ..	Parish	390	Glendale ..	"	District	13 211
nonby ..	York ..	Tnship.	80	Glendon.. ..	Northampton	Parish	63
norton ..	Leicester ..	Parish	853	Glenfield ..	Leicester ..	Parish	1 034
oes	" ..	Parish	12	Glenfield ..	"	Tnship.	522
land, St. Mary	Cumberland	Ecl. Dis.	224	Glenfield-Frith..	" ..	Parish	9
ton ..	Herts ..	Parish	270	Glenn Magna ..	" ..	Parish	827
ingham ..	Norfolk ..	Parish	332	Glenn Magna ..	" ..	Tnship.	785
ping..	Suffolk ..	Hamlet	76	Glenn Parva ..	" ..	Tnship.	119
lington, St. Philip	York ..	Ecl. Dis.	2 227	Glentham ..	Lincoln ..	Parish	516
sby	" ..	Tnship.	90	Glentworth ..	" ..	Parish	340
ton	Cambs ..	Parish	469	Glinton	Northampton	Parish	421
ton	Notts ..	Parish	188	Globe Road,St. Peter	Middlesex	Ecl. Dis.	12 139
burn.. ..	York ..	Sub-dis.	2 693	Glodwich ..	Lancaster ..	Ecl. Dis.	7 200
burn.. ..	" ..	Parish	1 756	Glooston ..	Leicester ..	Parish	157
burn.. ..	" ..	Tnship.	534	Glororum	Northumberland	Tnship.	39
burn Forest ..	" ..	Tnship.	301	Glossop ..	Derby ..	Sub-dis.	21 200
leham ..	Suffolk ..	Parish	267	Glossop.. ..	" ..	Union	21 200
lingham ..	" ..	Parish	623	Glossop.. ..	" ..	Parish	31 140
sing ..	Norfolk ..	Parish	481	**Glossop** ..	" ..	Town	19 126
tisham ..	Devon ..	Parish	355	Glossop-Dale ..	" ..	Tnship.	6 130
endale ..	York ..	Tnship.	40	Gloster Hill	Northumberland	Tnship.	46
endale, Great	" ..	Parish	86	Gloucester and Bristol		Diocese	568 574
endale, Great	" ..	Tnship.	60	Gloucestershire.. ..		County	485 770
destry ..	Radnor ..	Parish	350	Eastern Division ..		E. Div.	208 192
isdale ..	York ..	Tnship.	1 074	Western Division ..		W. Div.	277 578
morganshire . ..	..	County	317 752	Gloucester ..	Gloucester ..	L. Sub.	28 418
ndford ..	Norfolk ..	Parish	74	Gloucester ..	"	District	34 950
anford Brigg..	Lincoln ..	District	34 731	Gloucester, St. James	"	Ecl. Dis.	5 498
anford Brigg..	" ..	Tnship.	1 704	Gloucester, St. Mark	"	Ecl. Dis.	2 555
anogwen, Christch.	Carnv...	Ecl. Dis.	4 264	**Gloucester** ..	" ..	City	16 512
anton	Northumberland	Tnship.	619	Glusburn ..	York ..	Tnship.	1 475
apthorn ..	Northampton	Parish	396	Gluvias ..	Cornwall ..	Parish	4 760
apwell ..	Derby ..	Tnship.	103	Gluvias	" ..	—	1 213
asbury	Brecon & Radnor	Parish	1 264	Glympton	Oxon ..	Parish	153
asbury	" "	Tnship.	768	Glyn ..	Carmarthen	Hamlet	851
ascoed ..	Monmouth ..	Hamlet	253	Glyncorrwg ..	Glamorgan .	Parish	602
ascomb ..	Radnor ..	Parish	463	Glyncorrwg ..	" ..	Hamlet	322
ass Houghton .	York ..	Tnship.	489	Glynde ..	Sussex ..	Parish	321
asshouse Yard	Middlesex ..	Liberty	1 455	Glynfach ..	Brecon ..	Hamlet	55

G 2

Name of Place.	County.	Description.	Population.	Name of Place.	County.	Description.	Population.
Glynn	Brecon	Hamlet	273	Goltho	Lincoln	Tnship.	10?
Glynn Collwn	,,	Hamlet	342	Gomeldon	Wilts	Tithing	8?
Glyntaff	Glamorgan	Hamlet	2 724	Gomersal	York	Sub-dis.	11 23?
Glyntaff	,,	Ecl. Dis.	7 413	Gomersal	,,	Tnship.	11 23?
Glyntawe	Brecon	Hamlet	99	Gomersal	,,	Ecl. Dis.	3 50?
Glyntraian	Denbigh	Division	975	Gonalstone	Notts	Parish	107
Gnosall	Stafford	Sub-dis.	4 969	Gonerby, Great	Lincoln	Parish	1 14?
Gnosall	,,	Parish	2 400	Good-Easter	Essex	Parish	539
Goadby	Leicester	Tnship.	134	Gooderstone	Norfolk	Parish	57?
Goadby-Marwood	,,	Parish	195	Goodleigh	Devon	Parish	294
Goathill	Somerset	Parish	57	Goodmanham	York	Parish	294
Goathland	York	Tnship.	518	Goodmans Fields	Middlesex	Sub-dis.	11 16?
Goathurst	Somerset	Parish	304	Goodnestone, Faversham	Kent	Parish	78
Goatland	York	Tnship.	518	Goodnestone, Wingham	,,	Parish	344
Godalming	Surrey	Hund.	10 445	Goodrich	Hereford	Parish	796
Godalming	,,	Sub-dis.	6 472	Goodshaw	Lancaster	Ecl. Dis.	4 808
Godalming	,,	Parish	5 778	Goodworth Clatford	Hants	Parish	427
Godalming	,,	M. Bor.	2 321	Goole	York & Linc.	District	15 153
Goddington	Oxon	Parish	85	Goole	York	Sub-dis.	6 994
Godley	Cheshire	Tnship.	1 185	Goole	,,	Tnship.	3 479
Godley, &c.	,,	Ecl. Dis.	? 209	Goole	,,	Town	5 850
Godley	Surrey	Hund.	19 038	Goole, St. John	,,	Ecl. Dis.	5 613
Godmanchester	Hunts	Parish	2 438	Goosey	Berks	Chap.	202
Godmanchester	,,	M. Bor.	2 438	Goosnargh, &c.	Lancaster	Tnship.	1 307
Godmanstone	Dorset	Parish	175	Goostrey w. Barnshaw	Cheshire	Tnship.	268
Godmersham	Kent	Parish	388	Gopsall	Leicester	Parish	63
Godolphin	Cornwall	Ecl. Dis.	1 884	Gordon Sq., All Saints	Middlx.	Ecl. Dis.	6 780
Godsfield	Hants	Parish	9	Gore Wood	Dorset	Parish	6
Godshill	,, I. W.	Sub-dis.	8 020	Gore	Middlesex	Hund.	15 341
Godshill	,, I. W.	Parish	1 215	Gore	,,	L. Sub.	15 341
Godshill, Fordingbridge	Hant?	Parish	255	Goring	Oxon	Parish	947
Godstone	Surrey	L. Sub.	11 844	Goring	Sussex	Parish	535
Godstone	,,	District	9 642	Gorleston	Suffolk	Sub-dis.	6 339
Godstone	,,	Sub-dis.	9 642	Gorleston	,,	Parish	4 472
Godstone	,,	Parish	1 853	Gorleston	,,	—	2 758
Gogoyan	Cardigan	Tnship.	99	Gornal, Lower	Stafford	Ecl. Dis.	5 915
Golant	Cornwall	Parish	311	Gornal, Upper, St Peter	,,	Ecl. Dis.	4 044
Golborne	Lancaster	Parish	2 776	Gorran	Cornwall	Parish	1 054
Golbourn Bellow	Cheshire	Tnship.	108	Gorsedd	Flint	Ecl. Dis.	639
Golbourn David	,,	Tnship.	70	Gorton	Lancaster	Tnship.	9 897
Golcar	York	Sub-dis.	13 783	Gorton, St. James	,,	Ecl. Dis.	7 017
Golcar	,,	Tnship.	5 110	Gorwydd	Cardigan	Tnship.	667
Golcar St. John	,,	Ecl. Dis.	5 110	Gosbeck	Suffolk	Parish	301
Goldcliff	Monmouth	Parish	250	Gosberton	Lincoln	Sub-dis.	3 060
Golden Hill	Stafford	Ecl. Dis.	2 621	Gosberton	,,	Parish	2 107
Golden-square	Middlesex	Sub-dis.	13 966	Goscote, East	Leicester	Hund.	16 239
Goldhanger	Essex	Parish	545	Goscote, West	,,	Hund.	51 427
Goldington	Beds	Parish	609	Gosfield	Essex	Parish	620
Goldsborough	York	Parish	451	Gosford	Oxon	Hamlet	52
Goldsborough	,,	Tnship.	260	Gosforth	Cumberland	Parish	1 146
Goldshaw Booth	Lancaster	Tnship.	406	Gosforth	Northumberland	Parish	2 943
Golftyn	Flint	Tnship.	451	Gosforth, North	,,	Tnship.	197
Golon	Radnor	Tnship.	373	Gosforth, South	,,	Tnship.	248
Goltho	Lincoln	Parish	151	Gosport	Hants	—	11 269

Name of Place	County.	Description.	Population.	Name of Place.	County.	Description.	Population.
osport	Hants	Town	7 789	Grantham {	Lincoln {	M. Bor.	4 954
osport, Holy Trinity „		Ecl. Dis.	3 432			P. Bor.	11 121
osport, St. Matthew „		Ecl. Dis.	4 836	Grantley	York	Tnship.	235
oswell-street	Middlesex	Sub-dis.	16 200	Grappenhall	Cheshire	Parish	3 586
otham	Notts	Parish	771	Grappenhall	„	Tnship.	701
otherington	Gloucester	Hamlet	387	Grasby	Lincoln	Parish	433
oudhurst	Kent	Parish	2 778	Grasley	Berks	Tithing	72
ough Sq., Trinity	Middlesex	Ecl. Dis.	2 004	Grasmere	Westmoreland	Parish	2 347
oulsby	Lincoln	Parish	344	Grasmere	„	Tnship.	604
ourton	Denbigh	Tnship.	40	Grassendale, St.Mary	Lancaster	Ecl. Dis.	912
owdall	York	Tnship.	223	Grassington	York	Sub-dis.	2 764
ower	Glamorgan	District	8 316	Grassington	„	Tnship.	1 015
ower Eastern	„	Sub-dis.	4 962	Grassthorpe	Notts	Tnship.	75
ower Western	„	Sub-dis.	3 354	Grately	Hants	Parish	176
oxhill	Lincoln	Parish	1 192	Gratton	Derby	Tnship.	35
oxhill	York	Parish	63	Gratwich	Stafford	Parish	101
oytrey	Monmouth	Parish	668	Graveley	Cambs.	Parish	301
raby	Lincoln	Hamlet	19	Graveley	Herts	Parish	422
race Dieu Park	Monmouth	Parish	5	Graveney	Kent	Parish	234
rade	Cornwall	Parish	327	Gravenhurst, Lower	Beds	Parish	60
raffham	Hunts	Parish	328	Gravenhurst, Upper	„	Parish	337
raffham	Sussex	Parish	416	Gravesend	Kent	District	18 782
rafton	Cheshire	Tnship.	11	Gravesend	„	Sub-dis.	18 782
rafton	Hereford	Tnship.	93	Gravesend	„	Parish	7 885
rafton-Regis	Northampton	Parish	232	Gravesend	„	M. Bor.	18 782
rafton Underwood	„	Parish	294	Gravesend, St. James	„	Ecl. Dis.	3 215
rafton	Oxon	Tnship.	80	Graveship, Nether	Westmoreld.	Tnship.	441
rafton, East	Wilts	Ecl. Dis.	1 011	Grayingham	Lincoln	Parish	135
rafton Flyford	Worcester	Parish	225	Grayrigg	Westmoreland	Sub-dis.	4 026
rafton Manor	„	Parish	52	Grayrigg	„	Tnship.	251
raig	Monmouth	Hamlet	684	Grays	Essex	Sub-dis.	6 361
rain, St. James	Kent	Parish	255	Grays-Thurrock	„	Parish	2 209
rainsby	Lincoln	Parish	124	Grays Inn	Middlesex	Parish	308
rainthorpe	„	Parish	738	Grays Inn Lane	„	Sub-dis.	27 808
raizeley	Berks	Tithing	72	Gray's Inn Rd., Trinity	„	Ecl. Dis.	13 662
rampound	Cornwall	Sub-dis.	5 111	Gray's Inn Rd., St.Jude	„	Ecl. Dis.	8 427
rampound	„	Tnship.	573	Graysouthen	Cumberland.	Tnship.	758
ranby	Notts	Parish	479	Grazeley	Berks	Ecl. Dis.	648
randborough	Bucks	Parish	374	Greasbrough	York	Chap.	2 937
randborough	Warwick	Parish	462	Greasbrough, St. Mary	„	Ecl. Dis.	2 937
randpont	Berks	Tithing	487	Greasby	Cheshire	Tnship.	204
range	Cheshire	Tnship.	93	Greasley	Notts & Derby	Sub-dis.	18 028
range	Kent	Hamlet	206	Greasley	Notts	Parish	6 230
range de Lings	Lincoln	Parish	34	Great Abington	Cambs	Parish	330
ransmoor	York	Tnship.	108	Great Addington	Northampton	Parish	307
ransden, Little	Cambs	Parish	293	Great Alne	Warwick	Parish	347
ransden, Great	Hunts	Parish	641	Great Amwell	Herts	Parish	1 660
ranston	Pembroke	Parish	156	Gt. & L. Bourton	Oxon	Hamlet	560
rantchester	Cambs	Parish	696	Gt. & L. Carleton	Lancaster	Tnship.	363
rantham	Lincoln	L. Sub.	8 112	Gt. & L. Preston	York	Tnship.	541
rantham	{ Lincoln and Leicester }	District	28 886	Gt. & L. Singleton	Lancaster	Tnship.	338
				Gt. & L. Snarehill	Norfolk	Parish	46
rantham	Lincoln	Sub-dis.	16 270	Gt. & L. Usworth	Durham	Tnship.	3 677
rantham	„	Parish	11 116	Great Ashfield	Suffolk	Parish	408

Name of Place.	County.	Description.	Population.	Name of Place.	County.	Description.	Population.
Great Aycliffe	Durham	Tnship.	840	Great Claybrooke	Leicester	Parish	1 274
Great Ayton	York	Tnship.	1 450	Great Claybrooke	„	Tnship.	424
Great Baddow	Essex	Sub-dis.	6 857	Great Clifton	Cumberland	Tnship.	609
Great Baddow	„	Parish	2 061	Great Coates	Lincoln	Parish	206
Great Badminton	Gloucester	Parish	524	Great Coggeshall	Essex	Parish	3 679
Great Bardfield	Essex	Parish	1 065	Great Comberton	Worcester	Parish	247
Great Barford	Beds	Parish	907	Great Corby	Cumberland	Tnship.	323
Great Barlow	Derby	Chap.	682	Great Cornard	Suffolk	Parish	904
Great Barr	Stafford	Tnship.	1 075	Great Coxwell	Berks	Parish	371
Great Barrington	Gloucester	Parish	496	Great Creaton	Northampton	Parish	510
Great Bartlow	Cambs	Parish	120	Great Cressingham	Norfolk	Parish	530
Great Barton	Suffolk	Parish	848	Great Crosby	Lancaster	Chap.	3 794
Great Bavington	Nrthumberld.	Tnship.	61	Great Dalby	Leicester	Parish	484
Great Bealings	Suffolk	Parish	338	Great Doddington	Northampton	Parish	580
Great Beats	Lincoln	Parish	4	Great Driffield	York	Tnship.	4 405
Great Bedwin	Wilts	Parish	2 263	**Great Driffield**	„	Town	4 244
Great Bentley	Essex	Parish	1 033	Great Dunham	Norfolk	Parish	493
Great Berkhampstead	Herts	L. Sub.	13 872	Great Dunmow	Essex	Parish	2 976
Great Berkhampstead	„	Parish	3 585	Great Easton	„	Parish	891
Great Billing	Northampton	Parish	425	Great Easton	Leicester, &c.	Sub-dis.	3 135
Great Bircham	Norfolk	Parish	489	Great Easton	Leicester	Tnship.	590
Great Blakenham	Suffolk	Parish	291	Great Eccleston	Lancaster	Tnship.	641
Great Blencow	Cumberland	Tnship.	99	Great Edstone	York	Parish	152
Great Bolton	Lancaster	Tnship.	43 435	Great Edstone	„	Tnship.	135
Great Bookham	Surrey	Parish	1 106	Great Ellingham	Norfolk	Parish	717
Great Boughton	Ches. & Flint	District	58 501	Great Elm	Somerset	—	323
Great Boughton	Cheshire	Union	18 800	Great Eppleton	Durham	Tnship.	71
Great Boughton	„	Tnship.	1 387	Great Eversden	Cambs	Parish	314
Great Bowden	Leicester	Parish	3 697	Great Faringdon	Berks	Parish	3 702
Great Bowden	„	Tnship.	1 395	Great Faringdon	„	—	3 400
Great Bradley	Suffolk	Parish	460	Great Finborough	Suffolk	Parish	419
Great Bramshill	Hants	Tithing	141	Greatford	Lincoln	Parish	280
Great Braxted	Essex	Parish	384	Greatford	„	Tnship.	219
Great Bricett	Suffolk	Parish	207	Great Fransham	Norfolk	Parish	295
Great Brickhill	Bucks	Parish	590	Great Gaddesden	Herts	Parish	1 147
Great Bromley	Essex	Parish	758	Great Gidding	Hunts	Parish	543
Great Broughton	Cumberland	Tnship.	836	Great Givendale	York	Parish	86
Great Budworth	Cheshire	Parish	18 852	Great Givendale	„	Tnship.	60
Great Budworth	„	Tnship.	613	Great Glemham	Suffolk	Parish	354
Great Burdon	Durham	Tnship.	104	Great Glenn	Leicester	Parish	827
Great Burstead	Essex	Sub-dis.	4 803	Great Glenn	„	Tnship.	785
Great Burstead	„	Parish	2 095	Great Gonerby	Lincoln	Parish	1 145
Great Burstead	„	—	705	Great Gransden	Hunts	Parish	641
Great Busby	York	Tnship.	117	Great Greenford	Middlesex	Parish	557
Great Canfield	Essex	Parish	468	Great Grimsby	Lincoln	Sub-dis.	18 288
Great Carlton	Lincoln	Parish	338	Great Grimsby	„	Parish	11 067
Great Casterton	Rutland	Parish	323	**Great Grimsby**	„ {	M. Bor.	11 067
Great Catworth	Hunts	Parish	640			P. Bor.	15 060
Great Chalfield	Wilts	Parish	12	Great Habton	York	Tnship.	182
Great Chart	Kent	Parish	806	Great Hadham	Herts	Parish	1 172
Great Chesterford	Essex	Parish	1 027	Great Hale	Lincoln	Parish	1 059
Great Cheverell	Wilts	Parish	561	Great Hale	„	Tnship.	687
Great Chishall	Essex	Parish	473	Great Hallingbury	Essex	Parish	675
Great Clacton	„	Parish	1 280	Greatham	Durham	Parish	779

Name of Place.	County.	Description.	Population.	Name of Place.	County.	Description.	Population.
Greatham	Durham	Tnship.	724	Great Missenden	Bucks	Parish	2 250
Greatham	Hants	Parish	238	Great Mitton	York	Tnship.	184
Greatham	Sussex	Parish	51	Great Mollington	Cheshire	Tnship.	186
Great Hampden	Bucks	Parish	266	Great Mongeham	Kent	Parish	349
Great Hanwood	Salop	Parish	288	Great Moulton	Norfolk	Parish	442
Great Harrowden	Northampton	Parish	125	Great Munden	Herts	Parish	457
Great Harwood	Lancaster	Tnship.	4 070	Great Musgrave	Westmoreland	Parish	192
Great Harwood	„	Town	3 294	Great Ness	Salop	Parish	578
Great Haseley	Oxon	Parish	714	Great Neston	Cheshire	Tnship.	1 764
Great Haseley	„	Tnship.	498	Great Oakley	Essex	Parish	1 038
Great Hatfield	York	Tnship.	171	Great Oakley	Northampton	Parish	195
Great Hautbois	Norfolk	Parish	195	Great Ouseburn	York	District	11 534
Great Heaton	Lancaster	Tnship.	159	Great Ouseburn	„	Parish	655
Great Henny	Essex	Parish	363	Great Ouseburn	„	Tnship.	599
Great Heywood	Stafford	Ecl. Dis.	904	Great Oxendon	Northampton	Parish	238
Great Hinton	Wilts	Tithing	188	Great Packington	Warwick	Parish	336
Great Holland	Essex	Parish	467	Great Parndon	Essex	Parish	491
Great Horksley		Parish	769	Great Paxton	Hunts	Parish	411
Great Hormead	Herts	Parish	660	Great Plumstead	Norfolk	Parish	342
Great Horwood	Bucks	Parish	846	Great Pontou	Lincoln	Parish	561
Great Horwood	„	Tnship.	725	Great Poringland	Norfolk	Parish	464
Great Houghton	Northampton	Parish	365	Great Preston	York	Incor.	26 505
Great Houghton	York	Tnship.	309	Great Raveley	Hunts	Parish	318
Great Hucklow	Derby	Hamlet	242	Great Ribston, &c.	York	Tnship.	180
Great Ilford	Essex	Ward	4 523	Great Rissington	Gloucester	Parish	499
Great Ilford	„	Ecl. Dis.	3 688	Great Rollright	Oxon	Parish	410
Great Kelk	York	Tnship.	211	Great Rowsley	Derby	Tnship.	295
Great Kimble	Bucks	Parish	408	Great Ryburgh	Norfolk	Parish	556
Great Kyre	Worcester	Parish	152	Great Ryle	Nrthumbld.	Tnship.	99
Great Langton	York	Parish	239	Great Saling	Essex	Parish	361
Great Langton	„	Tnship.	137	Great Salkeld	Cumberland	Parish	502
Great Leighs	Essex	Parish	909	Great Salterns	Hants	Parish	29
Great Lever	Lancaster	Tnship.	722	Great Sampford	Essex	Parish	865
Gt. Lever, St. Michael	„	Ecl. Dis.	722	Great Sankey	Lancaster	Tnship.	563
Great Linford	Bucks	Parish	557	Great Saughall	Cheshire	Tnship.	545
Great Linstead	Suffolk	Parish	115	Great Saxham	Suffolk	Parish	270
Great Livermere	„	Parish	290	Great Shelford	Cambs	Sub-dis.	7 157
Great Longstone, &c.	Derby	Tnship.	683	Great Shelford	„	Parish	1 006
Great Lumley	Durham	Tnship.	1 555	Great Shurdington	Gloucester	Parish	164
Great Malvern	Worcester	L. Sub.	10 964	Great Smeaton	York	Parish	927
Great Malvern	„	Parish	6 245	Great Smeaton	„	Tnship.	208
Great Malvern	„	Tnship.	6 054	Great Snoring	Norfolk	Parish	594
Great Malvern	„	Town	4 484	Great Somerford	Wilts	Parish	532
Great Maplestead	Essex	Parish	462	Great Stainton	Durham	Parish	140
Great Marlow	Bucks	Sub-dis.	5 450	Great Stainton	„	Tnship.	110
Great Marlow	„	Parish	4 661	Great Stambridge	Essex	Parish	363
Great Marlow	Bucks & Berks	P. Bor.	6 496	Great Stanmore	Middlesex	Parish	1 318
Gt. Marsden, St.Jno.	Lancaster	Ecl. Dis.	3 057	Great Stanney	Cheshire	Tnship.	65
Great Marton	„	Hamlet	1 258	Great Staughton	Hunts	Parish	1 312
Great Massingham	Norfolk	Parish	934	Great Steeping	Lincoln	Parish	334
Great Melton	„	Parish	368	Great Stretton	Leicester	Tnship.	42
Great Meolse	Cheshire	Tnship.	184	Great Strickland	Westmoreland	Tnship.	308
Great Milton	Oxon	Parish	729	Great Stukeley	Hunts	Parish	453
Great Milton	„	Tnship.	630	Great Sturton	Lincoln	Parish	179

Name of Place.	County.	Description.	Population.	Name of Place.	County.	Description.	Population.
Great Sutton	Cheshire	Tnship	224	Greenhoe, South	Norfolk	Hund.	10 756
Great Tew	Oxon	Parish	454	Greenhoe, South	„	L. Sub.	10 756
Great Tey	Essex	Parish	818	Greenhow	York	Tnship.	155
Great Thurlow	Suffolk	Parish	423	Greenhow Hill, St. Mary „		Ecl: Dis.	748
Great Timble	York	Tnship.	175	Greenleighton	Nrthumberld.	Tnship.	29
Great Torrington	Devon	L. Sub.	13 344	Greens & Glantlees	„	Tnship.	22
Great Torrington	„	Sub-dis.	5 223	Greens-Norton	Northampton	Hund.	5 444
Great Torrington	„	Parish	3 298	Greens-Norton	„	Parish	903
Great Tosson, &c.	Nrthmberld.	Tnship.	113	Greenstead, Ongar	Essex	Parish	125
Great Totham	Essex	Parish	812	Greenstead, Colchester	„	Parish	789
Great Wakering	„	Sub-dis.	4 056	Greenstead St. James		Ecl. Dis.	659
Great Wakering	„	Parish	1 018	Greenwich	Kent & Surrey	District	127 670
Great Waldingfield	Suffolk	Parish	622	Greenwich East	Kent	Sub-dis.	18 306
Great Walsingham	Norfolk	Parish	512	Greenwich West	„	Sub-dis.	21 696
Great Waltham	Essex	Sub-dis.	5 595	Greenwich	„	Parish	40 002
Great Waltham	„	Parish	2 380	1. Church Ward		Ward	10 283
Great Warford	Cheshire	Tnship.	380	2. Ravensbourne Ward		Ward	9 760
Great Warley	Essex	Parish	1 220	3. Hospital Ward		Ward	13 748
Great Warley, Christch. „		Ecl. Dis.	1 734	4. Blackheath Ward		Ward	6 211
Great Washbourne	Gloucester	Parish	83	**Greenwich**	Kent & Surrey	P. Bor.	139 436
Great Weldon	Northampton	Parish	816	Greet	Salop	Parish	129
Great Weldon	„	—	302	Greet	„	Tnship.	26
Great Wenham	Suffolk	Parish	260	Greetham	Lincoln	Parish	152
Great Whelnetham	„	Parish	504	Greetham	Rutland	Parish	706
Great Whittington	Nrthmbld.	Tnship.	224	Greetwell	Lincoln	Parish	69
Great Wigborough	Essex	Parish	428	Greinton	Somerset	Parish	161
Great Wilbraham	Cambs	Parish	596	Grendon-Underwood	Bucks	Parish	451
Great Wishford	Wilts	Parish	381	Grendon-Bishop	Hereford	Parish	199
Great Witchingham	Norfolk	Parish	642	Grendon	Northampton	Parish	610
Great Witley	Worcester	Parish	445	Grendon	Warwick	Parish	561
Great Wolford	Warwick	Parish	534	Gresford	Denb. & Flint	Parish	4 417
Great Wolford	„	Tnship.	292	Gresford	Denbigh	Tnship.	658
Great Woolstone	Bucks	Parish	71	Gresham	Norfolk	Parish	345
Greatworth	Northampton	Parish	157	Gresley	Derby	Sub-dis.	9 039
Great Wratting	Suffolk	Parish	423	Gressenhall	Norfolk	Parish	991
Great Wymondley	Herts	Parish	314	Gressingham	Lancaster	Tnship.	158
Great Wyrley	Stafford	Tnship.	890	Gretton	Northampton	Parish	909
Great Wyrley, St. Mark „		Ecl. Dis.	2 067	Grewelthorpe	York	Tnship.	541
Great Yarmouth	Norfolk	L. Sub.	30 338	Grewelthorpe, St. James „		Ecl. Dis.	483
Great Yarmouth	„	Parish	30 338	Greys Forest	Northumberland	Tnship.	39
Great Yarmouth	Norf. & Suff.	Borough	34 810	Greystead	„	Parish	290
Great Yeldham	Essex	Parish	696	Greystoke	Cumberland	Sub-dis.	4 975
Green	Middlesex	Sub-dis.	31 789	Greystoke	„	Parish	2 885
Greenalgh, &c.	Lancaster	Tnship.	383	Greystoke	„	Tnship.	327
Greencroft	Durham	Tnship.	717	Greytree	Hereford	Hund.	13 882
Greenford, Great	Middlesex	Parish	557	Greywell	Hants	Parish	298
Greengate	Lancaster	Sub-dis.	37 534	Gribthorpe	York	Tnship.	41
Greenham	Berks	Tithing	1 167	Grimblethorpe	Lincoln	Parish	10
Greenham	„	Ecl. Dis.	593	Grimley	Worcester	Parish	776
Green Hammerton	York	Tnship.	333	Grimoldby	Lincoln	Parish	321
Greenhill	Lincoln	Parish	12	Grimsargh, &c.	Lancaster	Tnship.	247
Greenhithe, St. Mary	Kent	Ecl. Dis.	1 039	Grimsbury	Northampton	Hamlet	979
Greenhoe, North	Norfolk	Hund.	10 268	**Grimsby, Great**	Lincoln {	M. Bor.	11 067
Greenhoe, North	„	L. Sub.	10 268			P. Boro.	15 060

Name of Place.	County.	Description.	Population.	Name of Place.	County.	Description.	Population.
Grimsby, Great..	Lincoln ..	Parish	11 067	Guilden-Morden	Cambs ..	Parish	906
Grimsby, Little	,, ..	Parish	55	Guildford ..	Surrey ..	L. Sub.	46 372
Grimshoe ..	Norfolk ..	Hund.	7 554	Guildford ..	,, ..	District	29 330
Grimshoe w. Thetford ,, ..		L. Sub.	10 937	Guildford ..	,, ..	Sub-dis.	9 643
Grimstead, East	Wilts ..	Chap.	136	**Guildford** ..	,, ..	Borough	8 020
Grimstead, West	,, ..	Parish	251	Guildford ..	Sussex ..	Parish	152
Grimston ..	Leicester ..	Parish	190	Guilsborough ..	Northampton	Hund.	10 663
Grimston ..	York E. ..	Tnship.	64	Guilsborough ..	,,	Parish	996
Grimston ..	York W. ..	Tnship.	124	Guilsborough ..	,,	—	730
Grimston, North	York ..	Parish	181	Guilsfield ..	Montgomery	Parish	2 634
Grimstone ..	Norfolk ..	Parish	1 300	Guiltcross ..	Norfolk ..	Hund.	6 748
Grimstone ..	York ..	Tnship.	78	Guiltcross & Shropham ,, ..		L. Sub.	15 654
Grimsworth ..	Hereford ..	Hund	7 099	Guiltcross ..	,,	District	11 541
Grimthorpe ..	York ..	Tnship.	26	Guisbrough ..	York ..	District	22 128
Grindall ..	,, ..	Tnship.	174	Guisbrough ..	,, ..	Sub-dis.	4 762
Grindleton ..	,, ..	Tnship.	666	Guisbrough ..	,, ..	Parish	4 615
Grindleton ..	,, ..	Ecl. Dis.	920	Guisbrough ..	,, ..	Tnship.	4 084
Grindlow ..	Derby ..	Tnship.	75	**Guisbrough** ..	,, ..	Town	3 794
Grindon.. ..	Durham ..	Parish	343	Guiseley ..	,, ..	Parish	14 874
Grindon.. ..	,, ..	Tnship.	303	Guiseley ..	,, ..	Tnship.	2 566
Grindon..	Northumberland	Tnship.	128	**Guiseley** ..	,, ..	Town	2 226
Grindon.. ..	Stafford ..	Parish	371	Guist ..	Norfolk ..	Parish	361
Gringley ..	Notts ..	Sub-dis.	3 446	Guiting.. ..	Gloucester ..	Sub-dis.	5 974
Gringley on the Hill ,, ..		Parish	874	Guiting, Temple	,,	Parish	584
Grinsdale ..	Cumberland ..	Parish	100	Guiting, Temple	,, ..	Tnship.	573
Grinshill ..	Salop ..	Parish	317	Guldeford, East	Sussex ..	Parish	152
Grinstead, East .	Sussex ..	Parish	4 266	Gulval ..	Cornwall ..	Parish	1 743
Grinstead, West	,, ..	Parish	1 403	Gumfreston· ..	Pembroke ..	Parish	118
Grinton.. ..	York ..	Parish	4 537	Gumley.. ..	Leicester ..	Parish	214
Grinton.. ..	,, ..	Tnship.	611	Gunby, St. Nicholas	Lincoln ..	Parish	164
Gristhorpe ..	,, ..	Tnship.	207	Gunby, St. Peter	,, ..	Parish	82
Griston ..	Norfolk ..	Parish	257	Gunhouse ..	,, ..	Tnship.	197
Grittenham ..	Wilts ..	Tithing	192	Gunnerton,&c.	Northumberland	Tnship.	417
Grittleton ..	,, ..	Parish	349	Gunthorpe ..	Norfolk ..	Parish	249
Groby ..	Leicester ..	Hamlet	461	Gunthorpe ..	Northampton	Hamlet	66
Grondre ..	Pembroke ..	Hamlet	35	Gunthorpe ..	Notts ..	Tnship	331
Grosmont ..	Monmouth ..	Parish	743	Gunthorpe ..	Rutland ..	Hamlet	11
Grosmont, St. Matthew	York..	Ecl. Dis.	841	Gunthwaite ..	York ..	Tnship.	81
Groton	Suffolk ..	Parish	554	Gunton.. ..	Norfolk ..	Parish	78
Grouville ..	Isle of Jersey	Parish	2 628	Gunton.. ..	Suffolk ..	Parish	73
Grove	Berks ..	Tnship.	540	Gunwalloe ..	Cornwall ..	Parish	244
Grove	,, ..	Ecl. Dis.	540	Gussage, All Saints	Dorset ..	Parish	496
Grove	Bucks ..	Parish	19	Gussage, St. Michael	,, ..	Parish	311
Grove	Notts ..	Parish	113	Guston	Kent ..	Parish	436
Grovely Wood ..	Wilts ..	Parish	50	Guthlaxton ..	Leicester ..	Hund.	21 894
Grumbalds Ash .	Gloucester ..	Hund.	9 738	Guys Cliffe ..	Warwick ..	Parish	19
Grundisburgh ..	Suffolk ..	Parish	836	Guyson ..	Northumberland	Tnship.	217
Grunty-Fen ..	Cambs ..	—	19	Guyting, Lower	Gloucester ..	Parish	647
Grwynefawr ..	Brecon ..	Hamlet	19	Guyting, Temple	,, ..	Parish	584
Grwynefechan ..	,, ..	Hamlet	87	Guyting, Temple	,, ..	Tnship.	573
Gueldable ..	York ..	Tnship.	114	Guyzance	Northumberland	Tnship.	217
Guernsey, Isle of `		Island	29 804	Gwaenysgor ..	Flint ..	Parish	322
Guestling ..	Sussex ..	Parish	731	Gwarafog ..	Brecon ..	Hamlet	62
Guestwick ..	Norfolk ..	Parish	203	Gwastedin ..	Radnor ..	Tnship.	499

Name of Place.	County.	Description.	Population.	Name of Place.	County.	Description.	Population.
Gwehellog	Monmouth	Hamlet	331	Hackney, South	Middlesex	Sub-dis.	15 458
Gwenddwr	Brecon	Parish	528	Hackney	,,	Parish	76 687
Gwennap	Cornwall	Sub-dis.	12 895	1. Stamford Hill Ward		Ward	5 131
Gwennap	,,	Parish	10 537	2. West Ward		Ward	9 633
Gwennap, St. Days	,,	Ecl. Dis.	3 798	3. De Beauvoir Ward		Ward	10 997
Gwernafield	Flint	Tnship.	836	4. Dalston Ward		Ward	13 933
Gwernafield	,,	Ecl. Dis.	1 243	5. Hackney Ward		Ward	12 790
Gwernesney	Monmouth	Parish	57	6. Homerton Ward		Ward	9 272
Gwernhowel	Denbigh	Parish	107	7. South Ward		Ward	14 931
Gwernybwlch	Montgomery	Tnship.	545	Hackney, South	Middlesex	Ecl. Dis.	15 458
Gwersyllt	Denbigh	Tnship.	1 356	Hackney, West	,,	Ecl. Dis.	24 265
Gwersyllt	,,	Ecl. Dis.	1 593	Hackthorn	Lincoln	Parish	234
Gwinear	Cornwall	Parish	2 880	Haddenham	Bucks	Sub-dis.	4 652
Gwithian	,,	Parish	774	Haddenham	,,	Parish	1 623
Gwnnws	Cardigan	Sub-dis.	3 423	Haddenham	Cambs	Sub-dis.	3 998
Gwnnws	,,	Parish	1 295	Haddenham	,,	Parish	1 976
Gwnnws, Lower	,,	Tnship.	535	Haddington	Lincoln	Tnship.	131
Gwnnws, Upper	,,	Tnship.	760	Haddiscoe	Norfolk	Parish	355
Gwredog	Anglesey	Parish	42	Haddlesey, West	York	Tnship.	213
Gwsaney	Flint	Tnship.	252	Haddon, Nether	Derby	Parish	103
Gwyddelwern	Mer. & Denb.	Sub-dis.	5 479	Haddon, Over	,,	Tnship.	245
Gwyddelwern	Merioneth	Parish	1 541	Haddon	Hunts	Parish	146
Gwydir	Carnarvon	Tnship.	400	Haddon, East	Northampton	Parish	727
GwynfeQuarter Bach	Carm.	Hamlet	1 354	Haddon, West	,,	Parish	963
Gwynfil	Cardigan	Tnship.	386	Hadfield	Derby	Tnship.	2 722
Gwytherin	Denbigh	Parish	438	Hadham, Great	Herts	Parish	1 172
Gyffin	Carnarvon	Parish	715	Hadham, Little	,,	Parish	864
Gyffylliog	Denbigh	Sub-dis.	1 326	Hadleigh	Essex	Parish	451
Gyffylliog	,,	Parish	567	Hadleigh	Suffolk	Sub-dis.	9 634
				Hadleigh	,,	Parish	3 606
Habberley	Salop	Parish	112	Hadleigh	,,	Hamlet	180
Habblesthorpe	Notts	Parish	142	**Hadleigh**	,,	Town	2 779
Habergham-Eaves	Lancaster	Tnship.	18 013	Hadley	Berks	Tithing	230
All Saints	,,	Ecl. Dis.	2 822	Hadley	Middlesex	Parish	1 053
Trinity	,,	Ecl. Dis.	11 533	Hadley, Holy Trinity	Salop	Ecl. Dis.	1 654
Habrough	Lincoln	Parish	364	Hadlow	Kent	Parish	2 568
Habton, Great	York	Tnship.	182	Hadlow, St. Mark	Sussex	Ecl. Dis.	981
Habton, Little	,,	Tnship.	61	Hadnall	Salop	Chap.	456
Haburgh	Lincoln	Parish	364	Hadsor	Worcester	Parish	158
Haccombe	Devon	Parish	42	Hadspen	Somerset	Tithing	218
Hacconby	Lincoln	Parish	408	Hadstock	Essex	Parish	511
Hacconby	,,	Parish	318	Hadstone	Northumberland	Tnship.	92
Haceby	,,	Parish	66	Hagbourne	Berks	Parish	795
Hacheston	Suffolk	Tnship.	526	Hagbourne, East	,,	Liberty	631
Hackford by Reepham	Norf.	Parish	761	Hagbourne, West	,,	Liberty	164
Hackford by W'ndham	,,	Parish	222	Haggerstone, East	Middlesex	Sub-dis.	17 310
Hackforth	York	Tnship.	167	Haggerstone, West	,,	Sub-dis.	23 260
Hackington	Kent	Parish	616	Haggerstone, All Saints	,,	Ecl. Dis.	5 930
Hackleton	Northampton	Hamlet	535	Haggerstone, St. Mary	,,	Ecl. Dis.	30 436
Hackness	York	Parish	658	Haggerstone, St. Paul	,,	Ecl. Dis.	4 204
Hackness	,,	Tnship.	207	Hagley	Worcester	Parish	963
Hackney	Middlesex	District	83 295	Hagnaby	Lincoln	Parish	93
Hackney	,,	Sub-dis.	31 481	Hagworthingham	,,	Parish	666
Hackney Road	,,	Sub-dis.	26 298	Haigh	Lancaster	Tnship.	1 171

Name of Place.	County.	Description.	Population.	Name of Place.	County.	Description.	Population.
...igh and Aspull	Lancaster	Ecl. Dis.	5 461	Hallam, West	Derby	Parish	559
...aighton	„	Tnship.	222	Hallam, Nether	York	Tnship.	19 758
...aile	Cumberland	Parish	302	Hallam, Upper	„	Tnship.	1 643
...ailes	Gloucester	Parish	102	Hallaton	Leicester	Parish	696
...ailey	Oxon	Tnship.	1 316	Hallikeld	York	Wapen.	6 596
...ailsham	Sussex	L. Sub.	20 004	Hallikeld	„	L. Sub.	6 758
...ailsham	„	District	12 668	Halling	Kent	Parish	760
...ailsham	„	Sub-dis.	6 005	Hallingbury, Great	Essex	Parish	675
...ailsham	„	Parish	2 098	Hallingbury, Little	„	Parish	514
...ail-Weston	Hunts	Parish	440	Hallington	Lincoln	Parish	82
...ainford	Norfolk	Parish	643	Hallington	Northumberland	Tnship.	109
...ainton	Lincoln	Parish	302	Halliwell	Lancaster	Sub-dis.	6 908
...aisthorpe	York	Tnship.	157	Halliwell	„	Tnship.	5 953
...alam	Notts	Parish	382	Halliwell, St. Paul	„	Ecl. Dis.	2 712
...alberton	Devon	Hund.	2 765	Halliwell, St. Peter	„	Ecl. Dis.	3 241
...alberton	„	Parish	1 663	Halloughton	Notts	Parish	67
...aldenby	York	Tnship.	57	Hallow	Worcester	Parish	1 507
...alden, High	Kent	Parish	653	Halmer End	Stafford	Liberty	1 275
...ale	Cheshire	Tnship.	1 160	Halsall	Lancaster	Sub-dis.	1 952
...ale	Hants	Parish	158	Halsall	„	Parish	4 672
...ale	Lancaster	Sub-dis.	2 424	Halsall	„	Tnship.	1 204
...ale	„	Tnship.	648	Halse	Somerset	Parish	453
...ale	„	Ecl. Dis.	1 062	Halse Town	Cornwall	Ecl. Dis.	1 940
...ale, Great	Lincoln	Parish	1 059	Halsham	York	Parish	265
...ale, Great	„	Tnship.	687	Halstead	Essex	District	18 482
...ale, Little	„	Tnship.	372	Halstead	„	Sub-dis.	11 544
...ales	Norfolk	Parish	315	Halstead	„	Parish	6 917
...ales	Stafford	Hamlet	318	Halstead	„	Town	5 707
...ales, St. Mary	„	Ecl. Dis.	318	Halstead	Kent	Parish	323
...ale, St. John	Surrey	Ecl. Dis.	2 864	Halstead	Leicester	Tnship.	211
...alesowen	Worcester	L. Sub.	23 905	Halstock	Dorset	Parish	532
...alesowen	„	Sub-dis.	11 511	Halston	Salop	Parish	33
...alesowen	„	Parish	29 293	Halstow, High	Kent	Parish	363
...alesowen	„	Tnship.	2 911	Halstow, Lower	„	Parish	399
Halesowen	„	Town	2 911	Haltemprice	York	Parish	9
Halesworth	Suffolk	Sub-dis.	7 983	Haltham upon Bain	Lincoln	Parish	215
Halesworth	„	Parish	2 521	Halton	Bucks	Parish	147
Halesworth	„	Town	2 382	Halton	Cheshire	Tnship.	1 505
Halewood	Lancaster	Tnship.	1 205	Halton, St. Mary	„	Ecl. Dis.	1 541
Halewood, St. Nicholas	„	Ecl. Dis.	1 184	Halton	Lancaster	Parish	670
Haley Hill	York	Ecl. Dis.	5 235	Halton, East	Lincoln	Parish	727
Halford	Salop	Chap.	141	Halton Holegate	„	Parish	531
Halford	Warw. & Worc.	Sub-dis.	3 857	Halton, West	„	Parish	422
Halford	Warwick	Parish	814	Halton, West	„	Tnship.	315
Halfshire	Worcester	Hund.	157 244	Halton	Northumberland	Tnship.	45
Halghton	Flint	Tnship.	464	Halton Shields	„	Tnship.	69
Halifax	York	District	128 673	Halton, St. Clement	Sussex	Ecl. Dis.	1 035
Halifax	„	Sub-Dis.	36 437	Halton, East	York	Tnship.	94
Halifax	„	Parish	147 988	Halton-Gill	„	Tnship.	83
Halifax	„	Tnship.	28 990	Halton, West	„	Tnship.	131
Halifax, St. James	„	Ecl. Dis.	14 388	Haltwhistle	Northumberland	District	6 693
Halifax, St. John	„	Ecl. Dis.	1 667	Haltwhistle	„	Sub-dis.	6 693
Halifax	„	Borough	37 014	Haltwhistle	„	Parish	5 200
Halkin	Flint	Parish	1 334	Haltwhistle	„	Tnship.	1 749

Name of Place.	County.	Description.	Population.	Name of Place.	County.	Description.	Population.
Halvergate	Norfolk	Parish	541	Hampstead, St. Paul	Middlesex	Ecl. Dis.	2 333
Halwell, Harberton	Devon	Parish	357	Hampstead, South	„	Ecl. Dis.	2 945
Halwell, Blk. Torrington	„	Parish	257	Hampsthwaite	York	Parish	2 422
Ham, West	Essex	District	59 319	Hampsthwaite	„	Tnship.	513
Ham, West	„	Sub-dis.	25 195	Hampton	Cheshire	Tnship.	332
Ham, East	„	Parish	2 264	Hampton, High	Devon	Parish	386
Ham, West	„	Parish	38 331	Hampton Bishop	Hereford	Parish	1 047
Ham	Gloucester	Tithing	577	Hampton Bishop	„	—	245
Ham	Kent	Parish	47	Hampton Charles	„	Hamlet	87
Ham, High	Somerset	Parish	1 283	Hampton, New	„	Parish	8
Ham w. Hatch	Surrey	Hamlet	1 420	Hampton Wafer	„	Parish	11
Ham, St. Andrew	„	Ecl. Dis.	1 265	Hampton	Middlesex	Sub-dis.	6 538
Ham	Wilts	Parish	249	Hampton	„	Parish	5 355
Hambledon	Bucks	Parish	1 464	Hampton	„	—	3 361
Hambledon	Hants	Sub-dis.	5 221	Hampton Wick	„	Hamlet	1 994
Hambledon	„	Parish	1 891	Hampton Wick	„	Ecl. Dis.	1 994
Hambledon	Surrey & Sussex	District	13 907	Hampton Gay	Oxon	Parish	67
Hambledon	Surrey	Parish	557	Hampton Poyle	„	Parish	125
Hamble-le-Rice	Hants	Parish	509	Hampton Welsh	Salop	Parish	516
Hambleton	Lancaster	Chap.	366	Hampton and Claverton	Som.	Liberty	973
Hambleton	Rutland	Parish	323	Hampton in Arden	Warwick	Parish	3 161
Hambleton	York	Tnship.	544	Hampton in Arden	„	—	690
Hambridge, St. James	Somerset	Ecl. Dis.	556	Hampton Lucy	„	Parish	435
Hambrook, w. Frenchay	Glouc.	Tithing	1 621	Hampton	Worcester	Parish	513
Hameringham	Lincoln	Parish	188	Hampton Lovett	„	Parish	185
Hamerton	Hunts	Parish	167	Hamsey	Sussex	Parish	541
Hamfallow	Gloucester	Tithing	692	Hamstall, Ridware	Stafford	Parish	440
Hamfordshoe	Northampton	Hund.	10 898	Hamsterley	Durham	Sub-dis.	15 613
Haminiog	Cardigan	Tnship.	895	Hamsterley	„	Tnship.	522
Hammersmith, St. Paul	Midlx.	Sub-dis.	19 104	Hamworthy	Dorset	Parish	393
Hammersmith, St. Peter	„	Sub-dis.	5 415	Hanbury	Stafford	Parish	2 638
Hammersmith	„	Parish	24 519	Hanbury	„	Tnship.	543
St. John	„	Ecl. Dis.	3 918	Hanbury	Worcester	Parish	1 044
St. Peter	„	Ecl. Dis.	5 415	Hanby	Lincoln	Hamlet	67
St. Stephen	„	Ecl. Dis.	6 388	Hanchurch	Stafford	Tnship.	187
Hammerton, Green	York	Tnship.	333	Handborough	Oxon	Parish	1 059
Hammerwich	Stafford	Chap.	991	Handford	Stafford	Tnship.	832
Hammerwich	„	Ecl. Dis.	530	Handforth w. Bosden	Cheshire	Tnship.	2 408
Hammoon	Dorset	Parish	74	Handforth	„	Hamlet	629
Hampden, Great	Bucks	Parish	266	Handley	„	Parish	364
Hampden, Little	„	Parish	68	Handley	„	Tnship.	294
Hamphall Stubbs	York	Tnship.	11	Handley	Dorset	Parish	1 203
Hampnett	Gloucester	Parish	156	Handsworth	Stafford	Sub-dis.	11 459
Hampole	York	Tnship.	160	Handsworth	„	Parish	11 459
Hampreston	Dorset & Hants	Parish	1 341	Handsworth, St. Jas.	„	Ecl. Dis.	3 691
Hampshire		County	481 815	Handsworth w. Soho	„	—	10 398
Northern Division		N. Div.	157 495	Handsworth	York	Sub-dis.	3 951
Southern Division		S. Div.	268 958	Handsworth	„	Parish	3 951
Isle of Wight		Island	55 362	Hanford	Dorset	Parish	6
Hampstead Marshall	Berks	Parish	299	Hanford	Stafford	Ecl. Dis.	857
Hampstead Norris	„	Parish	1 358	Hang, East	York	Wapen.	10 378
Hampstead	Middlesex	District	19 106	Hang, West	„	Wapen.	14 788
Hampstead	„	Parish	19 106	Hang, East	„	L. Sub.	10 025
Hampstead, Christch.	„	Ecl. Dis.	2 557	Hang, West	„	L. Sub.	14 615

Name of Place.	County.	Description.	Population.	Name of Place.	County.	Description.	Population.
Hanging Heaton, St. Paul	York	Ecl. Dis.	2 219	Harborough, Market	Leicester	Chap.	2 302
Hanging-Houghton	Nrthptn.	Hamlet	96	Harborough Magna	Warwick	Parish	295
Hangleton	Sussex	Parish	51	Harbottle	Northumberland	Tnship.	159
Hanham	Gloucester	Tnship.	1 224	Harbridge	Hants	Parish	293
Hanham, Christch.	,,	Ecl. Dis.	1 271	Harbury	Warwick	Parish	1 206
Hankelow	Cheshire	Tnship.	197	Harby	Leicester	Parish	655
Hankerton	Wilts	Parish	393	Harby	Notts	Tnship.	428
Hankerton	,,	—	285	Hardenhuish	Wilts	Parish	117
Hanley	Stafford	Sub-dis.	16 848	Hardham	Sussex	Parish	87
Hanley	,,	Tnship.	14 678	Hardhorn w. Newton	Lancaster	Tnship.	386
Hanley	,,	M. Bor.	31 953	Hardingham	Norfolk	Parish	527
Hanley	Worcester	Sub-dis.	11 377	Hardingstone	Northampton	District	9 928
Hanley Castle	,,	Parish	1 733	Hardingstone	,,	Sub-dis.	3 657
Hanley Child or Low	,,	Chap.	199	Hardingstone	,,	Parish	1 915
Hanley William or Up	,,	Parish	120	Hardington	Somerset	Parish	22
Hanlith	York	Tnship.	40	Hardington-Mandeville	,,	Parish	668
Hanmer	Flint	Sub-dis.	2 519	Hardley	Norfolk	Parish	271
Hanmer	,,	Parish	2 519	Hardmead	Bucks	Parish	91
Hanmer	,,	Tnship.	491	Hardres, Lower	Kent	Parish	233
Hannah	Lincoln	Parish	140	Hardres, Upper	,,	Parish	271
Hanney	Berks	Parish	1 096	Hardwick	Lincoln	Tnship.	82
Hanningfield, East	Essex	Parish	453	Hardwick	Norfolk	Parish	227
Hanningfield, South	,,	Parish	235	Hardwick	Northampton	Parish	83
Hanningfield, West	,,	Parish	527	Hardwick	Oxon	Parish	59
Hannington	Hants	Parish	264	Hardwick	,,	Hamlet	134
Hannington	Northampton	Parish	226	Hardwick	Suffolk	Parish	25
Hannington	Wilts	Parish	378	Hardwick, East	York	Tnship.	213
Hanover-square	Middlesex	L. Sub.	87 771	Hardwick, West	,,	Tnship.	86
Hanover-square	,,	Sub-dis.	19 773	Hardwicke	Bucks	Parish	708
Hanover-sq., St. Geo.	,,	Parish	87 771	Hardwicke	,,	—	283
Hanover Chapel	,,	Ecl. Dis.	5 923	Hardwicke	Cambs	Parish	240
Hanover-sq., St. Mark	,,	Ecl. Dis.	4 972	Hardwicke	Gloucester	Parish	625
Hanslope	Bucks	Parish	1 792	Hardwicke	Monmouth	Hamlet	130
Hanthorpe	Lincoln	Hamlet	154	Hareby	Lincoln	Parish	93
Hanwell	Middlesex	Parish	2 687	Harefield	Middlesex	Parish	1 567
Hanwell	Oxon	Parish	285	Harehope	Northumberland	Tnship.	38
Hanwood, Great	Salop	Parish	288	Harescomb	Gloucester	Parish	138
Hanworth, Cold	Lincoln	Parish	91	Haresfield	,,	Sub-dis.	3 314
Hanworth	Middlesex	Parish	763	Haresfield	,,	Parish	612
Hanworth	Norfolk	Parish	227	Hareup	Northumberland	Tnship.	38
Happing	,,	Hund.	6 987	Harewood	Hereford	Parish	101
Happisburgh	,,	Parish	584	Harewood	York	Sub-dis.	2 762
Hapsford	Cheshire	Tnship.	84	Harewood	,,	Parish	2 396
Hapton	Lancaster	Tnship.	1 003	Harewood	,,	Tnship.	834
Hapton	Norfolk	Parish	196	Harewood's End	Hereford	L. Sub.	8 546
Harberton	Devon	Sub-dis.	2 575	Harford	Devon	Parish	158
Harberton	,,	Parish	1 221	Hargate Manor	Derby	Parish	7
Harbertonford	,,	Ecl. Dis.	533	Hargham	Norfolk	Parish	83
Harbledown	Kent	Parish	655	Hargrave	Northampton	Parish	310
Harborne	Stafford	Sub-dis.	16 996	Hargrave	Suffolk	Parish	520
Harborne	,,	Parish	16 996	Harkstead	,,	Parish	380
Harborne	,,	Tnship.	3 617	Harlaston	Stafford	Tnship.	289
Harborne Heath	,,	Ecl. Dis.	2 289	Harlaston	,,	Ecl. Dis.	255
Harborne North	,,	Ecl. Dis.	5 550	Harlaxton	Lincoln	Parish	488

Name of Place.	County.	Description.	Population.	Name of Place.	County.	Description.	Population.
Harle, Little	Northumberland	Tnship.	80	Harrogate, High	York	Ecl. Dis.	4 327
Harle, West	,,	Tnship.	17	Harrogate, Low	,,	Ecl. Dis.	993
Harleston	Norfolk	Sub-dis.	5 922	Harrold	Beds	Sub-dis.	3 238
Harleston	,,	Chap.	1 302	Harrold		Parish	1 119
Harleston	Suffolk	Parish	65	Harroldston, East	Pembroke	Parish	281
Harlestone	Northampton	Parish	651	Harroldston, West	,,	Parish	149
Harleton	Cambs	Parish	302	Harrow	Middlesex	Sub-dis.	7 374
Harley	Salop	Parish	220	Harrow on the Hill	,,	Parish	5 525
Harling, East	Norfolk	Parish	1 109	Harrow Weald	,,	Ecl. Dis.	1 119
Harling, West	,,	Parish	124	Harrowby	Lincoln	Tnship.	118
Harlington	Beds	Parish	529	Harrowden, Great	Northampton	Parish	125
Harlington	Middlesex	Parish	1 159	Harrowden, Little	,,	Parish	679
Harlow	Essex	Hund.	8 351	Harston	Cambs	Parish	782
Harlow	,,	Sub-dis.	5 544	Harston	Leicester	Parish	164
Harlow	,,	Parish	2 377	Harswell	York	Parish	89
Harlow, St. John	,,	Ecl. Dis.	694	Hart	Durham	Parish	1 420
Harlow Hill	Northumberland	Tnship.	113	Hart	,,	Tnship.	297
Harlsey, East	York	Parish	430	Hartburn, East	,,	Tnship.	163
Harlsey, West	,,	Tnship.	61	Hartburn	Northumberland	Parish	1 526
Harlthorpe	,,	Tnship.	99	Hartburn	,,	Tnship.	31
Harmby	,,	Tnship.	263	Hartburn-Grange	,,	Tnship.	90
Harmondsworth	Middlesex	Parish	1 385	Hartcliffe, &c.	Somerset	Hund.	6 879
Harmston	Lincoln	Parish	414	Hartest	Suffolk	Sub-dis.	6 428
Harnham	Northumberland	Tnship.	45	Hartest	,,	Parish	744
Harnham, East	Wilts	Ecl. Dis.	461	Hartfield	Sussex	Parish	1 451
Harnham, West	,,	Parish	285	Hartfield, North	,,	Division	449
Harnhill	Gloucester	Parish	88	Hartfield, South	,,	Division	1 002
Harpenden	Herts	Sub-dis.	7 000	Hartford	Cheshire	Tnship.	987
Harpenden	,,	Parish	2 164	Hartford	Hunts	Parish	341
Harpford	Devon	Parish	243	Hartford, East	Northumbld.	Tnship.	13
Harpham	York	Parish	274	Hartford, West	,,	Tnship.	62
Harpley	Norfolk	Parish	479	Hartgrove	Dorset	Tithing	185
Harpole	Northampton	Parish	833	Harthill	Cheshire	Parish	122
Harpsden	Oxon	Parish	261	Harthill	Derby	Tnship.	81
Harpswell	Lincoln	Parish	104	Harthill	York	Wapen.	51 296
Harpton, Lower	Hereford	Tnship.	85	Harthill w. Woodall	,,	Parish	673
Harpton, Upper	Radnor	Tnship.	186	Harting	Sussex	Sub-dis.	4 537
Harptree	Somerset	Sub-dis.	3 562	Harting	,,	Parish	1 247
Harptree, East	,,	Parish	657	Hartington	Derby	Sub-dis.	1 652
Harptree, West	,,	Parish	539	Hartington	,,	Parish	2 410
Harpurhey	Lancaster	Tnship.	827	Hartington Mid. Qr.	,,	Tnship.	326
Harpurhey w. Moston	,,	Ecl. Dis.	5 126	Hartington Nether Qr.	,,	Tnship.	399
Harraby	Cumberland	Tnship.	73	Hartington Town Qr.	,,	Tnship.	495
Harraton	Durham	Sub-dis.	13 423	Hartington Upper Qr.	,,	Tnship.	1 190
Harraton	,,	Tnship.	1 642	Hartington	Northumberland	Tnship.	81
Harrietsham	Kent	Parish	624	Hartington Hall	,,	Tnship.	25
Harrington	Cumberland	Sub-dis.	6 765	Hartismere	Suffolk	Hund.	15 235
Harrington	,,	Parish	1 788	Hartismere	,,	District	17 665
Harrington	Lincoln	Parish	104	Hartland	Devon	Hund.	4 197
Harrington	Northampton	Parish	222	Hartland	,,	Sub-dis.	3 774
Harringworth	,,	Parish	360	Hartland	,,	Parish	1 916
Harrogate	York	Sub-dis.	8 605	Hartle	Derby	Tnship.	81
Harrogate	,,	Town	4 737	Hartlebury	Worcester	Parish	2 115
Harrogate w. Bilton	,,	Tnship.	4 563	Hartlebury	,,	Tnship.	1 853

Name of Place.	County.	Description.	Population.	Name of Place.	County.	Description.	Population.
Hartlepool	Durham	District	29 153	Hascombe	Surrey	Parish	396
Hartlepool	,,	Sub-dis.	29 153	Haselbeech	Northampton	Parish	180
Hartlepool	,,	Parish	12 245	Haselbury Bryan	Dorset	Parish	761
Hartlepool	,,	M.Bor.	12 245	Haselbury Plucknett	Somerset	Parish	834
Hartlepool, Trinity	,,	Ecl. Dis.	5 638	Haseley	Warwick	Parish	209
Hartlepool, West, Christch.	,,	Ecl. Dis.	9 708	Haseley, Great	Oxon	Parish	714
Hartlepool, West	,,	Town	12 603	Haseley, Great	,,	—	498
Hartley	Kent	Parish	244	Haseley, Little	,,	Tnship.	127
Hartley	Northumberland	Tnship.	1 567	Haselor	Stafford	Parish	27
Hartley	Westmoreland	Tnship.	215	Haselor	Warwick	Parish	355
Hartleyburn	Northumberland	Tnship.	439	Hasfield	Gloucester	Parish	299
Hartley Dummer	Berks	Liberty	845	Hasguard	Pembroke	Parish	145
Hartley Mauditt	Hants	Parish	92	Hasketon	Suffolk	Parish	483
Hartley Westpall	,,	Parish	343	Hasland	Derby	Tnship.	1 999
Hartley Wintney	,,	District	11 480	Hasland, St. Paul	,,	Ecl. Dis.	1 107
Hartley Wintney	,,	Sub-dis.	4 965	Haslemere	Surrey	Parish	952
Hartley Wintney	,,	Parish	1 746	Haslingden	Lancaster	District	69 781
Hartlington	York	Tnship.	107	Haslingden	,,	Sub-dis.	10 320
Hartlip	Kent	Parish	319	Haslingden	,,	Tnship.	10 109
Hartoft	York	Tnship.	180	**Haslingden**	,,	Town	6 929
Harton	Durham	Tnship.	877	Haslingfield	Cambs	Parish	762
Harton	York	Tnship.	125	Haslington	Cheshire	Tnship.	1 215
Hartpury	Gloucester	Parish	843	Haslington, St. Matthew	,,	Ecl. Dis.	1 215
Harts Grounds	Lincoln	—	61	Hassall	,,	Tnship.	246
Hartshead	Lancaster	Sub-dis.	19 245	Hassingham	Norfolk	Parish	118
Hartshead	,,	Par. div.	12 454	Hassop	Derby	Tnship.	189
Hartshead	York	Hamlet	779	Hastingleigh	Kent	Parish	198
Hartsheath	Flint	Tnship.	188	Hastings	Sussex	Rape	39 294
Hartshill	Stafford	Ecl. Dis.	1 835	Hastings	,,	L. Sub.	16 274
Hartshill	Warwick	Hamlet	1 129	Hastings	,,	District	26 631
Hartshill, Trinity	,,	Ecl. Dis.	1 129	**Hastings**	,,	{ M. Bor.	22 837
Hartshorn	Derby & Leic.	Sub-dis.	6 207			P. Bor.	22 910
Hartshorn	Derby	Parish	1 541	Haswell	Durham	Tnship.	4 165
Hartwell	Bucks	Parish	137	Hatcham	Surrey	Manor	5 731
Hartwell	Northampton	Parish	542	Hatcham, St. Jas.	Sur. & Kent	Ecl. Dis.	9 887
Hartwell Lodge	,,	—	4	Hatch-Beauchamp	Somerset	Parish	324
Hartwith w. Winsley	York	Tnship.	1 227	Hatch, West	,,	Parish	432
Hartwith w. Winsley	,,	Ecl. Dis.	1 227	Hatcliffe	Lincoln	Parish	159
Harty	Kent	Parish	159	Hatfield	Essex	Sub-dis.	4 554
Harum	York	Tnship.	447	Hatfield, Broad Oak	,,	Parish	1 960
Harvington	Worcester	Parish	452	Hatfield Heath	,,	Ecl. Dis.	622
Harwell	Berks	Parish	876	Hatfield-Peverel	,,	Parish	1 311
Harwell	Notts	Hamlet	127	Hatfield	Hereford	Parish	180
Harwich	Essex	Sub-dis.	5 070	Hatfield	Herts	District	8 400
Harwich	,,	Borough	5 070	Hatfield	,,	Union	6 189
Harwood	Lancaster	Sub-dis.	10 220	Hatfield	,,	Sub-dis.	6 189
Harwood, Great	,,	Tnship.	4 070	Hatfield	,,	Parish	3 871
Harwood, Little	,,	Tnship.	270	Hatfield	York	Parish	2 564
Harwood	,,	Tnship.	2 055	Hatfield	,,	Tnship.	1 813
Harwood, Christch.	,,	Ecl. Dis.	1 525	Hatfield, Great	,,	Tnship.	171
Harwood	Northumberland	Tnship.	36	Hatfield, Little	,,	Tnship.	40
Harwood Dale	York	Tnship.	214	Hatford	Berks	Parish	122
Harworth	Notts	Parish	925	Hatherleigh	Devon	L. Sub.	9 767
Hasbury	Worcester	Tnship.	1 485	Hatherleigh	,,	Sub-dis.	3 986

Name of Place.	County.	Description.	Population.	Name of Place.	County.	Description.	Population.
Hatherleigh ..	*Devon* ..	Parish	1 645	Haverholme Priory *Lincoln* ..		Parish	15
Hatherley, Down	*Gloucester* ..	Parish	192	Havering atte Bower *Essex* ..		Liberty	9 260
Hatherley, Up ..	,, ..	Parish	68	Havering atte Bower ,, ..		Parish	429
Hathern ..	*Leicester* ..	Parish	1 112	Haveringland ..	*Norfolk* ..	Parish	131
Hatherop ..	*Gloucester* ..	Parish	323	Haversham ..	*Bucks* ..	Parish	288
Hathersage ..	*Derby* ..	Parish	2 391	Haverstock Hill, Trinity *Mdlx.*		Ecl. Dis.	16 821
Hathersage ..	,, ..	Tnship.	990	Haverthwaite ..	*Lancaster* ..	Ecl. Dis.	1 099
Hatherton ..	*Cheshire* ..	Tnship.	377	Hawarden	*Flint & Chesh.*	Union	9 528
Hatherton ..	*Stafford* ..	Tnship.	415	Hawarden .. ,, ,,		Sub-dis.	9 528
Hatley, East ..	*Cambs* ..	Parish	139	Hawarden ..	*Flint* ..	Parish	7 044
Hatley, St. George ,,	..	Parish	164	Hawarden .. ,, ..		Tnship.	652
Hattersley ..	*Cheshire* ..	Tnship.	400	Hawerby w. Beesby *Lincoln* ..		Parish	91
Hatton, Waverton ,,	..	Tnship.	146	Hawes	*York* ..	Sub-dis.	2 442
Hatton, Runcorn ,,	..	Tnship.	357	Hawes	,, ..	Tnship.	1 727
Hatton ..	*Derby* ..	Tnship.	346	Hawick ..	*Northumberland*	Tnship.	5
Hatton ..	*Lincoln* ..	Parish	199	Hawkchurch ..	*Dorset* ..	Parish	706
Hatton ..	*Warwick* ..	Parish	1 259	Hawkedon ..	*Suffolk* ..	Parish	321
Hatton ..	,, ..	Tnship.	674	Hawkesbury ..	*Gloucester* ..	Sub-dis.	4 156
Haugh ..	*Lincoln* ..	Parish	17	Hawkesbury ..	,, ..	Parish	2 173
Haugham ..	,, ..	Parish	115	Hawkesbury ..	,, ..	Tithing	466
Haughley ..	*Suffolk* ..	Parish	987	Hawkesdale ..	*Cumberland*	Tnship.	336
Haughmond Demesne *Salop* ..		Parish	141	Hawkhurst ..	*Kent* ..	Sub-dis.	6 724
Haughton ..	*Cheshire* ..	Tnship.	172	Hawkhurst ..	,, ..	Parish	2 715
Haughton ..	*Durham* ..	Tnship.	536	Hawkinge ..	,, ..	Parish	133
Haughton-le-Skerne ,,	..	Parish	1 473	Hawkley ..	*Hants* ..	Parish	312
Haughton ..	*Lancaster* ..	Tnship.	3 371	Hawkridge ..	*Somerset* ..	Parish	110
Haughton	*Northumberland*	Tnship.	105	Hawkshead ..	*Lancaster* ..	Sub-dis.	3 599
Haughton ..	*Notts* ..	Parish	61	Hawkshead ..	,, ..	Parish	2 081
Haughton ..	*Stafford* ..	Parish	516	Hawkshead, &c. ..	,, ..	Tnship.	1 144
Haukswell ..	*York* ..	Parish	273	Hawkswick ..	*York* ..	Tnship.	55
Haukswell, East. ,,	..	Tnship.	98	Hawksworth ..	*Notts* ..	Parish	176
Haukswell, West ,,	..	Tnship.	58	Hawksworth ..	*York* ..	Tnship.	237
Haulgh ..	*Lancaster* ..	Tnship.	2 018	Hawkwell ..	*Essex* ..	Parish	334
Haunton ..	*Stafford* ..	Hamlet	185	Hawkwell	*Northumberland*	Tnship.	165
Hautbois, Great . *Norfolk* ..		Parish	195	Hawley & Minley *Hants* ..		Tithing	1 119
Hautbois, Little . ,,	..	Parish	25	Hawley	,, ..	Ecl. Dis.	805
Hauxley	*Northumberland*	Tnship.	937	Hawling ..	*Gloucester* ..	Parish	171
Hauxton ..	*Cambs* ..	Parish	262	Hawn ..	*Worcester* ..	Tnship.	194
Havant ..	*Hants* ..	District	7 212	Hawnby ..	*York* ..	Parish	746
Havant ..	,, ..	Sub-dis.	7 212	Hawnby ..	,, ..	Tnship.	295
Havant ..	,, ..	Parish	2 470	Hawnes ..	*Beds* ..	Parish	932
Haven Bank, &c. *Lincoln* ..		Parish	37	Haworth ..	*York* ..	Sub-dis.	5 896
Havengore ..	*Essex* ..	Parish	25	Haworth ..	,, ..	Tnship.	5 896
Haverah Park ..	*York* ..	Parish	100	Hawridge ..	*Bucks* ..	Parish	276
Haverbrack ..	*Westmoreland*	Tnship.	77	Hawsker w. Stainsacre *York* ..		Tnship.	914
Havercroft, &c...	*York* ..	Tnship.	109	Hawstead ..	*Suffolk* ..	Parish	446
Haverfordwest ..	*Pembroke*	District	37 343	Hawthorn ..	*Durham* ..	Tnship.	227
Haverfordwest ..	,,	Sub-dis.	12 330	Hawthorpe ..	*Lincoln* ..	Hamlet	86
Haverfordwest, St. Thos. ,,		Parish	2 038	Hawton ..	*Notts* ..	Parish	246
Haverfordwest	,,	Borough	7 019	Haxby ..	*York* ..	Parish	597
Haverfordwest, P. Dis. of ,,		Boros.	9 821	Haxey ..	*Lincoln* ..	Parish	2 157
Havergate Island *Suffolk* ..		Parish	6	Hay ..	*Brecon* ..	L. Sub.	3 071
Haverhill ..	*Suff. & Essex*	Sub-dis.	7 328	Hay ..	*Brecon, &c.* ..	District	10 819
Haverhill .. ,, ,,		Parish	2 434	Hay ..	*Brecon & Heref.*	Sub-dis.	4 822

Name of Place.	County.	Description.	Population.	Name of Place.	County.	Description.	Population.
Hay	Brecon	Parish	1 998	Headley	Hants	Sub-dis.	3 128
Hay	"	—	680	Headley	"	Incor.	3 128
Hay	"	Town	1 318	Headley	"	Parish	1 320
Haydock	Lancaster	Tnship.	3 615	Headley	Surrey	Parish	322
Haydon	Dorset	Parish	131	Headon w. Upton	Notts	Parish	282
Haydon	Northumberland	Parish	2 221	Heage	Derby	Chap.	2 286
Haydor	Lincoln	Parish	565	Heage	"	Ecl. Dis.	2 286
Haydor	"	Tnship.	346	Healaugh	York	Parish	228
Hayes	Kent	Parish	598	Healey, Christch.	Lancaster	Ecl. Dis.	2 758
Hayes	Middlesex	Sub-dis.	9 157	Healey and Comb Hill	Nrthmb.	Tnship.	32
Hayes	"	Parish	7 134	Healey Mount	"	Tnship.	43
Hayes	"	—	2 650	Healey w. Sutton	York	Tnship.	317
Hayfield	Derby & Ches.	District	32 176	Healey, St. Paul.	"	Ecl. Dis.	900
Hayfield	" "	Sub-dis.	10 976	Healing	Lincoln	Parish	96
Hayfield	" "	Union	10 976	Healy	Northumberland	Tnship.	71
Hayfield	Derby	Tnship.	2 156	Healyfield	Durham	Tnship.	336
Hayfield	"	Ecl. Dis.	3 359	Heanor	Derby	Parish	8 080
Hayling, North.	Hants	Parish	262	Heanor	"	Tnship.	4 084
Hayling, South.	"	Parish	777	Heanton Punchardon	Devon	Parish	540
Hayridge	Devon	Hund.	12 413	Heap	Lancaster	Tnship.	17 353
Hayscastle	Pembroke	Parish	297	Heap, St. James.	"	Ecl. Dis.	7 633
Hayton	Cumberland	Sub-dis.	2 583	Heapey	"	Tnship.	396
Hayton	"	Parish	1 256	Heapham	Lincoln	Parish	129
Hayton	"	Tnship.	534	Heath and Reach	Beds	Hamlet	953
Hayton and Mealo	"	Tnship.	390	Heath	Derby	Parish	369
Hayton	Notts	Parish	258	Heath and Jay.	Hereford	Tnship.	62
Hayton	York	Parish	478	Heath, Charnock	Lancaster	Tnship.	772
Hayton	"	Tnship.	210	Heath	Salop	Tnship.	38
Haytor	Devon	Hund.	41 997	Heath Farm	"	—	6
Haywards Fields	Gloucester	Parish	5	Heather	Leicester	Parish	371
Haywood	Hereford	Parish	102	Heathfield	Somerset	Parish	124
Haywood Oaks	Notts	Parish	11	Heathfield	Sussex	Parish	1 892
Hazeleigh	Essex	Parish	106	Heathpool	Northumberland	Tnship.	21
Hazlebadge	Derby	Lordsp.	58	Heathylee	Stafford	Tnship.	504
Hazlegrove	Cheshire	Sub-dis.	4 917	Heaton	Lancaster	Tnship.	955
Hazlemere	Bucks	Ecl. Dis.	966	Heaton	"	Sub-dis.	3 455
Hazleton	Gloucester	Parish	308	Heaton w. Oxcliffe	"	Tnship.	165
Hazleton	"	—	185	Heaton, Great	"	Tnship.	159
Hazlewood	Derby	Tnship.	392	Heaton, Little	"	Tnship.	838
Hazlewood, St. John	"	Ecl. Dis.	719	Heaton Mersey	"	Ecl. Dis.	1 875
Hazlewood	Suffolk	Parish	91	Heaton Norris	"	Sub-dis.	17 696
Hazlewood and Storiths	York	Tnship.	185	Heaton Norris	"	Tnship.	16 333
Hazley Heath	Hants	Tithing	398	Heaton Norris Ch. ch.	"	Ecl. Dis.	9 625
Hazon	Northumberland	Tnship.	116	Heaton Norris St. Thos.	"	Ecl. Dis.	6 179
Heacham	Norfolk	Parish	990	Heaton	Northumberland	Tnship.	376
Headbourn Worthy	Hants	Parish	194	Heaton	Stafford	Tnship.	396
Headcorn	Kent	Sub dis.	5 286	Heaton	York	Tnship.	1 673
Headcorn	"	Parish	1 339	Heavitree	Devon	Sub-dis.	6 556
Headingley w. Burley	York	Tnship.	9 674	Heavitree	"	Parish	3 133
Headington	Oxon	District	17 185	Hebburn	Nrthumbld.	Parish	595
Headington	"	Parish	2 110	Hebburn	"	Tnship.	125
Headington Quarry	"	Ecl. Dis.	684	Hebburn (Chillingham P.)	"	Tnship.	77
Headlam	Durham	Tnship.	102	Hebden	York	Tnship.	435
Headless Cross	Warwick	Ecl. Dis.	1 743	Hebden Bridge	"	Sub-dis.	10 826

Name of Place.	County.	Description.	Population.	Name of Place.	County.	Description.	Population.
Hebden Bridge..	York ..	Ecl. Dis.	3 385	Helmsley ..	York ..	Parish	3 429
Heck	,, ..	Tnship.	278	Helmsley ..	,, ..	Tnship.	1 384
Heckfield ..	Hants ..	Parish	1 200	Helmsley Gate ..	,, ..	Parish	200
Heckfield ..	,, ..	—	570	Helmsley, Upper	,,	Parish	78
Heckingham ..	Norfolk ..	Parish	317	Helperby	,, ..	Tnship.	639
Heckington ..	Lincoln ..	Sub-dis.	4 366	Helperthorpe	,, ..	Parish	146
Heckington ..	,, ..	Parish	1 725	Helpringham ..	Lincoln ..	Parish	912
Heckmondwike..	York ..	Tnship.	6 344	Helpstone ..	Northampton	Parish	763
Heckmondwike	,,	Town	8 680	Helsby ..	Cheshire ..	Tnship.	570
Heckmondwike, St. Jas.	,,	Ecl. Dis.	6 344	Helsington ..	Westmoreland	Tnship.	302
Heddington ..	Wilts ..	Parish	362	Helston ..	Cornwall ..	District	30 036
Heddon, East	Northumberland	Tnship.	43	Helston ..	,, ..	Sub-dis.	5 499
Heddon on Wall	,,	Parish	744	Helston ..	,, ..	Chap.	3 843
Heddon on Wall	,,	Tnship.	385	**Helston** ..	,,	{ M. Bor.	3 843
Heddon, West ..	,,	Tnship.	36			{ P. Bor.	8 497
Hedenham ..	Norfolk ..	Parish	280	Helston ..	,,	Ecl. Dis.	3 841
Hedgeley	Northumberland	Tnship.	104	Helton ..	Westmoreland	Tnship.	180
Hedgerley ..	Bucks ..	Parish	153	Hemblington ..	Norfolk ..	Parish	219
Hedgerley Dean.	,, ..	Hamlet	227	Hemel Hempstead	Herts ..	L. Sub.	14 527
Hedingham ..	Essex ..	Sub-dis.	6 938	Hemel Hempstead	,,	District	13 922
Hedingham Castle	,, ..	Parish	1 203	Hemel Hempstead	,,	Sub-dis.	7 948
Hedingham, Sible	,, ..	Parish	2 123	Hemel Hempstead	,,	Parish	7 948
Hedley ..	Durham ..	Tnship.	44	**Hemel Hempstead**	,,	Town	2 974
Hedley Hope ..	,, ..	Tnship.	93	Hemingbrough..	York ..	Parish	2 297
Hedley ..	Northumberland	Tnship.	241	Hemingbrough..	,,	Tnship.	579
Hedley Woodside	,,	Tnship.	69	Hemingby ..	Lincoln ..	Parish	473
Hedon	York ..	Sub-dis.	2 053	Hemingford Abbotts	Hunts ..	Parish	518
Hedon	,, ..	Parish	975	Hemingford Grey	,, ..	Parish	1 103
Hedsor	Bucks ..	Parish	175	Hemingstone ..	Suffolk ..	Parish	395
Hedworth, &c...	Durham ..	Tnship.	6 494	Hemington ..	Leicester ..	Tnship.	385
Heeley	York ..	Hamlet	2 453	Hemington ..	Northampton	Parish	152
Heeley	,, ..	Ecl. Dis.	5 563	Hemington ..	Somerset ..	Parish	459
Heene	Sussex ..	Parish	194	Hemley ..	Suffolk ..	Parish	63
Heigham ..	Norfolk ..	Parish	13 894	Hemlingford	Warwick ..	Hund.	74 233
Heighington ..	Durham ..	Parish	1 323	Hemlington ..	York ..	Tnship.	94
Heighington ..	,, ..	Tnship.	668	Hempholme ..	,,	Tnship.	101
Heighington ..	Lincoln ..	Tnship.	624	Hempnall ..	Norfolk ..	Parish	1 094
Heighton, South	Sussex ..	Parish	104	Hempstead ..	Essex ..	Parish	797
Helhoughton ..	Norfolk ..	Parish	346	Hempstead ..	Gloucester ..	Parish	424
Helion-Bumpstead	Esx. & Cam.	Parish	887	Hempstead by Holt	Norfolk ..	Parish	280
Helland.. ..	Cornwall ..	Parish	224	Hempstead ..	,,	Parish	178
Hellesdon ..	Norfolk ..	Parish	496	Hempston, Little	Devon ..	Parish	244
Hellesdon ..	,, ..	Hamlet	393	Hempton & Patchway	Glouc...	Tithing	548
Hellidon ..	Northampton	Parish	449	Hempton ..	Norfolk ..	Parish	459
Hellifield ..	York ..	Tnship.	272	Hempton ..	Oxon ..	Hamlet	229
Hellingly ..	Sussex ..	Sub-dis.	6 663	Hemsby.. ..	Norfolk ..	Parish	664
Hellingly ..	,, ..	Parish	1 606	Hemswell ..	Lincoln ..	Parish	465
Helmdon ..	Northampton	Parish	602	Hemsworth ..	York ..	District	7 793
Helme	York ..	Ecl. Dis.	787	Hemsworth ..	,, ..	Sub-dis.	7 793
Helmingham ..	Suffolk ..	Parish	320	Hemsworth ..	,, ..	Parish	975
Helmington Row	Durham ..	Tnship.	3 469	Hemyock ..	Devon ..	Hund.	5 225
Helmsley ..	York ..	District	11 832	Hemyock ..	,, ..	Parish	1 068
Helmsley ..	,, ..	Union	6 093	Henbury w. Pexhall	Cheshire..	Tnship.	445
Helmsley ..	,, ..	Sub-dis.	3 969	Henbury, St. Thomas	,, ..	Ecl. Dis.	1 015

Name of Place.	County.	Description.	Population.	Name of Place.	County.	Description.	Population.
nbury	Gloucester	Hund.	7 377	Henstead	Norfolk	Sub-dis.	5 670
nbury	,,	Parish	2 482	Henstead	Suffolk	Parish	534
nbury	,,	Tithing	423	Henstridge	Somerset	Parish	1 173
nderskelf	York	Tnship.	157	Hentland	Hereford	Parish	647
ndford	Somerset	Ecl. Dis.	3 997	Henton	Oxon	Liberty	268
ndon, St. Paul	Durham	Ecl. Dis.	11 451	Henton, Christch.	Somerset	Ecl. Dis.	548
ndon	Middlesex	District	19 238	Hepple	Northumberland	Tnship.	74
ndon	,,	Sub-dis.	4 544	Hepple Demesne	,,	Tnship.	30
ndon	,,	Parish	4 544	Hepscott	,,	Tnship.	253
ndrebiffa	Flint	Tnship.	320	Heptonstall	York	Tnship.	3 497
ndred	Berks	Sub-dis.	4 369	Hepworth	Suffolk	Parish	594
ndred, East	,,	Parish	889	Hepworth	York	Tnship.	1 530
ndred, West	,,	Parish	351	Herbrandston	Pembroke	Parish	257
ndredenny	Glamorgan	Hamlet	555	Hereford		Diocese	232 401
neglwys	Anglesey	Parish	510	Herefordshire		County	123 712
nfield	Sussex	Parish	1 662	Hereford	Hereford	L. Sub.	27 755
nfynyw	Cardigan	Parish	1 067	Hereford	Heref. & Monm.	District	39 287
ngoed	Carmarthen	Hamlet	2 024	Hereford	Hereford	Union	29 768
ngoed	Glamorgan	Hamlet	578	Hereford City	,,	Sub-dis.	14 065
ngoed, St. Barnabas	Salop	Ecl. Dis.	672	Hereford	,,	City	15 585
ngrave	Suffolk	Parish	219	Hereford, Little	,,	Parish	458
nham	Essex	Parish	875	Hereford, Little	,,		360
nham	,,	—	732	Herm, Isle of	Channel Is.	Island	41
nham	Suffolk	Hamlet	161	Hermitage	Berks	Ecl. Dis.	434
nheads	Lancaster	Tnship.	211	Hermitage	Dorset	Parish	131
nhull	Cheshire	Tnship.	90	Herne	Kent	Sub-dis.	4 473
nley	Oxon	L. Sub.	14 602	Herne	,,	Parish	3 147
nley	Oxon, &c.	District	18 200	Herne Bay, Christch.	,,	Ecl. Dis.	1 503
nley	,,	Sub-dis.	13 791	Herne Hill, St. Paul	Surrey	Ecl. Dis.	911
nley on Thames	Oxon	Parish	3 676	Hernhill	Kent	Parish	701
nley on Thames	,,	Town	3 419	Herods Foot, All Saints	Cornw.	Ecl. Dis.	453
nley	Suffolk	Parish	293	Herriard	Hants	Parish	439
nley	Warwick	L. Sub.	7 545	Herringfleet	Suffolk	Parish	210
nley in Arden	,,	Tnship.	1 069	Herringswell	,,	Parish	203
nllan	Cardigan	Parish	133	Herrington, E. & Mid.	Durham	Tnship.	242
nllan	Denbigh	Parish	2 607	Herrington, West	,,	Tnship.	752
nllan	Pembroke	Hamlet	22	Hersham, Trinity	Surrey	Ecl. Dis.	1 766
nllanamgoed	Carmarthen	Parish	445	Herstmonceux	Sussex	Parish	1 287
nllanamgoed	Carmarthen	Hamlet	177	Hertfordshire		County	173 280
nllis	Monmouth	Parish	238	Hertford	Herts	Hund.	16 681
nllys	Cardigan	Tnship.	483	Hertford	,,	L. Sub.	17 027
nlow	Beds	Parish	1 011	Hertford	,,	District	15 301
nnock	Devon	Parish	1 004	Hertford	,,	Sub-dis.	11 163
nny, Great	Essex	Parish	363	Hertford	,,	Borough	6 769
nny, Little	,,	Parish	81	Hertingfordbury	,,	Parish	799
nry's Moat	Pembroke	Parish	287	Hesket in the Forest	Cumberld.	Parish	1 983
nsall	York	Tnship.	264	Hesket, Up. & Nether	,,	Tnship.	775
nsall, St. Paul	,,	Ecl. Dis.	633	Hesketh w. Becconsall	Lancaster	Parish	804
nshaw	Northumberland	Tnship.	550	Heskin	,,	Tnship.	439
nsingham	Cumberland	Chap.	1 538	Heslerton	York	Parish	603
nsington	Oxon	Hamlet	271	Heslerton, East	,,	Tnship.	262
nstead	Norfolk	Hund.	5 729	Heslerton, West	,,	Tnship.	341
nstead & Humbleyard	,,	L. Sub.	11 349	Hesley-Hurst	Northumberland	Tnship.	39
nstead	,,	District	11 290	Heslington St. Lawrence	York	Tnship.	307

Name of Place.	County.	Description	Population.	Name of Place.	County.	Description	Populati
Heslington St. Paul	York	Parish	233	Heytesbury	Wilts	Hund	5 57
Hessay	„	Tnship.	127	Heytesbury	„	Sub-dis.	4 37
Hessenford, St. Anne	Cornwall	Ecl. Dis.	963	Heytesbury	„	Parish	1 10
Hesset	Suffolk	Parish	454	Heythrop & Dunthrop	Oxon	Parish	12
Hessle	York	Sub-dis.	2 522	Heywood	Lancaster	Sub-dis.	17 59
Hessle	„	Parish	1 625	**Heywood**	„	Town	12 82
Hessle	„	Tnship.	125	Heywood, St. Luke	„	Ecl. Dis.	9 23
Heston	Middlesex	Parish	7 096	Heywood, Great	Stafford	Ecl. Dis.	90
Heswall	Chester	Parish	749	Hibaldstow	Lincoln	Parish	77
Heswall w. Oldfield	„	Tnship.	556	Hickleton	York	Parish	12
Hethe	Oxon	Parish	442	Hickling	Norfolk	Parish	76
Hethel	Norfolk	Parish	196	Hickling	Notts	Parish	64
Hethersett	„	Parish	1 169	Hidcote Bartrim	Gloucester	Hamlet	8
Hethersgill	Cumberland	Tnship.	712	Hiendley, South	York	Tnship.	28
Hett	Durham	Tnship.	241	High Abbotside	„	Tnship.	55
Hetton-le-Hole	„	Sub-dis.	10 535	Higham Gobion	Beds	Parish	12
Hetton-le-Hole	„	Tnship.	6 419	Higham	Derby	Hamlet	37
Hetton	York	Tnship.	124	Higham	Kent	Parish	1 06
Heugh	Northumberland	Tnship.	430	Higham, &c.	Lancaster	Tnship.	75
Heveningham	Suffolk	Parish	354	Higham on the Hill	Leicester	Parish	55
Hever	Kent	Parish	626	Higham Ferrers	Northampton	Hund.	11 50
Heversham	Westmoreland	Parish	4 300	Higham Ferrers	Nrptn. & Beds	Sub-dis.	7 10
Heversham, &c.	„	Tnship.	1 433	Higham Ferrers	Northampton	Parish	1 15
Hevingham	Norfolk	Parish	838	Higham Park	„	Parish	1
Hewelsfield	Gloucester	Parish	417	Higham Dykes	Nrthumberld.	Tnship.	2
Heworth	Durham	Sub-dis.	10 315	Higham	Suffolk	Parish	22
Heworth	„	Chap.	10 315	Higham Green	„	Hamlet	40
Heworth, St. Albans	„	Ecl. Dis.	2 635	Highampton	Devon	Parish	38
Heworth	York	Tnship.	437	High & Low Bishopside	York	Tnship.	2 05
Hexham	Northumberland	District	31 850	High & Low Trewhitt	Nrthmb.	Tnship.	10
Hexham	„	Sub-dis.	9 735	High Angerton	„	Tnship.	10
Hexham	„	Parish	6 479	High Barton	Westmoreland	Tnship.	30
Hexham	„	Tnship.	5 270	High Bickington	Devon	Sub-dis.	2 93
Hexham	„	Town	4 655	High Bickington	„	Parish	73
Hexhamshire:—				High Blackwell	Cumberland	Tnship.	34
High Quarter	„	Tnship.	243	High Bolton	„	Tnship.	33
Low Quarter	„	Tnship.	454	Highbray	Devon	Parish	29
Middle Quarter	„	Tnship.	255	High Buston	Northumberland	Tnship.	12
West Quarter	„	Tnship.	257	Highbury, Ch. ch.	Middlesex	Ecl. Dis.	3 22
Hexton	Herts	Parish	234	High Caldbeck	Cumberland	Tnship.	31
Hey, St. John	Lancaster	Ecl. Dis.	3 132	High Callerton	Northumberland	Tnship.	9
Heybridge	Essex	Parish	1 476	High Catton	York	Tnshp.	21
Heydon	„	Parish	270	Highclere	Hants	Sub-dis.	3 25
Heydon	Norfolk	Parish	302	Highclere	„	Parish	44
Heyford, Nether	Northampton	Parish	807	High Coniscliffe	Durham	Tnship.	23
Heyford, Upper	„	Parish	116	High Crosby	Cumberland	Tnship.	17
Heyford, Lower	Oxon	Parish	625	High Cross	Middlesex	Ward	3 20
Heyford, Upper	„	Parish	453	High Easter	Essex	Parish	94
Heyhouses	Lancaster	Tnship.	128	High Edge	Derby	Ecl. Dis.	2 28
Heyhouses, St. Nicholas	„	Ecl. Dis.	1 616	Higher Baglan	Glamorgan	Hamlet	25
Heyop	Radnor	Parish	283	Higher Bebington	Cheshire	Tnship.	2 08
Heyop	„	Tnship.	435	Higher Booth	Lancaster	Tnship.	5 13
Heysham	Lancaster	Parish	567	Higher Coychurch	Glamorgan	Hamlet	31
Heyshott	Sussex	Parish	396	Higher Coyty	„	Hamlet	51

Name of Place.	County.	Description.	Population.	Name of Place.	County.	Description.	Population.
Higher Kinnerton	*Flint* ..	Tnship.	411	Hildenly ..	*York* ..	Tnship.	42
Higher Llangynwyd	*Glamorgan*	Hamlet	2 187	Hildersham ..	*Cambs* ..	Parish	227
Higher Newcastle	" ..	Hamlet	1 357	Hilderstone ..	*Stafford* ..	Ecl. Dis.	448
Higher Wirral .	*Cheshire* ..	L. Sub.	10 228	Hilderthorpe ..	*York* ..	Tnship.	176
High Fotherly	*Northumberland*	Tnship.	104	Hilfield.. ..	*Dorset* ..	Parish	111
Highgate, St. Michael	*Mdlx.*	Ecl. Dis.	4 547	Hilgay	*Norfolk* ..	Parish	1 624
High Halden ..	*Kent* ..	Parish	653	Hill	*Gloucester* ..	Parish	216
High Halstow ..	" ..	Parish	363	Hill	*Lincoln* ..	Hund.	3 739
High Ham ..	*Somerset* ..	Parish	1 283	Hill, St. James..	*Warwick* ..	Ecl. Dis.	1 246
High Harrogate .	*York* ..	Ecl. Dis.	4 327	Hill	*Worcester* ..	Tnship.	1 328
Highhead ..	*Cumberland* .	Tnship.	126	Hill & Moor ..	" ..	Hamlet	346
High Hoyland ..	*York* ..	Sub-dis.	3 569	Hill Croome ..	" ..	Parish	198
High Hoyland ..	" ..	Parish	3 357	Hillam	*York* ..	Tnship.	319
High Hoyland ..	" ..	Tnship.	224	Hill Deverill ..	*Wilts* ..	Parish	149
High Ireby ..	*Cumberland* .	Tnship.	128	Hillesdon ..	*Bucks* ..	Parish	251
High Lane, St. Thos.	*Cheshire*	Ecl. Dis.	1 193	Hillesley ..	*Gloucester* ..	Tithing	451
High Laver ..	*Essex* ..	Parish	471	Hillesley, St. Giles	" ..	Ecl. Dis.	574
Highlaws	*Northumberland*	Tnship.	20	Hillfarrance ..	*Somerset* ..	Parish	582
Highlaws, High & Low	"	Tnship.	82	Hillhampton ..	*Worcester* ..	Hamlet	158
Highleadon ..	*Gloucester* ..	Hamlet	97	Hillingdon ..	*Middlesex* ..	Sub-dis.	8 844
High Leigh ..	*Cheshire* ..	Tnship.	1 004	Hillingdon ..	" ..	Parish	10 758
Highley ..	*Salop* ..	Parish	407	Hillingdon ..	" ..	—	7 522
Highley, St. Mary	*Devon* ..	Parish.	18	Hillington ..	*Norfolk* ..	Sub-dis.	4 543
Highlight ..	*Glamorgan* .	Parish	15	Hillington ..	" ..	Parish	330
High Littleton ..	*Somerset* ..	Parish	860	Hillington, Loddon	" ..	Parish	98
High Longtown .	*Cumberland*	Sub-dis.	3 291	Hillmarton ..	*Wilts* ..	Parish	787
Highlow ..	*Derby* ..	Lordsp.	50	Hillmorton ..	*Warwick* ..	Parish	978
High Melton ..	*York* ..	Parish	109	Hill-Top ..	*York* ..	Tnship.	82
Highmore, St. Paul	*Oxon* ..	Ecl. Dis.	333	Hill Top, St. James	*Stafford* ..	Ecl. Dis.	8 521
Highnam ..	*Gloucester* ..	Hamlet	218	Hilperton ..	*Wilts* ..	Parish	880
Highnam ..	" ..	Ecl. Dis.	357	Hilston	*York* ..	Parish	54
High Offley ..	*Stafford* ..	Parish	883	Hilton	*Derby* ..	Tnship	719
High Ongar ..	*Essex* ..	Parish	1 177	Hilton	*Dorset* ..	Parish	833
High Peak ..	*Derby* ..	Hund.	66 397	Hilton	*Durham* ..	Tnship.	98
High Peak ..	" .	L. Sub.	66 397	Hilton	*Hunts* ..	Parish	387
High Roothing .	*Essex* ..	Parish	469	Hilton	*Stafford* ..	Tnship.	82
High Sebergham	*Cumberland*	Tnship.	423	Hilton	*Westmoreland*	Tnship.	253
High Street ..	*Suffolk* ..	Parish	20	Hilton	*York* ..	Parish	127
High Toynton ..	*Lincoln* ..	Parish	210	Himbleton ..	*Worcester* ..	Parish	410
High Walton ..	*Cumberland*	Tnship.	144	Himley	*Stafford* ..	Parish	367
Highway ..	*Wilts* ..	Parish	121	Hincaster ..	*Westmoreland*	Tnship.	143
Highweek ..	*Devon* ..	Parish	1 571	Hinckford ..	*Essex* ..	Hund.	44 040
High Worsall ..	*York* ..	Chap.	109	Hinckford, North	" ..	L. Sub.	16 114
Highworth &c. ..	*Wilts* ..	Hund.	14 027	Hinckford, South	" ..	L. Sub.	28 056
Highworth ..	" ..	District	19 237	Hinckley	*Leic. & Warw*	District	16 374
Highworth ..	" ..	Sub-dis.	7 013	Hinckley ..	" "	Sub-dis.	7 658
Highworth ..	" ..	Parish	3 629	Hinckley ..	" "	Parish	7 315
Highworth ..	" ..	Tithing	631	Hinckley ..	*Leicester* ..	Tnship.	6 344
High Wycombe .	*Bucks* ..	Sub-dis.	11 583	Hinckley ..	" ..	Town	6 344
High Wycombe .	" ..	Parish	8 373	Hinckley, Trinity	" ..	Ecl. Dis.	1 862
Hilbeck.. ..	*Westmoreland*	Tnship.	76	Hinderclay ..	*Suffolk* ..	Parish	388
Hilborough ..	*Norfolk* ..	Parish	365	Hinders Lane ..	*Gloucester* ..	—	184
Hilbre, Isle of ..	*Cheshire* ..	Island	7	Hinderwell ..	*York* ..	Parish	2 805
Hildenborough..	*Kent* ..	Ecl. Dis.	1 049	Hinderwell ..	" ..	Tnship.	2 571

Name of Place.	County.	Description.	Population.	Name of Place.	County.	Description.	Population.
Hindley.. ..	Lancaster ..	Sub-dis.	17 654	Hockering ..	Norfolk ..	Parish	387
Hindley.. ..	,, ..	Tnship.	8 477	Hockerton ..	Notts ..	Parish	108
Hindley ..	,, ..	Town	8 477	Hockham ..	Norfolk ..	Parish	629
Hindolveston ..	Norfolk ..	Parish	705	Hockley.. ..	Essex ..	Parish	798
Hindon.. ..	Wilts ..	L. Sub.	18 626	Hockliffe ..	Beds ..	Parish	416
Hindon.. ..	,, ..	Sub-dis.	2 501	Hockwold w. Wilton	Norfolk ..	Parish	803
Hindon.. ..	,, ..	Parish	604	Hockworthy ..	Devon ..	Parish	373
Hindringham ..	Norfolk ..	Parish	731	Hoddesdon ..	Herts ..	Sub-dis.	4 895
Hingham ..	,, ..	Parish	1 605	Hoddesdon ..	,, ..	Hamlet	1 898
Hinksey, North .	Berks ..	Parish	438	Hoddesdon ..	,, ..	Ecl.Dis.	2 203
Hinksey, South .	,, ..	Parish	636	Hodgeston ..	Pembroke ..	Parish	43
Hinlip	Worcester ..	Parish	136	Hodnel, Lower .	Warwick ..	Parish	4
Hinstock ..	Salop ..	Parish	791	Hodnel, Upper .	,, ..	Parish	20
Hintlesham ..	Suffolk ..	Parish	613	Hodnet	Salop ..	Sub-dis.	5 095
Hinton Waldrist	Berks ..	Parish	829	Hodnet	,, ..	Parish	1 979
Hinton Martell..	Dorset ..	Parish	357	Hodnet	,, ..	Tnship.	1 714
Hinton Parva ..	,, ..	Parish	54	Hodsock ..	Notts ..	Lordsp.	207
Hinton, St. Mary	,, ..	Parish	342	Hoe	Norfolk ..	Parish	169
Hinton	Gloucester ..	Tithing	620	Hoff and Row ..	Westmoreland	Tnship.	107
Hinton on Green	,, ..	Parish	192	Hoggeston ..	Bucks ..	Parish	207
Hinton Ampner .	Hants ..	Parish	362	Hoghton ..	Lancaster ..	Tnship.	1 201
Hinton in Hedges	Northampton	Parish	178	Hoghton ..	,, ..	Ecl. Dis.	1 100
Hinton Blewett .	Somerset ..	Parish	302	Hognaston ..	Derby ..	Parish	295
Hinton, St. George	,, ..	Parish	761	Hogshaw w. Fulbrook	Bucks ..	Parish	50
Hinton, Great ..	Wilts ..	Tithing	188	Hogsthorpe ..	Lincoln ..	Parish	874
Hinton, Little ..	,, ..	Parish	298	Holbeach ..	,, ..	District	18 402
Hints	Stafford ..	Parish	200	Holbeach ..	,, ..	Sub-dis.	7 409
Hinxhill ..	Kent ..	Parish	128	Holbeach ..	,, ..	Parish	4 956
Hinxton ..	Cambs ..	Parish	396	Holbeach ..	,, ..	Town	2 088
Hinxworth ..	Herts ..	Parish	320	Holbeck.. ..	Notts ..	Tnship.	266
Hippenscombe ..	Wilts ..	Parish	42	Holbeck.. ..	York ..	Sub-dis.	19 935
Hipperholme, &c.	York ..	Tnship.	7 340	Holbeck.. ..	,, ..	Tnship.	15 824
Hipswell ..	,, ..	Tnship.	260	Holbeck, Little, St. John	,, ..	Ecl.Dis.	2 612
Hirnant.. ..	Montgomery	Parish	295	Holbeton ..	Devon ..	Parish	965
Hirst Courtney..	York ..	Tnship.	126	Holborn ..	Middlesex ..	Division	555 538
Hirst Temple ..	,, ..	Tnship.	104	Holborn ..	,, ..	L. Sub.	119 286
Histon	Cambs ..	Parish	971	Holborn ..	,, ..	District	44 862
Hitcham ..	Bucks ..	Parish	205	Holborn, St. Andrew	,, ..	Parish	28 721
Hitcham ..	Suffolk ..	Parish	991	Holbrook ..	Derby ..	Chap.	956
Hitchin ..	Herts & Beds	District	25 603	Holbrook ..	Suffolk ..	Sub-dis.	6 144
Hitchin ..	,, ,,	Sub-dis.	16 865	Holbrook ..	,, ..	Parish	903
Hitchin ..	Herts ..	Parish	7 677	Holcombe Burnell	Devon ..	Parish	242
Hitchin ..	,, ..	L. Sub.	16 036	Holcombe Rogus	,, ..	Parish	704
Hitchin ..	,, ..	Town	6 330	Holcombe ..	Lancaster ..	Sub-dis.	6 645
Hitchin ..	,, ..	Hund.	14 090	Holcombe ..	Somerset ..	Parish	388
Hittisleigh ..	Devon ..	Parish	156	Holcot	Northampton	Parish	517
Hixon, St. Peter	Stafford ..	Ecl. Dis.	710	Holcutt.. ..	Beds ..	Parish	71
Hoath	Kent ..	Parish	348	Holdenby ..	Northampton	Parish	184
Hoathley, East .	Sussex ..	Parish	615	Holdenhurst ..	Hants ..	Parish	2 488
Hoathley, West .	,, ..	Parish	1 120	Holderness ..	York ..	Wapen.	26 584
Hob Lench ..	Worcester ..	Hamlet	66	Holderness, Middle	,, ..	L. Sub.	8 774
Hoby	Leicester ..	Parish	869	Holderness, North	,, ..	L. Sub.	9 534
Hockenhull Stapleford	Cheshire	Tnship.	36	Holderness, South	,, ..	L. Sub.	8 276
Hockerill, All Saints	Herts ..	Ecl.Dis.	1 467	Holdfast ..	Worcester ..	Hamlet	90

Name of Place.	County.	Description.	Population.	Name of Place.	County.	Description.	Population.
Holdgate	Salop	Parish	196	Holme, South ..	York	Tnship.	68
Holdgate	,,	Tnship.	46	Holme on Wolds	,,	Parish	168
Holdingham	Lincoln	Hamlet	142	Holmebridge, St.David	,,	Ecl. Dis.	2 708
Holford	Somerset	Parish	170	Holmer	Hereford	Parish	1 237
Holgate	York	Tnship.	170	Holmer & Shelwick	,,	Tnship.	1 083
Holgate Road, St. Paul	,,	Ecl. Dis.	2 409	Holmesfield	Derby	Tnship.	529
Holker, Lower	Lancaster	Tnship.	1 160	Holmesley Walk	Hants	—	27
Holker, Upper	,,	Tnship.	1 035	Holmfirth	York	Sub-dis.	10 845
Holkham	Norfolk	Parish	603	Holmfirth	,,	Town	2 466
Hollacombe	Devon	Parish	87	Holmfirth, Trinity	,,	Ecl. Dis.	5 447
Holland, Great	Essex	Parish	467	Holm Lacy	Hereford	Parish	307
Holland, Little	,,	Parish	88	Holmpton	York	Parish	116
Hollesley	Suffolk	Parish	603	Holmside	Durham	Tnship.	1 048
Holleth	Lancaster	Tnship.	30	Holmwood	Surrey	Ecl. Dis.	1 211
Hollingbourn	Kent	District	13 584	Holne	Devon	Parish	348
Hollingbourn	,,	Sub-dis.	4 690	Holnest	Dorset	Parish	147
Hollingbourn	,,	Parish	1 190	Holsworthy	Devon	L. Sub.	9 849
Hollinghill	Northumberland	Tnship.	109	Holsworthy	Dev. & Cornw.	District	9 876
Hollington	Derby	Tnship.	296	Holsworthy	Devon	Sub-dis.	2 756
Hollington	Sussex	Parish	531	Holsworthy	,,	Parish	1 724
Hollingwood, St.Margaret	Lan.	Ecl. Dis.	6 298	Holt	Denbigh, &c.	Sub-dis.	4 452
Hollingworth	Cheshire	Tnship.	2 155	Holt	Denbigh	Parish	1 490
Hollinsclough	Stafford	Tnship.	393	Holt	,,	Tnship.	1 008
Hollis Croft	York	Ecl. Dis.	6 229	Holt	,,	P. Bor.	1 008
Holloway, Low. St. Jas.	Mdlsex.	Ecl. Dis.	10 563	Holt	Dorset	Tithing	1 394
Holloway, Up. St. John	,,	Ecl. Dis.	7 286	Holt	Leicester	Tnship.	33
Hollym	York	Parish	625	Holt	Norfolk	Hund.	9 942
Hollym	,,	Tnship.	423	Holt	,,	L. Sub.	9 942
Holme Abbey	Cumberland	Tnship.	982	Holt	,,	Sub-dis.	6 787
Holme Cultram	,,	Parish	3 867	Holt	,,	Parish	1 635
Holme, St. Cuthbert	,,	Tnship.	821	Holt	Wilts	Ecl. Dis.	809
Holme, St. Cuthbert	,,	Ecl. Dis.	821	Holt	Worcester	Sub-dis.	3 509
Holme, East Waver	,,	Tnship.	526	Holt	,,	Parish	503
Holme Eden	,,	Ecl. Dis.	1 107	Holt	,,	Tnship.	295
Holme, Low	,,	Tnship.	1 538	Holtby	York	Parish	165
Holme, Low, St.Paul	,,	Ecl. Dis.	1 521	Holton Beckering	Lincoln	Parish	179
Holme, East	Dorset	Parish	50	Holton-le-Clay	,,	Parish	297
Holme	Hunts	Chap.	644	Holton-le-Moor	,,	Chap.	180
Holme in Cliviger	Lancaster	Ecl. Dis.	1 770	Holton	Oxon	Parish	245
Holme, Isle of	,,	Island	3	Holton	Somerset	Parish	208
Holme	Lincoln	Tnship.	56	Holton	Suffolk	Parish	470
Holme Hale	Norfolk	Parish	464	Holton, St. Mary	,,	Parish	167
Holme by Runcton	,,	Parish	273	Holverstone	Norfolk	Parish	28
Holme by Sea	,,	Parish	305	Holwell	Beds	Parish	191
Holme	Notts	Parish	121	Holwell	Dorset	Parish	495
Holme Pierrepont	,,	Parish	150	Holwell	Leicester	Tnship.	147
Holme	Westmoreland	Tnship.	750	Holwell	Oxon	Tnship.	110
Holme, Trinity	,,	Ecl. Dis.	750	Holwell	,,	Ecl. Dis.	193
Holme Beacon	York	L. Sub.	10 263	Holwick	York	Tnship.	253
Holme	,,	Sub-dis.	1 913	Holybourne	Hants	Parish	643
Holme on Spalding Moor	,,	Parish	1 913	Holybourne	,,	—	586
Holme	,,	Tnship.	54	Holy Cross, Westgate	Kent	Parish	1 065
Holme (Almondbury P.)	,,	Tnship.	807	Westgate, Within	,,	—	249
Holme, North	,,	Tnship.	17	Westgate, Without	,,	—	816

Name of Place.	County.	Description.	Population.	Name of Place.	County.	Description.	Population.
Holy Cross & St. Giles	*Salop* ..	Parish	2 234	Honeychurch ..	*Devon* ..	Parish	44
Holy Cross ..	*Worcester* ..	Parish	2 578	Honily	*Warwick* ..	Parish	63
Holy Cross ..	,, ..	—	1 953	Honing	*Norfolk* ..	Parish	304
Holyfield ..	*Essex* ..	Hamlet	406	Honingham ..	,, ..	Parish	328
Holyhead ..	*Anglesey* ..	Sub-dis.	9 235	Honington ..	*Lincoln* ..	Parish	157
Holyhead ..	,, ..	Parish	8 773	Honington ..	*Suffolk* ..	Parish	363
Holyhead ..	,, ..	P. Bor.	6 193	Honington ..	*Warwick* ..	Parish	250
Holyhead ..	,, ..	Union	20 317	Honiton ..	*Devon* ..	L. Sub.	12 103
Holy Island	*Northumberland*	Parish	935	Honiton ..	,, ..	District	22 729
Holy Oakes ..	*Leicester* ..	Liberty	9	Honiton ..	,, ..	Sub-dis.	10 783
Holy Rood ..	*Hants* ..	Parish	1 571	Honiton ..	,, ..	Parish	3 301
Holy Sepulchre .	*Cambs* ..	Parish	547	**Honiton** ..	,, ..	Borough	3 301
Holystone	*Northumberland*	P. Chap.	426	Honiton Clist ..	,, ..	Parish	416
Holystone ..	,,	Tnship.	135	Honley ..	*York* ..	Sub-dis.	5 723
Holy Trinity ..	*Cambs* ..	Parish	1 949	Honley	,, ..	Tnship.	4 626
Holy Trinity ..	*Cheshire* ..	Parish	3 675	Hoo ..	*Kent* ..	District	2 861
Holy Trinity ..	,, ..	—	3 606	Hoo, St. Mary ..	,, ..	Parish	264
Holy Trinity ..	*Devon* ..	Parish	3 841	Hoo, St. Werburg	,, ..	Parish	1 065
Holy Trinity, Dorchester	*Dors.*	Parish	1 601	Hoo ..	*Suffolk* ..	Parish	182
Holy Trinity, Shaftesbury	,, ..	Parish	1 028	Hood-Grange ..	*York* ..	Parish	50
Holy Trinity, Wareham	,, ..	Parish	816	Hooe, St. John ..	*Devon* ..	Ecl. Dis.	1 082
Holy Trinity ..	*Dorset* ..	—	470	Hooe ..	*Sussex* ..	Parish	496
Holy Trinity ..	*Essex* ..	Parish	875	Hook ..	*Dorset* ..	Parish	247
Holy Trinity ..	*Gloucester* ..	Parish	539	Hook-Norton ..	*Oxon* ..	Parish	1 393
Holy Trinity, Minories	*Midsx.*	Parish	420	Hook ..	*Surrey* ..	Hamlet	248
Holy Trinity, Less	,,	Parish	553	Hook, St. Paul ..	,, ..	Ecl. Dis.	370
Holy Trinity ..	*Surrey* ..	Parish	1 708	Hook ..	*York* ..	Tnship.	2 958
Holy Trinity ..	*Sussex* ..	Parish	1 683	Hoole ..	*Cheshire* ..	Tnship.	1 596
Holy Trinity ..	*Warwick* ..	Sub-dis.	19 481	Hoole ..	*Lancaster* ..	Parish	1 132
Holy Trinity ..	,, ..	Parish	19 815	Hoole, Little	,, ..	Tnship.	424
Holy Trinity ..	,, ..	—	18 770	Hoole, Much	,, ..	Tnship.	708
Holy Trinity, Goodramgate	*York*	Parish	431	Hoon ..	*Derby* ..	Tnship.	43
Holy Trinity & St. Mary	,,	Parish	56 888	Hoose ..	*Cheshire* ..	Tnship.	664
Holy Trinity, Kings Court	,,	Parish	599	Hooton ..	,, ..	Tnship.	141
Holy Trinity, Micklegate	,,	Parish	1 907	Hooton Levett ..	*York* ..	Tnship.	84
Holy Trinity, Micklegate	,,	—	1 621	Hooton Pagnell .	,, ..	Parish	342
Holywell ..	*Flint & Denb.*	District	39 941	Hooton Pagnell .	,, ..	Tnship.	274
Holywell ..	,, ,,	Sub-dis.	12 100	Hooton Roberts .	,, ..	Parish	241
Holywell ..	*Flint* ..	Parish	10 292	Hope ..	*Derby* ..	Parish	5 107
Holywell ..	,, ..	P. Bor.	5 335	Hope ..	,, ..	Tnship.	398
Holywell ..	*Hunts* ..	Parish	826	Hope Woodlands	,, ..	Tnship.	227
Holywell ..	*Lincoln* ..	Chap.	91	Hope ..	*Flint & Denb.*	Sub-dis.	11 297
Holywell ..	*Middlesex* ..	Sub-dis.	17 313	Hope ..	*Flint* ..	Parish	3 121
Holywell ..	,, ..	Ward	2 625	Hope Mansell ..	*Hereford* ..	Parish	205
Holywell ..	*Northampton*	Hamlet	266	Hope under Dinmore	,, ..	Parish	662
Holywell, St. Jas.	,,	Ecl. Dis.	266	Hope, All Saints .	*Kent* ..	Parish	59
Holywell	*Northumberland*	Tnship.	1 261	Hope ..	*Montgomery* ..	Tnship	187
Holywell ..	*Oxon* ..	Parish	943	Hope ..	,,	Ecl. Dis.	1 829
Holywell Row ..	*Suffolk* ..	Watch	453	Hope Baggot ..	*Salop* ..	Parish	82
Home ..	*Kent* ..	L. Sub.	17 257	Hope, Bowdler ..	,, ..	Parish	178
Home Ystradyfodwg	*Glam.* ..	Hamlet	1 011	Hope ..	*Stafford* ..	Ecl. Dis.	4 380
Homersfield ..	*Suffolk* ..	Parish	208	Hope ..	*York* ..	Tnship.	43
Homerton, St. Barnab.	*Mdlx* ..	Ecl. Dis.	8 663	Hopebendrid ..	*Salop* ..	P. Div.	400
Homington ..	*Wilts* ..	Parish	155	Hopesay ..	,,	Parish	676

Name of Place.	County.	Description.	Population.	Name of Place.	County.	Description.	Population.
ppen..	Northumberland	Tnship.	26	Horninglow	Stafford	Tnship.	1 968
pton..	Derby	Tnship.	115	Horningsea	Cambs	Parish	402
pton Cangeford	Salop	Parish	30	Horningsham	Wilts	Parish	1 065
pton Castle..	"	Parish	138	Horningsheath	Suffolk	Parish	670
pton Wafers.	"	Parish	440	Horningtoft	Norfolk	Parish	248
pton & Coton.	Stafford	Tnship.	1 174	Hornsea	York	Sub-dis.	2 529
pton, Gorleston	Suffolk	Parish	297	Hornsea w. Burton	"	Parish	1 063
pton, Thetford	"	Parish	643	Hornsey	Middlesex	Sub-dis.	11 082
pton, Uppr. St. John	York	Ecl. Dis.	1 211	Hornsey	"	Parish	11 082
pwas..	Stafford	Hamlet	277	Hornton	Oxon	Parish	514
pwas, Hayes.	"	—	2	Horrington	Somerset	Ecl. Dis.	868
pwell	Derby	Hamlet	27	Horseheath	Cambs	Parish	497
pwood	Lancaster	Tnship.	2 281	Horseley	Stafford	Tnship.	532
rbling	Lincoln	Parish	546	Horsell..	Surrey	Parish	788
rbury	York	Sub-dis.	3 246	Horsemonden	Kent	Parish	1 385
rbury	"	Tnship.	3 246	Horsendon	Bucks	Parish	45
rderley Hall.	Salop	Parish	7	Horsepath	Oxon	Parish	334
rdle..	Hants	Parish	921	Horsey by the Sea	Norfolk	Parish	206
rdley	Salop	Parish	291	Horsford	"	Parish	665
rethorn	Somerset	Hund.	7 137	Horsforth	York	Sub-dis.	5 733
rfield	Gloucester	Parish	1 746	Horsforth	"	Tnship.	5 281
rham	Suffolk	Parish	396	Horsham, St. Faiths	Norfolk	Parish	918
rksley, Great.	Essex	Parish	769	Horsham	Sussex	L. Sub.	17 791
rksley, Little.	"	Parish	253	Horsham	"	District	15 313
rkstow	Lincoln	Parish	245	Horsham	"	Parish	6 747
rley..	Oxon	Parish	337	**Horsham**	"	P. Boro.	6 747
rley..	Surrey	Sub-dis.	6 405	Horsington	Lincoln	Parish	418
rley..	"	Parish	1 587	Horsington	Somerset	Parish	869
rmead, Great.	Herts	Parish	660	Horsley..	Derby	Sub Dis.	5 930
rmead, Little.	"	Parish	103	Horsley..	"	Parish	2 250
rmer..	Berks	Hund.	4 432	Horsley..	"	Tnship	467
rn..	Rutland	Parish	30	Horsley Woodhouse	"	Tnship.	832
rnblotton	Somerset	Parish	93	Horsley..	Gloucester	Sub-dis.	4 628
rnby..	Lancaster	Tnship.	317	Horsley..	"	Parish	2 558
rnby, St. Margaret	"	Ecl. Dis.	455	Horsley..	Northumberland	Tnship.	272
rnby..	York	Parish	360	Horsley, Long..	"	Parish	964
rnby, Leyburn	"	Tnship.	96	Horsley, East..	Surrey	Parish	228
rnby, Grt. Smeaton	"	Tnship.	229	Horsley, West..	"	Parish	706
rncastle	Lincoln	Soke	10 739	Horsleydown, St. John	"	Sub-dis.	11 393
rncastle	"	L. Sub.	43 696	Horsleydown, St. Mark	"	Ecl. Dis.	2 920
rncastle	"	District	24 718	Horstead, &c...	Norfolk	Parish	608
rncastle	"	Sub-dis.	9 112	Horsted Keynes.	Sussex	Parish	790
rncastle	"	Parish	4 944	Horsted, Little..	"	Parish	296
rncastle	"	Town	4 846	Horton..	Bucks	Parish	810
rnchurch	Essex	Sub-dis.	6 228	Horton by Malpas	Cheshire	Tnship.	122
rnchurch	"	Parish	2 227	Horton w. Peele.	"	Tnship.	40
rncliffe	Northumberland	Tnship.	299	Horton..	Dorset	Parish	431
rndean	Hants	Sub-dis.	2 497	Horton..	Gloucester	Parish	454
rndon, East..	Essex	Parish	475	Horton Kirby..	Kent	Parish	867
rndon, West.	"	Parish	94	Horton..	Northampton	Parish	76
rndon on the Hill,,		Parish	522	Horton..	Northumberland	Parish	6 787
rne w. Harrowsley	Surrey	Parish	637	Horton..	"	Tnship.	368
rning	Norfolk	Parish	441	Horton Grange..	"	Tnship.	85
rninghold	Leicester	Parish	105	Horton w. Studley	Oxon	Hamlet	347

Name of Place.	County.	Description.	Population.	Name of Place.	County.	Description.	Population.
Horton	*Stafford* ..	Parish	1 046	Hound	*Hants* ..	Parish	2 039
Horton & Horton Hay ,,	..	Tnship.	456	Houndsborough, &c.	*Somerset*	Hund.	7 872
Horton	*York* ..	Sub-dis.	43 078	Hounslow ..	*Middlesex* ..	Town	5 760
Horton	,,	Tnship.	30 189	Hounslow ..	,,	Ecl. Dis.	5 201
Horton, St. James	,,	Ecl. Dis.	1 985	Hove ..	*Sussex* ..	Parish	9 624
Horton	,,	Tnship.	129	Hoveringham ..	*Notts* ..	Parish	387
Horton in Ribblesdale ,,	..	Parish	417	Hoveton, St. John	*Norfolk* ..	Parish	285
Horwich ..	*Lancaster* ..	Sub-dis.	4 051	Hoveton, St. Peter	,,	Parish	131
Horwich ..	,,	Tnship.	3 471	Hovingham ..	*York* ..	Sub-dis.	2 198
Horwich, Holy Trinity ,,	..	Ecl. Dis.	3 471	Hovingham ..	,,	Parish	1 208
Horwood, Great	*Bucks* ..	Parish	846	Hovingham ..	,,	Tnship.	608
Horwood, Great	,,	Tnship.	725	Howard-street ..	*Lancaster* ..	Sub-dis.	24 816
Horwood, Little	,,	Parish	449	How Bound ..	*Cumberland*	Tnship.	219
Horwood ..	*Devon* ..	Parish	109	How Caple ..	*Hereford* ..	Parish	161
Hose	*Leicester* ..	Parish	477	Howdenshire ..	*York* ..	Wapen.	8 108
Hotham.. ..	*York* ..	Parish	333	Howdenshire ..	,,	L. Sub.	8 108
Hothersall ..	*Lancaster* ..	Tnship.	159	Howden.. ..	,,	District	15 001
Hothfield ..	*Kent* ..	Parish	336	Howden.. ..	,,	Sub-dis.	6 934
Hothorpe ..	*Northampton*	Hamlet	12	Howden.. ..	,,	Parish	5 209
Hoton	*Leicester* ..	Tnship.	401	Howden.. ..	,,	Tnship.	2 507
Hough	*Cheshire* ..	Tnship.	846	Howden ..	,,	Town	2 376
Hough on Hill ..	*Lincoln* ..	Parish	655	Howden Fee ..	,,	Manor	356
Hougham ..	*Kent* ..	Sub-dis.	8 242	Howdon Pans	*Northumberland*	Tnship.	1 313
Hougham ..	,,	Parish	3 372	Howdon Pans ..	,,	Ecl. Dis.	3 443
Hougham, Christch. ,,	..	Ecl. Dis.	1 803	Howe ..	*Norfolk* ..	Parish	113
Hougham ..	*Lincoln* ..	Parish	849	Howe ..	*York* ..	Tnship.	36
Houghton Conquest	*Beds* ..	Parish	784	Howell ..	*Lincoln* ..	Parish	72
Houghton Regis	,,	Parish	2 169	Howick..	*Lancaster* ..	Tnship.	93
Houghton ..	*Cumberland*	Tnship.	369	Howick..	*Monmouth* ..	Hamlet	32
Houghton ..	,,	Ecl. Dis.	865	Howick..	*Northumberland*	Parish	265
Houghton Winterborne	*Dorset*	Parish	284	Howsham ..	*York* ..	Tnship.	188
Houghton le Side	*Durham* ..	Tnship.	133	Howtell..	*Northumberland*	Tnship.	141
Houghton le Spring	,,	District	21 773	Hoxne ..	*Suffolk* ..	Hund.	15 673
Houghton le Spring	,,	Sub-dis.	11 238	Hoxne ..	,,	L. Sub.	18 905
Houghton le Spring	,,	Parish	22 582	Hoxne ..	*Suff. & Norf.*	District	14 694
Houghton le Spring	,,	Tnship.	4 741	Hoxne ..	*Suffolk* ..	Parish	1 218
Houghton le Spring ,,	..	Tow	3 824	Hoxton New Town	*Middlesex* .	Sub-dis.	26 516
Houghton ..	*Hants* ..	Parish	428	Hoxton Old Town	,,	Sub-dis.	25 777
Houghton ..	*Hunts* ..	Parish	484	Hoxton, Christch.	,,	Ecl. Dis.	14 610
Houghton, &c. ..	*Lancaster* ..	Tnship.	253	Hoxton, St. John	,,	Ecl. Dis.	24 879
Houghton, West	,,	Ecl. Dis.	3 879	Hoxton, Trinity .	,,	Ecl. Dis.	10 911
Houghton on Hill	*Leicester* ..	Parish	449	Hoylake, Trinity	*Cheshire* ..	Ecl. Dis.	1 017
Houghton on Hill	*Norfolk* ..	Parish	49	Hoyland, High..	*York* ..	Parish	3 357
Houghton, New .	,,	Parish	227	Hoyland, High..	,,	Tnship.	224
Houghton in Hole	,,	Parish	191	Hoyland, Nether	,,	Tnship.	5 352
Houghton, Great	*Northampton*	Parish	365	Hoyland Swaine	,,	Tnship.	689
Houghton, Little	,,	Parish	578	Hubberston ..	*Pembroke* ..	Parish	1 270
Houghton, &c.	*Northumberland*	Tnship.	147	Huby ..	*York* ..	Tnship.	572
Houghton, Little	,,	Tnship.	130	Hucclecote ..	*Gloucester* ..	Hamlet	460
Houghton, Long	,,	Parish	777	Hucclecote ..	,,	Ecl. Dis.	359
Houghton, Long	,,	Tnship.	491	Hucking ..	*Kent* ..	Parish	119
Houghton ..	*Sussex* ..	Parish	165	Hucklow, Great .	*Derby* ..	Hamlet	242
Houghton, Great	*York* ..	Tnship.	309	Hucklow, Little .	,,	Hamlet	237
Houghton, Little	,,	Tnship.	93	Hucknall, Ault..	,,	Parish	686

Name of Place.	County.	Description.	Population.	Name of Place.	County.	Description.	Population.
Iucknall Torkard	Notts ..	Parish	2 836	Humber	.. York ..	Sub-dis.	10 690
Iucknall un. Huthwaite	„ ..	Tnship.	1 160	Humber	.. „ ..	Ward	4 237
Iuddersfield	.. York ..	District	131 336	Humbershoe'	.. Beds ..	Hamlet	418
Iuddersfield	.. „ ..	Sub-dis.	34 877	Humberstone	.. Leicester ..	Parish	515
Iuddersfield	.. „ ..	Parish	52 254	Humberstone	.. Lincoln ..	Parish	277
Iuddersfield	.. „ ..	Tnship.	34 877	Humberton	.. York ..	Tnship.	57
Iuddersfield	.. „ ..	P. Bor.	34 877	Humbleton	Northumberland	Tnship.	152
Holy Trinity	.. „ ..	Ecl. Dis.	3 316	Humbleton	.. York ..	Sub-dis.	1 438
St. Paul	.. „ ..	Ecl. Dis.	5 219	Humbleton	.. „ ..	Parish	594
St. Thomas	.. „ ..	Ecl. Dis.	4 814	Humbleton	.. „ ..	Tnship.	138
Iuddington	.. Worcester ..	Parish	87	Humbleyard	.. Norfolk ..	Hund.	5 620
Iuddleston & Lumby	York ..	Tnship.	267	Humbleyard	.. „ ..	Sub-dis.	5 620
Iudswell	.. „ ..	Tnship.	249	Humby, Little	.. Lincoln ..	Hamlet	99
Iuggate	.. „ ..	Parish	589	Humshaugh	Northumberland	Tnship.	443
Iugglescote, &c.	Leicester ..	Tnship.	1 227	Huncoat	.. Lancaster ..	Tnship.	839
Iughenden	.. Bucks ..	Parish	1 653	Huncote	.. Leicester ..	Hamlet	440
Iughley	.. Salop ..	Parish	98	Hundersfield, St. Mary	Lanc...	Ecl. Dis.	10 610
Iugil	.. Westmoreland	Tnship.	391	Hunderthwaite	. York ..	Tnship.	304
Iuish	.. Devon ..	Parish	171	Hundleby	.. Lincoln ..	Parish	704
Iuish, North	.. „ ..	Parish	432	Hundon	.. Suffolk ..	Parish	1 132
Iuish, South	.. „ ..	Parish	346	Hundred House	. Worcester ..	L. Sub.	7 822
Iuish Champflower	Somerset..	Parish	444	Hungerford	.. Berks, &c...	District	19 882
Iuish Episcopi	.. „ ..	Parish	679	Hungerford	.. Berks & Wilts	Sub-dis.	9 830
Iuish	.. Wilts ..	Parish	133	Hungerford	.. „ „	Parish	3 001
Iulcott	.. Bucks ..	Parish	143	Hungerford	.. Berks ..	Tithing	1 153
Iull	.. York ..	District	56 888	**Hungerford**	.. „ ..	Town	2 031
Iull *(1866) 108,269.*	..	Borough	97 661	Hungerton	.... Leicester ..	Parish	302
St. Mark	.. „ ..	Ecl. Dis.	7 172	Hungerton	.. „ ..	—	196
St. Paul	.. „ ..	Ecl. Dis.	9 480	Hungry-Bentley	Derby ..	Liberty	82
St. Stephen	.. „ ..	Ecl. Dis.	11 428	Hunmanby	.. York ..	Sub-dis.	3 914
Iulland	.. Derby ..	Tithing	189	Hunmanby	.. „ ..	Parish	1 425
Iull & Appleton	Cheshire ..	Tnship.	1 828	Hunmanby	.. „ ..	Tnship.	1 387
Iulland Ward	.. Derby ..	Tnship.	330	Hunningham	.. Warwick ..	Parish	253
Iulland Ward Intakes	„ ..	Tnship.	44	Hunnington	.. Worcester ..	Tnship.	147
Iullavington	.. Wilts ..	Parish	700	Hunsdon	.. Herts ..	Parish	516
Iullavington	.. „ ..	—	659	Hunshelf	.. .. York	Tnship.	1 150
Iull Bridge	.. York ..	Hamlet	57	Hunsingore	.. .. „	Parish	561
Iulme Walfield	. Cheshire ..	Tnship.	111	Hunsingore	.. .. „	Tnship.	192
Iulme	.. Lancaster ..	Sub-dis.	71 128	Hunslet	.. .. „	District	102 649
Iulme	.. „ ..	Tnship.	68 433	Hunslet	.. .. „	Sub-dis.	25 763
Holy Trinity	.. „ ..	Ecl. Dis.	12 067	Hunslet	.. .. „	Dis. Par.	25 763
St. George	.. „ ..	Ecl. Dis.	27 795	Hunslet, St. Mary	.. „	Ecl. Dis.	17 368
St. John	.. „ ..	Ecl. Dis.	8 370	Hunsley Beacon, North	„	L. Sub.	14 560
St. Mark	.. „ ..	Ecl. Dis.	5 637	Hunsley Beacon, South	„	L. Sub.	13 770
St. Mary	.. „ ..	Ecl. Dis.	6 730	Hunsonby & Winskel	Cumb. ..	Tnship.	208
St. Paul	.. „ ..	Ecl. Dis.	6 375	Hunstanton	.. Norfolk ..	Parish	490
St. Philip	.. „ ..	Ecl. Dis.	8 711	Hunsterson	.. Cheshire ..	Tnship.	212
Iulne Park	Northumberland	Tnship.	117	Hunston	.. Suffolk ..	Parish	172
Iulse	.. Cheshire ..	Tnship.	65	Hunston	.. Sussex ..	Parish	176
Iulton	.. Lancaster ..	Sub-dis.	6 488	Hunstonworth	.. Durham ..	Parish	778
Iulton, Little	.. „ ..	Tnship.	3 390	Hunsworth	.. York ..	Tnship.	1 199
Iulton, Middle	. „ ..	Tnship.	790	Huntingdonshire	.. ..	County	64 250
Iulton, Over	.. „ ..	Tnship.	447	Huntingdon	.. Hunts ..	District	20 518
Iumber	.. Hereford ..	Parish	251	Huntingdon	.. „ ..	Sub-dis.	9 368

Name of Place.	County.	Description.	Population.	Name of Place.	County.	Description.	Populatio
Huntingdon	Hunts	M. Bor.	3 816	Hutton John	Cumberland.	Tnship.	3
		P. Bor.	6 254	Hutton Roof	,,	Tnship.	16
Huntingfield	Suffolk	Parish	369	Hutton Soil	,,	Tnship.	35
Huntington	Cheshire	Tnship.	113	Hutton Henry	Durham	Tnship.	39
Huntington	Hereford	Hund.	6 028	Hutton	Essex	Parish	40
Huntington	,,	Parish	279	Hutton	Lancaster	Tnship.	46
Huntington	,,	Tnship.	154	Hutton	Somerset	Parish	35
Huntington	Stafford	Tnship.	161	Hutton, New	Westmoreland	Tnship.	12
Huntington	York	Parish	671	Hutton, Old, &c.	,,	Tnship.	40
Huntington	,,	Tnship.	529	Hutton Roof	,,	Tnship.	28
Huntley	Gloucester	Sub-dis.	5 715	Hutton	York	Sub-dis.	2 52
Huntley	,,	Parish	533	Hutton Bonville	,,	Chap.	12
Hunton	Hants	Chap.	105	Hutton Bushell	,,	Sub-dis.	4 66
Hunton	Kent	Parish	935	Hutton Bushell	,,	Parish	91
Hunton	York	Tnship.	524	Hutton Bushell	,,	Tnship.	52
Huntsham	Devon	Parish	248	Hutton-Conyers	,,	Tnship.	158
Huntshaw	,,	Parish	233	Hutton Cranswick	,,	Parish	1 41
Huntspill & Puriton	Somerset	Hund.	2 299	Hutton Cranswick	,,	Tnship.	1 31
Huntspill	,,	Sub-dis.	4 003	Hutton Hang	,,	Tnship.	34
Huntspill	,,	Parish	1 695	Hutton le Hole	,,	Tnship.	27
Huntspill, All Saints	,,	Ecl. Dis.	678	Hutton Lowcross	,,	Tnship.	27
Hunwick, &c.	Durham	Tnship.	1 203	Hutton Magna	,,	Parish	26
Hunwick, St. Paul	,,	Ecl. Dis.	1 487	Hutton Magna	,,	Tnship.	18
Hunworth	Norfolk	Parish	206	Hutton Mulgrave	,,	Tnship.	7
Hurdsfield	Cheshire	Tnship.	3 836	Hutton Rudby	,,	Tnship.	76
Hurdsfield, Trinity	,,	Ecl. Dis.	3 836	Huttons Ambo	,,	Parish	44
Hurleston	,,	Tnship.	181	Hutton Sessay	,,	Tnship.	136
Hurley	Berks	Parish	1 184	Hutton Wandesley	,,	Tnship.	122
Hursley	Hants	Union	2 550	Huxham	Devon	Parish	134
Hursley	,,	Sub-dis.	2 550	Huxley	Cheshire	Tnship.	253
Hursley	,,	Parish	1 540	Huxloe	Northampton	Hund.	16 724
Hurst	Berks	Parish	2 630	Huyton	Lancaster	Sub-dis.	4 094
Hurst, Old	Hunts	Parish	174	Huyton	,,	Parish	4 054
Hurst	Kent	Parish	51	Huyton	,,	Tnship.	1 612
Hurst, St. John	Lancaster	Ecl. Dis.	6 214	Hyckham, North	Lincoln	Parish	464
Hurst	Northumberland	Tnship.	41	Hyckham, South	Lincoln	Parish	155
Hurstbourne Priors	Hants	Parish	437	Hyde, E. & West	Beds	Hamlet	869
Hurstbourne-Tarrant	Hants, &c.	Sub-dis.	2 875	Hyde, East	,,	Ecl. Dis.	419
Hurstbourne-Tarrant	Hants	Parish	839	Hyde	Cheshire	Sub-dis.	20 594
Hurstingstone	Hunts	Hund.	19 961	Hyde	,,	Tnship.	13 722
Hurstingstone	,,	L. Sub.	21 910	Hyde	,,	Town	13 722
Hurstley	Hereford	Tnship.	101	Hyde, St. George	,,	Ecl. Dis.	8 287
Hurstmonceux	Sussex	Parish	1 287	Hyde, St. Thomas	,,	Ecl. Dis.	5 435
St. John	,,	Ecl. Dis.	763	Hyde	Gloucester	Hamlet	11
Hurstpierpoint	,,	Sub-dis.	6 158	Hyde Common	Hants	Ecl. Dis.	837
Hurstpierpoint	,,	Parish	2 558	Hyde, West	Herts	Ecl. Dis.	466
Hurworth	Durham	Parish	1 525	Hydes, Pastures	Warwick	Hamlet	41
Hurworth	,,	Tnship.	1 192	Hylton	Durham	Tnship.	487
Husbands-Bosworth	Leicester	Parish	934	Hylton, South	,,	Ecl. Dis.	2 036
Husborne-Crawley	Beds	Parish	535	Hyson Green	Notts	Sub-dis.	3 561
Husthwaite	York	Parish	616	Hyson Green	,,	Ecl. Dis.	2 858
Husthwaite	,,	Tnship.	446	Hyssington	Montg. & Salop	Parish	341
Huttoft	Lincoln	Parish	710	Hyssington	Montgomery	—	284
Hutton in Forest	Cumberland	Parish	255	Hythe, St. John	Hants	Ecl. Dis.	654

Name of Place.	County.	Description.	Population.	Name of Place.	County.	Description.	Population.
...ne ..	Kent ..	Sub-dis.	5 743	Ilar, Upper ..	Cardigan ..	L. Sub.	10 454
...ne, St. Leonard	,,	Parish	2 871	Ilchester ..	Somerset ..	Sub-dis.	2 492
...ne, West ..	,,	Parish	130	Ilchester ..	,,	Parish	781
...he ..	,,	M. Bor.	3 001	Ilderton	Northumberland	Parish	571
		P. Bor.	21 367	Ilderton..	,,	Tnship.	124
...erton	Dorset ..	Parish	237	Ilford ..	Essex ..	L. Sub.	82 283
...	Derby ..	Tnship.	69	Ilford ..	,,	Sub-dis.	5 405
...ey ..	Hants ..	Parish	286	Ilford, Great ..	,,	Ward	4 523
...ock ..	Leicester ..	Sub-dis.	6 243	Ilford, Great ..	,,	Ecl. Dis.	3 688
...ock ..	,,	Parish	2 334	Ilford, Little ..	,,	Parish	594
...ck ..	,,	Tnship.	1 107	Ilfracombe ..	Devon	Sub-dis.	5 663
...one ..	Bucks & Oxon	Parish	325	Ilfracombe ..	,,	Parish	3 851
...mb ..	Gloucester ..	Parish	164	Ilfracombe ..	,,	Town	3 034
...mb ..	,,	Hamlet	12	St. Philip and St. James ,,		Ecl. Dis.	1 291
...nham	Middlesex ..	Parish	351	Ilkeston..	Derby & Notts	Sub-dis.	13 745
...ord ..	Bucks & Oxon	Parish	437	Ilkeston..	Derby ..	Parish	8 374
...ord ..	Bucks ..	—	416	Ilkeston ..	,,	Town	3 330
...am ..	Kent ..	Parish	588	Ilketshall, St. Andrew	Suffolk ..	Parish	515
...eford	Herts ..	Parish	546	Ilketshall, St. John	,,	Parish	77
...esham	Sussex ..	Parish	816	Ilketshall, St. Lawrence	,,	Parish	202
...eton..	Cambs ..	Parish	721	Ilketshall, St. Marg.	,,	Parish	326
...ingham	Suffolk ..	Parish	625	Ilkley ..	York ..	Parish	1 407
...vorth	,,	Parish	65	Ilkley ..	,,	Tnship.	1 043
...ary ..	Oxon ..	Parish	233	Illey ..	Worcester ..	Tnship.	88
...esleigh	Devon ..	Parish	529	Illington ..	Norfolk ..	Parish	88
...inshall	Cheshire ..	Liberty	22	Illmire ..	Bucks ..	Parish	79
...	Devon ..	Parish	665	Illogan ..	Cornwall ..	Sub-dis.	9 683
...ford ..	,,	Parish	358	Illogan ..	,,	Parish	9 683
...Hill, St. Mary	Kent ..	Ecl. Dis.	706	Illsfield ..	Hants ..	Parish	255
...n ..	Sussex ..	Parish	600	Ilmington	Warw. & Glouc.	Parish	1 000
...e ..	York ..	Sub-dis.	14 574	Ilmington ..	Warwick ..	Tnship.	979
...e ..	,,	Tnship.	9 155	Ilminster ..	Somerset ..	Sub-dis.	7 448
...cote..	Warwick ..	Parish	115	Ilminster ..	,,	Parish	3 241
...aiston	Wilts ..	Parish	542	Ilminster ..	,,	Town	2 194
...aiston	,,	Tithing	212	Ilsington ..	Devon ..	Parish	1 209
...idgehay & Alton	Derby ..	Tnship.	233	Ilsley ..	Berks ..	Sub-dis.	5 635
...idgehay, St. Jas.	,,	Ecl.Dis.	639	Ilsley, East ..	,,	Parish	746
...toue ..	Berks ..	Tithing	142	Ilsley, West ..	,,	Parish	432
...worth	Hants ..	Chap.	333	Ilston ..	Glamorgan .	Parish	295
...ey ..	Oxon ..	Parish	1 004	Ilston on Hill ..	Leicester ..	Tnship.	235
...ey ..	,,	Hamlet	770	Ilton ..	Somerset ..	Parish	492
...ld ..	Kent ..	Parish	88	Ilton w. Pott ..	York ..	Tnship.	200
...ld ..	Sussex ..	Parish	1 307	Imber ..	Wilts ..	Parish	382
...rd ..	,,	Parish	167	Immingham ..	Lincoln ..	Parish	261
...n ..	Monmouth ..	Parish	20	Impington ..	Cambs ..	Parish	335
...n-Rhyn ..	Salop ..	Tnship.	975	Ince ..	Cheshire ..	Parish	371
...orough ..	Norfolk ..	Parish	192	Ince Blundell ..	Lancaster ..	Tnship.	572
...tenhill-Park .	Lancaster ..	Tnship.	161	Ince in Makerfield	,,	Tnship.	8 266
...tfield ..	Salop ..	Parish	344	Ingarsby ..	Leicester ..	Hamlet	54
...tham ..	Kent ..	Parish	1 152	Ingatestone ..	Essex ..	Sub-dis.	6 573
...n ..	Suffolk ..	Parish	336	Ingatestone ..	,,	Parish	332
...n ..	Stafford ..	Parish	243	Ingbirchworth ..	York ..	Tnship.	368
... ..	Cardigan ..	Hund.	18 433	Ingerthorpe ..	,,	Tnship.	39
				Ingestre..	Stafford ..	Parish	151

Name of Place.	County.	Description.	Population.	Name of Place.	County.	Description.	Popul.
Ingham	Lincoln ..	Parish	646	Irnham	Lincoln ..	Tnship.	
Ingham.. ..	Norfolk ..	Parish	464	Iron Acton ..	Gloucester ..	Sub-dis.	5
Ingham.. ..	Suffolk ..	Parish	236	Iron Acton ..	,, ..	Parish	1
Ingleby ..	Derby ..	Tnship.	140	Ironbridge ..	Salop ..	Town	3
Ingleby Arncliffe	York ..	Parish	326	Ironbridge, St. Luke	,,	Ecl. Dis.	3
Ingleby Barwick .	,, ..	Tnship.	140	Ironville ..	Derby ..	Ecl. Dis.	2
Ingleby Greenhow	,, ..	Parish	481	Irstead	Norfolk ..	Parish	
Ingleby Greenhow	,, ..	Tnship	207	Irthington ..	Cumberland	Parish	
Inglesham ..	Wilts ..	Parish	119	Irthington ..	,,	Tnship.	
Ingleton.. ..	Durham ..	Tnship.	300	Irthlingborough .	Northampton	Parish	1
Ingleton, St. John	,, ..	Ecl. Dis.	667	Irton	Cumberland	Parish	
Ingleton ..	York ..	Tnship.	1 247	Irton	York ..	Tnship.	
Ingoe ..	Northumberland	Tnship.	243	Isaf	Carnarvon ..	Hund.	4 9
Ingoldisthorpe ..	Norfolk ..	Parish	372	Isaled	Denbigh ..	Hund.	11 8
Ingoldmells ..	Lincoln ..	Parish	319	Iscoyd	Flint ..	Tnship.	
Ingoldsby	,, ..	Parish	427	Isdulas	Denbigh ..	Hund.	13
Ingram ..	Northumberland	Parish	200	Isell	Cumberland	Parish	
Ingram, &c. ..	,,	Tnship.	37	Isell Old Park ..	,,	Tnship.	
Ingrave.. ..	Essex ..	Parish	516	Isfield	Sussex ..	Sub-dis.	2 4
Ingrow w. Hainworth	York ..	Ecl. Dis.	4 072	Isfield	,, ..	Parish	
Ingworth ..	Norfolk ..	Parish	153	Isgorfai	Carnarvon ..	Hund.	22 7
Inkberrow ..	Worcester ..	Parish	1 573	Isgraig	Merioneth ..	Tnship.	
Inkpen	Berks ..	Parish	748	Isham	Northampton	Parish	
Inner Temple ..	Middlesex ..	Parish	148	Ishlawrcoed ..	Monmouth ..	Hamlet	2 6
Inskip w. Sowerby	Lancaster ..	Tnship.	663	Iskennen ..	Carmarthen .	Commot	8 1
Inskip, St. Peter.	,, ..	Ecl.Dis.	780	Islandshire	Northumberland	Ward	4 9
Instow	Devon ..	Parish	614	Islandshire ..	,,	Sub-dis.	4 0
Intwood.. ..	Norfolk ..	Parish	68	Isle-Abbots ..	Somerset ..	Parish	3
Inwardleigh ..	Devon ..	Parish	635	Isle-Brewers ..	,, ..	Parish	3
Inworth.. ..	Essex ..	Parish	655	Isleham ..	Cambs ..	Parish	1 9
Ipersbridge ..	Hants ..	—	25	Islehampstead-Cheynes	Bucks .	Parish	4
Iping	Sussex ..	Parish	404	Isle of Alderney .	Channel Isle	Island	4 9
Ipplepen ..	Devon ..	Parish	977	,, Anglesey .	County ..	Island	54 6
Ipplepen ..	,, ..	—	808	,, Bardsey ..	Carnarvon..	Island	
Ippollitts ..	Herts ..	Parish	952	,, Barry ..	Glamorgan .	Island	
Ipsden	Oxon ..	Parish	623	,, Bryher ..	Scilly Isle ..	Island	1
Ipsley	Warwick ..	Parish	1 127	,, Caldy ..	Pembroke ..	Island	
Ipstones.. ..	Stafford ..	Sub-dis.	6 118	,, Chapel ..	Lancaster ..	Island	
Ipstones.. ..	,, ..	Parish	1 904	,, Coquet	Northumberland	Island	
Ipswich	Suffolk ..	L. Sub.	63 559	,, Elmley ..	Kent ..	Parish	1
Ipswich.. ..	,, ..	District	37 881	,, Fern, or Staples	Nrthbld.	Island	
Ipswich ..	,, ..	Borough	37 950	,, Guernsey .	Channel Isle	Island	29 8
Ipswich, Trinity .	,, ..	Ecl. Dis.	2 326	,, Herm ..	,,	Island	
Irby	Cheshire ..	Tnship.	177	,, Hilbre ..	Chester ..	Island	
Irby in Marsh ..	Lincoln ..	Parish	169	,, Holme ..	Lancaster ..	Island	
Irby upon Humber	,, ..	Parish	235	,, Holy Island	Nrthumbld.	Island	9
Irchester ..	Northampton	Parish	1 168	,, Jersey ..	Channel Isle	Island	55 6
Ireby	Cumberland	Parish	465	,, Jethou ..	,,	Island	
Ireby, High ..	,,	Tnship.	128	,, Looe ..	Cornwall ..	Island	
Ireby, Low ..	,,	Tnship.	337	,, Lundy ..	Devon ..	Island	
Ireby	Lancaster ..	Tnship.	113	,, Man ..	(Mainland)	Island	52 4
Ireton Wood ..	Derby ..	Tnship.	156	,, Calf of Man	..	Island	2
Irmingland ..	Norfolk ..	Parish	15	,, Peel ..	Lancaster ..	Island	
Irnham	Lincoln ..	Parish	347	,, Portland..	Dorset ..	Sub-dis.	8 4

Name of Place.	County.	Description.	Population.	Name of Place.	County.	Description.	Population.
Isle of Ramsey ..	Pembroke ..	Island	15	Itchingfield ..	Sussex ..	Parish	377
„ St. Agnes .	Scilly Isle ..	Island	200	Itchingswell ..	Hants ..	Parish	452
„ St. Martin	„ ..	Island	185	Itchington Bishops	Warwick ..	Parish	598
„ St. Mary..	„ ..	Island	1 532	Itchington, Long	„ ..	Parish	1 150
„ St. Michael's Mt.	Cornwl.	Island	132	Itonfield ..	Cumberland	Tnship.	241
„ Sark ..	Channel Isle	Island	583	Itteringham ..	Norfolk ..	Parish	364
„ Sheppey..	Kent ..	Island	18 494	Itton ..	Monmouth ..	Parish	196
„ Skerries ..	Anglesey ..	Island	6	Itton ..	„	Hamlet	164
„ Skoholm, or Shokham	Pembroke ..	Island	2	Ivegill ..	Cumberland	Tnship.	126
„ Thanet ..	Kent ..	Union	31 862	Ivenbrook-Grange	Derby ..	Tnship.	32
„ Trescoe ..	Scilly Isle ..	Island	399	Iver ..	Bucks ..	Sub-dis.	5 787
„ Walner	Lancaster ..	Island	294	Iver ..	„ ..	Parish	2 114
„ Wight ..	Hants, I. W.	Island	55 362	Ivestone..	Durham ..	Tnship.	3 327
„ Wight ..	„ „	Division	47 428	Ivinghoe ..	Bucks ..	Sub-dis.	2 477
Isleworth ..	Middlesex ..	Hund.	23 610	Ivinghoe ..	„	Parish	1 849
Isleworth ..	„ ..	Sub-dis.	15 533	Ivington, St. John	Hereford ..	Tnship.	750
Isleworth ..	„ ..	Parish	8 437	Ivington, St. John	„ ..	Ecl. Dis.	750
Isleworth, St. John	„ ..	Ecl. Dis.	1 387	Ivybridge, St. John	Devon ..	Ecl. Dis.	1 348
Isley-Walton ..	Leicester ..	Chap.	46	Ivychurch ..	Kent ..	Parish	273
Islington ..	Lancaster ..	Sub-dis.	41 241	Iwade ..	„ ..	Parish	182
Islington ..	Middlesex	District	155 341	Iwerne Courtnay	Dorset ..	Parish	620
Islington, East..	„	Sub-dis.	79 899	Iwerne Minster..	„ ..	Parish	712
Islington, West..	„	Sub-dis.	75 442	Iwerne, Steepleton	„ ..	Parish	59
Islington ..	„	Parish	155 341	Ixworth..	Suffolk ..	L. Sub.	48 409
1 Upper Holloway Ward	„	Ward	16 264	Ixworth..	„ ..	Sub-dis.	6 250
2 Lower Holloway Ward	„	Ward	21 269	Ixworth..	„ ..	Parish	1 074
3 Highbury Ward	„	Ward	18 366	Jacobstow ..	Cornwall ..	Parish	462
4 Thornhill Ward	„	Ward	24 088	Jacobstowe ..	Devon ..	Parish	232
5 Barnsbury Ward	„	Ward	17 450	Jarrow ..	Durham ..	Parish	52 925
6 St. Mary's Ward	„	Ward	12 971	Jeffreston ..	Pembroke ..	Parish	634
7 Canonbury Ward	„	Ward	18 527	Jersey, Isle of ..	Channel Isle	Island	55 613
8 St. Peter's Ward	„	Ward	26 406	Jesmond	Northumberland	Tnship.	2 230
All Saints ..	„	Ecl. Dis.	17 489	Jesmond ..	„	Ecl. Dis.	3 442
Christchurch..	„	Ecl. Dis.	3 229	Jethou, Isle of ..	Channel Isle	Island	5
St. Andrew ..	„	Ecl. Dis.	18 091	Jevington ..	Sussex ..	Parish	263
St. James ..	„	Ecl. Dis.	10 563	Jews Lane ..	Norfolk ..	Ward	650
St. John ..	„	Ecl. Dis.	7 286	Johnby..	Cumberland	Tnship.	92
St. Jude ..	„	Ecl. Dis.	6 620	Johnston ..	Pembroke ..	Parish	275
St. Luke ..	„	Ecl. Dis.	6 843	Jordanston ..	„ ..	Parish	131
St. Mark ..	„	Ecl. Dis.	6 873	Jurby ..	Isle of Man .	Parish	911
St. Matthew..	„	Ecl. Dis.	6 791	Kaber ..	Westmoreland	Tnship.	268
St. Paul ..	„	Ecl. Dis.	11 789	Kate Hill, St. John	Worcester .	Ecl. Dis.	6 370
St. Peter ·	„	Ecl. Dis.	13 509	Kea ..	Cornwall ..	Sub-dis.	6 360
St. Philip ..	„	Ecl. Dis.	9 015	Kea ..	„ ..	Parish	3 949
St. Stephen ..	„	Ecl. Dis.	7 321	Keadby..	Lincoln ..	Tnship.	551
Trinity ..	„	Ecl. Dis.	11 704	Keal, East ..	„ ..	Parish	393
Islip ..	Northampton	Parish	627	Keal, West ..	„ ..	Parish	511
Islip ..	Oxon ..	Parish	688	Kearby w. Netherby	York ..	Tnship.	207
Issayndre ..	Cardigan ..	Tnship.	360	Kearsley	Northumberland	Tnship.	20
Isygarreg ..	Montgomery	Tnship.	402	Keckwick ..	Cheshire ..	Tnship.	115
Itchenor West ..	Sussex ..	Parish	167	Keddington ..	Lincoln ..	Parish	138
Itchin Abbas ..	Hants ..	Parish	214	Kedington ..	Suff. & Essex	Parish	996
Itchin Stoke ..	„ ..	Parish	295				

111

Name of Place.	County.	Description.	Population.	Name of Place.	County.	Description.	Population.
Kedleston	Derby	Parish	116	Kempston	Norfolk	Parish	48
Keelby	Lincoln	Parish	842	Kemp Town	Sussex	Sub-dis.	13 589
Keele	Stafford	Parish	1 062	Kemsing	Kent	Parish	366
Keevil	Wilts	Parish	669	Kenardington	,,	Parish	221
Keevil	,,	Hamlet	429	Kenarth	Carm. & Pem.	Sub-dis.	8 072
Kegidog, St. Geo.	Denbigh	Parish	469	Kenarth	Carmarthen	Parish	1 744
Kegworth	Leicester	Parish	1 819	Kenchester	Hereford	Parish	100
Kegworth	,,	Tnship.	1 773	Kencott	Oxon	Parish	214
Keighley	York	District	43 122	Kendal	Westmoreland	Ward	19 234
Keighley	,,	Sub-dis.	21 859	Kendal Ward	,,	L. Sub.	27 680
Keighley	,,	Parish	18 819	Kendal	Westm. & Lanc.	District	37 463
Keighley	,,	Town	15 005	Kendal	Westmoreland	Sub-dis.	12 305
Keinton Mandeville	Somerset	Parish	538	Kendal	,,	Parish	18 600
Keisby	Lincoln	Tnship.	84	Kendal	,,	Tnship.	10 418
Kelby	,,	Chap.	99	**Kendal**	,,	Borough	12 029
Kelfield	York	Tnship.	388	Kendal, St. George	,,	Ecl. Dis.	3 144
Kelham	Notts	Parish	178	Kendal, St. Thomas	,,	Ecl. Dis.	2 092
Kelk, Great	York	Tnship.	211	Kenderchurch	Hereford	Parish	99
Kelk, Little	,,	Parish	57	Kenfigg	Glamorgan	Parish	278
Kellet, Nether	Lancaster	Tnship.	284	**Kenfigg**	,,	P. Bor.	442
Kellet, Over	,,	Tnship.	425	Kenilworth	Warwick	Sub-dis.	6 195
Kelling	Norfolk	Parish	211	Kenilworth	,,	Parish	3 680
Kellington	York	Parish	1 443	Kenilworth St. John	,,	Ecl. Dis.	1 027
Kellington	,,	Tnship.	300	**Kenilworth**	,,	Town	3 013
Kelloe	Durham	Parish	12 867	Kenley	Salop	Parish	235
Kelloe	,,	Tnship.	530	Kenn	Devon	Parish	1 064
Kelly	Devon	Parish	217	Kenn	Somerset	Parish	282
Kelmarsh	Northampton	Parish	167	Kennarth	Radnor	Tnship.	500
Kelmscott	Oxon	Tnship.	141	Kennerleigh	Devon	Parish	106
Kelsale	Suffolk	Parish	1 084	Kennet, East	Wilts	Parish	78
Kelsall	Cheshire	Tnship.	542	Kennett	Cambs	Parish	207
Kelsey, North	Lincoln	Parish	870	Kenninghall	Norfolk	Sub-dis.	6 025
Kelsey, South	,,	Parish	633	Kenninghall	,,	Parish	1 405
Kelshall	Herts	Parish	318	Kennington	Berks	Tnship.	138
Kelstern	Lincoln	Parish	196	Kennington	Kent	Parish	567
Kelstern	,,	Tnship.	134	Kennington First	Surrey	Sub-dis.	30 785
Kelsterton	Flint	Tnship.	107	Kennington Second	,,	Sub-dis.	20 440
Kelston	Somerset	Parish	212	Kennington, St. Barnab.	,,	Ecl. Dis.	9 722
Kelvedon	Essex	Sub-dis.	4 423	Kennington, St. Mark	,,	Ecl. Dis.	26 345
Kelvedon	,,	Parish	1 741	Kennythorpe	York	Tnship.	57
Kelvedon-Hatch	,,	Parish	454	Kensal Green, St. John	Mdlx.	Ecl. Dis.	4 662
Kelways	Wilts	Parish	18	Kensington	,,	L. Sub.	187 140
Kemberton	Salop	Parish	244	Kensington	,,	District	185 950
Kemble	Wilts	Parish	466	Kensington Town	,,	Sub-dis.	51 910
Kemerton	Gloucester	Parish	559	Kensington	,,	Parish	70 108
Kemes	Pembroke	Hund.	13 576	1 Holy Trinity Brompton Wd.		Ward	18 198
Kemes	,,	L. Sub.	14 384	2 St. John Notting Hill and and St. James Norland Ward		Ward	30 176
Kemeys Commander	Monmouth	Parish	76				
Kemeys Inferior	,,	Parish	122				
Kempley	Gloucester	Parish	311	3 St. Mary Abbotts Ward		Ward	21 734
Kempsey	Worcester	Sub-dis.	3 511	Kensington, St. Barnabas	,,	Ecl. Dis.	2 584
Kempsey	,,	Parish	1 433	Kenswick	Worcester	Parish	21
Kempsford	Gloucester	Parish	1 007	Kensworth	Herts	Parish	925
Kempston	Beds	Parish	2 191	Kent		County	733 887

Name of Place.	County.	Description.	Population.	Name of Place.	County.	Description.	Population.
Kent, Eastern Division		E. Div.	247 027	Kettlewell	Norfolk	Ward	1 163
„ Western Division		W. Div.	486 860	Kettlewell	York	Sub-dis.	1 141
Kentchurch	Heref. & Mon.	Sub-dis.	3 567	Kettlewell	„	Parish	646
Kentchurch	Hereford	Parish	325	Kettlewell	„	Tnship.	485
Kentford	Suffolk	Parish	210	Ketton	Rutland	Parish	1 053
Kentisbeare	Devon	Parish	1 068	Kew	Surrey	Parish	1 099
Kentisbury	„	Parish	385	Kewstoke	Somerset	Parish	550
Kentish Town	Middlesex	Sub-dis.	44 317	Kexborough	York	Tnship.	605
Kentish Town	„	Ecl. Dis.	11 595	Kexby	Lincoln	Tnship.	272
Kentmere	Westmoreland	Tnship.	186	Kexby	York	Tnship.	182
Kenton	Devon	Sub-dis.	5 442	Kexby, St. Paul	„	Ecl. Dis.	182
Kenton	„	Parish	1 961	Keyham	Leicester	Tnship.	122
Kenton	Northumberland	Tnship.	658	Keyingham	York	Parish	639
Kenton	Suffolk	Parish	308	Keymer	Sussex	Parish	1 612
Kent Road	Surrey	Sub-dis.	19 652	Keynsham	Somerset	Hund.	8 649
Kent Town, St. Paul	„	Ecl. Dis.	887	Keynsham	„	L. Sub.	7 012
Kenwyn	Cornwall	Sub-dis.	10 673	Keynsham	Som. & Glouc.	District	21 802
Kenwyn	„	Parish	10 639	Keynsham	Somerset	Sub-dis.	4 214
Kenyon	Lancaster	Tnship.	274	Keynsham	„	Parish	2 190
Kepwick	York	Tnship.	161	Keysoe	Beds	Parish	867
Kerdistone	Norfolk	Parish	207	Keyston	Hunts	Parish	223
Keresley	Warwick	Hamlet	567	Keythorpe	Leicester	Liberty	29
Keresley & Coundon	„	Ecl. Dis.	792	Keyworth	Notts	Parish	736
Kermincham	Cheshire	Tnship.	163	Kibblesworth	Durham	Tnship.	819
Kerrier	Cornwall	Hund.	49 033	Kibbor	Glamorgan	Hund.	10 724
Kerrier	„	L. Sub.	62 132	Kibbor	„	L. Sub.	13 470
Kerry	Montgomery	Sub-dis.	2 601	Kibworth-Beauchamp	Leicester	Parish	1 867
Kerry	„	Parish	2 075	Kibworth-Beauchamp	„	—	868
Kersall	Notts	Tnship.	83	Kibworth-Harcourt	„	Tnship.	466
Kersall Moor, St. Paul	Lanc.	Ecl. Dis.	976	Kidbrooke	Kent	Liberty	804
Kersey	Suffolk	Parish	604	Kidderminster	Worcester	L. Sub.	22 908
Kersley	Lancaster	Tnship.	5 003	Kidderminster	Worcester,&c.	District	30 307
Kesgrave	Suffolk	Parish	93	Kidderminster	Worcester	Sub-dis.	17 912
Kessingland	„	Sub-dis.	4 759	Kidderminster	„	Parish	20 870
Kessingland	„	Parish	872	Kidderminster	„	Borough	15 399
Keston	Kent	Parish	690	Kidderminster	„	Old.Bor.	13 979
Keswick	Cumberland	Sub-dis.	6 274	Kidderminster	„	Foreign	3 933
Keswick	„	Tnship.	2 610	Kiddington	Oxon	Parish	305
Keswick	„	Town	2 610	Kidland	Northumberland	Parish	71
Keswick, St. John	„	Ecl. Dis.	1 583	Kidlington	Oxon	Parish	1 507
Keswick	Norfolk	Parish	154	Kidlington	„	Hamlet	1 190
Keswick, East	York	Tnship.	468	Kidmore End, St. John	„	Ecl. Dis.	605
Kettering	Northampton	L. Sub.	21 121	Kidsgrove, St. Thomas	Stafford	Ecl. Dis.	3 697
Kettering	„	District	18 995	Kidwelly	Carmarthen	Commot	11 860
Kettering	„	Sub-dis.	8 606	Kidwelly	„	Parish	1 652
Kettering	„	Parish	5 845	St. Mary, Within	„	—	1 413
Kettering	„	Town	5 498	St. Mary, Without	„	—	239
Ketteringham	Norfolk	Parish	198	Kiftsgate	Gloucester	Hund.	15 533
Kettlebaston	Suffolk	Parish	198	Kilbourne	Derby	Tnship.	951
Kettleburgh	„	Parish	359	Kilburn	York	Parish	700
Kettleshulme	Cheshire	Tnship.	357	Kilburn	„	Tnship.	434
Kettlestone	Norfolk	Parish	223	Kilby	Leicester	Parish	362
Kettlethorpe	Lincoln	Parish	486	Kildale	York	Parish	221
Kettlethorpe	„	Tnship.	209	Kildwick	„	Sub-dis.	7 853

Name of Place.	County.	Description.	Population.	Name of Place.	County.	Description.	Popula
Kildwick	York	Parish	10 893	Kimble, Little ..	Bucks	Parish	1
Kildwick	,,	Tnship.	170	Kimblesworth ..	Durham	Parish	
Kilgerran	Pembroke	Hund.	4 859	Kimbolton	Hereford	Parish	7.
Kilgerran	,,	L. Sub.	4 859	Kimbolton	Hunts, &c...	Sub-dis.	9 3
Kilgerran	,,	Parish	1 236	Kimbolton	Hunts	Parish	1 6
Kilgwrrwg	Monmouth	Parish	121	Kimcote w. Walton Leicester		Parish	5
Kilham ..	Northumberland	Tnship.	209	Kimmeridge	Dorset	Parish	1.
Kilham ..	York	Parish	1 252	Kimpton	Hants	Parish	3
Kilie Aeron	Cardigan	Parish	301	Kimpton	Herts	Parish	1 0
Kilkhampton	Cornwall	Sub-dis.	2 066	Kinderton w. Hulme Cheshire .		Tnship.	4
Kilkhampton	,,	Parish	1 198	Kineton..	Warwick	Sub-dis.	2 3
Killamarsh	Derby	Parish	1 053	Kineton..	,,	Parish	1 3
Klllerby..	Durham	Tnship.	109	Kineton..	,,	Tnship.	1 0
Killerby..	York	Tnship.	56	Kinfare ..	Staff. & Salop	Sub-dis.	4 8
Killinghall		Tnship.	746	Kinfare ..	Stafford	Parish	3 5
Killingholme	Lincoln	Parish	736	Kinfare	,,	Town	2 1
Killingholme, North	,,	Tnship.	181	Kingerby	Lincoln	Parish	1
Killingholme, South	,,	Tnship.	555	Kingham	Oxon	Parish	6
Killington	Westmoreland	Tnship.	273	King Moor	Cumberland	Parish	4
Killingworth	Northumberland	Tnship.	1 781	Kingsbridge	Devon	District	19 3
Killpeck..	Hereford	Parish	267	Kingsbridge	,,	Sub-dis.	4 4
Killybcbill	Glamorgan .	Parish	1 346	Kingsbridge	,,	Parish	1 5
Kilmersdon	Somerset	Hund	7 358	Kingbridge	Wilts	Hund.	15 3
Kilmersdon	,,	Sub-dis.	3 999	Kings Bromley Hays Stafford .		Parish	
Kilmersdon	,,	Parish	2 194	Kingsbury	Middlesex	Parish	5
Kilmington	Devon	Parish	518	Kingsbury, East .	Somerset	Hund.	7 8
Kilmington	Somerset	Parish	587	Kingsbury, West	,,	Hund.	11 6
Kilmiston	Hants	Parish	193	Kingsbury Episcopi	,,	Parish	1 8
Kilndown, Christch. Kent		Ecl. Dis.	904	Kingsbury	Warwick	Parish	1 4
Kilnhurst, St. Thomas York		Ecl. Dis.	1 247	Kings Caple	Hereford	Parish	3
Kilnsea ..	,,	Parish	179	Kingsclere	Hants	Division	13 3
Kilnwick .	,,	Parish	693	Kingsclere	,,	L. Sub.	13 3
Kilnwick .	,,	Tnship.	272	Kingsclere	,,	District	8 5
Kilnwick Percy..	,,	Parish	132	Kingsclere	,,	Sub-dis.	5 26
Kilpin ..	,,	Tnship.	476	Kingsclere	,,	Parish	2 77
Kilrhedin	Carm. & Pemb.	Parish	1 074	Kings Cliffe	Northampton	Parish	1 36
Kilsby ..	Northampton	Parish	539	Kingscote	Gloucester	Parish	31
Kilton ..	Somerset	Parish	174	Kings Cross, St. Luke Middlesex		Ecl. Dis.	8 02
Kilton ..	York	Tnship.	93	Kings Cross	York	Ecl. Dis.	3 78
Kilve ..	Somerset	Parish	226	Kingsdon	Somerset	Parish	47
Kilverstone	Norfolk	Parish	39	Kingsdown	Kent	Parish	42
Kilvington	Notts	Parish	77	Kingsdown	,,	Parish	9
Kilvington	,,	Hamlet	37	Kingsdown, St. John ,,		Ecl. Dis.	50
Kilvington, North	York	Tnship.	87	Kingsey ..	Bucks & Oxon	Parish	23
Kilvington, South	,,	Parish	360	Kingsey ..	Bucks	—	17
Kilvington, South	,,	Tnship.	233	Kingsholm	Gloucester	Sub-dis.	7 30
Kilworth, North .	Leicester	Parish	409	Kingsholm, St. Catherine ,,		Hamlet	99
Kilworth, South .	,,	Parish	421	Kingsholm, St. Mary	,,	Hamlet	1 03
Kimberley	Norfolk	Parish	112	Kingskerswell	Devon	Parish	90
Kimberley	Notts	Ecl. Dis.	2 821	Kingsland	Hereford	Sub-dis.	4 85
Kimberworth	York	Sub-dis.	17 921	Kingsland	,,	Parish	1 15
Kimberworth	,,	Tnship.	10 610	Kings Langley	Herts	Sub-dis.	2 90
Kimberworth, St. Thos.	,,	Ecl. Dis.	3 848	Kings Langley ..	,,	Parish	1 50
Kimble, Great ..	Bucks	Parish	408	Kingsley	Cheshire	Tnship.	99

Name of Place.	County.	Description.	Population.
Kingsley, St. John	Cheshire	Ecl. Dis.	1 131
Kingsley	Hants	Parish	441
Kingsley	Stafford	Parish	2 040
Kingsley	"	Tnship.	1 332
Kings Lynn	Norfolk	L. Sub.	16 170
Kings Lynn	"	District	16 701
Kings Lynn Middle	"	Sub-dis.	5 955
Kings Lynn North	"	Sub-dis.	3 962
Kings Lynn South	"	Sub-dis.	6 784
Kings Lynn St. John	"	Ecl. Dis.	3 867
Kings Lynn	"	Borough	16 170
Kingsmarsh	Cheshire	Parish	58
Kings Meaburn	Westmoreland	Tnship.	189
Kingsnorth	Kent	Parish	416
Kings Norton	Leicester	Parish	154
Kings Norton	"	Tnship.	71
Kings Norton	Worcester,&c.	District	47 349
Kings Norton	Worcester	Sub-dis.	14 316
Kings Norton	"	Parish	13 634
Kings Nympton	Devon	Parish	697
Kings Pyon	Hereford	Parish	489
Kings Ripton	Hunts	Parish	267
Kings Shelsley	Worcester	Hamlet	267
Kings Sombourn	Hants	Parish	1 241
Kings Sq., St. Barnabas	Mdlx.	Ecl. Dis.	9 125
Kings Sutton	Northampton	Hund.	13 397
Kings Sutton	"	Parish	1 145
Kingstanley	Gloucester	Parish	2 038
Kingsteignton	Devon	Parish	1 652
King Sterndale	Derby	Ecl. Dis.	200
Kingsthorpe	Northampton	Parish	1 906
Kingston Bagpuize	Berks	Parish	283
Kingston Lisle	"	Chap.	236
Kingston	Cambs	Parish	313
Kingston	Devon	Parish	451
Kingston Russell	Dorset	Parish	63
Kingston	Hants	Sub-dis.	23 089
Kingston	" I. W.	Parish	68
Kingston upon Soar	Notts	Parish	197
Kingston	Somerset	Parish	892
Kingston Seymour	"	Parish	336
Kingston	Stafford	Parish	312
Kingston	Surrey	L. Sub.	31 673
Kingston	"	Hund.	22 967
Kingston	Surrey & Mdlx.	District.	36 479
Kingston	Surrey	Sub-dis.	18 112
Kingston on Thames	"	Parish	17 792
Kingston	"	—	16 124
Kingston on Thames	"	M. Bor.	9 790
Kingston Vale, St. John	"	Ecl. Dis.	270
Kingston	Sussex	Parish	45
Kingston by Lewes	"	Parish	137
Kingston by Sea	"	Parish	93
Kingston Deverill	Wilts	Parish	376
Kingston on Hull Boro.	York	L. Sub.	97 661
Kingston upon Hull	"	Borough	97 661
Kingstone	Hereford	Parish	460
Kingstone	Kent	Parish	273
Kingstone	Somerset	Parish	276
Kingstone Winslow	Berks	Hamlet	146
Kings Walden	Herts	Parish	1 183
Kingswear	Devon	Parish	274
Kings Weston	Gloucester	Tithing	216
Kingswinford	Stafford	L. Sub.	65 569
Kingswinford	"	Sub-dis.	34 257
Kingswinford	"	Parish	34 257
Kingswinford, St. Mary	"	Ecl. Dis.	4 029
Kingswood	Bucks	Hamlet	54
Kingswood	Cheshire	Tnship.	160
Kingswood	Gloucester	Parish	1 061
Kingswood, Trinity	"	Ecl. Dis.	4 699
Kingswood	Surrey	Liberty	273
Kingswood St. Andrew	"	Ecl. dis.	838
Kings Worthy	Hants	Parish	359
Kingthorpe	York	Tnship.	54
Kington Magna	Dorset	Parish	552
Kington	Gloucester	Tithing	1 156
Kington	Hereford	L. Sub.	9 158
Kington	Heref. & Radnor	Union	11 930
Kington	Hereford	Sub-dis.	6 296
Kington	"	Parish	3 076
Kington, Old & New	"	Tnship.	2 178
Kington	"	Tnship.	284
Kington	Warwick	Hund.	24 569
Kington	"	L. Sub.	14 428
Kington, St. Michael	Wilts	Parish	1 089
Kington, St. Michael	"	Tithing	530
Kington, West	"	Parish	405
Kington	Worcester	Parish	172
Kingwater	Cumberland	Tnship.	391
Kingweston	Somerset	Parish	172
Kinlet	Salop	Parish	424
Kinnerley	"	Parish	1 310
Kinnersley	Hereford	Parish	313
Kinnersley	Salop	Parish	208
Kinnerton, Lower	Cheshire	Tnship.	99
Kinnerton, Higher	Flint	Tnship.	411
Kinnerton, &c.	Radnor	Tnship.	193
Kinniside	Cumberland	Tnship.	245
Kinoulton	Notts	Parish	430
Kinsham, Lower	Hereford	Tnship.	44
Kinsham, Upper	"	Parish	88
Kinson	Dorset	Tithing	1 201
Kintbury	Berks, &c.	Sub-dis.	4 398
Kintbury	Berks	Parish	1 802
Kintbury Eagle	"	Hund.	8 096
Kinvaston	Stafford	Tnship.	10
Kinwalsey	Warwick	Hamlet	14

I 2

Name of Place.	County.	Description.	Population.	Name of Place	County.	Description.	Population
Kinwardstone ..	*Wilts* ..	Hund.	12 310	Kirkby, East ..	*Lincoln* ..	Parish	432
Kinwarton ..	*Warwick* ..	Parish	64	Kirkby Green ..	,, ..	Parish	175
Kiplin	*York* ..	Tnship.	114	Kirkby-le-Thorpe	,, ..	Parish	208
Kippax	,, ..	Sub-dis.	8 546	Kirkby Underwood	,, ..	Parish	189
Kippax	,, ..	Parish	2 901	Kirkby upon Bain	,, ..	Parish	683
Kippax	,, ..	Tnship.	1 656	Kirkby upon Bain	,, ..	Tnship.	363
Kirby, West ..	*Cheshire* ..	Parish	2 059	Kirkby in Ashfield	*Notts* ..	Parish	2 886
Kirby, West ..	,, ..	Tnship.	413	Kirkby Kendal	*Westmoreland*	Parish	18 600
Kirby-le-Soken..	*Essex* ..	Parish	879	Kirkby Kendal..	,,	Tnship.	10 418
Kirby-Bellars ..	*Leicester* ..	Parish	243	Kirkby Lonsdale	*Wes. & Lanc.*	Sub-dis.	6 734
Kirby-Frith ..	,, ..	Parish	24	Kirkby Lonsdale	*Westmoreland*	Parish	4 365
Kirby-Muxloe ..	,, ..	Chap.	315	Kirkby Lonsdale	,,	Tnship.	1 727
Kirby-Bedon ..	*Norfolk* ..	Parish	277	Kirkby Stephen .	,,	Sub-dis.	6 563
Kirby-Cane ..	,, ..	Parish	448	Kirkby Stephen .	,,	Parish	3 531
Kirby-Kendal ..	*Westmoreland*	Parish	18 600	Kirkby Stephen .	,,	Tnship.	1 715
Kirby-Kendal ..	,,	Tnship.	10 418	Kirkby Thore ..	,,	Parish	1 153
Kirby in Cleveland	*York* ..	Parish	804	Kirkby Thore ..	,,	Tnship.	455
Kirby in Cleveland	,, ..	Tnship.	227	Kirkby in Cleveland	*York* ..	Parish	804
Kirby-Grindalyth	,, ..	Parish	571	Kirkby in Cleveland	,, ..	Tnship.	227
Kirby-Grindalyth	,, ..	Tnship	249	Kirkby Fleetham	,, ..	Parish	606
Kirby-Hill ..	,, ..	Parish	462	Kirkby-Hall ..	,, ..	Tnship.	62
Kirby-Hill ..	,, ..	Tnship.	158	Kirkby Hill ..	,, ..	Tnship.	158
Kirby-Knowle ..	,, ..	Parish	504	Kirkby on Hill..	,, ..	Parish	1 248
Kirby-Knowle ..	,, ..	Tnship.	116	Kirkby on Hill..	,, ..	Tnship.	88
Kirby-Misperton	,, ..	Parish	1 002	Kirkby Malham.	,, ..	Sub-dis.	826
Kirby-Misperton	,, ..	Tnship.	215	Kirkby Malham.	,, ..	Tnship.	128
Kirby-Sigston ..	,, ..	Parish	257	Kirkby Malzeard	,, ..	Sub-dis.	3 269
Kirby-Sigston ..	,, ..	Tnship.	110	Kirkby Malzeard	,, ..	Parish	4 680
Kirby, South ..	,, ..	Parish	1 284	Kirkby Malzeard	,, ..	Tnship.	730
Kirby, South ..	,, ..	Tnship.	482	Kirkby Misperton	,, ..	Parish	1 002
Kirby-under-Dale	,, ..	Parish	333	Kirkby Misperton	,, ..	Tnship.	215
Kirby-Wiske ..	,, ..	Parish	866	Kirkby on Moor.	,, ..	Parish	462
Kirby-Wiske ..	,, ..	Tnship.	209	Kirkby Moorside	,, ..	Union	5 739
Kirdford ..	*Sussex* ..	Parish	1 784	Kirkby Moorside	,, ..	Sub-dis.	5 739
Kirk-Andrews on Eden	*Cumbld.*	Parish	120	Kirkby Moorside	,, ..	Parish	2 659
Kirk-Andrews on Esk	,,	Parish	2 383	Kirkby Moorside	,, ..	Tnship.	1 851
Middle Quarter ..	,,	Tnship.	352	Kirkby Overblow	,, ..	Parish	1 569
Moat Quarter . ..	,,	Tnship.	376	Kirkby Overblow	,, ..	Tnship.	280
Nether Quarter ..	,,	Tnship.	439	Kirkby Ravensworth	,, ..	Parish	1 248
Kirk-Bampton	,,	Parish	497	Kirkby, South ..	,, ..	Tnship.	482
Kirk-Bampton	,,	Tnship.	205	Kirkby under Dale	,, ..	Parish	333
Kirk-Bramwith .	*York* ..	Parish	226	Kirkby Wharf ..	,, ..	Parish	739
Kirkbride ..	*Cumberland*	Parish	311	Kirkby Wharf ..	,, ..	Tnship.	100
Kirkburn ..	*York* ..	Parish	581	Kirkdale ..	*Lancaster* ..	L. Sub.	489 416
Kirkburn ..	,, ..	Hamlet	129	Kirkdale ..	,, ..	Tnship.	16 135
Kirkburton ..	,, ..	Sub-dis.	12 501	Kirkdale, St. Mary	,, ..	Ecl. Dis.	14 730
Kirkburton ..	,, ..	Parish	20 526	Kirkdale ..	*York* ..	Parish	1 043
Kirkburton ..	,, ..	Tnship.	3 664	Kirk Deighton ..	,, ..	District	987
Kirkby ..	*Lancaster* ..	Tnship.	1 415	Kirk Deighton ..	,, ..	Sub-dis.	987
Kirkby-Ireleth ..	,, ..	Parish	3 138	Kirk Deighton ..	,, ..	Parish	485
Kirkby-Ireleth ..	,, ..	Tnship.	1 666	Kirk Deighton ..	,, ..	Tnship.	364
Kirkby Mallory .	*Leicester* ..	Parish	2 392	Kirk Ella ..	,, ..	Parish	1 148
Kirkby Mallory .	,, ..	Tnship.	216	Kirk Ella ..	,, ..	Tnship.	250
Kirkby w. Osgodby	*Lincoln* ..	Parish	477	Kirk Fenton ..	,, ..	Parish	711

Name of Place.	County.	Description.	Population.	Name of Place.	County.	Description.	Population.
Kirk Fenton	York	Tnship.	469	Kirton in Holland	Lincoln	Sub-dis.	5 028
Kirk-Hallam	Derby	Parish	536	Kirton	,,	Parish	2 255
Kirk-Hallam	,,	Tnship.	101	Kirton in Lindsey	,,	Parish	2 058
Kirkham	Lancaster	Sub-dis.	9 141	Kirton	Notts	Parish	170
Kirkham	,,	Parish	11 445	Kirton	Suffolk	Parish	541
Kirkham	,,	Tnship.	3 380	Kislingbury	Northampton	Parish	723
Kirkham	,,	Town	3 380	Kittisford	Somerset	Parish	133
Kirkham	York	Parish	56	Knaith	Lincoln	Parish	105
Kirk Hammerton	,,	Parish	400	Knaptoft	Leicester	Parish	841
Kirk Hammerton	,,	Tnship.	310	Knapton	Norfolk	Parish	310
Kirkharle	Northumberland	Parish	123	Knapton, Poppleton	York	Tnship.	110
Kirkhaugh	,,	Parish	223	Knapton, Wintringham	,,	Tnship.	271
Kirkheaton	,,	Parish	161	Knapwell	Cambs	Parish	156
Kirkheaton	York	Sub-dis.	11 923	Knaresborough	York	District	17 176
Kirkheaton	,,	Parish	11 923	Knaresborough	,,	Sub-dis.	8 571
Kirkheaton	,,	Tnship.	3 011	Knaresborough	,,	Parish	11 277
Kirk Ireton	Derby	Parish	671	Knaresborough	,,	Tnship.	4 848
Kirk Ireton	,,	Tnship.	515	Knaresborough	,,	P. Bor.	5 402
Kirkland	Cumberland	Parish	804	Knaresdale	Northumberland	Parish	532
Kirkland, &c.	,,	Tnship.	167	Knayton	York	Sub-dis.	1 758
Kirkland	Lancaster	Tnship.	388	Knayton w. Brawith	,,	Tnship.	368
Kirkland	Westmoreland	Tnship.	1 170	Knebworth	Herts	Parish	250
Kirk Langley	Derby	Parish	648	Knedlington	York	Tnship.	138
Kirk Leatham	York	Sub-dis.	8 178	Kneesall	Notts	Sub-dis.	11 370
Kirk Leatham	,,	Parish	2 034	Kneesall	,,	Parish	553
Kirk Leatham	,,	Tnship.	1 107	Kneesall	,,	Tnship.	360
Kirk Leavington	,,	Parish	543	Kneesworth	Cambs	Hamlet	280
Kirk Leavington	,,	Tnship.	182	Kneeton	Notts	Parish	116
Kirkley	Northumberland	Tnship.	181	Knelston	Glamorgan	Parish	113
Kirkley	Suffolk	Parish	1 129	Knettishall	Suffolk	Parish	84
Kirklington	Notts	Parish	241	Knightlow	Warwick	Hund.	83 858
Kirklington	York	Parish	471	Knighton, West	Dorset	Parish	268
Kirklington w. Upsland	,,	Tnship.	311	Knighton	Leicester	Chap.	641
Kirk Linton	Cumberland	Parish	1 749	Knighton	Radnor	Hund.	6 038
Kirk Newton	Northumberland	Parish	1 503	Knighton	Radnor, &c.	District	10 379
Kirk Newton	,,	Tnship.	79	Knighton	,,	Sub-dis.	6 009
Kirkoswald	Cumberland	Sub-dis.	5 815	Knighton	Radnor	Parish	1 853
Kirkoswald	,,	Parish	944	Knighton	,,	P. Bor.	1 655
Kirkoswald	,,	Tnship.	672	Knighton	Stafford	Tnship.	143
Kirk Sandall	York	Parish	233	Knighton on Teme	Worcester	Chap.	570
Kirk Smeaton	,,	Parish	333	Knightsbridge, All Snts.	Mdlx.	Ecl. Dis.	7 041
Kirkstall	,,	Sub-dis.	18 364	Knightsbridge, St. Paul	,,	Ecl. Dis.	14 501
Kirkstall, St. Stephen,	,,	Ecl. Dis.	3 345	Knights-Enham	Hants	Parish	159
Kirkstead	Lincoln	Parish	158	Knight-Thorpe	Leicester	Hamlet	58
Kirkton	Notts	Parish	170	Knightwick	Worcester	Parish	166
Kirkwhelpington	Northumbld.	Sub-dis.	2 833	Knill	Hereford	Parish	84
Kirkwhelpington	,,	Parish	644	Knipton	Leicester	Parish	369
Kirkwhelpington	,,	Tnship.	190	Kniveton	Derby	Parish	315
Kirmington	Lincoln	Parish	405	Knockholt	Kent	Parish	617
Kirmond-le-Mire	,,	Parish	73	Knockin	Salop	Sub-dis.	4 423
Kirstead	Norfolk	Parish	245	Knockin	,,	Parish	289
Kirtling	Cambs	Parish	820	Knodishall	Suffolk	Parish	442
Kirtlington	Oxon	Parish	725	Knoll & Basset House	Leicester	Parish	14
Kirton	Lincoln	Wapen.	18 938	Knook	Wilts	Parish	208

Name of Place.	County.	Description.	Population.	Name of Place.	County.	Description.	Population.
Knossington	Leicester	Parish	251	Lakenheath	Suffolk	Parish	1 797
Knotting	Beds	Parish	185	Laleham	Middlesex	Parish	613
Knottingley	York	Sub-dis.	10 058	Laleston	Glamorgan	Parish	536
Knottingley	,,	Chap.	4 379	Lamarsh	Essex	Parish	329
Knottingley, East	,,	Ecl. Dis.	2 181	Lambcroft	Lincoln	Hamlet	62
Knott Lanes	Lancaster	Sub-dis.	7 312	Lamberhurst	Sussex & Kent	Parish	1 605
Knowbury, St. Paul	Salop	Ecl. Dis.	655	**Lambeth**	Surrey	P. Bor.	294 883
Knowle	Warwick	Sub-dis.	2 819	Lambeth	,,	District	162 044
Knowle	,,	Hamlet	1 200	Lambeth Church First	,,	Sub-dis.	19 839
Knowle, St. John	,,	Ecl. Dis.	1 200	Lambeth Church Second	,,	Sub-dis.	29 542
Knowl-End	Stafford	Tnship.	255	Lambeth	,,	Parish	162 044
Knowle, St. Giles	Somerset	Parish	104	1 North Marsh Ward	,,	Ward	24 249
Knowl Hill	Berks	Ecl. Dis.	850	2 South Marsh Ward	,,	Ward	18 177
Knowlton	Kent	Parish	31	3 Bishop's Ward	,,	Ward	21 964
Knowsley	Lancaster	Tnship.	1 349	4 Prince's Ward	,,	Ward	29 870
Knowsley, St. Mary	,,	Ecl. Dis.	1 349	5 Vauxhall Ward	,,	Ward	27 149
Knowstone	Devon	Parish	511	6 Stockwell Ward	,,	Ward	15 746
Knoyle, East	Wilts	Parish	1 034	7 Brixton Ward	,,	Ward	14 895
Knoyle, West	,,	Parish	187	8 Norwood Ward	,,	Ward	9 994
Knucklas	Radnor	P. Bor.	377	All Saints	,,	Ecl. Dis.	5 452
Knutsford	Cheshire	Sub-dis.	7 377	St. Andrew	,,	Ecl. Dis.	8 467
Knutsford	,,	Parish	4 194	St. Mary Less	,,	Ecl. Dis.	16 305
Knutsford	,,	Town	3 575	St. Thomas	,,	Ecl. Dis.	9 660
Knutsford, Inferior	,,	Tnship.	3 485	Trinity	,,	Ecl. Dis.	7 079
Knutsford, Superior	,,	Tnship.	204	Lambley	Northumberland	Parish	357
Knutton	Stafford	Tnship.	4 464	Lambley	Notts	Parish	836
Kyloe	Northumberland	Tnship.	1 004	Lambourn	Berks	Hund.	3 118
Kyme, North	Lincoln	Tnship.	455	Lambourn	,,	L. Sub.	3 118
Kyme, South	,,	Parish	1 004	Lambourn	Berks & Wilts	Sub-dis.	5 654
Kyme, South	,,	Tnship.	549	Lambourn	Berks	Parish	2 529
Kyo	Durham	Tnship.	1 679	Lambourne	Essex	Parish	890
Kyre, Great	Worcester	Parish	152	Lambrigg	Westmoreland	Tnship.	165
Kyre, Little	,,	Hamlet	123	Lambston	Pembroke	Parish	216
				Lambton	Durham	Tnship.	13
Laceby	Lincoln	Parish	1 021	Lamerton	Devon	Parish	1 517
Lach Dennis	Cheshire	Tnship.	28	Lamesley	Durham	Chap.	2 233
Lache w. Saltney	,,	Ecl. Dis.	2 194	Lammas	Norfolk	Parish	291
Lackford	Suffolk	Hund.	15 077	Lamonby	Cumberland	Tnship.	258
Lackford	,,	Parish	197	Lamorran	Cornwall	Parish	92
Lacy Green, St. John	Bucks	Ecl. Dis.	952	Lampeter	Cardigan	District	9 994
Ladbrooke	Warwick	Parish	274	Lampeter	,,	Sub-dis.	2 710
Ladock	Cornwall	Parish	742	Lampeter Pont Stephen	,,	Parish	1 542
Lady St. Mary	Dorset	Parish	1 643	Lampeter	,,	—	1 426
Ladywood	Warwick	Sub-dis.	34 728	**Lampeter**	,,	P. Bor.	989
Ladywood, St. John	,,	Ecl. Dis.	9 389	Lampetervelfrey	Pembroke	Parish	951
Laindon	Essex	Parish	586	Lampha	Glamorgan	Hamlet	135
Laindon	,,	Hamlet	406	Lamphey	Pembroke	Parish	365
Laindon Hills	,,	Parish	289	Lamplugh	Cumberland	Parish	808
Lainston	Hants	Parish	33	Lamport	Northampton	Parish	291
Laira Green	Devon	Parish	67	Lamport	,,	Hamlet	195
Laithkirk	York	Ecl. Dis.	1 330	Lamyatt	Somerset	Parish	240
Lakenham	Norfolk	Parish	4 866	Lanarth	Cardigan	Parish	2 216
Lakenham, St. Mark	,,	Ecl. Dis.	3 808	Lancashire		County	2429 440
Lakenheath	Suffolk	Sub-dis.	5 890	Northern Division	,,	N. Div.	547 469

Name of Place.	County.	Description.	Population.	Name of Place.	County.	Description.	Population.
Southern Division	.. .. ..	S. Div.	1881971	Langford	.. Notts ..	Parish	161
Lancaster	Lancaster ..	District	35 297	Langford	.. Oxon ..	Parish	701
Lancaster	,, ..	Sub-dis.	18 347	Langford	.. ,, ..	Tnship.	449
Lancaster	,, ..	Union	24 004	Langford Budville	Somerset ..	Parish	457
Lancaster	,, ..	Parish	27 430	Langford, Little	Wilts ..	Parish	39
Lancaster	,, ..	Tnship.	14 324	Langham	.. Essex ..	Parish	862
Lancaster Castle	,, ..	—	163	Langham	.. Norfolk ..	Parish	399
Lancaster	,, {	M. Bor.	14 487	Langham	.. Rutland ..	Parish	636
Lancaster	,, {	P. Bor.	16 005	Langham	.. Suffolk ..	Parish	242
Lancaster, St. Anne	,, ..	Ecl. Dis.	3 032	Langho, St. Leonard	Lancaster	Ecl. Dis.	1 038
Lancaster, St. John	,, ..	Ecl. Dis.	1 885	Langley Marish..	Bucks ..	Parish	1 874
Lancaster, St. Thomas	,, ..	Ecl. Dis.	2 908	Langley..	.. Durham ..	Tnship.	129
Lancant..	.. Gloucester ..	Parish	9	Langley..	.. Essex ..	Parish	410
Lanchester	.. Durham ..	Sub-dis.	20 218	Langley & Swineshead	Glouc. ..	Hund.	18 350
Lanchester	.. ,, ..	Union	27 812	Langley..	.. Kent ..	Parish	386
Lanchester	.. ,, ..	Parish	22 338	Langley Priory..	Leicester ..	Parish	11
Lanchester & Hamlets	,, ..	Tnship.	876	Langley..	.. Norfolk ..	Parish	316
Lancing..	.. Sussex ..	Parish	950	Langley..	.. Oxon ..	Hamlet	53
Landbeach	.. Cambs ..	Parish	441	Langley..	.. Warwick ..	Hamlet	194
Landcross	.. Devon ..	Parish	109	Langley..	.. Wilts ..	Tithing	549
Landewednack..	Cornwall ..	Parish	429	Langley Burrell	,, ..	Parish	1 100
Landford	.. Wilts ..	Parish	278	Langley Burrell, St. Paul	,, ..	Ecl. Dis.	1 218
Landican	.. Cheshire ..	Tnship.	64	Langley Wood..	,, ..	Parish	15
Landkey	.. Devon ..	Parish	699	Langley..	.. Worcester ..	Ecl. Dis.	5 825
Landmoth w. Catto	York ..	Tnship.	32	Langleydale, &c.	Durham ..	Tnship.	220
Landport	.. Hants ..	Sub-dis.	41 426	Langoe ..	.. Lincoln ..	Wapen.	11 440
Landrake	.. Cornwall ..	Parish	714	Langport	.. Somerset ..	L. Sub.	18 077
Landscove, St. Matt.	Devon ..	Ecl. Dis.	399	Langport	.. ,, ..	District	18 077
Land S. of the Witham	Lincoln	Parish	6	Langport	.. ,, ..	Sub-dis.	7 091
Landulph	.. Cornwall ..	Parish	547	Langport Eastover	,, ..	Parish	1 133
Landwade	.. Cambs ..	Parish	36	Langridge	.. ,, ..	Parish	102
Lane Bridge, St. Paul	Lanc. ..	Ecl. Dis.	4 420	Langrigg, &c.	.. Cumberland	Tnship.	324
Laneast..	.. Cornwall ..	Parish	244	Langriville	.. Lincoln	Parish	312
Lane End	.. Bucks ..	Ecl. Dis.	1 162	Langsett	.. York ..	Tnship.	280
Lane End & Longton	Stafford .	Tnship.	16 690	Langthorne	.. ,, ..	Tnship.	147
Laneham	.. Notts ..	Parish	376	Langthorpe	.. ,, ..	Tnship.	252
Lanercost	.. Cumberland	Parish	1 519	Langthwaite w. Tilts	,, ..	Tnship.	38
Lanfair in Buallt	Brecon ..	Parish	1 110	Langtoft	.. Lincoln ..	Parish	746
Langar ..	.. Notts ..	Parish	320	Langtoft	.. York ..	Sub-dis.	4 259
Langbaurgh, E. & W.	York ..	Liberty	45 919	Langtoft	.. ,, ..	Parish	783
Langbaurgh, East	,, ..	L. Sub.	15 862	Langtoft	.. ,, ..	Tnship.	688
Langbaurgh, North	,, ..	L. Sub.	26 349	Langton Herring	Dorset ..	Parish	241
Langbaurgh, West	,, ..	L. Sub.	8 836	Langton Long ..	,, ..	Parish	174
Langcliffe	.. ,, ..	Tnship.	376	Langton-Maltravers	,, ..	Parish	733
Langcliffe, St. John	,, ..	Ecl. Dis.	413	Langton	.. Durham ..	Tnship.	116
Langdale	.. Westmoreland	Chap.	534	Langton Church	Leicester ..	Parish	842
Langdon, Hills ..	Essex ..	Parish	289	Langton, East ..	,, ..	Tnship.	303
Langdon, East ..	Kent ..	Parish	362	Langton, Thorpe	,, ..	Tnship.	120
Langdon, West..	,, ..	Parish	106	Langton, Tur ..	,, ..	Tnship.	337
Langenhoe	.. Essex ..	Parish	169	Langton, West ..	,, ..	Tnship.	82
Langfield	.. York ..	Tnship.	4 391	Langton by Spilsby	Lincoln ..	Parish	188
Langford	.. Beds ..	Parish	1 086	Langton by Wragby	,, ..	Parish	321
Langford	.. Essex ..	Parish	279	Langton by Horncastle	,, ..	Parish	226
Langford	.. Norfolk ..	Parish	62	Langton, St. Andrew	,, ..	Ecl. Dis.	610

Name of Place.	County.	Description.	Population.	Name of Place.	County.	Description.	Population.
Langton Woodhouse	Lincoln..	—	3	Laughton	Lincoln	Parish	515
Langton	York	Parish	264	Laughton	„	Tnship.	365
Langton	„	Tnship.	207	Laughton by Falkingham	„	Parish	71
Langton, Great .	„	Parish	239	Laughton	Sussex	Parish	742
Langton, Great .	„	Tnship.	137	Laughton en le Morthen	York	Parish	1 033
Langton, Little .	„	Tnship.	102	Laughton en le Morthen	„	Tnship.	736
Langtree	Devon	Parish	837	Launcells	Cornwall	Parish	693
Langtree	Oxon	Hund.	4 194	Launceston	Corn. & Devon	District	17 005
Langwathby	Cumberland	Parish	346	Launceston	Cornwall	Sub-dis.	3 125
Langwith, Upper	Derby	Parish	183	Launceston	„	Parish	2 069
Langwith	Notts	Tnship.	328	Launceston	„	M. Bor.	2 790
Langwith	York	Tnship.	47	Launceston	„	P. Bor.	5 140
Lanhydrock	Cornwall	Parish	197	Launde ..	Leicester	Parish	42
Lanivet ..	„	Parish	1 151	Launditch	Norfolk	Hund.	13 177
Lanlivery	„	Sub-dis.	5 118	Launditch	„	L. Sub.	13 177
Lanlivery	„	Parish	1 657	Launton	Oxon	Parish	711
Lannarth, Christch.	„	Ecl. Dis.	2 615	Lavant, East	Sussex	Parish	421
Lanreath	„	Parish	649	Lavant, Mid	„	Parish	257
Lansallos	„	Parish	659	Lavendon	Bucks	Parish	820
Lansdown	Somerset	Sub-dis.	15 008	Lavenham	Suffolk	Sub-dis.	7 742
Lanteglos	Cornwall	Parish	1 620	Lavenham	„	Parish	1 823
Lanteglos by Fowey	„	Parish	1 271	Laver, High	Essex	Parish	471
Lanton	Northumberland	Tnship.	74	Laver, Little	„	Parish	111
Lantwit by Neath	Glamorgan .	Parish	2 232	Laver, Magdalen	„	Parish	213
Lantwit, Lower .	„	Hamlet	1 367	Lavernock	Glamorgan .	Parish	89
Lantwit Major ..	„	Parish	1 122	Laversdale	Cumberland	Tnship.	428
Lapal ..	Worcester	Tnship.	360	Laverstock	Hants	Parish	122
Lapford..	Devon	Parish	677	Laverstoke	Wilts	Parish	470
Lapley ..	Stafford	Parish	828	Laverton	Somerset	Parish	164
Lapworth	Warwick	Parish	639	Laverton	York	Tnship.	387
Lark Stoke	Gloucester	Hamlet	21	Lavington	Lincoln	Parish	330
Larkton..	Cheshire	Tnship.	35	Lavington	„	Tnship.	108
Larling ..	Norfolk	Parish	181	Lavington, St. Mary	Sussex	Ecl. Dis.	172
Lartington	York	Tnship.	192	Lavington	Wilts	Sub-dis.	5 620
Larton ..	Cheshire	Tnship.	35	Lavington, East .	„	Parish	1 583
Lasham..	Hants	Parish	235	Lavington, East .	„	—	1 122
Laskill Pasture..	York	Tnship.	105	Lavington, West	„	Parish	1 589
Lassington	Gloucester	Parish	73	Lavington, West	„	—	974
Lancant..	„	Parish	9	Lawford	Essex	Parish	842
Lastingham	York	Sub-dis.	1 659	Lawford Church	Warwick	Parish	311
Lastingham	„	Parish	1 597	Lawford, Little..	„	Tnship.	64
Lastingham	„	Tnship.	216	Lawford, Long ..	„	Tnship.	601
Latchford	Cheshire	Sub-dis.	4 054	Lawfords Gate ..	Gloucester	L. Sub.	44 999
Latchford	„	Tnship.	2 885	Lawhitton	Cornwall	Parish	435
Latchford & Lobb	Oxon	Hamlet	43	Lawkland	York	Tnship.	338
Latchingdon	Essex	Parish	430	Lawrence Weston	Gloucester	Tithing	334
Lathbury	Bucks	Parish	147	Lawrenny	Pembroke	Parish	339
Lathom..	Lancaster	Sub-dis.	4 690	Lawress..	Lincoln	Wapen.	7 728
Lathom..	„	Tnship.	3 385	Lawshall	Suffolk	Parish	903
Lathom, St. James	„	Ecl. Dis.	914	Laxfield..	„	Parish	1 031
Latton ..	Essex	Parish	196	Laxton ..	Northampton	Parish	119
Latton ..	Wilts	Parish	308	Laxton ..	Notts	Parish	613
Laugharne	Carmarthen	Parish	1 868	Laxton ..	York	Tnship.	327
Laughton	Leicester	Parish	152	Laxton ..	„	Ecl. Dis.	790

Name of Place.	County.	Description.	Population.	Name of Place.	County.	Description.	Population.
aycock..	Wilts	Parish	1 499	Leaton, Holy Trinity	Salop	Ecl. Dis.	434
ayer Breton	Essex	Parish	298	Leaveland	Kent	Parish	94
ayer-de-la-Hay	,,	Parish	807	Leavening	York	Tnship.	408
ayer-Marney	,,	Parish	276	Leavesden, All Saints	Herts	Ecl. Dis.	756
ayham..	Suffolk	Parish	534	Lebberston	York	Tnship.	156
aysters	Hereford	Parish	283	Lechlade	Gloucester	Parish	1 328
ayston..	Herts	Parish	998	Leck	Lancaster	Tnship.	324
aytham	York	Tnship.	115	Leck	,,	Ecl. Dis.	324
ayton w. Warbreck	Lancaster	Tnship.	3 907	Leckford	Hants	Parish	279
ayton, East	York	Tnship.	133	Leckhampstead	Berks	Tithing	385
ayton, West	,,	Tnship.	82	Leckhampstead	Bucks. & Nptn.	Sub-dis.	4 098
azenby	,,	Parish	25	Leckhampstead	Bucks	Parish	482
azonby	Cumberland	Parish	896	Leckhampton	Gloucester	Parish	2 523
azonby	,,	Tnship.	570	Leckonfield w. Arram	York	Parish	348
ea (Backford P.)	Cheshire	Tnship.	85	Leckwith	Glamorgan	Parish	133
ea Newbold	,,	Tnship.	35	Ledbury	Hereford	L. Sub.	13 866
ea (Wybunbury P.)	,,	Tnship.	62	Ledbury	Heref. & Wor	District	14 880
ea Hall	Derby	Hamlet	21	Ledbury	,, ,,	Sub-dis.	10 295
ea	Gloucester	Tithing	51	Ledbury	Hereford	Parish	5 598
ea Bailey	,,	Tithing	231	Ledbury	,,	Tnship.	5 537
ea	Hereford	Parish	226	**Ledbury**	,,	Town	3 263
ea, &c...	Lancaster	Tnship.	911	Ledsham	Cheshire	Tnship.	93
ea	Lincoln	Parish	194	Ledsham	York	Parish	1 146
ea Marston	Warwick	Parish	261	Ledsham	,,	Tnship.	459
ea	Wilts	Parish	432	Ledstone	,,	Tnship.	229
eadbrook Major	Flint	Tnship.	106	Lee	Bucks	Parish	116
eadbrook Minor	,,	Tnship.	49	Lee Chapel	Essex	Liberty	6
eadenham	Lincoln	Sub-dis.	3 940	Lee	Kent	Sub-dis.	11 807
eadenham	,,	Parish	688	Lee	,,	Parish	6 162
eaden-Roothing	Essex	Parish	207	Lee Park, Christch.	,,	Ecl. Dis.	2 333
ead Hall	York	Tnship.	46	Lee, St. John	Northumberland	Parish	2 254
eafield..	Oxon	Chap.	868	Lee Ward	,,	Tnship.	86
eagrim..	Lancaster	Tnship.	111	Lee Brockhurst	Salop	Parish	133
eake	Lincoln	Parish	1 912	Leebotwood	,,	Parish	210
eake	Notts & Leic.	Sub-dis.	6 627	Leeds	Kent	Parish	656
eake, East	Notts	Parish	1 059	Leeds	York	District	117 566
eake, West	,,	Parish	171	Leeds *(1866) 236,746*		Parish	207 165
eake	York	Parish	1 092	Leeds	,,	Tnship.	117 566
eake	,,	Tnship.	17	All Saints	,,	Ecl. Dis.	10 288
eamington	Warwick	Sub-dis.	18 768	Christchurch..	,,	Ecl. Dis.	7 058
eamington	,,	Town	17 958	St. Andrew	,,	Ecl. Dis.	5 725
eamington Hastings	,,	Parish	450	St. George	,,	Ecl. Dis.	8 421
eamington Priors	,,	Parish	17 402	St. John	,,	Ecl. Dis.	5 198
eamington St. Mary	,,	Ecl. Dis.	3 981	St. Philip	,,	Ecl. Dis.	3 512
earchild	Northumberland	Tnship.	40	St. Saviour	,,	Ecl. Dis.	6 881
easingham	Lincoln	Parish	473	**Leeds**	,,	Borough	207 165
easingham	,,	Tnship.	381	Leegrave	Beds	Hamlet	426
eath	Cumberland	Ward	28 675	Leek	Stafford	L. Sub.	29 499
eath	,,	L. Sub.	28 726	Leek	,,	District	24 806
eatherhead	Surrey	Sub-dis.	6 160	Leek	,,	Union	23 651
eatherhead	,,	Parish	2 079	Leek	,,	Sub-dis.	12 341
eather-Market	,,	Sub-dis.	16 696	Leek Frith	,,	Sub-dis.	1 790
eathley	York	Parish	272	Leek	,,	Parish	14 326
eathley	,,	Tnship.	199	Leek and Lowe..	,,	Tnship.	9 057

Name of Place.	County.	Description.	Population.	Name of Place.	County.	Description.	Population.
Leek Frith	Stafford	Tnship.	763	Leighton Buzzard	Beds	L. Sub.	8 752
Leek, St. Luke	,,	Ecl. Dis.	5 081	Leighton Buzzard	Beds & Bucks	District	17 648
Leek	,,	Town	10 045	Leighton Buzzard	,, ,,	Sub-dis.	9 243
Leek-Wootton	Warwick	Parish	389	Leighton Buzzard	Beds	Parish	7 312
Leemailing	Northumberland	Tnship.	234	Leighton Buzzard	,,	Tnship.	4 882
Leese	Cheshire	Tnship.	121	Leighton Buzzard	,,	Town	4 330
Leesfield, St. Thomas	Lancaster	Ecl. Dis.	5 358	Leighton	Cheshire	Tnship.	217
Leeswood	Flint	Tnship.	1 190	Leighton (Neston P.)	,,	Tnship.	363
Leftwich	Cheshire	Tnship.	2 627	Leighton, &c.	,,	Ecl. Dis.	619
Legbourne	Lincoln	Parish	512	Leighton	Hunts	Parish	450
Legsby	,,	Parish	365	Leighton	Montgomery	Tnship.	431
Leicestershire		County	237 412	Leighton	Salop	Parish	340
Northern Division		N. Div.	92'078	Leightonstone	Hunts	Hund.	10 789
Southern Division		S. Div.	145 334	Leightonstone	,,	L. Sub.	16 286
Leicester	Leicester	L. Sub.	96 131	Leinthall Starkes	Hereford	Parish	144
Leicester	,,	District	68 190	Leintwardine	,,	Sub-dis.	2 556
Leicester, East	,,	Sub-dis.	41 194	Leintwardine	,,	Parish	1 812
Leicester, West	,,	Sub-dis.	26 996	Leintwardine	,,	Tnship.	615
Leicester	,,	Borough	68 056	Leire	Leicester	Parish	433
Leicester, Christch.	,,	Ecl. Dis.	12 909	Leiston	Suffolk	Parish	2 227
Leicester, St. George	,,	Ecl. Dis.	10 333	Lelley	York	Tnship.	159
Leicester, St. John	,,	Ecl. Dis.	4 684	Lemington, Lower	Gloucester	Parish	57
Leicester Abbey	,,	Parish	40	Lemmington	Northumberland	Tnship.	142
Leicester Forest, East	,,	Parish	82	Lemsford	Herts	Ecl. Dis.	490
Leicester Forest, West	,,	Parish	51	Lenborough	Bucks	Hamlet	53
Leicester Frith	,,	Parish	24	Lenham	Kent	Sub-dis.	3 608
Leigh, High	Cheshire	Tnship.	1 004	Lenham	,,	Parish	2 016
Leigh, Little	,,	Tnship.	409	Lenton	Lincoln	Parish	330
Leigh, Little	,,	Ecl. Dis.	914	Lenton	,,	Tnship.	108
Leigh, North	Devon	Parish	253	Lenton	Notts	Sub-dis.	5 678
Leigh, South	,,	Parish	331	Lenton	,,	Parish	5 829
Leigh	Dorset	Ecl. Dis.	465	Leominster	Hereford	L. Sub.	16 930
Leigh	,,	Chap.	465	Leominster	,,	District	15 494
Leigh	Essex	Parish	1 473	Leominster	,,	Sub-dis.	6 618
Leigh	Gloucester	Parish	428	Leominster	,,	Parish	5 658
Leigh	Kent	Parish	1 256	Leominster	,,	In-Par.	4 630
Leigh	Lancaster	District	37 700	Leominster	,,	Borough	5 658
Leigh	,,	Town	10 621	Leominster	Sussex	Parish	908
Leigh	,,	Parish	30 052	Leominster	,,	—	801
Leigh, West	,,	Tnship.	4 434	Leonard Stanley	Gloucester	Parish	864
Leigh, North	Oxon	Parish	738	Leppington	York	Tnship.	132
Leigh, South	,,	Parish	319	Lepton	,,	Tnship.	3 273
Leigh Field Forest	Rutland	Parish	32	Lerrin	Cornwall	Sub-Dis.	3 804
Leigh on Mendip	Somerset	Parish	534	Lesbury	Northumberland	Parish	1 202
Leigh	Stafford	Parish	986	Lesbury	,,	Tnship.	750
Leigh	,,	Tnship.	902	Lesnewth	Cornwall	L. Sub.	8 742
Leigh	Surrey	Parish	506	Lesnewth	,,	Hund.	8 151
Leigh	Wilts	Chap.	312	Lesnewth	,,	Parish	114
Leigh de la Mere	,,	Parish	113	Lessingham	Norfolk	Parish	175
Leigh	Worcester	Sub-dis.	4 981	Letchworth	Herts	Parish	68
Leigh	,,	Parish	3 330	Letcombe Bassett	Berks	Parish	283
Leigh	,,	Tnship.	3 060	Letcombe Regis	,,	Parish	1 014
Leighs, Great	Essex	Parish	909	Letcombe Regis	,,	Tnship.	431
Leighs, Little	,,	Parish	171	Letheringham	Suffolk	Parish	208

Name of Place.	County.	Description.	Population.	Name of Place.	County.	Description.	Population.
Letheringsett	Norfolk	Parish	323	Leybourn	Kent	Parish	289
Letterston	Pembroke	Parish	511	Leyburn	York	District	10 105
Letton	Hereford	Parish	238	Leyburn	,,	Sub-dis.	5 875
Letton	,,	Tnship.	137	Leyburn	,,	Tnship.	886
Letton	Norfolk	Parish	111	Leyland	Lancaster	Hund.	58 622
Letwell	York	Tnship.	139	Leyland	,,	L. Sub.	58 622
Leven	,,	Sub-dis.	1 469	Leyland	,,	Sub-dis.	8 768
Leven	,,	Parish	990	Leyland	,,	Parish	13 684
Leven	,,	Tnship.	889	Leyland	,,	Tnship.	3 755
Levens	Westmoreland	Tnship.	936	Leyland, St. James	,,	Ecl. Dis.	1 427
Levens, St. John	,,	Ecl. Dis.	804	Leysdown	Kent	Parish	215
Levenshulme	Lancaster	Tnship.	2 095	Leyton	Essex	Sub-dis.	7 536
Levenshulme, St. Peter	,,	Ecl. Dis.	2 538	Leyton, Low	,,	Parish	4 794
Lever	,,	Sub-dis.	6 683	Leytonstone	,,	Ecl. Dis.	2 396
Lever Bridge, St.Steph.	,,	Ecl. Dis.	2 844	Leyton w. Warbreck	Lancaster	Tnship.	3 907
Lever, Great	,,	Tnship.	722	Lezant	Cornwall	Parish	815
Lever, Great, St. Mich.	,,	Ecl. Dis.	722	Lezayre	Isle of Man	Parish	2 520
Lever, Little	,,	Chap.	3 890	Leziate	Norfolk	Parish	197
Leverington	Cambs	Sub-dis.	5 385	Liberty of Sluice	Sussex	—	73
Leverington	,,	Parish	2 143	Lichfield		Diocese	1221404
Leverington	,,	—	1 267	Lichfield	Stafford	District	27 541
Leverton	Lincoln	Parish	770	Lichfield	,,	Sub-dis.	15 628
Leverton, North	Notts	Parish	329	Lichfield	,,	City	6 893
Leverton, South	,,	Parish	494	Lichfield, St. Chad	,,	Parish	2 145
Leverton, South	,,	Tnship.	408	Lichfield, St. Michael	,,	Parish	5 112
Levington	Suffolk	Parish	228	Lichfield, St. Michael	,,	—	1 986
Levisham	York	Parish	148	Lichfield, Christch.	,,	Ecl. Dis.	726
Lew	Oxon	Hamlet	182	Lickey, Holy Trinity	Worcester	Ecl. Dis.	1 361
Lewanick	Cornwall	Parish	685	Liddiard Millicent	Wilts	Parish	588
Lewes	Sussex	Rape	53 895	Liddiard Tregooze	,,	Parish	795
Lewes	,,	L. Sub.	26 539	Liddington	Rutland	Parish	613
Lewes	,,	District	26 995	Liddington	Wilts	Parish	440
Lewes	,,	Sub-dis.	10 116	Lidford	Devon	Parish	2 815
Lewes	,,	Union	10 116	Lidgate	Suffolk	Parish	443
Lewes	,,	P. Boro.	9 716	Lidlington	Beds	Parish	845
Leweston	Dorset	Parish	17	Lidsing	Kent	Ville	30
Lewisham	Kent	District	65 757	Lidstone	Oxon	Hamlet	162
Lewisham Village	,,	Sub-dis.	7 372	Lifton	Devon	Hund.	15 433
Lewisham	,,	Parish	22 808	Lifton	,,	L. Sub.	9 318
1 Blackheath Ward		Ward	5 492	Lifton	,,	Sub-dis.	3 975
2 Sydenham Ward		Ward	8 322	Lifton	,,	Parish	1 441
3 Lewisham Ward		Ward	8 994	Lightcliffe, St. Matthew	York	Ecl. Dis.	2 347
Lewknor	Oxon	Hund.	5 456	Lighthorne	Warwick	Parish	391
Lewknor	,,	Sub-dis.	3 701	Lilbourne	Northampton	Parish	292
Lewknor	Oxon & Bucks	Parish	833	Lilburn, East	Nrthumberld.	Tnship.	85
Lewknor	Oxon	Hamlet	598	Lilburn, West	,,	Tnship.	245
Lewknor Uphill	Oxon & Bucks	Hamlet	235	Lilford w. Wigsthorpe	Nrthptn.	Parish	179
Lewtrenchard	Devon	Parish	353	Lilleshall	Salop	Parish	3 746
Lexden	Essex	Hund.	24 241	Lilley	Herts	Parish	480
Lexden	,,	District	22 950	Lillings Ambo	York	Tnship.	196
Lexden	,,	Parish	1 543	Lillingstone Dayrell	Bucks	Parish	198
Lexham, East	Norfolk	Parish	226	Lillingstone Lovell	,,	Parish	185
Lexham, West	,,	Parish	152	Lillington	Dorset	Parish	163
Lexington	Notts	Parish	613	Lillington	Warwick	Parish	480

Name of Place.	County.	Description.	Population.	Name of Place.	County.	Description.	Populatio
Lilstock ..	.. Somerset ..	Parish	71	Linstead, Great .	Suffolk ..	Parish	11
Lilwall ..	.. Hereford ..	Tnship.	346	Linstead, Little .	,, ..	Parish	22
Limber Magna ..	Lincoln ..	Parish	514	Linsted ..	.. Kent ..	Parish	1 02
Limbury w. Biscott	Beds ..	Hamlet	355	Linstock	.. Cumberland	Tnship.	20
Limehouse	.. Middlesex ..	Sub-dis.	27 161	Linthorpe	.. York ..	Tnship.	70
Limehouse	.. ,, ..	Parish	27 161	Linthwaite	.. ,, ..	Tnship.	4 300
Limehouse, St. John	,, ..	Ecl. Dis.	9 531	Linthwaite, Christch.	,, ..	Ecl. Dis.	3 14
Limington	.. Somerset ..	Parish	311	Linton ..	.. Cambs ..	L. Sub.	12 77
Limpenhoe	.. Norfolk ..	Parish	227	Linton ..	Cambs & Essex	District	13 51
Limpsfield	.. Surrey ..	Parish	1 216	Linton ..	.. ,, ,,	Sub-dis.	4 81
Linbriggs	Northumberland	Tnship.	69	Linton ..	.. Cambs ..	Parish	1 83
Linby ..	.. Notts ..	Parish	257	Linton, Kirk, Middle	Cumbld..	Tnship	472
Linch ..	.. Sussex ..	Parish	111	Linton, West ..	,, ..	Tnship.	565
Linchmere	.. ,, ..	Parish	283	Linton ..	.. Derby ..	Tnship.	365
Lincoln ..	.. .. ..	Diocese	706 026	Linton ..	.. Gloucester ..	Hamlet	34
Lincolnshire ..	.. ..	County	412 246	Linton ..	.. Hereford ..	Parish	915
Parts of Lindsey	.. ..	1st Part	229 816	Linton ..	.. ,, ..	Tnship.	547
Parts of Keste- } ven & Holland }	.. ..	2nd Part	182 430	Linton ..	.. Kent ..	Parish	873
				Linton ..	.. York ..	Parish	1 911
Lincoln ..	.. Lincoln ..	District	47 063	Linton ..	.. ,, ..	Tnship.	284
Lincoln Home ..	,, ..	Sub-dis.	24 917	Linton (Spofforth P.)	,, ..	Tnship.	166
Lincoln North-East	,, ..	Sub-dis.	8 541	Linton upon Ouse	,, ..	Tnship.	253
Lincoln South-West	,, ..	Sub-dis.	13 605	Linwood	.. Lincoln ..	Parish	201
Lincoln Castle ..	,, ..	—	16	Liscard ..	.. Cheshire ..	Tnship.	5 625
Co. Lunatic Asylum	,, ..	Parish	106	Liscard, St. John	,, ..	Ecl. Dis.	3 221
Lincoln	.. ,, ..	City	20 999	Liskeard	.. Cornwall ..	District	33 562
Lincoln's Inn ..	Middlesex ..	Tnship.	47	Liskeard	.. ,, ..	Sub-dis.	15 194
Lindeth w. Warton	Lancaster .	Tnship.	581	Liskeard	.. ,, ..	Parish	6 504
Lindfield	.. Sussex ..	Sub-dis.	4 213	Liskeard	.. ,, ..	—	1 815
Lindfield	.. ,, ..	Parish	1 917	Liskeard ..	,, {	M. Bor.	4 689
Lindhurst	.. Notts ..	Parish	11			P. Bor.	6 585
Lindley ..	.. York ..	Tnship.	108	Liss ..	.. Hants ..	Parish	806
Lindley w. Quarmby	,, ..	Tnship.	4 259	Lissett ..	.. York ..	Tnship.	112
Lindley, St. Stephen	,, ..	Ecl. Dis.	4 259	Lissington	.. Lincoln ..	Parish	245
Lindrick	.. ,, ..	Tnship.	49	Liston ..	.. Essex ..	Parish	95
Lindridge	.. Worcester ..	Parish	1 760	Lisvane ..	.. Glamorgan .	Parish	226
Lindridge	.. ,, ..	Tnship.	687	Litcham	.. Norfolk ..	Sub-dis.	5 413
Lindsell ..	.. Essex ..	Parish	385	Litcham	.. ,, ..	Parish	903
Lindsey ..	.. Suffolk ..	Parish	316	Litchborough ..	Northampton	Parish	449
Lineham	.. Wilts ..	Parish	1 034	Litchfield	.. Hants ..	Parish	102
Linford, Great ..	Bucks ..	Parish	557	Litchurch	.. Derby ..	Tnship.	6 560
Linford, Little ..	,, ..	Parish	58	Litherland	.. Lancaster ..	Sub-dis.	5 084
Lingards	.. York ..	Tnship.	783	Litherland	.. ,, ..	Tnship.	3 632
Lingen ..	.. Hereford ..	Parish	287	Litherland, Christch.	,, ..	Ecl. Dis.	2 046
Lingfield	.. Surrey ..	Parish	2 202	Litlington	.. Cambs ..	Parish	693
Lingwood	.. Norfolk ..	Parish	509	Little Abington .	,, ..	Parish	316
Linkenholt	.. Hants ..	Parish	88	Little Addington	Northampton	Parish	337
Linkinhorne	.. Cornwall ..	Parish	2 551	Little Amwell ..	Herts ..	Liberty	500
Link, St. Matthias	Worcester ..	Ecl. Dis.	1 670	Little Ayton ..	York ..	Tnship.	78
Linley ..	.. Salop ..	Parish	94	Little Baddow ..	Essex ..	Parish	605
Linmouth	Northumberland	Tnship.	17	Little Badminton	Gloucester ..	Tithing	113
Linsdale	.. Bucks ..	L. Sub.	14 196	Little Bampton .	Cumberland	Tnship.	172
Linsheeles	Northumberland	Tnship.	89	Little Bardfield .	Essex ..	Parish	429
Linslade	.. Bucks ..	Parish	1 511	Little Barford ..	Beds ..	Parish	91

Name of Place.	County.	Description.	Population.	Name of Place.	County.	Description.	Population.
Little Barlow	Derby	Tnship.	54	Little Compton	Warwick	Parish	398
Little Barningham	Norfolk	Parish	273	Little Corby	Cumberland	Tnship.	241
Little Barrington	Gloucester	Parish	151	Little Cornard	Suffolk	Parish	404
Little Bavington	Nrthumberld.	Parish	67	Little Cowarne	Hereford	Parish	186
Little Bealings	Suffolk	Parish	278	Little Coxwell	Berks	Tnship.	302
Little Beats	Lincoln	Parish	10	Little Creaton	Northampton	Hamlet	73
Little Bedwin	Wilts	Parish	496	Little Cressingham	Norfolk	Parish	243
Little Bentley	Essex	Parish	458	Little Crosby	Lancaster	Tnship.	418
Little Berkhampstead	Herts	Parish	450	Little Dalby	Leicester	Parish	183
Little Berwick	Salop	Ecl. Dis.	186	Little Dawley	Salop	Ecl. Dis.	2 327
Little Billing	Northampton	Parish	76	Little Dean	Gloucester	Parish	887
Little Birch	Hereford	Parish	336	Little Dean Hill	„	—	98
Little Bittering	Norfolk	Parish	30	Little Dewchurch	Hereford	Parish	322
Little Blakenham	Suffolk	Parish	146	Little Drayton	Salop & Staff.	Ecl. Dis.	2 162
Little Blencow	Cumberland	Tnship.	68	Little Driffield	York	Tnship.	197
Little Bolton	Lancaster	Sub-dis.	24 942	Little Dunham	Norfolk	Parish	327
Little Bolton	„	Tnship.	25 891	Little Dunmow	Essex	Parish	379
Little Bolton, St. John	„	Ecl. Dis.	5 233	Little Easton	„	Parish	357
Little Bookham	Surrey	Parish	219	Little Eaton	Derby	Chap.	775
Littleborough	Notts	Parish	60	Little Eccleston, &c.	Lancaster	Tnship.	209
Littlebourn	Kent	Parish	757	Little Edstone	York	Tnship.	21
Little Bowden	Northampton	L. Sub.	7 842	Little Ellingham	Norfolk	Parish	382
Little Bowden	„	Parish	486	Little Elm	Somerset	Hamlet	54
Little Bradley	Suffolk	Parish	28	Little Eppleton	Durham	Tnship.	26
Little Bramshill	Hants	Tithing	13	Little Eversden	Cambs	Parish	239
Little Braxted	Essex	Parish	111	Little Faringdon	Oxon	Tithing	136
Littlebredy	Dorset	Parish	199	Little Fenton	York	Tnship.	100
Little Brickhill	Bucks	Parish	423	Little Finborough	Suffolk	Parish	62
Little Bromley	Essex	Parish	371	Little Fransham	Norfolk	Parish	256
Little Bromwich	Warwick	Hamlet	405	Little Gaddesden	Herts	Parish	386
Little Broughton	Cumberland.	Tnship.	641	Little Gidding	Hunts	Parish	45
Little Budworth	Cheshire	Parish	582	Little Glemham	Suffolk	Parish	325
Little Burstead	Essex	Parish	186	Little Gransden	Cambs	Parish	293
Littlebury	„	Parish	974	Little Grimsby	Lincoln	Parish	55
Little Busby	York	Tnship.	38	Little Habton	York	Tnship.	61
Little Bytham	Lincoln	Parish	362	Little Hadham	Herts	Parish	864
Little Callerton	Northumbld.	Tnship.	20	Little Hale	Lincoln	Tnship.	372
Little Canfield	Essex	Parish	314	Little Hallingbury	Essex	Parish	514
Little Carlton	Lincoln	Parish	181	Littleham	Devon	Parish	408
Little Casterton	Rutland	Parish	118	Littleham by Exmouth	„	Parish	3 904
Little Catworth	Hunts	Hamlet	52	Littleham	„	—	243
Little Cawthorpe	Lincoln	Parish	223	Little Hampden	Bucks	Parish	68
Little Chalfield, &c.	Wilts	Parish	43	Littlehampton	Sussex	Sub-dis.	6 737
Little Chart	Kent	Parish	304	Littlehampton	„	Parish	2 350
Little Chester	Derby	Tnship.	431	Littlehampton	„	Town	2 350
Little Chesterford	Essex	Parish	276	Little Harle	Northumberland	Tnship.	80
Little Cheverell	Wilts	Parish	234	Little Harrowden	Northampton	Parish	679
Little Chishall	Essex	Parish	110	Little Harwood	Lancaster	Tnship.	270
Little Clacton	„	Parish	584	Little Haseley	Oxon	Tnship.	127
Little Claybrooke	Leicester	Tnship.	84	Little Hatfield	York	Tnship.	40
Little Clifton	Cumberland	Tnship.	476	Little Hautbois	Norfolk	Parish	25
Little Coates	Lincoln	Parish	59	Little Heaton	Lancaster	Tnship.	838
Little Coggeshall	Essex	Parish	429	Little Hempston	Devon	Parish	244
Little Comberton	Worcester	Parish	257	Little Henny	Essex	Parish	81

Name of Place.	County.	Description.	Population.	Name of Place.	County.	Description.	Population.
Little Hereford..	*Hereford* ..	Parish	458	Little Neston ..	*Cheshire* ..	Tnship.	580
Little Hereford..	,, ..	Tnship.	360	Little Newcastle	*Pembroke* ..	Parish	354
Little Hinton ..	*Wilts* ..	Parish	298	Little Oakley ..	*Essex* ..	Parish	306
Little Holbeck, St. John	*York* .	Ecl. Dis.	2 612	Little Oakley ..	*Northampton*	Parish	127
Little Holland ..	*Essex* ..	Parish	88	Little Ouseburn .	*York* ..	Parish	548
Little Hoole ..	*Lancaster* ..	Tnship.	424	Little Ouseburn	,, ..	Tnship.	281
Little Horksley..	*Essex* ..	Parish	253	Littleover ..	*Derby* ..	Tnship.	604
Little Hormead .	*Herts* ..	Parish	103	Little Packington	*Warwick* ..	Parish	124
Little Horsted ..	*Sussex* ..	Parish	296	Little Parndon..	*Essex* ..	Parish	71
Little Horwood .	*Bucks* ..	Parish	449	Little Paxton ..	*Hunts* ..	Parish	247
Little Houghton	*Northampton*	Parish	578	Little Peatling ..	*Leicester* ..	Parish	168
Little Houghton	*Nrthumbld.*..	Tnship.	130	Little Petherick .	*Cornwall* ..	Parish	236
Little Houghton	*York* ..	Tnship.	93	Little Plumstead	*Norfolk* ..	Parish	319
Little Hucklow..	*Derby* ..	Hamlet	237	Little Ponton ..	*Lincoln* ..	Parish	208
Little Hulton ..	*Lancaster* ..	Tnship.	3 390	Little Poringland	*Norfolk* ..	Parish	46
Little Humby ..	*Lincoln* ..	Hamlet	99	Littleport ..	*Cambs* ..	Sub-dis.	5 968
Little Ilford ..	*Essex* ..	Parish	594	Littleport ..	,, ..	Parish	3 728
Little Kelk ..	*York* ..	Parish	57	Little and Great Preston	*York*	Tnship.	541
Little Kimble ..	*Bucks* ..	Parish	182	Little Raveley ..	*Hunts* ..	Parish	60
Little Kyre ..	*Worcester* ..	Hamlet	123	Little Ribston ..	*York* ..	Tnship.	230
Little Langford .	*Wilts* ..	Parish	39	Little Rissington	*Gloucester*..	Parish	290
Little Langton..	*York* ..	Tnship.	102	Little Rollright .	*Oxon* ..	Parish	36
Little Laver ..	*Essex* ..	Parish	111	Little Ryburgh .	*Norfolk* ..	Parish	232
Little Lawford ..	*Warwick* ..	Tnship.	64	Little Ryle	*Northumberland*	Tnship.	35
Little Leigh ..	*Chester* ..	Tnship.	409	Little St. John & Hosp.	*Chesh.*	—	61
Little Leigh ..	,, ..	Ecl. Dis.	914	Little Salkeld ..	*Cumberland*	Tnship.	137
Little Leighs ..	*Essex* ..	Parish	171	Little Sampford .	*Essex* ..	Parish	477
Little Lever ..	*Lancaster* ..	Chap.	3 890	Little Saughall..	*Cheshire* ..	Tnship.	94
Little Linford ..	*Bucks* ..	Parish	58	Little Saxham ..	*Suffolk* ..	Parish	171
Little Linstead..	*Suffolk* ..	Parish	227	Little Shelford ..	*Cambs* ..	Parish	474
Little Livermere	,, ..	Parish	167	Little Shelsley ..	*Worcester* ..	Parish	57
Little London ..	*York* ..	Ecl. Dis.	4 490	Little Smeaton..	.. *York*	Tnship.	238
Little Longstone	*Derby* ..	Tnship.	185	Little Smeaton (Birkby P.)	,,	Tnship.	82
Little Lumley ..	*Durham* ..	Tnship.	373	Little Snoring ..	*Norfolk* ..	Parish	311
Little Malvern ..	*Worcester* ..	Parish	104	Little Sodbury ..	*Gloucester*..	Parish	143
Little Maplestead	*Essex* ..	Parish	325	Little Sombourn	*Hants* ..	Parish	87
Little Marcle ..	*Hereford* ..	Parish	168	Little Somerford	*Wilts* ..	Parish	335
Little Marlow ..	*Bucks* ..	Parish	790	Little Stainton..	*Durham* ..	Tnship.	73
Little Marsden..	*Lancaster* ..	Tnship.	5 162	Little Stambridge	*Essex* ..	Parish	125
Little Marton ..	,, ..	Hamlet	433	Little Stanmore .	*Middlesex* ..	Parish	891
Little Massingham	*Norfolk* ..	Parish	132	Little Stanney ..	*Cheshire* ..	Tnship.	204
Little Melton ..	,, ..	Parish	370	Little Staughton	*Beds* ..	Parish	572
Little Meolse ..	*Cheshire* ..	Tnship.	169	Little Steeping..	*Lincoln* ..	Parish	326
Little Milton ..	*Oxon* ..	Parish	411	Little Stonham..	*Suffolk* ..	Parish	391
Little Milton, St. James	,, ..	Ecl. Dis.	431	Little Stretton ..	*Leicester* ..	Tnship.	83
Little Missenden	*Bucks* ..	Parish	1 089	Little Strickland	*Westmoreland*	Tnship.	114
Little Mollington	*Cheshire* ..	Tnship.	29	Little Stukeley..	*Hunts* ..	Parish	385
Little Mongeham	*Kent* ..	Parish	138	Little Sutton ..	*Cheshire* ..	Tnship.	474
Lt. Moorfields, St.Barth.	*Mdlx.*	Ecl. Dis.	4 216	Little Tew ..	*Oxon* ..	Parish	262
Littlemore ..	*Oxon* ..	Ecl. Dis.	1 126	Little Tey ..	*Essex* ..	Parish	63
Littlemore ..	,, ..	Liberty	1 126	Little Thurlow..	*Suffolk* ..	Parish	369
Little Munden..	*Herts* ..	Parish	601	Little Thurrock .	*Essex* ..	Parish	294
Little Musgrave	*Westmoreland*	Tnship.	61	Little Timble ..	*York* ..	Tnship.	49
Little Ness ..	*Salop* ..	Tnship.	238	Little Tintern ..	*Monmouth* ..	Parish	335

Name of Place.	County.	Description.	Population.	Name of Place.	County.	Description.	Population.
Littleton	Cheshire	Tnship.	66	St. Anne	Lancaster	Ecl. Dis.	10 330
Littleton on Severn	Gloucester	Parish	195	St. Barnabas	„	Ecl. Dis.	7 544
Littleton, West	„	Parish	120	St. Bartholomew	„	Ecl. Dis.	8 777
Littleton	Hants	Parish	109	St. Bridget	„	Ecl. Dis.	3 954
Littleton	Middlesex	Parish	111	St. Catherine	„	Ecl. Dis.	9 679
Littleton, High	Somerset	Parish	860	St. David	„	Ecl. Dis.	7 442
Littleton	Wilts	Tithing	62	St. George	„	Ecl. Dis.	4 002
Littleton, Drew	„	Parish	233	St. John	„	Ecl. Dis.	5 561
Littleton-Pannell	„	Tithing	615	St. Mark	„	Ecl. Dis.	10 066
Littleton, St. Andrew	„	Parish	233	St. Martin	„	Ecl. Dis.	26 961
Littleton, North	Worcester	Parish	303	St. Michael	„	Ecl. Dis.	8 819
Littleton, South	„	Parish	294	St. Paul	„	Ecl. Dis.	7 637
Little Torrington	Devon	Parish	563	St. Saviour	„	Ecl. Dis.	4 615
Little Tosson	Northumberland	Tnship.	33	St. Silas	„	Ecl. Dis.	7 019
Little Totham	Essex	Parish	346	St. Simon	„	Ecl. Dis.	5 716
Little & Gt. Usworth	Durham	Tnship.	3 677	St. Thomas	„	Ecl. Dis.	4 984
Little Wakering	Essex	Parish	283	Liversedge	York	Sub-dis.	14 520
Little Waldingfield	Suffolk	Parish	412	Liversedge	„	Tnship.	8 176
Little Walsingham	Norfolk	Parish	1 069	Liversedge, Christch.	„	Ecl. Dis.	5 848
Little Waltham	Essex	Parish	684	Liverstock Green	Herts	Ecl. Dis.	1 247
Little Warley	„	Parish	485	Liverton	York	Tnship.	186
Little Washbourne	Gloucester	Hamlet	28	Livesey	Lancaster	Tnship.	3 581
Little Weldon	Northampton	Hamlet	514	Llan	Flint	Tnship.	334
Little Wenham	Suffolk	Parish	95	Llanaber	Merioneth	Parish	1 600
Little Wenlock	Salop	Parish	988	Llanaelhaiarn	Carnarvon	Parish	736
Little Whelnetham	Suffolk	Parish	194	Llanafan	Cardigan	Parish	567
Little Whittington	Nrthumbld.	Tnship.	19	Llanafanfawr	Brecon	Parish	936
Little Wigborough	Essex	Parish	92	Llanafanfechan	„	Parish	163
Little Wilbraham	Cambs	Parish	353	Llanallgo	Anglesey	Chap.	430
Little Witchingham	Norfolk	Parish	33	Llananno	Radnor	Parish	358
Little Witley	Worcester	Chap.	208	Llanarmon	Carnarvon	Parish	556
Little Wittenham	Berks	Parish	134	Llanarmon	Denbigh	Sub-dis.	3 196
Little Wolford	Warwick	Hamlet	242	Llanarmon	„	Parish	2 019
Little Woolstone	Bucks	Parish	125	Llanarmondyffrynceiriog	„	Parish	315
Little Woolton	Lancaster	Tnship.	1 062	Llanarmonmynyddmawr	„	Parish	140
Littleworth	Berks	Ecl. Dis.	337	Llanarth	Cardigan	Parish	2 216
Littleworth	Gloucester	Parish	501	Llanarth	Monmouth	Sub-dis.	1 884
Little Wratting	Suffolk	Parish	193	Llanarth	„	Parish	679
Little Wymondley	Herts	Parish	318	Llanarth	„	Tnship.	325
Little Yarmouth	Suffolk	Hamlet	1 714	Llanarthney	Carmarthen	Parish	2 001
Little Yeldham	Essex	Parish	307	Llanasa	Flint	Parish	2 682
Littlington	Sussex	Parish	134	Llanbabo	Anglesey	Parish	138
Litton	Derby	Hamlet	974	Llanbadarnfawr	Cardigan	Parish	13 724
Litton Cheney	Dorset	Parish	501	Llanbadarnfawr	Radnor	Parish	475
Litton & Cascob	Radnor	Tnship.	90	Llanbadarnfynydd	„	Parish	609
Litton	Somerset	Parish	313	Llanbadarnodwyn	Cardigan	Parish	527
Litton	York	Tnship.	93	Llanbadarntrefeglwys	„	Parish	948
Livermere, Great	Suffolk	Parish	290	Llanbadarnycroyddin Lo.	„	Tnship.	773
Livermere, Little	„	Parish	167	Llanbadarnycroyddin Up.	„	Tnship.	980
Liverpool	Lancaster	District	269 742	Llanbadarnygarreg	Radnor	Parish	59
Liverpool	„	Parish	269 742	Llanbaddock	Monmouth	Parish	452
Liverpool	500,676 (1864)	Borough	443 938	Llanbadrig	Anglesey	Parish	1 187
All Saints	„	Ecl. Dis.	9 204	Llanbeblig	Carnarvon	Parish	9 937
St. Aidan	„	Ecl. Dis.	12 718	Llanbeblig	„	Tnship.	1 425

Name of Place.	County.	Description.	Population.	Name of Place.	County.	Description.	Population.
Llanbedr	Brecon	Parish	280	Llandegla	Denbigh	Parish	425
Llanbedr	Merioneth	Parish	370	Llandegley	Radnor	Parish	382
Llanbedr	Denbigh	Parish	431	Llandegveth	Monmouth	Parish	116
Llanbedrgôch	Anglesey	Parish	356	Llandegwning	Carnarvon	Parish	142
Llanbedrog	Carnarvon	Parish	469	Llandeloy	Pembroke	Parish	208
Llanbedrpainscastle	Radnor	Parish	306	Llandenny	Monmouth	Parish	418
Llanbedrycennin	Carnarvon	Parish	489	Llandevenny	,,	Hamlet	42
Llanbedrycennin	,,	Tnship.	355	Llandewy	Glamorgan	Parish	149
Llanberis	,,	Parish	1 364	Llandewyfach	Radnor	Parish	115
Llanbeulan	Anglesey	Parish	315	Llandewyvelfrey	Pembroke	Parish	790
Llanbister	Radnor	Sub-dis.	4 370	Llandewyvelfrey	,,	Hamlet	768
Llanbister	,,	Parish	1 045	Llandewyystradenny	Radnor	Parish	669
Llanblethian	Glamorgan	Parish	753	Llandilo	Carmarthen	L. Sub.	15 075
Llanboidy	Carm. & Pem.	Sub-dis.	3 635	Llandilofawr	,,	District	17 222
Llanboidy	Carmarthen	Parish	1 744	Llandilo	,,	Sub-dis.	4 546
Llanbrynmair	Montgomery	Parish	2 061	Llandilofawr	,,	Parish	5 440
Llancadwalladr	Denbigh	Parish	223	Llandilo	Pembroke	Parish	126
Llancarvan	Glamorgan	Parish	668	Llandiloabercowin	Carmarthen	Parish	77
Llancillo	Hereford	Parish	74	Llandilograbau	Radnor	Parish	263
Llancwnlle	Cardigan	Parish	803	Llandilotalybont	Glamorgan	Sub-dis.	5 114
Llancynfelin	,,	Parish	967	Llandilotalybont	,,	Parish	1 331
Llandaff	..	Diocese	418 113	Llandilovane	Brecon	Parish	496
Llandaff	Glamorgan	Parish	6 585	Llandinabo	Hereford	Parish	63
Llandanwg	Merioneth	Parish	739	Llandinam	Montgomery	Parish	1 574
Llandawke	Carmarthen	Parish	38	Llandingat	Carmarthen	Sub-dis.	2 389
Llanddanielfab	Anglesey	Parish	442	Llandingat	,,	Parish	2 389
Llanddarog	Carmarthen	Parish	970	Llandinorwig	Carnarvon	Ecl. Dis.	3 346
Llanddausaint	Anglesey	Sub-dis.	5 388	Llandissilio	Cardigan	Sub-dis.	6 459
Llanddausaint	,,	Parish	565	Llandisiliogogo	,,	Parish	1 315
Llanddausaint	Carmarthen	Sub-dis.	848	Llandissilio	Carm. & Pem.	Sub-dis.	3 340
Llanddausaint	,,	Parish	848	Llandissilio	,, ,,	Parish	1 036
Llanddeiniolen	Carnarvon	Parish	5 747	Llandogo	Monmouth	Parish	648
Llanddeinol	Cardigan	Parish	260	Llandough	Glamorgan	Parish	119
Llandderfel	Merioneth	Parish	948	Llandough by Penarth	,,	Parish	234
Llanddewiaberarth	Cardigan	Parish	1 463	Llandovery	Carmarthen	L. Sub.	17 801
Llanddewiabergwessin	Brecon	Parish	111	Llandovery	Carm. & Brec.	District	14 775
Llanddewibrefi	Cardigan	Parish	2 754	Llandovery	Carmarthen	Tnship.	1 855
Llanddewircwn	Brecon	Parish	215	Llandovery	,,	M. Bor.	1 855
Llanddoget	Denbigh	Parish	276	Llandow	Glamorgan	Parish	133
Llanddona	Anglesey	Parish	567	Llandowror	Carmarthen	Parish	339
Llanddulas	Denbigh	Parish	619	Llandrillo	Merioneth	Parish	776
Llanddwywe	Merioneth	Parish	368	Llandrilloynrhos	Carn. & Denb.	Parish	1 321
Llanddyfnan	Anglesey	Parish	720	Llandrilloynrhos	Denbigh	Tnship.	1 026
Llandebie	Carmarthen	Sub-dis.	6 344	Llandrindod	Radnor	Parish	243
Llandebie	,,	Parish	2 821	Llandrinio	Montgomery	Parish	910
Llandecwyn	Merioneth	Parish	436	Llandrygarn	Anglesey	Parish	359
Llandefailogfach	Brecon	Parish	400	Llandudno	Carnarvon	Parish	2 316
Llandefailogfach	,,	Hamlet	222	Llandudwen	,,	Parish	94
Llandefailogtregraig	,,	Parish	38	Llandulas in Tyr Abbot	Brecon	Parish	124
Llandefalley	,,	Parish	687	Llandwrog	Carnarvon	Sub-dis.	8 518
Llandefeilog	Carmarthen	Parish	1 247	Llandwrog	,,	Parish	2 825
Llandegai	Carnarvon	Parish	3 381	Llandwrog, St. Thos.	,,	Ecl. Dis.	2 114
Llandegai, St. Anne	,,	Ecl. Dis.	1 745	Llandyfeisant	Carmarthen	Parish	258
Llandegfan	Anglesey	Parish	900	Llandyfodog	Glamorgan	Parish	254

Name of Place.	County.	Description.	Population.	Name of Place.	County.	Description.	Population.
landyfriog	Cardigan	Parish	807	Llanfairdyffrynclwyd	Denbigh	Parish	1 263
landyfrydog	Anglesey	Sub-dis.	4 580	Llanfairfechan	Carnarvon	Parish	1 199
landyfrydog	,,	Parish	706	Llanfair in Buallt	Brecon	Parish	1 110
landygwydd	Card. & Pem.	Sub-dis.	4 133	Llanfairisgaer	Carnarvon	Parish	1 060
landygwydd	Cardigan	Parish	1 028	Llanfair by Harlech	Merioneth	Parish	426
landyrnog	Denbigh	Sub-dis.	1 826	Llanf'rmathafarneithaf	Anglesey	Parish	757
landyrnog	,,	Parish	653	Llanfairnantgwyn	Pembroke	Parish	189
landysilio	Anglesey	Parish	1 359	Llanfairnantygof	,,	Parish	245
landysilio	Montgomery	Parish	689	Llanfairorllwyn	Cardigan	Parish	427
landyssil	Card. & Carm.	Sub-dis.	5 934	Llanfairpwllgwyngyll	Anglesey	Parish	695
landyssil	Cardigan	Parish	2 788	Llanfairtalhaiarn	Denbigh	Parish	1 309
landyssil	Montgomery	Parish	790	Llanfairtrefhelygen	Cardigan	Parish	81
lanedarn	Glamorgan	Parish	289	Llanfairyneubwll	Anglesey	Parish	357
lanedwen	Anglesey	Parish	273	Llanfairynghornwy	,,	Parish	293
lanedy	Carmarthen	Parish	1 086	Llanfairynycwmmwd	,,	Parish	37
lanegryn	Merioneth	Parish	652	Llanfallteg	Carm. & Pem.	Parish	353
lanegwad	Carmarthen	Parish	1 920	Llanfechan	Brecon	Parish	163
laneilian	Anglesey	Parish	1 282	Llanfechan	Montgomery	Parish	649
laneilian	Denbigh	Parish	548	Llanfechell	Anglesey	Parish	958
lanelidan	,,	Sub-dis.	2 684	Llanferras	Denbigh	Parish	754
lanelidan	,,	Parish	848	Llanffinan	Anglesey	Parish	138
lanelieu	Brecon	Parish	93	Llanfflewyn	,,	Parish	128
lanellen	Monmouth	Parish	373	Llanfigael	,,	Parish	121
lanelltyd	Merioneth	Parish	465	Llanfihangel	Brecon	Hamlet	246
lanelly	Brecon	Sub-dis.	9 603	Llanfihangel	Montgomery	Parish	950
lanelly	,,	Parish	9 603	,, aberbythych	Carmarthen	Parish	824
lanelly	Carmarthen	L. Sub.	25 089	,, abercowin	,,	Parish	893
lanelly	Carm. & Glam.	District	27 979	,, abergwessin	Brecon	Parish	355
lanelly	Carmarthen	Sub-dis.	14 619	,, ararth	Carmarthen	Parish	1 795
lanelly	,,	Parish	17 279	,, bachellaeth	Carnarvon	Parish	312
lanelly	,,	P. Bor.	11 446	,, beguildy	Radnor	Parish	1 203
lanelly, St. Paul	,,	Ecl. Dis.	5 009	,, brynpabuan	Brecon	Parish	341
lanelwedd	Radnor	Parish	227	,, cilfargen	Carmarthen	Parish	58
lanenddwyn	Merioneth	Parish	891	,, cwmdû	Brecon	Parish	1 056
lanengan	Carnarvon	Parish	1 021	,, esceifiog	Anglesey	Parish	1 026
lanerchayron	Cardigan	Parish	228	,, fechan	Brecon	Chap.	178
lanerchymedd, S. Mary	Angly.	Ecl. Dis.	1 164	,, geneurglynn	Cardigan	Parish	3 979
lanerchymedd	,,	Parish	67	,, glynmyfr	Denb. & Mer.	Parish	464
lanerfyl	Montgomery	Parish	885	,, glynmyfr	Denbigh	Hamlet	394
laneugrad	Anglesey	Parish	276	,, helygen	Radnor	Parish	110
lanfabon	Glamorgan	Parish	2 360	,, iledrod	Cardigan	Parish	1 125
lanfachreth	Anglesey	Parish	532	,, nantbrane	Brecon	Parish	453
lanfachreth	Merioneth	Parish	862	,, penbedw	Pembroke	Parish	287
lanfaelog	Anglesey	Parish	763	,, rhosycorn	Carmarthen	Parish	634
lanfaelrhys	Carnarvon	Parish	208	,, rhydithon	Radnor	Parish	378
lanfaes	Anglesey	Parish	243	,, rhydithon	,,	Tnship.	404
lanfaes	Brecon	Division	1 246	,, talyllyn	Brecon	Parish	149
lanfaethly	Anglesey	Parish	445	,, tre'rbeirdd	Anglesey	Parish	356
lanfaglan	Carnarvon	Parish	253	,, tynsylw	,,	Parish	54
lanfair	Montgomery	Sub-dis.	6 375	,, ycroyddin	Cardigan	Parish	2 774
lanfairarybryn	Carmarthen	Sub-dis.	1 559	,, ycroyddin, Low	,,	Tnship.	978
lanfairarybryn	,,	Parish	1 559	,, ycroyddin, Up.	,,	Tnship.	1 796
lanfaircaereinion	Montgomery	Parish	2 584	,, ynhowyn	Anglesey	Parish	222
lanfairclydogau	Cardigan	Parish	614	,, ypennant	Carnarvon	Parish	753

Name of Place.	County.	Description.	Population.	Name of Place.	County.	Description.	Popula
Llanfihypennant	Merioneth ..	Parish	368	Llangelynin ..	Carnarvon..	Parish	2
„ ystrad ..	Cardigan ..	Parish	1 162	Llangelynin ..	Merioneth ..	Parish	8
„ ytraethau	Merioneth ..	Sub-dis.	3 658	Llangendeirne ..	Carmarthen	Sub-dis.	9 0
„ ytraethau	„ ..	Parish	1 687	Llangendeirne ..	„	Parish	2 3
Llanfoist ..	Monmouth..	Parish	1 472	Llangennech ..	„	Parish	9
Llanfor	Merioneth ..	Parish	1 531	Llangennith ..	Glamorgan .	Parish	3
Llanfrothen ..	„ ..	Parish	830	Llangenny ..	Brecon ..	Parish	4
Llanfwrog ..	Anglesey ..	Parish	246	Llangerniew ..	Denbigh ..	Parish	1 2
Llanfwrog ..	Denbigh ..	Parish	1 425	Llangeview ..	Monmouth..	Parish	1
Llanfyllin ..	Montgomery	Hund.	7 545	Llangian ..	Carnarvon..	Parish	1 0
Llanfyllin ..	„	L. Sub.	7 545	Llangibby ..	Monmouth..	Sub-dis.	3 6
Llanfyllin ..	Mont. & Denb.	District	21 699	Llangibby ..	„ ..	Parish	5
Llanfyllin ..	Montgomery	Parish	1 880	Llanginning ..	Carmarthen	Parish	3
Llanfyllin ..	„	P. Bor.	1 068	Llanglydwen ..	„	Parish	2
Llanfynydd ..	Carmarthen	Sub-dis.	1 410	Llangoed ..	Anglesey ..	Parish	6
Llanfynydd ..	„	Parish	1 230	Llangoedmore ..	Cardigan ..	Parish	9
Llanfynydd, St.Michael	Flint..	Ecl. Dis.	1 133	Llangollen ..	Denbigh ..	L. Sub.	9 7
Llanfyrnach ..	Pembroke ..	Parish	934	Llangollen ..	„ ..	Parish	5 7
Llangadfan ..	Montgomery	Parish	1 028	Llangollentraian	„ ..	Division	4 8
Llangadock ..	Carmarthen	Sub-dis.	2 789	Llangolman ..	Pembroke ..	Parish	2
Llangadock ..	„	Parish	2 789	Llangorse ..	Brecon ..	Sub-dis.	2 9
Llangadwaladr ..	Anglesey ..	Parish	526	Llangorse ..	„ ..	Parish	4
Llangafelach ..	Glamorgan .	Hund.	17 923	Llangoven ..	Monmouth..	Parish	1
Llangafelach ..	„ ..	L. Sub.	26 305	Llangower ..	Merioneth ..	Parish	3
Llangafelach ..	„ ..	Sub-dis.	14 553	Llangranog ..	Cardigan ..	Parish	88
Llangafelach ..	„ ..	Parish	13 219	Llangristiolus ..	Anglesey ..	Parish	88
Llangaffo ..	Anglesey ..	Parish	122	Llangrwyddon ..	Cardigan ..	Parish	55
Llangain ..	Carmarthen	Parish	393	Llangstone ..	Monmouth..	Parish	2
Llangammarch ..	Brecon ..	Parish	1 078	Llangua.. ..	„ ..	Parish	1
Llangan..	Carm. & Pemb.	Parish	641	Llanguick ..	Glamorgan .	Parish	7 98
Llangan.. ..	Glamorgan .	Parish	223	Llangunider ..	Brecon ..	Sub-dis.	3 59
Llanganhafal ..	Denbigh ..	Parish	497	Llangunider ..	„ ..	Parish	3 59
Llanganten ..	Brecon ..	Parish	159	Llangunllo ..	Cardigan ..	Parish	58
Llangar.. ..	Merioneth ..	Parish	211	Llangunllo ..	Radnor ..	Parish	59
Llangarren ..	Hereford ..	Parish	1 215	Llangunllo ..	„ ..	Tnship.	44
Llangastytalyllyn	Brecon ..	Parish	200	Llangunnock ..	Carmarthen	Parish	71
Llangathen ..	Carmarthen	Sub-dis.	2 897	Llangunnor ..	„	Parish	1 25
Llangathen ..	„	Parish	977	Llangurig ..	Montgomery	Parish	1 64
Llangattock ..	Brecon ..	Sub-dis.	5 759	Llangwm ..	Denbigh ..	Parish	98
Llangattock ..	„ ...	Parish	5 759	Llangwm ..	Monmouth..	Parish	38
Llangattock ..	Monmouth	Parish	1 544	Llangwm ..	Pembroke ..	Parish	90
Llangattock ..	„	Tnship.	276	Llangwnadle ..	Carnarvon..	Parish	27
Llangattock-Llingoed	„	Parish	206	Llangwstennin ..	„	Parish	67
Llangattock by Usk	„	Parish	252	Llangwyfan ..	Anglesey ..	Parish	20
Llangattock-Vibon-Avel	„	Parish	497	Llangwyfan ..	Denbigh ..	Parish	24
Llangedwyn ..	Denbigh ..	Parish	297	Llangwyllog ..	Anglesey ..	Parish	20
Llangefni ..	Anglesey ..	Sub-dis.	5 431	Llangybi ..	Carnarvon..	Parish	62
Llangefni ..	„	Parish	1 696	Llangyby ..	Cardigan ..	Parish	29
Llangefni ..	„ ..	P. Bor.	1 317	Llangyniew ..	Montgomery	Parish	60
Llangeinor ..	Glamorgan .	Parish	363	Llangynog ..	Brecon ..	Parish	5
Llangeinwen ..	Anglesey ..	Parish	913	Llangynog ..	Montgomery	Parish	60
Llangeitho ..	Cardigan ..	Sub-dis.	3 336	Llangynwyd ..	Glamorgan .	Parish	7 00
Llangeitho ..	Cardigan ..	Parish	453	Llangynwyd, Higher	„ ..	Hamlet	2 18
Llangeler ..	Carmarthen	Parish	1 573	Llangynwyd, Lower	„ ..	Hamlet	88

Name of Place.	County.	Description.	Population.	Name of Place.	County.	Description.	Population.
Llangynwyd, Middle	Glamorgan	Hamlet	324	Llanrhaiadr ..	Denb. & Mntg	Sub-dis.	5 101
Llanhamlach ..	Brecon ..	Parish	304	Llanrhaiadr ..	Denbigh ..	Sub-dis.	2 611
Llanharan ..	Glamorgan .	Parish	299	Llanrhaiadr :—			
Llanhary ..	„ ..	Parish	275	„ in Kinmerch	„ ..	Parish	1 888
Llanhennock ..	Monmouth ..	Parish	228	„ ynmochnant	Dnb. & Mntg.	Parish	2 304
Llanhilleth ..	„ ..	Parish	1 020	Llanrhidian ..	Glamorgan .	Parish	1 993
Llanhowell ..	Pembroke ..	Parish	184	Llanrhidian Higher	„ ..	Hamlet	1 468
Llanidan ..	Anglesey ..	Sub-dis.	3 313	Llanrhidian Lower	„	Hamlet	525
Llanidan ..	„ ..	Parish	1 323	Llanrhwydrys ..	Anglesey ..	Parish	136
Llanidloes ..	Montgomery	Hund.	8 518	Llanrhychwyn ..	Carnarvon ..	Parish	532
Llanidloes ..	„	L. Sub.	11 645	Llanrhydd ..	Denbigh ..	Parish	965
Llanidloes, Lower	„	Sub-dis.	3 666	Llanrhyddlad ..	Anglesey ..	Parish	790
Llanidloes, Upper	„	Sub-dis.	3 663	Llanrhystyd ..	Cardigan ..	Sub-dis.	3 419
Llanidloes ..	„	Parish	3 987	Llanrhystyd ..	„ ..	Parish	1 533
Llanidloes ..	„	Borough	3 127	Llanrian ..	Pembroke ..	Parish .	1 017
Llaniestyn ..	Anglesey ..	Parish	212	Llanrithan ..	„ ..	Parish	188
Llaniestyn ..	Carnarvon ..	Parish	1 012	Llanrothall ..	Hereford ..	Parish	107
Llanigon ..	Brecon ..	Parish	484	Llanrug.. ..	Carnarvon ..	Sub-dis.	10 404
Llanigon ..	„ ..	Hamlet	429	Llanrug.. ..	„ ..	Parish	2 139
Llanilar.. ..	Cardigan ..	Parish	947	Llanrwst ..	Denbigh ..	L. Sub.	9 039
Llanilid.. ..	Glamorgan .	Parish	150	Llanrwst ..	Denb. & Carn.	District	12 770
Llanilterne ..	„ ..	Parish	150	Llanrwst ..	„ „	Sub-dis.	7 100
Llanina.. ..	Cardigan ..	Parish	498	Llanrwst ..	„ „	Parish	3 993
Llanina.. ..	„ ..	Hamlet	259	Llanrwst ..	Denbigh ..	Tnship.	3 593
Llanio	„ ..	Tnship.	122	Llansadurnen ..	Carmarthen	Parish	194
Llanishen ..	Glamorgan .	Parish	449	Llansadwrn ..	Anglesey ..	Parish .	419
Llanishen ..	Monmouth ..	Parish	320	Llansadwrn ..	Carmarthen	Sub-dis.	1 710
Llanllawddog ..	Carmarthen	Parish	696	Llansadwrn ..	„	Parish	1 099
Llanllawer ..	Pembroke ..	Parish	117	Llansaintffraid ..	Cardigan ..	Sub-dis.	7 081
Llanllechid ..	Carnarvon ..	Sub-dis.	9 127	Llansaintffraid ..	„ ..	Parish	1 309
Llanllechid ..	„ ..	Parish	7 346	Llansaintffraid ..	Montgomery	Sub-dis.	10 223
Llanlleonvel ..	Brecon ..	Parish	250	Llansaintffraid ..	„	Parish	1 255
Llanlleonvel ..	„ ..	Hamlet	188	„ glanconway	Denbigh ..	Parish	1 304
Llanllibio ..	Anglesey ..	Parish	59	„ glynceiriog	„ ..	Parish	738
Llanllowell ..	Monmouth ..	Parish	87	„ glyndyfrdwy	Merioneth..	Parish	161
Llanllugan ..	Montgomery	Parish	304	Llansaintfraed ..	Brecon ..	Parish	255
Llanllwch ..	Carmarthen	Ecl. Dis.	896	Llansaintfraed ..	Monmouth ..	Parish	16
Llanllwchaiarn .	Cardigan ..	Parish	1 976	Llansaintfraed in Elvel	Radnor	Parish	340
Llanllwchaiarn ..	Montgomery	Parish	2 394	Llansamlet ..	Glamorgan .	Sub-dis.	5 103
Llanllwny ..	Carmarthen	Parish	776	Llansamlet ..	„ ..	Parish	5 103
Llanllyfni ..	Carnarvon ..	Parish	2 362	LlansamletHigher	„ ..	Hamlet	1 860
Llanmadock ..	Glamorgan .	Parish	225	Llansamlet Lower	„ ..	Hamlet	3 243
Llanmaes ..	„ ..	Parish	164	Llansannan ..	Denbigh ..	Parish	1 256
Llanmartin ..	Monmouth ..	Parish	181	Llansannor ..	Glamorgan .	Parish	197
Llanmerewig ..	Montgomery	Parish	148	Llansawel ..	Carmarthen	Parish	1 003
Llanmihangel ..	Glamorgan .	Parish	29	Llansilin ..	Denbigh ..	L. Sub.	4 302
Llanefydd ..	Denbigh ..	Parish	1 136	Llansilin ..	Denb. & Salop	Sub-dis.	4 128
Llannon ..	Carmarthen	Sub-dis.	3 593	Llansilin ..	„ „	Parish	2 002
Llannon ..	„ ..	Parish	1 656	Llansilin ..	Denbigh ..	Tnship.	1 795
Llannor.. ..	Carnarvon ..	Parish	1 023	Llansoy.. ..	Monmouth ..	Parish	168
Llanover ..	Monmouth ..	Parish	4 290	Llanspyddid ..	Brecon ..	Parish	408
Llanover, Lower	„ ..	Division	348	Llanspyddid ..	„ ..	Hamlet	172
Llanover, Upper	„ ..	Division	3 942	Llanstadwell ..	Pembroke ..	Parish	1 745
Llanpumpsaint..	Carmarthen	Parish	543	Llanstephan ..	Carmarthen	Parish	1 229

Name of Place.	County.	Description.	Population.	Name of Place.	County.	Description.	Population.
Llanstephan	Radnor	Parish	231	Llanwenog	Cardigan	Parish	1 521
Llanstinan	Pembroke	Parish	174	Llanwern	Monmouth	Parish	15
Llanthetty	Brecon	Parish	631	Llanwinio	Carmarthen	Parish	944
Llanthew	,,	Parish	292	Llanwnda	Carnarvon	Parish	1 660
Llanthewyrhytherch	Monmouth	Parish	339	Llanwnda	Pembroke	Parish	1 138
Llanthewyskirrid	,,	Parish	88	Llanwnen	Cardigan	Parish	344
Llanthewyvach	,,	Parish	172	Llanwnog	Montgomery	Sub-dis.	4 802
Llantilliocrosenny	,,	Parish	748	Llanwnog	,,	Parish	1 631
Llantilliopertholey	,,	Parish	984	Llanwonno	Glamorgan	Parish	8 702
Llantood	Pembroke	Parish	264	Llanwrda	Carmarthen	Parish	611
Llantrisaint	Anglesey	Parish	488	Llanwrin	Montgomery	Parish	720
Llantrisaint	Glamorgan	Sub-dis.	12 904	Llanwrthwl	Brecon	Parish	556
Llantrisaint	,,	Parish	5 492	Llanwrtyd	,,	Sub-dis.	731
Llantrisaint	,,	P. Bor.	1 493	Llanwrtyd	,,	Parish	607
Llantrissent	Monmouth	Parish	308	Llanwyddelan	Montgomery	Parish	476
Llantrithyd	Glamorgan	Parish	204	Llanyblodwell	Salop	Parish	1 008
Llantwitvairdre	,,	Parish	4 415	Llanybyther	Carmarthen	Sub-dis.	2 541
Llantysilio	Denbigh	Parish	1 129	Llanybyther	,,	Parish	1 131
Llanuwchyllyn	Merioneth	Parish	1 145	Llanycefn	Pembroke	Parish	416
Llanvaches	Monmouth	Parish	235	Llanychaer	,,	Parish	194
Llanvair Discoed	,,	Parish	187	Llanychaiarn	Cardigan	Parish	580
Llanvair Discoed	,,	Tnship.	150	Llanychan	Denbigh	Parish	107
Llanvairkilgidin	,,	Parish	296	Llanychlwydog	Pembroke	Parish	206
Llanvair-Waterdine	Salop	Parish	611	Llanycil	Merioneth	Parish	2 383
Llanvapley	Monmouth	Parish	156	Llanycrwys	Carmarthen	Parish	524
Llanvareth	Radnor	Parish	155	Llanymowddwy	Merioneth	Parish	595
Llanvedw	Glamorgan	Hamlet	309	Llanymynech	Salop & Mont.	Parish	951
Llanvetherine	Monmouth	Parish	222	Llanymynech	Salop	Tnship.	551
Llanveynoe	Hereford	Tnship.	283	Llanynghenedl	Anglesey	Parish	427
Llanvigan	Brecon	Parish	674	Llanynys	Brecon	Parish	152
Llanvihangel	Monm. & Her.	Sub-dis.	1 860	Llynynys	Denbigh	Parish	723
,, crucorney	Monmouth	Parish	479	Llanyre	Radnor	Parish	744
,, crucorney	,,	—	372	Llanystymdwy	Carnarvon	Parish	1 126
,, lantarnam	,,	Parish	1 301	Llanywern	Brecon	Parish	139
,, nantmellan	Radnor	Parish	348	Llawhaden	Pembroke	Parish	647
,, nantmellan	,,	Tnship.	258	Llay	Denbigh	Tnship.	489
,, nr. Roggiett	Monmouth	Parish	36	Llechgwenfarwydd	Anglesey	Parish	366
,, nigh Usk	,,	Parish	112	Llechryd	Cardigan	Parish	454
,, pontymoile	,,	Parish	300	Llechwedd-Isaf	Carnarvon	Sub-dis.	2 037
,, torymynydd	,,	Parish	197	Llechweddor	Brecon	Hamlet	320
,, ysternllewern	,,	Parish	183	Llechylched	Anglesey	Parish	635
Llanvillo	Brecon	Parish	263	Lledrod Lower	Cardigan	Tnship.	588
Llanvithin	Glamorgan	Parish	28	Lledrod Upper	,,	Tnship.	537
Llanvrechva	Monmouth	Parish	2 554	Llowes	Radnor	Parish	324
Llanvrechva Lower	,,	Tnship.	933	Lloyndu	Monmouth	Hamlet	155
Llanvrechva Upper	,,	Tnshp.	1 621	Llwydiarth, St. Mary	Montgry.	Ecl. Dis.	322
Llanvrynach	Brecon	Parish	352	Llwynegrin	Flint	Tnship.	160
Llanwarne	Hereford	Parish	383	Llyfon	Anglesey	Hund.	6 378
Llanwddyn	Montgomery	Parish	529	Llysdanhunedd	Flint	Tnship.	83
Llanwenarth	Monmouth	Parish	2 326	Llysdinam	Brecon	Hamlet	242
Llanwenarth Citra	,,	Division	230	Llysfaen	Carnarvon	Parish	908
Llanwenarth, Ultra	,,	Division	2 096	Llyswen	Brecon	Parish	226
Llanwenllwyfo	Anglesey	Parish	546	Llysworney	Glamorgan	Parish	189
Llanwenog	Cardigan	Sub-dis.	1 865	Llysycoed	Flint	Tnship.	74

Name of Place.	County.	Description.	Population.	Name of Place.	County.	Description.	Population.
lysyfrâne	Pembroke	Parish	168	London, Little, St. Matt.	York.	Ecl. Dis.	4 490
lywell	Brecon	Parish	1 503	Londonthorpe	Lincoln	Parish	228
oan End	Northumberland	Tnship.	139	Long Acre	Middlesex	Sub-dis.	11 618
obthorpe	Lincoln	Hamlet	62	Long Ashton	Somerset	Sub-dis.	5 864
ockeridge	Wilts	Tithing	274	Long Ashton	,,	Parish	2 000
ockerley	Hants	Parish	581	Long Bennington	Lincoln	Parish	1 066
ocking	Somerset	Parish	152	Longbenton	Northumberland	Sub-dis.	13 304
ockinge, East	Berks	Parish	318	Longbenton	,,	Parish	13 304
ockinge, West	,,	Hamlet	66	Longbenton	,,	Tnship.	2 222
ockington	Leicester	Parish	571	Longborough	Gloucester	Parish	655
ockington	,,	Tnship.	186	Longbredy	Dorset	Parish	250
ockington	York	Sub-dis.	3 163	Longbridge Deverell	Wilts	Sub-dis.	3 927
ockington	,,	Parish	486	Longbridge Deverell	,,	Parish	1 197
ockington	,,	Tnship.	451	Long Buckby	Northampton	Sub-dis.	5 757
ockington (Kilnwick P.)	,,	Tnship.	135	Long Buckby	,,	Parish	2 500
ockton	,,	Sub-dis.	544	Longburgh	Cumberland	Tnship.	146
ockton	,,	Chap.	396	Longburton	Dorset	Parish	336
ockwood	,,	Sub-dis.	9 488	Long Clawson	Leicester	Parish	820
ockwood	,,	Tnship.	6 755	Long Compton	Warwick	Parish	703
ockwood, Emmanuel	,,	Ecl. Dis.	8 783	Longcott	Berks	Tnship.	446
oddington	Kent	Hamlet	42	Long Crendon	,,	Parish	1 570
oddington	Leicester	Parish	142	Long Critchell	Dorset	Parish	145
oddington	Northampton	Parish	289	Longcross	Surrey	Ecl. Dis.	133
oddiswell	Devon	Parish	899	Long Ditton	,,	Parish	1 445
oddon	Norfolk	Hund.	7 509	Longdon	Stafford	Parish	1 220
oddon & Clavering	,,	L. Sub.	14 183	Longdon	Worcester	Parish	626
oddon	,,	District	14 242	Longdon upon Tern	Salop	Parish	88
oddon	,,	Sub-dis.	5 072	Long Drax	York	Tnship.	162
oddon	,,	Parish	1 153	Long Eaton	Derby	Tnship.	1 551
oders	Dorset	Parish	1 053	Long Eaton	,,	Ecl. Dis.	1 551
odge on Wolds	Notts	Parish	4	Longfield	Kent	Parish	188
odsworth	Sussex	Parish	629	Longfleet	Dorset	Tithing	1 417
oes	Suffolk	Hund.	13 033	Longfleet, St. Mary	,,	Ecl. Dis.	1 598
ofthouse	York	Sub-dis.	2 339	Longford	Derby	Parish	1 157
ofthouse	,,	Parish	1 103	Longford	,,	Tnship.	50C
ofthouse w. Carlton	,,	Tnship.	2 028	Longford	Salop	Parish	214
ofthouse Christch.	,,	Ecl. Dis.	2 099	Longford St. Cather.	Gloucester	Hamlet	213
olworth	Cambs	Parish	133	Longford St. Mary	,,	Hamlet	418
onan	Isle of Man	Parish	2 909	Long Framlington	Nrthumbld.	Tnship.	447
Londesborough	York	Parish	306	Long Grove Christch.	Hereford	Ecl. Dis.	742
LONDON		**Metro.**	**2803989**	Longham	Norfolk	Parish	320
London Middlesex *Part of*		Metro.	2030814	Longhirst	Northumberland	Tnship.	253
London Surrey	,,	Metro.	579748	Longhope	Gloucester	Parish	1 104
London Kent	,,	Metro.	193427	Long Horsley	Northumberland	Parish	964
London		Diocese	2570079	Long Houghton	,,	Parish	777
London	Middlesex	M. City	112 063	Long Houghton	,,	Tnship.	491
London City	,,	District	45 555	Long Itchington	Warwick	Parish	1 150
London City, N. East	,,	Sub-dis.	11 544	Long Lane Christch.	Derby	Ecl. Dis.	332
London City, N. West	,,	Sub-dis.	9 020	Long Langton	Dorset	Parish	174
London City, South	,,	Sub-dis.	8 570	Long Lawford	Warwick	Tnship.	601
London City, S. East	,,	Sub-dis.	8 659	Long Marston	York	Parish	586
London City, S.West	,,	Sub-dis.	7 762	Long Marston	,,	Tnship.	405
London Road	Lancaster	Sub-dis.	28 817	Long Marton	Westmoreland	Parish	762
London Road	Surrey	Sub-dis.	19 190	Long Melford	Suffolk	Parish	2 870

Name of Place.	County.	Description.	Population.	Name of Place.	County.	Description.	Population.
Long Newnton	*Wilts*	Parish	277	Longworth	*Berks*	Parish	1 131
Long Newton	*Durham*	Parish	353	Longworth	,,	—	629
Longney	*Gloucester*	Parish	486	Longworth	*Lancaster*	Tnship.	154
Longnor	*Salop*	Parish	244	Lonsdale	,,	Hund.	56 704
Longnor	*Stafford*	Sub-dis.	5 041	Lonsdale	,,	L. Sub.	71 164
Longnor	,,	Tnship.	514	Lonsdale	*Westmoreland*	Ward	6 071
Longparish	*Hants*	Sub-dis.	4 284	Lonsdale Ward	,,	L. Sub.	6 071
Longparish	,,	Parish	803	Looe	*Cornwall*	Sub-dis.	5 665
Long Preston	*York*	Sub-dis.	1 358	Looe Island	,,	Island	8
Long Preston	,,	Parish	1 206	Looe, East and West	,,	Ecl. Dis.	1 860
Long Preston	,,	Tnship	536	Looe, East	,,	Tnship.	1 154
Longridge, St. Law.	*Lancaster*	Ecl. Dis.	2 057	Looe, West	,,	Tnship.	770
Longridge	*Northumberland*	Tnship.	57	Loose	*Kent*	Sub-dis.	5 867
Long Riston	*York*	Parish	401	Loose	,,	Parish	1 573
Long Sandall	,,	Tnship.	130	Lopen	*Somerset*	Parish	419
Longsdon, Endon, &c.	*Stafford*	Tnship.	1 241	Lopham, North	*Norfolk*	Parish	771
Longshaws	*Northumberland*	Tnship.	30	Lopham, South	,,	Parish	630
Longsight, St. John	*Lancaster*	Ecl. Dis.	2 927	Loppington	*Salop*	Parish	575
Long Sleddale	*Westmoreland*	Tnship.	137	Lorbottle	*Northumberland*	Tnship.	110
Long Stanton :—				Lorton	*Cumberland*	Parish	658
All Saints	*Cambs*	Parish	440	Lorton	,,	Tnship.	456
St. Michael	,,	Parish	145	Loscoe	*Derby*	Hamlet	670
Long Stanton	*Salop*	Parish	234	Lostock	*Lancaster*	Tnship.	580
Longstock	*Hants*	Parish	445	Lostock-Gralam	*Cheshire*	Tnship.	467
Longstone, Great, &c.	*Derby*	Tnship.	683	Lostock-Gralam	,,	Ecl. Dis.	1 294
Longstone, Little	,,	Tnship.	185	Lostwithiel	*Cornwall*	Parish	1 017
Longstow	*Cambs*	Hund.	6 456	Lothersdale Christch.	*York*	Ecl. Dis.	819
Longstow	,,	Parish	264	Lotherton w. Aberford	,,	Tnship.	547
Long Stow	*Hunts*	Parish	208	Lothingland & Mutford	*Suffolk*	Hund.	19 578
Long Stow	,,	Hamlet	156	Loughborough	*Leicester*	L. Sub.	35 663
Long Stratton, St. Mary	*Norf.*	Parish	743	Loughborough	*Leic. & Notts*	District	24 210
Long Sutton	*Hants*	Parish	301	Loughborough	*Leicester*	Sub-dis.	17 583
Long Sutton	*Lincoln*	Sub-dis.	7 999	Loughborough	,,	Parish	10 955
Long Sutton	,,	Parish	6 124	Loughborough	,,	Tnship.	10 830
Long Sutton	*Somerset*	Parish	958	Loughborough	,,	Town	10 830
Longthorpe	*Northampton*	Hamlet	294	Loughborough, Emml.	,,	Ecl. Dis.	4 554
Longthorpe	,,	Ecl. Dis.	294	Loughor	*Glam. & Carm.*	Sub-dis.	3 970
Longton	*Lancaster*	Sub-dis.	6 620	Loughor	*Glamorgan*	Parish	1 238
Longton	,,	Tnship.	1 637	Loughor	,,	Hamlet	362
Longton	*Stafford*	Sub-dis.	16 857	Loughor	,,	P. Bor.	876
Longton Town	,,	Tnship.	16 690	Loughton	*Bucks*	Parish	386
Longton St. James	,,	Ecl. Dis	12 706	Loughton	*Essex*	Parish	1 527
Longtown	*Cumberland*	District	10 469	Loughton	*Salop*	Chap.	100
Longtown, High	,,	Sub-dis.	3 291	Lound	*Notts*	Tnship.	458
Longtown, Low	,,	Sub-dis.	7 178	Lound	*Suffolk*	Parish	466
Longtown	,,	Tnship.	2 863	Louth	*Lincoln*	District	34 711
Longtown	,,	Town	2 717	Louth	,,	Sub-dis.	14 442
Longtown	*Hereford*	Tnship.	892	Louth	,,	Parish	10 667
Longtree	*Gloucester*	Hund.	16 260	Louth	,,	M. Bor.	10 560
Long Whatton	*Leicester*	Parish	779	Louth Eske	,,	Hund.	8 791
Long Wittenham	*Berks*	Parish	583	Louth Park	,,	Tnship.	107
Long Witton	*Northumberland*	Tnship.	152	Loveden	,,	Wapen.	14 600
Longwood	*York*	Tnship.	3 402	Loversall	*York*	Parish	175
Longwood, St. Mark	,,	Ecl. Dis.	3 402	Loveston	*Pembroke*	Parish	122

Name of Place.	County.	Description.	Population.	Name of Place.	County.	Description.	Population.
Lovington	Somerset	Parish	239	Lower Michaelstone	Glam.	Hamlet	5 323
Low Abbotside	York	Tnship.	163	Lower Millom	Cumberland	Tnship.	392
Low Angerton	Northumberland	Tnship.	80	Lower Mitton	Worcester	Sub-dis.	2 958
Low Blackwell	Cumberland	Tnship.	183	Lower Mitton	„	Hamlet	2 958
Low Bolton, &c.	„	Tnship.	718	Lower Mitton	„	Ecl. Dis.	2 958
Low Bowland Forest	York	Tnship.	319	Lower Neath	Glamorgan	Hamlet	174
Low Buston	Northumberland	Tnship.	129	Lower Newcastle	„	Hamlet	887
Low Caldbeck	Cumberland	Tnship.	675	Lower Penderyn	Brecon	Hamlet	1 134
Low Catton	York	Tnship.	179	Lower Penn	Stafford	Tnship	306
Low Coniscliffe, &c.	Durham	Tnship.	200	Lower Radbourn	Warwick	Parish	17
Low Crosby	Cumberland	Tnship.	125	Lower Sapey	Worcester	Parish	218
Lowdham	Notts	Parish	1 503	Lower Shuckburgh	Warwick	Parish	152
Lowdham	„	Tnship.	868	Lower Slaughter	Gloucester	Parish	212
Low Dinsdale	Durham	Parish	208	Lower Swell	„	Parish	449
Lower Allithwaite	Lancaster	Tnship.	933	Lower Tockington	„	Tithing	464
Lower Baglan	Glamorgan	Hamlet	456	Lower Tooting	Surrey	Parish	2 055
Lower Bebington	Chester	Tnship.	2 485	Lower Tythegston	Glamorgan	Hamlet	106
Lower Bedwas	Monmouth	Hamlet	422	Lower Vainor	Cardigan	Tnship.	198
Lower Beeding	Sussex	Parish	1 149	Lower Whitley	Cheshire	Tnship.	211
Lower Boddington	Northptn.	Parish	315	Lower Whitley	„	Ecl. Dis.	578
Lower Booths	Lancaster	Tnship.	4 655	Lower Whitley	York	Tnship.	1 042
Lower Brixham	Devon	Ecl. Dis.	4 586	Lower Whitley	„	Ecl. Dis.	1 042
Lower Bullingham	Hereford	Parish	255	Lower Withington	Cheshire	Tnship.	578
Lower Coychurch	Glamorgan	Hamlet	295	Low. Ystradgunlais	Brecon	Hamlet	3 801
Lower Coyty	„	Hamlet	2 174	Low. Ystradvelltey	„	Hamlet	299
Lower Darwen	Lancaster	Tnship.	3,301	Lowesby	Leicester	Parish	259
Lower Darwen St. James	„	Ecl. Dis.	2 081	Lowesby	„	Tnship.	121
Lower Dunsforth	York	Tnship.	144	Lowestoft	Suffolk	Sub-dis.	12 952
Lower Dyffrin Honddu	Brecon	Hamlet	196	Lowestoft	„	Parish	9 534
Lower Dylais	Glamorgan	Hamlet	348	Lowestoft	„	Town	10 663
Lower End	Berks	Hamlet	114	Lowestoft, St. John	„	Ecl. Dis.	2 829
Lower Gornal	Stafford	Ecl. Dis.	5 915	Lowswater	Cumberland	P. Chap.	392
Lower Gravenhurst	Beds	Parish	60	Low Harrogate	York	Ecl. Dis.	993
Lower Guyting	Gloucester	Parish	647	Low Holme	Cumberland	Tnship.	1 538
Lower Gwnnws	Cardigan	Tnship.	535	Low Holme, St. Paul	„	Ecl. Dis.	1 521
Lower Halstow	Kent	Parish	399	Lowick	Lancaster	Tnship.	468
Lower Hanley	Worcester	Chap.	199	Lowick	Northampton	Parish	427
Lower Hardres	Kent	Parish	233	Lowick	Northumberland	Parish	1 946
Lower Harpton	Hereford	Tnship.	85	Low Ireby	Cumberland	Tnship.	337
Lower Heyford	Oxon	Parish	625	Low Leyton	Essex	Parish	4 794
Lower Hodnel	Warwick	Parish	4	Low Longtown	Cumberland	Sub-dis.	7 178
Lower Holker	Lancaster	Tnship.	1 160	Low Moor, St. Mark	York	Ecl. Dis.	1 563
Low. Holloway, St. Jas.	Mddlx.	Ecl. Dis.	10 563	Low Oulton	Cheshire	Tnship.	53
Lower Kinnerton	Cheshire	Tnship.	99	Low Quarter	Northumberland	Tnship.	454
Lower Kinsham	Hereford	Tnship.	44	Low Sebergham	Cumberland	Tnship.	322
Lower Lantwit	Glamorgan	Hamlet	1 367	Lowside Quarter	„	Tnship.	264
Lower Lemington	Gloucester	Parish	57	Lowside	Durham	Tnship.	1 563
Lw. Llanbadarnycroyddin	Card.	Tnship.	773	Lowther	Westmoreland	Sub-dis.	3 860
Lower Llangynwyd	Glamorgan	Hamlet	337	Lowther	„	Parish	427
Lower Llanidloes	Montgomery	Sub-dis.	3 666	Lowthorpe	York	Parish	171
Lower Llansamlet	Glamorgan	Hamlet	3 243	Lowton	Lancaster	Sub-dis.	5 434
Lower Lledrod	Cardigan	Tnship.	588	Lowton	„	Parish	2 384
Lower Machen	Monmouth	Hamlet	963	Low Town	Northumberland	Ecl. Dis.	6 314
Lower Merthyr Tydfil	Glam.	Sub-dis.	25 300	Low Toynton	Lincoln	Parish	155

Name of Place.	County.	Description.	Population.	Name of Place.	County.	Description.	Population.
Low Walton	Cumberland	Tnship.	263	Lulworth, East	Dorset	Parish	45?
Low Winder	Westmoreland	Tnship.	12	Lulworth, West	"	Parish	44?
Low Worsall	York	Tnship.	212	Lumb, St. Michael	Lancaster	Ecl. Dis.	2 64?
Loxbear	Devon	Parish	126	Lumley, Great	Durham	Tnship.	1 55?
Loxhore	"	Parish	250	Lumley, Little	"	Tnship.	37?
Loxley	Warwick	Parish	368	Lund	Lancaster	Ecl. Dis.	73?
Loxton	Somerset	Parish	154	Lund	York	Parish	50?
Lozells	Warwick	Ecl. Dis.	10 923	Lundy Island	Devon	Parish	4?
Lubbesthorpe	Leicester	Chap.	64	Lune	York	Ecl. Dis.	1 33?
Lubenham	"	Parish	640	Lunedale	"	Tnship.	38?
Lucker	Northumberland	Tnship.	281	Lunt	Lancaster	Tnship.	7?
Luckham	Somerset	Parish	474	Luppitt	Devon	Parish	714
Luckington	Wilts	Parish	316	Lupton	Westmoreland	Tnship.	22?
Lucton	Hereford	Parish	174	Lurgashall	Sussex	Parish	727
Ludborough	Lincoln	Wapen.	1 892	Lusby	Lincoln	Parish	132
Ludborough	"	Parish	401	Lustleigh	Devon	Parish	322
Ludchurch	Pembroke	Parish	264	Luston	Hereford	Tnship.	431
Luddenden	York	Sub-dis.	5 850	Lutley	Worcester	Tnship.	130
Luddenham	Kent	Parish	264	Luton	Beds	L. Sub.	28 309
Luddesdown	"	Parish	279	Luton	Beds & Herts	District	30 712
Luddington	Lincoln	Parish	1 264	Luton	"	Sub-dis.	21 419
Luddington	"	Tnship.	684	Luton	Beds	Parish	17 821
Luddington	Npln. & Hunts	Parish	128	Luton	"	Tnship.	15 329
Luddington	Warwick	Hamlet	121	**Luton**	"	Town	15 329
Ludford Magna	Lincoln	Parish	356	Luton, Christchurch	"	Ecl. Dis.	6 658
Ludford Parva	"	Parish	462	Luton, Christchurch	Kent	Ecl. Dis.	2 730
Ludford	Salop & Heref.	Parish	319	Lutterworth	Leicester	L. Sub.	14 407
Ludgershall	Bucks	Parish	536	Lutterworth	Leicester, &c.	District	15 515
Ludgershall	"	—	482	Lutterworth	Leicester	Parish	2 289
Ludgershall	Wilts & Hants	Sub-dis.	3 538	**Lutterworth**	"	Town	2 289
Ludgershall	Wilts	Parish	595	Lutton	Nthptn. & Hunts	Parish	196
Ludgvan	Cornwall	Parish	3 480	Lutton, East & West	York	Tnship.	432
Ludham	Norfolk	Sub-dis	3 682	Luxborough	Somerset	Parish	521
Ludham	"	Parish	884	Luxulion	Cornwall	Parish	1 329
Ludlow	Salop	L. Sub.	5 178	Lydbrook	Monm. & Glouc.	Ecl. Dis.	1 776
Ludlow	Salop & Heref.	District	17 721	Lydbury	Salop	Sub-dis.	1 903
Ludlow	" "	Sub-dis.	8 801	Lydbury, North	"	Parish	1 025
Ludlow Castle	Salop	Parish	7	Lydd	Kent	Sub-dis.	2 826
Ludlow St. Lawrence	"	Parish	5 171	Lydd	"	Parish	1 667
Ludlow {	Salop & Heref.	M. Bor.	5 178	Lydden	Kent	Parish	198
{	"	P. Bor.	6 033	Lydeard	Somerset	Parish	664
Ludworth	Derby	Tnship.	1 640	Lydford, East	"	Parish	178
Luffenham, North	Rutland	Parish	491	Lydford, West	"	Parish	320
Luffenham, South	"	Parish	400	Lydgate, St. Anne	York	Ecl. Dis.	6 124
Luffield Abbey	Bucks	—	18	Lydham	Salop & Mont.	Parish	205
Luffincott	Devon	Parish	71	Lydham	Salop	Tnship.	143
Lufton	Somerset	Parish	31	Lydiate	Lancaster	Chap.	848
Lugwardine	Hereford	Parish	748	Lydlinch	Dorset	Parish	404
Lullingstone	Kent	Parish	63	Lydney	Gloucester	Sub-dis.	5 907
Lullington	Derby	Parish	625	Lydney	"	Parish	2 889
Lullington	"	Tnship.	272	Lydney	"	Tnship.	2 285
Lullington	Somerset	Parish	137	Lye	Worcester	Tnship.	5 255
Lullington	Sussex	Parish	16	Lye, Christchurch	"	Ecl. Dis.	6 772
Lulsley	Worcester	Tnship.	149	Lyford	Berks	Chap.	149

Name of Place.	County.	Description.	Population.	Name of Place.	County.	Description.	Population.
yford	Berks	Ecl. Dis.	149	Macclesfield Hyde	Cheshire	L. Sub.	68 834
yme-Handley	Cheshire	Tnship.	237	Macclesfield Prestbury	„	L. Sub.	65 290
yme	Dorset & Devon	Sub-dis.	4 204	Macclesfield Stockport	„	L. Sub.	65 302
yme-Regis	Dorset	Parish	2 537	Macclesfield	„	District	61 543
Lyme-Regis	„ {	M. Bor.	2 318	Macclesfield East	„	Sub-dis.	10 901
		P. Bor.	3 215	Macclesfield West	„	Sub-dis.	16 574
yminge	Kent	Parish	938	Macclesfield	„	Tnship.	27 475
ymington	Hants	Division	22 539	Macclesfield	„	Borough	36 101
ymington	„	L. Sub.	25 160	St. Michael	„	Ecl. Dis.	19 744
ymington	„	District	12 094	St. Paul	„	Ecl. Dis.	5 451
ymington	„	Sub-dis.	8 070	St. Peter	„	Ecl. Dis.	1 710
ymington	„	Parish	4 098	Macclesfield Forest	„	Tnship.	242
Lymington	„ {	M. Bor.	2 621	Macefen	„	Tnship.	47
		P. Bor.	5 179	Machen	Monm. & Glam.	Parish	2 700
Lymm	Cheshire	Sub-dis.	7 395	Machen, Lower	Monmouth	Hamlet	963
Lymm	„	Parish	3 769	Machen, Upper	„	Hamlet	1 414
Lympne	Kent	Parish	540	Machynlleth	Montgomery	Hund.	8 402
Lympsham	Somerset	Parish	496	Machynlleth	„	L. Sub.	8 513
Lympston	Devon	Parish	1 122	Machynlleth	Montgomery,&c.	District	12 395
Lynby	Notts	Parish	257	Machynlleth	Montg. & Card.	Sub-dis.	4 068
Lyncombe	Somerset	Sub-dis.	9 900	Machynlleth	Montgomery	Parish	2 396
Lyncombe & Widcombe	„	Parish	9 900	Machynlleth	„	Tnship.	1 640
Lyncombe	„	Ecl. Dis.	4 592	Machynlleth	„	P. Bor.	1 645
Lyndhurst	Hants & Wilts	Sub-dis.	3 355	Mackworth	Derby	Parish	525
Lyndhurst	Hants	Parish	1 522	Mackworth	„	Tnship.	278
Lyndon	Rutland	Parish	126	Maddington	Wilts	Parish	396
Lyneham	Oxon	Hamlet	237	Madehurst	Sussex	Parish	208
Lyneham	Wilts	Parish	1 034	Madeley	Salop	District	30 403
Lynesack & Softley	Durham	Tnship.	1 120	Madeley	„	Sub-dis.	10 733
Lynesack, St. John	„	Ecl. Dis.	1 120	Madeley	„	Parish	9 469
Lyneside	Cumberland	Tnship.	116	Madeley	Stafford	Parish	1 940
Lynford	Norfolk	Parish	95	Madeley	„	Tnship.	1 725
Lyng	„	Parish	590	Madingley	Cambs	Parish	279
Lyng	Somerset	Parish	390	Madley	Hereford	Sub-dis.	3 088
Lynn, North	Norfolk	Parish	62	Madley	„	Parish	970
Lynn, South	„	Parish	4 534	Madresfield	Worcester	Parish	271
Lynn, West	„	Parish	469	Madron	Cornwall	Parish	11 926
Lynton	Devon	Parish	1 043	Madron	„	—	2 512
Lyonshall	Hereford	Parish	900	Maenan	Carnarvon	Tnship.	373
Lytchett	Dorset	Sub-dis.	2 050	Maenclochog	Pembroke	Parish	396
Lytchett Maltravers	„	Parish	855	Maenclochog	„	—	367
Lytchett Minster	„	Parish	802	Maentwrog	Merioneth	Parish	883
Lytham	Lancaster	Sub-dis.	3 627	Maer	Stafford	Parish	473
Lytham	„	Parish	3 194	Maescar	Brecon	Hamlet	637
Lytham	„	Town	2 556	Maesgwyn	Radnor	Tnship.	384
Lytham, St. John	„	Ecl. Dis.	1 579	Maesmynis	Brecon	Parish	239
Lythe	York	Sub-dis.	4 923	Maesteg	Glamorgan	Sub-dis.	8 562
Lythe	„	Parish	3 233	Maesygroes	Flint	Tnship.	154
Lythe	„	Tnship.	1 053	Magdalen Place	Durham	Parish	18
				Magdalen Laver	Essex	Parish	213
Mabe	Cornwall	Parish	613	Maghull	Lancaster	Chap.	1 144
Mablethorpe St. Mary	Lincoln	Parish	336	Magor	Monmouth	Parish	740
Mablethorpe St. Peter	„	Parish	82	Magor	„	Tnship.	451
Macclesfield	Cheshire	Hund.	104 352	Maiden Bradley	Wilts & Som.	Parish	653

Name of Place.	County.	Description.	Population.	Name of Place	County.	Description.	Population.
Maiden Bradley .	*Wilts* ..	—	592	Maltby ..	.. York	Parish	858
Maidenhead ..	*Berks* ..	L. Sub.	15 184	Maltby ..	.. ,,	Tnship.	774
Maidenhead ..	,, ..	M. Bor.	3 895	Malton ..	.. ,,	District	23 483
Maiden Newton .	*Dorset* ..	Sub-dis.	5 603	Malton ..	.. ,,	L. Sub.	10 630
Maiden Newton .	,, ..	Parish	844	Malton ..	.. ,,	Sub-dis.	9 972
Maidford ..	*Northampton*	Parish	344	Malton New, St. Leonard ,,		Parish	2 221
Maids-Moreton..	*Bucks* ..	Parish	543	Malton New, St. Michael ,,		Parish	1 566
Maidstone ..	*Kent* ..	District	38 670	Malton, Old ..	.. ,,	Parish	1 302
Maidstone ..	,, ..	Parish	23 058	**Malton**..	.. ,,	P. Bor.	8 072
Maidstone ..	,, {	M. Bor.	23 016	Maltraeth	.. *Anglesey* ..	Hund.	4 741
		P. Bor.	23 058	**Malvern, Great**	*Worcester* ..	Parish	6 245
St. Peter ..	,, ..	Ecl. Dis.	3 610	Malvern, Great..	,, ..	Town	4 484
Trinity ..	,, ..	Ecl. Dis.	12 729	Malvern, Little..	,, ..	Parish	104
Maidwell ..	*Northampton*	Parish	290	Malvern Wells, St.Pet. ,,	..	Ecl. Dis.	558
Mainsforth ..	*Durham* ..	Tnship.	58	Mamble..	.. ,,	Parish	307
Mainstone	*Salop & Montg.*	Parish	365	Mamhead ..	*Devon* ..	Parish	218
Mainstone ..	*Salop* ..	Tnship.	220	Mamhilad ..	*Monmouth* ..	Parish	339
Maisemore ..	*Gloucester* ..	Parish	516	Manaccan ..	*Cornwall* ..	Parish	505
Maisey Hampton	,, ..	Parish	852	Manafon ..	*Montgomery*	Parish	701
Maker ..	.. *Cornwall* ..	Parish	2 986	Manaton ..	*Devon* ..	Parish	415
Maker ..	.. ,, ..	—	1 759	Manby ..	.. *Lincoln* ..	Parish	210
Marlborough ..	*Devon* ..	Parish	2 388	Mancetter ..	*Warwick* ..	Parish	5 408
Marlborough in Vines	*Worc.*..	Parish	20	Mancetter ..	.. ,, ..	Tnship.	355
Malden..	.. *Surrey* ..	Parish	320	Manchester ..	.. .. ..	Diocese	1679326
Maldon..	.. *Essex* ..	District	22 556	Manchester ..	.. *Lancaster* ..	L. Sub.	575 636
Maldon ..	,, }	M. Bor.	4 785	Manchester ..	.. ,, ..	District	243 988
		P. Bor.	6 261	Manchester ..	.. ,, ..	Parish	529 245
Malew ..	.. *Isle of Man.*	Parish	5 065	Manchester ..	.. ,, ..	Tnship.	185 410
Malham..	.. *York* ..	Tnship.	184	**Manchester** (*1865*) *3,96,535*		M.City	338 722
Malham Moor ..	,, ..	Tnship.	115			P. City	357 979
Malins Lee ..	*Salop* ..	Ecl. Dis.	4 512	St. Anne ..	,, ..	Ecl. Dis.	1 416
Mallerstang ..	*Westmoreland*	Tnship.	232	St. Barnabas..	,, ..	Ecl. Dis.	8 232
Malling..	.. *Kent* ..	L. Sub.	25 420	St. Catherine .	,, ..	Ecl. Dis.	7 618
Malling..	.. ,, ..	District	21 447	St. George ..	,, ..	Ecl. Dis.	24 212
Malling, East ..	,, ..	Parish	1 974	St. James ..	,, ..	Ecl. Dis.	4 074
Malling, West ..	,, ..	Parish	2 086	St. John ..	,, ..	Ecl. Dis.	12 469
Malling, South ..	*Sussex* ..	Parish	716	St. Jude ..	,, ..	Ecl. Dis.	12 868
Mallwyd	*Merion. & Montg.*	Parish	1 049	St. Mary ..	,, ..	Ecl. Dis.	3 507
Mallwyd ..	*Merionsth* ..	Tnship.	938	St. Matthew..	,, ..	Ecl. Dis.	11 257
Malmsbury ..	*Wilts* ..	Hund.	14 145	St. Michael ..	,, ..	Ecl. Dis.	11 525
Malmsbury ..	,, ..	L. Sub.	15 212	St. Paul ..	,, ..	Ecl. Dis.	6 609
Malmsbury ..	,, ..	District	14 556	St. Peter ..	,, ..	Ecl.Dis.	2 904
Malmsbury Eastern	,, ..	Sub-dis.	7 475	St. Simon & St.Jude ,,	..	Ecl. Dis.	4 515
Malmsbury Western	,, ..	Sub-dis.	7 081	Mancott..	.. *Flint* ..	Tnship.	276
Malmsbury, St. Paul	,, ..	Parish	2 400	Mancroft ..	*Norfolk* ..	Sub-dis.	14 397
Malmsbury ..	,, ..	P. Bor.	6 881	Manea ..	.. *Cambs* ..	Chap.	1 206
Malpas ..	.. *Cheshire* ..	Sub-dis.	3 621	Manerdivy ..	*Pembroke* ..	Parish	896
Malpas ..	*Cheshire & Flint*	Parish	5 598	Manfield ..	*York* ..	Parish	405
Malpas ..	.. *Cheshire* ..	Tnship.	1 037	Manfield ..	.. ,, ..	Tnship.	351
Malpas, St. Chad	,, ..	Ecl.Dis.	871	Mangotsfield ..	*Gloucester* ..	Parish	4 222
Malpas ..	.. *Monmouth* ..	Parish	304	Manhood ..	*Sussex* ..	Sub-dis.	3 418
Maltby ..	.. *Durham* ..	Tnship.	141	Man, Isle of ..	..	Island	52 469
Maltby-le-Marsh	*Lincoln* ..	Parish	332	Manley ..	.. *Cheshire* ..	Tnship.	294
Maltby ..	.. .. *York* ..	Sub-dis.	2 588	Manley ..	.. *Lincoln* ..	Wapen.	29 534

138

Name of Place.	County.	Description.	Population.	Name of Place.	County.	Description.	Population.
Manmoel	Monmouth	Hamlet	11 510	March	Cambs	Town	3 600
Manningford Abbots	Wilts	Parish	139	Marcham	Berks	Parish	1 111
Manningford Bohun	,,	Tithing	254	Marcham	,,	—	778
Manningford Bruce	,,	Parish	252	Marchington	Stafford	Tnship.	484
Manningham	York	Tnship.	12 889	Marchington Woodlands	,,	Tnship.	339
St. Jude	,,	Ecl. Dis.	5 891	Marchington Woodlands	,,	Ecl. Dis.	339
St. Paul	,,	Ecl. Dis.	5 283	Marchwiel	Denbigh	Parish	536
Mannington	Norfolk	Parish	6	Marchwood	Hants	Ecl. Dis.	1 185
Manningtree	Essex	Sub-dis.	5 223	Marcle, Little	Hereford	Parish	168
Manningtree	,,	Parish	881	Marcle, Much	,,	Parish	1 209
Manor and Rake	Flint	Tnship.	88	Marcle, Much	,,	Tnship.	984
Manorbier	Pembroke	Parish	715	Marcross	Glamorgan	Parish	91
Manorowen	,,	Parish	186	Marden	Hereford	Parish	929
Mansell Gamage	Hereford	Parish	131	Marden	,,	Tnship.	899
Mansell-Lacy	,,	Parish	331	Marden	Kent	Sub-dis.	4 905
Mansergh	Westmoreland	Tnship.	190	Marden	,,	Parish	2 295
Mansfield	Notts	L. Sub.	27 060	Marden	Wilts	Parish	235
Mansfield	Notts & Derby	District	30 593	Marden, East	Sussex	Parish	63
Mansfield	Notts	Sub-dis.	10 225	Marden, North	,,	Parish	28
Mansfield	,,	Parish	10 225	Marden, Up.	,,	Parish	366
Mansfield	,,	Town	8 346	Marefield	Leicester	Tnship.	28
Mansfield, St. John	,,	Ecl. Dis.	4 192	Mareham-le-Fen	Lincoln	Parish	937
Mansfield Woodhouse	,,	Parish	2 263	Mareham on Hill	,,	Parish	215
Manshead	Beds	Hund.	28 340	Maresfield	Sussex	Sub-dis.	5 563
Mansriggs	Lancaster	Tnship.	69	Maresfield	,,	Parish	1 911
Manston	Dorset	Parish	152	Marfleet	York	Parish	176
Manston	York	Ecl. Dis.	606	Margam	Glamorgan	Sub-dis.	16 815
Manthorpe	Lincoln	Hamlet	107	Margam	,,	Parish	5 528
Manthorpe, &c.	,,	Tnship.	2 241	Margaret Marsh	Dorset	Parish	71
Manthorpe, St. John	,,	Ecl. Dis.	434	Margaret Roothing	Essex	Parish	236
Manton	,,	Parish	281	Margaretting	,,	Parish	483
Manton	,,	Tnship.	106	Margate	Kent	Sub-dis.	10 019
Manton	Rutland	Parish	274	Margate	,,	Parish	10 019
Manuden	Essex	Parish	740	Margate	,,	M. Bor.	8 874
Maperton	Somerset	Parish	207	Margate Trinity	,,	Ecl. Dis.	4 818
Maplebeck	Notts	Parish	136	Marham	Norfolk	Parish	870
Maplederwell	Hants	Parish	223	Marhamchurch	Cornwall	Parish	581
Mapledurham	Oxon	Parish	486	Marholm	Northampton	Parish	172
Maplestead, Great	Essex	Parish	462	Mariansleigh	Devon	Parish	281
Maplestead, Little	,,	Parish	325	Marishes	York	Tnship.	287
Maplewell Longdale	Leicester	Parish	12	Mark	Somerset	Parish	1 217
Mapperley	Derby	Tnship.	435	Mark Beech, Trinity	Kent	Ecl. Dis.	289
Mapperton	Dorset	Parish	92	Markby	Lincoln	Parish	111
Mappleton	Derby	Parish	185	Market Bosworth	Leicester	L. Sub.	26 258
Mappleton	York	Parish	475	Market Bosworth	,,	District	13 428
Mappleton	,,	Hamlet	163	Market Bosworth	,,	Sub-dis.	7 185
Mappowder	Dorset	Parish	238	Market Bosworth	,,	Parish	2 376
Marazion	Cornwall	Sub-dis.	5 098	Market Bosworth	,,	Tnship.	997
Marazion	,,	Chap.	1 545	Market Deeping	Lincoln	Parish	1 337
Marbury	Cheshire	Tnship.	17	Market Downham	Norfolk	Parish	3 133
Marbury	,,	Parish	779	Market Drayton	Salop, &c.	District	14 260
Marbury w. Quoisley	,,	Tnship.	387	Market Drayton	,, ,,	Sub-dis.	5 242
March	Cambs	Sub-dis.	6 569	Market Drayton	,, ,,	Parish	5 242
March	,,	Chap.	5 455	Market Drayton	Salop	Town	3 661

Name of Place.	County.	Description.	Population.	Name of Place.	County.	Description.	Population.
Market Harborough	*Leicester* .	L. Sub.	11 697	Marsden, Gt. & Lit.	*Lancaster*	Tnship.	5 162
Market Harborough	*Leic.*, &c. .	District	16 059	Marsden, Gt. St. John	,,	Ecl. Dis.	3 057
Market Harborough	*Leicester* .	Chap.	2 302	Marsden	*York* ..	Tnship.	2 689
Market Harborough	,, ..	Town	2 302	Marsham	*Norfolk* ..	Parish	622
Market Lavington	*Wilts* ..	Parish	1 583	Marsh Chapel ..	*Lincoln* ..	Parish	671
Market Lavington	,, ..	—	1 122	Marshfield	*Gloucester* ..	Sub-dis.	4 103
Market Overton .	*Rutland* ..	Parish	429	Marshfield ..	,, ..	Parish	1 742
Market Rasen ..	*Lincoln* ..	Sub-dis.	10 224	Marshfield ..	*Monmouth* ..	Parish	509
Market Rasen ..	,, ..	Parish	2 563	Marsh Gibbon ..	*Bucks* ..	Parish	858
Market Rasen .	,, ..	Town	2 468	Marshwood ..	*Dorset* ..	Parish	473
Market Stainton	,, ..	Parish	108	Marske ..	*York* ..	Sub-dis.	4 803
Market Street ..	*Lancaster* ..	Sub-dis.	23 526	Marske by Redcar	,, ..	Parish	2 314
Market Weighton	*York* ..	Sub-dis.	5 254	Marske ..	,, ..	Tnship.	1 470
Market Weighton	,, ..	Parish	2 589	Marske ..	,, ..	Parish	263
Market Weighton, &c.	,, ..	Tnship.	2 178	Marston Moretaine	*Beds* ..	Parish	1 270
Market Weighton	,, ..	Town	2 178	Marston, North .	*Bucks* ..	Parish	644
Market Weston .	*Suffolk* ..	Parish	303	Marston ..	*Cheshire* ..	Tnship.	745
Markfield ..	*Leicester* ..	Parish	1 391	Marston Montgomery	*Derby* .	Parish	405
Markham, East .	*Notts* ..	Parish	807	Marston upon Dove	,, ..	Parish	1 211
Markham, West .	,, ..	Parish	193	Marston upon Dove	,, ..	Tnship.	103
Markheaton ..	*Derby* ..	Tnship.	247	Marston Sicca ..	*Gloucester* ..	Parish	371
Markingfield Hall	*York* ..	—	15	Marston..	*Lincoln* ..	Parish	403
Markington, &c.	,, ..	Tnship.	496	Marston, St. Lawr.	*Nrthmpton.*	Parish	535
Markington, St. Mich.,	,, ..	Ecl. Dis.	535	Marston-Trussell	,.	Parish	219
Marksbury ..	*Somerset* ..	Parish	307	Marston ..	*Oxon* ..	Parish	452
Markshall ..	*Essex* ..	Parish	42	Marston Bigott .	*Somerset* ..	Parish	379
Markshall ..	*Norfolk* ..	Parish	34	Marston Magna .	,, ..	Parish	379
Marks Tey ..	*Essex* ..	Parish	396	Marston ..	*Stafford* ..	Tnship.	345
Marland Peters .	*Devon* ..	Parish	332	Marston (Pottern P.)	*Wilts* ..	Tithing	190
Marlboro' & Ramsbury	*Wilts* .	L. Sub.	20 869	Marston Maisey .	,, ..	Parish	215
Marlborough ..	,,	District.	9 774	Marston, South .	,, ..	Tithing	370
Marlborough ..	,, {	M. Bor.	3 684	Marston, Long ..	*York* ..	Parish	586
		P. Bor.	4 893	Marston, Long ..	,, ..	Tnship.	405
Marlborough, St. Mary	,,	Parish	1 903	Marstow ..	*Hereford* ..	Parish	142
Marlboro', St. Peter, &c.	,,	Parish	1 781	Marsworth ..	*Bucks* ..	Parish	549
Marldon ..	*Devon* ..	Parish	554	Marthall ..	*Cheshire* ..	Tnship.	253
Marlesford ..	*Suffolk* ..	Parish	412	Marthall, All Saints	,, ..	Ecl. Dis.	525
Marlingford ..	*Norfolk* ..	Parish	224	Martham ..	*Norfolk* ..	Parish	1 092
Marloes ..	*Pembroke* ..	Parish	443	Martin ..	*Lincoln* ..	Parish	56
Marlow, Great ..	*Bucks* ..	Sub-dis.	5 450	Martin ..	,, ..	Hamlet	909
Marlow, Great ..	,, ..	Parish	4 661	Martin ..	*Wilts* ..	Parish	574
Marlow Great .	,, ..	P. Boro.	6 496	Martindale ..	*Westmoreland*	Chap.	174
Marlow, Little ..	,, ..	Parish	790	Martinhoe ..	*Devon* ..	Parish	219
Marlow ..	*Hereford* ..	Tnship.	107	Martin Hussingtree	*Worcester*	Parish	170
Marlston w. Leach	*Cheshire* ..	Tnship.	163	Martinsley ..	*Rutland* ..	Hund.	4 431
Marnham ..	*Notts* ..	Parish	348	Martinsthorpe ..	,, ..	Parish	6
Marnham ..	,, ..	Tnship.	273	Martlesham ..	*Suffolk* ..	Parish	465
Marnhall ..	*Dorset* ..	Parish	1 444	Martletwy ..	*Pembroke* ..	Parish	703
Marown ..	*Isle of Man*	Parish	1 161	Martley ..	*Worcester* ..	District	15 098
Marple ..	*Cheshire* ..	Sub-dis	5 128	Martley ..	,, ..	Sub-dis.	3 128
Marple ..	,, ..	Tnship.	3 333	Martley ..	,, ..	Parish	1 298
Marr ..	*York* ..	Parish	222	Martley ..	,, ..	Tnship.	1 140
Marrick ..	,, . ..	Parish	462	Martock ..	*Somerset* ..	Hund.	3 155
Marros ..	*Carmarthen*	Parish	130	Martock ..	,, ..	Sub-dis.	5 979

Name of Place.	County.	Description.	Population.	Name of Place.	County.	Description.	Population.
Martock	Somerset	Parish	3 155	Massingham, Little *Norfolk*		Parish	132
Marton	Cheshire	Tnship.	639	Masters Close *Northumberland*		Parish	3
Marton (Prestbury P.) ,,		Tnship.	296	Matching	Essex	Parish	665
Marton, Great	Lancaster	Hamlet	1 258	Matfen, East *Northumberland*		Tnship.	147
Marton, Little	,,	Hamlet	433	Matfen, Holy Trinity ,,		Ecl. Dis.	751
Marton	Lincoln	Sub-dis.	2 091	Matfen, West	,,	Tnship.	354
Marton	,,	Parish	487	Matherne	Monmouth	Parish	450
Marton, St. Mark	Salop	Eol. Dis.	328	Mathon	Worcester	Parish	1 014
Marton	Warwick	Parish	410	Mathon, St. Jas. *Heref. & Wor.*		Ecl. Dis.	1 417
Marton, Long	Westmoreland	Parish	762	Mathrafal	Montgomery	Hund.	5 677
Marton	York E.	Tnship.	117	Mathrafal	,,	L. Sub.	5 566
Marton	York N.	Parish	587	Mathry	Pembroke	Parish	976
Marton	,,	Tnship.	243	Matlask	Norfolk	Parish	163
Marton w. Grafton *York W.*		Parish	454	Matley	Cheshire	Tnship.	231
Marton	,,	Parish	256	Matlock	Derby	Sub-dis.	9 815
Marton in Forest *York*		Parish	168	Matlock	,,	Parish	4 252
Marton-le-Moor	,,	Tnship.	205	Matlock Bath, Trinity ,,		Ecl. Dis.	1 258
Martyr Worthy	Hants	Parish	259	Matson	Gloucester	Parish	32
Marwood	Devon	Parish	1 009	Matterdale	Cumberland	Chap.	420
Marwood	Durham	Tnship.	241	Mattersey	Notts	Parish	436
Marylebone	Middlesex	L. Sub.	161 680	Mattingley	Hants	Hamlet	232
Marylebone	,,	District	161 680	Mattishall	Norfolk	Sub-dis.	4 340
Marylebone	,,	P. Boro.	436 252	Mattishall	,,	Parish	971
Marylebone	,,	Parish	161 680	Mattishall Burgh	,,	Parish	191
1 Hamilton's Terrace Ward		Ward	7 224	Maugersbury	Gloucester	Hamlet	562
2 St. John's Wd. Ter. Ward		Ward	11 992	Maughold	Isle of Man	Parish	4 545
3 New Church Street Ward		Ward	32 154	Maulden	Beds	Parish	1 563
4 Dorset Sq. & Rgt's. Pk. Wd.		Ward	15 304	Maunby	York	Tnship.	250
5 Bryanstone Ward ,,		Ward	22 493	Mautby	Norfolk	Parish	68
6 Portman Ward ,,		Ward	26 692	Mavesyn Ridware *Stafford*		Parish	462
7 Portland Place Ward ,,		Ward	25 707	Mavis Enderby	Lincoln	Parish	186
8 Cavendish Sq. Ward ,,		Ward	20 114	Mawdesley	Lancaster	Tnship.	912
All Saints	,,	Ecl. Dis.	2 981	Mawdesley St. Peter	,,	Ecl. Dis.	1 189
All Saints, St. J. Wood ,,		Ecl. Dis.	5 481	Mawgan in Meneage *Cornwall*		Parish	895
All Souls	,,	Ecl. Dis.	15 268	Mawgan in Pyder	,,	Parish	731
Christchurch	,,	Ecl. Dis.	29 999	Mawnan	,,	Parish	572
Holy Trinity	,,	Ecl. Dis.	13 951	Mawr	Glamorgan	Hamlet	733
St. Andrew	,,	Ecl. Dis.	5 143	Mawsley	Northampton	Parish	11
St. Mark	,,	Ecl. Dis.	4 756	Maxey	,,	Parish	643
S. Mary	,,	Ecl. Dis.	27 678	Maxey	,,	Hamlet	419
St. Matthew	,,	Ecl. Dis.	7 972	Maxstoke	Warwick	Parish	322
St. Stephen	,,	Ecl. Dis.	9 621	May Fair	Middlesex	Sub-dis.	12 885
St. Thomas	,,	Ecl. Dis.	9 732	Mayfield	Staff. & Derby	Sub-dis.	3 446
Maryport	Cumberland	Sub-dis.	13 707	Mayfield	Stafford	Parish	1 426
Maryport	,,	Chap.	6 150	Mayfield	,,	Tnship.	1 005
Maryport	,,	Town	6 037	Mayfield	Sussex	Parish	2 688
Marystow	Devon	Parish	448	Mayland	Essex	Parish	225
Mary Tavy, St.	,,	Parish	1 202	Maylor	Flint	Hund.	9 719
Masham	York	Sub-dis.	2 650	Meanwood	York	Ecl. Dis.	1 321
Masham	,,	Parish	2 438	Meare	Somerset	Parish	1 640
Masham	,,	Tnship.	1 079	Mearley	Lancaster	Tnship.	47
Mashbury	Essex	Parish	120	Mears Ashby	Northampton	Parish	525
Mason	Northumberland	Tnship.	113	Measham	Derby & Leic.	Sub-dis.	4 109
Massingham, Great *Norfolk*		Parish	934	Measham	Derby	Parish	1 639

Name of Place.	County.	Description.	Population.	Name of Place.	County.	Description.	Population.
Measham	*Derby*	Tnship.	1 569	Mellor	*Lancaster*	Sub-dis.	2 863
Meaux	*York*	Tnship.	86	Mellor	,,	Tnship.	1 398
Meavy	*Devon*	Parish	269	Mellor, St. Mary	,,	Ecl. Dis.	1 718
Mechlas	*Flint*	Tnship.	128	Mells & Leigh	*Somerset*	Liberty	1 506
Medbourne	*Leicester*	Parish	613	Mells	,,	Parish	972
Medbourne	,,	Tnship.	580	Melmerby	*Cumberland*	Parish	307
Medlar w. Wesham	*Lancaster*	Tnship.	563	Melmerby	*York N.*	Tnship.	123
Medmendham	*Bucks*	Parish	380	Melmerby	,, *W.*	Tnship.	285
Medomsley	*Durham*	Tnship.	1 296	Melplaish, Christch.	*Dorset*	Ecl. Dis.	464
Medstead	*Hants*	Parish	497	Melsonby	*York*	Parish	471
Medway	*Kent*	District	51 805	Meltham	,,	Sub-dis.	6 840
Meerbrook, St. Matt.	*Stafford*	Ecl. Dis.	553	Meltham	,,	Tnship.	4 046
Meering	*Notts*	Parish	7	Meltham Mills	,,	Ecl. Dis.	1 196
Meesden	*Herts*	Parish	163	Melton Mowbray	*Leicester*	L. Sub.	20 559
Meeth	*Devon*	Parish	287	Melton Mowbray	*Leic. & Notts*	District	20 171
Mefenydd	*Cardigan*	Tithing	638	Melton Mowbray	*Leicester*	Sub-dis.	6 375
Meifod	*Montgomery*	Parish	1 806	Melton Mowbray	,,	Parish	4 936
Melbecks	*York*	Tnship.	1 622	**Melton Mowbray**	,,	Town	4 047
Melbecks	,,	Ecl. Dis.	2 173	Melton Ross	*Lincoln*	Parish	168
Melbourne	*Cambs*	Sub-dis.	8 450	Melton Constable, &c.	*Norfolk*	Parish	118
Melbourne	,,	Parish	1 637	Melton, Great	,,	Parish	368
Melbourne	*Derby & Leic.*	Sub-dis.	4 694	Melton, Little	,,	Parish	370
Melbourne	*Derby*	Parish	2 621	Melton	*Suffolk*	Parish	1 084
Melbourne	,,	Town	2 194	Melton	*York*	Tnship.	175
Melbourne	*York*	Tnship.	568	Melton, High	,,	Parish	109
Melbury Abbas	*Dorset*	Parish	412	Meltonby	,,	Tnship.	66
Melbury Bubb	,,	Parish	136	Melverley	*Salop*	Parish	214
Melbury Osmond	,,	Parish	329	Membury	*Devon*	Parish	751
Melbury-Sampford	,,	Parish	60	Menai	*Anglesey*	Hund.	8 068
Melchbourn	*Beds*	Parish	251	Mendham	*Suff. & Norf.*	Parish	779
Melchet Park	*Wilts*	Parish	29	Mendlesham	*Suffolk*	Sub-dis.	5 830
Melcombe Horsey	*Dorset*	Parish	208	Mendlesham	,,	Parish	1 316
Melcombe Regis	,,	Parish	6 498	Menheniot	*Cornwall*	Parish	2 423
Meldon	*Northumberland*	Parish	144	Mennethorpe	*York*	Tnship.	124
Meldreth	*Cambs*	Parish	735	Menstone	,,	Tnship.	318
Melford	*Suffolk*	L. Sub	58 260	Menthorpe w. Bowthorpe	,,	Tnship.	69
Melford	*Suff. & Essex*	Sub-dis.	5 574	Mentmore	*Bucks*	Parish	399
Melford, Long	*Suffolk*	Parish	2 870	Menwith w. Darley	*York*	Tnship.	650
Meliden	*Flint*	Parish	1 250	Meole, Brace	*Salop*	Parish	1 215
Melindwr	*Cardigan*	Tnship.	1 311	Meolse, Great	*Cheshire*	Tnship.	184
Meline	*Pembroke*	Parish	414	Meolse, Little	,,	Tnship.	169
Melkridge	*Northumberland*	Tnship.	299	Meols, North	*Lancaster*	Parish	15 947
Melksham	*Wilts*	Hund.	17 696	Meols, North	,,	Tnship.	14 661
Melksham	,,	District	17 233	Meon, East	*Hants*	Parish	1 486
Melksham	,,	Sub-dis.	5 866	Meon Stoke	,,	Parish	429
Melksham	,,	Parish	5 337	Meon, West	,,	Parish	842
Melksham	,,	—	4 251	Meopham	*Kent*	Parish	1 123
Melksham	,,	Town	2 452	Mepal	*Cambs*	Parish	510
Melling	*Lancaster*	Parish	2 013	Meppershall	*Beds*	Parish	541
Melling & Wrayton	,,	Tnship.	169	Mercaston	*Derby*	Tnship.	135
Melling	,,	Tnship.	728	Mere	*Cheshire*	Tnship.	556
Mellis	*Suffolk*	Parish	598	Mere	*Lincoln*	Parish	39
Mellor	*Derby*	Tnship.	1 733	Mere	*Wilts*	Hund.	4 449
Mellor	,,	Ecl. Dis.	3 373	Mere	*Wilts, &c.*	District	8 057

Name of Place.	County.	Description.	Population.	Name of Place.	County.	Description.	Population.
Mere ...	Wilts	Parish	2 929	Michael..	Isle of Man	Parish	1 314
Mere Town	,,	Tithing	1 210	Michaelchurch-Eskley	Hereford	Parish	448
Merevale	Warw. & Leic.	Parish	212	Michaelchurch ..	Radnor	Parish	138
Mereworth	Kent	Parish	835	Michaelstone on Avon	Glam..	Parish	6 184
Merford, &c.	Flint	Lordship	257	Michaelstone, Lower	,,	Hamlet	5 323
Meriadog	Denbigh	Tnship.	335	Michaelstone, Upper	,,	Hamlet	861
Meriden	Warwick	District	11 290	Michaelstone-le-Pit	,,	Parish	73
Meriden	,,	Sub-dis.	6 387	Michaelstone on Ely	,,	Parish	49
Meriden	,,	Parish	968	Michaelstoneyvedw	Monm., &c.	Parish	512
Merionethshire..	..	County	38 963	Michaelstoneyvedw	Monmouth	Hamlet	203
Merrington	Durham	Parish	4 046	Michaelstow ..	Cornwall	Parish	219
Merrington	,,	Tnship.	926	Michelmersh ..	Hants & Wilts	Sub-dis.	3 976
Merriott	Somerset	Parish	1 413	Michelmersh ..	Hants	Parish	1 099
Merrow..	Surrey	Parish	363	Mickfield	Suffolk	Parish	259
Mersea, East	Essex	Parish	305	Mickleby ..	York	Tnship.	177
Mersea, West	,,	Parish	944	Micklefield	,,	Tnship.	435
Mersham	Kent	Parish	752	Micklegate	,,	Sub-dis.	13 790
Merstham	Surrey	Parish	846	Mickleham ..	Surrey	Parish	721
Merston..	Sussex	Parish	79	Micklehurst ..	Cheshire	Hamlet	800
Merther..	Cornwall	Parish	384	Mickleover ..	Derby	Parish	2 104
Merthyr	Brecon	Hund.	3 174	Mickleover	,,	Tnship	1 101
Merthyr	,,	L. Sub.	3 133	Micklethwaite ..	York	Parish	66
Merthyr Cynog .	,,	Sub-dis.	1 593	Mickleton ..	Gloucester	Parish	743
Merthyr Cynog .	,,	Parish	800	Mickleton ..	,,	—	622
Merthyr	Carmarthen	Parish	287	Mickleton ..	York	Tnship.	688
Merthyr Dovan .	Glamorgan .	Parish	143	Mickle-Trafford .	Cheshire	Tnship.	265
Merthyr Mawr..	,,	Parish	174	Mickley..	Northumberland	Tnship.	1 208
Merthyr Tydfil .	Glam. & Brec.	District	107 105	Mickley, St. John	York	Ecl. Dis.	210
Merthyr Tydfil Lower	Glam...	Sub-dis.	25 300	Middle ..	Middlesex	Ward	3 148
Merthyr Tydfil Up.	Glm. & Br.	Sub-dis.	27 478	Middle ..	Salop	Parish	1 258
Merthyr Tydfil .	Glamorgan .	Parish	49 794	Middle ..	,,	Tnship.	802
Merthyr Tydfil	Glam. & Bre.	P. Bor.	83 875	Middle Aston ..	Oxon	Tnship.	86
Merton ..	Devon	Parish	820	Middle Chinnock	Somerset	Parish	238
Merton ..	Norfolk	Parish	194	Middle Claydon .	Bucks	Parish	146
Merton ..	Oxon	Parish	204	Middleham ..	York	Sub-dis.	4 230
Merton ..	Surrey	Parish	1 822	Middleham ..	,,	Parish	922
Meshaw..	Devon	Parish	250	Middle Hulton,.	Lancaster	Tnship.	790
Messing..	Essex	Parish	813	Middle Llangynwyd	Glam.	Hamlet	324
Messingham	Lincoln	Parish	1 362	Middle Neath ..	,,	Hamlet	222
Messingham	,,	Tnship.	1 086	Middle Quarter	Nrthumberland	Tnship.	255
Metfield..	Suffolk	Parish	663	Middle Q., K. Andrews	Cumbd.	Tnship.	352
Metham	York	Tnship.	91	Middle Q., K. Linton	,,	Tnship.	472
Metheringham ..	Lincoln	Parish	1 532	Middle Rasen ...	Lincoln	Parish	1 063
Methley..	York	Parish	2 472	Middlesborough	York	Parish	19 416
Methop, &c.	Westmoreland	Tnship.	76	Middlesborough	,,	Tnship.	18 714
Methwold	Norf. & Suff.	Sub-dis.	8 869	**Middlesborough**	,,	M. Bor.	18 992
Methwold	Norfolk	Parish	1 509	Middlesceugh,&c.	Cumberland	Hamlet	159
Mettingham	Suffolk	Parish	387	Middlesex ..	..	County	2206485
Metton ..	Norfolk	Parish	78	Middlestone ..	Durham	Tnship.	497
Mevagissey	Cornwall	Sub-dis.	4 575	Middle Temple..	Middlesex	Parish	81
Mevagissey	,,	Parish	1 914	Middlethorpe ..	York	Tnship.	135
Mexborough	York	Parish	2 665	Middleton & Smerril	Derby	Tnship.	244
Mexborough	,,	Tnship.	2 462	Middleton ..	,,	Tnship.	964
Meyllteyrn	Carnarvon	Parish	265	Middleton, Holy Trinity	,,	Ecl. Dis.	133

Name of Place.	County.	Description.	Population.	Name of Place.	County.	Description.	Population.
Middleton in Teesdale	*Durham*	Parish	4 557	Midgley..	.. *York* ..	Tnship.	2 842
Middleton in Teesdale	,,	Tnship.	2 266	Midhurst	.. *Sussex* ..	L. Sub.	10 485
Middleton, St. George	,,	Parish	294	Midhurst	.. ,, ..	District	12 581
Middleton	.. *Essex* ..	Parish	138	Midhurst	.·. ,, ..	Sub-dis.	5 258
Middleton on Hill	*Hereford* ..	Parish	415	Midhurst	.·. ,, ·	Parish	1 340
Middleton	.. *Lancaster* ..	L. Sub.	212 176	**Midhurst**	.. ,,	P. Bor.	6 405
Middleton, Heaton	,, ..	Tnship.	182	Midland Roborough	*Devon* ..	L. Sub.	71 408
Middleton	.. ,, ..	Sub-dis.	10 299	Mid Lavant	.. *Sussex* ..	Parish	257
Middleton	.. ,, ..	Parish	19 635	Midley ..	.. *Kent* ..	Parish	42
Middleton	.. ,, ..	Tnship.	9 876	Midloe ..	.. *Hunts* ..	Parish	47
Middleton	.. ,, ..	Town	9 876	Midsomer Norton	*Somerset* ..	Sub-dis.	9 074
Middleton	.. *Norfolk* ..	Sub-dis.	2 239	Midsomer Norton	,, ..	Parish	3 836
Middleton	.. ,, ..	Parish	894	Midville	.. *Lincoln* ..	P. Tp.	152
Middleton	.. *Northampton*	Tnship.	421	Milborne Port	..*Somerset* ..	Sub-dis.	5 395
Middleton Cheney	,,	Parish	1 250	Milborne Port	.. ,, ..	Parish	1 814
Middleton-Malzor	,,	Parish	668	Milborne, St. Andrew	*Dorset* ..	Parish	327
Middleton	*Northumberland.*	Tnship.	112	Milborne Stileham	,, ..	Hamlet	288
Middleton Hall .	,,	Tnship.	73	Milbourn	.. *Wilts* ..	Tithing	117
Middleton, North, Morpeth ,,		Tnship.	94	Milbourne	.. *Westmoreland*	Chap.	324
Middleton, North, Ilderton ,,		Tnship.	113	Milbrook	.. *Hants* ..	Sub-dis.	11 246
Middleton, South, Morpeth ,,		Tnship.	22	Milbrook	.. ,, ..	Parish	10 107
Middleton, South, Ilderton ,,		Tnship.	75	Milburn..	*Northumberland*	Tnship.	86
Middleton-Stoney	*Oxon* ..	Parish	259	Milburn-Grange	,,	Tnship.	39
Middleton, Trinity	*Salop* ..	Ecl. Dis.	740	Milby ..	.. *York* ..	Tnship.	108
Middleton-Scriven	,, ..	Parish	111	Milcomb	.. *Oxon* ..	Tnship.	241
Middleton	.. *Suffolk* ..	Parish	589	Milcomb	.. ,, ..	Ecl. Dis.	241
Middleton	.. *Sussex* ..	Parish	89	Milcote ..	.. *Warwick* ..	Lordship	57
Middleton	.. *Warwick* ..	Parish	484	Milden ..	.. *Suffolk* ..	Parish	159
Middleton	.. *Westmoreland*	Tnship.	366	Mildenhall	.. ,, ..	District	9 595
Middleton	.. *York E.* ..	Parish	701	Mildenhall	.. ,, ..	Parish	4 046
Middleton	.. *York & Durh.*	Sub-dis.	7 079	Mildenhall High Town	,,	—	1 615
Middleton	.. *York N.* ..	Parish	2 100	Mildenhall	.. *Wilts* ..	Parish	466
Middleton	.. ,, ..	Tnship.	283	Mildmay Park ..	*Middlesex* ..	Ecl. Dis.	6 620
Middleton	.. *York W.*	Tnship.	176	Mile End St. Michael	*Essex* ..	Parish	880
Middleton (Rothwell P.) ,,		Tnship.	902	Mile End New Town	*Middlesex*	Sub-dis.	15 392
Middleton, St. Mary	*York* ..	Ecl. Dis.	1 360	Mile End New Town	,,	Hamlet	10 845
Middleton-Quernhow	,, ..	Tnship.	129	Mile End N. Tn. All Snts. ,,		Ecl. Dis.	10 845
Middleton Tyas .	,, ..	Parish	775	Mile End Old Town	,,	District	73 064
Middleton Tyas, &c.	,, ..	Tnship.	531	Mile End O. Tn., Eastern ,,		Sub-dis.	39 317
Middleton upon Leven	,, ..	Tnship.	108	Mile End O. Tn.,Western ,,		Sub-dis.	33 747
Middletown	.. *Montgomery*	Tnship.	216	Mile End Old Town	,,	Hamlet	73 064
Middlewich	.. *Cheshire* ..	Sub-dis.	5 644	1. North Ward	.. ,,	Ward	15 412
Middlewich	.. ,, ..	Parish	4 752	2. East Ward	.. ,,	Ward	9 570
Middlewich	.. ,, ..	Tnship.	1 203	3. West Ward	.. ,,	Ward	14 805
Middlewich ..	,, ..	Town	3 146	4. Centre Ward	.. ,,	Ward	18 392
Middle Ystradyfodwg	*Glam.* ..	Hamlet	1 203	5. South Ward	.. ,,	Ward	14 885
Middlezoy	.. *Somerset* ..	Sub-dis.	2 737	Mileham	.. *Norfolk* ..	Parish	546
Middlezoy	.. ,, ..	Parish	725	Miles Platting, St. John	*Lanc.*	Ecl. Dis.	5 153
Middop ..	.. *York* ..	Tnship.	57	Milfield ..	*Northumberland*	Tnship.	225
Middridge	.. *Durham* ..	Tnship.	313	Milford ..	.. *Derby* ..	Ecl. Dis.	1 770
Middridge-Grange	,, ..	Tnship.	56	Milford ..	.. *Hants* ..	Sub-dis.	4 024
Midgham	.. *Berks* ..	Tithing	233	Milford ..	.. ,, ..	Parish	1 784
Midgham	.. ,, ..	Ecl. Dis.	233	Milford ..	.. *Pembroke* ..	Sub-dis.	9 771
Midgholm	.. *Cumberland* ..	Parish	82	**Milford** ..	,, ..	P. Bor.	3 007

Name of Place.	County.	Description.	Population.	Name of Place.	County.	Description.	Population.
Milford, St. John	Surrey	Ecl. dis.	717	Milverton	Somerset	Sub-dis.	4 214
Milford	Wilts	Tithing	631	Milverton	"	Parish	1 895
Milford, South	York	Tnship.	823	Milverton	Warwick	Parish	1 366
Milford, South, St. Mary	"	Ecl. Dis.	1 059	Milwich	Stafford	Parish	567
Milland	Hants	Ville	211	Mimms, North	Herts	Parish	1 095
Millbrook	Beds	Parish	430	Mimms, South	Middlesex	L. Sub.	4 291
Mill Hill, St. Paul	Middlesex	Ecl. Dis.	1 188	Mimms, South	"	Parish	3 238
Millhill Ward	York	—	5 312	Minchinhampton	Gloucester	Sub-dis.	4 147
Millington	Cheshire	Tnship.	338	Minchinhampton	"	Parish	4 147
Millington	York	Parish	275	Mindtown	Salop	Parish	48
Millmece	Stafford	Tnship.	114	Minehead	Somerset	Sub-dis.	3 480
Millom	Cumberland	Parish	2 015	Minehead	"	Parish	1 582
Millom Above	"	Tnship.	508	Minera	Denbigh	Tnship.	1 221
Millom Below	"	Tnship.	392	Minera	"	Ecl. Dis.	1 714
Milnsbridge, St. Luke	York	Ecl. Dis.	2 903	Minety	Wilts	Parish	812
Milnthorpe	Westmoreland	Sub-dis.	5 994	Miningsby	Lincoln	Parish	477
Milnthorpe St. Thomas	"	Ecl. Dis.	1 073	Minshull Vernon	Cheshire	Tnship.	402
Milson	Salop	Parish	157	Minshull Vernon	"	Ecl. Dis.	619
Milstead	Kent	Parish	245	Minskip	York	Tnship.	220
Milston	Wilts	Parish	130	Minstead	Hants	Parish	905
Milthorpe	Lincoln	Hamlet	87	Minster	Cornwall	Parish	505
Milton Bryant	Beds	Parish	345	Minster	Kent	Sub-dis.	16 937
Milton Earnest	"	Parish	485	Minster in Sheppey	"	Parish	15 964
Milton	Berks	Parish	429	Minster	"	Sub-dis.	3 836
Milton Keynes	Bucks	Parish	346	Minster in Thanet	"	Parish	1 588
Milton	Cambs	Parish	494	Minster Close Prec.	Northmptn.	Parish	238
Milton Abbot	Devon	Sub-dis.	4 728	Minsterley	Salop	Chap.	890
Milton Abbot	"	Parish	1 062	Minster-Lovell	Oxon	Parish	586
Milton Damerel	"	Sub-dis.	2 542	Minsterworth	Gloucester	Parish	463
Milton Damerel	"	Parish	684	Minster Yd. w. Beddern	York	Parish	944
Milton, South	"	Parish	363	Mint	Kent	Parish	85
Milton Abbas	Dorset	Sub-dis.	6 285	Mintern Magna	Dorset	Parish	374
Milton Abbas	"	Parish	1 014	Minting	Lincoln	Parish	422
Milton	Hants	Parish	1 295	Mintlyn	Norfolk	Parish	46
Milton, St. James	"	Ecl. Dis.	3 896	Minty	Wilts	Parish	812
Milton by Gravesend	Kent	Parish	10 897	Mint Yard	York	Liberty	90
Christchurch	"	Ecl. Dis.	5 631	Minwere	Pembroke	Parish	99
Holy Trinity	"	Ecl. Dis.	3 642	Minworth	Warwick	Hamlet	319
Milton	"	District	14 775	Mirfield	York	Sub-dis.	9 263
Milton	"	Sub-dis.	14 775	Mirfield	"	Parish	9 263
Milton by Sittingbourne	"	Parish	2 731	Miserden	Gloucester	Parish	503
Milton	"	Town	2 731	Miskin	Glamorgan	Hund.	57 347
Milton Chapel	"	Parish	11	Miskin, Higher	"	L. Sub.	44 858
Milton	Northampton	Sub-dis	2 857	Miskin, Lower	"	L. Sub.	12 017
Milton	"	Parish	668	Missenden	Bucks	Sub-dis.	2 366
Milton by Adderbury	Oxon	Hamlet	172	Missenden, Great	"	Parish	2 250
Milton	"	Tnship.	895	Missenden, Little	"	Parish	1 089
Milton, Great	"	Parish	729	Misson	Notts & York	Parish	803
Milton, Great	"	Tnship.	630	Misterton	Leicester	Parish	554
Milton, Little	"	Parish	411	Misterton	Notts	Sub-dis.	3 151
Milton, Little, St. James	"	Ecl. Dis.	431	Misterton	"	Parish	1 627
Milton Clevedon	Somerset	Parish	210	Misterton	"	Tnship.	1 089
Milton Lilborne	Wilts	Parish	697	Misterton	Som. & Dorset	Sub-dis.	1 630
Milverton	Somerset	Hund.	4 002	Misterton	Somerset	Parish	588

Name of Place.	County.	Description.	Population.	Name of Place.	County.	Description.	Populat
Mistley ..	Essex	Parish	1 539	Mongewell	Oxon	Parish	1
Mitcham	Surrey	Sub-dis.	9 381	Monington	Pembroke	Parish	1
Mitcham	,,	Parish	5 078	Monk Bretton ..	York	Tnship.	19
Mitcheldever	Hants	Sub-dis.	2 347	Monk Bretton ..	,,	Ecl. Dis.	2 4
Mitcheldever	,,	Parish	1 041	Monken Hadley	Middlesex	Parish	1 0
Mitchel Dean ..	Gloucester	Parish	689	Monk Frystone .	York	Parish	1 1
Mitchel Troy ..	Monmouth	Parish	385	Monk Frystone .	,,	Tnship.	5
Mitford..	Norfolk	Hund.	11 452	Monk Hesledon .	Durham	Parish	2 0
Mitford..	,,	L. Sub.	11 452	Monk Hesledon .	,,	Tnship.	1 5
Mitford..	,,	District.	28 020	Monkhill	York	Tnship.	
Mitford..	Northumberland	Parish	646	Monkhopton ..	Salop	Parish	1
Mitford..	,,	Tnship.	210	Monkland	Hereford	Parish	2.
Mithian..	Cornwall	Ecl. Dis.	2 085	Monkleigh	Devon	Parish	6
Mitton, &c.	Lancaster	Tnship.	62	Monknash	Glamorgan	Parish	1
Mitton, Lower, &c.	Worcester	Hamlet	2 958	Monk Okehampton	Devon	Parish	2
Mitton, Lower ..	,,	Ecl. Dis.	2 958	Monkridge Ward	Nrthumbld..	Tnship.	8
Mitton, Upper ..	,,	Hamlet	262	Monks Coppenhall	Cheshire	Tnship.	8 1
Mitton	York & Lanc.	Parish	3 403	Monkseaton	Northumberland	Tnship.	4
Mitton, Great ..	York	Tnship.	184	Monks Eleigh ..	Suffolk	Parish	6
Mixbury	Oxon	Parish	381	Monk Sherborne	Hants	Parish	64
Moat Quarter ..	Cumberland	Tnship.	376	Monks Horton..	Kent	Parish	1 5
Mobberley	Cheshire	Parish	1 245	Monkshouse	Northumberland	—	
Moccas ..	Hereford	Parish	196	Monks Kirby ..	Warwick	Parish	1 93
Modbury	Devon	Sub-dis.	3 679	Monks Kirby ..	,,	Tnship.	59
Modbury	,,	Parish	1 621	Monks Liberty..	Lincoln	Parish	2
Modrydd	Brecon	Hamlet	117	Monksilver	Somerset	Parish	30
Moggerhanger ..	Beds	Ecl. Dis.	503	Monk Soham ..	Suffolk	Parish	4
Mold	Flint	Hund.	19 517	Monks Risborough	Bucks	Parish	98
Mold	,,	L. Sub.	19 260	Monks Risbridge	Suffolk	Parish	
Mold	,,	Sub-dis.	11 719	Monkswood ..	Monmouth	Parish	17
Mold	,,	Parish	12 216	Monkton	Devon	Parish	12
Mold	,,	Tnship.	3 735	Monkton	Kent	Parish	37
Mold	,,	P. Bor.	3 735	Monkton, West .	Somerset	Parish	1 15
Moldash	Kent	Parish	328	Monkton Farleigh	Wilts	Parish	35
Molescroft	York	Tnship.	143	Monkton Moor..	York	Parish	38
Molesden	Northumberland	Tnship.	47	Monkton Moor..	,,	Tnship.	25
Molesworth	Hunts	Parish	256	Monk Wearmouth	Durham	Sub-dis.	23 44
Molland	Devon	Parish	598	Monk Wearmouth	,,	Parish	23 44
Mollington,Great	Cheshire	Tnship.	186	Monk Wearmouth	,,	Tnship.	3 34
Mollington, Little	,,	Tnship.	29	Monk Wearmouth, All Sts.	,,	Ecl. Dis.	3 49
Mollington	Oxon & War.	Chap.	372	Monk Wearmouth Shore	,,	Tnship.	15 13
Molton, North ..	Devon	Parish	1 842	Monmouthshire		County	174 63
Molton, South ..	,,	District	19 209	Monmouth ..	Monmouth	L. Sub.	6 82
Molton, South ..	,,	Sub Dis.	8 698	Monmouth	Monmouth, &c.	District	30 24
Molton, South ..	,,	Parish	3 830	Monmouth	Monmouth	Sub-dis.	6 02
Molton, South .	,,	M. Bor.	3 830	Monmouth	,,	Parish	5 27
Monachlogddu..	Pembroke	Parish	471	Monmouth	,,	M. Bor.	5 78
Monckton Wyld	Dorset	Ecl. Dis.	362	Monmouth, Parl. Dist. of	,,	Boros.	30 57
Monckton	Pembroke	Parish	1 708	Monmouth, St. Thos.	,,	Ecl. Dis.	1 14
Monckton Combe	Somerset	Parish	1 271	Monnington on Wye	Hereford.	Parish	10
Monckton Deverill	Wilts	Parish	180	Montacute	Somerset	Parish	99
Monewden ..	Suffolk	Parish	223	Montford	Salop	Sub-dis.	1 16
Mongeham, Great	Kent	Parish	349	Montford	,,	Parish	46
Mongeham, Little	,,	Parish	138	Montgomeryshire		County	66 91

Name of Place.	County.	Description.	Population.	Name of Place.	County.	Description.	Population.
Montgomery	Montgomery	Hund.	5 523	Moreton Hampstead	Devon ..	Sub-dis.	2 718
Montgomery, Lower	„ ..	L. Sub.	2 922	Moreton Hampstead	„ ..	Parish	1 468
Montgomery, Upper	„ ..	L. Sub.	2 601	Moreton	.. Dorset ..	Parish	283
Montgomery	Mont. & Salop	District	19 097	Moreton	.. Essex ..	Parish	497
Montgomery & Pool	„ „	Incor.	17 468	Moreton	.. Glouc., &c...	Sub-dis.	6 086
Montgomery	„ „	Sub-dis.	6 121	Moreton in Marsh	Gloucester .	Parish	1 420
Montgomery	Montg.	Parish	1 276	Moreton Valence	„ ..	Parish	337
Montgomery ..	.. „	P. Bor.	1 276	Moreton on Lugg	Hereford ..	Parish	77
Montgomery, Parl. Dist. of	„	Boros.	18 036	Moreton Corbet	Salop ..	Parish	255
Montpelier	.. Gloucester ..	Ecl. Dis.	6 101	Moreton Say ..	Salop, &c...	Sub-dis.	3 923
Monxton	.. Hants ..	Parish	275	Moreton Say .,	Salop ..	Parish	679
Monyash	.. Derby ..	Tnship.	460	Moreton, St. Mary	Stafford ..	Ecl. Dis.	679
Moor ..	.. Flint ..	Tnship.	110	Moreton Morrell	Warwick ..	Parish	266
Moor Allerton ..	York ..	Ecl. Dis.	697	Morice ..	.. Devon ..	Sub-dis.	14 089
Moorby..	.. Lincoln ..	Parish	128	Morland	.. Westmoreland	Sub-dis.	4 212
Moore ..	.. Cheshire ..	Tnship.	269	Morland	.. „ ..	Parish	1 927
Moore Critchell .	Dorset ..	Parish	342	Morleston & Litchurch	Derby	Hund.	57 563
Mooresbarrow, &c.	Cheshire ..	Tnship.	25	Morleston & Litchurch	„	L. Sub.	100 654
Mooresholm w. Gerrick	York..	Tnship.	305	Morley ..	.. „	Parish	951
Moorfields	.. „ ..	Ecl. Dis.	6 254	Morley ..	.. „	Tnship.	230
Moorfields, Little	Middlesex ..	Ecl. Dis.	4 216	Morley, St. Botolph	Norfolk ..	Parish	278
Moorhay, &c. ..	Northampton	Lodges	28	Morley, St. Peter	„ ..	Parish	147
Moorhouse ..	Cumberland	Tnship.	306	Morley ..	.. York ..	L. Sub.	383 026
Moorhouse ..	Durham ..	Tnship.	94	Morley ..	.. „ ..	Sub-dis.	6 840
Moorlinch ..	Somerset ..	Parish	2 329	Morley ..	.. „ ..	Tnship.	6 840
Moorlinch ..	„ ..	Hamlet	334	Morley, St. Peter	„ ..	Ecl. Dis.	8 404
Moorsley ..	Durham ..	Tnship.	973	Morningthorpe..	Norfolk ..	Parish	140
Moorthwaite ..	Cumberland	Tnship.	144	Morpeth	Northumberland	Ward	14 291
Moortown	Northumberland	Tnship.	543	Morpeth Ward .	„ ..	L. Sub.	27 140
Moor Town ..	York ..	Tnship.	27	Morpeth	.. „ ..	District	24 003
Moor, West ..	Somerset ..	—	31	Morpeth	.. „ ..	Sub-dis.	8 426
Moorwinstow ..	Cornwall ..	Parish	868	Morpeth	.. „ ..	Parish	5 612
Morborn ..	Hunts ..	Parish	132	Morpeth	.. „ ..	Tnship.	4 521
Morchard Bishop	Devon ..	Sub-dis.	4 569	**Morpeth** ..	.. „ .	M. Bor.	4 296
Morchard Bishop	„ ..	Parish	1 658			P. Bor.	13 794
Morcott..	.. Rutland ..	Parish	494	Morpeth Castle .	„ ..	Tnship.	180
Morden, Guilden	Cambs ..	Parish	906	Morrick..	.. „ ..	Tnship.	71
Morden, Steeple.	„ ..	Parish	913	Morston	.. Norfolk ..	Parish	153
Morden..	.. Dorset ..	Parish	939	Morthoe	.. Devon ..	Parish	347
Mordiford ..	Hereford ..	Parish	691	Mortimer	Berks & Hants	Sub-dis.	4 931
Mordon..	.. Durham ..	Tnship.	179	Mortlake	.. Surrey ..	Sub-dis.	6 137
Mordon..	.. Surrey ..	Parish	654	Mortlake	.. „ ..	Parish	3 778
More ..	.. Salop ..	Parish	227	Morton ..	.. Derby ..	Parish	911
Morebath ..	Devon ..	Parish	430	Morton ..	.. „ ..	Tnship.	594
Moreleigh ..	„ ..	Parish	122	Morton East ..	Durham ..	Tnship.	2 104
Moresby ..	Cumberland	Parish	1 222	Morton Grange .	„ ..	Tnship.	220
Moresby ..	„ ..	Tnship.	463	Morton Palms ..	„ ..	Tnship.	59
Morestead ..	Hants ..	Parish	112	Morton Tinmouth	„ ..	Tnship.	27
Moreton ..	Berks ..	Hund.	6 487	Morton Jefferies.	Hereford ..	Parish	41
Moreton, North .	„ ..	Parish	352	Morton ..	.. Lincoln ..	Tnship.	623
Moreton, South .	„ ..	Parish	371	Morton, St. Paul	„ ..	Ecl. Dis.	616
Moreton, Maids .	Bucks ..	Parish	543	Morton, Lincoln	„ ..	Parish	8
Moreton w. Alcumlow	Cheshire ..	Tnship.	119	Morton, Bourn	„ ..	Parish	1 008
Moreton w. Lingham	„ ..	Tnship.	361	Morton ..	.. „ ..	Tnship.	854

Name of Place.	County.	Description.	Population.	Name of Place.	County.	Description.	Population.
Morton on Hill .	Norfolk	Parish	149	Mount ..	Cardigan	Parish	146
Morton Pinkney.	Northampton	Parish	570	Mount Bures ..	Essex	Parish	301
Morton ..	Notts	Parish	142	Mountfield ..	Sussex	Parish	585
Morton ..	Salop	Ecl. Dis.	823	Mount Hawke ..	Cornwall	Ecl. Dis.	2 226
Morton Baggott .	Warwick	Parish	139	Mount Healey	Northumberland	Tnship.	43
Morton ..	York N.	Tnship.	47	Mountnessing ..	Essex	Parish	844
Morton ..	,, ,,	Parish	34	Mounton ..	Monmouth	Parish	90
Morton ..	,, W.	Tnship.	2 113	Mounton ..	Pembroke	Parish	40
Morton ..	,, ,,	Ecl. Dis.	2 432	Mount Pellon, Christch.	York .	Ecl. Dis.	2 021
Morton upon Swale	,, N.	Tnship.	286	Mount Pleasant .	Cumberland	Ecl. Dis.	4 131
Morvah ..	Cornwall	Parish	380	Mount Pleasant .	Lancaster	Sub-dis.	47 410
Morval ..	,,	Parish	765	Mountsorrel Nth. End	Leicester	Tnship.	857
Morvil ..	Pembroke	Parish	125	Mountsorrel Sth. End	,,	Tnship.	897
Morvill ..	Salop	Parish	507	Mountsorrel, Christch.	,,	Ecl. Dis.	897
Morvill ..	,,	Tnship.	422	Mousel Lane ..	Gloucester	—	4
Morwick	Northumberland	Tnship.	71	Mouson..	Northumberland	Tnship.	82
Mosedale ..	Cumberland	Tnship.	51	Mowcop, St. Thomas	Stafford	Ecl. Dis.	2 135
Moseley, St. Mary	Worcester	Ecl. Dis.	2 591	Mowsley ..	Leicester	Chap.	241
Mosley, Holy Trinity	Cheshire	Ecl. Dis.	949	Moxley ..	Stafford	Ecl. Dis.	3 857
Moss ..	York	Tnship.	242	Moyddyn ..	Cardigan	Hund.	15 553
Mosser ..	Cumberland	Tnship.	88	Moyddyn, Upper	,,	L. Sub.	5 408
Moss Side ..	Lancaster	Tnship.	2 695	Moylgrove ..	Pembroke	Parish	429
Moss Side Christch.	,,	Ecl. Dis.	6 114	Mucclestone ..	Staff. & Salop	Parish	1 610
Mosterton ..	Dorset	Parish	380	Mucclestone ..	Stafford	Tnship.	177
Moston ..	Cheshire	Tnship.	15	Much Birch ..	Hereford	Parish	496
Moston (Warmingham P.)	,,	Tnship.	170	Much Cowarne..	,,	Parish	563
Moston ..	Lancaster	Tnship.	1 199	Much Dewchurch	,,	Parish	608
Mostyn ..	Flint	Ecl. Dis.	1 640	Muchelney ..	Somerset	Parish	308
Motcombe ..	Dorset	Parish	1 433	Much Hadham .	Herts	L. Sub.	3 931
Motherby & Gill	Cumberland	Tnship.	117	Much Hadham .	,,	Parish	1 172
Mottingham ..	Kent	Hamlet	142	Much Hoole ..	Lancaster	Tnship.	708
Mottisfont ..	Hants	Parish	496	Much Marcle ..	Hereford	Parish	1 209
Mottiston ..	,, I.W.	Parish	160	Much Marcle ..	,,	Tnship.	984
Mottram ..	Cheshire	Sub-dis.	7 652	Much Wenlock..	Salop	Sub-dis.	2 494
Mottram ..	,,	Parish	22 495	Much Wenlock..	,,	Parish	2 494
Mottram ..	,,	Tnship.	3 406	Much Woolton..	Lancaster	Sub-dis.	4 608
Mottram, St. Andrew	,,	Tnship.	460	Much Woolton..	,,	Tnship.	3 546
Moughtre ..	Montgomery	Parish	526	**Much Woolton**	,,	Town	3 296
Mouldsworth ..	Cheshire	Tnship.	175	Much Woolton..	,,	Ecl. Dis.	3 538
Moulsey, East ..	Surrey	Parish	1 568	Mucking ..	Essex	Parish	253
Moulsey, West..	,,	Parish	459	Mucklewick ..	Salop	Tnship.	57
Moulsford ..	Berks	Parish	180	Muckton ..	Lincoln	Parish	106
Moulsham, St. John	Essex	Ecl. Dis.	4 229	Mudford ..	Somerset	Parish	421
Moulsoe ..	Bucks	Parish	234	Muggerhanger ..	Beds	Hamlet	503
Moulton ..	Cheshire	Tnship.	395	Muggerhanger St. John	,,	Ecl. Dis.	503
Moulton ..	Lincoln	Sub-dis.	2 893	Mugginton ..	Derby	Parish	689
Moulton ..	,,	Parish	2 143	Mugginton ..	,,	Tnship.	261
Moulton ..	Norfolk	Parish	259	Muggleswick ..	Durham	Parish	788
Moulton, Great .	,,	Parish	442	Muker ..	York	Sub-dis.	2 627
Moulton ..	Northampton	Sub-dis.	4 890	Muker ..	,,	Tnship.	1 005
Moulton ..	,,	Parish	1 840	Muker, St. Mary	,,	Ecl. Dis.	1 005
Moulton Park ..	,,	Parish	8	Mulbarton ..	Norfolk	Parish	525
Moulton ..	Suffolk	Parish	518	Mullion..	Cornwall	Parish	679
Moulton ..	York	Tnship.	244	Mumby..	Lincoln	Parish	786

Name of Place.	County.	Description.	Population.	Name of Place.	County.	Description.	Population.
Muncaster ..	Cumberland	Sub-dis.	2 282	Myton upon Swale	York ..	Parish	155
Muncaster ..	,,	Parish	580				
Munden, Great .	Herts ..	Parish	457	**Naburn** ..	York ..	Tnship.	471
Munden, Little..	,, ..	Parish	601	Nackington ..	Kent ..	Parish	165
Mundford ..	Norfolk ..	Parish	376	Nacton	Suffolk ..	Parish	580
Mundham ..	,, ..	Parish	282	Nafferton	Northumberland	Tnship.	53
Mundham, North	Sussex ..	Parish	426	Nafferton ..	York ..	Parish	1 535
Mundon ..	Essex ..	Parish	322	Nafferton ..	,,	Tnship.	1 311
Mundsley ..	Norfolk ..	Parish	437	Nailsea	Somerset ..	Parish	2 278
Mungrisdale ..	Cumberland	Tnship.	202	Nailsea, Christchurch	,,	Ecl. Dis.	955
Munsley ..	Hereford ..	Parish	234	Nailstone ..	Leicester ..	Parish	639
Munslow ..	Salop ..	Hund.	10 978	Nailstone ..	,, ..	Tnship.	302
Munslow, Lower	,, ..	L. Sub.	7 746	Nannerch ..	Flint & Denb.	Parish	333
Munslow, Upper	,, ..	L. Sub.	5 384	Nannerch ..	Flint	Tnship.	275
Munslow ..	,, ..	Sub-dis.	2 051	Nant-Conway ..	Carnarvon ..	Hund.	4 556
Munslow ..	,, ..	Parish	712	Nantcwnlle ..	Cardigan ..	Parish	803
Mursley ..	Bucks ..	Parish	482	Nantddu ..	Brecon ..	Chap.	95
Murston ..	Kent ..	Parish	572	Nantglyn ..	Denbigh ..	Parish	320
Murton ..	Northumberland	Tnship.	543	Nantmel ..	Radnor ..	Sub-dis.	3 177
Murton.. ..	Westmoreland	Tnship.	218	Nantmel ..	,, ..	Parish	1 453
Murton	York ..	Tnship.	154	Nantmor ..	Merioneth ..	Hamlet	309
Musbury ..	Devon ..	Parish	493	Nantwich ..	Cheshire ..	Hund.	34 292
Musbury ..	Lancaster ..	Tnship.	997	Nantwich ..	,, ..	L. Sub.	34 292
Musbury ..	,,	Ecl. Dis.	2 724	Nantwich ..	,, ..	District	40 955
Muscoates ..	York ..	Tnship.	64	Nantwich ..	,, ..	Sub-dis.	10 062
Musden Grange .	Stafford ..	Parish	14	Nantwich ..	,, ..	Parish	6 763
Musgrave, Great	Westmoreland	Parish	192	Nantwich ..	,, ..	Tnship.	6 225
Musgrave, Little	,,	Tnship.	61	**Nantwich** ..	,, ..	Town	6 225
Muskham, North	Notts ..	Parish	848	Nantyglo ..	Monmouth ..	Ecl. Dis.	4 450
Muskham, North	,, ..	Tnship.	614	Nappa	York ..	Tnship.	31
Muskham, South	,, ..	Parish	277	Napton on Hill..	Warwick ..	Parish	978
Muston.. ..	Leicester ..	Parish	360	Narberth ..	Pembroke ..	Hund.	13 276
Muston.. ..	York ..	Parish	391	Narberth ..	,, ..	L. Sub.	15 980
Muswell Hill, St. Jas.	Mddlsx.	Ecl. Dis.	919	Narberth	Pemb. & Carm.	District	21 344
Mutford & Lothingland	Suffolk	Hund.	19 578	Narberth ..	,, ,,	Sub-dis.	3 620
Mutford	,,	District	24 050	Narberth ..	Pembroke ..	Parish	2 546
Mutford	,,	Parish	386	**Narberth** ..	,, ..	P. Bor.	1 209
Myddelton Sq., St. Mark	Mdlx.	Ecl. Dis.	10 417	Narberth, North.	,,	Division	1 717
Myddfai ..	Carmarthen	Sub-dis.	1 118	Narberth, South.	,,	Division	829
Myddfai ..	,, ..	Parish	1 118	Narborough ..	Leicester ..	Parish	1 156
Mydrim.. ..	,, ..	Parish	992	Narborough ..	,, ..	Tnship.	716
Myerscough ..	Lancaster ..	Tnship.	426	Narburgh ..	Norfolk ..	Parish	387
Myfod	Montgomery	Parish	1 806	Narford	,, ..	Parish	123
Mylor	Cornwall ..	Sub-dis.	3 730	Naseby	Northampton	Parish	811
Mylor	,, ..	Parish	2 213	Nash	Bucks ..	Hamlet	462
Mynachty ..	Carmarthen	Hamlet	214	Nash	Glamorgan .	Parish	11
Mynyddyslwyn .	Mon. & Glam.	Sub-dis.	10 596	Nash	Monmouth ..	Parish	284
Mynyddyslwyn .	Monmouth ..	Parish	6 877	Nash	Pembroke ..	Parish	171
Mynyddmaen ..	,,	Hamlet	1 782	Nash	,,	Hamlet	147
Mystyrrhoesllowdy	Radnor ..	Tnship.	202	Nash	Salop ..	Tnship.	269
Mytholmroyd ..	York ..	Ecl. Dis.	3 063	Nassaburgh ..	Northampton	Hund.	21 287
Myton	,, ..	Sub-dis.	40 066	Nassington ..	,,	Parish	718
Myton, North ..	,, ..	Ward	15 485	Nateby	Lancaster ..	Tnship.	385
Myton, South ..	,, ..	Ward	24 581	Nateby	Westmoreland	Tnship.	159

Name of Place.	County.	Description.	Population.	Name of Place.	County.	Description.	Population.
Nately Scures ..	*Hants* ..	Parish	271	Neswick.. ..	*York* ..	Tnship.	66
Nately Up ..	" ..	Parish	99	Nether Alderley.	*Cheshire* ..	Tnship.	617
Natland ..	*Westmoreland*	Tnship.	276	Netheravon ..	*Wilts* ..	Sub-dis.	5 471
Naughton ..	*Suffolk* ..	Parish	155	Netheravon ..	" ..	Parish	516
Naunton ..	*Gloucester* ..	Parish	535	Nether Broughton	*Leicester* ..	Parish	519
Naunton Beauchamp	*Worcester*	Parish	157	Netherbury ..	*Dorset* ..	Sub-dis.	4 971
Navenby ..	*Lincoln* ..	Parish	1 170	Netherbury ..	" ..	Parish	1 875
Navestock ..	*Essex* ..	Parish	928	Netherby ..	*Cumberland*	Tnship.	395
Navisford ..	*Northampton*	Hund.	3 075	Nether Cerne ..	*Dorset* ..	Parish	95
Naworth ..	*Cumberland*	Tnship.	557	Nether Compton	" ..	Parish	376
Nawton	*York* ..	Tnship.	358	Nethercot ..	*Northampton*	Hamlet	97
Nayland ..	*Suffolk* ..	Parish	1 061	Nether Denton..	*Cumberland*	Parish	302
Nazeing	*Essex* ..	Parish	763	Nether Exe ..	*Devon* ..	Parish	78
Neasham ..	*Durham* ..	Tnship.	333	Nether Graveship	*Westmoreld.*	Tnship.	441
Neat Enstone ..	*Oxon* ..	Hamlet	414	Nether Haddon .	*Derby* ..	Parish	103
Neath	*Glamorgan* .	Hund.	22 993	Nether Hallam..	*York* ..	Sub-dis.	17 305
Neath ..	*Glam. & Brecon*	District	58 533	Nether Hallam..	" ..	Tnship.	19 758
Neath	*Glamorgan* .	Sub-dis.	13 462	Netherhampton .	*Wilts* ..	Parish	132
Neath	" ..	Parish	6 734	Nether Heyford .	*Northampton*	Parish	80
Neath	" ..	Borough	6 810	Nether Hoyland .	*York* ..	Tnship.	5 352
Neath, Lower ..	" ..	Hamlet	174	Nether Kellet ..	*Lancaster* ..	Tnship.	284
Naath, Middle ..	" ..	Hamlet	222	Nether Padley ..	*Derby* ..	Hamlet	40
Neath, Upper ..	" ..	Hamlet	1 637	Nether Peover ..	*Cheshire* ..	Tnship.	258
Neatham ..	*Hants* ..	Tithing	57	Nether Pool ..	" ..	Tnship.	25
Neatishead ..	*Norfolk* ..	Parish	580	Nether Poppleton	*York* ..	Parish	311
Nechells, St. Clement	*Warwick*	Ecl. Dis.	6 675	Nether Poppleton	" ..	Tnship.	262
Necton ..	*Norfolk* ..	Parish	948	Nether Quarter..	*Cumberland*	Tnship.	439
Nedging.. ..	*Suffolk* ..	Parish	171	Nether Quarter..	*Derby* ..	Tnship.	399
Needham ..	*Norfolk* ..	Parish	395	Nether & Over Seal	*Leicester* ..	Tnship.	1 246
Needham-Market	*Suffolk* ..	Sub-dis.	7 694	Nether Silton ..	*York* ..	Chap.	178
Needham-Market	" ..	Hamlet	1 377	Nether Staveley	*Westmoreland*	Tnship.	294
Neen Savage ..	*Salop* ..	Parish	452	Nether Stowey..	*Somerset* ..	Parish	876
Neen Sollars ..	" ..	Parish	189	Netherthong ..	*York*..	Tnship.	1 097
Neenton.. ..	" ..	Parish	110	Netherthong, All Saints	" ..	Ecl. Dis.	1 640
Neithrop ..	*Oxon* ..	Tnship.	5 081	Netherthorpe, St. Steph.	" ..	Ecl. Dis.	4 097
Nempnett-Thrubwell	*Somerset.*	Parish	259	Netherton ..	*Lancaster* ..	Tnship.	286
Nenthead ..	*Cumberland*	Chap.	2 039	Netherton ..	*Worcester* ..	Hamlet	91
Nenthead, St. John	" ..	Ecl. Dis.	2 039	Netherton, St. Andrew	" ..	Ecl. Dis.	10 426
Nerquis.. ..	*Flint* ..	Tnship.	482	Netherton, Nth. Side	*Nthmbld.*	Tnship.	76
Nerquis.. ..	" ..	Ecl. Dis.	842	Netherton, Sth. Side	" ..	Tnship.	75
Nesbit ..	*Northumberland*	Tnship.	62	Nether Wallop..	*Hants* ..	Parish	946
Nesbit (Stamfordham P.)	"	Tnship.	41	Nether Wasdale .	*Cumberland*	Chap.	192
Nesbitt	*Durham* ..	Tnship.	12	Nether Whitacre	*Warwick* ..	Parish	479
Nesfield w. Langbar	*York* ..	Tnship.	188	Nether Winchendon	*Bucks* ..	Parish	316
Ness	*Cheshire* ..	Tnship.	346	Nether Witton..	*Northumbld.*	Parish	486
Ness	*Lincoln* ..	Wapen.	7 450	Nether Witton..	" ..	Tnship.	301
Ness, Great ..	*Salop* ..	Parish	573	Nether Worton..	*Oxon* ..	Parish	61
Ness, Little ..	" ..	Tnship.	238	Nether Wyersdale	*Lancaster*..	Tnship.	667
Ness, East ..	*York* ..	Tnship.	49	Netley, St. Matthew	*Hants* ..	Ecl. Dis.	1 081
Ness, West ..	" ..	Tnship.	57	Netteswell ..	*Essex* ..	Parish	335
Neston ..	*Cheshire* ..	Sub-dis.	5 223	Nettlebed ..	*Oxon* ..	Parish	737
Neston	" ..	Parish	4 049	Nettlecombe ..	*Somerset* ..	Parish	327
Neston, Great ..	" ..	Tnship.	1 764	Nettleden ..	*Bucks* ..	Hamlet	124
Neston, Little ..	" ..	Tnship.	580	Nettleham ..	*Lincoln* ..	Parish	919

Name of Place.	County.	Description.	Population.	Name of Place.	County.	Description.	Population.
Nettlestead	Kent	Parish	575	New Brentford..	Middlesex	Tp. or P.	1 995
Nettlestead	Suffolk	Parish	105	**New Brighton**. Cheshire		Town	2 404
Nettleton	Lincoln	Parish	536	New Brighton, St. Jas. „		Ecl. Dis.	2 404
Nettleton	Wilts	Parish	632	Newbrough	Northumberland	Parish	703
Nevendon	Essex	Parish	205	New Buckenham	Norfolk	Parish	656
Nevern ..	Pembroke	Parish	1 436	Newburgh	York	Tnship.	138
Nevill Holt	Leicester	Tnship.	33	Newburn	Northumberland	Parish	4 619
Nevin ..	Carnarvon	Sub-dis.	4 938	Newburn	„	Tnship.	1 008
Nevin ..	„	Parish	1 818	Newburn Hall ..	„	Tnship.	703
Nevin ..	„	P. Bor.	1 818	Newbury	Berks	L. Sub.	30 156
New Accrington.	Lancaster	Tnship.	11 853	Newbury	Berks & Hants	District	19 999
New Accrington, Ch. ch. „		Ecl. Dis.	5 322	Newbury	„ „	Sub-dis.	7 193
Newall w. Clifton	York	Tnship.	209	Newbury	Berks	Parish	6 161
New Alresford ..	Hants	Parish	1 546	**Newbury** ..	„	M. Bor.	6 161
Newark..	Northampton	Hamlet	307	Newbury, St. John „		Ecl. Dis.	2 008
Newark ..	Notts	Wapen.	8 613	Newby ..	Cumberland	Tnship.	128
Newark ..	„	L. Sub.	27 323	Newby ..	Westmoreland	Tnship.	284
Newark ..	Notts & Linc.	District	30 186	Newby ..	York	Tnship.	129
Newark ..	Notts	Sub-dis.	11 498	Newby (Scalby P.) „		Tnship.	50
Newark ..	„	Borough	11 515	Newby Wiske ..	„	Tnship.	223
Newark upon Trent „		Parish	11 498	Newby w. Mulwith	„	Tnship.	60
Newark, Christch. „		Ecl. Dis.	3 679	Newcastle in Emlyn	Carmthn.	L. Sub.	6 744
Newarke	Leicester	Liberty	1 341	Newcastle Emlyn	Carm., &c.	District	19 081
Newbald	York	Parish	910	Newcastle, Trinity Crm. & Crd.		Ecl. Dis.	2 426
Newbald, North .	„	Tnship.	699	Newcastle ..	Glamorgan	Hund.	24 575
Newbald, South .	„	Tnship.	211	Newcastle & Ogmore	„	L. Sub.	28 751
Newball..	Lincoln	Tnship.	88	Newcastle ..	„	Parish	2 244
New Basford	Notts	Ecl. Dis.	3 241	Newcastle, Higher	„	Hamlet	1 357
New Bewick	Northumberland	Tnship.	78	Newcastle, Lower	„	Hamlet	887
Newbiggen ..	„	Tnship.	69	Newcastle on Tyne	Northumbld.	L. Sub.	109 108
Newbiggen ..	York	Tnship.	121	Newcastle on Tyne	„	District	110 968
Newbiggin ..	Cumberland	Tnship.	321	Newcastle, All Saints	„	Parish	37 529
Newbiggin ..	Durham	Tnship.	641	**Newcastle on Tyne** (1842)		Borough	109 108
Newbiggin, E. & W. „		Tnship.	33	Newcastle, St. Anne	„	Ecl. Dis.	4 537
Newbiggin	Northumberland	Tnship.	948	Newcastle, St. Peter	„	Ecl. Dis.	4 559
Newbiggin (Newburn P.) „		Tnship.	51	Newcastle, Little	Pembroke	Parish	354
Newbiggin ..	Westmoreland	Parish	107	Newcastle ..	Salop	Division	314
Newbold Astbury	Cheshire	Tnship.	741	Newcastle, St. John „		Ecl. Dis.	580
Newbold w. Dunston	Derby	Tnship.	3 283	Newcastle ..	Stafford	L. Sub.	90 477
Newbold w. Dunston	„	Ecl. Dis.	2 362	Newcastle under Lyme	„	District	24 567
Newbold Verdon	Leicester	Parish	708	Newcastle under Lyme	„	Sub-dis.	15 640
Newbold Verdon	„	Tnship.	668	Newcastle under Lyme	„	Parish	12 638
Newbold Pacey..	Warwick	Parish	360	**Newcastle under Lyme** „		Borough	12 938
Newbold Revel..	„	Hamlet	12	Newcastle, St. George	„	Ecl. Dis.	6 807
Newbold upon Avon	„	Parish	1 169	New Catton, Christch.	Norfolk	Ecl. Dis.	2 991
Newbold upon Avon	„	Tnship.	456	New Chapel, St. Jas.	Stafford	Ecl. Dis.	3 440
Newbold, &c. ..	Worcester	Hamlet	498	Newchurch ..	Carmarthen	Parish	782
New Bolingbroke	Lincoln	Ecl. Dis.	947	Newchurch ..	Hants I.W.	Parish	14 008
Newborough ..	Northampton	Parish	806	New Church, St. Peter „ „		Ecl. Dis.	394
Newborough ..	Stafford	Tnship.	788	New Church ..	Kent	Parish	332
Newborough ..	Anglesey	Parish	918	Newchurch ..	Lancaster	Sub-dis.	24 413
Newbottle ..	Durham	Tnship.	2 674	Newchurch, &c..	„	Tnship.	24 413
Newbottle ..	Northampton	Parish	527	**Newchurch** ..	„	Town	3 115
Newbourn ..	Suffolk	Parish	168	Newchurch Kenyon	„	Parish	2 488

Name of Place.	County.	Description.	Population.	Name of Place.	County.	Description.	Population.
Newchurch	Monmouth	Parish	729	Newlands	Cumberland	Chap.	211
Newchurch	Radnor	Parish	132	Newlands	Northumberland	Tnship.	138
New Conduit	Norfolk	Ward	829	Newland Side, &c.	Durham	Tnship.	559
Newdigate	Surrey	Parish	608	Newlyn	Cornwall	Sub-dis.	3 593
Newenden	Kent	Parish	137	Newlyn	,,	Parish	1 641
Newent	Gloucester	L. Sub.	8 930	Newlyn, St. Peter	,,	Ecl. Dis.	3 086
Newent	Gloucester, &c.	District	12 420	New Malton, St. Leond.	York	Parish	2 221
Newent	Glouc. & Heref.	Sub-dis.	6 689	New Malton, St. Michael	,,	Parish	1 566
Newent	Gloucester	Parish	3 182	Newmarket	Cambs	L. Sub.	18 885
Newfield	Durham	Tnship.	1 024	Newmarket	Cambs & Suff.	District	28 675
New Fishbourne	Sussex	Parish	341	Newmarket	,, ,,	Sub-dis.	5 967
New Forest	Hants & Wilts	District	13 509	Newmarket, All Saints	Cambs	Parish	1 259
New Forest	Hants	Union	13 053	Newmarket	Cambs & Suff.	Town	4 069
New Forest	York	Tnship.	53	Newmarket	Flint	Parish	520
New Found Pool	Leicester	Parish	75	Newmarket, St. Mary	Suffolk	Parish	2 002
Newhall	Cheshire	Tnship.	28	Newmill	York	Sub-dis.	6 322
Newhall	,,	Tnship.	826	Newmill, Christch.	,,	Ecl. Dis.	2 803
Newhall	Derby	Ecl. Dis.	2 246	New Mills, St. George	Derby	Ecl. Dis.	4 822
Newham	Northumberland	Tnship.	328	Newminster Abbey	Nrthumbld.	Tnship.	140
Newham (Whalton P.)	,,	Tnship.	48	New Moat	Pembroke	Parish	311
New Hampton	Hereford	Parish	8	Newnham	Gloucester	L. Sub.	19 075
Newhaven	Sussex	Union	5 605	Newnham	,,	Sub-dis.	14 474
Newhaven	,,	Sub-dis.	3 213	Newnham	,,	Parish	1 325
Newhaven	,,	Parish	1 886	Newnham	Hants	Parish	367
Newholm w. Dunsley	York	Tnship.	382	Newnham	Herts	Parish	135
New Houghton	Norfolk	Parish	227	Newnham	Kent	Parish	409
New Hutton	Westmoreland	Tnship.	127	Newnham	Northampton	Parish	514
Newick	Sussex	Parish	991	Newnham Murren	Oxon	Parish	231
Newington	Kent	Parish	854	Newnham Regis	Warwick	Parish	129
Newington by Hythe	,,	Parish	523	Newnton, Long	Wilts	Parish	277
Newington, Stoke	Middlesex	Parish	6 608	Newnton, North	,,	Parish	376
Newington	Oxon	Parish	446	New Parks	Leicester	Parish	52
Newington	,,	Hamlet	403	Newport	Bucks	Hund.	30 226
Newington, North	,,	Tnship.	428	Newport Pagnell	,,	L. Sub.	11 079
Newington, South	,,	Parish	400	Newport Pagnell	,,	District	24 855
Newington	Surrey	L. Sub.	543 997	Newport Pagnell	,,	Sub-dis.	3 823
Newington	,,	District	82 220	Newport Pagnell	,,	Parish	3 823
Newington	,,	Parish	82 220	Newport Pagnell	,,	Town	3 676
1 St. Mary's Ward	,,	Ward	15 082	Newport	Devon	Ecl. Dis.	1 027
2 Trinity Ward	,,	Ward	17 731	Newport	Essex	Sub-dis.	5 040
3 St. Paul's Ward	,,	Ward	15 260	Newport	,,	Parish	886
4 St. Peter's Ward	,,	Ward	34 147	Newport	Hants, I.W.	Sub-dis.	13 761
St. John	,,	Ecl. Dis.	7 426	Newport	,, ,,	Parish	3 819
St. Paul	,,	Ecl. Dis.	11 770	Newport	,, ,,	Borough	7 934
St. Peter	,,	Ecl. Dis.	32 011	Newport	Monmouth	L. Sub.	34 708
Trinity	,,	Ecl. Dis.	17 731	Newport	Mon. & Glam.	District	51 412
Newington-Bagpath	Gloucester	Parish	242	Newport	Monmouth	Sub-dis.	24 756
New Inn	Middlesex	—	30	Newport	,,	Old Bor.	9 060
Newland	Berks	Liberty	339	Newport, St. Paul	,,	Ecl. Dis.	12 879
Newland	Gloucester	Parish	5 147	Newport	,,	Borough	23 249
Newland	,,	Tithing	676	Newport	Pembroke	Sub-dis.	5 566
Newland	Worcester	Chap.	191	Newport	,,	Parish	1 575
Newland	York	Tnship.	301	Newport	Salop & Staff.	District	15 447
Newland w. Woodhouse	,,	Parish	78	Newport	Salop	Sub-dis.	10 478

Name of Place.	County.	Description.	Population.	Name of Place.	County.	Description.	Population.
ewport	Salop	Parish	3 051	Newton Poppleford	Devon	Tithing	661
ewport	,,	Town	2 856	Newton St. Cyres	,,	Parish	1 083
ewport	York	Sub-dis.	4 046	Newton St. Petrock	,,	Parish	231
ewport & Wallingfen	,,	Tnship.	348	Newton Tracey	,,	Parish	136
ew Radford, Christch.	Notts	Ecl. Dis.	5 145	Newton Bewley	Durham	Tnship.	134
ew Radnor	Radnor	Parish	490	Newton Cap	,,	Tnship.	404
ew Radnor	,,	—	463	Newton, Long	,,	Parish	353
ew Radnor	,,	P. Bor.	2 262	Newton Nottage	Glamorgan	Parish	1 082
ew Romney	Kent	Sub-dis.	2 882	Newton Valence	Hants	Parish	340
ew Romney	,,	Parish	1 062	Newton	Hereford	Tnship.	263
ew Seaham	Durham	Ecl. Dis.	2 489	Newton St. John	,,	Ecl. Dis.	263
ewsham	,,	Tnship.	50	Newton	,,	Tnship.	100
ewsham	Northumberland	Tnship.	948	Newton	Lancaster	Sub-dis.	19 311
ewsham	York	Sub-dis.	1 413	Newton	,,	Tnship.	14 907
ewsham	,,	Tnship.	366	Newton Heath, All Saints	,,	Ecl. Dis.	11 241
ewsham w. Breckenbro'	,,	Tnship.	184	Newton in Makerfield	,,	Sub-dis.	9 524
ewsholme	,,	Tnship.	52	Newton in Makerfield	,,	Parish	5 909
ew Shoreham	Sussex	Parish	3 351	Newton in Makerfield	,,	Town	5 909
ew Shoreham	,,	P. Bor.	32 622	Newton St. Peter	,,	Ecl. Dis.	2 122
ew Sleaford	Lincoln	Parish	3 467	Newton w. Scales	,,	Tnship.	286
ew Sleaford	,,	Tnship.	3 325	Newton-Harcourt	Leicester	Tnship.	207
ewstead	,,	Parish	53	Newton	Lincoln	Parish	228
ewstead	Northumberland	Tnship.	116	Newton by Toft	,,	Parish	81
ewstead Priory	Notts	Liberty	108	Newton-le-Wold	,,	Parish	189
ew Swindon	Wilts	Town	4 167	Newton-upon-Trent	,,	Parish	325
ew Swindon, St. Mark	,,	Ecl. Dis.	4 167	Newton, Dixton	Monmouth	Parish	753
ewthorpe	York	Tnship.	88	Newton by Castleacre	Norfolk	Parish	84
ewtimber	Sussex	Parish	162	Newton Flotman	,,	Parish	328
ewton Blossomville	Bucks	Parish	277	Newton St. Faiths	,,	Parish	273
ewton Longville	,,	Parish	547	Newton, West	,,	Parish	268
ewton, Grt. Shelford	Cambs.	Parish	216	Newton	Northampton	Parish	84
ewton, Leverington	,,	Parish	431	Newton Bromshold	,,	Parish	163
ewton	Cheshire	Tnship.	1 657	Newton	Northumberland	Tnship	126
ewton in Mottram	,,	Tnship.	6 440	Newton by Sea	,,	Tnship.	238
ewton	,,	Tnship.	85	Newton Hall	,,	Tnship.	73
ewton	,,	Sub-dis.	7 625	Newton on Moor	,,	Tnship.	291
ewton by Chester	,,	Tnship.	298	Newton Park	,,	Tnship.	18
ewton by Daresbury	,,	Tnship.	191	Newton Underwood	,,	Tnship.	78
ewton by Frodsham	,,	Tnship.	136	Newton, West	,,	Tnship.	95
ewton by Tattenhall	,,	Tnship.	121	Newton Purcell	Oxon	Parish	105
ewton-cum-Larton	,,	Tnship.	62	Newton, North	Pembroke	Parish	56
ewton by Malpas	,,	Tnship.	23	Newton	Somerset	Sub-dis.	2 426
ewton St. Mary	,,	Ecl. Dis.	5 416	Newton, St. Loe	,,	Parish	401
ewton Arlosh	Cumberland	Ecl. Dis.	526	Newton	Stafford	Liberty	139
ewton Regny	,,	Parish	253	Newton by Sudbury	Suffolk	Parish	529
ewton Regny	,,	Tnship.	141	Newton, Old	,,	Parish	718
ewton W. & Allonby	,,	Tnship.	649	Newton & Biggin	Warwick	Tnship.	282
ewton West	,,	Ecl. Dis.	422	Newton Regis	,,	Parish	442
ewton Grange	Derby	Hamlet	51	Newton, South	Wilts	Parish	717
ewton Solney	,,	Parish	406	Newton Toney	,,	Parish	351
ewton-Abbot	Devon	District	59 063	Newton	York	Chap.	243
ewton-Abbot	,,	Sub-dis.	10 467	Newton	,,	Tnship.	394
Newton Abbot	,,	Town	5 221	Newton, East	,,	Tnship.	31
ewton Ferrers	,,	Parish	670	Newton, West	,,	Tnship.	220

Name of Place.	County.	Description.	Population.	Name of Place.	County.	Description.	Population.
Newton, East, &c.	York	Tnship.	84	Norbury	Salop	Tnship.	392
Newton in Cleveland	„	Parish	122	Norbury	Cheshire	Tnship.	1 305
Newton Kyme, &c.	„	Parish	162	Norbury, St. Thomas	„	Ecl. Dis.	994
Newton-le-Willows	„	Tnship.	388	Norbury	Derby	Parish	476
Newton Morrel .	„	Tnship.	33	Norbury	Salop	Sub-dis.	1 636
Newton Mulgrave	„	Tnship.	111	Norbury	„	Parish	412
Newton Out	„	Tnship.	66	Norbury	Stafford	Parish	364
Newton-on-Derwent	„	Tnship.	246	Norbury	„	Tnship.	217
Newton-upon-Ouse	„	Parish	931	Norfolk ..		County	434 798
Newton-upon-Ouse	„	Tnship.	590	Eastern Division		E. Div.	254 027
Newtown	Cumberland	Tnship.	197	Western Division		W. Div.	180 771
Newtown, I.W.	Hants	Borough	99	Norham..	Northumberland	Parish	3 783
Newtown near Newbury	„	Parish	276	Norham..	„	Tnship.	919
New Town, Trinity	„	Ecl. Dis.	635	Norham Mains..	„	Tnship.	117
Newtown, St. Luke	„	Ecl. Dis.	3 348	Norhamshire ..	„	Ward	3 783
New Town Trinity	Herts	Ecl. Dis.	1 543	Norhamshire ..	„	Sub-dis.	3 783
Newtown	Montgomery	Hund.	12 447	Norland, St. James	Middlesex	Ecl. Dis.	7 800
Newtown	„	L. Sub.	12 579	Norland..	York	Tnship.	1 718
Newtown	„	District	21 732	Norley ..	Cheshire	Tnship.	728
Newtown	„	Sub-dis.	6 086	Norley, St. John	„	Ecl. Dis.	728
Newtown	„	Parish	8 692	Normacot	Stafford	Ecl. Dis.	1 097
Newtown	„	P. Bor.	5 916	Normacot	„	Liberty	1 011
Newtown, Chillingham	Nthmld.	Tnship.	104	Normanby	Lincoln	Parish	478
Newtown, Rothbury	„	Tnship.	62	Normanby	„	Hamlet	28
Newtown Linford	Leicester	Parish	500	Normanby-on-Wolds	„	Parish	138
Newtown or St. John's	Sussex	Parish	143	Normanby (Ormseby P.)	York	Tnship.	2 204
New Village	York	Parish	144	Normanby	„	Parish	234
New Winchester	Hants	Union	23 785	Normanby	„	Tnship.	199
New Windsor	Berks	Parish	6 728	Norman Cross	Hunts	Hund	12 324
New Windsor	„	—	6 533	Norman Cross	„	L. Sub.	12 324
New Windsor, Trinity	„	Ecl. Dis.	3 055	Normandy	Surrey	Tithing	409
New Wortley, St. John	York	Ecl. Dis.	7 334	Normanton	Derby	Parish	437
Nibley, North	Gloucester	Parish	1 020	Normanton, South	„	Parish	1 805
Nicholaston	Glamorgan	Parish	109	Normanton Temple	„	Tnship.	130
Nichol Forest	Cumberland	Chap.	1 216	Normanton-le-Heath	Leicester	Chap.	178
Nidd	York	Parish	141	Normanton Turville	„	Tnship.	19
Nidon	Somerset	—	41	Normanton	Lincoln	Parish	172
Ninfield..	Sussex	Parish	587	Normanton upon Soar	Notts	Parish	360
Niton, I.W.	Hants	Parish	700	Normanton upon Trent	„	Parish	402
Nixons ..	Cumberland	Tnship.	161	Normanton on Wolds	„	Tnship.	193
Nobottle Grove	Northampton	Hund.	10 211	Normanton	Rutland	Parish	59
Nocton ..	Lincoln	Parish	537	Normanton	York	Parish	1 923
Noctorum	Cheshire	Tnship.	31	Normanton	„	Tnship.	563
Noddfa ..	Montgomery	Tnship.	680	Northallerton	„	District	12 174
Noke	Oxon	Parish	116	Northallerton	„	Sub-dis.	9 222
Nolton ..	Pembroke	Parish	205	Northallerton	„	Parish	4 980
No Mans Heath	Warwick	Parish	75	Northallerton	„	Tnship.	2 970
No Mans Land..	Cheshire	—	25	Northallerton..	„	P. Bor.	4 755
No Mans Land..	Devon	Parish	67	Northam	Devon	Sub-dis.	4 460
No Mans Land..	Essex	—	6	Northam	„	Parish	3 687
No Mans Land..	Wilts	Parish	149	Northam, Christch.	Hants	Ecl. Dis.	3 246
Nonington	Kent	Parish	896	North Ambersham	Sussex	Tithing	111
Nook	Northumberland	Tnship.	53	Northamptonshire		County	227 704
Norbiton, St. Peter	Surrey	Ecl. Dis.	5 041	Northern Division		N. Div.	104 262

Name of Place.	County.	Description.	Population.	Name of Place.	County.	Description.	Population.
Southern Division	..	S. Div.	123 442	North Curry	Somerset	Sub-dis.	5 999
Northampton	Northampton	L. Sub.	65 148	North Curry	„	Parish	1 839
Northampton	„	District	41 160	North Dalton	York	Parish	486
Northampton	„	Borough	32 813	North Deighton	„	Tnship.	121
St. Andrew	„	Ecl. Dis.	5 601	North Dissington	Northumbld.	Tnship.	76
St. Edmund	„	Ecl. Dis.	6 445	North Duffield	York	Tnship.	470
St. Katharine	„	Ecl. Dis.	2 638	North Eling, St. Mary	Hants	Ecl. Dis.	1 239
North Aston	Oxon	Parish	296	North Elkington	Lincoln	Parish	108
Northaw	Herts	Parish	551	North Elmham	Norfolk	Sub-dis.	4 626
North Aylesford	Kent	District	19 121	North Elmham	„	Parish	1 251
North Baddesley	Hants	Parish	258	North Elmsall	York	Tnship.	236
North Bailey	Durham	Parish	800	Northen	Cheshire	Parish	1 430
North Barrow	Somerset	Parish	114	Northen	„	Tnship.	709
North Barsham	Norfolk	Parish	57	North End, St. Mary	Middlesex	Ecl. Dis.	3 702
North Bedburn	Durham	Tnship.	1 771	North End	Norfolk	Ward	1 324
North Benfleet	Essex	Parish	285	North Fambridge	Essex	Parish	191
North Bierley	York	Union	85 775	North Ferriby	York	Parish	948
North Bierley	„	Sub-dis.	12 500	North Ferriby	„	Tnship.	434
North Bierley	„	Tnship.	12 500	Northfield	Worcester	L. Sub.	23 232
N. Bishop Wearmouth	Durham	Sub-dis.	23 749	Northfield	„	Parish	3 130
Northborough	Northampton	Parish	240	Northfleet	Kent	Sub-dis.	9 600
Northbourne	Kent	Parish	890	Northfleet	„	Parish	5 743
North Bovey	Devon	Parish	513	North Forty-foot-Bank	Lincoln	Parish	300
North Bradley	Wilts	Parish	2 196	North Frodingham	York	Parish	837
North Bradley	„	Tithing	955	North Gosforth	Northumbld.	Tnship.	197
North Brewham	Somerset	Parish	321	North Grimston	York	Parish	181
North Burton	York	Parish	525	North Hamlet	Gloucester	Parish	490
North Bury	Lancaster	Sub-dis.	15 375	North Harborne	Stafford	Ecl. Dis.	5 550
North Cadbury	Somerset	Parish	997	North Hayling	Hants	Parish	262
North Carlton	Lincoln	Parish	163	North Hinckford	Essex	L. Sub.	16 114
North Carlton	Notts	Tnship.	699	North Hinksey	Berks	Parish	438
North Cave	York	Parish	1 281	Northholme	Lincoln	Parish	162
North Cave	„	Tnship.	976	North Holme	York	Tnship.	17
North Cerney	Gloucester	Parish	692	North Horsham	Sussex	Sub-dis.	10 799
North Chapel	Sussex	Parish	785	North Huish	Devon	Parish	432
North Charford	Hants	Parish	70	North Hyckham	Lincoln	Parish	464
North Charlton	Northumberld.	Tnship.	184	Northiam	Sussex	Parish	1 260
North Cheriton	Somerset	Parish	302	Northill	Beds	Parish	1 366
Northchurch	Herts	Parish	1 638	Northill	„	Hamlet	523
North Cleobury	Salop	Parish	168	Northill	Cornwall	Sub-dis.	5 508
North Cliff	York	Tnship	76	Northill	„	Parish	1 263
North Clifton	Notts	Parish	1 110	Northington	Hants	Parish	283
North Clifton	„	Tnship.	269	North Kelsey	Lincoln	Parish	870
North Coates	Lincoln	Parish	290	North Killingholme	„	Tnship.	181
North Cockerington	„	Parish	265	North Kilvington	York	Tnship.	87
North Collingham	Notts & Linc.	Sub-dis.	5 683	North Kilworth	Leicester	Parish	409
North Collingham	Notts	Parish	1 010	North Kyme	Lincoln	Tnship.	455
Northcott	Devon	Hamlet	97	Northleach	Gloucester	L. Sub.	8 115
Northcourt	Berks	Hamlet	290	Northleach	„	District	10 895
North Cove	Suffolk	Parish	200	Northleach	„	Parish	1 404
North Cowton	York	Tnship.	312	Northleach	„	Tnship.	962
North Crawley	Bucks	Parish	981	North Leeds	York	Sub-dis.	41 136
North Cray	Kent	Parish	578	North Leigh	Devon	Parish	253
North Creake	Norfolk	Parish	708	North Leigh	Oxon	Parish	738

Name of Place.	County.	Description.	Population.	Name of Place.	County.	Description.	Population.
North Leverton	Notts	Parish	329	North Rode, St. Michael	Chesh.	Ecl. Dis.	285
Northlew	Devon	Parish	930	North Runcton	Norfolk	Parish	304
North Lincoln	Lincoln	L. Sub.	17 380	North Savernake	Wilts	Parish	108
North Littleton	Worcester	Parish	303	North Scarle	Lincoln	Parish	595
North Lopham	Norfolk	Parish	771	Northsceugh	Cumberland	Tnship.	163
North Luffenham	Rutland	Parish	491	North Seaton	Northumberland	Tnship.	1 262
North Lydbury	Salop	Parish	1 025	North Sheffield	York	Sub-dis.	33 994
North Lynn, St. Edmd.	Norfolk	Parish	62	North Shields	Northumberland	Sub-dis.	17 138
North Marden	Sussex	Parish	28	North Shields	„	Tnship.	9 595
North Marston	Bucks	Parish	644	North Shoebury	Essex	Parish	193
North Meols	Lancaster	Sub-dis.	14 661	North Skirlaugh	York	Tnship.	323
North Meols	„	Parish	15 947	North Somercotes	Lincoln	Parish	1 178
North Meols	„	Tnship.	14 661	N. Stainley w. Sleningfd.	York	Tnship.	445
North Middleton	Nrthumberld.	Tnship.	113	North Stainley, St. Mary	„	Ecl. Dis.	514
North Middleton	„	Tnship.	94	North Stoke	Lincoln	Tnship.	104
North Mimms	Herts	Parish	1 095	North Stoke	Oxon	Parish	177
North Molton	Devon	Parish	1 842	North Stoke	Somerset	Parish	160
Northmoor	Oxon	Parish	364	North Stoke	Sussex	Parish	58
Northmoor Green	Somerset	Ecl. Dis.	760	North Stoneham	Hants	Parish	963
North Moreton	Berks	Parish	352	Northstow	Cambs	Hund.	4 925
North Mundham	Sussex	Parish	426	North Sunderland	Nrthumbld.	Tnship.	1 008
North Muskham	Notts	Parish	848	North Sunderland	„	Ecl. Dis.	1 178
North Muskham	„	Tnship.	614	North Tamerton	Cornwall	Parish	486
North Myton	York	Ward	15 485	N. Tawton & Winkleigh	Devon	Hund.	12 666
North Narberth	Pembroke	Division	1 717	North Tawton	„	Sub-dis.	4 322
North Newbald	York	Tnship.	699	North Tawton	„	Parish	1 849
North Newington	Oxon	Hamlet	428	North Thoresby	Lincoln	Parish	824
North Newnton	Wilts	Parish	376	North Thurmaston	Leicester	Tnship.	209
North Newton	Pembroke	Parish	56	North Tidworth	Wilts	Parish	345
North Nibley	Gloucester	Parish	1 020	North Tuddenham	Norfolk	Parish	437
North Ockendon	Essex	Parish	341	Northumberland		County	343 025
Northolt	Middlesex	Parish	658	Northern Division		N. Div.	93 041
Northop	Flint	Parish	3 657	Southern Division		S. Div.	249 984
Northop	„	Tnship.	753	North Walsham	Norfolk	Sub-dis.	6 942
North Ormsby	Lincoln	Parish	155	North Walsham	„	Parish	2 896
Northorpe	„	Parish	194	North Walsham	„	Town	2 896
North Otterington	York	Parish	630	North Waltham	Hants	Parish	484
North Otterington	„	Tnship.	66	North Leeds	York	Ward	14 554
Northover	Somerset	Parish	122	North East Leeds	„	Ward	26 582
North Owersby	Lincoln	Parish	421	North West Leeds	„	Ward	16 561
Northowram	York	Sub-dis.	19 240	North Weald	Essex	Parish	1 842
Northowram	„	Tnship.	16 178	North Wheatley	Notts	Parish	711
North Perrott	Somerset	Parish	374	Northwich	Cheshire	Hund.	47 268
North Petherton	„	Sub-dis.	5 305	Northwich	„	L. Sub.	47 208
North Petherton	„	Parish	3 943	Northwich	„	District	33 338
North Petherwin	Devon & Corn.	Sub-dis.	2 269	Northwich	„	Sub-dis.	12 941
North Petherwin	Devon	Parish	945	Northwich	„	Tnship.	1 190
North Pickenham	Norfolk	Parish	287	Northwick & Redwick	Glouc.	Tithing	267
North Piddle	Worcester	Parish	131	North Widcombe	Somerset	Tithing	101
North Poorton	Dorset	Parish	92	North Willingham	Lincoln	Parish	203
North Rauceby	Lincoln	Parish	279	North Wingfield	Derby	Parish	7 339
North Repps	Norfolk	Parish	625	North Wingfield	„	Tnship.	785
North Reston	Lincoln	Parish	44	N. Div. of Witchford	Cambs	L. Sub.	14 791
North Rode	Cheshire	Tnship.	285	North Witchford	„	District	14 791

Name of Place.	County.	Description.	Population.	Name of Place.	County.	Description.	Population.
rth Witham ..	Lincoln, ..	Parish	278	Norton-le-Clay ..	York ..	Tnship.	14 ᵇ
rth Witham ..	,, ..	Tnship.	216	Norwell ..	Notts ..	Parish	1 020
rthwold ..	Norfolk ..	Parish	1 370	Norwell ..	,, ..	Tnship.	601
rth Wood ..	Essex ..	Parish	12	Norwell Woodhouse ,,		Tnship.	135
rthwood ..	Hants, I. W.	Parish	6 534	Norwich ..	..	Diocese	667 704
rthwood	Mddlx. & Herts.	Ecl. Dis.	451	Norwich ..	Norfolk ..	L. Sub.	74 891
rthwood ..	Stafford ..	Ecl. Dis.	6 099	Norwich ..	,, ..	District	74 440
rth Wootton .	Dorset ..	Parish	76	Norwich ℞ ..	,, ..	City	74 891
rth Wootton .	Norfolk ..	Parish	247	Norwood ..	Middlesex ..	Precinct	4 484
rth Wootton .	Somerset ..	Parish	322	Norwood ..	Surrey ..	Sub-dis.	7 462
rth Worcester	Worcester ..	Sub-dis.	10 725	Norwood, All Saints ,,		Ecl. Dis.	4 060
rth Wraxhall .	Wilts ..	Parish	466	Norwood, St. Luke ,,		Ecl. Dis.	7 098
rton ..	Cheshire ..	Tnship.	380	Norwood S., St.Mark ,,		Ecl. Dis.	1 489
rton ..	Derby ..	Sub-dis.	2 440	Noseley ..	Leicester ..	Parish	48
rton ..	,, ..	Parish	2 318	Notgrove ..	Gloucester ..	Parish	162
rton ..	Durham ..	Parish	2 317	Nottinghamshire ..	..	County	293 867
rton-Mandeville	Essex ..	Parish	129	Northern Division ..	..	N. Div.	210 909
rton ..	Gloucester ..	Parish	458	Southern Division ..	..	S. Div.	82 958
rton Canon ..	Hereford	Parish	334	Nottingham ..	Notts .	L. Sub.	97 572
rton w. Brockhmptn.	,,	Tnship.	623	Nottingham ..	,, ..	District	75 765
rton ..	Herts ..	Parish	352	Nottingham ..	,, ..	Union	74 693
rton ..	Kent ..	Parish	124	Nottingham ..	,, ■ ..	Borough	74 693
rton, East ..	Leicester ..	P. Chap.	139	St. John Baptist	,, ..	Ecl. Dis.	5 892
rton by Twycross	,, ..	Parish	451	St. Mark ..	,, ..	Ecl. Dis.	12 119
rton by Twycross	,, ..	Tnship.	335	St. Matthew ..	,, ..	Ecl. Dis.	5 455
rton Disney ..	Lincoln ..	Parish	196	St. Paul ..	,, ..	Ecl. Dis.	6 817
rton-Folgate..	Middlesex ..	Liberty	1 873	Trinity ..	,, ..	Ecl. Dis.	9 239
rton-Subcourse	Norfolk ..	Parish	376	Notting Hill, St. John	Middlesex	Ecl. Dis.	15 662
rton ..	Northampton	Parish	480	,, St.Peter	,,	Ecl. Dis.	6 660
rton ..	Notts ..	Tnship.	320	Notton ..	York ..	Tnship.	286
rton-Cuckney	,, ..	Parish	1 454	Nowhere ..	Norfolk ..	—	16
rton, Over ..	Oxon ..	Hamlet	373	Nowhere House .	Suffolk ..	—	2
rton ..	Radnor ..	Parish	313	Nowton ..	,, ..	Parish	186
rton in Hales	Salop ..	Parish	309	Nuffield ..	Oxon ..	Parish	259
rton-Ferris ..	Somerset ..	Hund.	5 441	Nunburnholme..	York ..	Parish	281
rton-Fitzwarren	,, ..	Parish	634	Nunburnholme..	,, ..	Tnship.	248
rton-Hawkfield	,, ..	Ville	42	Nuneaton ..	Warwick ..	District	13 054
rton-Malreward	,, ..	Parish	108	Nuneaton ..	,, ..	Sub-dis.	13 054
rton St. Philip	,, ..	Parish	672	Nuneaton ..	,, ..	Parish	7 666
rton un. Hambdon	,, ..	Parish	467	Nuneaton ..	,, ..	Town	4 645
rton ..	Stafford ..	Sub-dis.	5 634	Nuneham-Courtney	Oxon ..	Sub-dis.	3 500
rton in Moors	,, ..	Parish	4 393	Nuneham-Courtney	,, ..	Parish	314
rton in Moors	,, ..	Tnship.	4 135	Nunkeeling w. Bewholme	York	Parish	271
rton und. Cannock	,, ..	Parish	1 628	Nun-Monkton ..	.. ,,	Parish	323
rton ..	Suffolk ..	Parish	948	Nunney ..	Somerset ..	Sub-dis.	4 589
rton-Lindsey .	Warwick ..	Parish	157	Nunney ..	,, ..	Parish	1 088
rton Bavant..	Wilts ..	Parish	261	Nunnington ..	York ..	Parish	423
rton-Coleparle	,, ..	Parish	112	Nunny-Kirk	Northumberland	Tnship.	31
rton ..	Worcester ..	Parish	396	Nunriding ..	,,	Tnship.	25
rton by Bredon	,, ..	Hamlet	243	Nunthorpe ..	York ..	Tnship.	160
rton by Kempsey	,, ..	Parish	661	Nunton w. Bodenham	Wilts ..	Parish	282
rton ..	York ..	Parish	2 983	Nunwick w.Howgrave	York ..	Tnship.	41
rton ..	,, ..	Tnship.	633	Nursling ..	Hants ..	Parish	947
rton-Conyers .	,, ..	Tnship.	97	Nursted..	Kent ..	Parish	57

Name of Place.	County.	Description.	Population.	Name of Place.	County.	Description.	Population.
Nutfield..	Surrey	Parish	997	Ockendon, North	Essex	Parish	341
Nuthall..	Notts	Parish	842	Ockendon, South	„	Parish	1 267
Nuthampstead..	Herts	Hamlet	281	Ockham..	Surrey	Parish	682
Nuthurst..	Sussex	Parish	767	Ocker Hill	Stafford	Ecl. Dis.	3 787
Nuthurst..	Warwick	Hamlet	117	Ockley ..	Surrey	Parish	683
Nutley ..	Hants	Parish	141	Ocle-Pitchard..	Hereford	Parish	299
Nutley, St. James	Sussex	Ecl. Dis.	731	Odcombe	Somerset	Parish	652
Nyland ..	Somerset	Parish	40	Oddingley	Worcester	Parish	202
Nymet-Rowland	Devon	Parish	111	Oddington	Gloucester	Parish	588
Nymet-Tracey ..	„	Parish	904	Oddington	Oxon	Parish	169
Nymphsfield ..	Gloucester	Parish	373	Odd-Rode	Cheshire	Tnship.	2 503
Nympton, Bishops	Devon	Parish	1 198	Odd-Rode	„	Ecl. Dis.	2 476
Nympton, St. George	„	Parish	258	Odell ..	Beds	Parish	494
Nympton, Kings	„	Parish	697	Odiham..	Hants	Division	36 838
Nynehead ..	Somerset	Parish	321	Odiham..	„	L. Sub.	36 838
				Odiham..	„	Sub-dis.	6 515
Oadby ..	Leicester	Parish	1 254	Odiham..	„	Parish	2 833
Oake ..	Somerset	Parish	155	Odsey ..	Herts	Hund.	8 174
Oaken ..	Stafford	Tnship.	314	Odstock..	Wilts	Parish	184
Oakengates, Trinity	Salop	Ecl. Dis.	1 821	Odstone..	Berks	Tithing	32
Oakes, Holy ..	Leicester	Liberty	9	Odstone..	Leicester	Hamlet	184
Oakfield, St. John	Hants, I. W.	Ecl. Dis.	1 547	Offchurch	Warwick	Parish	304
Oakford..	Devon	Parish	629	Offcote & Underwood	Derby	Liberty	506
Oakham Soke ..	Rutland	Hund.	4 990	Offenham	Worcester	Parish	461
Oakham	Rutld. & Leic.	District	11 112	Offerton..	Cheshire	Tnship.	297
Oakham	Rutland	Parish	2 959	Offerton..	Derby	Hamlet	21
Oakham ..	„	Town	2 948	Offerton..	Durham	Tnship.	172
Oakham-Deanshold	„	Manor	689	Offham ..	Kent	Parish	411
Oakham-Lordshold	„	Manor	2 091	Offley ..	Herts	Parish	1 215
Oakington	Cambs	Parish	592	Offley, High ..	Stafford	Parish	883
Oakington	„	Hamlet	514	Offlow ..	„	Hund.	214 246
Oakley ..	Beds	Parish	443	Offord-Cluney ..	Hunts	Parish	326
Oakley ..	Bucks	Parish	420	Offord-Darcy ..	„	Parish	437
Oakley, Great ..	Essex	Parish	1 038	Offton ..	Suffolk	Parish	394
Oakley, Little ..	„	Parish	306	Offwell ..	Devon	Parish	393
Oakley, Great ..	Northampton	Parish	195	Ogbourne, St. Andrew	Wilts	Parish	518
Oakley, Little ..	„	Parish	127	Ogbourne, St. George	„	Parish	534
Oakley, Tamworth	Stafford	Tnship.	28	Ogle ..	Northumberland	Tnship.	117
Oakley, Moreton Say	„	Tnship.	79	Ogley Hay ..	Stafford	Parish	1 357
Oakley ..	Suffolk	Parish	332	Ogley Hay, St. James	„	Ecl. Dis.	2 490
Oakmere ..	Cheshire	Tnship.	284	Ogmore..	Glamorgan	Hund.	4 176
Oakridge, St. Barthol.	Glouc.	Ecl. Dis.	875	Ogwell, East ..	Devon	Parish	275
Oaks Ch. Charnwood	Leicester	Ecl. Dis.	702	Ogwell, West ..	„	Parish	51
Oaksey ..	Wilts	Parish	450	Okeford-Fitzpaine	Dorset	Parish	685
Oakthorpe ..	Derby	Hamlet	654	Okehampton ..	Devon	District	18 580
Oakworth ..	York	Ecl. Dis.	1 979	Okehampton ..	„	Sub-dis.	5 026
Oare ..	Kent	Parish	217	Okehampton ..	„	Parish	1 929
Oare ..	Somerset	Parish	60	Okeover..	Stafford	Parish	61
Oborne ..	Dorset	Parish	150	Okewood, St. John	Surrey	Ecl. Dis.	703
Oby ..	Norfolk	Parish	80	Old ..	Northampton	Parish	472
Occlestone	Cheshire	Tnship.	110	Old Accrington .	Lancaster	Tnship.	5 835
Occold ..	Suffolk	Parish	570	Old Alresford ..	Hants	Parish	526
Ock ..	Berks	Hund.	7 198	Old Artillery Ground	Middlsx.	Liberty	2 168
Ockbrook ..	Derby	Parish	1 506	Oldberrow	Worcester	Parish	53

Name of Place.	County.	Description.	Population.	Name of Place.	County.	Description.	Population.
l Bewick	Northumberland	Tnship.	204	Old Street, St. Mark	Middlesex	Ecl. Dis.	5 479
l Brentford ..	Middlesex ..	Chap.	6 748	Oldswinford	Worc. & Staff.	Parish	22 958
l Brentford ..	,, ..	Ecl. Dis.	6 720	Old Tower Without	Middlesex	Precinct	626
l Buckenham	Norfolk ..	Parish	1 214	Old Trafford ..	Lancaster ..	Ecl. Dis.	2 184
lbury on Hill	Gloucester..	Parish	440	Old Warden ..	Beds ..	Parish	597
lbury on Severn	,, ..	Tithing	707	Old Warren House	Berks ..	—	10
lbury ..	Salop ..	Parish	207	Old Weston ..	Hunts ..	Parish	426
lbury ..	Warwick ..	Hamlet	47	Oldwick.. ..	Bucks ..	Parish	3
lbury ..	Worcester ..	Sub-dis.	17 258	Old Windsor ..	Berks ..	Parish	1 835
lbury ..	,, ..	Tnship.	15 703	Old Withington	Cheshire ..	Tnship.	169
lbury ..	,, ..	Town	15 615	Old Wood, St. Mich.	Wor. & Hfd.	Ecl. Dis.	561
lbury ..	,, ..	Ecl. Dis.	9 780	Ollerton.. ..	Cheshire ..	Tnship.	272
d Byland ..	York ..	Parish	157	Ollerton.. ..	Notts ..	Tnship.	932
dcastle ..	Cheshire ..	Tnship.	100	Ollerton.. ..	Salop ..	Tnship.	166
d Castle ..	Kent ..	Parish	42	Olney	Bucks ..	L. Sub.	6 159
dcastle ..	Monmouth ..	Parish	60	Olney	,, ..	Sub-dis.	10 579
d Castle ..	Wilts ..	Parish	7	Olney	,, ..	Parish	2 347
d Cleeve ..	Somerset ..	Parish	1 529	Olney	,, ..	—	2 273
dcott	Stafford ..	Tnship.	2 238	Olney	,, ..	Town	2 258
d Ford, St. Stephen	Middlesex	Ecl. Dis.	7 158	Olney Park Farm	,, ..	Parish	11
ldham.. ..	Lancaster ..	District	111 276	Olveston ..	Gloucester ..	Parish	1 699
ldham above Town	,, ..	Sub-dis.	30 563	Ombersley ..	Worcester ..	Sub-dis.	5 181
ldham below Town	,, ..	Sub-dis.	41 770	Ombersley ..	,, ..	Parish	2 463
ldham.. ..	,, ..	Tuship.	72 333	Ompton.. ..	Notts ..	Tnship	110
ldham ..	,,	M. Bor.	72 333	Onecot ..	Stafford ..	Tnship.	463
ldham ..	,,	P. Bor.	94 344	Onehouse ..	Suffolk ..	Parish	336
ldham, St. James	,, ..	Ecl.Dis.	17 520	Ongar ..	Essex ..	Hund.	16 393
ldham, St. Mary	,, ..	Ecl. Dis.	16 576	Ongar	,, ..	L. Sub.	10 982
ldham, St. Peter	,, ..	Ecl. Dis.	7 094	Ongar	,, ..	District	11 317
ldham Road, St. Peter	,, ..	Ecl. Dis.	11 128	Ongar, Chipping	,, ..	Parish	867
ld Hurst ..	Hunts ..	Parish	174	Ongar, High ..	,, ..	Parish	1 177
ld Hutton, &c.	Westmoreland	Tnship.	406	Onibury ..	Salop ..	Parish	375
ldland.. ..	Gloucester ..	Sub-dis.	10 091	Onneley.. ..	Stafford ..	Tnship.	215
ldland.. ..	,, ..	Hamlet	5 869	Onston ...	Cheshire ...	Tnship.	98
ldland.. ..	,, ..	Ecl. Dis.	1 618	Openshaw ..	Lancaster ..	Tnship.	8 623
ld Laund Booth	Lancaster ..	Tnship.	423	Openshaw, St. Barnab.	,, ..	Ecl. Dis.	8 623
ld Malton ..	York ..	Parish	1 302	Orby ..	Lincoln ..	Parish	357
ldmoor	Northumberland	Tnship.	69	Orchard, East ..	Dorset ..	Parish	227
ld Newton ..	Suffolk ..	Parish	718	Orchard, West..	,, ..	Parish	103
ld Park ..	Durham ..	Tnship.	23	Orchardleigh ..	Somerset ..	Parish	34
ld Radnor	Radn. & Heref.	Parish	1 349	Orchard Portman	,, ..	Parish	66
ld Radnor and Burlingjobb	} Radnor ..	Tnship.	350	Orcheston ..	Wilts ..	Sub-dis.	2 454
				Orcheston St. George	,, ..	Parish	236
ld Romney ..	Kent ..	Parish	151	Orcheston St. Mary	,, ..	Parish	177
ld St. Pancras	Middlesex ..	Ecl. Dis.	11 161	Orcop ..	Hereford ..	Parish	583
ld Sarum ..	Wilts ..	Parish	7	Ord ..	Northumberland	Tnship.	762
ld Shoreham ..	Sussex ..	Parish	282	Ordsall ..	Notts ..	Parish	1 911
ld Sleaford ..	Lincoln ..	Parish	372	Ore ..	Sussex ..	Sub-dis.	3 188
ld Sodbury ...	Gloucester ..	Parish	809	Ore	,, ..	Parish	1 636
ldstead ..	York ..	Tnship.	113	Orell & Ford ..	Lancaster ..	Tnship.	358
ld Stratford ..	Warw. & Glo.	Sub-dis.	5 931	Orford ..	Suffolk ..	Sub-dis.	3 281
ld Stratford ..	Warwick ..	Parish	6 823	Orford ..	,, ..	Parish	948
ld Stratford ..	,,	Tnship.	2 995	Orgarswick ..	Kent ..	Parish	10
ld Street ..	Middlesex ..	Sub-Dis.	11 504	Orgreave ..	Stafford ..	Tnship.	175

Name of Place.	County.	Description.	Population.	Name of Place.	County.	Description.	Population.
Orgreave	York	Tnship.	72	Ossett w. Gawthorpe	York	Tnship.	7 950
Orlestone	Kent	Parish	390	Ossett w. Gawthorpe	,,	Ecl. Dis.	4 932
Orleton	Hereford	Parish	600	Ossett, South	York	Ecl. Dis.	3 018
Orleton	Worcester	Chap.	99	Ossington	Notts	Parish	231
Orlingbury	Northampton	Hund.	6 629	Ossulstone	Middlesex	Hund.	1963630
Orlingbury	,,	Parish	307	Oswaldkirk	York	Sub-dis.	2 124
Ormesby, St. Margaret	Norfolk	Parish	777	Oswaldkirk	,,	Parish	524
Ormesby, St. Michael	,,	Parish	311	Oswaldkirk	,,	Tnship	219
Ormesby	York	Parish	6 299	Oswaldslow	Worcester	Hund.	41 442
Ormesby	,,	Tnship.	1 105	Oswaldtwisle	Lancaster	Sub-dis.	12 454
Ormsby, North	Lincoln	Parish	155	Oswaldtwisle	,,	Tnship.	7 701
Ormsby, South	,,	Parish	261	Oswaldtwisle	,,	Ecl. Dis.	6 103
Ormside	Westmoreland	Parish	188	Oswestry	Salop	Hund.	15 192
Ormskirk	Lancaster	L. Sub.	42 319	Oswestry Hundred	,,	L. Sub.	15 192
Ormskirk	,,	District	46 252	Oswestry Town	,,	L. Sub.	5 414
Ormskirk	,,	Sub-dis.	6 426	Oswestry	Salop & Denb.	District	23 817
Ormskirk	,,	Parish	17 049	Oswestry	Salop	Sub-dis.	9 357
Ormskirk	,,	Tnship.	6 426	Oswestry	,,	Parish	9 357
Ormskirk	,,	Town	6 426	Oswestry rural part	,,	—	3 943
Orpington	Kent	Parish	1 727	**Oswestry**	,,	M. Bor.	5 414
Orrell	Lancaster	Tnship.	2 932	Oswestry, Trinity	,,	Ecl. Dis.	2 683
Orsett	Essex	L. Sub.	11 601	Otford	Kent	Parish	804
Orsett	,,	District	11 595	Otham	,,	Parish	294
Orsett	,,	Sub-dis.	5 234	Othery	Somerset	Parish	698
Orsett	,,	Parish	1 531	Otley	Suffolk	Parish	615
Orston	Notts	Parish	424	Otley	York	District	18 669
Orton	Cumberland	Parish	468	Otley	,,	Sub-dis.	15 907
Orton Longville	Hunts	Parish	311	Otley	,,	Parish	13 040
Orton Waterville	,,	Parish	299	Otley	,,	Tnship.	4 714
Orton on Hill	Leicester	Parish	334	**Otley**	,,	Town	4 458
Orton	Northampton	Chap.	69	Otterbourne	Hants	Parish	573
Orton	Westmoreland	Sub-dis.	3 319	Otterburn Ward	Northumberld.	Tnship.	378
Orton	,,	Parish	1 615	Otterburn	York	Tnship.	59
Orwell	Cambs	Parish	645	Otterden	Kent	Parish	194
Osbaldeston	Lancaster	Tnship.	238	Otterford	Somerset	Parish	476
Osbaldwick	York	Parish	342	Otterham	Cornwall	Parish	160
Osbaldwick	,,	Tnship.	188	Otterhampton	Somerset	Parish	235
Osbaston	Leicester	Tnship.	228	Otterington, North	York	Parish	630
Osbournby	Lincoln	Parish	613	Otterington, North	,,	Tnship.	66
Osgathorpe	Leicester	Parish	351	Otterington, South	,,	Parish	353
Osgodby	Lincoln	Tnship.	71	Otterton	Devon	Parish	1 140
Osgodby	York	Tnship.	225	Ottery, St. Mary	,,	Hund.	4 340
Osgodby (Cayton P.)	,,	Tnship.	77	Ottery	,,	L. Sub.	12 963
Osgoldcross	,,	Wapen.	37 031	Ottery St. Mary	,,	Sub-dis.	11 946
Osgoldcross	,,	L. Sub.	42 377	Ottery St. Mary	,,	Parish	4 340
Osleston, &c.	Derby	Tnship.	350	**Ottery St. Mary**	,,	Town	2 429
Osmaston by Derby	,,	Parish	152	Ottery Venn	,,	Parish	101
Osmaston	,,	Parish	289	Ottringham	York	Parish	644
Osmington	Dorset	Parish	448	Oughterby	Cumberland	Tnship.	120
Osmotherley	Lancaster	Tnship.	419	Oughterside, &c.	,,	Tnship.	705
Osmotherley	York	Parish	1 320	Oulston	York	Tnship.	214
Osmotherley	,,	Tnship.	995	Oulton, Low	Cheshire	Tnship.	53
Ospringe	Kent	Parish	1 111	Oulton	Cumberland	Tnship.	416
Ossett	York	Sub-dis.	7 950	Oulton	Norfolk	Parish	357

Name of Place.	County.	Description.	Population.	Name of Place.	County.	Description.	Population.
ulton	Suffolk ..	Parish	747	Overs	Salop ..	Hund.	2 615
ulton	York ..	Sub-dis.	3 879	Overs	,, ..	L. Sub.	2 615
ulton w. Woodlesford	,, ..	Tnship.	1 851	Over Silton ..	York ..	Parish	255
undle	Northampton	L. Sub.	15 377	Over Silton ..	,, ..	Tnship.	94
undle ..	Nrthptn. & Hunts	District	15 463	Oversley ..	Warwick ..	Hamlet	295
undle ..	,, ,,	Sub-dis.	6 669	Over Stavely ..	Westmoreland	Tnship.	705
undle	Northampton	Parish	3 217	Overstone ..	Northampton	Parish	206
undle	,, ..	Tnship.	3 040	Over Stowey ..	Somerset ..	Parish	613
undle.. ..	,, ..	Town	2 450	Overstrand ..	Norfolk ..	Parish	251
usby	Cumberland	Parish	294	Over Tabley, St. Paul	Cheshire	Ecl. Dis.	792
usden	Suffolk ..	Parish	346	Overton.. ..	,,	Tnship.	107
use & Derwent	York ..	Wapen.	11 844	Overton.. ..	Flint ..	Sub-dis.	1 779
use & Derwent	,, ..	L. Sub.	11 844	Overton.. ..	,, ..	Parish	1 397
useburn, Great	,, ..	District	11 534	Overton ..	,, ..	P. Boro.	1 397
useburn, Great	,, ..	Parish	655	Overton.. ..	Hants ..	Parish	1 460
useburn, Great	,, ..	Tnship.	599	Overton & Sunderland	Lanc..	Tnship.	305
useburn, Little	,, ..	Parish	543	Overton, Cold ..	Leicester ..	Parish	97
useburn, Little	,, ..	Tnship.	281	Overton, Market	Rutland ..	Parish	429
usefleet ..	,, ..	Tnship.	233	Overton.. ..	Wilts ..	Parish	910
uston	Durham ..	Tnship.	320	Overton Heath..	,, ..	Parish	19
uston	Leicester ..	Parish	169	Overton, West..	,, ..	Tnship.	429
uston ..	Northumberland	Tnship.	23	Overton.. ..	York ..	Parish	763
utchester ..	,, ..	Tnship.	116	Overton.. ..	,, ..	Tnship.	68
ut-Newton ..	York ..	Tnship.	66	Over Wallop ..	Hants ..	Parish	508
ut-Rawcliffe ..	Lancaster ..	Tnship.	771	Over Whitacre..	Warwick ..	Parish	285
ut-Rawcliffe ..	,, ..	Ecl. Dis.	771	Over Whitley ..	Cheshire ..	Tnship.	367
utseats ..	Derby ..	Tnship.	251	Over Worton ..	Oxon ..	Parish	82
utwell..	Norf. & Cambs	Parish	1 265	Over Wyersdale.	Lancaster ..	Tnship.	524
utwood ..	York ..	Ecl. Dis.	2 335	Oving ..	Bucks ..	Parish	436
venden ..	,, ..	Sub-dis.	11 067	Oving ..	Sussex ..	Parish	949
venden ..	,, ..	Tnship.	11 067	Ovingdean ..	,, ..	Parish	121
venden, St. John	,, ..	Ecl. Dis.	2 171	Ovingham	Northumberland	Parish	5 014
ver	Cambs ..	Parish	1 146	Ovingham ..	,, ..	Tnship.	277
ver	Cheshire ..	Sub-dis.	8 304	Ovington ..	Essex ..	Parish	145
ver	,, ..	Parish	3 454	Ovington ..	Hants ..	Parish	152
ver	,, ..	Tnship.	3 774	Ovington ..	Norfolk ..	Parish	291
ver	Gloucester ..	Hamlet	144	Ovington	Northumberland	Tnship.	420
ver	,, ..	Tithing	74	Ovington ..	York ..	Tnship.	142
ver Alderley ..	Cheshire ..	Tnship.	421	Owermoigne ..	Dorset ..	Parish	420
verbury	Worc. & Glouc.	Sub-dis.	2 970	Owersby, North.	Lincoln ..	Parish	421
verbury ..	,, ,,	Parish	925	Owersby, South.	,, ..	Parish	76
verbury ..	Worcester ..	Tnship.	483	Owlpen.. ..	Gloucester ..	Parish	91
verchurch ..	Cheshire ..	Parish	293	Owmby.. ..	Lincoln ..	Parish	314
ver Compton ..	Dorset ..	Parish	150	Owram, North ..	York ..	Tnship.	16 178
ver Darwen ..	Lancaster ..	Tnship.	16 492	Owram, South ..	,, ..	Tnship.	7 245
ver Darwen..	,, ..	Town	14 327	Owslebury ..	Hants ..	Parish	843
ver Darwen, Trinity	,, ..	Ecl. Dis.	14 101	Owsthorpe ..	York ..	Tnship.	17
ver Darwen, St. James	,, ..	Ecl. Dis.	4 045	Owston	Lincoln ..	Sub-dis.	4 649
ver Dinsdale ..	York ..	Tnship.	82	Owston	,, ..	Parish	2 520
ver Haddon ..	Derby ..	Tnship.	245	Owston	,, ..	Tnship.	1 585
ver Hulton ..	Lancaster ..	Tnship.	447	Owston	York ..	Parish	454
ver Kellet ..	,, ..	Tnship.	425	Owston	,, ..	Tnship.	269
ver Norton ..	Oxon ..	Hamlet	373	Owstwick ..	,, ..	Tnship.	99
ver Pool ..	Cheshire ..	Tnship.	88	Owthorne ..	,, ..	Parish	704

Name of Place.	County.	Description.	Population.	Name of Place.	County.	Description.	Population.
Owthorne	York	Tnship.	424	Paddock, All Saints	York	Ecl. Dis.	3 940
Owthorpe	Notts	Parish	112	Padfield	Derby	Tnship.	1 619
Oxborough	Norfolk	Parish	225	Padgate, Christch.	Lancaster	Ecl. Dis.	1 510
Oxcombe	Lincoln	Parish	27	Padiham	,,	Sub-dis.	9 906
Oxendon, Great	Northampton	Parish	238	Padiham	,,	Tnship.	5 911
Oxenhall	Gloucester	Parish	272	**Padiham**	,,	Town	5 675
Oxenhope	York	Ecl. Dis.	2 880	Padley Nether	Derby	Hamlet	40
Oxenton	Gloucester	Parish	136	Padstow	Cornwall	Sub-dis.	6 649
Oxford		Diocese	515 083	Padstow	,,	Parish	2 489
Oxfordshire		County	170 944	Padworth	Berks	Parish	298
Oxford	Oxon	L. Sub.	48 093	Pagham	Sussex	Parish	988
Oxford	Oxon & Berks	District	20 037	Paglesham	Essex	Parish	474
Oxford	,, ,,	City	27 560	Paignton	Devon	L. Sub.	32 459
Oxford, St. Paul	Oxon	Ecl. Dis.	2 915	Paignton	,,	Sub-dis.	4 266
Oxford, Trinity	,,	Ecl. Dis.	2 609	Paignton	,,	Parish	3 090
Oxhey	Herts	Hamlet	733	**Paignton**	,,	Town	2 628
Oxhill	Warwick	Parish	373	Pailton	Warwick	Hamlet	704
Oxnead	Norfolk	Parish	57	Painscastle	Radnor	Hund.	3 587
Oxney	Kent	Parish	12	Painscastle	,,	L. Sub.	3 587
Oxon & Shelton	Salop	Ecl. Dis.	430	Painswick	Gloucester	Sub-dis.	4 334
Oxspring	York	Tnship.	346	Painswick	,,	Parish	3 229
Oxted	Surrey	Parish	1 074	Pakefield	Suffolk	Parish	768
Oxton	Cheshire	Tnship.	2 670	Pakenham	,,	Parish	1 130
Oxton, St. Saviour	,,	Ecl. Dis.	2 945	Palace	Sussex	Sub-dis.	21 948
Oxton	Notts	Parish	738	Palgrave	Suffolk	Parish	739
Oxton	York	Tnship.	71	Palling by Sea	Norfolk	Parish	442
Oxwich	Glamorgan	Parish	328	Pamber	Hants	Parish	677
Oxwick	Norfolk	Parish	66	Pampisford	Cambs	Parish	347
Oystermouth	Glamorgan	Parish	2 460	Pancras	Middlesex	District	198 788
Ozleworth	Gloucester	Parish	130	Pancras, All Saints	,,	Ecl. Dis.	6 780
				Pancras, Christch.	,,	Ecl. Dis.	9 867
Packington	Leic. & Derby	Parish	1 190	Pancras, Old	,,	Ecl. Dis.	11 161
Packington	,, ,,	Tnship.	595	Pancras, St. Anne	,,	Ecl. Dis.	491
Packington, Great	Warwick	Parish	336	Pancras, St. Barthol.	,,	Ecl. Dis.	5 318
Packington, Little	,,	Parish	124	Pancras, St. John	,,	Ecl. Dis.	17 779
Packwood	,,	Parish	292	Pancras, St. Mark	,,	Ecl. Dis.	6 986
Padbury	Bucks	Parish	550	Pancras, St. Mary	,,	Ecl. Dis.	5 116
Paddington	Lancaster	Ecl. Dis.	6 488	Pancrasweek	Devon	Parish	378
Paddington	Middlesex	L. Sub.	75 784	Panfield	Essex	Parish	308
Paddington, St. John	,,	Sub-dis.	36 769	Pangbourn	Berks	Parish	753
Paddington, St. Mary	,,	Sub-dis.	39 015	Pannal	York	Parish	1 587
Paddington	,,	Parish	75 784	Panteague	Monmouth	Parish	2 823
Ward No. 1	,,	Ward	17 120	Panton	Lincoln	Parish	172
Ward No. 2	,,	Ward	26 254	Panxworth	Norfolk	Parish	121
Ward No. 3	,,	Ward	15 707	Papcastle	Cumberland	Tnship.	736
Ward No. 4	,,	Ward	16 703	Paperhaugh	Northumberland	Tnship.	69
Paddington, All Saints	,,	Ecl. Dis.	6 337	Papplewick	Notts	Parish	270
Paddington, Christch.	,,	Ecl. Dis.	4 019	Papworth	Cambs	Hund.	6 670
Paddington, H. Trinity	,,	Ecl. Dis.	16 497	Papworth—			
Paddington, St. John	,,	Ecl. Dis.	9 974	St. Agnes	Cambs & Hunts	Parish	165
Paddington, St. Mary	,,	Ecl. Dis.	10 646	St. Everard	Cambs	Parish	133
Paddington, St. Saviour	,,	Ecl. Dis.	7 787	Par	Cornwall	Ecl. Dis.	2 327
Paddlesworth	Kent	Parish	57	Paracombe	Devon	Sub-dis.	2 839
Paddock Wood	,,	Ecl. Dis.	898	Paracombe	,,	Parish	410

Name of Place.	County.	Description.	Population.	Name of Place.	County.	Description.	Population.
aradise	Norfolk	Ward	2 276	Pattishall	Northampton	Parish	885
arbold	Lancaster	Tnship.	474	Pattiswick	Essex	Parish	324
arcel Canol	Cardigan	Tnship.	604	Patton	Westmoreland	Tnship.	92
arham	Suffolk	Parish	470	Paul	Cornwall	Parish	5 072
arham	Sussex	Parish	71	Paul	York	Parish	844
ark Quarter	Durham	Tnship.	1 091	Paul	"	Tnship.	552
ark	Glamorgan	Hamle	132	Paulerspury	Northampton	Parish	1 233
ark House	Hants	—	7	Paulton	Somerset	Parish	1 958
arks, New	Leicester	Parish	52	Pauntley	Gloucester	Parish	233
ark Grace Dieu	Monmouth	Parish	5	Pavenham	Beds	Parish	536
ark	Notts	Sub-dis.	6 095	Pawlett	Somerset	Parish	555
ark Leys	"	Parish	10	Paxton, Great	Hunts	Parish	411
ark-End	Stafford	Tnship.	75	Paxton, Little	"	Parish	247
arkham	Devon	Sub-dis.	2 794	Payhembury	Devon	Parish	532
arkham	"	Parish	886	Paythorne	York	Tnship.	126
arkhold	Hereford	Tnship.	61	Peak Forest	Derby	Parish	542
arkhurst Forest	Hants, I. W.	—	15	Peakirk	Northampton	Parish	246
arkstone	Dorset	Tithing	1 134	Peals	Northumberland	Tnship.	64
arkstone	"	Ecl. Dis.	1 134	Peasemore	Berks	Parish	332
arley, West	"	Parish	268	Peasenhall	Suffolk	Parish	875
arlington	York	Tnship.	195	Peasmarsh	Sussex	Parish	906
arndon, Great	Essex	Parish	491	Peatling Magna	Leicester	Parish	272
arndon, Little	"	Parish	71	Peatling Parva	"	Parish	168
arr	Lancaster	Tnship.	8 253	Pebmarsh	Essex	Parish	653
arr, St. Peter	"	Ecl. Dis.	4 712	Pebworth	Gloucester	Parish	736
arson Drove	Cambs	Chap.	876	Pebworth	"	Hamlet	506
artington	Cheshire	Tnship.	445	Peckforton	Cheshire	Tnship.	221
artney	Lincoln	Parish	487	Peckham, East	Kent	Parish	2 341
arton, &c.	Cumberland	Tnship.	97	Peckham, East, Trinity	"	Ecl. Dis.	1 918
arton, Moresby	"	Tnship.	759	Peckham, West	"	Parish	446
artrishow	Brecon	Parish	73	Peckham	Surrey	Sub-dis.	28 135
arwich	Derby	Parish	521	Peckham	"	Hamlet	28 135
assenham	Northampton	Parish	1 105	Peckham St. Mary Mag.	"	Ecl. Dis.	8 154
aston	Norfolk	Parish	286	Peckleton	Leicester	Parish	378
aston	Northampton	Parish	1 071	Pedmore	Worcester	Parish	297
aston	"	Hamlet	99	Peel, Isle of	Lancaster	Island	4
aston	Northumberland	Tnship.	189	Peel	Isle of Man	Town	2 848
atcham	Sussex	Parish	638	Pegsworth	Northumberland	Tnship.	193
atching	"	Parish	275	Peldon	Essex	Sub-dis.	4 685
ateley Bridge	York	District	9 534	Peldon	"	Parish	501
ateley Bridge	"	Sub-dis.	3 349	Pelham, Brent	Herts	Parish	286
atney	Wilts	Parish	154	Pelham, Furneux	"	Parish	620
atrick	Isle of Man	Parish	2 778	Pelham, Stocking	"	Parish	126
atrick Brompton	York	Parish	1 216	Pelhams Lands	Lincoln	Parish	54
atrick Brompton	"	Tnship.	205	Pelsall	Stafford	Tnship.	1 892
atrington	"	District	9 681	Pelton	Durham	Tnship.	2 787
atrington	"	Sub-dis.	9 681	Pelton	"	Ecl. Dis.	4 344
atrington	"	Parish	1 724	Pelynt	Cornwall	Parish	729
atrixbourne	Kent	Parish	228	Pemberton	Lancaster	Sub-dis.	10 435
atshull	Stafford	Parish	194	Pemberton	"	Tnship.	6 870
atterdale w. Hartsop	Westmld.	Chap.	693	Pemberton	"	Ecl. Dis.	8 853
attesley	Norfolk	Parish	10	Pembrey	Carmarthen	Sub-dis.	5 797
attingham	Staff. & Salop	Parish	1 126	Pembrey	"	Parish	4 145
attingham	Stafford	Tnship.	959	Pembridge	Hereford	Parish	1 500

Name of Place.	County.	Description.	Population.	Name of Place	County.	Description.	Population.
Pembrokeshire ..	.. ..	County	96 278	Penketh..	.. Lancaster ..	Tnship.	784
Pembroke ..	Pembroke	District	29 003	Penkhull	.. Stafford ..	Tnship.	10 865
Pembroke ..	,,	Sub-dis.	16 559	Penkhull	.. ,, ..	Ecl. Dis.	2 110
Pembroke ..	,,	Borough	15 071	Penkridge	.. ,, ..	Lt. Sub.	19 103
Pembroke Parl. Dist. of	,,	Boros.	21 773	Penkridge	.. ,, ..	District	18 662
Pembroke Dock .	,,	Ecl. Dis.	10 190	Penkridge	.. ,, ..	Sub-dis.	4 260
Pembuallt	.. Brecon ..	Hamlet	604	Penkridge	.. ,, ..	Parish	3 146
Pembury	.. Kent ..	Parish	1 257	Penkridge	.. ,, ..	Tnship	2 510
Penally ..	.. Pembroke ..	Parish	545	Penley ..	.. Flint ..	Chap.	382
Penalt ..	.. Brecon ..	Parcel	732	Penllech	.. Carnarvon ..	Parish	261
Penalt ..	.. Monmouth ..	Parish	458	Penlline..	.. Glamorgan.	Parish	286
Penarth..	.. Cardigan ..	Hund.	6 965	Penllyn ..	.. Merioneth ..	Hund.	6 352
Penarth..	.. ,, ..	L. Sub.	7 314	Penllyn ..	.. ,, ..	L. Sub.	6 352
Penarth..	.. Glamorgan .	Parish	1 406	Penmachno	.. Carnarvon ..	Parish	1 425
Penbedw	.. Denbigh ..	Tnship.	58	Penmaen	.. Glamorgan .	Parish	123
Penbiddle	.. Monmouth ..	Hamlet	107	Penmaen	.. Monmouth ..	Hamlet	2 686
Penboyr..	.. Carmarthen	Parish	1 146	Penmaen	.. ,, ..	Ecl. Dis.	2 686
Penbryn	.. Cardigan ..	Sub-dis.	5 075	Penmark	.. Glamorgan .	Parish	529
Penbryn	.. ,, ..	Parish	1 575	Penmon..	.. Anglesey ..	Parish	240
Pencarreg	.. Carm. & Card.	Sub-dis.	2 878	Penmorfa	.. Carnarvon ..	Parish	1 104
Pencarreg	.. Carmarthen	Parish	1 208	Penmynydd	.. Anglesey ..	Parish	446
Pencoed..	.. Glamorgan .	Hamlet	604	Penn ..	.. Bucks ..	Parish	1 096
Pencombe	.. Hereford ..	Parish	415	Penn Street	.. ,,	Ecl. Dis.	693
Pencoyd..	.. ,,	Parish	219	Penn ...	.. Stafford ..	Parish	1 765
Pendeen	.. Cornwall ..	Ecl. Dis.	3 513	Penn, Lower ..	.. ,,	Tnship.	306
Penderry	.. Glamorgan .	Hamlet	1 330	Penn, Upper ..	.. ,,	Tnship.	1 459
Penderyn	.. Brecon ..	L. Sub.	4 983	Penn, Upper, St. Philip,	..	Ecl. Dis.	852
Penderyn	.. ,, ..	Parish	1 331	Pennal ..	Merion. & Montg.	Sub-dis.	4 167
Penderyn, Lower	,, ..	Hamlet	1 134	Pennal ..	.. Merioneth ..	Parish	588
Penderyn, Upper	,, ..	Hamlet	197	Pennant	.. Montgomery	Parish	712
Pendine..	.. Carmarthen	Parish	175	Pennard	.. Glamorgan .	Parish	321
Pendle ..	.. Lancaster ..	Sub-dis.	1 784	Pennard, East ..	Somerset ..	Parish	631
Pendlebury	.. ,, ..	Tnship.	3 548	Pennard, West..	,, ..	Parish	836
Pendlebury, Christch.	,,	Ecl. Dis.	3 170	Pennington	.. Hants ..	Ecl. Dis.	753
Pendlebury, St. John	,,	Ecl. Dis.	2 610	Pennington	.. Lancaster ..	Parish	879
Pendleton	.. ,, ..	Tnship.	1 446	Pennington	.. ,, ..	Tnship.	5 015
Pendleton	.. ,, ..	Sub-dis.	24 448	Pennington, Christch. ,,	..	Ecl. Dis.	2 803
Pendleton	.. ,, ..	Tnship.	20 900	Pennycross	.. Devon ..	Chap.	315
Pendleton, St. George	,,	Ecl. Dis.	5 361	Penponds	.. Cornwall ..	Ecl. Dis.	2 012
Pendock..	.. Worcester ..	Parish	329	Penpont	.. Brecon ..	Hamlet	119
Pendomer	.. Somerset ..	Parish	96	Penrhos..	.. Carnarvon ..	Parish	104
Pendoylon	.. Glamorgan .	Parish	380	Penrhos, Trinity	Montgomery	Ecl. Dis.	976
Penegoes	.. Montgomery	Parish	1 126	Penrhoslligwy ..	Anglesey ..	Parish	473
Penge ..	.. Surrey ..	Hamlet	5 015	Penrhyn	.. Merioneth ..	Ecl. Dis.	1 315
Penhow..	.. Monmouth ..	Parish	293	Penrice ..	.. Glamorgan .	Parish	307
Penhurst	.. Sussex ..	Parish	105	Penrith ..	.. Cumberland	District	22 322
Penistone	.. York ..	Union	14 419	Penrith ..	.. ,, ..	Sub-dis.	11 532
Penistone	.. ,, ..	Sub-dis.	6 025	Penrith ..	.. ,, ..	Parish	7 948
Penistone	.. ,, ..	Parish	7 149	Penrith ..	.. ,, ..	Town	7 189
Penistone	.. ,, ..	Tnship.	860	Penrith ..	.. Pembroke ..	Parish	370
Penkelly	.. Brecon ..	Hund.	6 465	Penrith ..	.. ,, ..	—	205
Penkelly	.. ,, ..	L. Sub.	2 776	Penrose..	.. Monmouth ..	Parish	378
Penkelly	.. ,, ..	Sub-dis.	1 657	Penryn ..	.. Cornwall ..	Sub-dis.	4 760
Penkelly	.. ,, ..	Hamlet	332	Penryn..	.. ,, ..	M. Bor.	3 547

Name of Place.	County.	Description.	Population.	Name of Place.	County.	Description.	Population.
nryn & Falmouth	*Cornw.*	P. Bor.	14 485	Pershore	*Worcester* ..	Hund.	33 695
nsax ..	*Worcester* ..	Chap.	503	Pershore	,,	L. Sub.	14 354
nsby ..	*Cheshire* ..	Tnship.	38	Pershore	,,	District	13 865
pselwood	*Somerset* ..	Parish	442	Pershore	,,	Sub-dis.	6 507
nsford, St. Thos.	,,	Parish	312	**Pershore**	,,	Town	2 905
nsham	*Worcester* ..	Hamlet	106	Pertenhall	*Beds* ..	Parish	404
nshaw	*Durham* ..	Tnship.	2 075	Pertwood, Upper	*Wilts* ..	Parish	30
nshaw	,,	Ecl. Dis.	3 537	Peterborough	..	Diocese	486 977
nshurst	*Kent*	Sub-dis.	7 288	Peterborough	*Northampton*	L. Sub.	22 893
nshurst	,,	Parish	1 698	Peterborough	*Nrthptn., &c.*	District	33 178
nsnett	*Stafford* ..	Ecl. Dis.	5 639	Peterborough	,,	Sub-dis.	17 158
nsthorpe	*Norfolk* ..	Parish	12	**Peterborough**	*Northampton*	P. City	11 735
nstrowed	*Montgomery*	Parish	142	Peterborough, St. John	,,	Parish	11 497
nterry	*Monmouth* ..	Parish	28	Peterborough, St. Mark	,,	Ecl. Dis.	3 170
ntlow	*Essex* ..	Parish	397	Peterchurch	*Hereford* ..	Parish	710
ntney..	*Norfolk* ..	Parish	642	Petersfield	*Hants* ..	Division	11 474
nton-Grafton	*Hants* ..	Parish	444	Petersfield	,,	L. Sub.	11 474
nton-Mewsey	,,	Parish	277	Petersfield	,,	District	7 853
ntonville	*Middlesex* ..	Sub-dis.	13 079	Petersfield	,,	Sub-dis.	5 172
ntonville, St. Jas.	,,	Ecl. Dis.	11 974	Petersfield	,,	Parish	1 950
ntraeth	*Anglesey* ..	Parish	962	Petersfield	,,	—	1 466
ntrebach, St. John	*Glam.* ..	Ecl. Dis.	5 288	**Petersfield**	,,	P. Bor.	5 655
ntrevoelas	*Denbigh* ..	Parish	534	Petersham	*Surrey* ..	Parish	637
ntrich	*Derby* ..	Parish	5 829	Peterstone on Ely	*Glamorgan* .	Parish	235
ntrich	,,	Tnship.	585	Peterstone	,,	Chap.	216
ntridge	*Dorset* ..	Parish	295	Peterstone	*Monmouth* ..	Parish	180
ntrobbin	*Flint* ..	Tnship.	942	Peterstow	*Hereford* ..	Parish	276
ntyrch	*Glamorgan* .	Parish	2 110	Petham..	*Kent* ..	Parish	596
nwerris	*Cornwall* ..	Ecl. Dis.	882	Petherick, Little	*Cornwall* ..	Parish	236
nwith.	,,	Hund.	88 953	Petherton, North	*Somerset* ..	Hund.	7 663
nwith	,,	L. Sub.	105 394	Petherton, North	,,	Parish	3 943
nwortham	*Lancaster* ..	Parish	5 488	Petherton, South	,,	Hund.	6 196
nwortham	,,	Tnship.	1 506	Petherton, South	,,	Parish	2 423
nyclawdd	*Monmouth* ..	Parish	53	**Petherton, South**	,,	Town	2 031
nzance	*Cornwall* ..	District	54 554	Petherwin, South	*Cornwall* ..	Parish	876
nzance	,,	Sub-dis.	18 741	Petherwin, North	*Devon* ..	Parish	945
nzance	,,	M. Bor.	9 414	Petrockstow	,,	Parish	613
opleton	*Worcester* ..	Parish	326	Petsoe Manor	*Bucks* ..	Parish	8
eover Inferior	*Cheshire* ..	Tnship.	109	Pett	*Sussex* ..	Parish	320
eover, Nether..	,,	Tnship.	258	Pettaugh	*Suffolk* ..	Parish	275
eover Superior	,,	Tnship.	531	Petteril-Crooks..	*Cumberland*	Tnship.	528
epper Harrow	*Surrey* ..	Parish	104	Pettistree	*Suffolk* ..	Parish	290
ercy ..	*Northumberland*	Ecl. Dis.	3 953	Petton ..	*Salop* ..	Parish	45
erfedd..	*Carmarthen*	Hund.	7 787	Petworth	*Sussex* ..	L. Sub.	16 913
erivale..	*Middlesex* ..	Parish	48	Petworth	,,	District	9 397
erlethorpe	*Notts* ..	Tnship.	98	Petworth	,,	Sub-dis.	5 152
erranarwothal	*Cornwall* ..	Parish	1 517	Petworth	,,	Parish	3 368
erranuthnoe	,,	Parish	1 507	**Petworth**	,,	Town	2 326
erranzabuloe	,,	Parish	2 959	Pevensey	,,	Rape	56 922
erridge	*Devon* ..	Farm	12	Pevensey	,,	Parish	385
errott, South	*Dorset* ..	Parish	363	Pewsey ..	*Wilts* ..	District	12 466
errott, North	*Somerset* ..	Parish	374	Pewsey ..	,,	Sub-dis.	6 995
erry Barr	*Stafford* ..	Hamlet	1 061	Pewsey ..	,,	Parish	2 027
ershall..	,,	Tnship.	101	Pewsham	,,	—	462

Name of Place.	County.	Description.	Population.	Name of Place.	County.	Description.	Populat
Phillack..	Cornwall ..	Sub-dis.	9 035	Pimperne ..	Dorset ..	Parish	49
Phillack..	,,	Parish	5 381	Pinchbeck ..	Lincoln ..	Sub-dis.	3 05
Philleigh ..	,,	Parish	363	Pinchbeck ..	,,	Parish	2 98
Phillyholme ..	Dorset ..	Tithing	490	Pinchbeck, West	,,	Ecl. Dis.	1 41
Pickenham, North	Norfolk ..	Parish	287	Pinchingthorpe .	York ..	Tnship,	7
Pickenham, South	,,	Parish	159	Pinhoe ..	Devon ..	Parish	50
Pickering ..	York ..	District	10 549	Pinley ..	Warwick ..	Tnship.	2
Pickering ..	,,	Sub-dis.	4 701	Pinner ..	Middlesex ..	Parish	1 84
Pickering ..	,,	Parish	4 501	Pinnock & Hyde	Gloucester ..	Tnship.	5
Pickering ..	,,	Tnship.	3 399	Pinvin ..	Worcester ..	Chap.	26
Pickering ..	,,	Town	2 640	Pinxton..	Derby ..	Parish	1 36
Pickering-Lythe .	,,	Wapen.	17 866	Pipehill..	Stafford ..	Tnship.	15
Pickering-Lythe, East	,,	L. Sub.	26 030	Pipe Ridware ..	,,	Parish	9
Pickering-Lythe, West	,,	L. Sub.	10 353	Pipe w. Lyde ..	Hereford ..	Parish	20
Pickhill..	Denbigh ..	Tnship.	175	Pipton ..	Brecon ..	Hamlet	11
Pickhill..	York ..	Sub-dis.	1 557	Pirbright ..	Surrey ..	Parish	59
Pickhill..	,,	Parish	783	Pirehill ..	Stafford ..	Hund.	149 73
Pickhill w. Roxby	,,	Tnship.	416	Pirton ..	Herts ..	Parish	1 02
Pickmere ..	Cheshire ..	Tnship.	247	Pirton ..	Oxon ..	Hund.	3 61
Pickton..	,,	Tnship.	108	Pirton ..	,,	Parish	70
Pickton..	York ..	Tnship.	96	Pirton ..	Worcester ..	Parish	21
Pickwell ..	Leicester ..	Parish	169	Pishill ..	Oxon ..	Parish	21
Pickworth ..	Lincoln ..	Parish	253	Pistill ..	Carnarvon ..	Parish	49
Pickworth ..	Rutland ..	Parish	151	Pitchcombe ..	Gloucester ..	Parish	17
Piddinghoe ..	Sussex ..	Parish	243	Pitchcott ..	Bucks ..	Parish	3
Piddington ..	Northampton	Parish	1 102	Pitchford ..	Salop ..	Parish	18
Piddington ..	,,	Tnship.	567	Pitcombe ..	Somerset ..	Parish	44
Piddington ..	Oxon ..	Parish	389	Pitcombe ..	,,	—	22
Piddle, North ..	Worcester ..	Parish	131	Pitminster ..	Som. & Devon	Sub-dis.	4 95
Pidley w. Fenton	Hunts ..	Parish	569	Pitminster ..	Somerset ..	Parish	1 57
Pierse Bridge ..	Durham ..	Tnship.	211	Pitney ..	,,	Hund.	1 81
Pigdon ..	Northumberland	Tnship.	54	Pitney ..	,,	Parish	37
Pilham ..	Lincoln ..	Parish	89	Pitsea ..	Essex ..	Parish	26
Pilkington ..	Lancaster ..	Sub-dis.	12 303	Pitsford..	Northampton	Parish	60
Pilkington ..	,,	Tnship.	12 303	Pitsmoor ..	York ..	Ecl. Dis.	8 92
Pillaton..	Cornwall ..	Parish	349	Pitstone..	Bucks ..	Parish	58
Pillerton Hersey	Warwick ..	Parish	242	Pitstone..	,,	Tnship.	45
Pillerton, Priors	,,	Parish	190	Pitt ..	Devon ..	Quarter	89
Pilleth ..	Radnor ..	Parish	104	Pittington ..	Durham ..	Parish	5 69
Pilling ..	Lancaster ..	Tnship.	1 388	Pittington ..	,,	Tnship.	2 15
Pilsdon ..	Dorset ..	Parish	86	Pitton ..	Wilts ..	Chap.	39
Pilsgate..	Northampton	Hamlet	152	Pixley ..	Hereford ..	Parish	11
Pilsley ..	Derby..	Tnship.	320	Plainmellor	Northumberland	Tnship.	14
Pilsley (N. Wingfield P.)	,,	Tnship.	628	Plaistow & Church St.	Essex ..	Wards	22 33
Pilsworth ..	Lancaster ..	Tnship.	343	Plaistow, St. Mary	,,	Ecl. Dis.	11 21
Pilton ..	Devon ..	Parish	1 863	Plaitford ..	Wilts ..	Parish	24
Pilton ..	Northampton	Parish	144	Plashetts & Tynehead	Nrthmb.	Tnship.	49
Pilton ..	Rutland ..	Parish	72	Platt, St.Mary ..	Kent ..	Ecl. Dis.	1 02
Pilton ..	Somerset ..	Parish	1 202	Plawsworth ..	Durham ..	Tnship.	68
Pimhill ..	Salop ..	Hund.	11 462	Plaxtole..	Kent ..	Ecl. Dis.	1 14
Pimhill ..	,,	L. Sub.	10 486	Playden..	Sussex ..	Parish	30
Pimlico, St. Gabriel	Middlesex	Ecl. Dis.	15 658	Playford ..	Suffolk ..	Parish	27
Pimlico, St. Michael	,,	Ecl. Dis.	10 373	Pleasington ..	Lancaster ..	Tnship.	42
Pimlico, St. Peter	,,	Ecl. Dis.	14 328	Pleasley..	Derby & Notts	Sub-dis.	2 48

Name of Place.	County.	Description.	Population.	Name of Place.	County.	Description.	Population.
?leasley..	Derby	Parish	613	Polebrook	Northampton	Parish	488
?leck & Bescot..	Stafford	Ecl. Dis.	3 220	Polebrook	,,	Hamlet	465
?ledgdon	Essex	Hamlet	143	Polesworth	Warwick	Parish	2 451
?lemonstall	Cheshire	Parish	2 019	Poling ..	Sussex	Parish	203
?leshy ..	Essex	Parish	342	Pollards-Lands..	Durham	Tnship.	355
?lomesgate	Suffolk	Hund.	11 113	Pollington	York	Tnship.	501
?lomesgate	,,	District	20 720	Pollington w. Balne	,,	Ecl. Dis.	863
?lompton	York	Tnship.	219	Polstead	Suffolk	Parish	922
?loughley	Oxon	Hund.	14 747	Poltimore	Devon	Parish	348
?luckley & Pevington	Kent	Parish	777	Ponsonby	Cumberland	Parish	175
?lucknett, Haslebury	Somerset	Parish	834	Pont Blyddyn ..	Flint	Ecl. Dis.	1 378
?lucknett, Preston	,,	Parish	363	Pont Dolanog ..	Montgomery	Ecl. Dis.	390
?lumbland	Cumberland	Parish	726	Pontefract	York	District	34 794
?lumbley	Cheshire	Tnship.	365	Pontefract	,,	Sub-dis.	14 181
?lumpton Street	Cumberland	Tnship.	170	Pontefract	,,	Parish	10 971
?lumpton Wall .	,,	Tnship.	326	Pontefract	,,	Tnship.	5 346
?lumpton	Northampton	Parish	42			M. Bor.	5 346
?lumpton	Sussex	Parish	404	Pontefract .. ,, {		P. Bor.	11 736
?lumstead	Kent	Sub-dis.	32 974	Pontefract, All Saints	,,	Ecl. Dis.	1 392
?lumstead	,,	Parish	24 502	Pontefract Park .	,,	Parish	74
?lumstead	Norfolk	Parish	178	Ponteland	Northumberland	Sub-dis.	7 190
?lumstead, Great	,,	Parish	342	Ponteland	,,	Parish	1 089
?lumstead, Little	,,	Parish	319	Ponteland	,,	Tnship.	488
Plumtree	Notts	Parish	551	Pontesbury	Salop	Sub-dis.	3 866
Plumtree	,,	Tnship.	285	Pontesbury	,,	Parish	3 466
Plungar..	Leicester	Parish	251	Pontfadog, St. John	Denbigh	Ecl. Dis.	1 499
Plymouth	Devon	District	62 599	Pontfaen	Pembroke	Parish	32
Plymouth	,,	Borough	62 599	Pontisbright	Essex	Parish	370
Christchurch..	,,	Ecl. Dis.	3 984	Pontnewynydd..	Monmouth	Ecl. Dis.	2 753
Holy Trinity..	,,	Ecl. Dis.	3 809	Ponton, Great ..	Lincoln	Parish	561
St. James	,,	Ecl. Dis.	3 163	Ponton, Little ..	,,	Parish	208
St. Peter	,,	Ecl. Dis.	10 325	Pont Robert, St. John	Montg.	Ecl. Dis.	612
Plympton	,,	Hund.	10 285	Pontypool	Monmouth	L. Sub.	27 887
Plympton St. Mary	,,	District	20 502	Pontypool	,,	District	30 288
Plympton	,,	Sub-dis.	11 293	Pontypool	,,	Sub-dis.	22 633
Plympton Earls .	,,	Parish	900	Pontypool .. ,,		Town	4 661
Plympton St. Mary	,,	Parish	3 026	Pontyrhun, St. John	Glam.	Ecl. Dis.	5 288
Plymstock	,,	Parish	2 997	Pool, Nether	Cheshire	Tnship.	25
Plymtree	,,	Parish	462	Pool, Over	,,	Tnship.	88
Pockley..	York	Tnship.	199	Pool, South	Devon	Parish	413
Pocklington	,,	District	16 710	Pool	Montgomery	Hund.	2 895
Pocklington	,,	Sub-dis.	6 954	Pool	,,	L. Sub.	6 652
Pocklington	,,	Parish	2 923	Pool	,,	Sub-dis.	7 220
Pocklington	,,	Tnship.	2 671	Pool	,,	Parish	4 844
Pocklington ..	,,	Town	2 671	Pool	,,	Division	725
Pockthorpe	Norfolk	Hamlet	2 055	Pool, Lower	,,	Division	1 478
Podimore Milton	Somerset	Parish	131	Pool, Middle	,,	Division	2 644
Podington	Beds	Parish	643	Pool, Upper	,,	Division	658
Podmore	Stafford	Tnship.	38	Poole	Cheshire	Tnship.	187
Pointington	Somerset	Parish	174	Poole	Dorset	District	13 742
Pointon..	Lincoln	Hamlet	510	Poole	,,	Sub-dis.	9 366
Pokesdown, St. James	Hants..	Ecl. Dis.	457	Poole, St. James	,,	Parish	6 815
Polden Hill	Somerset	Sub-dis.	3 704	Poole ..	,,	Borough	9 759
Polebrook	Northampton	Hund.	5 723	Poole Keynes ..	Wilts	Parish	180

Name of Place.	County.	Description.	Population.	Name of Place.	County.	Description.	Population.
Poole	York	Tnship.	337	Potter Heigham	Norfolk	Parish	439
Pool Meadow	Gloucester	Parish	62	Potterne & Cannings	Wilts	Hund.	8 095
Poorstock	Dorset	Parish	1 067	Potterne	,,	Parish	1 826
Poorton, North	,,	Parish	92	Potterne	,,	—	1 235
Popham	Hants	Parish	124	Potter-Newton	York	Tnship.	1 878
Poplar	Middlesex	District	79 196	Potter's Bar, St. John	Mddlx.	Ecl. Dis.	959
Poplar	,,	Sub-dis.	43 529	Potters-Marston	Leicester	Hamlet	15
Poplar	,,	Parish	43 529	Potterspury	Nptn. & Bucks	District	11 632
Poplar, Christchurch	,,	Ecl. Dis.	8 579	Potterspury	Northampton	Parish	1 710
Poppleton	York	Sub-dis.	2 742	Potterspury	,,	Tnship.	1 060
Poppleton, Nether	,,	Parish	311	Pottery Field, St. Jude	York	Ecl. Dis.	6 052
Poppleton, Nether	,,	Tnship.	262	Potto	,,	Tnship.	194
Poppleton, Upper	,,	Chap.	355	Potton	Beds	Sub-dis.	9 280
Porchester	Hants	Parish	771	Potton	,,	Parish	1 944
Poringland, Gt. or E.	Norfolk	Parish	464	Pott-Shrigley	Cheshire	Tnship.	450
Poringland, Lit. or W.	,,	Parish	46	Poughill	Cornwall	Parish	363
Porlock	Somerset	Parish	835	Poughill	Devon	Parish	356
Portbury	,,	Hund.	11 558	Poulshot	Wilts	Parish	334
Portbury	,,	Parish	677	Poulton	Cheshire	Tnship.	132
Porteynon	Glamorgan	Parish	297	Poulton w. Seacombe	,,	Tnship.	3 683
Portgate	Nrthumberld.	Tnship.	74	Poulton w. Spittle	,,	Tnship.	360
Porthkerry	Glamorgan	Parish	168	Poulton	Gloucester	Parish	454
Porthleven, St. Barth.	Cornwall	Ecl. Dis.	1 259	Poulton	Kent	Parish	28
Portingscale	Cumberland	Tnship.	261	Poulton	Lancaster	Tnship.	2 236
Portington & Cavil	York	Tnship.	120	Poulton, Trinity	,,	Ecl. Dis.	2 228
Portisham	Dorset	Parish	704	Poulton-le-Fylde	,,	Sub-dis.	12 914
Portishead	Somerset	Parish	1 201	Poulton-le-Fylde	,,	Parish	8 665
Portland	Dorset	Parish	8 468	Poulton-le-Fylde	,,	Tnship.	1 141
Portland Tn., St. Steph.	Mddlx.	Ecl. Dis.	9 621	Poulton w. Fearnhead	,,	Tnship.	642
Portlemouth, East	Devon	Parish	403	Pounden	Bucks	Hamlet	95
Portmadoc	Carnarvon	L. Sub.	7 308	Poundstock	Cornwall	Parish	534
Porton	Wilts	Chap.	176	Powder	,,	Hund.	60 024
Portscuett	Monmouth	Parish	175	Powder	,,	L. Sub.	81 067
Portsea Island	Hants	District	94 828	Powderham	Devon	Parish	238
Portsea Town	,,	Sub-dis.	19 967	Powick	Worcester	Parish	2 222
Portsea	,,	Parish	83 966	Pownall Fee	Cheshire	Tnship.	2 181
Portsea, All Saints	,,	Ecl. Dis.	18 478	Poxwell	Dorset	Parish	82
Portsea, St. John	,,	Ecl. Dis.	6 606	Poynings	Sussex	Parish	261
Portsea, St. Paul	,,	Ecl. Dis.	21 310	Poynton	Cheshire	Tnship.	1 284
Portsea, Trinity	,,	Ecl. Dis.	10 315	Prebend End	Bucks	Precinct	884
Portslade	Sussex	Parish	1 103	Preen, Church	Salop	Parish	97
Portsmouth, Borough	Hants	L. Sub.	94 799	Prees	,,	Sub-dis.	3 362
Portsmouth Town	,,	Sub-dis.	10 346	Prees	,,	Parish	3 097
Portsmouth	,,	Parish	10 833	Preesall w. Hackinsall	Lanc.	Tnship.	812
Portsmouth	,,	Borough	94 799	Prendergast	Pembroke	Parish	1 540
Portswood	,,	Tithing	3 546	Prendwick	Northumberland	Tnship.	87
Portswood, Christch.	,,	Ecl. Dis.	2 386	Prenton	Cheshire	Tnship.	123
Portwood	Cheshire	Ecl. Dis.	5 346	Prescot	Lancaster	L. Sub.	79 298
Posenhall	Salop	Parish	22	Prescot	,,	District	73 127
Poslingford	Suffolk	Parish	350	Prescot	,,	Sub-dis.	12 377
Postling	Kent	Parish	139	Prescot	,,	Parish	63 540
Postwick	Norfolk	Parish	291	Prescot	,,	Tnship.	5 136
Potsgrove	Beds	Parish	298	Prescot	,,	Town	6 066
Potter Hanworth	Lincoln	Parish	413	Prescot, St. Helens	,,	Ecl. Dis.	20 176

Name of Place.	County.	Description.	Population.	Name of Place.	County.	Description.	Population.
rescott..	Gloucester ..	Parish	63	Preston, East ..	Sussex ..	Incor.	15 384
rescott..	Oxon ..	Lordship	19	Preston, East ..	„ ..	Parish	320
reshute	Wilts ..	Parish	1 209	Preston Bagot ..	Warwick ..	Parish	220
restatyn	Flint ..	Hund.	5 872	Preston Patrick	Westmoreland	Tnship.	488
restatyn & Rhuddlan	„ ..	L. Sub.	17 436	Preston Richard	„	Tnship.	504
restatyn	„ ..	Ecl. Dis.	700	Preston ..	York ..	Parish	1 061
restbury	Cheshire ..	Sub-dis.	5 197	Preston ..	„ ..	Tnship.	902
restbury	„ ..	Parish	55 680	Preston, Great ..	„ ..	Incor.	26 505
restbury	„ ..	Tnship.	358	Preston. Gt. & Lit.	„ ..	Tnship.	541
restbury	Gloucester ..	Parish	1 297	Preston, Long ..	„ ..	Parish	1 206
resteigne	Radn. & Heref.	District	15 671	Preston, Long ..	„ ..	Tnship.	536
resteigne	„ „	Sub-dis.	3 741	Preston under Scar	„ ..	Tnship.	434
resteigne	„ „	Union	3 741	Prestwich	Lancaster ..	Union	58 578
resteigne	„ „	Parish	2 383	Prestwich	„ ..	Sub-dis	6 285
resteigne	„ „	P. Boro.	1 743	Prestwich	„ ..	Tnship.	5 288
reston Bisset ..	Bucks ..	Parish	469	Prestwich	„ ..	Parish	117 961
reston on Hill .	Cheshire ..	Tnship.	596	Prestwich	Northumberland	Tnship.	177
reston Quarter .	Cumberland	Tnship.	5 471	Prestwold	Leicester ..	Parish	969
reston ..	Dorset ..	Parish	723	Prestwold	„ ..	Tnship.	72
reston-le-Skerne	Durham ..	Tnship.	146	Prestwood	Bucks ..	Ecl. Dis.	947
reston on Tees .	„ ..	Tnship.	111	Prestwood	Stafford ..	Tnship.	55
reston by Ledbury	Gloucester	Parish	78	Priddy ..	Somerset ..	Parish	251
reston ..	„ ..	Parish	217	Priest-Hutton ..	Lancaster ..	Tnship.	218
reston on Stour	„ ..	Parish	376	Primethorpe, &c.	Leicester ..	Tnships.	431
reston-Candover	Hants ..	Parish	476	Prince's Park, St. Paul	Lanc...	Ecl. Dis.	7 116
reston on Wye .	Hereford ..	Parish	277	Princes Risboro .	Bucks & Oxon	Sub-dis.	5 907
reston-Wynne .	„ ..	Chap.	182	Princes Risborough	Bucks ..	Parish	2 392
reston by Faversham	Kent ..	Parish	1 535	Prince's Road St. Mary	Surrey	Ecl. Dis.	16 305
reston by Wingham	„ ..	Parish	557	Princethorpe ..	Warwick ..	Tnship.	319
reston ..	Lancaster ..	District	110 523	Prinknash Park .	Gloucester ..	Parish	17
reston ..	„ ..	Sub-dis.	82 985	Prion ..	Denbigh ..	Ecl. Dis.	479
reston ..	„ ..	Parish	85 699	Priors Dean	Hants ..	Parish	129
reston ..	„ ..	Tnship.	81 101	Priors Lee ..	Salop ..	Ecl. Dis.	2 461
reston	„ ..	Borough	82 985	Priors Hardwick	Warwick ..	Parish	323
All Saints ..	„ ..	Ecl. Dis.	4 481	Priors Marston..	„ ..	Parish	698
Christchurch .	„ ..	Ecl. Dis.	8 340	Priory St. Andrew	Northampton	Parish	6 411
Holy Trinity..	„ ..	Ecl. Dis.	4 287	Priory ..	Sussex ..	Parish	1 683
St. George ..	„ ..	Ecl. Dis.	3 337	Prisk & Carfan..	Cardigan ..	Tnship	145
St. James ..	„ ..	Ecl. Dis.	8 052	Prisk & Killey ..	Brecon ..	Parcel	5 027
St. Luke ..	„ ..	Ecl. Dis.	4 316	Priston ..	Somerset ..	Parish	292
St. Mary ..	„ ..	Ecl. Dis.	9 025	Prittlewell ..	Essex ..	Sub-dis.	5 394
St. Paul ..	„ ..	Ecl. Dis.	10 443	Prittlewell ..	„ ..	Parish	3 427
St. Peter ..	„ ..	Ecl. Dis.	16 506	Privett ..	Hants ..	Parish	258
St. Thomas ..	„ ..	Ecl. Dis.	8 053	Probus ..	Cornwall ..	Sub-dis.	3 702
reston-Capes ..	Northampton	Parish	320	Probus ..	„ ..	Parish	1 449
reston-Deanery	„ ..	Parish	80	Provosts Fee ..	York ..	Manor	262
reston, Tynemouth	Nthmld.	Tnship.	1 456	Prudhoe	Northumberland	Tnship.	471
reston, Ellingham	„ ..	Tnship.	67	Prudhoe Castle..	„ ..	Tnship.	490
reston ..	Rutland ..	Parish	349	Pryors ..	Devon ..	Quarter	494
reston-Gubbals	Salop ..	Parish	478	Pryors Hayes ..	Cheshire ..	Parish	15
reston on Wild Moors	„ ..	Parish	228	Publow..	Somerset ..	Parish	643
reston-Plucknett	Somerset ..	Parish	363	Puckington	„ ..	Parish	260
reston ..	Suffolk ..	Parish	848	Pucklechurch ..	Gloucester ..	Hund.	5 121
reston ..	Sussex ..	Parish	1 044	Pucklechurch ..	„ ..	Parish	1 265

Name of Place.	County.	Description.	Population.	Name of Place.	County.	Description.	Population.
Pudding-Norton	Norfolk	Parish	17	Pyrford	Surrey	Parish	381
Puddington	Beds	Parish	643	Pyrton	Oxon	Hund.	3 615
Puddington	Cheshire	Tnship.	160	Pyrton	,,	Parish	705
Puddington	Devon	Parish	210	Pytchley	Northampton	Parish	536
Puddlehinton	Dorset	Parish	414	Pyworthy	Devon	Parish	567
Puddlestone	Hereford	Parish	349				
Puddletown	Dorset	Sub-dis.	4 143	**Quadring**	Lincoln	Parish	1 001
Puddletown	,,	Parish	1 241	Quainton	Bucks	Parish	929
Puddletrenthide	,,	Parish	793	Quainton	,,	Tnship.	864
Pudsey	York	Sub-dis.	12 912	Quantoxhead, East	Somerset	Parish	339
Pudsey	,,	Tnship.	12 912	Quantoxhead, West	,,	Parish	223
Pudsey, St. Paul	,,	Ecl. Dis.	1 976	Quarles Farm	Norfolk	Parish	30
Puffin	Anglesey	Island	7	Quarley	Hants	Parish	182
Pulborough	Sussex	Sub-dis.	3 378	Quarlton	Lancaster	Tnship.	253
Pulborough	,,	Parish	1 852	Quarndon	Derby	Parish	496
Pulford	Cheshire	Parish	354	Quarnford	Stafford	Tnship.	549
Pulford	,,	Tnship.	222	Quarrendon	Bucks	Parish	58
Pulham	Dorset	Parish	302	Quarrington	Durham	Tnship.	1 056
Pulham :—				Quarrington	Lincoln	Parish	299
St. Mary Magdalen	Norfolk	Parish	1 279	Quarry Bank	Stafford	Ecl. Dis.	4 790
St. Mary Virgin	,,	Parish	863	Quatford	Salop	Parish	598
Pulloxhill	Beds	Parish	704	Quatford	,,	Tnship.	228
Pulverbatch	Salop	Parish	534	Quatt	,,	Parish	485
Puncheston	Pembroke	Parish	231	Quatt Jervis	,,	Tnship.	285
Puncknowle	Dorset	Parish	502	Quatt Malvern	,,	Tnship.	200
Purbrook, St. John	Hants	Ecl. Dis.	335	Quedgeley	Gloucester	Parish	408
Puriton	Somerset	Parish	604	Quedgeley	,,	Tnship.	353
Purleigh	Essex	Parish	1 095	Queenborough	Kent	Parish	973
Purley	Berks	Parish	193	Queen Camel	Somerset	Parish	734
Purslow	Salop	Hund.	9 536	Queen Charlton	,,	Parish	141
Purslow	,,	L. Sub.	6 817	Queenhill	Worcester	Hamlet	106
Purston-Jaglin	York	Tnship.	263	Queeniborough	Leicester	Parish	511
Purton	Wilts	Parish	2 087	Queen's Head	York	Ecl. Dis.	5 850
Purton	,,	—	2 038	Quenby	Leicester	Hamlet	26
Pusey	Berks	Parish	134	Quendon	Essex	Parish	165
Putford, East	Devon	Parish	190	Quenington	Gloucester	Parish	426
Putford, West	,,	Parish	362	Quernmore	Lancaster	Tnship.	563
Putley	Hereford	Parish	197	Quernmore, St. Peter	,,	Ecl. Dis.	563
Putney	Surrey	Sub-dis.	6 481	Quethiock	Cornwall	Parish	728
Putney	,,	Parish	6 481	Quiddenham	Norfolk	Parish	111
Puttenham	Herts	Parish	135	Quinton	Gloucester	Parish	557
Puttenham	Surrey	Parish	402	Quinton	,,	Tnship.	396
Puxton	Somerset	Parish	147	Quinton	Northampton	Parish	119
Pwllcrochan	Pembroke	Parish	264	Quinton	Worcester	Ecl. Dis.	2 495
Pwllheli	Carnarvon	L. Sub.	20 139	Quorndon	Leicester	Sub-dis.	5 089
Pwllheli	,,	District	20 908	Quorndon	,,	Tnship.	1 622
Pwllheli	,,	Sub-dis.	6 579				
Pwllheli	,,	Borough	2 818	**Raby**	Cheshire	Tnship.	214
Pwllywrach	Brecon	Hamlet	132	Raby & Keverstone	Durham	Tnship.	295
Pyder	Cornwall	Hund.	27 978	Rackenford	Devon	Parish	486
Pyder	,,	L. Sub.	17 121	Rackham	Sussex	Hamlet	194
Pyecombe	Sussex	Parish	283	Rackheath	Norfolk	Parish	271
Pyle	Glamorgan	Parish	1 192	Racton	Sussex	Parish	95
Pylle	Somerset	Parish	207	Radbourne	Derby	Parish	225

Name of Place.	County.	Description.	Population.	Name of Place.	County.	Description.	Population.
Radbourn, Lower	Warwick ..	Parish	17	Rainhill, St. Ann	Lancaster ..	Ecl. Dis.	2 608
Radbourn, Upper	,, ..	Parish	15	Rainow	Cheshire ..	Sub-dis.	3 478
Radcliffe ..	Lancaster ..	Sub-dis.	8 972	Rainow	,, ..	Tnship.	1 550
Radcliffe ..	,, ..	Parish	8 838	Rainton, East ..	Durham ..	Tnship.	1 505
Radcliffe, St. Thomas	,, ..	Ecl. Dis.	5 115	Rainton, West ..	,, ..	Tnship.	1 447
Radclive ..	Bucks ..	Parish	356	Rainton, West ..	,, ..	Ecl. Dis.	4 096
Radcot	Oxon ..	Hamlet	36	Rainton w. Newby	York ..	Tnship.	380
Raddington ..	Somerset ..	Parish	121	Raisthorpe & Birdhall	,,	Tnship.	87
Radfield ..	Cambs ..	Hund.	5 306	Raithby	Lincoln ..	Parish	217
Radford.. ..	Notts ..	District	30 479	Raithby w. Maltby	,, ..	Parish	145
Radford.. ..	,, ..	Sub-dis.	10 192	Rakes Farm ..	,, ..	Parish	4
Radford.. ..	,, ..	Parish	13 495	Rame	Cornwall ..	Parish	792
Radford, New Christch.	,, ..	Ecl. Dis.	5 145	Rampisham ..	Dorset ..	Parish	356
Radford.. ..	Oxon ..	Hamlet	100	Rampton ..	Cambs ..	Parish	240
Radford.. ..	Warwick ..	Hamlet	711	Rampton ..	Notts ..	Parish	496
Radford.. ..	,, ..	Sub-dis.	4 049	Ramsbottom ..	Lancaster ..	Ecl. Dis.	4 134
Radford-Semele .	,, ..	Parish	527	Ramsbury ..	Wilts ..	Hund.	3 629
Radipole ..	Dorset ..	Parish	691	Ramsbury	,,	Parish	2 533
Radley	Berks ..	Parish	484	Ramsbury Town	,,	Tithing	1 850
Radley	,, ..	Hamlet	407	Ramsden Bellhouse	Essex ..	Parish	430
Radlow	Hereford ..	Hund.	16 316	Ramsden-Crays .	,, ..	Parish	262
Radnage ..	Bucks ..	Parish	478	Ramsden ..	Oxon ..	Tnship.	455
Radnorshire ..	.. ..	County	25 382	Ramsey ..	Essex ..	Parish	605
Radnor	Cheshire ..	Tnship.	25	Ramsey ..	Hunts ..	Sub-dis.	5 266
Radnor	Radnor ..	Hund.	4 914	Ramsey	,, ..	Parish	4 500
Radnor	,, ..	L. Sub.	2 652	Ramsey	,, ..	Town	2 354
Radnor ..	Radn. & Heref.	Sub-dis.	3 567	Ramsey, St. Mary	,, ..	Ecl. Dis.	1 088
Radnor, New ..	Radnor ..	Parish	490	Ramsey ..	Isle of Man .	Town	2 891
Radnor, New ..	,, ..	Tnship.	463	Ramsey, Isle of..	Pembroke ..	Island	15
Radnor, New ..	,, ..	P. Boro.	2 262	Ramsgate ..	Kent ..	L. Sub.	5 881
Radnor, Old	Radn. & Heref.	Parish	1 349	Ramsgate ..	,, ..	Sub-dis.	18 007
Radnor, Old, &c.	Radnor ..	Tnship.	350	Ramsgate ..	,, ..	Parish	11 865
Radnor, Parl. Dis. of	Radn., &c.	Boros.	7 106	Ramsgate ..	,, ..	Town	11 865
Radstock ..	Somerset ..	Parish	2 227	Ramsgate, Christch.	,, ..	Ecl. Dis.	2 622
Radstone ..	Northampton	Parish	168	Ramsgate, Trinity	,, ..	Ecl. Dis.	1 351
Radway.. ..	Warwick ..	Parish	375	Ramsgill ..	York ..	Sub-dis.	1 189
Radwell.. ..	Beds ..	Hamlet	202	Ramsgill, St. Mary	,, ..	Ecl. Dis.	523
Radwell.. ..	Herts ..	Parish	102	Ramsgrave ..	Lancaster ..	Tnship.	820
Radwinter ..	Essex ..	Sub-dis.	5 035	Ramsholt ..	Suffolk ..	Parish	186
Radwinter ..	,, ..	Parish	946	Ramshope ..	Northumberland	Parish	6
Radyr	Glamorgan .	Parish	472	Ramshorn ..	Stafford ..	Tnship.	118
Ragdale.. ..	Leicester ..	Parish	120	Ranby	Lincoln ..	Parish	142
Ragland ..	Monmouth ..	Hund.	8 024	Rand	,,	Parish	165
Ragland ..	,, ..	L. Sub.	3 430	Rand	,,	Tnship.	92
Ragland ..	,, ..	Parish	905	Rands Grange ..	York ..	Tnship.	21
Ragnall ..	Notts ..	Parish	204	Randwick ..	Gloucester ..	Parish	1 060
Rainford ..	Lancaster ..	Sub-dis.	2 784	Rangeworthy ..		Chap.	250
Rainford	,, ..	Tnship.	2 784	Ranmore, St. Barnabas	Surrey	Ecl. Dis.	275
Rainham ..	Essex ..	Parish	924	Ranscliff ..	Stafford ..	Tnship.	1 443
Rainham ..	Kent ..	Parish	1 422	Ranskill.. ..	Notts ..	Tnship.	337
Rainham, East ..	Norfolk ..	Parish	139	Ranton ..	Stafford ..	Parish	283
Rainham, South	,, ..	Parish	129	Ranton Abbey ..	,, ..	Parish	13
Rainham, West .	,, ..	Parish	369	Ranworth ..	Norfolk ..	Parish	282
Rainhill ..	Lancaster ..	Tnship.	2 130	Rapsgate ..	Gloucester ..	Hund.	3 998

Name of Place.	County.	Description.	Population	Name of Place.	County.	Description.	Population
Rasen, Market ..	Lincoln ..	Parish	2 563	Rawreth ..	Essex ..	Parish	386
Rasen, Middle ..	,, ..	Parish	1 063	Rawtenstall, St. Mary	Lanc...	Ecl. Dis.	7 823
Rasen, West ..	,, ..	Parish	245	Raydon ..	Suffolk ..	Parish	561
Raskelf ..	York ..	Chap.	577	Rayleigh ..	Essex ..	Sub-dis.	4 937
Rastrick ..	,, ..	Sub-dis.	4 904	Rayleigh ..	,, ..	Parish	1 433
Rastrick ..	,, ..	Tnship.	4 516	Rayne ..	,, ..	Parish	401
Ratby ..	Leicester ..	Parish	1 264	Reach ..	Cambs ..	Hamlet	448
Ratby ..	,, ..	Tnship.	690	Read ..	Lancaster ..	Tnship.	531
Ratchwood	Northumberland	Tnship.	14	Reading ..	Berks ..	Hund.	9 912
Ratcliff ..	Middlesex ..	Sub-dis.	16 874	Reading ..	,, ..	L. Sub.	40 321
Ratcliff ..	,, ..	Hamlet	16 874	Reading ..	,, ..	District	25 876
Ratcliff, St. James	,, ..	Ecl. Dis.	8 445	**Reading** ..	,, ..	Borough	25 045
Ratcliffe, Culey..	Leicester ..	Chap.	208	Rearsby ..	Leicester ..	Parish	468
Ratcliff on Wreak	,, ..	Parish	126	Reavely ..	Northumberland	Tnship.	66
Ratcliffe on Soar	Notts ..	Parish	165	Rectory ..	Middlesex ..	Sub-dis.	26 692
Ratcliffe on Trent	,, ..	Sub-dis.	7 791	Reculver ..	Kent ..	Parish	254
Ratcliffe on Trent	,, ..	Parish	1 371	Redbank St. Thomas	Lancaster	Ecl. Dis.	8 167
Rathmell ..	York ..	Tnship.	304	Redberth ..	Pembroke ..	Parish	107
Rathmell Trinity	,, ..	Ecl. Dis.	342	Redbornestoke ..	Beds ..	Hund.	15 984
Ratley ..	Warwick ..	Parish	476	Redbourn ..	Herts ..	Parish	2 043
Ratlinghope ..	Salop ..	Parish	285	Redbourne ..	Lincoln ..	Parish	320
Rattery ..	Devon ..	Parish	396	Redcar ..	York ..	Tnship.	1 330
Rattlesden ..	Suffolk ..	Sub-dis.	6 551	Redcliff, St. Mary	Gloucester ..	Parish	7 467
Rattlesden ..	,, ..	Parish	1 117	Reddall Hill ..	Stafford ..	Ecl. Dis.	10 349
Rauceby, North .	Lincoln ..	Parish	279	Reddish ..	Lancaster ..	Tnship.	1 363
Rauceby, South .	,, ..	Parish	474	Redditch ..	Worcester ..	Tnship.	5 441
Raughton & Gaitsgill	Cumbld.	Tnship.	271	**Redditch** ..	Worc. & War.	Town	5 571
Raunds ..	Nthptn. & Hunts	Sub-dis.	6 606	Redditch, St. Stephen	Worc...	Ecl. Dis.	5 441
Raunds ..	Northampton	Parish	2 337	Redenhall ..	Norfolk ..	Parish	1 736
Raveley, Great..	Hunts ..	Parish	318	Redenhall ..	,, ..	Hamlet	434
Raveley, Little..	,, ..	Parish	60	Redgrave ..	Suffolk ..	Parish	1 266
Ravendale, East .	Lincoln ..	Parish	144	Redgrave ..	,, ..	Hamlet	686
Ravendale, East .	,, ..	Hamlet	94	Redhill ..	Hants ..	Ecl. Dis.	343
Ravendale, West	,, ..	Chap.	50	Redisham ..	Suffolk ..	Parish	182
Ravenfield ..	York ..	Parish	183	Redlingfield ..	,, ..	Parish	203
Raveningham ..	Norfolk ..	Parish	264	Redlynch ..	Somerset ..	Tithing	61
Ravenscroft ..	Cheshire ..	Tnship.	32	Redlynch, St. Mary	Wilts ..	Ecl. Dis.	1 170
Ravensdale Park	Derby ..	Hamlet	66	Redmarley	Worc. & Glouc.	Sub-dis.	5 731
Ravensden ..	Beds ..	Parish	477	Redmarley D'Abitot	Worcester	Parish	1 265
Ravensthorpe ..	Northampton	Parish	701	Redmarshall ..	Durham ..	Parish	278
Ravensthorpe ..	,, ..	Tnship.	489	Redmarshall ..	,, ..	Tnship.	62
Ravenstone ..	Bucks ..	Parish	400	Redmile ..	Leicester ..	Parish	521
Ravenstone ..	Leic. & Derby	Parish	392	Redmire ..	York ..	Tnship.	440
Ravenstone Dale	Westmoreland	Parish	1 264	Redmore ..	Norfolk ..	—	18
Ravensworth ..	Durham ..	Tnship.	138	Redruth ..	Cornwall ..	District	57 173
Ravensworth ..	York ..	Tnship.	257	Redruth ..	,, ..	Sub-dis.	11 504
Raventhorpe ..	Lincoln ..	Hamlet	26	Redruth ..	,, ..	Parish	11 504
Raw ..	Northumberland	Tnship.	67	**Redruth** ..	,, ..	Town	7 919
Rawcliffe, Out ..	Lancaster ..	Tnship.	771	Redwick & Northwick	Glouc...	Tithing	267
Rawcliffe, Upper, &c.	,, ..	Tnship.	682	Redwick ..	Monmouth ..	Chap.	289
Rawcliffe ..	York N. ..	Tnship.	115	Redworth ..	Durham ..	Tnship.	325
Rawcliffe ..	,, W. ..	Tnship.	1 630	Reed ..	Herts ..	Parish	224
Rawden ..	York ..	Tnship.	2 576	Reed ..	Suffolk ..	Parish	245
Rawmarsh ..	,, ..	Parish	4 374	Reedham ..	Norfolk ..	Parish	836

Name of Place.	County.	Description.	Population.	Name of Place.	County.	Description.	Population.
edley-Hallows, &c.	Lancaster	Tnship.	423	Rhandir Abbot	Carmarthen	Hamlet	553
edness	York	Tnship.	601	Rhandir Canol	„	Hamlet	297
epham	Lincoln	Parish	436	Rhandir Isaf	„	Hamlet	433
epham	Norfolk	Parish	346	Rhandir Uchaf	„	Hamlet	276
eeth	York	District	6 196	Rhayader	Radnor	Hund.	4 853
eeth	„	Sub-dis.	3 569	Rhayader	„	L. Sub.	4 853
eeth	„	Tnship.	1 299	Rhayader	Radn. & Brec.	District	6 816
egent Road	Lancaster	Sub-dis.	33 468	Rhayader	„ „	Sub-dis.	3 639
egents Park	Middlesex	Sub-dis.	34 927	Rhayader	Radnor	Parish	846
egent Square, St. Peter	„	Ecl. Dis.	9 777	Rhayader	„	P. Bor.	1 030
eigate	Surrey	Hund.	19 143	Rheidol	Cardigan	Sub-dis.	8 635
eigate	„	L. Sub.	19 143	Rhesycae	Flint	Ecl. Dis.	627
eigate	„	District	20 109	Rhigos	Glamorgan	Hamlet	822
eigate	„	Sub-dis.	13 704	Rhinefield	Hants	—	23
eigate	„	Parish	9 975	Rhiw	Carnarvon	Parish	370
eigate	„	P. Bor.	9 975	Rhiwrhiad	Radnor	Tnship.	141
eigate	„	Old Bor.	2 008	Rhodogeidio	Anglesey	Parish	284
eigate	„	Foreign	7 967	Rhosbeirio	„	Parish	26
eighton	York	Parish	251	Rhoscilly	Glamorgan	Parish	294
einden	Kent	—	4	Rhoscolyn	Anglesey	Parish	462
emenham	Berks	Parish	493	Rhoscrowther	Pembroke	Parish	202
empstone	Notts	Parish	377	Rhosferig	Brecon	Hamlet	95
endcombe	Gloucester	Parish	246	Rhosgoch	Montgomery	Tnship.	48
endham	Suffolk	Parish	384	Rhos Llannerchrugog	Denbigh	Ecl. Dis.	6 620
endlesham	„	Parish	359	Rhos-y-Gwalia	Merioneth	Ecl. Dis.	356
enhold	Beds	Parish	513	Rhosymedre	Denbigh	Ecl. Dis.	5 305
ennington	Northumberland	Tnship.	263	Rhostie	Cardigan	Parish	122
enwick	Cumberland	Parish	266	Rhuddlan	Flint	Hund.	11 564
epham	Lincoln	Parish	436	Rhuddlan, &c.	„	L. Sub.	17 436
epps, North	Norfolk	Parish	625	Rhuddlan	„	Parish	4 397
epps, South	„	Parish	816	Rhuddlan	„	P. Bor.	1 406
epps w. Bastwick	„	Parish	293	Rhulen	Radnor	Parish	111
epton & Gresley	Derby	Hund.	23 859	Rhydgwern	Glamorgan	Hamlet	323
epton & Gresley	„	L. Sub	23 859	Rhydyboithan	„	Hamlet	1 925
epton	„	Sub-dis.	6 484	Rhydycroesau	Salop & Denb.	Ecl. Dis.	328
epton	„	Parish	2 177	Rhyl	Flint	Ecl. Dis.	2 965
epton	„	Tnship.	1 853	Rhymney	Monmouth	Ecl. Dis.	7 630
esolven	Glamorgan	Hamlet	762	Rhyndwyclydach	Glamorgan	Hamlet	1 720
eston, North	Lincoln	Parish	44	Ribbesford	Worcester	Parish	3 158
eston, South	„	Parish	235	Ribbesford	„	Tnship.	253
etford	Notts	L. Sub.	29 593	Ribbleton	Lancaster	Tnship.	175
etford, East	„	Parish	2 982	Ribby w. Wrea	„	Tnship.	444
etford, East	„	M. Bor.	2 982	Ribchester	„	Parish	3 885
		P. Bor.	47 330	Ribchester	„	Tnship.	1 357
etford, West	„	Parish	637	Ribston Gt. w. Walshford	York	Tnship.	180
ettendon	Essex	Parish	785	Ribston, Little	„	Tnship.	230
evelstoke	Devon	Parish	505	Ribton	Cumberland	Tnship.	18
evesby	Lincoln	Parish	614	Riby	Lincoln	Parish	242
ewe	Devon	Parish	260	Riccall	York	Sub-dis.	3 487
ewe	„	Hamlet	163	Riccall	„	Parish	783
eydon	Suffolk	Parish	294	Richards Castle	Salop & Heref.	Parish	710
eymerston	Norfolk	Parish	21	Richmond	Surrey	L. Sub.	18 802
eynoldston	Glamorgan	Parish	270	Richmond	„	District	18 802
eynoldston	Pembroke	Parish	106	Richmond	„	Sub-dis.	12 665

Name of Place.	County.	Description.	Population.	Name of Place.	County.	Description.	Population.
Richmond	_Surrey_	Parish	10 926	Ringwould	_Kent_	Parish	846
Richmond	,,	Town	7 423	Ripe	_Sussex_	Parish	358
Richmond, St. John	,,	Ecl. Dis.	4 721	Ripley	_Derby_	Sub-dis.	12 185
Richmond	_York_	District	13 457	Ripley	,,	Chap.	5 244
Richmond	,,	Sub-dis.	7 174	Ripley	,,	Ecl. Dis.	5 199
Richmond	,,	Parish	4 290	Ripley	_Surrey_	Sub-dis.	2 591
Richmond	,,	M. Bor.	4 290	Ripley	,,	Chap.	933
Richmond	,,	P. Bor.	5 134	Ripley	_York_	Parish	1 558
Rickerby	_Cumberland_	Tnship.	97	Ripley	,,	Tnship.	330
Rickergate	,,	Tnship.	3 564	Riplington	_Northumberland_	Tnship.	16
Rickinghall, Inferior	_Suffolk_	Parish	437	Ripon	,,	Diocese	1167288
Rickinghall, Superior	,,	Parish	742	Ripon	_York_	District	15 742
Rickling	_Essex_	Parish	502	Ripon	,,	Sub-dis.	8 979
Rickmansworth	_Herts_	Sub-dis.	5 609	Ripon	,,	Parish	15 165
Rickmansworth	,,	Parish	4 873	Ripon	,,	Tnship.	5 619
Riddles Quarter	_Nrthumbld._	Tnship.	205	Ripon	,,	City	6 172
Riddlesworth	_Norfolk_	Parish	97	Ripon, Holy Trinity	,,	Ecl. Dis.	2 848
Riddings, St. James	_Derby_	Ecl. Dis.	4 145	Rippingale	_Lincoln_	Parish	569
Ridgacre	_Worcester_	Tnship.	492	Ripple	_Essex_	Ward	515
Ridge	_Herts_	Parish	437	Ripple	_Kent_	Parish	254
Ridge	_Wilts_	Tithing	176	Ripple	_Worcester_	Parish	1 045
Ridgmont	_Beds_	Parish	1 029	Ripplesmere	_Berks_	Hund.	8 873
Ridgway, St. John	_Derby_	Ecl. Dis.	1 745	Ripponden	_York_	Sub-dis.	6 620
Ridgwell	_Essex_	Parish	795	Risbridge	_Suffolk_	Hund.	17 604
Riding	_Northumberland_	Tnship.	142	Risbridge	_Suff. & Essex_	District	17 432
Ridley	_Cheshire_	Tnship.	129	Risby	_Suffolk_	Parish	427
Ridley	_Denbigh_	Tnship.	25	Risby	_York_	Hamlet	46
Ridley	_Kent_	Parish	101	Risca	_Monmouth_	Parish	2 744
Ridley	_Northumberland_	Tnship.	232	Rise	_York_	Parish	188
Ridlington	_Norfolk_	Parish	236	Riseholme	_Lincoln_	Parish	93
Ridlington	_Rutland_	Parish	282	Riseley	_Beds_	Sub-dis.	2 778
Rigsby	_Lincoln_	Parish	102	Riseley	,,	Parish	1 026
Rigton	_York_	Tnship.	501	Rishangles	_Suffolk_	Parish	229
Rillington	,,	Sub-dis.	4 287	Rishton	_Lancaster_	Tnship.	1 198
Rillington	,,	Parish	1 132	Rishworth	_York_	Tnship.	1 244
Rillington	,,	Tnship.	884	Risley	_Derby_	Chap.	203
Rilston	,,	Tnship.	107	Rissington, Great	_Gloucester_	Parish	499
Rimmington	,,	Tnship.	501	Rissington, Little	,,	Parish	290
Rimpton	_Somerset_	Parish	282	Rissington-Wick	,,	Parish	206
Rimswell	_York_	Tnship.	137	Riston, Long	_York_	Parish	401
Ringland	_Norfolk_	Parish	360	Ritton Colt Park	_Nrthumberld._	Tnship.	69
Ringmer	_Sussex_	Parish	1 522	Ritton Whitehouse	,,	Tnship.	22
Ringmore	_Devon_	Parish	271	Rivaulx	_York_	Tnship.	229
Ringsash	,,	Parish	842	Rivenhall	_Essex_	Parish	719
Ringsfield	_Suffolk_	Parish	324	River	_Kent_	Parish	445
Ringshall	,,	Parish	359	River Green	_Northumberland_	Parish	50
Ringstead	_Northampton_	Parish	831	Riverhead	_Kent_	Liberty	1 800
Ringstead	_Norfolk_	Parish	522	Rivington	_Lancaster_	Sub-dis.	3 493
Ringwood	_Hants_	Division	20 911	Rivington	,,	Tnship.	369
Ringwood	,,	L. Sub.	20 911	Rixton	,,	Sub-dis.	1 920
Ringwood	,,	Union	5 151	Rixton w. Glazebrook	,,	Tnship.	752
Ringwood	,,	District	5 357	Road	_Somerset_	Sub-dis.	3 573
Ringwood	,,	Sub-dis.	5 357	Road	,,	Parish	663
Ringwood	,,	Parish	3 751	Road Hill, Christch.	_Wilts_	Ecl. Dis.	408

Name of Place.	County.	Description.	Population.	Name of Place.	County.	Description.	Population.
Roade	Northampton	Parish	664	Rode, North ..	Cheshire ..	Tnship.	285
Roath	Glamorgan .	Parish	3 044	Rode, North, St. Michael „ ..		Ecl. Dis.	285
Robert Twn., All Saints	York ..	Ecl. Dis.	2 256	Rodington ..	Salop ..	Parish	481
Robeston Wathen	Pembroke ..	Parish	362	Rodmarton ..	Gloucester ..	Parish	401
Robeston, West .	„ ..	Parish	159	Rodmell ..	Sussex ..	Parish	292
Roborough ..	Devon ..	Hund.	27 803	Rodmersham ..	Kent ..	Parish	294
Roborough ..	„ ..	L. Sub.	64 783	Rodney Stoke ..	Somerset ..	Parish	323
Roborough ..	„ ..	Parish	478	Rodsley ..	Derby ..	Tnship.	197
Roby	Lancaster ..	Tnship.	467	Roeburndale ..	Lancaster ..	Tnship.	144
Roby, St. Bartholomew „ ..		Ecl. Dis.	715	Roecliffe ..	York ..	Ecl. Dis.	231
Rocester.. ..	Stafford ..	Parish	1 175	Roecliffe ..	„ ..	Tnship.	231
Roch	Pembroke ..	Parish	679	Roehampton Trinity	Surrey ..	Ecl. Dis.	974
Rochdale ..	Lancaster ..	District	91 754	Roel	Gloucester ..	Parish	50
Rochdale ..	Lanc. & York	Parish	119 531	Rofford.. ..	Oxon ..	Liberty	18
		M. Bor.	38 114	Rogate	Sussex ..	Parish	990
Rochdale ..	Lancaster {	P. Bor.	38 184	Rogerstone ..	Monmouth ..	Hamlet	1 210
Rochdale St. Alban „ ..		Ecl. Dis.	5 391	Roggiett ..	„ ..	Parish	36
Rochdale, St. James „ ..		Ecl. Dis.	7 130	Rokeby.. ..	York ..	Parish	151
Roche ..	Cornwall ..	Parish	1 882	Rollesby ..	Norfolk ..	Parish	531
Rochester	..	Diocese	608 914	Rolleston ..	Leicester ..	Tnship.	42
Rochester ..	Kent ..	L. Sub.	92 796	Rolleston ..	Notts ..	Parish	587
Rochester ..	„ ..	Sub-dis.	17 550	Rolleston ..	„ ..	Tnship.	268
Rochester ..	„ ..	City	16 862	Rolleston ..	Stafford ..	Parish	956
Rochester St. Peter „ ..		Ecl. Dis.	4 361	Rolleston ..	„ ..	Tnship.	608
Rochester Ward .	Northumbld.	Tnship.	406	Rollright, Great	Oxon ..	Parish	410
Rochford ..	Essex ..	Hund.	17 178	Rollright, Little .	„ ..	Parish	36
Rochford ..	„ ..	L. Sub.	18 282	Rolls, The ..	Middlesex ..	Liberty	2 274
Rochford ..	„ ..	District	18 282	Rolls Lib. St. Thos.	„ ..	Ecl. Dis.	2 274
Rochford ..	„ ..	Sub-dis.	3 895	Rollstone ..	Wilts ..	Parish	52
Rochford ..	„ ..	Parish	1 696	Rolvenden ..	Kent ..	Sub-dis.	4 331
Rochford ..	Worcester ..	Parish	315	Rolvenden ..	„ ..	Parish	1 483
Rock ..	Northumberland	Tnship.	230	Romald Kirk ..	York ..	Parish	2 417
Rock ..	Worcester ..	Parish	1 379	Romald Kirk ..	„ ..	Tnship.	327
Rockbeare ..	Devon ..	Parish	540	Romanby ..	„ ..	Tnship.	362
Rock Bedwelty ..	Monmouth ..	Sub-dis.	2 962	Romansleigh ..	Devon ..	Parish	230
Rockbourn ..	Hants ..	Parish	507	Romford ..	Essex ..	District	26 965
Rockferry ..	Cheshire ..	Ecl. Dis.	2 086	Romford ..	„ ..	Sub-dis.	9 741
Rockfield ..	Monmouth ..	Parish	270	Romford ..	„ ..	Parish	6 604
Rockhampton ..	Gloucester ..	Parish	248	Romford ..	„ ..	Town	4 361
Rockingham ..	Northampton	Parish	211	Romiley.. ..	Cheshire ..	Tnship.	1 468
Rockingham Forest „ ..		Lodge	9	Romney Marsh .	Kent ..	District	5 708
Rockland All Saints	Norfolk ..	Parish	373	Romney New ..	„ ..	Parish	1 062
Rockland St. Andrew „ ..		Parish	111	Romney, Old ..	„ ..	Parish	151
Rockland St. Peter „ ..		Parish	386	Romsey.. ..	Hants ..	Division	12 015
Rockland St. Mary „ ..		Parish	476	Romsey.. ..	„ ..	L. Sub.	14 131
Rockliff.. ..	Cumberland	Parish	949	Romsey.. ..	Hants & Wilts	District	10 771
Rocksavage ..	Cheshire ..	Tnship.	30	Romsey.. ..	Hants ..	Sub-dis.	6 795
Rodborne Cheney	Wilts ..	Parish	670	Romsey.. ..	„ ..	Parish	5 848
Rodborough ..	Gloucester ..	Sub-dis.	5 019	Romsey ..	„ ..	M. Bor.	2 116
Rodborough ..	„ ..	Parish	2 165	Romsley ..	Salop ..	Liberty	136
Rodbourn ..	Wilts ..	Tithing	162	Romsley ..	Worcester ..	Tnship.	377
Rodd, &c. ..	Hereford ..	Tnship.	153	Romsley St. Kenelm „ ..		Ecl. Dis.	377
Roddam ..	Northumberland	Tnship.	118	Rookwith ..	York ..	Tnship.	49
Rodden ..	Somerset ..	Parish	234	Roos ..	„ ..	Parish	652

Name of Place.	County.	Description.	Population.	Name of Place.	County.	Description.	Population.
Roosdown	Devon	Parish	13	Christchurch	Surrey	Ecl. Dis.	4 616
Roose	Pembroke	Hund.	16 197	Trinity	,,	Ecl. Dis.	3 448
Roose	,,	L. Sub.	21 623	Rothersthorpe	Northampton	Parish	289
Roose	,,	Sub-dis.	3 225	Rotherwick	Hants	Parish	386
Roothing, Abbots	Essex	Parish	220	Rothley	Leicester	Sub-dis.	4 796
Roothing, Aythorp	,,	Parish	269	Rothley	,,	Parish	2 213
Roothing, Beauchamp	,,	Parish	226	Rothley	,,	Tnship.	939
Roothing, Berners	,,	Parish	94	Rothley Temple	,,	Parish	80
Roothing, High	,,	Parish	469	Rothley	Northumberland	Tnship	174
Roothing, Leaden	,,	Parish	207	Rothwell	Lincoln	Parish	267
Roothing, Margaret	,,	Parish	236	Rothwell	Northampton	Hund.	9 231
Roothing, White	,,	Parish	466	Rothwell	,,	Sub-dis.	6 179
Rope	Cheshire	Tnship.	88	Rothwell	,,	Parish	2 354
Ropley	Hants	Sub-dis.	3 508	Rothwell	,,	Tnship.	2 263
Ropley	,,	Parish	796	Rothwell	York	Sub-dis.	4 122
Ropsley	Lincoln	Parish	845	Rothwell	,,	Parish	8 072
Ropsley	,,	Tnship.	746	Rothwell	,,	Tnship.	3 220
Rose Ash	Devon	Parish	549	Rotsea	,,	Tnship.	41
Rosedale, East Side	York	Tnship.	446	Rottingdean	Sussex	Sub-dis.	2 392
Rosedale, West Side	,,	Tnship.	338	Rottingdean	,,	Parish	1 016
Roseden	Northumberland	Tnship.	68	Rottington	Cumberland	Tnship.	44
Rosemarket	Pembroke	Parish	451	Rouchester	Northumberland	Tnship.	58
Rosherville St. Mark	Kent	Ecl. Dis.	1 498	Roudham	Norfolk	Parish	132
Rosley	Cumberland	Tnship.	252	Rougham	,,	Parish	409
Rosliston	Derby	Parish	382	Rougham	Suffolk	Sub-dis.	6 185
Ross	Hereford	L. Sub.	11 788	Rougham	,,	Parish	988
Ross	Heref. & Glouc.	District	16 306	Roughdown	Hants	—	60
Ross	,, ,,	Sub-dis.	9 032	Roughlee Booth	Lancaster	Tnship.	424
Ross	Hereford ,,	Parish	4 346	Roughton	Lincoln	Parish	131
Ross	,, ,,	Town	3 715	Roughton	Norfolk	Parish	412
Ross	Northumberland	Tnship.	64	Roundhay	York	Tnship.	570
Rossendale	Lancaster	Sub-dis.	12 637	Rounton, East	,,	Tnship.	114
Rosset Christchurch	Denbigh	Ecl. Dis.	1 371	Rounton, West	,,	Parish	222
Rossington	York	Parish	400	Rouse Lench	Worcester	Parish	306
Rostherne	Cheshire	Parish	4 058	Rousham	Oxon	Parish	131
Rostherne	,,	Tnship.	393	Routh	York	Parish	172
Rothbury	Northumberland	District	7 147	Rowberrow	Somerset	Parish	241
Rothbury	,,	Sub-dis.	5 310	Row-Bound	Cumberland	Tnship.	96
Rothbury	,,	Parish	2 387	Rowde	Wilts	Parish	1 142
Rothbury	,,	Tnship.	798	Rowell	Gloucester	Parish	50
Rotherby	Leicester	Parish	134	Rowington	Warwick	Parish	995
Rotherfield-Greys	Oxon	Parish	1 629	Rowington	,,	Tnship.	974
Rotherfield-Peppard	,,	Parish	437	Rowland	Derby	Tnship.	70
Rotherfield Trinity	,,	Ecl. Dis.	1 235	Rowlands Marsh	Lincoln	—	38
Rotherfield	Sussex	Sub-dis.	6 101	Rowley Regis	Stafford	Sub-dis.	19 785
Rotherfield	,,	Parish	3 413	Rowley Regis	,,	Parish	19 785
Rotherham	York & Derby	District	44 350	Rowley	York	Parish	476
Rotherham	York	Sub-dis.	12 094	Rowley, &c.	,,	Hamlet	373
Rotherham	,,	Parish	24 003	Rowlstone	Hereford	Parish	145
Rotherham	,,	Tnship.	8 390	Rowlstone	York	Hamlet	50
Rotherham	,,	Town	7 598	Rowner	Hants	Parish	147
Rotherhithe	Surrey	District	24 502	Rownham, St. John	,,	Ecl. Dis.	393
Rotherhithe	,,	Parish	24 502	Rowsley, Great	Derby	Tnship.	295
All Saints	,,	Ecl. Dis.	6 212	Rowsley, St. Catherine	,,	Ecl. Dis.	616

Name of Place.	County.	Description.	Population.	Name of Place.	County.	Description.	Population.
wston	Lincoln	Parish	224	**Rugby**	Warwick	Town	7 818
wton	Cheshire	Tnship.	163	Rugby, St. Matthew	,,	Ecl. Dis.	2 919
xby w. Risby	Lincoln	Parish	348	Rugeley	Stafford	L. Sub.	9 014
xby	York	Tnship.	234	Rugeley	,,	Sub-dis.	7 148
xham	Norfolk	Parish	58	Rugeley	,,	Parish	4 362
xholme	Lincoln	Hamlet	92	**Rugeley**	,,	Town	4 362
xton	Beds	Parish	688	Ruishton	Somerset	Parish	506
xwell	Essex	Parish	986	Ruislip	Middlesex	Parish	1 365
ydon	,,	Parish	910	Rumbolds-Wyke	Sussex	Parish	582
ydon, near Diss	Norfolk	Parish	607	Rumburgh	Suffolk	Parish	405
ydon, ur. Freebge. Lynn	,,	Parish	196	Rumney	Monmouth	Parish	356
yston	Herts	L. Sub.	8 748	Rumworth	Lancaster	Tnship.	1 861
yston	Herts, &c.	District	25 014	Runcorn	Cheshire	District	26 792
yston	,, ,,	Sub-dis.	10 175	Runcorn	,,	Sub-dis.	13 590
yston	,, ,,	Union	18 625	Runcorn	,,	Parish	16 457
yston	Herts & Cambs	Parish	1 882	Runcorn	,,	Tnship.	10 063
ystone	York	Parish	4 210	**Runcorn**	,,	Town	10 434
ystone	,,	Tnship.	545	Runcorn, Holy Trinity,	,,	Ecl. Dis.	3 515
yton	Denbigh	Tnship.	94	Runcton, North	Norfolk	Parish	304
yton	Lancaster	Sub-dis.	9 520	Runcton, South	,,	Parish	139
yton	,,	Tnship.	7 493	Runhall	,,	Parish	246
yton, St. Paul	,,	Ecl. Dis.	7 493	Runham	,,	Parish	396
xabon	Denbigh	L. Sub.	14 570	Runnington	Somerset	Parish	100
xabon	Denb. & Flint	Sub-dis.	14 680	Runton	Norfolk	Parish	510
xabon	Denbigh	Parish	14 343	Runwell	Essex	Parish	366
xan-Lanihorne	Cornwall	Parish	325	Ruscomb	Berks	Parish	264
xan Major	,,	Parish	141	Rushall	Norfolk	Parish	242
xan Minor	,,	Parish	260	Rushall	Stafford	Parish	2 842
xardean	Gloucester	Parish	1 054	Rushall	Wilts	Parish	224
uckinge	Kent	Parish	429	Rushbrooke	Suffolk	Parish	185
uckland	Lincoln	Parish	46	Rushbury	Salop	Parish	576
uckley & Langley	Salop	Tnship.	78	Rushcliffe	Notts	Wapen.	11 777
udbaxton	Pembroke	Parish	586	Rushden	Herts	Parish	291
udby in Cleveland	York	Parish	1 147	Rushden	Northampton	Parish	1 748
udby in Cleveland	,,	Tnship.	69	Rushen	Isle of Man	Parish	3 300
udchester	Northumberland	Tnship.	58	Rushford	Norf. & Suff.	Parish	170
uddington	Notts	Parish	2 283	Rushmere	Suffolk	Parish	121
udford	Gloucester	Parish	202	Rushmere, St. Andrew	,,	Parish	678
udford	,,	Tnship.	105	Rushock	Worcester	Parish	159
udge	Salop	Tnship.	167	Rusholme	Lancaster	Tnship.	5 380
udgwick	Sussex	Parish	1 068	Rusholme, Holy Trinity	,,	Ecl. Dis.	2 508
udham, East	Norfolk	Parish	956	Rushton	Cheshire	Tnship.	342
udham, East	,,	Tnship.	940	Rushton	Northampton	Parish	484
udham, West	,,	Parish	487	Rushton Grange	Stafford	Ville	2 652
udheath	Cheshire	Tnship.	411	Rushton James	,,	Tnship.	273
udry	Glamorgan	Parish	329	Rushton Spencer	,,	Tnship.	358
udston	York	Parish	605	Ruskington	Lincoln	Parish	1 089
udyard	Stafford	Tnship.	94	Rusland	Lancaster	Ecl. Dis.	178
ufford	Lancaster	Parish	865	Rusper	Sussex	Parish	590
ufford	Notts	Liberty	420	Rustington	,,	Parish	340
ufforth	York	Parish	297	Ruston, East	Norfolk	Parish	757
ugby	Warwick, &c.	District	24 436	Ruston, South	,,	Parish	102
ugby	Warwick	Sub-dis.	13 601	Ruston Parva	York	Parish	161
ugby	,,	Parish	7 818	Ruswarp	,,	Tnship.	2 995

Name of Place.	County.	Description.	Population.	Name of Place.	County.	Description.	Population
Ruthin	*Denbigh* ..	Hund.	7 363	Saffron Walden .	*Essex* ..	District	19 721
Ruthin	,, ..	L. Sub.	12 850	Saffron Walden .	,, ..	Sub-dis.	9 646
Ruthin	,, ..	District	16 083	Saffron Walden .	,, ..	Parish	5 474
Ruthin	,, ..	Sub-dis.	4 438	**Saffron Walden**	,, ..	M. Bor.	5 474
Ruthin	,, ..	Parish	1 299	Saham Toney ..	*Norfolk* ..	Sub-dis.	7 231
Ruthin.. ..	,, ..	Borough	3 372	Saham Toney ..	,, ..	Parish	1 286
Rutlandshire ..	..	County	21 861	Saighton ..	*Cheshire* ..	Tnship.	272
Ryton ..	*Salop* ..	Parish	1 200	St. Agnes ..	*Scilly Isle* ..	Island	200
Ryall ..	*Northumberland*	Tnship.	101	St. Agnes ..	*Cornwall* ..	Sub-dis.	9 509
Ryarsh ..	*Kent* ..	Parish	447	St. Agnes ..	,, ..	Parish	6 550
Ryburgh, Great .	*Norfolk* ..	Parish	556	St. Albans ..	*Herts* ..	Liberty	40 733
Ryburgh, Little .	,, ..	Parish	232	St. Albans ..	,, ..	L. Sub.	18 926
Rycote	*Oxon* ..	Liberty	46	St. Albans ..	,, ..	District	18 926
Rydall & Loughrigg	*Westmld.*	Tnship.	414	St. Albans ..	,, ..	Sub-dis.	11 926
Ryde	*Hants, I.W.*	Sub-dis.	17 175	St. Albans ..	,, ..	Parish	3 679
Ryde, Holy Trinity	,, ,,	Ecl. Dis.	3 051	**St. Albans** ..	,, ..	M. Bor.	7 675
Ryde	,, ,,	Town	9 269	St. Albans, Christch.	,,	Ecl. Dis.	677
Rye	*Sussex* ..	L. Sub.	6 862	St. Alban, Wood-st.	*Middlesex* .	Parish	276
Rye	*Sussex & Kent*	District	11 927	St. Alban ..	*Worcester* ..	Parish	323
Rye	,, ,,	Sub-dis.	6 353	St. Aldate ..	*Gloucester* ..	Parish	710
Rye	*Sussex* ..	Parish	4 288	St. Aldate ..	*Oxon & Berks*	Parish	1 911
Rye	,, {	M. Bor.	3 738	St. Alkmond ..	*Salop* ..	Parish	1 444
		P. Bor.	8 202	St. Alkmund ..	*Derby* ..	Sub-dis.	17 817
Ryedale.. ..	*York* ..	Wapen.	19 834	St. Alkmund ..	,, ..	Parish	18 582
Ryedale.. ..	,, ..	L. Sub.	11 950	St. Allen ..	*Cornwall* ..	Parish	687
Ryhall	*Rutland* ..	Parish	847	St. Alphage ..	*Kent* ..	Parish	1 152
Ryhill	*York E.* ..	Tnship.	214	St. Alphage ..	*Middlesex* ..	Parish	699
Ryhill	,, *W.* ..	Tnship.	160	St. Andrew Great	*Cambs* ..	Sub-dis.	6 078
Ryhope.. ..	*Durham* ..	Tnship.	2 082	St. Andrew Great	,, ..	Parish	2 633
Ryhope, St. Paul	,, ..	Ecl. Dis.	2 271	St. Andrew Less	,, ..	Sub-dis.	11 848
Ryle, Great	*Northumberland*	Tnship.	99	St. Andrew Less	,, ..	Parish	11 848
Ryle, Little ..	,, ..	Tnship.	35	St. Andrew ..	*Devon* ..	Sub-dis.	39 209
Ryme-Intrinseca	*Dorset* ..	Parish	217	St. Andrew ..	,, ..	Parish	39 524
Rymer	*Suffolk* ..	Parish	19	St. Andrew ..	*Glamorgan* .	Parish	570
Ryston	*Norfolk* ..	Parish	29	St. Andrew Minor	,, ..	Parish	12
Ryther	*York* ..	Parish	372	St. Andrew ..	*Isle of Guern.*	Parish	1 049
Ryther & Ossendike	,, ..	Tnship.	326	St. Andrew ..	*Herts* ..	Parish	2 184
Ryton	*Durham* ..	Parish	3 052	St. Andrew ..	*Kent* ..	Parish	523
Ryton	,, ..	Tnship.	1 140	St. Andrew Eastern	*Middlesex*	Sub-dis.	12 947
Ryton Woodside	,, ..	Tnship.	1 051	St. Andrew, Holborn	,, ..	Parish	28 721
Ryton	*Salop* ..	Parish	213	Above Bars ..	,, ..	—	22 384
Ryton on Dunsmore	*Warwick*	Parish	557	Below Bars ..	,, ..	—	6 337
Ryton	*York* ..	Tnship.	226	St. Andrew Hubbard	,, ..	Parish	205
				St. Andrew Undershaft	,, ..	Parish	1 071
Sacomb ..	*Herts* ..	Parish	314	St. Andrew Wardrobe	,, ..	Parish	682
Sadberge ..	*Durham* ..	Tnship.	355	St. Andrew ..	*Norfolk* ..	Parish	978
Sadberge ..	,, ..	Ecl. Dis.	414	St. Andrew	*Northumberland*	Sub-dis.	17 100
Saddington ..	*Leicester* ..	Parish	259	St. Andrew ..	,, ..	Parish	22 720
Saddlewood, &c. ..	*Gloucester* ..	Tithing	368	St. Andrew ..	,, ..	—	17 100
Saddleworth ..	*York* ..	District	18 631	St. Andrew ..	*Somerset* ..	Liberty	326
Saddleworth ..	,, ..	Tnship.	18 631	St. Andrew, Chichester E.	*Sussex*	Parish	613
Saffron Hill ..	*Middlesex* ..	Sub-dis.	12 012	St. Andrew, Hastings	,, ..	Parish	84
Saffron Hill, &c. ..	,, ..	Liberty	7 148	St. Andrew, Droitwich	*Worc...*	Parish	1 008
Saffron Hill, St. Peter	,, ..	Ecl. Dis.	7 148	St. Andrew, Pershore	,, ..	Parish	2 483

Name of Place.	County.	Description.	Population.	Name of Place.	County.	Description.	Population.
St. Andrew	Worcester	—	976	St. Botolph	Lincoln	Parish	1 027
St. Andrew, Worcester	„	Parish	1 768	St. Botolph	Middlesex	Sub-dis.	20 990
St. Andrew	York	Parish	280	St. Botolph Aldersgate	„	Parish	6 199
St. Ann	Isle of Man	Parish	693	St. Botolph Aldersgate	„	—	4 744
St. Ann & St. Agnes	Middlesex	Parish	362	St. Botolph Aldgate	„	Parish	9 421
St. Anne Blackfriars	„	Parish	2 615	St. Botolph Aldgate	„	Liberty	4 000
St. Anne Soho	„	Sub-dis.	17 426	St. Botolph Billingsgate	„	Parish	222
St. Anne, Soho	„	Parish	17 426	St. Botolph Bishopsgate	„	Parish	11 569
St. Ann	Notts	Sub-dis.	20 079	St. Brelade	Isle of Jersey	Parish	2 354
St. Ann	Sussex	Parish	980	St. Breock	Cornwall	Parish	1 866
St. Antholin	Middlesex	Parish	263	St. Breward	„	Parish	705
St. Anthony Meneage	Cornwall	Parish	252	St. Briavels	Gloucester	Hund.	28 215
St. Anthony Roseland	„	Parish	169	St. Briavels	„	Parish	1 261
St. Anthony Stratford	Wilts	Parish	161	St. Brides	Glamorgan	Hamlet	351
St. Arvans	Monmouth	Parish	379	St. Brides Major	„	Parish	826
St. Arvans Grange	„	Farm	12	St. Brides Minor	„	Parish	879
St. Asaph		Diocese	246 337	St. Brides Minor	„	—	534
St. Asaph	Flint & Denb.	District	27 518	St. Bride super Ely	„	Parish	122
St. Asaph	„ „	Sub-dis.	11 922	St. Bride	Middlesex	Parish	5 660
St. Asaph	„ „	Parish	3 592	St. Brides Netherwent	Monm.	Parish	171
St. Asaph	Flint	—	2 979	St. Brides Netherwent	„	Tnship.	129
St. Asaph	Flint	P. Bor.	2 063	St. Brides Wentlloog	„	Parish	241
St. Athan	Glamorgan	Parish	357	St. Brides	Pembroke	Parish	151
St. Aubyn	Devon	Sub-dis.	7 239	St. Bridget	Cheshire	Parish	1 040
St. Augustine	Gloucester	Sub-dis.	15 398	St. Bridget Beckermet	Cumbld.	Parish	657
St. Augustine	„	Parish	10 476	St. Budeaux	Devon	Parish	1 376
St. Augustine, &c.	Kent	Parish	380	Saintbury	Gloucester	Parish	121
St. Augustine	Middlesex	Parish	110	St. Buryan	Cornwall	Sub-dis.	2 488
St. Augustine	Norfolk	Parish	1 890	St. Buryan	„	Parish	1 428
St. Austell	Cornwall	District	33 797	St. Catherine	Gloucester	Parish	2 478
St. Austell	„	Sub-dis.	14 768	St. Catherine	Somerset	Parish	84
St. Austell	„	Parish	11 893	St. Chad	Salop	Sub-dis.	9 533
St. Austell	„	Town	3 825	St. Chad	„	Parish	8 318
St. Barthol. Hyde	Hants	Parish	953	St. Chad	Stafford	Parish	2 145
St. Bartholomew	Kent	Parish	51	St. Christoph. Stock	Middlesex	Parish	23
St. Barthol. Exchange	Mddlx.	Parish	236	St. Clears	Carmarthen	L. Sub.	12 610
St. Bartholomew, Great	„	Parish	3 426	St. Clears	„	Sub-dis.	6 862
St. Bartholomew, Less	„	Parish	849	St. Clears	„	Parish	1 129
St. Bartholomew	Suffolk	Parish	7	St. Cleer	Cornwall	Parish	3 931
St. Bartholomew	Sussex	Parish	373	St. Clement	Cambs	Parish	907
St. Bees	Cumberland	Sub-dis.	8 681	St. Clement	Cornwall	Sub-dis.	8 089
St. Bees	„	Parish	23 901	St. Clement	„	Parish	3 731
St. Bees	„	Tnship.	1 031	St. Clement	Isle of Jersey	Parish	1 448
St. Benedict	Cambs	Parish	967	St. Clement	Kent	Parish	889
St. Benedict	Hunts	Parish	821	St. Clement Danes	Middlesex	Sub-dis.	15 207
St. Benedict	Lincoln	Parish	653	St. Clement Danes	„	Parish	15 592
St. Benedict	Norfolk	Parish	1 381	St. Clement, Eastcheap	„	Parish	198
St. Benet Fink	Middlesex	Parish	213	St. Clement	Norfolk	Parish	3 961
St. Benet Gracech. St.	„	Parish	278	St. Clement	Oxon	Sub-dis.	13 506
St. Benet Paul's Wharf	„	Parish	537	St. Clement	„	Parish	2 286
St. Benet Sherehog	„	Parish	114	St. Clement	Suffolk	Sub-dis.	8 911
St. Blazey	Cornwall	Parish	4 224	St. Clement	„	Parish	7 061
St. Botolph	Cambs	Parish	758	St. Clement	Sussex	Parish	4 073
St. Botolph	Essex	Parish	6 228	St. Clement	Worcester	Parish	2 434

Name of Place.	County.	Description.	Population.	Name of Place.	County.	Description.	Population.
St. Clether	*Cornwall*	Parish	229	St. Faith	*Hants*	Parish	1 39
St. Columb	„	District	16 754	St. Faith	*Middlesex*	Parish	76
St Columb	„	Sub-dis.	6 512	St. Faiths	*Norfolk*	District	11 74
St. Columb Major	„	Parish	2 879	St. Faiths	„	Sub-dis.	5 63
St. Columb Minor	„	Parish	2 067	St. Feock	*Cornwall*	Parish	2 41
St. Cross Hosp. Prec. *Hants*		Parish	36	St. Florenco	*Pembroke*	Parish	45
St. Cross Mill	„	Parish	7	St. Gabriel	*Middlesex*	Parish	17
St. Crux	*York*	Parish	905	St. Gennys	*Cornwall*	Parish	57
St. Cuthbert	*Beds*	Parish	787	St. George	*Denbigh*	Parish	46
St. Cuthbert	*Cumberland*	Sub-dis.	14 127	St. George	*Devon*	Parish	59
St. Cuthbert	„	Parish	13 961	St. George	*Glamorgan*	Parish	21
St. Cuthbert	*Norf. & Suff.*	Parish	1 695	St. George	*Gloucester*	Sub-dis.	10 27
St. Cuthbert	*Somerset*	Parish	7 120	St. George	„	Parish	10 27
St. Cuthbert In	„	—	3 546	St. George Martyr *Kent*		Parish	1 24
St. Cuthbert Out	„	—	3 574	St. George	*Lancaster*	Sub-dis.	16 82
St. Cuthbert	*York*	Parish	2 091	St. George	„	Sub-dis.	48 05
St. David		Diocese	435 912	St. George	*Lincoln*	Parish	1 88
St. David	*Brecon*	Parish	1 418	St. Geo. Bloomsbury *Middlesex*		Sub-dis.	17 39
St. David	*Devon*	Sub-dis.	15 212	St. Geo. Bloomsbury	„	Parish	17 39
St. David	„	Parish	4 486	St. Geo. Botolph-lane	„	Parish	21
St. Davids	*Pembroke*	Sub-dis.	7 347	St. George East	„	District	48 89
St. Davids	„	Parish	2 199	St. George East	„	Parish	48 89
St. Davids Cathedral Close,	„	Parish	37	1 North Ward	„	Ward	15 52
St. Decumans	*Somerset*	Parish	3 196	2 South Ward	„	Ward	33 36
St. Denis Walmgate *York*		Parish	1 463	Christchurch	„	Ecl. Dis.	13 14
St. Dennis	*Cornwall*	Parish	993	St. Mary	„	Ecl. Dis.	5 51
St. Devereux	*Hereford*	Parish	242	St. Matthew	„	Ecl. Dis.	3 24
St. Dionis	*Middlesex*	Parish	534	St. Geo. Hanover-square	„	District	87 77
St. Dogmells	*Pembroke*	Parish	2 438	St. Geo. Hanover-square	„	Parish	87 77
St. Dogwells	„	Parish	436	1 Dover Ward	„	Ward	3 17
St. Dominick	*Cornwall*	Parish	862	2 Conduit Ward	„	Ward	5 21
St. Donats	*Glamorgan*	Parish	126	3 Grosvenor Ward	„	Ward	7 75
St. Dunstan	*Kent*	Parish	1 520	4 Brook Ward	„	Ward	10 81
St. Dunstan East *Middlesex*		Parish	971	5 Curzon Ward	„	Ward	5 69
St. Dunstan West	„	Parish	2 511	6 Knightsbridge Ward	„	Ward	19 68
St. Ebbe	*Oxon*	Parish	4 909	7 Out Ward	„	Ward	35 42
St. Edmund	*Devon*	Parish	1 525	St. George Martyr	„	Sub-dis.	19 90
St. Edmund King *Middlesex*		Parish	333	St. George Martyr	„	Parish	9 86
St. Edmund	*Norfolk*	Parish	753	St. George Colegate *Norfolk*		Parish	1 60
St. Edmund	*Wilts*	Parish	4 458	St. George Tombland	„	Parish	68
St. Edrens	*Pembroke*	Parish	118	St. George	*Somerset*	Sub-dis.	4 81
St. Edward	*Cambs*	Parish	605	St. George	*Surrey*	Sub-dis.	20 33
St. Elvis	*Pembroke*	Parish	33	St. George	„	Ecl. Dis.	20 32
St. Enoder	*Cornwall*	Parish	1 151	St. Geo. Southwark	„	District	55 51
St. Erne	„	Parish	554	St. Geo.	„	Parish	55 51
St. Erney	„	Parish	79	St. Michael Ward	„	Ward	24 778
St. Erth	„	Parish	2 558	St. Paul Ward	„	Ward	12 83
St. Ervan	„	Parish	437	St. George Ward	„	Ward	17 899
St. Ethelburga	*Middlesex*	Parish	606	St. George	*Warwick*	Sub-dis.	44 405
St. Etheldred	*Norfolk*	Parish	614	St. George	*York*	Parish	2 218
St. Eval	*Cornwall*	Parish	295	St. Germans	*Cornwall*	District	17 631
St. Ewe	„	Parish	1 434	St. Germans	„	Sub-dis.	3 513
St. Ewin	*Gloucester*	Parish	76	St. Germans	„	Parish	2 842
St. Fagans	*Glamorgan*	Parish	506	St. Giles	*Berks*	Sub-dis.	10 200

Name of Place.	County.	Description.	Population.	Name of Place.	County.	Description.	Population.
Giles	Berks	Parish	10 200	St. James Tregony	Cornwall	Parish	699
Giles	,,	—	9 456	St. James, Pool..	Dorset	Parish	6 815
Giles	Cambs	Sub-dis.	4 142	St. James, Shaftesbury	,,	Parish	931
Giles	,,	Parish	2 119	St. James	,,	—	589
Giles on Heath	Devon	Parish	342	St. James	Essex	Parish	1 959
Giles in Wood	,,	Parish	962	St. James	Gloucester	Sub-dis.	10 325
Giles	Durham	Parish	6 135	St. James	,,	In.-Par.	10 325
Giles	Essex	Parish	2 736	St. James & St. Paul	,,	Out-Par	9 944
Giles	Middlesex	District	54 076	St. James	Kent	Sub-dis.	12 419
Giles North..	,,	Sub-dis.	17 201	St James	,,	Parish	4 122
Giles South..	,,	Sub-dis.	19 483	St. James Grain.	,,	Parish	255
Giles Cripplegate	,,	Parish	13 498	St. James	Middlesex	L. Sub.	53 105
Giles in Fields	,,	Parish	36 684	St. James Clerkenwell	,,	Sub-dis.	19 152
Giles	Norfolk	Parish	1 586	St. James, Duke's Place	,,	Parish	851
Giles	Northampton	Sub-dis.	23 682	St. James Garlick	,,	Parish	461
Giles	,,	Parish	6 314	St. James's Square	,,	Sub-dis.	10 753
Giles	Oxon	Parish	5 025	St. James Westminster	,,	District	35 326
Giles in Suburbs	York	Parish	2 241	St. James	,,	Parish	35 326
Gluvias	Cornwall	Parish	4 760	1 Pall Mall Ward	,,	Ward	4 753
Gluvias	,,	—	1 213	2 Golden Square Ward	,,	Ward	9 483
t. Gregory	Kent	Ville	1 426	3 Church Ward	,,	Ward	6 769
t. Gregory by St. Paul	Middlx.	Parish	1 154	4 Great Marlboro' Wd.	,,	Ward	14 321
t. Gregory	Norfolk	Parish	934	St. James	Norfolk	Parish	3 408
t. Gregory	Suffolk	Parish	2 781	St. James	,,	—	1 853
t. Harmon	Radnor	Parish	902	St. James	Northampton	Parish	768
t. Helen	Berks	Parish	5 958	St. James	Somerset	Parish	5 788
t. Helen	,,	—	5 317	St. James	Suffolk	Parish	6 714
t. Helens	Hants, I. W.	Parish	2 586	St. James Berdmondsey	Surrey	Sub-dis.	25 154
t. Helens	Lancaster	Sub-dis.	37 961	St. James	Sussex	Parish	54
St. Helens	,,	Town	18 396	St. James	Wilts	Chap.	2 773
St. Helen Bishopsgate	Mddlesx.	Parish	558	St. John	Beds	Parish	465
St. Helen	Norfolk	Parish	507	St. John Evangelist	Brecon	Parish	4 129
St. Helen	Suffolk	Parish	2 748	St. John..	Cheshire	Parish	9 835
St. Helen	Worcester	Parish	1 484	St. John, &c., Little	,,	Parish	61
St. Helen Stonegate	York	Parish	547	St. John..	Cornwall	Parish	213
St. Helen on Walls	,,	Parish	436	St. John Beckermet	Cumberland	Parish	492
St. Helier	Isle of Jersey	Town	29 528	St. John Castlerigg, &c.	,,	Tnship.	605
St. Hilary	Cornwall	Parish	3 459	St. John..	Devon	Parish	653
St. Hilary	,,	—	1 914	St. John..	Durham	Sub-dis.	5 691
St. Hilary	Glamorgan	Parish	139	St. John, Cardiff	Glamorgan	Parish	8 666
St. Ishmaels	Carmarthen	Parish	1 211	St. John, Swansea	,,	Parish	2 738
St. Ishmaels	Pembroke	Parish	469	St. John..	Gloucester	Parish	960
St. Issells	,,	Parish	2 022	St. John Baptist.	,,	Sub-dis.	7 798
St. Issells Harroldston	,,	Parish	281	St. John Baptist.	,,	Parish	3 682
St. Issey	Cornwall	Parish	756	St. John, Winchester	Hants	Parish	1 160
St. Ive ..	,,	Parish	2 593	St. John, Southampton	,,	Parish	733
St. Ives ..	,,	Sub-dis.	8 967	St. John..	Hereford	Parish	1 419
St. Ives ..	,,	Parish	7 027	St. John..	Herts	Parish	2 388
St. Ives	,,	M. Bor.	7 027	St. John..	Hunts	Parish	1 462
St. Ives	,,	P. Bor.	10 353	St. John..	Isle of Jersey	Parish	1 815
St. Ives ..	Hunts	District	19 654	St. John's Hospital	Kent	Parish	27
St. Ives ..	,,	Sub-dis.	8 144	St. John..	Lincoln	Parish	1 199
St. Ives ..	,,	Parish	3 395	St. John Newport	,,	Parish	285
St. Ives	,,	Town	3 321	St. John, Westminster	Middlesex	Sub-dis.	37 483

Name of Place.	County.	Description.	Population.	Name of Place.	County.	Description.	Population.
St. John, St. Geo. E.	*Middlesex*	Sub-dis.	9 695	St. Lawrence	*Hants, I. W.*	Parish	359
St. John Evangelist	,,	Parish	27	St. Lawrence	,,	Parish	238
St. John Paddington	,,	Sub-dis.	36 769	St. Lawrence	*Kent* ,,	Parish	3 287
St. John Savoy	,,	Precinct	380	St. Lawrence Jewry	*Middlesex*	Parish	410
St. John Walbrook	,,	Parish	132	St. Lawrence Pountney	,,	Parish	233
St. John Wapping	,,	Parish	4 038	St. Lawrence	*Norfolk*	Parish	877
St. John Westminster	,,	Parish	37 483	St. Lawrence	*Pembroke*	Parish	205
Ward No. 1	,,	Ward	11 049	St. Lawrence	*Suffolk*	Parish	502
Ward No. 2	,,	Ward	15 513	St. Lawrence	*Worcester*	Parish	1 699
Ward No. 3	,,	Ward	10 921	St. Lawrence	*York*	Parish	2 220
St. John's Wood	,,	Sub-dis.	32 540	St. Leonard	*Berks*	Parish	1 030
,, All Saints	,,	Ecl. Dis.	5 481	St. Leonards	*Bucks*	Hamlet	189
St. John Zachary	,,	Parish	132	St. Leonard	*Devon*	Parish	1 576
St. John Maddrmrkt.	*Norfolk*	Parish	537	St. Leonard	*Essex*	Parish	1 492
St. John Sepulchre	,,	Parish	2 219	St. Leonard	*Gloucester*	Parish	104
St. John Timberhill	,,	Parish	1 802	St. Leonard	*Kent*	Parish	2 871
St. John Baptist.	*Northampton*	Parish	11 497	St. Leonard, &c.	*Leicester*	Parish	441
St. John Baptist.	,,	—	10 321	St. Leonard	*Middlesex*	Sub-dis.	19 188
St. John Lee	*Northumberland*	Parish	2 254	St. Leonard Eastcheap	,,	Parish	111
St. John	,,	Parish	46 533	St. Leonard Foster-lane	,,	Parish	297
St. John	*Oxon*	Parish	187	St. Leonard	*Salop*	Parish	3 044
St. John Horsleydown	*Surrey*	Sub-dis.	11 393	St. Leonards	*Sussex*	Parish	1 693
St. John Horsleydown	,,	Parish	11 393	St. Leonard New,	*York*	Parish	2 221
St. John Southover	*Sussex*	Parish	1 344	St. Levan	*Cornwall*	Parish	447
St. John und. Castle	,,	Parish	2 308	St. Luke	*Middlesex*	District	57 073
St. John	*Warwick*	Sub-dis.	22 166	St. Luke	,,	Parish	57 073
St. John w. St. Michl.	,,	Parish	22 166	1 City Road West Wd.	,,	Ward	9 413
St. John Baptist.	*Wilts*	Parish	1 906	2 Old Street Ward	,,	Ward	8 044
St. John Bedwardine	*Worcester*	Parish	2 974	3 City Road East Wd.	,,	Ward	11 907
St. John	*York*	Parish	1 315	4 West Finsbury Ward	,,	Ward	20 651
St. John Delpike	,,	Parish	428	5 East Finsbury Ward	,,	Ward	7 058
St. John Micklegate	,,	Parish	872	St. Lythans	*Glamorgan*	Parish	136
St. Julian	*Norfolk*	Parish	1 361	St. Mabyn	*Cornwall*	Sub-dis.	3 085
St. Julian	*Salop*	Parish	4 832	St. Mabyn	,,	Parish	714
St. Juliot	*Cornwall*	Parish	226	St. Magnus Martyr	*Middlesex*	Parish	197
St. Just	,,	Sub-dis.	4 737	St. Margaret	*Hereford*	Parish	343
St. Just in Penwith	,,	Sub-dis.	10 903	St. Margaret	*Kent*	Parish	8 130
St. Just in Penwith	,,	Parish	9 290	St. Margaret	,,	Parish	660
St. Just in Roseland	,,	Parish	1 546	St. Margaret Cliffe	,,	Parish	831
St. Katharine Tower	*Middlesex*	Prec.	208	St. Margaret	*Leicester*	Parish	41 835
St. Katharine Coleman	,,	Parish	444	St. Margaret	,,	—	41 194
St. Katharine Cree	,,	Parish	1 794	St. Margaret's Close	*Lincoln*	Parish	452
St. Kerrian	*Devon*	Parish	479	St. Margaret	*Middlesex*	L. Sub.	67 890
St. Keverne	*Cornwall*	Sub-dis.	4 904	St. Margaret Lothbury	,,	Parish	164
St. Keverne	,,	Parish	1 892	St. Margaret Moses	,,	Parish	137
St. Kew	,,	Parish	1 182	St. Marga. New Fish-st.	,,	Parish	317
St. Keyne	,,	Parish	181	St. Margaret Pattens	,,	Parish	103
St. Kingsmark	*Monmouth*	Parish	5	St. Margaret	,,	Sub-dis.	30 730
St. Lawrence	*Berks*	Sub-dis.	4 736	Ward No. 1	,,	Ward	7 558
St. Laurence	*Isle of Jersey*	Parish	2 255	Ward No. 2	,,	Ward	13 737
St. Lawrence	*Berks*	Parish	4 736	Ward No. 3	,,	Ward	9 435
St. Lawrence	*Devon*	Parish	561	St. Margaret	,,	Parish	30 407
St. Lawrence	*Essex*	Parish	184	St. Margaret, Lynn	*Norfolk*	Parish	11 636
St. Lawrence	*Hants, I. W.*	Parish	85	St. Margaret, Norwich	,,	Parish	664

Name of Place	County	Description	Population
. Margaret	Suffolk	Sub-dis.	12 942
. Margaret	,,	Parish	8 108
. Margaret Walmgate	York	Parish	1 704
. Mark	Lincoln	Parish	722
.. Martha on Hill	Surrey	Parish	168
. Martin	Cheshire	Parish	694
. Martin	Cornwall	Parish	1 497
.. Martin	,,	—	343
. Martin in Meneage	,,	Parish	419
. Martin	Devon	Parish	207
.. Martin	Dorset	Parish	617
.. Martin	Essex	Parish	994
.. Martin	Isle of Guern.	Parish	2 000
.. Martin	Isle of Jersey	Parish	3 558
.. Martin	Hereford	Parish	1 457
.. Martin	Kent	Parish	199
t. Martin	Lancaster	Sub-dis.	81 228
t. Martin	Leicester	Parish	2 778
t. Martin	Lincoln	Parish	2 332
t. Martin in Fields	Middlesex	District	22 689
t. Martin in Fields	,,	Parish	22 689
Ward No. 1	,,	Ward	5 744
Ward No. 2	,,	Ward	11 618
Ward No. 3	,,	Ward	5 327
St. John	,,	Ecl. Dis.	2 983
St. Michael	,,	Ecl. Dis.	3 324
t. Martin Ludgate	,,	Parish	1 080
t. Martin Orgars	,,	Parish	296
t. Martin Outwich	,,	Parish	165
t. Martins Pomroy	,,	Parish	185
t. Martins Vintry	,,	Parish	244
t. Martin at Oak	Norfolk	Parish	2 546
t. Martin at Palace	,,	Parish	1 085
t. Martin	Northampton	Parish	1 606
t. Martin	Oxon	Parish	377
t. Martin	Pembroke	Parish	2 120
t. Martin	Salop & Denb.	Sub-dis.	5 909
t. Martin	Salop	Parish	2 351
t. Martin	Isle of Scilly	Island	185
t. Martin	Sussex	Parish	277
t. Martin	Warwick	Sub-dis.	30 252
t. Martin	Wilts	Parish	2 997
t. Martin	Worcester	Parish	5 601
t. Martin	York	Parish	53
t. Martin	,,	Parish	4 413
t. Martin, Coney St.	,,	Parish	460
t. Martin, Micklegate	,,	Parish	727
t. Mary	Beds	Parish	1 869
t. Mary	Berks	Sub-dis.	10 940
t. Mary	,,	Parish	10 940
t. Mary	,,	—	10 853
t. Mary-le-More	,,	Parish	1 198
t. Mary	Brecon	Chap.	2 107
t. Mary Great	Cambs	Sub-dis.	4 293
St. Mary Great	Cambs	Parish	758
St. Mary Less	,,	Parish	800
St. Mary	Cardigan	Parish	2 706
St. Mary Kidwelly	Carmarthen	Parish	1 652
St. Mary Within	,,	—	1 413
St. Mary Without	,,	—	239
St. Mary on Hill	Cheshire	Parish	5 464
St. Mary	Scilly Isles	Parish	2 431
St. Mary, Launceston	Cornwall	Parish	2 069
St. Mary	Cumberland	Sub-dis.	17 648
St. Mary	,,	Parish	18 762
St. Mary Within	,,	—	4 312
St. Mary Arches	Devon	Parish	652
St. Marychurch	,,	Parish	3 231
St. Mary Major	,,	Parish	3 409
St. Mary Steps	,,	Parish	1 422
St. Mary Tavy	,,	Parish	1 202
St. Mary	Dorset	Parish	1 643
St. Mary-le-Bow	Durham	Parish	300
St. Mary Less	,,	Parish	106
St. Mary	Essex	Parish	1 278
St. Mary Magdalen	,,	Parish	473
St. Mary at Walls	,,	Parish	1 505
St. Mary	Glamorgan	Parish	24 288
St. Mary Church	,,	Parish	119
St. Mary Hill	,,	Parish	252
St. Mary Crypt	Gloucester	Parish	953
St. Mary Grace	,,	Parish	251
St. Mary Lode	,,	Parish	8 616
St. Mary Lode	,,	—	950
St. Mary-le-Port	,,	Parish	196
St. Mary Redcliff	,,	Sub-dis.	14 335
St. Mary Redcliff	,,	Parish	7 467
St. Mary	Hants	Parish	28 514
Ss. Mary Bourne	,,	Parish	1 188
St. Mary's & Win. Col.	,,	Parish	41
St. Mary Extra	,,	Sub-dis.	5 675
St. Mary Extra	,,	Parish	2 468
St. Mary Kalender	,,	Parish	896
St. Mary	Hunts	Parish	1 103
St. Mary	Isle of Jersey	Parish	1 040
St. Mary de Castro	Is. of Guern.	Parish	2 071
St. Mary	Kent	Sub-dis.	10 914
St. Mary, Dover	,,	Parish	10 914
St. Mary, Romney	,,	Parish	175
St. Mary, Hoo	,,	Parish	264
St. Mary Bredin	,,	Parish	889
St. Mary Bredman	,,	Parish	360
St. Mary Cray	,,	Parish	1 464
St. Mary Magdalen	,,	Parish	429
St. Mary Northgate	,,	Parish	4 865
St. Mary Sandwich	,,	Parish	919
St. Mary	Leicester	Parish	13 264
St. Mary	Lincoln	Parish	359

Name of Place.	County.	Description.	Population.	Name of Place.	County.	Description.	Population.
St. Mary Magdalen *Lincoln* ..		Parish	625	St. Mary Stoke.. *Suffolk* ..		Parish	2 518
St. Mary-le-Wigford	,, ..	Parish	1 746	St. Mary Magdalen *Surrey*		Sub-dis.	16 505
St. Mary, St. Geo. E. *Middlesex*		Sub-dis.	18 181	St. Mary Newington	,, ..	Sub-dis.	15 082
St. Mary, Marylebone	,, ..	Sub-dis.	22 493	St. Mary	.. ,, ..	Parish	1 713
St. Mary Abchurch	,, ..	Parish	264	St. Mary Bulverhithe *Sussex* ..		Parish	68
St. Mary Aldermanbury	,, ..	Parish	443	St. Mary in Castle	,, ..	Sub-dis.	15 884
St. Mary Aldermary	,, ..	Parish	232	St. Mary in Castle	,, ..	Parish	4 809
St. Mary Bothaw	,, ..	Parish	161	St. Mary Magdalen	,, ..	Parish	7 106
St. Mary-le-Bow	,, ..	Parish	317	St. Mary	.. *Warwick* ..		Sub-dis.	17 477
St. Mary Colechurch	,, ..	Parish	164	St. Mary	.. ,, ..	Parish	6 071
St. Mary at Hill	,, ..	Parish	738	St. Mary	.. *Wilts* ..		Parish	2 685
St. Marylebone..	,, ..	Parish	161 680	St. Mary	.. *York* ..		Sub-dis.	6 132
1 Hamilton-terrace	,, ..	Ward	7 224	St. Mary	.. ,, ..	Parish	3 831
2 St. John's-wood	,, ..	Ward	11 992	St. Mary Bishpshll. Jun. ,, ..		Parish	5 278
3 New Church-street	,, ..	Ward	32 154	St. Mary Bishpshll. Sen. ,, ..		Parish	2 427
4 Dorset-sq. & Regent's Park		Ward	15 304	St. Mary Castlegate	,, ..	Parish	994
5 Bryanstone	,, ..	Ward	22 493	St. Mary North..	,, ..	Ward	6 132
6 Portman	,, ..	Ward	26 692	St. Matthew Friday-st. *Mddlx.*		Parish	167
7 Portland-place	,, ..	Ward	25 707	St. Matthew	.. *Suffolk* ..		Sub-dis.	16 028
8 Cavendish-square	,, ..	Ward	20 114	St. Matthew	.. ,, ..	Parish	6 216
St. Mary Milk-street	,, ..	Parish	125	St. Matthew Brixton *Surrey* ..		Ecl. Dis.	10 305
St. Mary Mounthaw	,, ..	Parish	474	St. Maughans .. *Monmouth* ..		Parish	191
St. Mary Old Fish-street	,, ..	Parish	732	St. Maurice .. *Hants* ..		Parish	2 254
St. Mary Paddington	,, ..	Sub-dis.	39 015	St. Maurice in Suburbs *York*..		Parish	4 327
St. Mary Somerset	,, ..	Parish	271	St. Mellion .. *Cornwall* ..		Parish	299
St. Mary Staining	,, ..	Parish	161	St. Mellons .. *Monmouth* ..		Parish	688
St. Mary-le-Strand	,, ..	Sub-dis.	10 346	St. Merryn .. *Cornwall* ..		Parish	570
St. Mary-le-Strand	,, ..	Parish	2 072	St. Mewan .. ,, ..		Parish	1 237
St. Mary Bow ..	,, ..	Parish	11 590	St. Michael .. *Cambs* ..		Parish	376
St. Mary Woolchurch	,, ..	Parish	102	St. Michael .. *Cheshire* ..		Parish	922
St. Mary Woolnoth	,, ..	Parish	291	St. Michael Carhayes *Cornwall*		Parish	173
St. Mary .. *Norf. & Suff.*		Parish	1 256	St. Michael's Mount	,, ..	Par. Is.	132
St. Mary Coslany *Norfolk* ..		Parish	1 498	St. Michael Penkivel	,, ..	Parish	194
St. Mary in Marsh	., ..	Parish	451	St. Michael .. *Derby* ..		Parish	1 519
St. Mary .. *Notts* ..		Sub-dis.	6 659	St. Michael Mile-End *Essex* ..		Parish	880
St. Mary .. ,, ..		Parish	64 553	St. Michael, Bristol *Gloucester*		Parish	4 922
St. Mary Magdalen *Oxon* ..		Parish	2 680	St. Michael, Gloucester ,, ..		Parish	3 687
St. Mary Virgin . *Oxon, &c.* ..		Parish	1 274	St. Michael, Southampton *Hants*		Parish	1 992
St. Mary, Haverfordwest *Pmb.*		Parish	1 525	St. Michael, Winchester ,,		Parish	542
St. Mary, Pembroke ,,		Parish	12 559	St. Michael .. *Herts* ..		Parish	2 303
St. Mary Tenby . ,,		Parish	3 197	St. Michael on Wyre *Lancaster*		Sub-dis.	3 359
St. Mary Tenby . ,, ..		In Lib.	2 982	St. Michael on Wyre ,, ..		Parish	4 509
St. Mary Tenby . ,, ..		Out Lib.	215	St. Michael, Lincoln *Lincoln*		Parish	1 296
St. Mary .. *Salop* ..		Sub-dis.	16 251	St. Michael, Stamford ,, ..		Parish	1 305
St. Mary .. ,, ..		Parish	8 360	St. Michl. Bassishaw *Middlesex*		Parish	501
St. Mary Magdalen ,, ..		Parish	2 683	St. Michael Cornhill ,, ..		Parish	371
St. Mary .. *Scilly Isle* ..		Island	1 532	St. Michl. Crooked-lane ,, ..		Parish	323
St. Mary .. *Stafford* ..		Parish	2 683	St. Michael le Quern ,, ..		Parish	74
St. Mary & St. Chad ,,		Parish	13 206	St. Michael Queenhithe ,, ..		Parish	548
St. Mary & St. Chad ,, ..		—	10 996	St. Michael Royal ,, ..		Parish	169
St. Mary .. *Suffolk* ..		Parish	6 604	St. Michael Wood-street ,, ..		Parish	217
St. Mary at Elms ,, ..		Parish	1 178	St. Michael Coslany *Norfolk* ..		Parish	1 365
St. Mary at Quay ,, ..		Parish	1 017	St. Michael at Plea ,, ..		Parish	379
St. Mary at Tower ,, ..		Parish	984	St. Michael at Thorn ,, ..		Parish	2 121

Name of Place.	County.	Description.	Population.	Name of Place.	County.	Description.	Population.
Michael	Oxon	Parish	971	St. Nicholas, Droitwich	Worc.	Parish	707
Michael	Pembroke	Parish	1 501	St. Nicholas, Worcester	,,	Parish	1 933
Michael	Somerset	Parish	2 951	St. Nicholas	York	Parish	1 410
Michaelchurch	,,	Parish	29	St. Nicholas in Suburbs	,,	Parish	236
Michael	Stafford	Parish	5 112	St. Olave	Cheshire	Parish	480
Michael	Sussex	Parish	1 076	St. Olave	Devon	Parish	945
Michael on Rock	,,	Parish	441	St. Olave Hart-st.	Middlesex	Parish	757
Mich. w. S. John	Warwick	Parish	22 733	St. Olave Old Jewry	,,	Parish	143
Mich. Bedwardine	Worcester	Parish	570	St. Olave Silver-st.	,,	Parish	527
Michael Belfry	York	Parish	939	St. Olave Southwark	Surrey	District	19 056
Michael	,,	Parish	1 566	St. Olave	,,	Sub-dis.	7 663
Mich. Spurrier Gate	,,	Parish	486	St. Olave	,,	Parish	6 197
Mildred	Kent	Parish	2 281	St. Olave	Sussex	Parish	247
Mildred Bread-st.	Middlesex	Parish	86	St. Olave Marygate	York	Parish	3 917
Mildred Poultry	,,	Parish	257	St. Olave Marygate	,,	Tnship.	966
Minver	Cornwall	Parish	1 111	St. Oswald	Cheshire	Parish	9 845
Minver Highlands	,,	—	626	St. Oswald	,,	—	7 534
Minver Lowlands	,,	—	485	St. Oswald	Durham	Sub-dis.	18 714
Neot..	,,	Parish	1 584	St. Oswald	,,	Parish	12 964
Neots	Hunts, &c...	District	18 965	St. Osyth	Essex	Sub-dis.	6 072
Neots	,, ,,	Sub-dis.	9 616	St. Osyth	,,	Parish	1 638
Neots	Hunts	Parish	3 321	St. Owen	Isle of Jersey	Parish	2 320
Neots	,,	Town	3 090	St. Owen	Gloucester	Parish	830
Nicholas	Berks	Parish	742	St. Owen	Hereford	Parish	2 171
Nicholas	Devon	Parish	1 148	St. Pancras	Devon	Parish	345
Nicholas	Durham	Sub-dis.	23 748	St. Pancras	Middlesex	L. Sub.	198 788
Nicholas	,,	Parish	2 606	St. Pancras	,,	Parish	198 788
Nicholas	Essex	Parish	1 096	Ward No. 1	,,	Ward	19 749
Nicholas Harwich	,,	Parish	3 839	Ward No. 2	,,	Ward	14 666
Nicholas	Glamorgan	Sub-dis.	4 705	Ward No. 3	,,	Ward	26 894
Nicholas	,,	Parish	354	Ward No. 4	,,	Ward	18 017
Nicholas	Gloucester	Sub-dis.	7 416	Ward No. 5	,,	Ward	23 270
Nicholas, Gloster.	,,	Parish	2 348	Ward No. 6	,,	Ward	39 013
Nicholas, Bristol	,,	Parish	1 935	Ward No. 7	,,	Ward	25 916
Nich. in Castle	Hants, I. W.	Parish	265	Ward No. 8	,,	Ward	31 263
Nicholas	Hereford	Parish	1 533	St. Pancras, Old	,,	Ecl. Dis.	11 161
Nicholas	Kent	Parish	3 442	St. Pancras Soper-lane	,,	Parish	76
Nicholas Deptford	,,	Sub-dis.	8 139	St. Pancras	Sussex	Parish	1 087
Nicholas Deptford	,,	Parish	8 139	St. Paul	Beds	Parish	7 410
Nicholas Hospital	,,	Parish	40	St. Paul	Devon	Parish	1 308
Nicholas Wade	,,	Parish	590	St. Paul	Gloucester	Sub-dis.	15 775
Nicholas	Leicester	Parish	1 662	St. Paul	,,	In Par.	11 397
Nicholas	Lincoln	Parish	1 515	St. Paul & St. James	,,	Out Par.	9 944
Nicholas Acons	Middlesex	Parish	168	St. Pauls Walden	Herts	Parish	1 123
Nicholas Cole Abbey	,,	Parish	230	St. Paul	Kent	Parish	1 653
Nicholas Olave	,,	Parish	355	St. Pauls Cray	,,	Parish	532
Nicholas	Northumberland	Sub-dis.	16 632	St. Paul Deptford	Kent & Sur.	Sub-dis.	37 834
Nicholas	,,	Parish	7 487	St. Paul Deptford	,, ,,	Parish	37 834
Nicholas	Notts	Parish	5 154	1 North Ward	,, ,,	Ward	8 395
Nicholas	Pembroke	Parish	284	2 South Ward	,, ,,	Ward	10 162
Nicholas	Suffolk	Parish	1 912	3 East Ward	,, ,,	Ward	13 472
Nicholas	Surrey	Parish	2 005	4 West Ward.	,, ,,	Ward	5 805
Nicholas	,,	—	1 061	St. Paul Deptford	Kent	—	32 103
Nicholas	Warwick	Parish	4 499	St. Paul..	Lincoln	Parish	789

Name of Place	County	Description	Population	Name of Place	County	Description	Population
St. Paul..	Middlesex	Sub-dis.	21 015	St. Peter Walworth	Surrey	Sub-dis.	44 463
St. Paul Covent Garden	,,	Parish	5 154	St. Peter	Sussex	Sub-dis.	42 156
St. Paul Hammersmith	,,	Sub-dis.	19 104	St. Peter the Great	,,	Parish	5 325
St. Paul Shadwell	,,	Parish	8 499	St. Peter the Less	,,	Parish	344
St. Paul..	Norfolk	Parish	2 907	St. Peter & St. Mary	,,	Parish	980
St. Paul..	Warwick	Sub-dis.	9 489	St. Peter	Warwick	Sub-dis.	14 806
St. Peter	Beds	Parish	2 882	St. Peter & St. Paul	Wilts	Parish	1 781
St. Peter	Berks	Parish	472	St. Peter, Droitwich	Worcester	Parish	854
St. Peter	Cambs	Parish	569	St. Peter, Worcester	,,	Parish	6 055
St. Peter	Carmarthen	Parish	9 798	St. Peter Bengeworth	,,	Parish	1 259
St. Peter	Cheshire	Parish	798	St. Peter the Little	York	Parish	407
St. Peter	Derby	Sub-dis.	33 232	St. Peter-le-Willows	,,	Parish	526
St. Peter	,,	Parish	20 234	St. Petrock	Devon	Parish	220
St. Peter	,,	—	18 450	St. Petrox	,,	Parish	885
St. Peter's Close	Devon	Precinct	595	St. Petrox	Pembroke	Parish	78
St. Peter Tavy..	,,	Parish	469	St. Philip & Jacob	Gloucester	Sub Dis.	31 753
St. Peter, Dorchester	Dorset	Parish	1 213	St. Philip & Jacob	,,	In Par.	4 378
St. Peter, Shaftesbury	,,	Parish	1 001	St. Philip & Jacob	,,	Out Par.	31 753
St. Peter, Colchester	Essex	Parish	2 127	St. Philip	Warwick	Sub-dis.	9 375
St. Peter	,,	Sub-dis.	6 741	St. Pierre & Runstone	Monm	Parish	92
St. Peter, Maldon	,,	Parish	2 550	St. Pinnock	Cornwall	Parish	571
St. Peter	Gloucester	Parish	1 472	St. Runwald	Essex	Parish	320
St. Peter Cheesehill	Hants	Parish	752	St. Sampson	Cornwall	Parish	311
St. Peter Colebrook	,,	Parish	704	St. Sampson	Is. Guernsey	Parish	2 781
St. Peter	Hereford	Parish	8 053	St. Sampson	York	Parish	702
St. Peter	Herts	Parish	4 158	St. Saviour	Devon	Parish	2 171
St. Peter	,,	—	2 720	St. Saviour	Is. Guernsey	Parish	942
St. Peter	Is. Jersey	Parish	2 671	St. Saviour	Isle of Jersey	Parish	3 723
St. Peter, Thanet	Kent	Parish	2 855	St. Saviour	Norfolk	Parish	1 532
St. Peter, Canterbury	,,	Parish	1 188	St. Saviour Southwark	Surrey	District	36 170
St. Peter Sandwich	,,	Parish	1 085	St. Saviour	,,	Sub-dis.	19 101
St. Peter Arches	Lincoln	Parish	562	St. Saviour	,,	Parish	19 101
St. Peter-du-Bois	Is. Guernsey	Parish	1 141	St. Saviour	York	Parish	2 779
St. Peter Eastgate	Lincoln	Parish	1 028	St. Sepulchre	Middlesex	Parish	12 084
St. Peter Gowts .	,,	Parish	2 055	Middlesex part	,,	—	4 609
St. Peter's Close	Middlesex	Parish	323	Without Newgate	,,	—	7 475
St. Peter Cornhill	,,	Parish	533	St. Sepulchre	Northampton	Parish	9 814
St. Peter Hammersmith	,,	Sub-Dis.	5 415	St. Sidwell	Devon	Sub-dis.	18 530
St. Peter Paul's Wharf	,,	Parish	410	St. Sidwell	,,	Parish	10 478
St. Peter-le-Poer	,,	Parish	540	St. Simon & St. Jude	Norfolk	Parish	288
St. Peter-Port	Is. Guernsey	Town	16 388	St. Stephen	Corn.& Devon	Sub-dis.	3 607
St. Peter Westcheap	Middlesex	Parish	148	St. Stephen, Launstn.	Cornwall	Parish	873
St. Peter Hungate	Norfolk	Parish	399	St. Stephen, St. Austell	,,	Parish	3 045
St. Peter Mancroft	,,	Parish	2 575	St. Stephen by Saltash	,,	Parish	3 287
St. Peter Mountergate	,,	Parish	2 868	St. Stephen	Devon	Parish	407
St. Peter Southgate	,,	Parish	457	St. Stephen	Gloucester	Parish	2 680
St. Peter, Brackley	Nthampton.	Parish	1 615	St. Stephen	Herts	Parish	1 786
St. Peter, Nthampton.	,,	Parish	1 216	St. Stph. Coleman-st.	Middlesex	Parish	8 324
St. Peter	Notts	Parish	4 986	St. Stph. Walbrook	,,	Parish	300
St. Peter-le-Bailey	Oxon	Parish	1 153	St. Stephen	Norfolk	Parish	4 191
St. Peter East ..	,,	Parish	1 174	St. Stephen	Suffolk	Parish	679
St. Peter & St. Paul	Somerset	Parish	2 347	St. Stithians	Cornwall	Parish	2 358
St. Peter, Ipswich	Suffolk	Parish	3 639	St. Swithin	Hants	Parish	170
St. Peter, Sudbury	,,	Parish	1 880	St. Swithin	Lincoln	Parish	4 665

Name of Place.	County.	Description.	Population.	Name of Place.	County.	Description.	Population.
. Swithin	Middlesex	Parish	297	Salford	Lancaster	Tnship.	71 002
. Swithin	Norfolk	Parish	699	Salford (1668) 117,162		Borough	102 449
. Swithin	Worcester	Parish	764	Christchurch	,,	Ecl. Dis.	9 414
t. Teath	Cornwall	Parish	1 980	St. Bartholomew	,,	Ecl. Dis.	10 893
t. Thomas Apostle	,,	Parish	887	St. Matthias	,,	Ecl. Dis.	7 194
t. Thomas-street	,,	Hamlet	621	St. Philip	,,	Ecl. Dis.	11 415
i. Thomas	Devon	District	48 405	St. Simon	,,	Ecl. Dis.	6 957
t. Thomas	,,	Sub-dis.	6 053	St. Stephen	,,	Ecl. Dis.	12 031
t. Thomas Apostle	,,	Parish	4 533	Trinity	,,	Ecl. Dis.	12 192
t. Thomas	Glamorgan	Hamlet	3 325	Salford	Oxon	Parish	397
t. Thomas	Gloucester	Parish	1 276	Salford	Warwick	Parish	858
t. Thomas	Hants	Parish	4 738	Salhouse	Norfolk	Parish	684
t. Thomas	Lancaster	Sub-dis.	29 142	Saling, Great	Essex	Parish	361
t. Thomas Apostle	Middlesex	Parish	112	Salisbury & Amesbury	Wilts	L. Sub.	41 713
t. Thomas	Oxon	Parish	5 059	Salisbury		Diocese	377 337
t. Thomas	Pembroke	Parish	2 088	Salisbury	Wilts	District	9 039
t. Thomas	,,	—	1 876	Salisbury	,,	Sub-dis.	9 039
t. Thomas	,,	Hamlet	162	Salisbury	,,	City	12 278
t. Thomas Pensford	Somerset	Parish	312	Salkeld, Great	Cumberland	Parish	502
t. Thomas	Surrey	Parish	1 466	Salkeld, Little	,,	Tnship.	137
t. Thomas Apostle	Sussex	Parish	719	Sall	Norfolk	Parish	241
t. Thomas at Cliffe	,,	Parish	1 568	Salmonby	Lincoln	Parish	101
t. Thomas	Warwick	Sub-dis.	32 269	Salperton	Gloucester	Parish	189
t. Thomas	Wilts	Parish	2 215	Salt	Stafford	Ecl. Dis.	808
t. Tudy	Cornwall	Parish	570	Salt & Enson	,,	Tnship.	509
t. Twinell	Pembroke	Parish	220	Saltash	Cornwall	Sub-dis.	6 240
t. Vedast	Middlesex	Parish	278	Saltash	,,	Chap.	1 900
t. Veep	Cornwall	Parish	628	Saltby	Leicester	Parish	292
t. Wenn	,,	Parish	580	Salter w. Eskat.	Cumberland	Parish	43
t. Weonards	Hereford	Sub-dis.	3 633	Salterforth	York	Tnship.	424
t. Weonards	,,	Parish	690	Salterhebble	,,	Ecl. Dis.	4 258
t. Werburgh	Derby	Parish	18 222	Salterns, Great	Hants	Parish	29
t. Werburgh	Gloucester	Parish	40	Saltfleet	Lincoln	Sub-dis.	5 503
t. Werburgh	Kent	Parish	1 065	Saltfleetby, All Saints	,,	Parish	195
t. Wilfred	York	Parish	262	Saltfleetby, St. Clement	,,	Parish	139
t. Winnow	Cornwall	Parish	1 115	Saltfleetby, St. Peter	,,	Parish	308
t. Woollos	Mon. & Glam.	Sub-dis.	8 445	Saltford	Somerset	Parish	373
t. Woollos	Monmouth	Parish	24 756	Salthouse	Norfolk	Parish	268
St. Wollos	,,	Tnship.	15 696	Saltley	Warwick	Ecl. Dis.	2 842
St. Whites	Gloucester	—	21	Saltley & Washwood	,,	Hamlet	2 842
Salcey and Hartwell	Nrthmptn.	Lodges	14	Saltmarsh	Hereford	Parish	10
Salcombe	Devon	Ecl. Dis.	1 658	Saltmarshe	York	Tnship.	136
Salcombe Regis	,,	Parish	434	Saltney	Flint	Tnship.	1 325
Salcott	Essex	Parish	188	Salton	York	Parish	384
Sale	Cheshire	Tnship.	3 031	Salton	,,	Tnship.	169
Sale, St. Anne	,,	Ecl. Dis.	3 031	Saltwood	Kent	Parish	643
Saleby	Lincoln	Parish	244	Salwarpe	Worcester	Parish	442
Salehurst	Sussex	Sub-dis.	3 181	Sambourn	Warwick	Hamlet	635
Salehurst	,,	Parish	2 014	Sambrook, St. Luke	Salop	Ecl. Dis.	552
Salesbury	Lancaster	Tnship.	331	Samford	Suffolk	Hund.	12 721
Salesbury, St. Peter	,,	Ecl. Dis.	1 292	Samford	,,	District	12 736
Salford	Beds	Parish	264	Samlesbury	Lancaster	Tnship.	1 215
Salford	Lancaster	Hund.	435 423	Sampford Courtnay	Devon	Parish	991
Salford	,,	District	105 335	Sampford Peverell	,,	Parish	720

Name of Place.	County.	Description.	Population.	Name of Place.	County.	Description.	Population.
Sampford Spiney	*Devon* ..	Parish	565	Sapley ..	.. *Hunts* ..	Parish	17
Sampford, Great	*Essex* ..	Parish	865	Sapperton	.. *Gloucester* ..	Parish	600
Sampford, Little	,, ..	Parish	477	Sapperton	.. ,, ..	Tithing	363
Sampford Arundell	*Somerset* ..	Parish	425	Sapperton	.. *Lincoln* ..	Parish	51
Sampford Brett .	,, ..	Parish	280	Saredon..	.. *Stafford* ..	Tnship.	236
Sancreed	.. *Cornwall* ..	Parish	1 233	Sarisbury	.. *Hants* ..	Ecl. Dis.	1 406
Sancton ..	.. *York* ..	Parish	476	Sark Isles	.. *Channel Is* ..	Island	583
Sancton & Houghton	,, ..	Tnship.	400	Sarn, Trinity	.. *Montgomery*	Ecl. Dis.	641
Sandal ..	.. ,, ..	Sub-dis.	7 588	Sarnesfield	.. *Hereford* ..	Parish	120
Sandall Long ..	.. ,, ..	Tnship.	130	Sarratt ..	.. *Herts* ..	Parish	736
Sandal Magna ..	.. ,, ..	Parish	4 214	Sarre ..	.. *Kent* ..	Ville	169
Sandal Magna ..	.. ,, ..	Tnship.	1 590	Sarsden ..	.. *Oxon* ..	Parish	166
Sandbach	.. *Cheshire* ..	Sub-dis.	12 690	Sarum, Old	.. *Wilts* ..	Parish	7
Sandbach	.. ,, ..	Parish	9 046	Satley ..	.. *Durham* ..	Chap.	139
Sandbach	.. ,, ..	Tnship.	4 989	Satterleigh	.. *Devon* ..	Parish	79
Sandbach	.. ,, ..	Town	3 252	Satterthwaite	.. *Lancaster* ..	Tnship.	397
Sandcroft	.. *Suffolk* ..	Parish	238	Saughall, Great .	*Cheshire* ..	Tnship.	545
Sanden Fee	.. *Berks* ..	Tithing	846	Saughall, Little .	,, ..	Tnship.	94
Sanderingham ..	*Norfolk* ..	Parish	56	Saughall Massey	,, ..	Tnship.	202
Sanderstead	.. *Surrey* ..	Parish	206	Saul ..	.. *Gloucester* ..	Parish	607
Sandford	.. *Berks* ..	Tnship.	113	Saundby	.. *Notts* ..	Parish	86
Sandford	.. *Devon* ..	Parish	1 842	Saunderton	.. *Bucks* ..	Parish	428
Sandford, Woodstock	*Oxon* ..	Parish	476	Sausthorpe	.. *Lincoln* ..	Parish	144
Sandford, Abingdon	,, ..	Parish	376	Savernake, North	*Wilts* ..	Parish	108
Sandford Orcas..	*Somerset* ..	Parish	318	Savernake, South, &c.	,, ..	Parish	230
Sandgate	.. *Kent* ..	Ecl. Dis.	1 669	Savernake	.. ,, ..	Ecl. Dis.	345
Sandhoe	*Northumberland*	Tnship.	266	Sawbridgeworth .	*Herts & Essex*	Sub-dis.	4 278
Sandhurst	.. *Berks* ..	Sub-dis.	1 271	Sawbridgeworth .	*Herts* ..	Parish	2 701
Sandhurst	.. ,, ..	Parish	1 271	Sawdon	.. *York* ..	Tnship.	166
Sandhurst	.. *Gloucester* ..	Parish	549	Sawley ..	.. *Derby* ..	Parish	2 633
Sandhurst	.. *Kent* ..	Parish	1 231	Sawley w. Wilsthorpe	,, ..	Tnship.	1 082
Sand Hutton, York	*York* ..	Tnship.	200	Sawley ..	.. *York* ..	Parish	254
Sand Hutton, Thirsk	,, ..	Tnship.	297	Sawley ..	.. ,, ..	Tnship.	446
Sandiacre	.. *Derby* ..	Parish	1 012	Sawston	.. *Cambs* ..	Parish	1 363
Sandleford	.. *Berks* ..	Parish	45	Sawtry ..	.. *Hunts* ..	Sub-dis.	2 329
Sandon ..	.. *Essex* ..	Parish	512	Sawtry All Saints	,, ..	Parish	650
Sandon ..	.. *Herts* ..	Parish	771	Sawtry, St. Andrew	,, ..	Parish	386
Sandon ..	.. *Stafford* ..	Parish	590	Sawtry, St. Judith	,, ..	Parish	272 .
Sandown	.. *Hants, I. W.*	Ecl. Dis.	1 743	Saxby ..	.. *Leicester* ..	Parish	117
Sandridge	.. *Herts* ..	Parish	833	Saxby, Lincoln..	*Lincoln* ..	Parish	112
Sandwich	.. *Kent* ..	Sub-dis.	8 759	Saxby, Glandford Brigg	,, ..	Parish	293
Sandwich	.. ,, .. {	M. Bor.	2 944	Saxelby..	.. *Leicester* ..	Parish	120
		P. Bor.	13 750	Saxelby w. Ingleby	*Lincoln* ..	Parish	1 174
Sandwith	.. *Cumberland*	Tnship.	333	Saxham, Great ..	*Suffolk* ..	Parish	270
Sandy ..	.. *Beds* ..	Parish	2 118	Saxham, Little..	,, ..	Parish	171
Sandy ..	.. ,, ..	Tnship.	1 754	Saxlingham	.. *Norfolk* ..	Parish	156
Sankey ..	.. *Lancaster* ..	Sub-dis.	2 529	Saxlingham, Nethergate	,, ..	Parish	586
Sankey. Great ..	,, ..	Tnship.	563	Saxlingham Thorpe	,, ..	Parish	141
Santon ..	.. *Norfolk* ..	Parish	55	Saxmundham ..	*Suffolk* ..	Sub-dis.	3 109
Santon Downham	*Suffolk* ..	Parish	81	Saxmundham ..	,, ..	Parish	1 222
Sapcote ..	.. *Leicester* ..	Parish	668	Saxondale	.. *Notts* ..	Tnship.	95
Sapey, Upper ..	*Hereford* ..	Parish	357	Saxtead..	.. *Suffolk* ..	Parish	448
Sapey, Lower ..	*Worcester* ..	Parish	218	Saxthorpe	.. *Norfolk* ..	Parish	328
Sapiston	.. *Suffolk* ..	Parish	255	Saxton ..	.. *York* ..	Parish	461

Name of Place.	County.	Description.	Population.	Name of Place.	County.	Description.	Population.
axton, &c.	York	Tnship.	360	Scotby	Cumberland	Ecl. Dis.	520
cackleton	„	Tnship.	175	Scotforth	Lancaster	Tnship.	955
caftworth	Notts	Tnship.	117	Scothern	Lincoln	Parish	579
cagglethorpe	York	Tnship.	315	Scotland	Lancaster	Ward	81 228
calby	York E.	Tnship.	114	Scotter	Lincoln	Sub-dis.	4 706
calby	„ N.	Parish	1 876	Scotter	„	Parish	1 167
calby	„ „	Tnship.	643	Scotton	„	Parish	482
caldwell	Northampton	Parish	396	Scotton	„	Tnship.	320
caleby	Cumberland	Parish	548	Scotton	York N.	Tnship.	111
caleby, East	„	Tnship.	206	Scotton	„ W.	Tnship.	321
caleby, West	„	Tnship.	342	Scottow	Norfolk	Parish	454
calford	Leicester	Parish	553	Scot-Willoughby	Lincoln	Parish	19
calthwaiterigg, &c.	Westmld.	Tnship.	504	Scoulton	Norfolk	Parish	329
camblesby	Lincoln	Parish	471	Scrafield	Lincoln	Parish	47
cammonden	York	Tnship.	1 012	Scrafton, West	York	Tnship.	112
campston	„	Tnship.	248	Scraptoft	Leicester	Parish	108
campton	Lincoln	Parish	235	Scratby	Norfolk	Parish	309
carborough	York	District	30 425	Scray	Kent	Lathe	68 961
carborough	„	Sub-dis.	20 467	Scrayingham	York	Parish	480
carborough	„	Parish	18 377	Scrayingham	„	Tnship.	160
carborough	„	Tnship.	17 204	Scredington	Lincoln	Parish	397
Scarborough	„	Borough	18 377	Scremby	„	Parish	184
carborough St. Thos.	„	Ecl. Dis.	2 821	Scremerston	Northumberland	Ecl. Dis.	1 227
carcliff	Derby	Parish	548	Screnwood	„	Tnship.	52
carcroft	York	Tnship.	292	Screveton	Notts	Parish	241
cargill	„	Tnship.	93	Scrivelsby	Lincoln	Parish	168
carisbrick	Lancaster	Sub-dis.	4 573	Scriven w. Tentergate	York	Tnship.	1 426
carisbrick	„	Tnship.	2 112	Scrooby	Notts	Parish	256
Scarle North	Lincoln	Parish	595	Scropton	Staff. & Derby	Parish	520
Scarle, South	Notts	Parish	513	Scropton	„ „	Tnship.	281
Scarle, South	„	Tnship.	175	Scruton	York	Parish	408
Scarning	Norfolk	Parish	693	Sculcoates	„	District	51 956
Scarrington	Notts	Parish	231	Sculcoates	„	Parish	27 167
Scarsdale	Derby	Hund.	79 978	Sculthorpe	Norfolk	Parish	680
Scarsdale	„	L. Sub.	89 814	Scunthorpe	Lincoln	Tnship.	278
Scartho	Lincoln	Parish	188	Scyborycoed	Cardigan	Tnship.	546
Scattergate	Westmoreland	Tnship.	171	Seaborough	Somerset	Parish	123
Scawby w. Sturton	Lincoln	Parish	1 570	Seabridge	Stafford	Tnship.	123
Scawton	York	Parish	148	Seacombe, St. Paul	Cheshire	Ecl. Dis.	3 683
School Aycliffe	Durham	Tnship.	25	Seacourt	Berks	Parish	39
Scilly Islands	Cornwall	District	2 431	Seacroft	York	Tnship.	1 235
Bryher	„	Island	115	Seacroft, St. James	„	Ecl. Dis.	1 306
St. Agnes	„	Island	200	Seaford	Sussex	Parish	1 084
St. Martin	„	Island	185	Seagrave	Leicester	Parish	443
St. Mary	„	Island	1 532	Seagry	Wilts	Parish	263
Trescoe	„	Island	399	Seaham	Durham	Parish	2 827
Scisset	York	Ecl. Dis.	3 131	Seaham	„	Tnship.	2 591
Scole	Norfolk	Parish	677	Seaham Harbour	„	Town	6 137
Scopwick	Lincoln	Parish	383	Seaham Harbour	„	Ecl. Dis.	6 137
Scorborough	York	Parish	89	Seaham, New	„	Ecl. Dis.	2 489
Scorton	„	Tnship.	476	Seal	Kent	Parish	1 505
Sco-Ruston	Norfolk	Parish	102	Seal	Leicester	Parish	1 576
Scosthrop	York	Tnship.	64	Seal	„	Tnship.	1 246
Scotby	Cumberland	Tnship.	520	Seal w. Tongham	Surrey	Parish	669

Name of Place.	County.	Description.	Population.	Name of Place.	County.	Description.	Populati
Sealand	Flint	Tnship.	390	Seighford	Stafford	Parish	8(0
Seamer, Stokesley	York	Parish	260	Seisdon	,,	Hund.	135 48
Seamer, Scarborough	,,	Parish	1 305	Seisdon	,,	Union	15 86
Seamer	,,	Tnship.	774	Selattyn	Salop	Parish	1 1
Searby w. Owmby	Lincoln	Parish	263	Selborne	Hants	Parish	1 1
Seasalter	Kent	Parish	1 378	Selby	York	District	16 0(
Seasoncote	Gloucester	Parish	81	Selby	,,	Union	14 91
Seathwaite	Lancaster	Hamlet	171	Selby	,,	Sub-dis.	10 09
Seaton	Cumberland	Tnship.	1 102	Selby	,,	Parish	5 4
Seaton	Devon	Parish	1 966	Selby	,,	Town	5 27
Seaton	,,	Tnship.	809	Selbys Forest	Northumberland	Tnship.	5
Seaton & Slingley	Durham	Tnship.	236	Selham	Sussex	Parish	12
Seaton Carew	,,	Tnship.	884	Selkley	Wilts	Hund.	7 0(
Seaton Carew	,,	Ecl. Dis.	884	Sellack	Hereford	Parish	34
Seaton Delaval	Northumberland	Tnship.	2 876	Selling	Kent	Parish	57
Seaton Ho. w. Boulmer	,,	Tnship.	156	Sellinge	,,	Parish	58
Seaton, North	,,	Tnship.	1 262	Selmeston	Sussex	Parish	19
Seaton	Rutland	Parish	422	Selsey	,,	Parish	90
Seaton	,,	Tnship.	345	Selside & Whitwell	Westmoreld.	Tnship.	25
Seaton & Wassand	York	Tnship.	443	Selston	Notts	Parish	2 62
Seaton Ross	,,	Parish	549	Selworthy	Somerset	Parish	43
Seavington St. Mary	Somerset	Parish	330	Semer	Suffolk	Parish	42
Seavington St. Michael	,,	Parish	244	Semington	Wilts	Chap.	42
Sebergham	Cumberland	Parish	745	Semley	,,	Parish	69
Sebergham, High	,,	Tnship.	423	Semperingham	Lincoln	Parish	63
Sebergham, Low	,,	Tnship.	322	Semperingham	,,	Tnship.	5
Seckington	Warwick	Parish	108	Send	Surrey	Parish	1 74
Sedbergh	York	District	4 391	Sennen	Cornwall	Parish	61
Sedbergh	,,	Sub-dis.	2 346	Senny	Brecon	Hamlet	24
Sedbergh	,,	Parish	4 391	Serjeants Inn, Fleet-st.	Middlx.	Parish	7
Sedbergh	,,	Tnship.	2 346	Sessay	York	Parish	45
Sedgeberrow	Worcester	Parish	354	Sessay	,,	Tnship.	32(
Sedgebrook	Lincoln	Parish	269	Sesswick	Denbigh	Tnship.	12
Sedgefield	Durham	Union	11 774	Setchey	Norfolk	Parish	9
Sedgefield	,,	Sub-dis.	11 774	Setmurthy	Cumberland	Tnship.	16(
Sedgefield	,,	Parish	2 656	Settle	York	District	12 52
Sedgefield	,,	Tnship.	1 808	Settle	,,	Sub-dis.	4 50
Sedgeford	Norfolk	Parish	742	Settle	,,	Tnship.	1 58(
Sedgeford Lane	,,	Ward	2 245	Settle, Ascension	,,	Ecl. Dis.	1 58(
Sedgehill	Northumberland	Tnship.	1 801	Settrington	,,	Parish	87
Sedghill	Wilts	Parish	194	Settrington	,,	Tnship.	55(
Sedgley	Stafford	Sub-dis.	36 637	Sevenhampton	Gloucester	Parish	54
Sedgley	,,	Parish	36 637	Sevenhampton	Wilts	Tithing	21
Sedgmoor, West	Somerset	—	6	Sevenoaks	Cheshire	Tnship.	159
Sedgwick	Westmoreland	Tnship.	194	Sevenoaks	Kent	L. Sub.	14 751
Sedlescomb	Sussex	Parish	703	Sevenoaks	,,	District	22 039
Seend	Wilts	Chap.	1 086	Sevenoaks	,,	Sub-dis.	9 568
Seer-Green	Bucks	Hamlet	334	Sevenoaks	,,	Parish	4 695
Seer-Green	,,	Ecl. Dis.	334	Sevenoaks	,,	—	2 071
Seething	Norfolk	Parish	431	Severn Stoke	Worcester	Parish	679
Sefton	Lancaster	Parish	10 159	Sevington	Kent	Parish	113
Sefton	,,	Tnship.	430	Sewardstone	Essex	Hamlet	744
Seghill	Northumberland	Tnship.	1 801	Sewerby	York	Ecl. Dis.	342
Seghill	,,	Ecl. Dis.	4 588	Sewerby w. Marton	,,	Tnship.	342

Name of Place.	County.	Description.	Population.	Name of Place.	County.	Description.	Population.
stern	Leicester	Chap.	307	Shaw Chapel	Lancaster	Ecl. Dis.	3 618
ow	York	Tnship.	42	Shaw	Wilts	Ecl. Dis.	596
ncote	Gloucester	Parish	81	Shawbury	Salop	Parish	1 027
obington	Bucks	Parish	371	Shawdon	Northumberland	Tnship.	96
kerstone	Leicester	Parish	462	Shawell	Leicester	Parish	205
kerstone	,,	Tnship.	278	Shearsby	,,	Chap.	306
lforth	Durham	Tnship.	1 164	Shebbear	Devon	Hund.	15 726
lforth, St. Cuthbert	,,	Ecl. Dis.	2 490	Shebbear	,,	Sub-dis.	3 063
lingfield	Suffolk	Parish	209	Shebbear	,,	Parish	1 109
loxhurst	Kent	Parish	194	Sheen	Stafford	Parish	427
lwell	Middlesex	Sub-dis.	12 537	Sheepscar, St. Luke	York	Ecl. Dis.	3 552
lwell	,,	Parish	8 499	Sheepscombe	Gloucester	Ecl. Dis.	510
lwell	York	Tnship.	399	Sheepshed	Leicester	Parish	3 626
lwell	,,	Ecl. Dis.	442	Sheepstor	Devon	Parish	98
tesbury	Dorset	L. Sub.	15 274	Sheepwash	,,	Parish	527
tesbury	,,	District	12 986	Sheepwash, &c.	Northumberld.	Tnship.	76
tesbury	,,	Sub-dis.	4 940	Sheepy Magna	Leicester	Parish	647
ftesbury { ,,		M. Bor.	2 497	Sheepy Magna	,,	Tnship.	439
ftesbury { Dorset & Wilts		P. Bor.	8 983	Sheepy Parva	,,	Parish	114
toe, East	Northumberland	Tnship.	32	Sheering	Essex	Parish	499
toe, West	,,	Tnship.	31	**Sheerness**	Kent	Town	12 015
ton	York	Tnship.	224	Sheerness, Trinity	,,	Ecl. Dis.	13 186
bourn	Berks & Wilts	Parish	1 012	Sheet	Hants	Tithing	484
lden	Hants	Parish	185	Sheffield	York	District	128 951
fleet	,,	Parish	1 196	Sheffield Park	,,	Sub-dis.	18 737
ford	Essex	Parish	760	Sheffield	,,	Parish	185 172
ford	Surrey	Parish	1 293	Sheffield	,,	Tnship.	87 718
lstone	Bucks	Parish	243	**Sheffield** (1864) 252362	,,	Borough	185 172
mblehurst	Hants	Tithing	1 754	Sheffield, St. George	,,	Ecl. Dis.	10 538
ngton	Leicester	Parish	82	Sheffield, St. James	,,	Ecl. Dis.	4 659
nklin	Hants	Parish	479	Sheffield, St. John	,,	Ecl. Dis.	9 014
p	Westmoreland	Parish	991	Sheffield, St. Mary	,,	Ecl. Dis.	16 224
pwick	Dorset	Parish	446	Sheffield, St. Paul	,,	Ecl. Dis.	6 965
pwick	Somerset	Parish	407	Sheffield, St. Philip	,,	Ecl. Dis.	18 461
rdlow	Derby, &c.	District	31 113	Shefford	Beds	Tnship.	1 015
rdlow	Derby	Sub-dis.	4 454	Shefford Hardwick	,,	Parish	56
rdlow	,,	Parish	945	Shefford, East	Berks	Parish	79
reshill	Stafford	Parish	531	Shefford, West	,,	Parish	538
reshill	,,	Tnship.	295	Sheldon	Derby	Tnship.	178
rleston	York	Tnship.	262	Sheldon	Devon	Parish	180
rnbrook	Beds	Sub-dis.	2 894	Sheldon	Warwick	Parish	434
rnbrook	,,	Parish	867	Sheldwich	Kent	Parish	616
rnford	Leicester	Parish	589	Shelf	York	Tnship.	3 062
row	York	Tnship.	256	Shelf, St. Michael	,,	Ecl. Dis.	3 311
row	,,	Ecl. Dis.	738	Shelfanger	Norfolk	Parish	370
rpenhoe	Beds	Hamlet	175	Shelford, Great	Cambs	Parish	1 006
rperton	Northumberland	Tnship.	92	Shelford, Little	,,	Parish	474
rples	Lancaster	Sub-dis.	4 243	Shelford	Notts	Parish	692
rples	,,	Tnship.	3 294	Shelford	,,	Tnship.	597
rrington	Norfolk	Parish	257	Shell	Worcester	Parish	54
ston	Dorset	Division	12 777	Shelland	Suffolk	Parish	99
ugh Prior	Devon	Parish	570	Shelley	Essex	Parish	178
vington w. Gresty	Cheshire	Tnship.	629	Shelley	Suffolk	Parish	142
w w. Donnington	Berks	Parish	680	Shelley	York	Tnship.	1 901

Name of Place.	County.	Description.	Population.	Name of Place.	County.	Description.	Population.
Shellingford	*Berks*	Parish	308	Sherburn	*York W.*	Tnship.	1 465
Shellow-Bowells	*Essex*	Parish	110	Shere	*Surrey*	Parish	1 503
Shelsley Beauchamp	*Worcester*	Parish	556	Shereford	*Norfolk*	Parish	62
Shelsley Beauchamp	„	Tnship.	289	Sherfield English	*Hants*	Parish	342
Shelsley Kings	„	Hamlet	267	Sherfield on Loddon	„	Parish	693
Shelsley Little, or Shelsley Walsh	„	Parish	57	Sherford	*Devon*	Parish	404
				Sheriff Hales	*Salop & Staff.*	Parish	966
Shelswell	*Oxon*	Parish	44	Sheriff Hales	„ „	Tnship.	816
Shelton	*Beds*	Parish	143	Sheriff Hutton	*York*	Parish	1 397
Shelton	*Norfolk*	Parish	192	Sheriff Hutton	„	Hamlet	892
Shelton	*Notts*	Parish	127	Sheringham	*Norfolk*	Parish	1 289
Shelton & Oxon	*Salop*	Ecl. Dis.	430	Shermanbury	*Sussex*	Parish	464
Shelton	*Stafford*	Sub-dis.	18 331	Shermans Grounds	*Leicester*	Parish	24
Shelton	„	Tnship.	18 831	Shernborne	*Norfolk*	Parish	144
Shelton, St. Mark	„	Ecl. Dis.	8 617	Sherrington	*Bucks*	Parish	839
Shelve	*Salop*	Parish	78	Sherrington	*Wilts*	Parish	187
Shenfield	*Essex*	Parish	1 149	Sherston Magna	„	Parish	1 503
Shenington	*Oxon*	Parish	415	Sherston Parva	„	Parish	156
Shenley	*Bucks*	Parish	492	Sherwill	*Devon*	Hund.	4 392
Shenley	*Herts*	Parish	1 304	Sherwill	„	Parish	609
Shenstone	*Stafford*	L. Sub.	11 368	Sherwood Villa	„	Parish	11
Shenstone	„	Parish	2 131	Sherwood	*Notts*	Sub-dis.	12 572
Shenton	*Leicester*	Chap.	206	Shevington	*Lancaster*	Tnship.	1 115
Shephall	*Herts*	Parish	243	Sheviock	*Cornwall*	Parish	671
Shepley	*York*	Tnship.	1 432	Shidfield, St. John	*Hants*	Ecl. Dis.	937
Shepley, St. Paul	„	Ecl. Dis.	1 432	Shields, South	*Durham*	Tnship.	8 973
Shepperton	*Middlesex*	Parish	849	**Shields, South**	„	Borough	35 239
Sheppey, Isle of	*Kent*	Dis. Is.	18 494	Shields, S., St. Hilda	„	Ecl. Dis.	12 133
Shepreth	*Cambs*	Parish	339	Shields, S., St. Stephen	„	Ecl. Dis.	6 252
Shepscombe	*Gloucester*	Tithing	510	Shields, S. Trinity	„	Ecl. Dis.	16 807
Shepton Beauchamp	*Somerset*	Parish	658	Shields, North	*Northumbld.*	Sub-dis.	17 138
Shepton Mallet	„	District	16 619	Shields, North	„	Tnship.	9 595
Shepton Mallet	„	L. Sub.	16 619	Shiffnal	*Salop & Staff.*	District	11 994
Shepton Mallet	„	Sub-dis.	8 152	Shiffnal	„ „	Sub-dis.	7 849
Shepton Mallet	„	Parish	5 347	Shiffnal	*Salop*	Parish	5 923
Shepton Mallet	„	Town	4 868	**Shiffnal**	„	Town	2 046
Shepton Montague	„	Parish	433	Shifford	*Oxon*	Hamlet	41
Shepway	*Kent*	Lathe	51 826	Shilbottle	*Northumberland*	Parish	1 267
Sheraten	*Durham*	Hamlet	139	Shilbottle	„	Tnship.	570
Sherborne	*Dorset*	Division	18 556	Shildon	*Durham*	Tnship.	2 947
Sherborne	„	L. Sub.	11 575	Shildon	„	Ecl. Dis.	4 458
Sherborne	*Dorset & Som.*	District	13 463	Shillingford	*Devon*	Parish	64
Sherborne	*Dorset*	Sub-dis.	5 793	Shilling Okeford	*Dorset*	Parish	509
Sherborne	„	Parish	5 793	Shillingstone	„	Parish	509
Sherborne	„	Town	5 523	Shillington	*Beds*	Sub-dis.	4 188
Sherborne	*Gloucester*	Parish	584	Shillington	„	Parish	1 788
Sherborne, St. John	*Hants*	Parish	675	Shilton	*Oxon*	Parish	298
Sherborne, W., or Monk	„	Parish	649	Shilton	*Warwick*	Parish	487
Sherbourne	*Warwick*	Parish	167	Shilvington	*Northumberland*	Tnship.	94
Sherburn	*Durham*	Tnship.	2 380	Shimpling	*Norfolk*	Parish	219
Sherburn Hospital	„	Parish	186	Shimpling	*Suffolk*	Parish	500
Sherburn	*York E.*	Sub-dis.	1 564	Shincliffe	*Durham*	Tnship.	1 544
Sherburn	„	Parish	744	Shincliffe	„	Ecl. Dis.	1 620
Sherburn	*York W.*	Parish	3 944	Shineton	*Salop*	Parish	175

Name of Place.	County.	Description.	Population.	Name of Place.	County.	Description.	Population.
-field	Berks	Parish	1 195	Shoby ..	Leicester	Parish	39
-field	,,	—	850	Shocklach	Cheshire	Parish	414
-gay	Cambs	Parish	128	Shocklach Church	,,	Tnship.	180
-gham	Norfolk	Parish	62	Shocklach Oviatt	,,	Tnship.	168
-borne	Kent	Parish	476	Shocks Coppice .	Oxon	—	10
-brook	Cheshire	Tnship.	94	Shoebury, North	Essex	Parish	193
-dham	Norfolk	Sub-dis.	2 777	Shoebury, South	,,	Parish	1 502
-dham	,,	Parish	1 644	Shokham Island	Pembroke	Parish	2
-ham	Somerset	Parish	520	Sholden..	Kent	Parish	407
-lake	Oxon	Parish	621	Shopland	Essex	Parish	80
-ley ..	Derby	Tnship.	688	Shoreditch	Middlesex	District	129 364
-ley ..	Northumberland	Tnship.	110	Shoreditch ..	,,	Parish	129 364
-ley ..	Sussex	Parish	1 212	1 Moorfields Ward	,,	Ward	18 918
-ley ..	York ..	Sub-dis.	8 773	2 Church Ward	,,	Ward	25 404
-ley ..	,,	Tnship.	7 100	3 Hoxton Ward	,,	Ward	18 778
-ley w. Heaton	,,	Ecl. Dis.	8 773	4 Wenlock Ward	,,	Ward	15 719
-meadow	Suffolk	Parish	334	5 Whitmore Ward	,,	Ward	16 186
-pon	Berks	Tnship.	211	6 Kingsland Ward	,,	Ward	13 010
-ston	Salop	Parish	186	7 Haggerstone Ward	,,	Ward	11 215
-ston on Stour	Worc., &c...	District	19 852	8 Acton Ward	,,	Ward	10 134
-ston on Stour	Wor. & War.	Sub-dis.	5 064	Shoreham	Kent	Sub-dis.	5 183
-ston on Stour	Worcester ..	Parish	1 760	Shoreham	,,	Parish	1 253
-ton Lee ..	Bucks	Hamlet	65	Shoreham	Sussex	Sub-dis.	18 369
-ton George..	Dorset	Parish	413	Shoreham, New	,,	Parish	3 351
-ton Moyne..	Gloucester ..	Parish	407	Shoreham, New	,,	P. Bor.	32 622
-ton Oliffe ..	,,	Parish	255	Shoreham, Old..	,,	Parish	282
-ton Sollars..	,,	Parish	80	Shoreswood	Northumberland	Tnship.	412
-ton Bellinger	Hants	Parish	270	Shorncote	Wilts	Parish	19
-ton on Cherwell	Oxon	Parish	131	Shorne & Merston	Kent	Parish	963
-ton un. Wychwood	,,	Parish	3 163	Shortflatt	Northumberland	Tnship.	44
-ton un. Wychwood	,,	Tnship.	655	Shorthampton	Oxon	Chap.	257
-ton ..	York E.	Tnship.	411	Shorwell	Hants, I. W.	Parish	612
-ton ..	,, N.	Tnship.	440	Shoston..	Northumberland	Tnship.	85
-ton ..	York	Ecl. Dis.	440	Shotley ..	,,	Parish	1 180
-burn	Oxon	Parish	292	Shotley H. Quar.	,,	Tnship.	474
-ebrook, Trinity	Derby	Ecl. Dis.	342	Shotley Lo. Quar.	,,	Tnship.	637
-e Hall Yard.	Suffolk	Parish	305	Shotley ..	Suffolk	Parish	582
-ehampton ..	Gloucester ..	Tithing	731	Shotover	Oxon	Parish	79
-e-Newton ..	Monmouth ..	Sub-dis.	4 893	Shotover Hill Place	,,	Parish	78
-e-Newton ..	,,	Parish	886	Shotswell	Warwick	Parish	307
-eshead, St. Paul	Lancaster	Ecl. Dis.	397	Shotter Mill	Surrey	Ecl. Dis.	579
-land	Derby	Parish	1 426	Shottesbrook	Berks	Parish	148
-land	,,	Tnship.	1 048	Shottesham			
-ley ..	,,	Parish	596	All Saints	Norfolk	Parish	484
-ley ..	,,	Tnship.	301	SS. Mary & Martin	,,	Parish	369
-ley, St. James	Hants	Ecl. Dis.	4 941	Shottisham	Suffolk	Parish	317
-ley, St. John	Surrey	Ecl. Dis.	642	Shottle & Postern	Derby	Tnship.	427
-ley, St. James	Worcester ..	Ecl. Dis.	1 062	Shotton ..	Durham	Tnship.	1 871
-lington H. Quar.	Northmb.	Tnship.	93	Shotton ..	Flint	Tnship.	336
-lington L. Quar.	,,	Tnship.	61	Shotwick	Cheshire	Parish	931
-lington	York	Tnship.	2 022	Shotwick	,,	Tnship.	98
-terton	Dorset	Tithing	147	Shotwick Park ..	,,	Parish	4
-bdon	Hereford	Parish	503	Shouldham	Norfolk	Parish	727
-brooke	Devon	Parish	630	Shouldham Thorpe	,,	Parish	298

Name of Place.	County.	Description	Population.	Name of Place.	County.	Description.	Populat
Shrawardine	Salop	Parish	161	Siddington	Gloucester	Parish	4⁷
Shrawley	Worcester	Parish	549	Side	„	Parish	8
Shrewley	Warwick	Hamlet	812	Sidestrand	Norfolk	Parish	14
Shrewsbury	Salop	Hund.	6 080	Sidlesham	Sussex	Parish	96
Shrewsbury	„	L. Sub.	24 569	Sidmonton	Hants	Parish	14
Shrewsbury	„	District	25 784	Sidmouth	Devon	Parish	3 35
Shrewsbury	„	Borough	22 163	Sidmouth	„	Town	2 57
St. George	„	Ecl. Dis.	2 581	Sigglesthorne	York	Parish	81
St. Giles	„	Ecl. Dis.	575	Sigglesthorne	„	Tnship.	21
St. Michael	„	Ecl. Dis.	3 681	Sigston Kirby	„	Parish	25
Shrewton	Wilts	Parish	710	Sigston Kirby	„	Tnship.	11
Shripple	„	Tithing	52	Silchester	Hants	Parish	48
Shrivenham	Berks	Hund.	5 684	Sileby	Leicester	Parish	1 57
Shrivenham	Berks & Wilts	Sub-dis.	4 521	Silian	Cardigan	Parish	34
Shrivenham	Berks	Parish	2 258	Silkstone	York	Parish	25 28
Shrivenham	„	Tnship.	784	Silkstone	„	Tnship.	1 15
Shropham	Norfolk	Hund.	8 906	Silksworth	Durham	Tnship.	28
Shropham	„	Parish	510	Silk Willoughby	Lincoln	Parish	23
Shropshire		County	240 959	Silpho	York	Tnship.	6
Northern Division		N. Div.	136 410	Silsden	„	Tnship.	2 58
Southern Division		S. Div.	104 549	Silsoe	Beds.	Hamlet	71
Shroton	Dorset	Parish	620	Silsoe	„	Ecl. Dis.	71
Shuckburgh, Lower	Warwick	Parish	152	Silton	Dorset	Parish	30
Shuckburgh, Upper	„	Parish	60	Silton, Nether	York	Chap.	178
Shudy-Camps	Cambs	Parish	351	Silton, Over	„	Parish	255
Shurdington, Great	Gloucester	Parish	164	Silton, Over	„	Tnship.	94
Shurlach	Cheshire	Tnship.	150	Silverdale	Lancaster	Tnship.	294
Shustoke	Warwick	Parish	558	Silverdale	Stafford	Ecl. Dis.	4 673
Shustoke	„	Tnship.	325	Silverstone	Northampton	Parish	1 166
Shute	Devon	Parish	610	Silverton	Devon	Sub-dis.	5 120
Shutford, East	Oxon	Tnship.	26	Silverton	„	Parish	1 260
Shutford, West	„	Tnship.	360	Silvington	Salop	Parish	47
Shutlanger	Northampton	Hamlet	394	Simmondley	Derby	Tnship.	565
Shuttington	Warwick	Parish	194	Simonburn	Northumberland	Parish	1 042
Shuttleworth, St. John	Lancaster	Ecl. Dis.	2 889	Simonburn	„	Tnship.	494
Sibbertoft	Northampton	Parish	394	Simonstone	Lancaster	Tnship.	325
Sibbertswold	Kent	Parish	411	Simonswood	„	Tnship.	461
Sibdon Carwood	Salop	Parish	69	Simon Weir	Lincoln	Parish	10
Sibford-Ferris	Oxon	Tnship.	314	Simpson	Bucks	Parish	562
Sibford-Gower	„	Tnship.	482	Sinderby	York	Tnship.	126
Sibford, Trinity	„	Ecl. Dis.	796	Sinfin Moor	Derby	Parish	16
Sible Hedingham	Essex	Parish	2 123	Singleborough	Bucks	Hamlet	121
Sibsey	Lincoln	Sub-dis.	3 259	Singleton, Gt. & Lit.	Lancaster	Tnship.	338
Sibsey	„	Parish	1 297	Singleton	Sussex	Sub-dis.	1 846
Sibson	Leicester	Parish	480	Singleton	„	Parish	556
Sibson	„	Tnship.	242	Singleton	„	—	340
Sibstone	„	Parish	242	Sinnington	York	Sub-dis.	1 119
Sibthorpe	Notts	Parish	142	Sinnington	„	Parish	607
Sibton	Suffolk	Parish	489	Sinnington	„	Tnship.	343
Sicklinghall	York	Tnship.	292	Sisland	Norfolk	Parish	76
Sidbury	Devon	Parish	1 682	Sissinghurst	Kent	Ecl. Dis.	1 133
Sidbury	Salop	Parish	60	Siston	Gloucester	Parish	938
Sidcup, St. John	Kent	Ecl. Dis.	976	Sithney	Cornwall	Parish	3 306
Siddington	Cheshire	Tnship.	433	Sittingbourne	Kent	Parish	4 301

Name of Place.	County.	Description.	Population.	Name of Place.	County.	Description.	Population.
xhills	Lincoln ..	Parish	164	Skipton on Swale	York ..	Tnship.	143
xeeby ..	York ..	Tnship.	180	Skipwith ..	„ ..	Parish	769
xeffington ..	Leicester ..	Parish	244	Skipwith ..	„ ..	Tnship.	299
xeffling ..	York ..	Parish	205	Skirbeck ..	Lincoln ..	Wapen.	7 327
xegby ..	Notts ..	Parish	805	Skirbeck ..	„	Parish	2 878
xegness ..	Lincoln ..	Parish	322	Skirbeck Quarter	„	Hamlet	642
xelbrooke ..	York	Tnship.	87	Skircoat.. ..	York	Tnship.	7 447
xelden.. ..	„	Tnship.	37	Skirlaugh ..	„	District	9 654
xellingthorpe ..	Lincoln ..	Parish	662	Skirlaugh ..	„	Sub-dis.	2 336
xellow ..	York ..	Tnship.	185	Skirlaugh, North	„	Tnship.	323
xelmersdale ..	Lancaster ..	Tnship.	1 028	Skirlaugh, South	„	Tnship.	364
xelmersdale, St. Paul	„	Ecl. Dis.	1 028	Skirmage ..	Salop ..	—	4
xelsmergh ..	Westmoreland	Tnship.	325	Skirpenbeck ..	York	Parish	198
xelton	Cumberland	Parish	719	Skirwith ..	Cumberland	Tnship.	314
xelton	„ ..	Tnship.	282	Skoholme Isle ..	Pembroke ..	Island	2
xelton	York E. ..	Sub-dis.	1 533	Skutterskelf ..	York ..	Tnship.	45
xelton	„ „	Tnship.	305	Skyrack.. ..	„	Wapen.	60 225
xelton	„ N.	Parish	1 457	Skyrack w. Leeds Boro.	„	L. Sub.	267 390
xelton	„ „	Tnship.	1 034	Slad, Trinity ..	Gloucester..	Ecl. Dis.	874
xelton	„ „	Parish	61	Slaidburn ..	Lanc. & York	Sub-dis.	1 799
xelton	„ „	Tnship.	316	Slaidburn ..	York ..	Parish	1 480
xelton	„ W.	Tnship.	282	Slaidburn ..	„	Tnship.	579
xendleby ..	Lincoln	Parish	299	Slaithwaite ..	„	Sub-dis.	7 971
xenfreth ..	Monmouth..	Hund.	3 910	Slaithwaite ..	„	Tnship.	2 932
xenfreth ..	„ ..	L. Sub.	3 142	Slaley ..	Northumberland	Parish	561
xenfreth ..	„ ..	Parish	666	Slapton.. ..	Bucks	Parish	325
xer ..	Glamorgan .	Parish	14	Slapton.. ..	Devon	Parish	681
xerne ..	York .:	Parish	207	Slapton.. ..	Northampton	Parish	240
xerries Islands .	Anglesey ..	Islands	6	Slaugham ..	Sussex ..	Parish	1 518
xerton ..	Lancaster ..	Tnship.	1 556	Slaughter ..	Gloucester..	Hund.	9 365
xerton, St. Luke	„	Ecl. Dis.	1 556	Slaughter, Lower	„	Parish	212
xetchley ..	Leicester ..	Hamlet	64	Slaughter, Upper	„	Parish	241
xetty, St. Paul .	Glamorgan .	Ecl. Dis.	1 312	Slaughterford ..	Wilts	Parish	141
xewen		Ecl. Dis.	3 173	Slawston ..	Leicester	Parish	246
xeyton.. ..	Norfolk	Parish	341	Sleaford.. ..	Lincoln ..	L. Sub.	40 467
xidbrook, &c. ..	Lincoln	Parish	361	Sleaford.. ..	„	District	24 919
xidby w. Skidby Carr	York ..	Parish	384	Sleaford.. ..	„	Sub-dis.	8 131
xiddaw ..	Cumberland	Parish	15	Sleaford ..	„	Town	3 745
xilgate.. ..	Somerset ..	Parish	214	Sleaford, New ..	„	Parish	3 467
xillington ..	Lincoln ..	Parish	466	Sleaford, New ..	„	Tnship.	3 325
xiningrove ..	York ..	Tnship.	86	Sleaford, Old ..	„	Parish	372
xinnand ..	Lincoln ..	Parish	24	Sleagill.. ..	Westmoreland	Tnship.	135
xiplam.. ..	York ..	Tnship.	87	Slebech	Pembroke ..	Sub-dis.	3 171
xipsea	„	Sub-dis.	1 939	Slebech	„	Parish	280
xipsea	„	Parish	844	Sleddale, Long..	Westmoreland	Tnship.	137
xipsea	„	Tnship.	444	Sledmere w. Croom	York ..	Parish	486
xipton.. ..	„	District	31 343	Sleep	Herts	Hamlet	818
xipton.. ..	„	Union	31 155	Slimbridge ..	Gloucester..	Parish	789
xipton.. ..	„	Sub-dis.	8 590	Slindon	Stafford ..	Tnship.	135
xipton.. ..	„	Parish	7 734	Slindon	Sussex ..	Parish	543
xipton.. ..	„	Tnship.	5 454	Slinfold.. ..	„	Parish	755
xipton ..	„	Town	4 533	Slingsby ..	York ..	Parish	707
xipton, Christch.	„	Ecl. Dis.	1 749	Slipton	Northampton	Parish	144
xipton Bridge..	„ ..	Ecl. Dis.	247	Sloley	Norfolk ..	Parish	258

Name of Place.	County.	Description.	Population.	Name of Place.	County.	Description.	Population.
Slough : ..	Bucks ..	Town	3 425	Snibston ..	Leicester ..	Hamlet	595
Slyne w. Hest ..	Lancaster ..	Tnship.	312	Snilesworth ..	York ..	Tnship.	100
Smalesmouth	Northumberland	Tnship.	211	Snitter ..	Northumberland	Tnship.	134
Smallbridge, St. John	Lancaster	Ecl. Dis.	5 644	Snitterby ..	Lincoln ..	Parish	286
Smallburgh ..	Norfolk ..	Sub-dis.	4 229	Snitterfield ..	Warwick ..	Parish	881
Smallburgh ..	,, ..	Parish	559	Snodland ..	Kent ..	Parish	1 078
Smalley.. ..	Derby ..	Tnship.	721	Snoreham ..	Essex ..	Parish	219
Smallthorne, St. Sav.	Stafford .	Ecl. Dis.	1 727	Snoring, Great ..	Norfolk ..	Parish	594
Smallwood ..	Cheshire ..	Tnship.	590	Snoring, Little ..	,, ..	Parish	311
Smallwood, St. John	,, ..	Ecl. Dis.	590	Snowshill ..	Gloucester ..	Parish	235
Smannell w. Hatherden	Hants .	Ecl. Dis.	638	Snydale.. ..	York ..	Tnship.	150
Smardale ..	Westmoreland	Tnship.	44	Soberton ..	Hants ..	Parish	1 136
Smarden ..	Kent ..	Parish	1 130	Sockbridge & Tirril	Westmld. .	Tnship.	245
Smeaton, Great .	York N. ..	Parish	927	Sockburn ..	Durh. & York	Parish	231
Smeaton, Great .	,, ,, ..	Tnship.	208	Sockburn ..	Durham ..	Tnship.	59
Smeaton, Little .	,, ,, ..	Tnship.	82	Sock Dennis ..	Somerset ..	Parish	26
Smeaton, Kirk..	,, W. ..	Parish	333	Sodbury ..	Gloucester ..	L. Sub.	15 048
Smeaton, Little .	,, ,, ..	Tnship.	238	Sodbury, Chipping	,, ..	Parish	1 112
Smeeth	Kent ..	Parish	486	Sodbury, Little .	,, ..	Parish	143
Smeeton Westerby	Leicester ..	Tnship.	533	Sodbury, Old ..	,, ..	Parish	809
Smethcott ..	Salop ..	Parish	318	Sodor and Man		Diocese	52 469
Smethwick ..	Stafford	Hamlet	13 379	Soham	Cambs ..	Sub-dis.	9 400
Smethwick ..	,, ..	Ecl. Dis.	1 058	Soham	,, ..	Parish	4 278
Smethwick, St. Matthew	,, ..	Ecl. Dis.	3 935	Soho, St. Mary..	Middlesex ..	Ecl. Dis.	6 003
Smethwick,West, St.Paul	,, ..	Ecl. Dis.	2 817	Sokeholme ..	Notts ..	Tnship.	52
Smilesworth ..	York ..	Tnship.	100	Solihull..	Warw. & Worc.	District	13 231
Smisby	Derby ..	Parish	304	Solihull.. ..	,, ,,	Sub-dis.	7 383
Smithdon ..	Norfolk	Hund.	9 689	Solihull.. ..	Warwick ..	Parish	3 329
Smithdon&Brothercross	,,	L. Sub.	14 303	Sollershope ..	Hereford ..	Sub-dis.	3 641
Smithfield, East .	Middlesex ..	Liberty	4 000	Sollershope ..	,, ..	Parish	166
Snailwell ..	Cambs ..	Parish	257	Solport	Cumberland	Tnship.	277
Snainton ..	York ..	Tnship.	713	Sombourne, Kings	Hants ..	Parish	1 241
Snaith	,, ..	Sub-dis.	4 117	Sombourne,Little	,, ..	Parish	87
Snaith	,, ..	Parish	12 772	Somerby ..	Leicester ..	Sub-dis.	3 892
Snaith	,, ..	Hamlet	914	Somerby	,, ..	Parish	506
Snape	Suffolk ..	Parish	554	Somerby ..	Lincoln ..	Parish	234
Snape	York ..	Tnship.	592	Somerby by Brigg	,, ..	Parish	120
Snareshill, Gt. &Lit.	Norfolk ..	Parish	46	Somercotes, North	,, ..	Parish	1 178
Snarestone ..	Leicester ..	Parish	355	Somercotes, South	,, ..	Parish	419
Snarford ..	Lincoln ..	Parish	97	Somerford ..	Cheshire ..	Tnship.	82
Snargate ..	Kent ..	Parish	71	Somerford, Booths	,, ..	Tnship.	220
Snave	,, ..	Parish	97	Somerford, Great	Wilts ..	Parish	532
Snead	Montgomery	Parish	59	Somerford, Keynes	,, ..	Parish	386
Sneaton.. ..	York ..	Parish	268	Somerford, Little	,, ..	Parish	335
Snelland ..	Lincoln ..	Parish	138	Somerleyton ..	Suffolk ..	Parish	621
Snelson.. ..	Cheshire ..	Tnship.	158	Somersall-Herbert	Derby ..	Parish	116
Snelston ..	Derby ..	Parish	317	Somersby ..	Lincoln ..	Parish	72
Snenton.. ..	Notts ..	Sub-dis.	11 048	Somersetshire		County	444 873
Snenton.. ..	,, ..	Parish	11 048	Eastern Division ..		E. Div.	259 335
Snetterton ..	Norfolk ..	Parish	237	Western Division ..		W. Div.	185 538
Snettisham ..	,, ..	Sub-dis.	5 702	Somersham ..	Hunts ..	Sub-dis.	4 480
Snettisham ..	,, ..	Parish	1 173	Somersham ..	,, ..	Parish	1 621
Sneyd	Stafford ..	Hamlet	1 128	Somersham ..	Suffolk ..	Parish	366
Sneyd, Trinity..	,, ..	Ecl. Dis.	3 071	Somers Town ..	Middlesex ..	Sub-dis.	39 099

Name of Place.	County.	Description.	Population.	Name of Place.	County.	Description.	Population.
Somerton, East	Norfolk	Parish	62	South Bersted	Sussex	—	605
Somerton, West	"	Parish	244	South Biddick	Durham	Tnship.	48
Somerton	Oxon	Parish	335	South Blyth	Northumberland	Tnship.	1 953
Somerton	Somerset	Hund.	5 929	Southborough	Kent	Ecl. Dis.	2 038
Somerton	"	Sub-dis.	5 797	South Bradon	Somerset	Parish	38
Somerton	"	Parish	2 266	South Brent	Devon	Parish	1 205
Somerton	Suffolk	Parish	153	South Brent	Somerset	Parish	905
Sompting	Sussex	Parish	628	South Brewham	"	Parish	519
Sonning	Berks	Hund.	8 268	Southbroom	Wilts	Chap.	2 773
Sonning	Berks & Oxon	Parish	2 747	South Burgh	Norfolk	Parish	317
Sonningtown	Berks	Liberty	465	Southburn	York	Tnship.	90
Soothill	York	Sub-dis.	6 238	South Bury	Lancaster	Sub-dis.	15 726
Soothill	"	Tnship.	6 238	South Cadbury	Somerset	Parish	287
Sopley	Hants	Parish	908	South Carlton	Lincoln	Parish	181
Sopworth	Wilts	Parish	214	South Carlton	Notts	Tnship.	336
Sotby	Lincoln	Parish	164	South Cave	York	Sub-dis.	3 390
Sotherton	Suffolk	Parish	187	South Cave	"	Parish	1 377
Sotterley	"	Parish	231	South Cave	"	Tnship.	894
Sotwell	Berks	Parish	149	South Cerney	Gloucester	Parish	1 006
Soughton	Flint	Tnship.	557	South Charford	Hants	Parish	70
Soughton	Salop	Tnship.	207	South Charlton	Nrthumberld.	Tnship.	153
Soulbury	Bucks	Parish	589	South Charlton	"	Ecl. Dis.	261
Soulby	Cumberland	Tnship.	66	Southchurch	Essex	Parish	494
Soulby	Westmoreland	Tnship.	453	South Clay	Notts	Division	8 072
Souldern	Oxon	Parish	587	South Cliff	York	Tnship.	119
Souldrop	Beds	Parish	276	South Clifton	Notts	Tnship.	319
Sound	Cheshire	Tnship.	246	Southcoates	York	Tnship.	2 804
Sourton	Devon	Parish	543	South Cockerington	Lincoln	Parish	300
Southacre	Norfolk	Parish	92	South Collingham	Notts	Parish	863
Southall Green	Middlesex	Ecl. Dis.	474	Southcot	Berks	Tithing	87
Southam, &c.	Gloucester	Hamlet	248	South Cove	Suffolk	Parish	187
Southam	Warw. & Nrthptn.	District	10 392	South Cowton	York	Chap.	167
Southam	Warwick	Parish	1 674	South Creake	Norfolk	Parish	1 058
South Ambersham	Sussex	Tithing	143	South Crosland	York	Tnship.	2 794
Southampton	(Hants)	County	481 815	South Crosland, Trinity	"	Ecl. Dis.	2 259
Northern Division		N. Div.	157 495	South Croxton	Leicester	Parish	311
Southern Division		S. Div.	268 958	South Dalton	York	Parish	338
Isle of Wight		Island	55 362	South Damerham	Wilts	Hund.	3 008
Southampton	Hants	Division	21 996	South Damerham	"	Parish	697
Southampton	"	L. Sub.	21 996	South Darley, St. Mary	Derby	Ecl. Dis.	582
Southampton Town	"	L. Sub.	46 960	South Dissington	Northumbld.	Tnship.	63
Southampton	"	District	43 414	South Duffield	York	Tnship.	236
Southampton	"	Borough	46 960	Southease	Sussex	Parish	84
Southampton, Trinity	"	Ecl. Dis.	5 421	South-East Leeds	York	Sub-dis.	29 196
Southampton, St. James	"	Ecl. Dis.	6 883	South Elkington	Lincoln	Parish	333
Southampton, St. Peter	"	Ecl. Dis.	1 550	South Elmham—			
South Baddesley St. Mary	"	Ecl. Dis.	561	All Saints	Suffolk	Parish	197
South Bailey	Durham	Parish	106	St. Cross	"	Parish	238
South Banbury	Oxon	Ecl. Dis.	4 043	St. James	"	Parish	294
South Barrow	Somerset	Parish	140	St. Margaret	"	Parish	152
South Bedburn	Durham	Tnship.	332	St. Michael	"	Parish	156
South Benfleet	Essex	Parish	573	St. Nicholas	"	Parish	103
South Bersted	Sussex	Sub-dis.	3 128	St. Peter	"	Parish	88
South Bersted	"	Parish	3 128	South Elmsall	York	Tnship.	468

Name of Place.	County.	Description.	Population.	Name of Place.	County.	Description.	Population.
Southend, St. John	Essex	Ecl. Dis.	1716	South Mimms	Middlesex	L. Sub.	4291
Southend, St. Peter	Surrey	Ecl. Dis.	2932	South Mimms	Mdlx. & Herts	Sub-dis.	5381
Southernby Bound	Cumberland	Tnship.	123	South Mimms	Middlesex	Parish	3238
Southerndown	Glamorgan	Hamlet	340	Southminster	Essex	Sub-dis.	4639
Southery	Norfolk	Parish	1164	Southminster	,,	Parish	1424
South Fambridge	Essex	Parish	104	South Molton	Devon	Hund.	9092
South Ferriby	Lincoln	Parish	573	South Molton	,,	L. Sub.	27906
Southfleet	Kent	Parish	717	South Molton	,,	District	19209
South Frodingham	York	Tnship.	59	South Molton	,,	Sub-dis.	8698
Southgate	Middlesex	Ecl. Dis.	2226	South Molton	,,	Parish	3830
South Gosforth	Nrthumberld.	Tnship.	248	South Molton	,,	M. Bor.	3830
South Hackney	Middlesex	Sub-dis.	15458	South Moreton	Berks	Parish	371
South Hackney	,,	Ecl. Dis.	15458	South Muskham	Notts	Parish	277
South Hamlet	Gloucester	Sub-dis.	12427	South Myton	York	Ward	24581
South Hamlet	,,	Parish	2248	South Narberth	Pembroke	Division	829
South Hampstead	Middlesex	Ecl. Dis.	2945	South Newbald	York	Tnship.	211
South Hanningfield	Essex	Parish	235	South Newington	Oxon	Parish	400
South Hayling	Hants	Parish	777	South Newton	Wilts	Parish	717
South Heighton	Sussex	Parish	104	South Normanton	Derby	Parish	1805
South Hiendley	York	Tnship.	282	Sth. Norwood, St. Mark	Surrey	Ecl. Dis.	1489
South Hinckford	Essex	L. Sub.	28056	South Ockendon	Essex	Parish	1267
Southill	Beds	Parish	1391	Southoe	Hunts	Parish	281
Southill	,,	Tnship.	619	Southolt	Suffolk	Parish	193
Southill	Cornwall	Parish	691	South Ormsby	Lincoln	Parish	261
South Hinksey	Berks	Parish	636	Southorpe	,,	Parish	44
South Holme	York	Tnship.	68	Southorpe	Northampton	Hamlet	227
South Horsham	Sussex	Sub-dis.	4514	South Osset	York	Ecl. Dis.	3018
South Huish	Devon	Parish	346	South Otterington	,,	Parish	853
South Hyckham	Lincoln	Parish	155	South Owersby	Lincoln	Parish	76
South Hylton	Durham	Ecl. Dis.	2036	Southowram	York	Sub-dis.	7245
South Kelsey	Lincoln	Parish	633	Southowram	,,	Tnship.	7245
South Killingholme	,,	Tnship.	555	South Perrot	Dorset	Parish	363
South Kilvington	York	Parish	360	South Petherton	Somerset	Hund.	6196
South Kilvington	,,	Tnship.	233	South Petherton	,,	Sub-dis.	3862
South Kilworth	Leicester	Parish	421	South Petherton	,,	Parish	2423
South Kirby	York	Parish	1284	South Petherton	,,	Town	2031
South Kirby	,,	Tnship.	482	South Petherwin	Cornwall	Parish	876
South Kyme	Lincoln	Parish	1004	South Pickenham	Norfolk	Parish	159
South Leigh	Devon	Parish	331	South Pool	Devon	Parish	413
Southleigh	Oxon	Parish	319	Southport	Lancaster	Town	8940
South Leverton	Notts	Parish	494	South Rainham	Norfolk	Parish	129
South Leverton	,,	Tnship.	408	South Rauceby	Lincoln	Parish	474
South Lincoln	Lincoln	L. Sub.	43781	South Repps	Norfolk	Parish	816
South Littleton	Worcester	Parish	294	South Reston	Lincoln	Parish	235
South Lopham	Norfolk	Parish	630	Southrop	Gloucester	Parish	362
South Luffenham	Rutland	Parish	400	South Runcton	Norfolk	Parish	139
South Lynn	Norfolk	Parish	4534	South Ruston	,,	Parish	102
South Malling	Sussex	Parish	716	South Savernake, &c.	Wilts	Parish	230
South Marston	Wilts	Tithing	370	South Scarle	Notts	Parish	513
S. Middleton, Ilberton	Nrthmb.	Tnship.	75	South Scarle	,,	Tnship.	175
South Middleton, Morpeth	,,	Tnship.	22	Southsea, St. Jude	Hants	Ecl. Dis.	6301
South Milford	York	Tnship.	823	South Sheffield	York	Sub-dis.	17680
South Milford, St. Mary	,,	Ecl. Dis.	1059	South Shields	Durham	District	44849
South Milton	Devon	Parish	863	South Shields	,,	Sub-dis.	15467

Name of Place.	County.	Description.	Population.	Name of Place.	County.	Description.	Population.
uth Shields ..	Durham	Tnship.	8 973	South Wingfield .	Derby ..	Parish	1 241
uth Shields .	,, ..	Borough	85 239	South Witham ..	Lincoln ..	Parish	531
uth Shields, St. Hilda	,, ..	Ecl. Dis.	12 133	Southwold ..	Suffolk ..	Parish	2 032
a. Shields. St. Stephen	,, ..	Ecl. Dis.	6 252	Southwold ..	,, ..	M. Bor.	2 032
uth Shields, Trinity	,, ..	Ecl. Dis.	16 807	Southwood ..	Norfolk ..	Parish	39
uth Shoebury .	Essex ..	Parish	1 502	South Wootton..	,, ..	Parish	150
uth Skirlaugh .	York ..	Tnship.	364	South Worcester	Worcester ..	Sub-dis.	11 651
uth Somercotes	Lincoln ..	Parish	419	Southworth w. Croft	Lancaster ..	Parish	1 094
uth Stainley, &c.	York ..	Parish	259	Sowe ..	Warwick ..	Sub-dis.	4 670
uth Stoke ..	Lincoln ..	Tnship.	140	Sowe ..	,, ..	Parish	1 667
uth Stoke ..	Oxon ..	Parish	810	Sowerby ..	York W. ..	Sub-dis.	13 945
uth Stoke ..	Somerset ..	Parish	375	Sowerby	,, ..	Tnship.	8 753
uth Stoke ..	Sussex ..	Parish	111	Sowerby Bridge	,, ..	Town	5 382
uth Stoneham.	Hants ..	District	25 542	Sowerby, St. George	,, ..	Ecl. Dis.	2 707
uth Stoneham	,, ..	Sub-dis.	8 621	Sowerby, St.Mary	,, ..	Ecl. Dis.	1 902
uth Stoneham	,, ..	Parish	7 761	Sowerby ..	York N. ..	Tnship.	1 248
uth Tawton ..	Devon ..	Parish	1 541	Sowerby w. Cotcliffe	,, ..	Tnship.	50
uth Thoresby .	Lincoln ..	Parish	162	Sowton ..	Devon ..	Parish	382
uth Thurmaston	Leicester ..	Tnship.	893	Soyland..	York ..	Tnship.	3 373
uth Tidmouth.	Hants ..	Parish	208	Spalding ..	Lincoln ..	L. Sub.	37 928
uth Town ..	Suffolk ..	Hamlet	1 714	Spalding ..	,, ..	District	20 949
uth Walsham .	Norfolk ..	Sub-dis.	5 734	Spalding ..	,, ..	Sub-dis.	9 253
. Walsham, St. Lawr.	,, ..	Parish	220	Spalding ..	,, ..	Parish	8 723
. Walsham, St. Mary	,, ..	Parish	336	Spalding ..	,, ..	Town	7 032
Southwark ..	Surrey ..	P. Boro.	193 593	Spaldington ..	York ..	Tnship.	363
Southwark, St. Geo.	,, ..	Parish	55 510	Spaldwick ..	Hunts ..	Sub-dis.	3 555
St. Jude	,, ..	Ecl. Dis.	6 968	Spaldwick ..	,, ..	Parish	470
St. Mary	,, ..	Ecl. Dis.	9 283	Spalford..	Notts ..	Hamlet	94
St. Paul	,, ..	Ecl. Dis.	7 699	Spa & Westhay .	Northampton	Lodges	28
St. Peter	,, ..	Ecl. Dis.	5 044	Spanby ..	Lincoln ..	Parish	75
St. Stephen ..	,, ..	Ecl. Dis.	5 260	Sparham ..	Norfolk ..	Parish	353
Trinity ..	,, ..	Ecl. Dis.	17 731	Sparkenhoe ..	Leicester ..	Hund.	37 579
South Warnborough	Hants ..	Parish	369	Sparkford ..	Somerset ..	Parish	305
Southwater —				Sparsholt ..	Berks ..	Parish	863
Holy Innocents	Sussex ..	Ecl. Dis.	703	Sparsholt ..	,, ..	Tnship.	493
Holy Trinity..	,, ..	Ecl. Dis.	1 037	Sparsholt ..	Hants ..	Parish	395
South Weald ..	Essex ..	Parish	5 209	Spaunton ..	York ..	Tnship.	111
South Weald ..	,, ..	—	2 116	Spaxton..	Somerset ..	Parish	1 057
Southwell ..	Notts ..	Division	7 869	Speen ..	Berks ..	Sub-dis.	7 580
Southwell ..	,, ..	L. Sub.	8 875	Speen ..	,, ..	Parish	3 311
Southwell ..	,, ..	District	24 425	Speenhamland ..	,, ..	Ecl. Dis.	1 767
Southwell ..	,, ..	Sub-dis.	13 055	Speeton..	York ..	Tnship.	140
Southwell ..	,, ..	Parish	3 469	Speke ..	Lancaster ..	Tnship.	571
Southwell ..	,, ..	Town	3 095	Speldhurst ..	Kent ..	Parish	3 598
Southwell Tinity	,, ..	Ecl. Dis.	852	Spelhoe ..	Northampton	Hund.	7 089
South Weston ..	Oxon ..	Parish	92	Spelsbury ..	Oxon ..	Parish	516
South Wheatley .	Notts ..	Parish	32	Spelthorne ..	Middlesex ..	Hund.	19 440
Southwick ..	Durham ..	Tnship.	4 263	Spelthorne ..	,, ..	L. Sub.	19 440
Southwick ..	,, ..	Ecl. Dis.	4 683	Spennithorne ..	York ..	Parish	852
Southwick ..	Hants ..	Parish	609	Spennithorne ..	,, ..	Tnship.	198
Southwick ..	Northampton	Parish	130	Spernall..	Warwick ..	Parish	91
Southwick ..	Sussex ..	Parish	1 358	Spetchley ..	Worcester ..	Parish	140
Southwick ..	Wilts ..	Tithing	1 241	Spetisbury ..	Dorset ..	Parish	688
South Willingham	Lincoln ..	Parish	340	Spexhall ..	Suffolk ..	Parish	181

199

Name of Place.	County.	Description.	Population.	Name of Place.	County.	Description.	Popula
Spilsby ..	*Lincoln*	District	28 799	Stafford..	*Stafford*	District	24 4
Spilsby ..	,,	Sub-dis.	8 421	Stafford..	,,	Sub-dis.	14 7
Spilsby ..	,,	Parish	1 467	**Stafford**	,,	Borough	12 5
Spindlestone	*Northumberland*	Tnship.	113	Stafford Christch.	,,	Ecl. Dis.	5 4
Spitalfields	*Middlesex*	Sub-dis.	15 700	Stagsden	*Beds*	Parish	7
Spitalfields	,,	Parish	20 593	Stainbrough	*York*	Tnship.	4
Spitalfields, St. Stephen	,,	Ecl. Dis.	5 090	Stainburn	*Cumberland*	Tnship.	1
Spital-sq., St. Mary	,,	Ecl. Dis.	4 041	Stainburn	*York*	Tnship.	2
Spittal	*Northumberland*	Tnship.	1 768	Stainby ..	*Lincoln*	Parish	1
Spittal ..	*Pembroke*	Parish	392	Staincliffe & Ewecross	*York*	Wapen.	75 8
Spittle Boughton	*Cheshire*	Parish	163	Staincliffe & Ewecross E.	,,	L. Sub.	52 5
Spittle (Ovingham P.)	*Nrthmb.*	Tnship.	13	Staincliffe & Ewecross W.	,,	L. Sub.	23 3
Spittle Hill	,,	Tnship.	9	Staincross	,,	Wapen.	57 9
Spittlegate, &c...	*Lincoln*	Tnship.	3 803	Staincross	,,	L. Sub.	57 9
Spittlegate, St. John	,,	Ecl. Dis.	3 803	Staindrop	*Durh. & York*	Sub-dis.	5 24
Spixworth	*Norfolk*	Parish	44	Staindrop	*Durham*	Parish	2 40
Spofforth	*York*	Parish	3 733	Staindrop	,,	Tnship.	1 3
Spofforth w. Stockeld	,,	Tnship.	1 017	Staine ..	*Cambs*	Hund.	5 0
Spondon	*Derby*	Sub-dis.	7 238	Staines ..	*Middlesex*	District	15 9
Spondon	,,	Parish	2 057	Staines ..	,,	Sub-dis.	8 6
Spondon	,,	Tnship.	1 523	Staines ..	,,	Parish	2 74
Spoonbed	*Gloucester*	Tithing	669	**Staines..**	,,	Town	2 5
Sporle w. Palgrave	*Norfolk*	Parish	806	Stainfield	*Lincoln*	Hamlet	9
Spotland	*Lancaster*	Tnship.	30 378	Stainfield	,,	Parish	16
Spotland Far Side	,,	Sub-dis.	6 505	Stainforth	*York*	Tnship.	1
Spotland, Near Side	,,	Sub-dis.	9 867	Stainforth, St. Peter	,,	Ecl. Dis	2
Spotland, St. Clement	,,	Ecl. Dis.	11 016	Stainforth (Hatfield P.)	,,	Tnship.	7
Spratton	*Northampton*	Sub-dis.	5 914	Stainland	,,	Tnship.	4 65
Spratton	,,	Parish	1 086	Stainland, St. Andrew	,,	Ecl. Di.	4 65
Spratton	,,	Tnship.	1 013	Stainley w. Sleningford	,,	Tnship	44
Spreyton	*Devon*	Parish	358	Stainley, North..	,,	Ecl. Di.	51
Spridlington	*Lincoln*	Parish	311	Stainley, South..	,,	Parish	25
Springfield	*Essex*	Parish	2 566	Stainmore	*Westmoreland*	Chap.	67
Spring Grove, St. Mary	*Mddlx.*	Ecl. Dis.	782	Stainton (Dacre P.)	*Cumberland*	Tnship.	33
Springthorpe	*Lincoln*	Parish	260	Stainton (Stanwix P.)	,,	Tnship.	6
Sproatley	*York*	Parish	455	Stainton, Great .	*Durham*	Parish	14
Sproston	*Cheshire*	Tnship.	163	Stainton, Great .	,,	Tnship.	11
Sprotborough	*York*	Parish	504	Stainton Little..	,,	Tnship.	7
Sprotborough	,,	Tnship.	339	Stainton w. Streatlam	,,	Tnship.	35
Sproughton	*Suffolk*	Parish	598	Stainton by Langworth	*Lincoln*	Parish	21
Sprowston	*Norfolk*	Sub-dis.	6 119	Stainton by Langworth	,,	Tnship.	12
Sprowston	,,	Parish	1 407	Stainton le Vale..	,,	Parish	19
Sproxton	*Leicester*	Parish	455	Stainton	*Westmoreland*	Tnship.	35
Sproxton	*York*	Tnship.	182	Stainton	*York*	Parish	3 85
Spurstow	*Cheshire*	Tnship.	514	Stainton, Yarm..	,,	Tnship.	35
Stackpole Elidor	*Pembroke*	Parish	273	Stainton, Richmond	,,	Tnship.	2
Stadhampton	*Oxon*	Parish	329	Stainton w. Hellaby	,,	Parish	26
Stadmoreslow	*Stafford*	Tnship.	525	Stainton Dale ..	,,	Tnship.	34
Staffield..	*Cumberland*	Tnship.	272	Stalbridge	*Dorset*	Sub-dis.	4 42
Staffordshire		County	746 943	Stalbridge	,,	Parish	1 92
Northern Division ..		N. Div.	289 663	Staley ..	*Lancaster*	Tnship.	6 18
Southern Division ..		S. Div.	457 280	Stalham..	*Norfolk*	Sub-dis.	4 03
Stafford, West ..	*Dorset*	Parish	220	Stalham..	,,	Parish	75
Stafford..	*Stafford*	L. Sub.	41 716	Stalisfield	*Kent*	Parish	33

Name of Place.	County.	Description.	Population.	Name of Place.	County.	Description.	Population.
.llingborough	Lincoln ..	Parish	433	Stanford Rivers..	Essex ..	Parish	992
.lmine ..	Lancaster ..	Sub-dis.	3 037	Stanford Bishop	Hereford ..	Parish	234
.lmine & Stainall	„ ..	Tnship.	471	Stanford ..	Norfolk ..	Parish	200
.lybridge	Chesh. & Lanc.	M. Bor.	24 921	Stanford ..	Northampton	Parish	42
.lybridge, New St. Geo.	Lanc.	Ecl. Dis.	4 047	Stanford on Soar	Notts ..	Parish	140
.lybridge St. Paul	Cheshire..	Ecl. Dis.	6 919	Stanford on Teme	Worcester ..	Parish	201
.mborough ..	Devon ..	Hund.	14 807	Stanghow ..	York ..	Tnship.	118
.mborough & Coleridge	„ ..	L. Sub.	33 279	Stanhoe.. ..	Norfolk ..	Parish	468
.mbourne ..	Essex ..	Parish	537	Stanhope ..	Durham ..	Sub-dis.	5 196
.mbridge, Little	„ ..	Parish	125	Stanhope ..	„ ..	Parish	9 654
.mbridge, Great	„ ..	Parish	363	Stanhope Quarter	„ ..	Tnship.	2 918
.mford ..	Lincoln, &c..	District	18 213	Stanion.. ..	Northampton	Parish	351
.mford ..	„ ..	Sub-dis.	12 521	Stanley	Derby ..	Tnship.	534
.mford	Linc. & Nrthptn.	Borough	8 047	Stanley	„ ..	Ecl. Dis.	534
All Saints ..	Lincoln ..	Parish	2 070	Stanley-Pontlarge	Gloucester ..	Parish	57
St. George ..	„ ..	Parish	1 881	Stanley St. Leonard	„ ..	Parish	864
St. John ..	„ ..	Parish	1 199	Stanley	York ..	Sub-dis.	8 237
St. Mary ..	„ ..	Parish	359	Stanley w. Wrenthorpe	„ ..	Tnship.	8 237
St. Michael ..	„ ..	Parish	1 305	Stanley	„ ..	Ecl. Dis.	2 924
.mford Hill ..	Middlesex ..	Sub-dis.	5 483	Stanlow.. ..	Cheshire ..	Parish	14
.mford Hill St. Thos.	„ ..	Ecl. Dis.	5 483	Stanmer.. ..	Sussex ..	Parish	147
.mford-Baron .	Northampton	Parish	1 606	Stanmore, Great .	Middlesex ..	Parish	1 318
.mford-Baron .	„ ..	—	1 530	Stanmore, Little .	„ ..	Parish	891
.mford	Northumberland	Tnship.	108	Stanney, Great..	Cheshire ..	Tnship.	65
.mford Bridge East	York ..	Sub-dis.	4 502	Stanney, Little ..	„ ..	Tnship.	204
.mford Bridge East	„ ..	Tnship.	417	Stanningfield ..	Suffolk ..	Parish	351
.mford Bridge, &c.	„ ..	Tnship.	196	Stannington	Northumberland	Parish	1 058
.mfordham	Northumberland	Sub-dis.	7 753	Stannington, N. East	„ ..	Quarter	503
.mfordham ..	„ ..	Parish	1 800	Stannington, N. West	„ ..	Quarter	178
.anage ..	Radnor ..	Lordship	162	Stannington, South	„ ..	Quarter	377
.anbridge ..	Beds ..	Hamlet	554	Stannington Christch.	York ..	Ecl. Dis.	2 909
.anbridge ..	Dorset ..	Parish	54	Stansfield ..	Suffolk ..	Parish	549
.ancill w. Wellingley	York ..	Tnship.	65	Stansfield ..	York ..	Tnship.	8 174
.and All Saints	Lancaster ..	Ecl. Dis.	8 758	Stanstead ..	Herts ..	Sub-dis.	2 431
.andard Hill, &c.	Notts ..	Parish	1 072	Stanstead Abbots	„ ..	Parish	980
.anderwick ..	Somerset ..	Parish	60	Stanstead, St. Margaret	„ ..	Parish	93
.andford ..	Kent ..	Parish	294	Stanstead ..	Kent ..	Parish	403
.andground	Hunts & Cambs	Parish	1 839	Stanstead ..	Suffolk ..	Parish	382
.andground ..	„	Tnship.	1 061	Stanstead Christch.	Sussex ..	Ecl. Dis.	317
.andish ..	Gloucester ..	Parish	525	Stansted ..	Essex ..	Sub-dis.	5 040
.andish ..	Lancaster ..	Sub-dis.	6 894	Stansted Mountfitchet	„ ..	Parish	1 769
.andish ..	„ ..	Parish	10 410	Stansted Mountfitchet	„ ..	Hamlet	1 240
.andish w. Langtree	„ ..	Tnship.	3 054	Stansty ..	Denbigh ..	Tnship.	410
.andlake ..	Oxon ..	Parish	822	Stanthorne ..	Cheshire ..	Tnship.	161
.anlinch ..	Wilts ..	Parish	90	Stanton.. ..	Derby ..	Tnship.	716
.andon.. ..	Herts ..	Sub-dis.	3 303	Stanton & Newhall	„ ..	Tnship.	2 413
.andon.. ..	„ ..	Parish	2 245	Stanton by Bridge	„ ..	Parish	185
.andon High Cross	„ ..	Ecl. Dis.	819	Stanton by Dale ..	„ ..	Parish	499
.andon.. ..	Stafford ..	Parish	347	Stanton St. Gabriel	Dorset ..	Parish	75
.anfield ..	Norfolk ..	Parish	195	Stanton.. ..	Gloucester ..	Parish	280
.anford ..	Beds ..	Hamlet	385	Stanton upon Arrow	Hereford .	Parish	387
.anford Dingley	Berks ..	Parish	145	Stanton und. Bardon	Leicester ..	Tnship.	312
.tanford in Vale .	„ ..	Parish	1 277	Stanton ..	Northumberland	Tnship.	112
.tanford le Hope	Essex ..	Parish	504	Stanton on Wolds	Notts ..	Parish	158

Name of Place.	County.	Description.	Population.	Name of Place.	County.	Description.	Population.
Stanton Harcourt	Oxon	Parish	661	Stapleton	York W.	Tnship.	130
Stanton St. John	,,	Parish	518	Staploe	Cambs	Hund.	11 887
Stanton Lacy	Salop	Parish	1 598	Starbotton	York	Tnship.	161
Stanton Long	,,	Parish	234	Starcross	Devon	Ecl. Dis.	1 192
Stanton on Hineheath	,,	Parish	648	Starston	Norfolk	Parish	481
Stanton Drew	Somerset	Parish	523	Startforth	York	Parish	802
Stanton Prior	,,	Parish	136	Startforth	,,	Tnship.	565
Stanton	Stafford	Tnship.	403	Statfold	Stafford	Parish	26
Stanton	Suffolk	Parish	1 045	Stathern	Leicester	Parish	524
Stanton Fitzwarren	Wilts	Parish	205	Staughton, Little	Beds	Parish	572
Stanton St. Bernard	,,	Parish	358	Staughton, Great	Hunts	Parish	1 312
Stanton St. Quintin	,,	Parish	338	Staunton	Gloucester	Parish	202
Stantonbury	Bucks	Parish	29	Staunton on Wye	Hereford	Parish	675
,, w. New Bradwell	,,	Ecl. Dis.	1 207	Staunton-Harrold	Leicester	Tnship.	352
Stanway	Essex	Sub-dis.	4 663	Staunton	Notts	Parish	151
Stanway	,,	Parish	964	Staunton	,,	Tnship.	87
Stanway, All Saints	,,	Ecl. Dis.	513	Staunton	Worcester	Parish	507
Stanway	Gloucester	Parish	378	Staveley	Derby	Parish	7 513
Stanwell	Middlesex	Parish	1 714	Staveley	,,	Tnship.	6 831
Stanwick	Northampton	Parish	669	Staveley	,,	Town	2 400
Stanwick St. John	York	Parish	768	Staveley	Lancaster	Tnship.	409
Stanwick St. John	,,	Tnship.	53	Staveley, Nether	Westmoreland	Tnship.	294
Stanwix	Cumberland	Sub-dis.	3 801	Staveley, Over	,,	Tnship.	705
Stanwix	,,	Parish	2 356	Staveley	York	Parish	342
Stanwix	,,	Tnship.	935	Staverton	Devon	Parish	949
Stapeley	Cheshire	Tnship.	578	Staverton	Gloucester	Parish	315
Stapenhill	Derby	Parish	3 077	Staverton	Northampton	Parish	486
Stapenhill	,,	Tnship.	1 111	Staverton	Wilts	Ecl. Dis.	580
Staple by Wingham	Kent	Parish	520	Stawell	Somerset	Hamlet	173
Staple Inn	Middlesex	Parish	42	Stawley	,,	Parish	188
Staple Fitzpaine	Somerset	Parish	264	Staxton	York	Tnship.	307
Staplefield, St. Mark	Sussex	Ecl. Dis.	798	Stayley	Cheshire	Sub-dis.	7 218
Stapleford	Cambs	Parish	465	Stayley	,,	Tnship.	6 187
Stapleford-Abbots	Essex	Parish	502	Staythorpe	Notts	Tnship.	62
Stapleford-Tawney	,,	Parish	273	Stean	Northampton	Parish	25
Stapleford	Herts	Parish	226	Stebbing	Essex	Sub-dis.	4 956
Stapleford	Leicester	Parish	109	Stebbing	,,	Parish	1 346
Stapleford	Lincoln	Parish	204	Stedham	Sussex	Parish	530
Stapleford	Notts & Derby	Sub-dis.	8 952	Steen	Northampton	Parish	25
Stapleford	Notts	Parish	1 729	Steep	Hants & Sussex	Parish	903
Stapleford	Wilts	Parish	260	Steep	Hants	Hamlet	649
Staplegate	Kent	Ville	283	Steeping, Great	Lincoln	Parish	334
Staplegrove	Somerset	Parish	469	Steeping, Little	,,	Parish	326
Staplehurst	Kent	Parish	1 695	Steeple	Dorset	Parish	262
Staples or Fern	Northumberld.	Islands	23	Steeple	Essex	Parish	559
Stapleton	Cumberland	Parish	984	Steeple Ashton	Wilts	Parish	1 767
Stapleton	,,	Tnship.	462	Steeple Ashton	,,	Tithing	776
Stapleton Preston	Dorset	Parish	59	Steeple Aston	Oxon	Parish	736
Stapleton	Gloucester	Sub-dis.	9 184	Steeple Aston	,,	Tnship.	650
Stapleton	,,	Parish	5 355	Steeple Barton	,,	Parish	859
Stapleton	Hereford	Tnship.	159	Steeple Bumpstead	Essex	Parish	1 158
Stapleton	Leicester	Chap.	240	Steeple Claydon	Bucks	Parish	946
Stapleton	Salop	Parish	281	Steeple Gidding	Hunts	Parish	118
Stapleton	York N.	Tnship.	152	Steeple Langford	Wilts	Parish	628

Name of Place.	County.	Description.	Population.	Name of Place.	County.	Description.	Population.
Steeple Morden	Cambs	Parish	913	Stock	Essex	Parish	657
Steepleton-Iwerne	Dorset	Parish	59	Stock & Bradley	Worcester	Chap.	310
Steeton	York N.	Tnship.	75	Stockbridge	Hants & Wilts	District	7 286
Steeton w. Eastburn	„ W.	Tnship.	1 341	Stockbridge	Hants	Sub-dis.	3 577
Stella	Durham	Tnship.	542	Stockbridge	„	Parish	935
Stella St. Cuthbert	„	Ecl. Dis.	3 751	Stockbridge & Tirril	Westmld.	Tnship.	245
Stelling	Kent	Parish	309	Stockbury	Kent	Parish	613
Stelling Minnis	„	Parish	82	Stockcross, St. John	Berks	Ecl. Dis.	815
Stelling	Northumberland	Tnship.	27	Stockdalewath Bound	Cumbld.	Tnship.	247
Stembridge	Glamorgan	Parish	10	Stockerston	Leicester	Parish	50
Stenigot	Lincoln	Parish	96	Stock Gayland	Dorset	Parish	50
Stepney	Middlesex	District	56 572	Stockham	Cheshire	Tnship.	42
Stepney	„	Parish	98 836	Stockingford	Warwick	Ecl. Dis.	1 610
Stepney, Trinity	„	Ecl. Dis.	10 478	Stocking Pelham	Herts	Parish	126
Stepney, St. Philip	„	Ecl. Dis.	14 805	Stockland	Devon	Parish	1 123
Steppingley	Beds	Parish	865	Stockland Bristol	Somerset	Parish	142
Sternfield	Suffolk	Parish	208	Stockleigh English	Devon	Parish	114
Stert	Wilts	Tithing	184	Stockleigh Pomeroy	„	Parish	188
Stetchworth	Cambs	Parish	671	Stockley	Durham	Tnship.	282
Stevenage	Herts	L. Sub.	12 388	Stocklinch Magdalen	Somerset	Parish	116
Stevenage	„	Parish	2 352	Stocklinch Ottersay	„	Parish	69
Steventon	Beds	Parish	606	Stockport	Chesh. & Lanc.	District	94 360
Steventon	Berks	Parish	886	Stockport First	„ „	Sub-dis.	28 224
Steventon	Hants	Parish	167	Stockport, Second	„ „	Sub-dis.	12 860
Stewkley	Bucks	Parish	1 453	Stockport	Cheshire	Parish	98 005
Stewton	Lincoln	Parish	73	Stockport	„	Tnship.	30 746
Steyning	Sussex	L. Sub.	15 670	Stockport	Chesh. & Lanc.	Borough	54 681
Steyning	„	District	24 053	Stockport Etchells	Cheshire	Tnship.	860
Steyning	„	Sub-dis.	5 684	Stockport St. Matthew	„	Ecl. Dis.	5 535
Steyning	„	Parish	1 620	Stockport St. Peter	„	Ecl. Dis.	4 455
Steynton	Pembroke	Parish	3 710	Stockport St. Thomas	„	Ecl. Dis.	12 670
Stibbard	Norfolk	Parish	451	Stocksfield Hall	Nrthumberld.	Tnship.	48
Stibbington	Hunts	Parish	721	Stockton	Cheshire	Tnship.	27
Stickford	Lincoln	Parish	357	Stockton Heath, St.Thos.	„	Ecl. Dis.	1 763
Stickney	„	Sub-dis.	2 131	Stockton	Durham	Ward	31 643
Stickney	„	Parish	851	Stockton Ward	„	L. Sub.	57 245
Stiffkey	Norfolk	Parish	513	Stockton	„	District	57 099
Stifford	Essex	Parish	281	Stockton	„	Union	45 325
Stillingfleet	York	Parish	964	Stockton	„	Sub-dis.	20 246
Stillingfleet w. Moreby	„	Tnship.	422	Stockton on Tees	„	Parish	13 761
Stillington	Durham	Tnship.	40	Stockton on Tees	„	Tnship.	13 487
Stillington	York	Sub-dis.	2 846	Stockton	„	M. Bor.	13 357
Stillington	„	Parish	738	Stockton, Trinity	„	Ecl. Dis.	4 267
Stilton	Hunts	Sub-dis.	5 797	Stockton	Norfolk	Parish	129
Stilton	„	Parish	724	Stockton	Salop	Parish	490
Stinchcombe	Gloucester	Parish	340	Stockton	Warwick	Parish	548
Stinsford	Dorset	Parish	357	Stockton	Wilts	Parish	288
Stirchley	Salop	Parish	310	Stockton	Worcester	Parish	129
Stirton w. Thorlby	York	Tnship.	127	Stockton on Forest	York	Parish	449
Stisted	Essex	Parish	821	Stockwell, St. Michael	Surrey	Ecl. Dis.	7 265
Stittenham	York	Tnship.	81	Stockwith, East	Lincoln	Tnship.	313
Stivichall	Warwick	Parish	72	Stockwith, E., St Peter	„	Ecl. Dis.	378
Stixwould	Lincoln	Parish	269	Stockwith, West	Notts	Tnship.	538
Stoborough	Dorset	Liberty	346	Stockwood	Dorset	Parish	60

Name of Place.	County.	Description.	Population.	Name of Place.	County.	Description.	Population.
Stodden..	*Beds*	Hund.	6 393	Stoke Holy Cross	*Norfolk* ..	Parish	446
Stodmarsh	*Kent*	Parish	145	Stokesby w. Herringby	,,	Parish	418
Stody ..	*Norfolk*	Parish	160	Stoke Albany ..	*Northampton*	Parish	344
Stogumber	*Somerset*	Sub-dis.	3 789	Stoke Bruerne ..	,,	Parish	824
Stogumber	,,	Parish	1 398	Stoke Bruerne ..	,,	Hamlet	430
Stogursey	,,	Sub-dis.	2 677	Stoke Doyle ..	,,	Parish	149
Stogursey	,,	Parish	1 455	Stoke Bardolph .	*Notts*	Tnship.	174
Stoke ..	*Bucks*	Hund.	17 693	Stoke, East ..	,,	Parish	490
Stoke ..	,,	L. Sub.	22 353	Stoke, East ..	,,	Tnship.	280
Stoke Goldington	,,	Parish	963	Stokeham ..	,,	Parish	53
Stoke Hammond	,,	Parish	401	Stoke Lyne ..	*Oxon*	Parish	625
Stoke Mandeville	,,	Parish	477	Stoke Lyne ..	,,	—	425
Stoke Poges ..	,,	Parish	1 600	Stokenchurch ...	,,	Parish	1 508
Stoke Poges ..	,,	—	1 505	Stoke, North ..	,,	Parish	177
Stoke ..	*Cheshire*	Parish	431	Stoke, South, &c.	,,	Parish	810
Stoke ..	,,	Tnship.	102	Stoke Talmage ..	,,	Parish	113
Stoke (Acton P.)	,,	Tnship.	171	Stoke Row, St. John	,,	Ecl. Dis.	386
Stokeclimsland ..	*Cornwall*	Parish	2 554	Stoke Dry ..	*Rutl. & Leic.*	Parish	53
Stoke ..	*Derby*	Tnship.	68	Stoke Dry ..	*Rutland*	Tnship.	44
Stoke Damerel ..	*Devon*	District	50 440	Stoke ..	*Salop*	Tnship.	47
Stoke ..	,,	Sub-dis.	9 034	Stoke, St. Milborough	,,	Parish	573
Stoke Damerel ..	,,	Parish	50 440	Stoke, St. Milborough	,,	Tnship.	535
Stoke Canon ..	,,	Parish	452	Stokesay ..	,,	Parish	559
Stokefleming ..	,,	Parish	661	Stoke on Tern ..	,,	Parish	961
Stoke Gabriel ..	,,	Parish	622	Stoke on Tern ..	,,	Tnship.	403
Stokeinteignhead	,,	Parish	628	Stoke Lane ..	*Somerset*	Sub-dis.	3 326
Stokenham ..	,,	Sub-dis.	3 877	Stoke Lane ..	,,	Parish	734
Stokenham ..	,,	Parish	1 566	Stoke, North ..	,,	Parish	160
Stoke Rivers ..	,,	Parish	242	Stoke Pero ..	,,	Parish	51
Stoke Abbott ..	*Dorset*	Parish	703	Stoke, St. Gregory	,,	Parish	1 617
Stoke, East ..	,,	Parish	594	Stoke, St. Mary .	,,	Parish	266
Stoke Wake ..	,,	Parish	112	Stoke, South ..	,,	Parish	375
Stoke Gifford ..	*Gloucester*	Parish	445	Stoke Trister ..	,,	Parish	395
Stoke Bishop ..	,,	Tithing	5 623	Stoke un Hamdon	,,	Parish	1 395
Stoke Bishop, St. Mary	,,	Ecl. Dis.	554	Stoke upon Trent	*Stafford*	L. Sub.	71 036
Stoke Orchard ..	,,	Hamlet	201	Stoke upon Trent	,,	District	71 308
Stoke, Bishop ..	*Hants*	Parish	1 390	Stoke upon Trent	,,	Sub-dis.	11 390
Stoke Charity ..	,,	Parish	130	Stoke upon Trent	,,	Parish	71 308
Stoke, Itchin ..	,,	Parish	295	**Stoke upon Trent**	,,	P. Bor.	101 207
Stoke Meon ..	,,	Parish	429	Stoke Ash ..	*Suffolk*	Parish	371
Stoke Bliss ..	*Heref. & Wor.*	Parish	298	Stoke by Clare ..	,,	Parish	863
Stoke Edith ..	*Hereford*	Parish	506	Stoke by Nayland	,,	Parish	1 275
Stoke Edith ..	,,	Tnship.	332	Stoke D'Abernon	*Surrey*	Parish	368
Stoke Lacy ..	,,	Parish	348	Stoke by Guildford	,,	Parish	3 797
Stoke Prior ..	,,	Parish	448	Stoke, North ..	*Sussex*	Parish	58
Stoke ..	*Kent*	Parish	557	Stoke, South ..	,,	Parish	111
Stoke Golding ..	*Leicester*	Chap.	638	Stoke, West ..	,,	Parish	94
Stoke ..	*Lincoln*	Parish	394	Stoke ..	*Warwick*	Parish	1 555
Stoke, North ..	,,	Tnship.	104	Stoke Bliss ..	*Wor. & Heref.*	Parish	298
Stoke, South ..	,,	Tnship.	140	Stoke Prior ..	*Worcester*	Parish	1 622
Stoke Newington	*Middlesex*	Sub-dis.	6 608	Stokesley ..	*York*	District	10 381
Stoke Newington	,,	Parish	6 608	Stokesley ..	,,	Sub-dis.	7 853
St. Matthias ..	,,	Ecl. Dis.	6 738	Stokesley ..	,,	Parish	2 401
Stoke Ferry ..	*Norfolk* ..	Parish	791	Stokesley ..	,,	Tnship.	1 993

Name of Place.	County.	Description.	Population.	Name of Place.	County.	Description.	Population.
onar	Kent ..	Parish	42	Stotfold	York ..	—	7
ondon, Upper .	Beds ..	Parish	66	Stottesden ..	Salop ..	Hund.	12 218
ondon Massey .	Essex ..	Purish	273	Stottesden-Chelmarsh ,, ..		L. Sub.	5 691
one	Bucks ..	Parish	1 094	Stottesden-Cleobury ,, ..		L. Sub.	6 462
one	Gloucester ..	Chap.	277	Stottesden .. ,, ..		Sub-dis.	2 790
one	Kent ..	Parish	422	Stottesden .. ,, ..		Parish	1 518
one by Dartford ,, ..		Parish	1 013	Stottesden .. ,, ..		Tnship.	1 214
one by Faversham ,, ..		Parish	91	Stoughton ..	Leicester ..	Tnship.	119
one	Somerset ..	Hund.	2 119	Stoughton ..	Sussex ..	Parish	633
one	Stafford ..	District	21 926	Stoulton ..	Worcester ..	Parish	410
one	,, ..	Sub-dis.	9 528	Stourbridge ..	,, ..	L. Sub.	29 192
one	,, ..	Parish	9 382	Stourbridge ..	Worc. & Staff.	District	68 726
tone	,, ..	Town	4 509	Stourbridge ..	,, ,,	Sub-dis.	22 958
tone Christchurch ,, ..		Ecl. Dis.	4 629	Stourbridge ..	Worcester ..	Tnship.	8 783
tone	Worcester ..	Parish	475	**Stourbridge** ..	,, ..	Town	8 166
onebeck, Down	York ..	Tnship.	400	Stourmouth ..	Kent ..	Parish	294
onebeck, Upper	,, ..	Tnship.	374	Stourpaine ..	Dorset ..	Parish	658
one Easton ..	Somerset ..	Parish	431	Stourport ..	Worcester ..	L. Sub.	9 659
onegate ..	Norfolk ..	Ward	1 719	Stourton-Caundle	Dorset ..	Parish	395
onegate, St. Peter	Sussex ..	Ecl. Dis.	444	Stourton ..	Warwick ..	Hamlet	202
onegrave ..	York ..	Parish	290	Stourton ..	Wilts & Som.	Parish	660
onegrave ..	,, ..	Tnship.	149	Stourton ..	Wilts ..	—	365
oneham, North	Hants ..	Parish	968	Stouting ..	Kent ..	Parish	213
oneham, South	,, ..	Parish	7 761	Stoven	Suffolk ..	Parish	161
oneham Aspall	Suffolk ..	Parish	694	Stow w. Quy ..	Cambs ..	Parish	368
onehouse, East	Devon ..	Parish	14 343	Stow-Maries ..	Essex ..	Parish	265
onehouse ..	Gloucester ..	Sub-dis.	4 538	Stow on Wold ..	Gloucester ..	L. Sub.	12 588
onehouse ..	,, ..	Parish	2 609	Stow on Wold ..	Glo. & Worc.	District	9 687
onelands ..	Oxon ..	—	8	Stow on Wold ..	,, ,,	Sub-dis.	5 063
oneleigh ..	Warwick ..	Parish	1 283	Stow on Wold ..	Gloucester ..	Parish	2 077
oneraise ..	Cumberland	Tnship.	349	Stow on Wold ..	,, ..	Tnship.	1 374
onesby ..	Leicester ..	Parish	271	Stow, Long ..	Hunts ..	Parish	208
onesfield ..	Oxon ..	Parish	650	Stow, Long ..	,, ..	Hamlet	156
oneton ..	Northampton	Parish	20	Stow Bardolph ..	Norfolk ..	Parish	1 090
toney Middleton	Derby ..	Chap.	608	Stow-Bedon ..	,, ..	Parish	343
toney Stanton ..	Leicester ..	Parish	703	Stow Wood ..	Oxon ..	Parish	27
tonham, Little .	Suffolk ..	Parish	391	Stow	Suffolk ..	Hund.	9 817
tonnall	Stafford ..	Ecl. Dis.	966	Stow	,, ..	District	20 908
tonton Wyville .	Leicester ..	Parish	102	Stowmarket ..	,, ..	Sub-dis.	8 367
tony Stratford ..	Bucks ,.	L. Sub.	11 893	Stowmarket ..	,, ..	Parish	3 639
tony Stratford, E. Side ,, ..		Parish	649	Stowmarket ..	,, ..	—	3 563
tony Stratford, W. Side ,, ..		Parish	1 356	**Stowmarket** ..	,, ..	Town	3 531
tony Stratford ,, ..		Town	2 005	Stow Upland ..	,, ..	Parish	986
toodleigh ..	Devon ..	Parish	499	Stow Upland, Trinity ,, ..		Ecl. Dis.	793
topham ..	Sussex ..	Parish	130	Stow, West ..	,, ..	Parish	238
topsley	Beds ..	Hamlet	842	Stowe ..	Bucks ..	Parish	352
topsley	,, ..	Ecl. Dis.	842	Stowe	,, ..	—	332
toreton ..	Cheshire ..	Tnship.	256	Stowe ..	Lincoln ..	Parish	1 070
torkhill w. Sandholme	York .	Tnship.	70	Stowe	,, ..	Tnship.	404
torridge, St. John	Hereford ..	Ecl. Dis.	375	Stowe, Stamford	,, ..	Parish	11
torrington ..	Sussex ..	Parish	1 104	Stowe Nine Churches	Nthmptn.	Parish	353
tortford, Bishop	Herts ..	Parish	5 390	Stowe ..	Salop ..	Parish	161
torthwaite ..	York ..	Tnship.	104	Stowe ..	Stafford ..	Parish	1 267
totfold	Beds ..	Parish	2 071	Stowell ..	Gloucester ..	Parish	41

Name of Place.	County.	Description.	Population.	Name of Place.	County.	Description.	Population.
Stowell	Somerset ..	Parish	183	Stratton.. ..	Dorset ..	Parish	351
Stower, East ..	Dorset ..	Parish	426	Stratton.. ..	Gloucester ..	Parish	596
Stower-Provost..	„ ..	Parish	889	Stratton, East ..	Hants ..	Parish	365
Stower, West ..	„ ..	Parish	215	Stratton.. ..	Norfolk ..	Sub-dis.	6 065
Stowey	Somerset ..	Sub-dis.	4 977	Stratton, Long ..	„ ..	Parish	743
Stowey	„ ..	Parish	181	Stratton St. Michael	„ ..	Parish	251
Stowey, Nether..	„ ..	Parish	876	Stratton Strawless	„ ..	Parish	202
Stowey, Over ..	„ ..	Parish	613	Stratton Audley .	Oxon ..	Parish	378
Stowford ..	Devon ..	Parish	471	Stratton on Fosse	Somerset ..	Parish	335
Stowick.. ..	Gloucester ..	Tithing	517	Stratton Hall Farm	Suffolk ..	Parish	22
Stowlangtoft ..	Suffolk ..	Parish	204	Stratton St. Margaret	Wilts ..	Parish	1 642
Stowood ..	Oxon ..	Parish	27	Streatham ..	Surrey ..	Sub-dis.	10 082
Stradbroke ..	Suff. & Norf.	Sub-dis.	7 692	Streatham ..	„ ..	Parish	8 027
Stradbroke ..	Suffolk ..	Parish	1 537	Streatham, Christch.	„ ..	Ecl. Dis.	2 037
Stradishall ..	„ ..	Parish	425	Streatham, Emmanuel	„ ..	Ecl. Dis.	1 247
Stradsett ..	Norfolk ..	Parish	180	Streatham, St. Mary	„ ..	Ecl. Dis.	1 786
Strafforth & Tickhill	York	Wapen.	108 509	Streatley ..	Beds ..	Parish	341
Strafforth & Tickhill, Lower	„	L. Sub.	40 988	Streatley ..	„ ..	Tnship.	166
Strafforth & Tickhill, Upper	„	L. Sub.	269 099	Streatley ..	Berks ..	Parish	552
Stragglethorpe ..	Lincoln ..	Parish	90	Street	Somerset ..	Parish	1 898
Stramshall, St. Mich.	Stafford .	Ecl. Dis.	332	Street	Sussex ..	Parish	190
Strand	Middlesex ..	L. Sub.	41 975	Streethay ..	Stafford ..	Tnship.	137
Strand	„ ..	District	42 979	Strelley	Notts ..	Parish	253
Stranton ..	Durham ..	Parish	14 515	Strensall ..	York ..	Parish	406
Stranton	„ ..	Tnship.	13 601	Strensham ..	Worcester ..	Parish	279
Strata-Florida ..	Cardigan ..	Tnship.	868	Stretford ..	Hereford ..	Hund.	9 079
Stratfield Mortmr.	Bks. & Hts.	Parish	1 419	Stretford ..	„ ..	Parish	50
Stratfield Mortimer	Berks ..	—	844	Stretford ..	Lancaster ..	Sub-dis.	10 807
Strathfieldsaye	Hants & Berks	Parish	827	Stretford	„ ..	Tnship.	8 757
Strathfieldsaye ..	Hants ..	—	567	Stretford St. Matthew	„ ..	Ecl. Dis.	3 882
Stratfield Turgis .	„ ..	Parish	195	Strethall ..	Essex ..	Parish	41
Stratford Fenny .	Bucks ..	Tnship.	1 199	Stretham ..	Cambs ..	Parish	1 462
Stratford, Water .	„ ..	Parish	179	Stretham	„ ..	—	1 156
Stratford ..	Essex ..	Sub-dis.	15 994	Stretton.. ..	Cheshire ..	Tnship.	373
Stratford ..	„ ..	Ward	15 994	Stretton.. ..	„ ..	Ecl. Dis.	833
Stratford ..	„ ..	Town	15 994	Stretton.. ..	„ ..	Tnship.	94
Stratford Marsh, Christch.	„ ..	Ecl. Dis.	3 219	Stretton.. ..	Derby ..	Tnship.	524
Stratford, St. John	„ ..	Ecl. Dis.	12 764	Stretton-en-le-Field	„	Parish	384
Stratford, St. Andrew	Suffolk ..	Parish	181	Stretton-en-le-Field	„	Tnship.	108
Stratford, St. Mary	„ ..	Parish	655	Stretton Grandsome	Hereford	Parish	130
Stratford ..	Warwick ..	L. Sub.	23 363	Stretton-Sugwas.	„	Parish	209
Stratford, Old ..	War. & Glos.	Sub-dis.	5 931	Stretton, Great..	Leicester ..	Tnship.	42
Stratford, Old ..	Warwick ..	Parish	6 823	Stretton, Little..	„ ..	Tnship.	83
Stratford, Old ..	„ ..	Tnship.	2 995	Stretton.. ..	Rutland ..	Parish	189
Stratford on Avon	Warwick, &c.	District	21 249	Stretton.. ..	Stafford ..	Chap.	273
Stratford on Avon	„ ..	Sub-dis.	6 117	Stretton.. ..	„ ..	Tnship.	472
Stratford on Avon	Warwick	M. Bor.	3 672	Stretton-Baskerville	Warwick .	Parish	74
Stratford, St. Anthony	Wilts ..	Parish	161	Stretton on Dunsmore	„ ..	Parish	1 064
Stratford un. Castle	„ ..	Parish	332	Stretton on Dunsmore	„ ..	Tnship.	745
Stratton.. ..	Cornwall ..	Hund.	7 787	Stretton on Foss	„ ..	Parish	435
Stratton.. ..	„ ..	L. Sub.	7 787	Stretton under Foss	„ ..	Hamlet	331
Stratton.. ..	„ ..	District	8 028	Strickland, Great	Westmoreld.	Tnship.	308
Stratton.. ..	„ ..	Sub-dis.	3 392	Strickland Kettle	„ ..	Tnship.	484
Stratton.. ..	„ ..	Parish	1 755	Strickland, Little	„ ..	Tnship.	114

Name of Place.	County.	Description.	Population.	Name of Place.	County.	Description.	Population.
Strickland Roger	Westmoreld.	Tnship.	421	Suckley ..	Worcester ..	Tnship.	584
Stringston	Somerset ..	Parish	144	Sudborough	Northampton	Parish	321
Strixton..	Northampton	Parish	61	Sudbourne	Suffolk ..	Parish	525
Strood ..	Kent ..	Sub-dis.	9 521	Sudbrooke	Lincoln	Parish	75
Strood ..	,, ..	Parish	4 057	Sudbury	Derby & Suff.	Sub-dis.	3 803
Strood, Extra ..	,, ..	—	142	Sudbury	Derby	Parish	587
Strood Intra & Media	,, ..		3 915	Sudbury	Suff. & Essex	District	31 415
Stroud ..	Gloucester ..	L. Sub.	36 095	Sudbury	,, ,, ..	Sub-dis.	8 918
Stroud ..	,, ..	District	36 448	**Sudbury**	,, ,, ..	M. Bor.	6 879
Stroud ..	,, ..	Sub-dis.	9 090	All Saints	Suffolk ..	Parish	1 350
Stroud ..	,, ..	Parish	9 090	St. Gregory ..	,, ..	Parish	2 781
Stroud ..	,, ..	P. Bor.	35 517	St. Peter ..	,, ..	Parish	1 880
Stroud-end ..	,, ..	Tithing	874	Sudeley Manor..	Gloucester ..	Parish	98
Stroxton ..	Lincoln ..	Parish	107	Suffield ..	Norfolk ..	Parish	212
Strubby..	,, ..	Parish	295	Suffield w. Everley	York ..	Tnship.	120
Strumpshaw	Norfolk ..	Parish	386	Suffolk ..	.. ..	County	337 070
Stubbings, St. James	Berks ..	Ecl. Dis.	363	Eastern Division	.. ..	E. Div.	189 255
Stublach	Cheshire ..	Tnship.	47	Western Division	.. ..	W. Div.	147 815
Stubton..	Lincoln ..	Parish	157	Sugley ..	Northumberland	Tnship.	224
Studham	Beds & Herts	Parish	882	Sugnall Gt. & Lit.	Stafford ..	Tnships.	151
Studham ..	,, ,,	Tnship.	464	Sulby ..	Northampton	Parish	87
Studland ..	Dorset ..	Parish	595	Sulehay & Lock's	,, ..	Lodges	15
Studley ..	Oxon ..	Hamlet	73	Sulgrave	Nptn. & Bucks	Sub-dis.	5 815
Studley ..	War. & Worc.	Sub-dis.	4 274	Sulgrave	Northampton	Parish	565
Studley ..	Warwick ..	Parish	2 230	Sulham ..	Berks ..	Parish	118
Studley, St. John	Wilts ..	Ecl. Dis.	329	Sulhampstead Abbots	,, ..	Parish	357
Studley Roger ..	York ..	Tnship.	159	Sulhampstead-Bannister	,, ..	Parish	261
Stukeley, Great .	Hunts ..	Parish	453	,, Lower End	,, ..	Hamlet	114
Stukeley, Little..	,, ..	Parish	385	,, Upper End	,, ..	Hamlet	147
Sturmere ..	Essex ..	Parish	326	Sullington	Sussex ..	Parish	241
Sturminster	Dorset ..	Division	11 455	Sully ..	Glamorgan .	Parish	192
Sturminster ..	,, ..	L. Sub.	11 455	Summerhouse ..	Durham ..	Tnship.	184
Sturminster ..	,, ..	District	10 334	Summers Town .	Surrey ..	Ecl. Dis.	920
Sturminster ..	,, ..	Sub-dis.	5 912	Summertown ..	Oxon ..	Ecl. Dis.	1 088
Sturminster-Marshall	,, ..	Parish	850	Sunbury ..	Middlesex ..	Sub-dis.	7 289
Sturminster-Newton	,, ..	Parish	1 880	Sunbury ..	,, ..	Parish	2 332
Sturry ..	Kent ..	Sub-dis.	6 467	Sunderland ..	Cumberland	Tnship.	70
Sturry ..	,, ..	Parish	1 044	Sunderland ..	Durham ..	District	90 704
Sturston ..	Derby ..	Tnship.	674	Sunderland, East	,, ..	Sub-dis.	9 915
Sturston ..	Norfolk ..	Parish	75	Sunderland, West	,, ..	Sub-dis.	8 517
Sturton ..	Lincoln ..	Tnship.	560	Sunderland ..	,, ..	Parish	17 107
Sturton Great ..	,, ..	Parish	179	**Sunderland** ..	,, ..	M. Bor.	78 211
Sturton Grange .	Nrthumberld.	Tnship.	122			P. Bor.	85 797
Sturton ..	Notts ..	Parish	583	Sunderland Bridge	,, ..	Tnship.	227
Sturton Grange .	York ..	Tnship.	55	Sunderland North	Nrthumberld.	Tnship.	1 008
Stuston ..	Suffolk ..	Parish	232	Sunderland North	,, ..	Ecl. Dis.	1 178
Stutchbury ..	Northampton	Parish	23	Sunderlandwick ..	York ..	Tnship.	59
Stutton ..	Suffolk ..	Parish	531	Sundon ..	Beds ..	Parish	450
Stydd ..	Derby ..	Tnship.	32	Sundridge ..	Kent ..	Parish	1 495
Styford ..	Northumberland	Tnship.	90	Sunk Island ..	York ..	Parish	376
Styrrup ..	Notts ..	Tnship.	862	Sunningdale	Berks & Sur.	Ecl. Dis.	709
Subberthwaite ..	Lancaster ..	Tnship.	152	Sunninghill ..	Berks ..	Parish	1 596
Subdeanry ..	Sussex ..	Parish	5 325	Sunningwell ..	,, ..	Parish	364
Suckley ..	Worcester ..	Parish	1 207	Surbiton ..	Surrey ..	Ecl. Dis.	4 69?

Name of Place	County.	Description.	Population.	Name of Place.	County.	Description.	Population.
Surfleet	Lincoln ..	Parish	953	Sutton St. Edmund	Lincoln ..	Hamlet	730
Surlingham ..	Norfolk ..	Parish	465	Sutton St. Nicholas	,, ..	Hamlet	817
Surrendel ..	Wilts ..	Tithing	41	Sutton Bridge ..	,, ..	Ecl. Dis.	1 565
Surrey	..	County	831 093	Sutton	Norfolk ..	Parish	338
Eastern Division ..	..	E. Div.	713 527	Sutton	Northampton	Chap.	112
Western Division ..	..	W. Div.	117 566	Sutton Basset ..	,, ..	Parish	147
Sussex	..	County	363 735	Sutton	Notts ..	Tnship.	458
Eastern Division ..	..	E. Div.	254 379	Sutton in Ashfield	,, ..	Sub-dis.	8 455
Western Division ..	..	W. Div.	109 356	Sutton in Ashfield	,, ..	Parish	7 643
Sustead.. ..	Norfolk ..	Parish	136	Sutton in Ashfield	,, ..	Tnship.	6 483
Sutcombe ..	Devon ..	Parish	441	Sutton Bonnington :—			
Sutterby ..	Lincoln ..	Parish	40	St. Anne ..	,, ..	Parish	381
Sutterton ..	,, ..	Parish	1 338	St. Michael ..	,, ..	Parish	638
Sutton	Beds ..	Parish	438	Sutton w. Lound	,, ..	Parish	916
Sutton Courtney	Berks & Oxon	Sub-dis.	3 975	Sutton on Trent .	,, ..	Parish	1 147
Sutton Courtney	Berks ..	Parish	1 581	Sutton	Salop ..	Parish	75
Sutton Courtney	,, ..	—	974	Sutton Maddock	,, ..	Parish	420
Sutton-Wick ..	,, ..	Tnship.	319	Sutton Bingham	Somerset ..	Parish	67
Sutton	Cambs ..	Sub-dis.	4 025	Sutton Long ..	,, ..	Parish	958
Sutton	,, ..	Parish	1 731	Sutton Mallet ..	,, ..	Chap.	139
Sutton	Cheshire	Sub-dis.	7 392	Sutton Montis ..	,, ..	Parish	155
Sutton	,, ..	Tnship.	6 756	Sutton	Suffolk ..	Parish	618
Sutton St. George	,, ..	Ecl. Dis.	5 308	Sutton	Surrey ..	Parish	3 186
Sutton St. James	,, ..	Ecl. Dis.	1 448	Sutton	Sussex ..	Incor.	6 522
Sutton (Middlewich P.)	,, ..	Tnship.	26	Sutton	,, ..	Sub-dis.	2 763
Sutton (Runcorn P.)	,, ..	Tnship.	356	Sutton	,, ..	Parish	364
Sutton Great ..	,, ..	Tnship.	224	Sutton Coldfield.	Warwick ..	Sub-dis.	5 527
Sutton Guilden..	,, ..	Parish	223	Sutton Coldfield .	,, ..	Parish	4 662
Sutton Little ..	,, ..	Tnship.	474	Sutton un. Brails	,, ..	Parish	227
Sutton	Denbigh ..	Tnship.	173	Sutton Benger ..	Wilts ..	Parish	406
Sutton, &c. ..	Derby ..	Parish	507	Sutton Mandeville	,, ..	Parish	289
Sutton on Hill ..	,, ..	Parish	545	Sutton-Veney ..	,, ..	Parish	794
Sutton on Hill ..	,, ..	Tnship.	149	Sutton	Worcester ..	Hamlet	170
Sutton on Plym.	Devon ..	Ecl. Dis.	6 237	Sutton	York E. ..	Sub-dis.	8 348
Sutton-Waldron	Dorset ..	Parish	248	Sutton & Stoneferry	,, ..	Parish	8 348
Sutton	Essex ..	Parish	148	Sutton on Derwent	York ..	Parish	385
Sutton, Bishop..	Hants ..	Parish	537	Sutton	York N. ..	Sub-dis.	1 431
Sutton, Long ..	,, ..	Parish	301	Sutton on Forest	York ..	Parish	1 224
Sutton St. Michael	Hereford ..	Parish	95	Sutton on Forest	,, ..	Tnship.	652
Sutton St. Nicholas	,, ..	Parish	251	Sutton un. Whitstone	,, ..	Tnship.	349
Sutton at Hone .	Kent ..	Lathe	262 419	Sutton	York W. ..	Tnship.	1 699
Sutton at Hone .	,, ..	Parish	1 563	Sutton (Brotherton P.)	,, ..	Tnship.	51
Sutton by Dover	,, ..	Parish	141	Sutton (Campsall P.)	,, ..	Tnship.	112
Sutton, East ..	,, ..	Parish	385	Sutton Grange..	York ..	Tnship.	69
Sutton-Valence..	,, ..	Parish	1 056	Sutton Howgrave	,, ..	Tnship.	122
Sutton	Lancaster ..	Tnship.	9 223	Sutton w. Hazlewood	,, ..	Tnship.	446
Sutton	,, ..	Ecl. Dis.	4 071	Swaby	Lincoln ..	Parish	498
Sutton Cheney ..	Leicester ..	Chap.	352	Swadlincote ..	Derby ..	Tnship.	1 076
Sutton in Marsh	Lincoln ..	Parish	368	Swadlincote Emmanuel	,, ..	Ecl. Dis.	1 553
Sutton, Long, or ⎫ Sutton St. Mary . ⎬	,, ..	Parish	6 124	Swaffham Bulbeck	Cambs ..	Parish	873
				Swaffham Prior.	,, ..	Parish	1 329
Sutton St. Mary .	,, ..	Hamlet	4 051	Swaffham ..	Norfolk ..	District	13 747
Sutton St. James	,, ..	Hamlet	526	Swaffham ..	,, ..	Sub-dis.	6 516
Sutton Bourne ..	,, ..	Hamlet	817	Swaffham ..	,, ..	Parish	3 559

Name of Place.	County.	Description.	Population.	Name of Place.	County.	Description.	Population.
waffham	Norfolk	Town	2 974	Swettenham	Cheshire	Tnship.	187
wafield	,,	Parish	172	Swilland	Suffolk	Parish	243
wainby w. Allerthorpe	York	Tnship.	52	Swillington	York	Parish	662
wainsthorpe	Norfolk	Parish	338	Swimbridge	Devon	Parish	1 532
wainswick	Somerset	Parish	632	Swinbrook	Oxon	Parish	191
walcliffe	Oxon & War.	Sub-dis.	6 219	Swinden	York	Tnship.	25
walcliffe	Oxon	Parish	1 919	Swinden	,,	Hamlet	46
walcliffe	,,	Tnship.	379	Swinderby	Lincoln	Parish	572
walecliff	Kent	Parish	168	Swindon	Gloucester	Parish	227
wallow	Lincoln	Parish	239	Swindon	Wilts	Sub-dis.	12 224
wallowcliffe	Wilts	Parish	317	Swindon	,,	Parish	6 856
wallowfield	Berks	Parish	1 265	Swindon, New, St. Mark	,,	Ecl.Dis.	4 167
wallwell	Durham	Tnship.	1 479	Swindon, New	,,	Town	4 167
wanage	Dorset	Sub-dis.	3 682	Swine	York	Parish	1 823
wanage	,,	Parish	2 004	Swine	,,	Tnship.	182
wanborough	Wilts	Hund.	9 653	Swinefleet	York & Linc.	Sub-dis.	4 042
wanbourne	Bucks	Parish	603	Swinefleet	York	Tnship.	1 149
wanland	York	Tnship.	514	Swineshead, &c.	Gloucester	Hund.	18 350
wanmore	Hants	Ecl. Dis.	849	Swineshead	Hunts	Parish	275
wannington	Leicester	Tnship.	1 276	Swineshead	Lincoln	Sub-dis.	5 583
wannington	Norfolk	Parish	385	Swineshead	,,	Parish	1 903
wanscombe	Kent	Parish	2 323	Swinethorpe	,,	Parish	64
wansea	Glamorgan	Hund.	14 371	Swinfen & Packington	Stafford	Hamlets	109
wansea	,,	L. Sub.	47 595	Swinford	Leicester	Parish	402
wansea	,,	District	51 260	Swinford, Old	Worcester	Parish	22 958
wansea	,,	Sub-dis.	31 593	Swinford, Upper	,,	Tnship.	2 749
wansea	,,	Parish	33 972	Swingfield	Kent	Parish	418
wansea, Higher	,,	Division	2 379	Swinhoe	Northumberland	Tnship.	153
wansea, Lower	,,	Division	1 107	Swinhope	Lincoln	Parish	105
wansea town & franch.	,,	—	27 161	Swinnerton	Stafford	Parish	880
wansea	,,	Borough	41 606	Swinstead	Lincoln	Parish	396
wansea, Parl. Dist. of	,,	Boros.	57 488	Swinton	York N.	Tnship.	381
wansea, Holy Trinity	,,	Ecl. Dis.	4 305	Swinton	,, W.	Tnship.	3 190
wanton Abbott	Norfolk	Parish	523	Swinton w. Warthermask	York	Tnship.	202
wanton Morley	,,	Parish	769	Swithland	Leicester	Parish	255
wanton Novers	,,	Parish	315	Swydd, &c.	Radnor	Tnship.	339
warby	Lincoln	Parish	188	Swyncombe	Oxon	Parish	446
wardeston	Norfolk	Parish	385	Swyre	Dorset	Parish	277
warkeston	Derby	Parish	307	Sychtyn	Salop	Tnship.	207
warland	Northumberland	Tnship.	164	Sydenham Damerel	Devon	Parish	603
warraton	Hants	Parish	100	Sydenham	Kent	Sub-dis.	10 595
waton	Lincoln	Parish	297	Sydenham	,,	Chap.	10 595
wavesey	Cambs	Sub-dis.	3 675	,, St. Bartholomew	,,	Ecl. Dis.	5 955
wavesey	,,	Parish	1 371	Sydenham	Oxon	Parish	397
way	Hants	Ecl. Dis.	694	Syderstone	Norfolk	Parish	528
wayfield	Lincoln	Parish	263	Sydling, St. Nicholas	Dorset	Parish	692
weethope	Northumberland	Tnship.	11	Syerscote	Stafford	Tnship.	37
wefling	Suffolk	Parish	318	Syerston	Notts	Parish	196
well, Lower	Gloucester	Parish	449	Sykehouse	York	Tnship.	623
well, Upper	,,	Parish	65	Sykehouse, Trinity	,,	Ecl. Dis.	623
well	Somerset	Parish	110	Syleham	Suffolk	Parish	357
wepstone	Leicester	Parish	566	Symondsbury	Dorset	Parish	1 352
werford	Oxon	Parish	402	Syresham	Northampton	Parish	1 047
wettenham	Cheshire	Parish	350	Sysonby	Leicester	Chap.	67

Name of Place.	County.	Description.	Population.	Name of Place.	County.	Description.	Population.
Syston	*Leicester* ..	Sub-dis.	4 749	Tamworth Castle	*Warwick* ..	Liberty	170
Syston	,,	Parish	1 656	Tandridge ..	*Surrey* ..	Hund.	11 844
Syston	*Lincoln* ..	Parish	238	Tandridge	,, ..	Parish	621
Sywell	*Northampton*	Parish	241	Tanfield.. ..	*Durham* ..	Sub-dis.	7 594
				Tanfield.. ..	,, ..	Chap.	4 593
Tabley Inferior	*Cheshire* ..	Tnship.	130	Tanfield, East ..	*York* ..	Tnship.	38
Tabley Superior .	,, ..	Tnship.	490	Tanfield, West ..	,, ..	Parish	623
Tabley Over, St.Paul	,,	Ecl. Dis.	792	Tangley.. ..	*Hants* ..	Parish	270
Tachbrook Mallory	*Warwick* ..	Hamlet	63	Tangmere ..	*Sussex* ..	Parish	201
Tackley	*Oxon* ..	Parish	626	Tankersley ..	*York* ..	Parish	2 524
Tacolnestone ..	*Norfolk* ..	Parish	452	Tankersley ..	,, ..	Tnship.	1 403
Tadcaster ..	*York* ..	District	18 118	Tannington ..	*Suffolk* ..	Parish	246
Tadcaster ..	,, ..	Sub-dis.	4 390	Tanshelf ..	*York* ..	Tnship.	776
Tadcaster ..	,, ..	Parish	3 126	Tansley	*Derby* ..	Tnship.	622
Tadcaster, East .	,, ..	Tnship.	920	Tansley, Holy Trinity	,, ..	Ecl. Dis.	622
Tadcaster, West	,, ..	Tnship.	1 646	Tansor	*Northampton*	Parish	248
Tadcaster ..	,, ..	Town	2 327	Tanworth ..	*Warwick* ..	Sub-dis.	3 029
Taddington w. Priestcliffe	*Dby.*	Tnship.	507	Tanworth ..	,, ..	Parish	1 946
Tadley	*Hants* ..	Parish	900	Tanworth, St. Patrick	,, ..	Ecl. Dis.	1 143
Tadlow	*Cambs* ..	Parish	214	Taplow	*Bucks* ..	Parish	811
Tadmarton ..	*Oxon* ..	Parish	411	Tapton	*Derby* ..	Tnship.	257
Takeley	*Essex* ..	Parish	1 000	Tarbock.. ..	*Lancaster* ..	Tnship.	626
Talachddû ..	*Brecon* ..	Parish	193	Tardebigg ..	*Worcester* ..	Sub-dis.	8 896
Talbenny ..	*Pembroke* ..	Parish	204	Tardebigg ..	,, ..	Parish	7 010
Talgarth ..	*Brecon* ..	Hund.	7 685	Tarleton ..	*Lancaster* ..	Sub-dis.	3 656
Talgarth	,, ..	L. Sub.	4 281	Tarleton ..	,, ..	Parish	1 987
Talgarth	,, ..	Sub-dis.	2 476	Tarnacre w. Rawcliffe	,, ..	Tnship.	682
Talgarth	,, ..	Parish	1 330	Tarporley ..	*Cheshire* ..	Parish	2 577
Talgarth Borough	,, ..	Hamlet	684	Tarporley ..	,, ..	Tnship.	1 212
Talkin	*Cumberland*	Tnship.	310	Tarraby.. ..	*Cumberland*	Tnship.	106
Talk-o'-th'-Hill..	*Stafford* ..	Tnship.	2 406	Tarrant Crawford	*Dorset* ..	Parish	67
Talk-o'-th'-Hill..	,, ..	Ecl. Dis.	2 089	Tarrant Gunville	,, ..	Parish	441
Talland	*Cornwall* ..	Parish	1 570	Tarrant Hinton .	,, ..	Parish	258
Talland	,, ..	—	800	Tarrant Keynston	,, ..	Parish	309
Tallaton.. ..	*Devon* ..	Parish	437	Tarrant Launceston	,, ..	Parish	107
Tallentire ..	*Cumberland*	Tnship.	248	Tarrant Monckton	,, ..	Parish	243
Talley	*Carmarthen*	Sub-dis.	2 025	Tarrant Rawston	,, ..	Parish	53
Talley	,, ..	Parish	1 022	Tarrant Rushton	,, ..	Parish	173
Tallington ..	*Lincoln* ..	Parish	239	Tarretburn	*Northumberland*	Tnship.	206
Talworth ..	*Surrey* ..	Hamlet	434	Tarring-Neville..	*Sussex* ..	Parish	84
Talybolion ..	*Anglesey* ..	Hund.	14 312	Tarring, West ..	,, ..	Parish	806
Talybont & Mowddy	*Merioneth*	Hund.	7 395	Tarrington ..	*Hereford* ..	Parish	543
Talyllyn.. ..	*Merion. & Mont.*	Sub-dis.	4 839	Tarset, West	*Northumberland*	Tnship.	412
Talyllyn.. . ..	*Merioneth* ..	Parish	1 284	Tarvin	*Cheshire* ..	Parish	3 319
Tamar	*Devon* ..	Sub-dis.	9 416	Tarvin w. Oscroft	,, ..	Tnship.	1 074
Tamerton, North	*Cornwall* ..	Parish	486	Tasburgh ..	*Norfolk* ..	Parish	446
Tamerton Foliott	*Devon* ..	Parish	1 164	Tasley	*Salop* ..	Parish	78
Tamhorn ..	*Stafford* ..	Parish	23	Tatenhill ..	*Stafford* ..	Parish	2 600
Tamworth ..	*Stafford, &c.*	District	15 504	Tatenhill ..	,, ..	Tnship.	619
Tamworth ..	,, ..	Sub-dis.	8 647	Tatham.. ..	*Lancaster* ..	Parish	588
Tamworth ..	*War. & Staff.*	Parish	10 190	Tathwell ..	*Lincoln* ..	Parish	405
Tamworth ..	,, ,,	Tnship	4 326	Tatsfield ..	*Surrey* ..	Parish	162
Tamworth ..	,, ,, {	M. Boro.	4 326	Tattenhall ..	*Cheshire* ..	Sub-dis.	7
		P. Boro.	10 192	Tattenhall ..	,, ..	Parish	1

Name of Place.	County.	Description.	Population.	Name of Place.	County.	Description.	Population.
Tattenhall	Cheshire	Tnship.	1 033	Teignbridge	Devon	L. Sub.	38 197
Tattenhoe	Bucks	Parish	64	Teignmouth	,,	Sub-dis.	11 184
Tatterford	Norfolk	Parish	70	Teignmouth, East	,,	Parish	2 059
Tattersett	,,	Parish	205	Teignmouth, West	,,	Parish	3 963
Tattershall	Lincoln	Sub-dis.	6 609	Teignmouth	,,	Town	6 022
Tattershall	,,	Parish	848	Teingrace	,,	Parish	172
Tattershall	,,	Tnship.	547	Tellisford	Somerset	Parish	119
Tattershall Thorpe	,,	Tnship.	301	Telscombe	Sussex	Parish	156
Tattingstone	Suffolk	Parish	626	Telsford	Somerset	Parish	119
Tatton	Cheshire	Tnship.	109	Telych	Carmarthen	Hamlet	179
Taunton, &c.	Somerset	Hund.	26 740	Temple	Cornwall	Parish	12
Taunton	,,	L. Sub.	34 024	Temple	Gloucester	Parish	5 592
Taunton	Som. & Devon	District	35 601	Temple Bruer, &c.	Lincoln	Parish	104
Taunton, St. James	Somerset	Sub-dis.	10 339	Temple Grafton	Warwick	Parish	403
Taunton, St. James	,,	Parish	5 239	Temple Guiting	Gloucester	Parish	584
Taunton, St. Mary	,,	Sub-dis.	11 283	Temple Guiting	,,	Tnship.	573
Taunton, St. Mary	,,	Parish	8 481	Temple Hirst	York	Tnship.	104
Taunton	,,	P. Boro.	14 667	Templenewsam	,,	Tnship.	1 806
Taunton, Trinity	,,	Ecl. Dis.	2 786	Temple Sowerby	Westmoreland	Tnship.	374
Taverham	Norfolk	Hund.	8 343	Templeton	Devon	Parish	217
Taverham	,,	L. Sub.	8 343	Tempsford	Beds	Parish	566
Taverham	,,	Parish	212	Tenbury	Worcester	L. Sub.	4 372
Tavistock	Devon	Hund.	10 155	Tenbury	Worcester, &c.	District	7 366
Tavistock	,,	L. Sub.	21 513	Tenbury	,,	Sub-dis.	4 320
Tavistock	,,	District	35 265	Tenbury St. Mich.	Wor. & Herf.	Ecl. Dis.	561
Tavistock	,,	Sub-dis.	17 864	Tenbury	Worcester	Parish	1 947
Tavistock	,,	Parish	8 965	Tenbury Foreign, &c.	,,	Hamlet	372
Tavistock	,,	P. Boro.	8 857	**Tenbury**	,,	Town	1 171
Tavistock, St. Paul	,,	Ecl. Dis.	1 323	Tenby	Pembroke	Sub-dis.	9 219
Tavy, St. Mary	,,	Parish	1 202	Tenby, St. Mary	,,	Parish	3 197
Tavy, St. Peter	,,	Parish	469	**Tenby**	,,	Borough	2 982
Tawstock	,,	Parish	1 257	Tendring	Essex	Hund	24 620
Tawton, North, &c.	,,	Hund.	12 666	Tendring	,,	L. Sub.	27 105
Tawton, North	,,	Sub-dis.	4 322	Tendring	,,	District	27 105
Tawton, North	,,	Parish	1 849	Tendring	,,	Parish	929
Tawton, South	,,	Parish	1 541	Tenterden	Kent	District	10 947
Taxall	Cheshire	Parish	1 329	Tenterden	,,	Sub-dis.	6 616
Taxall	,,	Tnship.	277	Tenterden	,,	Parish	3 656
Taynton	Gloucester	Parish	689	**Tenterden**	,,	M. Bor.	3 762
Taynton	Oxon	Parish	341	Terling	Essex	Parish	902
Tealby	Lincoln	Parish	863	Terrington St. Clement	Norfolk	Sub-dis.	5 355
Tean, Upper, Christch.	Stafford	Ecl. Dis.	1 171	Terrington St. Clement	,,	Parish	2 303
Tedburn, St. Mary	Devon	Parish	768	Terrington St. John	,,	Parish	793
Teddesley Hay	Stafford	Parish	117	Terrington	York	Parish	833
Teddington	Middlesex	Parish	1 183	Terrington, &c.	,,	Tnship.	724
Teddington	Worcester	Hamlet	132	Terwick	Sussex	Parish	106
Tedstone-Delamere	Hereford	Parish	205	Testerton	Norfolk	Parish	12
Tedstone-Wafer	,,	Parish	74	Teston	Kent	Parish	267
Teesdale	Durh. & York	District	20 880	Tetbury	Gloucester	L. Sub.	8 214
Teeton	Northampton	Hamlet	108	Tetbury	Glouc. & Wilts	District	6 110
Teffont Evias	Wilts	Parish	163	Tetbury	,, ,,	Sub-dis.	4 640
Teffont Magna	,,	Parish	292	Tetbury	Gloucester	Parish	3 274
Teigh	Rutland	Parish	128	**Tetbury**	,,	Town	2 285
Teignbridge	Devon	Hund.	14 120	Tetcott	Devon	Parish	289

Name of Place.	County.	Description.	Population.	Name of Place.	County.	Description.	Population.
Tetford	Lincoln	Sub-dis.	4 460	Thelbridge	Devon	Parish	259
Tetford	,,	Parish	793	Thelnetham	Suffolk	Parish	516
Tetney	,,	Sub-dis.	5 655	Thelveton	Norfolk	Parish	160
Tetney	,,	Parish	917	Thelwall	Cheshire	Tnship.	468
Tetsworth	Oxon	Parish	481	Themelthorpe	Norfolk	Parish	68
Tettenhall	Staff. & Salop	Sub-dis.	6 046	Thenford	Northampton	Parish	112
Tettenhall	Stafford	Parish	3 716	Therfield	Herts	Parish	1 222
Tetton	Cheshire	Tnship.	170	Thetford	Cambs	Hamlet	306
Tetworth	Hunts	Parish	261	Thetford w. Grimshoe	Norfolk	L. Sub.	10 937
Teversall	Notts	Parish	351	Thetford	Norf. & Suff.	District	18 712
Teversham	Cambs	Parish	231	Thetford	,, ,,	Sub-dis.	9 843
Tew, Great	Oxon	Parish	454	Thetford, St. Cuthb.	,, ,,	Parish	1 695
Tew, Little	,,	Parish	262	Thetford, St. Mary	,, ,,	Parish	1 256
Tewin	Herts	Parish	547	Thetford, St. Peter	Norfolk	Parish	1 257
Tewkesbury	Gloucester	Hund.	4 529	Thetford	Norf. & Suff.	Borough	4 208
Tewkesbury	,,	L. Sub.	13 229	Thickley, East	Durham	Tnship.	1 142
Tewkesbury	Glouc. & Wor.	District	14 908	Thimbleby	Lincoln	Parish	477
Tewkesbury	Gloucester	Sub-dis.	7 709	Thimbleby	York	Tnship.	180
Tewkesbury	,,	Parish	5 876	Thingoe	Suffolk	Hund.	6 820
Tewkesbury	,,	Borough	5 876	Thingoe	,,	District	18 224
Tey, Great	Essex	Parish	818	Thingwall	Lancaster	Hamlet	40
Tey, Little	,,	Parish	63	Thingwell	Cheshire	Tnship.	114
Teynham	Kent	Sub-dis.	4 061	Thirkleby	York	Tnship.	50
Teynham	,,	Parish	919	Thirkleby	,,	Parish	299
Thakeham	Sussex	District	7 567	Thirlby	,,	Tnship.	102
Thakeham	,,	Parish	559	Thirlwall	Northumberland	Tnship.	360
Thame	Oxon	Hund.	4 949	Thirn	York	Tnship.	142
Thame	Oxon & Bucks	District	15 305	Thirne	Norfolk	Parish	210
Thame	,, ,,	Sub-dis.	5 958	Thirsk	York	District	12 299
Thame	Oxon	Parish	3 245	Thirsk	,,	Sub-dis.	5 743
Thame	,,	Town	2 917	Thirsk	,,	Parish	4 815
Thames Ditton	Surrey	Parish	2 253	Thirsk	,,	Tnship.	2 956
Thames Nav. Toll-house	,,	—	3	Thirsk	,,	P. Boro.	5 350
Thanet	Kent	District	31 862	Thirston, &c.	Northumberland	Tnship.	294
Thanington	,,	Parish	446	Thirtleby	York	Tnship.	68
Tharston	Norfolk	Parish	351	Thistleton, &c.	Lancaster	Tnship.	383
Thatcham	Berks	Sub-dis.	5 226	Thistleton	Rutland	Parish	142
Thatcham	,,	Parish	4 129	Thixendale	York	Tnship.	279
Thatcham	,,	—	2 729	Thockrington	Northumberland	Parish	166
Thavies Inn	Middlesex	Parish	185	Thockrington	,,	Tnship.	47
Thaxted	Essex	Sub-dis.	4 563	Tholthorpe	York	Tnship.	280
Thaxted	,,	Parish	2 302	Thomley	Oxon	Hamlet	31
Theakstone	York	Tnship.	57	Thompson	Norfolk	Parish	475
Theale	Berks	Hund.	6 108	Thompsons Walls, &c.	Nrthmb.	Tnship.	30
Theale	Somerset	Ecl. Dis.	743	Thoralby	York	Tnship.	271
Thearne	York	Tnship.	113	Thoresby, North	Lincoln	Parish	824
Theberton	Suffolk	Parish	541	Thoresby, South	,,	Parish	162
Theddingworth	Leic. & Nthptn.	Parish	281	Thoresby, &c.	York	Tnship.	345
Theddingworth	Leicester	—	269	Thoresway	Lincoln	Parish	196
Theddlethorpe:—				Thorganby, Caistor	,,	Parish	140
All Saints	Lincoln	Parish	300	Thorganby	York	Parish	407
St. Helen	,,	Parish	426	Thorington	Suffolk	Parish	121
Thedwestry	Suffolk	Hund.	11 199	Thorley	Hants	Parish	143
The Forest	Berks	L. Sub.	17 781	Thorley	Herts	Parish	388

Name of Place.	County.	Description.	Population.	Name of Place.	County.	Description.	Population.
ornanby	York	Parish	147	Thornley w. Wheatley	Lancaster	Tnship.	409
ornaby	"	Tnship.	3 126	Thornthwaite	Cumberland	Tnship.	153
ornaby	"	Ecl. Dis.	3 117	Thornthwaite	"	Ecl. Dis.	530
ornage	Norfolk	Parish	358	Thornthwaite	York	Sub-dis.	1 925
ornborough	Bucks	Parish	694	Thornthwaite	"	Tnship.	257
ornbrough	Northumberland	Tnship.	74	Thornton	Bucks	Parish	111
ornbrough	York	Tnship.	23	Thornton w. Nash	"	Ecl. Dis.	573
ornbury	Devon	Parish	365	Thornton Hough	Cheshire	Tnship.	349
ornbury	Gloucester	Hund.	7 917	Thornton-le-Moors	"	Parish	913
ornbury	"	L. Sub.	11 606	Thornton-le-Moors	"	Tnship.	206
ornbury	"	District	16 499	Thornton w. Fleetwood	Lanc...	Tnship.	5 084
ornbury	"	Sub-dis.	5 870	Thornton (Sefton P.)	"	Tnship.	291
ornbury	"	Parish	4 494	Thornton	Leicester	Parish	1 292
ornbury	"	Borough	1 497	Thornton	"	Tnship.	446
ornbury	Hereford	Parish	224	Thornton	Lincoln	Parish	281
ornby	Northampton	Parish	252	Thornton Curtis.	"	Parish	483
orncombe	Dorset	Parish	1 277	Thornton-le-Fen	"	Parish	193
orncote	Beds	Hamlet	252	Thornton-le-Moor	"	Parish	127
orndon, All Saints	Suffolk	Parish	674	Thornton	Northumberland	Tnship.	121
orne Coffin	Somerset	Parish	99	Thornton, East..	"	Tnship.	65
orne Falcon	"	Parish	196	Thornton, West .	"	Tnship.	62
orne, St. Margaret	"	Parish	144	Thornton	York E.	Parish	851
orne	York & Linc.	District	16 011	Thornton	" "	Tnship.	179
orne	York	Sub-dis.	7 153	Thornton	" W.	Sub-dis.	13 282
orne	"	Parish	3 381	Thornton	" "	Tnship.	7 627
horne	"	Town	2 591	Thornton Bridge	York	Tnship.	66
orner..	"	Parish	1 500	Thornton Dale ..	"	Parish	893
orner..	"	Tnship.	809	Thornton in Craven	"	Parish	2 112
ornes..	"	Ecl. Dis.	1 798	Thornton Lonsdale	Yk. & Lanc.	Parish	1 151
orney	Cambs	Sub-dis.	2 219	Thornton in Lonsdale	York	Tnship.	441
orney	"	Parish	2 219	Thornton-le-Beans	"	Tnship.	240
orney	Notts	Parish	395	Thornton-le-Clay	"	Tnship.	270
orney	"	Tnship.	175	Thornton-le-Moor	"	Tnship.	324
orney, West..	Sussex	Parish	93	Thornton-le-Street	"	Parish	241
orneyburn	Northumberland	Parish	514	Thornton-le-Street	"	Tnship.	154
orneyburn	"	Tnship.	402	Thornton w. Baxby	"	Tnship.	97
ornford	Dorset	Parish	415	Thornton Risebrough	"	Tnship.	35
orngrafton	Northumberland	Tnship.	321	Thornton Rust ..	"	Tnship.	147
orngumbald	York	Tnship.	292	Thornton Steward	"	Parish	253
ornham	Kent	Parish	531	Thornton Watlass	"	Parish	440
ornham	Lancaster	Tnship.	2 027	Thornton Watlass	"	Tnship.	206
ornham	Norfolk	Parish	728	Thornville	"	Tnship.	16
ornham Magna	Suffolk	Parish	282	Thoroton	Notts	Parish	210
ornham Parva	"	Parish	124	Thorp Arch	York	Parish	388
ornhaugh	Northampton	Parish	243	Thorp Audlin	"	Tnship.	304
ornhill	Derby	Tnship.	129	Thorpe ..	Derby	Parish	204
ornhill	York	Sub-dis.	4 521	Thorpe Bulmer .	Durham	Tnship.	28
ornhill	"	Parish	7 633	Thorpe ..	Essex	Sub-dis.	5 776
ornhill	"	Tnship.	3 479	Thorpe le Soken .	"	Parish	1 159
ornhill Lees ..	"	Ecl. Dis.	1 553	Thorpe Arnold ..	Leicester	Parish	124
ornholme	"	Tnship.	114	Thorpe Satchville	"	Chap.	171
ornley	Durham	Tnship.	3 306	Thorpe on Hill..	Lincoln	Parish	427
ornley	"	Ecl. Dis.	3 454	Thorpe, St. Peter	"	Parish	598
ornley, St. Barthol.	"	Ecl. Dis.	3 264	Thorpe Tilney ..	"	Hamlet	120

Name of Place.	County.	Description.	Population.	*Name* of Place.	County.	Description.	Population.
Thorpe, West ..	Lincoln ..	Parish	54	Thrigby..	.. Norfolk ..	Parish	45
Thorpe ..	.. Norfolk ..	Hamlet	2 388	Thrimby	.. Westmoreland	Tnship.	87
Thorpe-Abbots..	,, ..	Parish	256	Thringstone	.. Leicester ..	Tnship.	1 404
Thorpe Market..	,, ..	Parish	215	Thrintoft	.. York ..	Tnship.	162
Thorpe by Haddiscoe	,, ..	Parish	84	Thriplow	.. Cambs ..	Hund.	5 388
Thorpe by Norwich	,, ..	Parish	3 841	Thriplow	,, ..	Parish	502
Thorpe by Norwich	,, ..	—	1 453	Thrislington	.. Durham ..	Tnship.	38
Thorpe Parva ..	,, ..	Parish	21	Throapham, St. John	York ..	Tnship.	75
Thorpe, St. Matthew	,, ..	Ecl. Dis.	2 378	Throcking	.. Herts ..	Parish	97
Thorpe, St. Andrew	,, ..	Parish	3 841	Throckley	Northumberland	Tnship.	278
Thorpe, St. Andrew	,, ..	—	1 453	Throckmorton	.. Worcester ..	Chap.	152
Thorpe-Achurch	Northampton	Parish	209	Throphill	Northumberland	Tnship.	42
Thorpe Lubenham	,, ..	—	25	Thropton	.. ,, ..	Tnship.	253
Thorpe Malsor..	,, ..	Parish	251	Throston	.. Durham ..	Tnship.	745
Thorpe Mandeville	,, ..	Parish	164	Throwleigh	.. Devon ..	Parish	327
Thorpe Underwood	,, ..	Hamlet	22	Throwley	.. Kent ..	Parish	635
Thorpe ..	.. Notts ..	Parish	107	Throxenby	.. York ..	Tnship.	45
Thorp Bochart..	,, ..	Parish	36	Thrumpton	.. Notts ..	Parish	144
Thorpe by Water	Rutland ..	Hamlet	77	Thrup ..	.. Oxon ..	Hamlet	150
Thorpe Constantine	Stafford..	Parish	54	Thrupp and Wick	Berks ..	Liberty	16
Thorpe by Ixworth	Suffolk ..	Parish	139	Thruscross	.. York ..	Tnship.	363
Thorpe Morieux	,, ..	Parish	447	Thrussington	.. Leicester ..	Parish	574
Thorpe ..	.. Surrey ..	Parish	552	Thruxton	.. Hants ..	Parish	247
Thorpe ..	.. York · E. ..	Tnship.	33	Thruxton	.. Hereford ..	Parish	65
Thorpe ..	.. ,, W. ..	Tnship.	71	Thrybergh	.. York ..	Parish	330
Thorpe (Burnsall P.)	,, ..	Tnship.	53	Thrybergh	.. ,, ..	Tnship.	235
Thorpe Bassett ..	York ..	Parish	219	Thundersley	.. Essex ..	Parish	531
Thorpe Brantingham	,, ..	Tnship.	79	Thundridge	.. Herts ..	Parish	489
Thorpe Hesley ..	,, ..	Ecl. Dis.	1 966	Thurcaston	.. Leicester ..	Parish	1 095
Thorpe in Balne	,, ..	Tnship.	107	Thurcaston	.. ,, ..	Tnship.	248
Thorpe le Street	,, ..	Tnship.	33	Thurgarton	.. Norfolk ..	Parish	264
Thorpe le Willows	,, ..	Tnship.	24	Thurgarton	.. Notts ..	Wapen.	37 500
Thorpe-Salvin ..	,, ..	Parish	337	Thurgarton	.. ,, ..	Parish	361
Thorpe Stapleton	,, ..	Tnship.	44	Thurgoland	.. York ..	Tnship.	1 783
Thorpe Underwoods	,, ..	Tnship.	167	Thurgoland, Trinity	,, ..	Ecl. Dis.	1 783
Thorpe Willoughby	,, ..	Tnship.	150	Thurlaston	.. Leicester ..	Parish	698
Thorp-Langton..	Leicester ..	Tnship.	120	Thurlaston	.. ,, ..	Tnship.	679
Thorrington ..	Essex ..	Parish	424	Thurlaston	.. Warwick ..	Tnship.	328
Thorverton ..	Devon ..	Parish	1 211	Thurlbear	.. Somerset ..	Parish	192
Thoydon Bois ..	Essex ..	Parish	610	Thurlby, Bassingham	Lincoln..	Parish	142
Thoydon Garnon	,, ..	Parish	1 095	Thurlby, Bourn	,, ..	Parish	833
Thoydon Mount	,, ..	Parish	154	Thurleigh	.. Beds ..	Parish	666
Thrandeston ..	Suffolk ..	Parish	364	Thurleston	.. Devon ..	Parish	437
Thrapston ..	Northampton	L. Sub.	11 029	Thurlow, Great..	Suffolk ..	Parish	423
Thrapston	Nthptn. & Hunts	District	14 056	Thurlow, Little..	,, ..	Parish	369
Thrapston ..	Northampton	Sub-dis.	7 459	Thurloxton	.. Somerset ..	Parish	207
Thrapston ..	,, ..	Parish	1 257	Thurlstone	.. York ..	Tnship.	2 251
Threapwood	.. Flint & Chesh.	Parish	335	Thurlton	.. Norfolk ..	Parish	420
Threckingham ..	Lincoln ..	Parish	189	Thurmaston, North	Leicester ..	Tnship.	209
Thredling ..	Suffolk ..	Hund.	3 232	Thurmaston, South	,, ..	Tnship.	893
Three Farms ..	Stafford ..	Tnship.	118	Thurnby ..	.. ,, ..	Parish	375
Threlkeld ..	Cumberland ..	Chap.	380	Thurnby ..	.. ,, ..	Tnship.	196
Threshfield ..	York ..	Tnship.	· 177	Thurnham	.. Lancaster ..	Tnship.	717
Threxton ..	Norfolk ..	Parish	80	Thurning	Hunts & Nrthptn.	Parish	214

Name of Place.	County.	Description.	Population.	Name of Place.	County.	Description.	Population.
Thurning	Norfolk	Parish	178	Tidworth, North	Wilts	Parish	345
Thurnscoe	York	Parish	196	Tidworth, South	Hants	Parish	208
Thurrock, Grays	Essex	Parish	2 209	Tiffield	Northampton	Parish	214
Thurrock, Little	,,	Parish	294	Tilbrook	Beds	Parish	329
Thurrock, West	,,	Parish	1 039	Tilbury	Essex	Parish	232
Thursby	Cumberland	Parish	568	Tilbury, East	,,	Parish	403
Thursby	,,	Tnship.	366	Tilbury, West	,,	Parish	885
Thursfield	Stafford	Tnship.	979	Tilehurst	Berks & Oxon	Sub-dis.	5 308
Thursford	Norfolk	Parish	322	Tilehurst	Berks	Parish	2 330
Thurshelton	Devon	Parish	484	Tillingham	Essex	Parish	1 040
Thursley	Surrey	Parish	805	Tillington	Hereford	Tnship.	523
Thurstable	Essex	Hund.	7 163	Tillington	Stafford	Parish	79
Thurstaston	Cheshire	Parish	162	Tillington	Sussex	Parish	908
Thurstaston	,,	Tnship.	123	Tilmanstone	Kent	Parish	405
Thurston	Suffolk	Parish	740	Tilney All Saints	Norfolk	Parish	510
Thurstonland	York	Tnship.	1 116	Tilney w. Islington	,,	Parish	295
Thurton	Norfolk	Parish	246	Tilney St. Lawrence	,,	Parish	855
Thuxton	,,	Parish	132	Tilshead	Wilts	Parish	500
Thwaite by Aylsham	,,	Parish	147	Tilsop	Salop	Tnship.	104
Thwaite by Bungay	,,	Parish	136	Tilstock	,,	Ecl. Dis.	656
Thwaite	Suffolk	Parish	147	Tilston	Cheshire	Parish	817
Thwaites	Cumberland	Chap.	350	Tilston	,,	Tnship.	382
Thwing	York	Parish	416	Tilstone-Fearnall	,,	Tnship.	173
Tibaldstone	Gloucester	Hund.	1 076	Tilstone, St. Jude	,,	Ecl. Dis.	1 407
Tibberton	,,	Parish	391	Tilsworth	Beds	Parish	348
Tibberton	Salop	Tnship.	352	Tilton	Leicester	Parish	432
Tibberton, All Saints	,,	Ecl. Dis.	538	Tilton	,,	—	180
Tibberton	Worcester	Parish	309	Tilty	Essex	Parish	83
Tibenham	Norfolk	Parish	729	Timberland	Lincoln	Parish	1 618
Tiberton	Hereford	Parish	153	Timberland	,,	Tnship.	589
Tibshelf	Derby	Parish	863	Timberscombe	Somerset	Parish	434
Tibthorpe	York	Tnship.	309	Timble, Great	York	Tnship.	175
Ticehurst	Sussex & Kent	District	14 626	Timble, Little	,,	Tnship.	49
Ticehurst	Sussex	Sub-dis.	4 901	Timperley	Cheshire	Tnship.	1 571
Ticehurst	,,	Parish	2 758	Timperley, Christch.	,,	Ecl. Dis.	2 256
Tickencote	Rutland	Parish	104	Timsbury	Hants	Parish	207
Tickenham	Somerset	Parish	401	Timsbury	Somerset	Parish	1 551
Tickenhurst	Kent	Hamlet	28	Timworth	Suffolk	Parish	222
Tickhill	York	Sub-dis.	6 950	Tincleton	Dorset	Parish	154
Tickhill	,,	Parish	1 980	Tingewick	Bucks	Sub-dis.	3 671
Tickhill	,,	Tnship.	1 915	Tingewick	,,	Parish	914
Ticknall	Derby	Parish	1 068	Tingrith	Beds	Parish	226
Tickton	York	Hamlet	215	Tinsley	York	Tnship.	697
Tidcombe	Devon	Quarter	576	Tintagel	Cornwall	Parish	900
Tidcombe	Wilts	Parish	274	Tintern, Little	Monmouth	Parish	335
Tiddington	Oxon	Hamlet	141	Tintinhull	Somerset	Hund.	4 123
Tidebrook, St. John	Sussex	Ecl. Dis.	710	Tintinhull	,,	Parish	437
Tideford, St. Luke	Cornwall	Ecl. Dis.	913	Tintwistle	Cheshire	Tnship.	1 691
Tidenham	Gloucester	Parish	1 652	Tintwistle, Christch.	,,	Ecl. Dis.	3 585
Tideswell	Derby	Sub-dis.	9 016	Tinwell	Rutland	Parish	235
Tideswell	,,	Parish	3 512	Tipton, St. John	Devon	Ecl. Dis.	470
Tideswell	,,	Tnship.	2 057	Tipton	Stafford	Sub-dis.	28 870
Tidmarsh	Berks	Parish	179	Tipton	,,	Parish	28 870
Tidmington	Worcester	Parish	69	Tipton, St. John	,,	Ecl. Dis.	2 856

Name of Place.	County.	Description.	Population.	Name of Place.	County.	Description.	Population.
Tipton, St. Paul.	*Stafford* ..	Ecl. Dis.	10 028	Toft	*Cheshire* ..	Tnship.	16
Tiptree Heath ..	*Essex* ..	Ecl. Dis.	853	Toft, St. John ..	,, ..	Ecl. Dis.	24
Tirevan	*Denbigh* ..	Tnship.	352	Toft & Lound ..	*Lincoln* ..	Hamlets	20
Tirley	*Gloucester* ..	Parish	539	Toft next Newton	,, ..	Parish	8
Tisbury	*Wilts* ..	District	9 862	Toft Monks ..	*Norfolk* ..	Parish	42
Tisbury	,, ..	Sub-dis.	3 207	Toftrees	,, ..	Parish	6
Tisbury, East ..	,, ..	Parish	940	Tofts, West .. ●	,, ..	Parish	19
Tisbury, West ..	,, ..	Parish	653	Togstone	*Northumberland*	Tnship.	22
Tissington ..	*Derby* ..	Parish	403	Tolland	*Somerset* ..	Parish	13
Tisted, East ..	*Hants* ..	Parish	221	Tollard Royal	*Wilts & Dorset*	Parish	59
Tisted, West ..	,, ..	Parish	282	Tollard Royal ..	*Wilts* ..	—	37
Titchborne ..	,, ..	Parish	308	Toller Fratrum ..	*Dorset* ..	Parish	4
Titchfield ..	,, ..	Sub-dis.	5 224	Toller Porcorum	,, ..	Parish	50
Titchfield ..	,, ..	Parish	4 043	Tollerton ..	*Notts* ..	Parish	14
Titchmarsh ..	*Northampton*	Parish	893	Tollerton ..	*York* ..	Tnship.	54
Titchwell ..	*Norfolk* ..	Parish	146	Tollesbury ..	*Essex* ..	Sub-dis.	3 63
Titley	*Hereford* ..	Parish	373	Tollesbury	,, ..	Parish	1 46
Titlington	*Northumberland*	Tnship.	77	Tolleshunt D'Arcy	,, ..	Parish	80
Titsey	*Surrey* ..	Parish	167	Tolleshunt-Knights	,, ..	Parish	38
Tittenhanger ..	*Herts* ..	Hamlet	620	Tolleshunt-Major	,, ..	Parish	43
Tittenley ..	*Cheshire* ..	Tnship.	27	Tollington Park .	*Middlesex* ..	Ecl. Dis.	6 87
Tittesworth ..	*Stafford* ..	Tnship.	1 227	Tolpuddle ..	*Dorset* ..	Parish	40
Tittleshall w. Godwick	*Norfolk*	Parish	544	Tong	*Kent* ..	Parish	27
Tiverton ..	*Cheshire* ..	Tnship.	704	Tong	*Salop* ..	Parish	53
Tiverton ..	*Devon* ..	Hund.	904	Tong	*York* ..	Tnship.	3 03
Tiverton	,, ..	Union	30 875	Tonge w. Haulgh	*Lancaster* ..	Sub-dis.	7 15
Tiverton ..	,, ..	District	31 305	Tonge	,, ..	Tnship.	1 52
Tiverton	,, ..	Sub-dis.	10 447	Tonge St. James	,, ..	Ecl. Dis.	2 884
Tiverton	,, ..	Parish	10 447	Tonge (Prestwich P.)	,, ..	Tnship.	4 606
Tiverton Town ..	,, ..	Quarter	7 947	Tonge w. Alkrington	,, ..	Ecl. Dis.	5 029
Tiverton	,, ..	Borough	10 447	Tooting	*Surrey* ..	Parish	2 055
Tivetshall St. Margr.	*Norfolk* ..	Parish	375	Tooting, Trinity .	,, ..	Ecl. Dis.	1 055
Tivetshall St. Mary	,, ..	Parish	362	Topcliffe ..	*York* ..	Sub-dis.	1 810
Tixall	*Stafford* ..	Parish	289	Topcliffe ..	,, ..	Parish	2 800
Tixover	*Rutland* ..	Parish	129	Topcliffe ..	,, ..	Tnship.	676
Tockenham ..	*Wilts* ..	Parish	157	Topcroft ..	*Norfolk* ..	Parish	418
Tocketts	*York* ..	Tnship.	55	Toppesfield ..	*Essex* ..	Parish	1 045
Tockholes ..	*Lancaster* ..	Tnship.	820	Topsham ..	*Devon* ..	Sub-dis.	4 777
Tockholes, St. Stephen	,, ..	Ecl. Dis.	2 542	Topsham	,, ..	Parish	3 503
Tockington, Lower	*Gloucester* .	Tithing	464	**Topsham**	,, ..	Town	2 772
Tockwith ..	*York* ..	Tnship.	535	Torbock ..	*Lancaster* ..	Tnship.	626
Todbere ..	*Dorset* ..	Parish	122	Torbrian ..	*Devon* ..	Parish	205
Todburn	*Northumberland*	Tnship.	17	Torkington ..	*Cheshire* ..	Tnship.	218
Toddington ..	*Beds* ..	Sub-dis.	4 913	Torksey ..	*Lincoln* ..	Parish	379
Toddington ..	,, ..	Parish	2 433	Torksey ..	,, ..	Tnship.	205
Toddington ..	*Gloucester* ..	Parish	153	Tormarton ..	*Gloucester* ..	Parish	454
Todenham ..	,, ..	Parish	408	Tormoham ..	*Devon* ..	Parish	16 419
Todmorden ..	*Lanc. & York*	District	31 113	Torpenhow ..	*Cumberland*	Parish	1 083
Todmorden ..	,, ,,	Sub-dis.	20 287	Torpenhow & Whitrigg	,, ..	Tnship.	324
Todmorden ..	,, ,,	Town	11,797	Torquay ..	*Devon* ..	Sub-dis.	21 585
Todmorden & Walsden	*Lanc.* ..	Tnship.	9 146	**Torquay**	,, ..	Town	16 419
Todridge	*Northumberland*	Tnship.	4	Torrington, Black	,, ..	Hund.	18 295
Todwick ..	*York* ..	Parish	187	Torrington ..	,, ..	District	16 876
Toft	*Cambs* ..	Parish	359	Torrington, Great	,, ..	Parish	3 298

Name of Place.	County.	Description.	Population.	Name of Place.	County.	Description.	Population.
orrington, Little	Devon	Parish	563	Town, Bethnal Grn.	Middlesex	Sub-dis.	21 486
orrington	,,	M. Bor.	3 298	Town Close	Norfolk	Liberty	249
orrington, East	Lincoln	Parish	120	Town Part	Northampton	Parish	6 411
orrington, West	,,	Parish	165	Town-Quarter	Derby	Tnship.	495
orteval	Is. Guernsey	Parish	365	Townstall	Devon	Parish	1 337
ortington	Sussex	Parish	112	Towthorpe, Driffield	York	Tnship.	62
ortworth	Gloucester	Parish	235	Towthorpe, Huntingdon	,,	Tnship.	45
orver	Lancaster	Tnship.	194	Towton	,,	Tnship.	101
orwood	Devon	Ecl. Dis.	2 491	Towyn	Merioneth	Parish	2 859
orworth	Notts	Tnship.	237	Toxteth Park	Lancaster	Sub-dis.	69 284
oseland	Hunts	Hund.	14 922	Toxteth Park	,,	Parish	69 284
oseland	,,	L. Sub.	13 730	Toxteth Park, St. Clement	,,	Ecl. Dis.	7 637
oseland	,,	Parish	217	Toxteth Park, St. James	,,	Ecl. Dis.	13 345
osside	York	Parish	96	Toxteth Park, St. John	,,	Ecl. Dis.	17 534
osson & Rye-hill	Nrthumberld.	Tnship.	113	Toxteth Park, St. Matth.	,,	Ecl. Dis.	5 681
osson, Little	,,	Tnship.	33	Toxteth Park, St. Thos.	,,	Ecl. Dis.	20 692
ostock	Suffolk	Parish	382	Toyd Farm, &c.	Wilts	Parish	12
otham, Great	Essex	Parish	812	Toynton, All Saints	Lincoln	Parish	471
otham, Little	,,	Parish	346	Toynton, High	,,	Parish	210
othill	Lincoln	Parish	61	Toynton, Low	,,	Parish	155
othill Fields	Middlesex	Ecl. Dis.	9 761	Toynton, St. Peter	,,	Parish	433
otley	Derby	Tnship.	396	Trafford, Old, St. Thos.	Lanc.	Ecl. Dis.	2 184
otmonslow	Stafford	Hund.	53 398	Traian-Glas	Brecon	Hamlet	614
Totnes	Devon	District	32 942	Traian-Mawr, &c.	,,	Hamlet	584
Totnes	,,	Sub-dis.	5 881	Trallong	,,	Parish	278
Totnes	,,	Parish	3 409	Tranmere	Cheshire	Sub-dis.	14 485
Totnes	,,	Borough	4 001	Tranmere	,,	Tnship.	9 918
Toton	Notts	Tnship.	200	Tranmere, St. Cath.	,,	Ecl. Dis.	5 672
Tottenham Court	Middlesex	Sub-dis.	29 371	Tranwell, &c.	Northumberland	Tnship.	103
Tottenham	,,	Sub-dis.	13 240	Trawden	Lancaster	Tnship.	2 087
Tottenham	,,	Parish	13 240	Trawden, St. Mary	,,	Ecl. Dis.	1 516
Tottenham, St. Paul	,,	Ecl. Dis.	2 265	Trawsfyndd	Merioneth	Parish	1 517
Tottenham, Trinity	,,	Ecl. Dis.	6 061	Trawsgoed	Brecon	Hamlet	67
Tottenhill	Norfolk	Parish	342	Treals, &c.	Lancaster	Tnship.	632
Tottenhoe	Beds	Parish	652	Treborough	Somerset	Parish	183
Totteridge	Herts	Parish	573	Trebrys	Denbigh	Tnship.	121
Tottington High End	Lancaster	Tnship.	3 726	Trecefel	Cardigan	Tnship.	128
Tottington Lower End	,,	Sub-dis.	5 119	Trecoed	Radnor	Tnship.	211
Tottington Lower End	,,	Tnship.	11 764	Tredegar	Monmouth	Sub-dis.	28 548
Tottington, St. Anne	,,	Ecl. Dis.	5 119	**Tredegar**	,,	Town	9 383
Tottington	Norfolk	Parish	308	Tredegar, St. George	,,	Ecl. Dis.	20 318
Tovil, St. Stephen	Kent	Ecl. Dis.	897	Tredington	Gloucester	Parish	117
Towcester	Northampton	Hund.	5 163	Tredington	Worcester	Parish	1 100
Towcester	,,	L. Sub.	19 666	Tredington	,,	Tnship.	239
Towcester	,,	District	13 004	Tredunnock	Monmouth	Parish	164
Towcester	,,	Sub-dis.	7 531	Treeton	York	Parish	612
Towcester	,,	Parish	2 715	Treeton	,,	Tnship.	368
Towcester	,,	Town	2 417	Trefdraeth	Anglesey	Parish	921
Towednack	Cornwall	Parish	1 007	Trefecca	Brecon	Hamlet	236
Tower Hamlets	Middlesex	L. Sub.	647 845	Trefeglwys	Montgomery	Parish	1 701
Tower Hamlets	,,	P. Bor.	647 845	Trefeirig	Cardigan	Tnship.	1 095
Tower of London	,,	—	783	Treffgarne	Pembroke	Parish	86
Tower, Old	,,	Precinct	626	Trefilan	Cardigan	Parish	313
Towersey	Bucks	Parish	449	Treflis	Brecon	Hamlet	474

Name of Place.	County.	Description.	Population.	Name of Place.	County.	Description.	Population.
Treflys ..	Carnarvon ..	Parish	91	Treworgan, &c. ..	Monmouth ..	Parish	
Treflynn	Cardigan ..	Tnship.	147	Treyford	Sussex ..	Parish	12:
Trefnant	Denbigh ..	Ecl. Dis.	639	Trigg ..	Cornwall ..	Hund.	10 06!
Trefonen	Salop ..	Ecl. Dis.	1 248	Trigg ..	,, ..	L. Sub.	13 70:
Trefriw ..	Carnarvon ..	Parish	483	Trindon..	Durham ..	Parish	2 97!
Trefycoed	Cardigan ..	Hamlet	116	Trimmingham ..	Norfolk ..	Parish	18!
Tregaian	Anglesey ..	Parish	160	Trimley, St. Martin	Suffolk ..	Parish	58:
Tregare ..	Monmouth ..	Parish	319	Trimley, St. Mary	,, ..	Parish	38!
Tregaron	Cardigan ..	L. Sub.	7 314	Tring ..	Herts & Bucks	Sub-dis.	7 47!
Tregaron	,, ..	District	10 737	Tring ..	Herts ..	Parish	4 84!
Tregaron	,, ..	Sub-dis.	3 978	**Tring** ..	,, ..	Town	3 13(
Tregavethan	Cornwall ..	Parish	34	Trinity, Holy ..	Cheshire ..	Parish	3 67!
Tregony..	,, ..	Parish	699	Trinity, Holy ..	,, ..	—	3 60(
Tregoyd & Velindre	Brecon ..	Hamlets	385	Trinity Hall ..	Norfolk ..	Ward	60!
Tregynon	Montgomery	Sub-dis.	2 914	Trinity ..	Isle of Jersey	Parish	2 27:
Tregynon	,, ..	Parish	703	Trinity, Newington	Surrey ..	Sub-dis.	22 67!
Treleacharbettws	Carmarthen	Parish	1 456	Trinity ..	York ..	Ward	2 24(
Treleigh	Cornwall ..	Ecl. Dis.	2 349	Tritlington	Northumberland	Tnship.	142
Tre-Llan	Flint ..	Tnship.	334	Troedyraur ..	Cardigan ..	Hund.	11 671
Trelleck..	Monmouth ..	L. Sub.	3 581	Troedyraur Low. Div.	,, ..	L. Sub.	4 317
Trelleck..	,, ..	Sub-dis.	4 797	Troedyraur Upp. Div.	,, ..	L. Sub.	9 214
Trelleck..	,, ..	Parish	1 128	Troedyraur	,, ..	Parish	974
Trelleck..	,, ..	Tnship.	128	Troston ..	Suffolk ..	Parish	322
Trelleck, parish part	,, ..	—	863	Trostrey ..	Monmouth ..	Parish	190
Trelleck Grange	,, ..	Chap.	137	Trotterscliffe ..	Kent ..	Parish	293
Trellynian	Flint ..	Tnship.	35	Trotton ..	Sussex ..	Parish	452
Trelystan	Montgomery	Tnship.	94	Trough ..	Cumberland	Tnship.	134
Trelystan	,, ..	Ecl. Dis.	573	Troughend Ward	Northumbld.	Tnship.	262
Tremadoc	Merioneth ..	Sub-dis.	6 848	Troutbeck ..	Westmoreland	Tnship.	428
Tremain	Cardigan ..	Parish	282	Troutsdale ..	York ..	Tnship.	67
Tremaine	Cornwall ..	Parish	109	Trowbridge ..	Wilts ..	Sub-dis.	11 367
Treneglos	,, ..	Parish	138	Trowbridge ..	,, ..	Parish	10 487
Trent ..	Somerset ..	Parish	512	**Trowbridge** ..	,, ..	Town	9 626
Trentham	Stafford ..	Sub-dis.	6 259	Trowbridge, Trinity	,, ..	Ecl. Dis.	2 374
Trentham	,, ..	Parish	4 611	Trowell ..	Notts ..	Parish	343
Trentham	,, ..	Tnship.	645	Trowse ..	Norfolk ..	Parish	1 404
Trentishoe	Devon ..	Parish	123	Trowse Millgate, &c.	,, ..	Hamlets	687
Trent Vale, St. John	Stafford..	Ecl. Dis.	2 183	Trull ..	Somerset ..	Parish	779
Trescoe Isle	Scilly Isles	Island	399	Trumpington ..	Cambs ..	Parish	(illegible)
Treslothan, St. John	Cornwall	Ecl. Dis.	1 804	Trunch ..	Norfolk ..	Parish	(illegible)
Tresmeer	,, ..	Parish	148	Truro ..	Cornwall ..	District	43 070
Treswell	Notts ..	Parish	270	**Truro** ..	,, ..	Borough	11 337
Tretire w. Michl.-ch.	Hereford	Parish	147	Truro, St. Clement	,,	Parish	3 731
Tretower	Brecon ..	Parcel	296	Truro, St. Mary .	,,	Parish	3 117
Trevalga	Cornwall ..	Parish	158	Truro, St. George	,,	Eel. Dis.	2 846
Treverbyn	,, ..	Ecl. Dis.	2 109	Trusham ..	Devon ..	Parish	223
Trevethin, &c. ..	Monmouth ..	Parish	18 146	Trusley ..	Derby ..	Parish	99
Treville..	Hereford ..	Parish	145	Trusthorpe ..	Lincoln ..	Parish	332
Trewalchmai	Anglesey ..	Parish	768	Tryddyn ..	Flint ..	Chap.	1 525
Trewin ..	Cornwall ..	Parish	178	Trysull ..	Stafford ..	Parish	610
Trewern..	Montgomery	Tnship.	507	Tubney ..	Berks ..	Parish	180
Trewern & Gwythla	Radnor ..	Tnship.	108	Tuckingmill ..	Cornwall ..	Ecl. Dis.	3 769
Trewhitt, H. & Low	Northmbld.	Tnship.	108	Tuddenham, East	Norfolk ..	Parish	512
Trewick..	,, ..	Tnship.	24	Tuddenham, North	,, ..	Parish	437

Name of Place.	County.	Description.	Population.	Name of Place.	County.	Description.	Population.
Tuddenham, Carlford	Suffolk	Parish	394	Turnworth	Dorset	Parish	150
Tuddenham, Worlington	,,	Parish	413	Turton	Lancaster	Sub-dis.	5 459
Tudeley	Kent	Parish	547	Turton	,,	Tnship.	4 513
Tudhoe	Durham	Tnship.	1 359	Turvey	Beds	Sub-dis.	2 407
Tuffley	Gloucester	Hamlet	138	Turvey	,,	Parish	1 093
Tufton	Hants	Parish	142	Turville	Bucks	Parish	437
Tugby	Leicester	Parish	360	Turweston	,,	Parish	335
Tugby	,,	—	331	Tushingham, &c.	Cheshire	Tnship.	324
Tugford	Salop	Parish	119	Tusmore	Oxon	Parish	45
Tughall	Northumberland	Tnship.	109	Tutbury	Staff. & Derby	Sub-dis.	6 797
Tulse Hill, Trinity	Surrey	Ecl. Dis.	2 334	Tutbury	Stafford	Parish	1 982
Tumby	Lincoln	Tnship.	320	Tutnall & Cobley	Worcester	Hamlets	508
Tunbridge	Kent	L. Sub.	35 548	Tuttington	Norfolk	Parish	202
Tunbridge Wells	,,	L. Sub.	5 963	Tuxford	Notts	Sub-dis.	4 998
Tunbridge	,,	District	34 271	Tuxford	,,	Parish	1 034
Tunbridge	,,	Sub-dis.	11 129	Tweedmouth	Northumberland	Parish	5 414
Tunbridge Wells	,,	Sub-dis.	17 656	Tweedmouth	,,	Tnship.	2 884
Tunbridge	,,	Parish	21 004	Twemlow	Cheshire	Tnship.	151
Tunbridge	,,	Town	5 919	Twerton	Somerset	Sub-dis.	6 953
Tunbridge Wells	Kent & Sus.	Town	13 807	Twerton	,,	Parish	3 012
Tunbridge, Christch.	Kent	Ecl. Dis.	2 452	Twickenham	Middlesex	Sub-dis.	8 077
Tunbridge, H. Trinity	,,	Ecl. Dis.	7 146	Twickenham	,,	Parish	8 077
Tunbridge, St. John	,,	Ecl. Dis.	1 821	Twickenham, Trinity	,,	Ecl. Dis.	3 985
Tunbridge, St. Stephen	,,	Ecl. Dis.	3 899	Twigmore	Lincoln	Tnship.	66
Tunstall	Durham	Tnship.	94	Twigworth	Gloucester	Hamlet	178
Tunstall	Kent	Parish	207	Twigworth, St. Matthew	,,	Ecl. Dis.	552
Tunstall	Lancaster	Sub-dis.	916	Twineham	Sussex	Parish	339
Tunstall	,,	Parish	803	Twining	Gloucester	Parish	992
Tunstall	,,	Tnship.	138	Twinstead	Essex	Parish	193
Tunstall	Norfolk	Parish	112	Twiston	Lancaster	Tnship.	141
Tunstall	Stafford	Sub-dis.	22 466	Twitchen	Devon	Parish	227
Tunstall	,,	Tnship.	11 207	Twizel	Northumberland	Tnship.	305
Tunstall (Adbaston P.)	,,	Tnship.	72	Twizell	,,	Tnship.	52
Tunstall Christch.	,,	Ecl. Dis.	11 150	Two Mile Hill	Gloucester	Ecl. Dis.	3 622
Tunstall	Suffolk	Parish	701	Twrcelyn	Anglesey	Hund.	10 345
Tunstall	York	Parish	166	Twycross	Leicester	Parish	336
Tunstall	,,	Tnship.	293	Twyford	Bucks	Parish	694
Tunstead, Trinity	Lancaster	Ecl. Dis.	4 681	Twyford	,,	—	429
Tunstead	Norfolk	Hund.	10 425	Twyford & Stenson	Derby	Tnship.	212
Tunstead & Happing	,,	L. Sub.	17 412	Twyford	Hants	Sub-dis.	4 203
Tunstead	,,	District	14 516	Twyford	,,	Parish	1 301
Tunstead	,,	Parish	405	Twyford	Leicester	Parish	543
Tunworth	Hants	Parish	118	Twyford	,,	Tnship.	372
Tupholme	Lincoln	Parish	81	Twyford	Lincoln	Hamlet	194
Tupsley	Hereford	Tnship.	802	Twyford-Abbey	Middlesex	Parish	18
Tupton	Derby	Tnship.	1 004	Twyford	Norfolk	Parish	60
Turkdean	Gloucester	Parish	291	Twywell	Northampton	Parish	336
Tur-Langton	Leicester	Tnship.	837	Tybroughton	Flint	Tnship.	194
Turnastone	Hereford	Parish	54	Tydd St. Giles	Cambs	Parish	924
Turnditch	Derby	Tnship.	350	Tydd St. Mary	Lincoln	Parish	977
Turnditch	,,	Ecl. Dis.	824	Tydweiliog	Carnarvon	Parish	371
Turners Puddle	Dorset	Parish	111	Tyldesley	Lancaster	Town	3 950
Turnham Green	Middlesex	Ecl. Dis.	2 623	Tyldesley w. Shackerley	,,	Tnship.	6 029
Turnhill	York	—	8	Tyldesley w. Shackerley	,,	Ecl. Dis.	6 029

Name of Place.	County.	Description.	Population.	Name of Place.	County.	Description.	Population.
Tyndaethy	*Anglesey*	Hund.	8 207	Ulceby, Alford	*Lincoln*	Parish	212
Tynedale Ward	*Northumbld.*	L. Sub.	48 723	Ulceby, Barton	,,	Parish	1 048
Tyneham	*Dorset*	Parish	272	Ulcombe	*Kent*	Parish	621
Tynemouth	*Northumberland*	District	77 955	Uldale	*Cumberland*	Parish	294
Tynemouth	,,	Sub-dis.	18 266	Uley	*Gloucester*	Sub-dis.	2 471
Tynemouth	,,	Parish	35 404	Uley	,,	Parish	1 230
Tynemouth	,,	Tnship.	16 560	Ulgham	*Northumberland*	Parish	362
Tynemouth	,,	Borough	34 021	Ullenhall	*Warwick*	Chap.	508
Tyringham	*Bucks*	Parish	226	Ulleskelf	*York*	Tnship.	515
Tyrley	*Stafford*	Tnship.	814	Ullesthorpe	*Leicester*	Hamlet	600
Tyrymynach	*Cardigan*	Tnship.	405	Ulley	*York*	Tnship.	165
Tysoe	*Warwick*	Parish	1 035	Ulley Trinity	,,	Ecl. Dis.	165
Tythby	*Notts*	Parish	718	Ullingswick	*Hereford*	Parish	318
Tythby	,,	Tnship.	114	Ullock	*Cumberland*	Tnship.	353
Tythegston	*Glamorgan*	Parish	1 678	Ulnes Walton	*Lancaster*	Tnship.	488
Tythegston Upper	,,	Hamlet	1 572	Ulpha	*Cumberland*	Chap.	360
Tythegston Lower	,,	Hamlet	106	Ulrome	*York*	Tnship.	212
Tytherington	*Cheshire*	Tnship.	395	Ulting	*Essex*	Parish	169
Tytherington	*Gloucester*	Parish	447	Ulverscroft	*Leicester*	Parish	104
Tytherington	*Wilts*	Parish	111	Ulverston	*Lancaster*	District	35 738
Tytherley, East	*Hants*	Parish	352	Ulverston	,,	Sub-dis.	8 781
Tytherley, West	,,	Parish	469	Ulverston	,,	Parish	11 464
Tytherton Kelways	,,	Parish	18	Ulverston	,,	Tnship.	7 414
Tythrop	*Oxon*	Liberty	66	Ulverston	,,	Town	6 630
Tywardreath	*Cornwall*	Parish	3 379	Ulverston, Trinity	,,	Ecl. Dis.	2 116
				Underbarrow, &c.	*Westmoreld.*	Tnship.	478
Ubbeston	*Suffolk*	Parish	206	Underditch	*Wilts*	Hund.	1 307
Ubley	*Somerset*	Parish	307	Undermilbeck	*Westmoreland*	Tnship.	1 702
Uchaf	*Carnarvon*	Hund.	13 894	Underskiddaw	*Cumberland*	Tnship.	482
Uchayndre	*Cardigan*	Tnship.	439	Undy	*Monmouth*	Parish	411
Uchygarreg	*Montgomery*	Tnship.	354	Unstone	*Derby*	Tnship.	879
Uckerby	*York*	Tnship.	56	Unthank	*Cumberland*	Tnship.	179
Uckfield	*Sussex*	L. Sub.	11 159	Unthank	*Northumberland*	Tnship.	37
Uckfield	,,	District	17 260	Uny-Lelant	*Cornwall*	Sub-dis.	8 357
Uckfield	,,	Parish	1 740	Uny-Lelant	,,	Parish	2 319
Uckington	*Gloucester*	Hamlet	195	Upavon	*Wilts*	Parish	508
Udimore	*Sussex*	Parish	444	Up Cerne	*Dorset*	Parish	75
Uffculme	*Devon*	Sub-dis.	5 229	Upchurch	*Kent*	Parish	468
Uffculme	,,	Parish	2 020	Up Exe	*Devon*	Tithing	97
Uffington	*Berks*	Parish	1 081	Upham	*Hants*	Parish	589
Uffington	,,	Tnship.	644	Uphatherley	*Gloucester*	Parish	68
Uffington	*Lincoln*	Parish	510	Uphaven	*Wilts*	Parish	508
Uffington	*Salop*	Parish	180	Uphill	*Somerset*	Parish	447
Ufford	*Northampton*	Parish	307	Upholland	*Lancaster*	Sub-dis.	6 982
Ufford	,,	Tnship.	192	Upholland	,,	Tnship.	3 463
Ufford	*Suffolk*	Parish	656	Upleadon	*Gloucester*	Parish	237
Ufton	*Warwick*	Parish	201	Upleatham	*York*	Parish	1 007
Ufton Nervet	*Berks*	Parish	367	Upleatham	,,	Tnship.	521
Ugborough	*Devon*	Sub-dis.	3 778	Uplowman	*Devon*	Parish	444
Ugborough	,,	Parish	1 482	Uplyme	,,	Parish	989
Uggeshall	*Suffolk*	Parish	272	Upmarden	*Sussex*	Parish	366
Ugglebarnby	*York*	Tnship.	437	Upminster	*Essex*	Parish	1 342
Ugley	*Essex*	Parish	404	Up Nately	*Hants*	Parish	99
Ugthorpe	*York*	Tnship.	256	Upottery	*Devon*	Parish	940

Name of Place.	County.	Description.	Population.	Name of Place.	County.	Description.	Population.
Upper Allithwaite	Lancaster ..	Tnship.	729	Upper Radbourn	Warwick ..	Parish	15
Upper Arley ..	Stafford ..	Parish	886	Upper Rawcliffe, &c.	Lancaster	Tnship.	682
Upper Bedwas ..	Monmouth ..	Hamlet	597	Upper Sapey ..	Hereford ..	Parish	357
Upper Beeding..	Sussex ..	Parish	553	Upper Shuckburgh	Warwick ..	Parish	60
Up. & Low. Bentley	Worcester	Tnship.	238	Upper Slaughter	Gloucester ..	Parish	241
Upper Boddington	Nrthamptn.	Parish	409	Upper Stondon..	Beds ..	Parish	66
Upper Broughton	Notts ..	Parish	406	Upper Stonebeck	York ..	Tnship.	374
Upper & Lower Coton	Stafford	Tnship.	446	Upper Swell ..	Gloucester ..	Parish	65
Upper Bullingham	Hereford..	Parish	83	Upper Swinford .	Worcester ..	Tnship.	2 749
Upperby ..	Cumberland	Tnship.	595	Upper Tean, Christch.	Stafford	Ecl. Dis.	1 171
Upperby, St. John	,, ..	Ecl. Dis.	1 898	Upperthong ..	York ..	Tnship.	2 690
Up. Chelsea, St. Jude	Middlesex	Ecl. Dis.	4 561	Upperthong ..	,, \ ..	Ecl. Dis.	2 690
Up. Chelsea, St. Saviour	,, ..	Ecl. Dis.	8 837	Upper Tythegston	Glamorgan	Hamlet	1 572
Up. Chelsea, St. Simon	,, ..	Ecl. Dis.	3 959	Upper Vainor ..	Cardigan ..	Tnship.	426
Upper Clatford..	Hants ..	Parish	703	Upper Whitley .	York ..	Tnship.	947
Upper Denton ..	Cumberland	Parish	100	Upper Winchendon	Bucks ..	Parish	220
Up. Dicker Common	Sussex ..	Ecl. Dis.	550	Up. Ystradgunlais	Brecon ..	Hamlet	544
Upper Dunsforth, &c.	York ..	Tnship.	151	Up. Ystradvelltey	,, ..	Hamlet	369
Up. Dyffrin Honddu	Brecon ..	Hamlet	187	Uppingham ..	Rutland, &c.	District	12 367
Upper Dylais ..	Glamorgan .	Hamlet	622	Uppingham ..	,, ,,	Sub-dis.	5 345
Upper Edmonton	Middlesex ..	Ecl. Dis.	2 945	Uppingham ..	Rutland ..	Parish	2 186
Up. Gornal, St. Peter	Stafford	Ecl. Dis.	4 044	Uppingham ..	,, ..	Town	2 176
Upper Gravenhurst	Beds ..	Parish	337	Uppington ..	Montgomery	Tnship.	112
Upper Gwnnws .	Cardigan ..	Tnship.	760	Uppington ..	Salop ..	Parish	95
Upper Hallam ..	York & Derby	Sub-dis.	2 649	Upsall	York ..	Tnship.	104
Upper Hallam ..	York ..	Tnship.	1 643	Upsall (Ormesby P.)	,, ..	Tnship.	108
Upper Hanley ..	Worcester ..	Parish	120	Upshire.. ..	Essex ..	Hamlet	961
Upper Hardres..	Kent ..	Parish	271	Upton	Berks ..	Hamlet	306
Upper Harpton .	Radnor ..	Tnship.	186	Upton w. Chalvey	Bucks ..	Parish	4 688
Upper Helmsley	York ..	Parish	78	Upton	Cheshire ..	Parish	293
Upper & N. Hesket	Cumberld.	Tnship.	775	Upton (St. Mary P.)	,, ..	Tnship.	758
Upper Heyford..	Northampton	Parish	116	Upton (Prestbury P.)	,, ..	Tnship.	171
Upper Heyford..	Oxon ..	Parish	453	Upton	Devon ..	Ecl. Dis.	6 774
Upper Hodnel ..	Warwick ..	Parish	20	Upton Helions..	,, ..	Parish	111
Upper Holker ..	Lancaster ..	Tnship.	1 035	Upton Pyne ..	,, ..	Parish	455
Upper Holloway	Middlesex ..	Ecl. Dis.	7 286	Upton	Gloucester ..	Tithing	775
Upper Hopton..	York ..	Ecl. Dis.	1 211	Upton St. Leonards	,, ..	Parish	1 035
Upper Kinsham.	Hereford ..	Parish	88	Upton Gray ..	Hants ..	Parish	371
Upper Lambourn	Berks ..	Tithing	409	Upton	Hereford ..	Tnship.	98
Upper Langwith	Derby ..	Parish	183	Upton Bishop ..	,, ..	Parish	716
Upper Llanidloes	Montgomery	Sub-dis.	3 663	Upton	Hunts ..	Parish	152
Upper Lledrod..	Cardigan ..	Tnship.	537	Upton	Leicester ..	Tnship.	145
Upper Machen..	Monmouth ..	Hamlet	1 414	Upton	Lincoln ..	Parish	527
U. Merthyr Tydfil	Glm. & Bre.	Sub-dis.	27 478	Upton	,, ..	Tnship.	255
Upper Michaelstone	Glamorgan	Hamlet	861	Upton	Norfolk ..	Parish	601
Upper Mill ..	York ..	Sub-dis.	8 877	Upton	Northampton	Parish	36
Upper Mitton ..	Worcester ..	Hamlet	262	Upton	,, ..	Chap.	100
Upper Neath ..	Glamorgan .	Hamlet	1 637	Upton	Notts ..	Parish	587
Upper Penderyn	Brecon ..	Hamlet	197	Upton and Signet	Oxon ..	Hamlet	214
Upper Penn ..	Stafford ..	Tnship.	1 459	Upton	Pembroke ..	Hamlet	24
Upper Penn, St. Philip	,, ..	Ecl. Dis.	852	Upton Cressett..	Salop ..	Parish	72
Upper Pertwood	Wilts ..	Parish	30	Upton Magna ..	,, ..	Parish	452
Upper Poppleton	York ..	Chap.	355	Upton Parva ..	,, ..	Parish	206
				Upton	Somerset ..	Parish	314

Name of Place.	County.	Description.	Population.	Name of Place.	County.	Description.	Population.
Upton Noble	Somerset	Parish	217	Vainor	Radnor	Tnship.	315
Upton Lovell	Wilts	Parish	210	Vale	Isle of Guernsey	Parish	2 455
Upton Scudamore	,,	Parish	381	Van	Glamorgan	Hamlet	62
Upton	Worcester	L. Sub.	13 143	Vange	Essex	Parish	160
Upton on Severn	,,	District	21 010	Vaultershome	Cornwall	Tithing	1 227
Upton on Severn	,,	Sub-dis.	6 122	Vauxhall	Lancaster	Ecl. Dis.	8 512
Upton on Severn	,,	Parish	2 676	Vauxhall Rd., Trinity	Mddlesx.	Ecl. Dis.	6 365
Upton Snodsbury	,,	Sub-dis.	3 130	Vaynore-Glare	Radnor	Tnship.	246
Upton Snodsbury	,,	Parish	358	Venn Ottery	Devon	Parish	101
Upton Warren	,,	Parish	338	Vennyvach	Brecon	Hamlet	140
Upton	York	Tnship.	221	Ventnor	Hants, I. W.	Ecl. Dis.	3 267
Upwaltham	Sussex	Parish	71	Ventnor	,, ,,	Town	3 208
Upway	Dorset	Sub-dis.	3 968	Vernhams-Dean	,, ,,	Parish	727
Upway	,,	Parish	646	Verwick	Cardigan	Parish	319
Upwell	Norf. & Cambs	Sub-dis.	4 947	Veryan	Cornwall	Parish	1 399
Upwell w. Welney	,, ,,	Parish	4 783	Virginia Water, Ch. Ch.	Surrey	Ecl. Dis.	877
Upwell	,, ,,	Chap.	3 682	Virginstow	Devon	Parish	141
Upwood	Hunts	Parish	388	Virley	Essex	Parish	67
Urchfont	Wilts	Parish	1 459	Vobster, St. Edmund	Somerset	Ecl. Dis.	182
Urchfont	,,	—	898	Vorlan	Pembroke	Hamlet	29
Urmston	Lancaster	Tnship.	748	Vowchurch	Hereford	Parish	333
Urpeth	Durham	Tnship.	1 123	Vro	Brecon	Hamlet	313
Urswick	Lancaster	Parish	1 080	Vro	,,	Parcel	549
Ushlawrcoed	Monmouth	Hamlet	17 038				
Usk	,,	Hund.	13 859	**Waberthwaite**	Cumberland	Parish	198
Usk	,,	L. Sub.	4 005	Wackerfield	Durham	Tnship.	160
Usk	,,	Sub-dis.	4 035	Wacton	Hereford	Parish	123
Usk	,,	Parish	2 112	Wacton	Norfolk	Parish	244
Usk	,,	—	1 528	Wadborough	Worcester	Hamlet	183
Usk	,,	P. Bor.	1 545	Waddesdon	Bucks	Sub-dis.	5 430
Usselby	Lincoln	Parish	76	Waddesdon	,,	Parish	1 786
Usworth, Gt. & Lit.	Durham	Tnship.	3 677	Waddesdon	,,	Tnship.	1 470
Utkinton	Cheshire	Tnship.	558	Waddingham	Lincoln	Parish	812
Utterby	Lincoln	Parish	326	Waddington	,,	Parish	909
Uttlesford	Essex	Hund.	12 646	Waddington	York	Tnship.	513
Uttoxeter	Stafford	L. Sub.	14 180	Waddingworth	Lincoln	Parish	82
Uttoxeter	Staff. & Derby	District	14 787	Wadenhoe	Northampton	Parish	270
Uttoxeter	,, ,,	Sub-Dis.	8 008	Wadhurst	Sussex & Kent	Sub-dis.	4 075
Uttoxeter	Stafford ,,	Parish	4 847	Wadhurst	Sussex	Parish	2 470
Uttoxeter	,,	Town	3 645	Wadsworth	York	Tnship.	4 141
Uwchgorfai	Carnarvon	Hund.	9 254	Wadsley	,,	Ecl. Dis.	3 849
Uwchgraig	Merioneth	Tnship.	104	Wadworth	,,	Parish	656
Uxbridge	Middlesex	L. Sub.	21 745	Wainfleet	Lincoln	Sub-dis.	5 502
Uxbridge	,,	District	23 155	Wainfleet All Saints	,,	Parish	1 392
Uxbridge	,,	Sub-dis.	5 154	Wainfleet St. Mary	,,	Parish	730
Uxbridge	,,	Tnship.	3 236	Waitby	Westmoreland	Tnship.	93
Uxbridge	,,	Town	3 815	Waith	Lincoln	Parish	43
Uxbridge Moor, St. John	,,	Ecl. Dis.	1 299	Wakefield	York	District	55 049
Uxbridge St. Margaret	,,	Ecl. Dis.	3 235	Wakefield	,,	Union	53 126
Uzmaston	Pembroke	Parish	610	Wakefield	,,	Sub-dis.	17 611
				Wakefield	,,	Parish	35 739
Vainor	Brecon	Parish	2 984	Wakefield	,,	Tnship.	17 611
Vainor, Lower	Cardigan	Tnship.	198	**Wakefield**	,,	M. Bor.	23 350
Vainor, Upper	,,	Tnship.	426			P. Bor.	23 150

Name of Place.	County.	Description.	Population.	Name of Place.	County.	Description.	Population.
Wakefield, St. Andrew	York	Ecl. Dis.	2 118	Wallasey	Cheshire	Parish	10 723
Wakefield, St. John	„	Ecl. Dis.	4 232	Wallasey	„	Tnship.	1 415
Wakefield, St. Mary	„	Ecl. Dis.	2 340	Wallbottle	Northumberland	Tnship.	792
Wakefield, Trinity	„	Ecl. Dis.	3 719	Wallerscote	Cheshire	Tnship.	6
Wakely	Herts	Parish	4	Wallingford	Berks	L. Sub.	5 704
Wakering, Great	Essex	Parish	1 018	Wallingford	Berks & Oxon	District	14 017
Wakering, Little	„	Parish	283	Wallingford	„ „	Sub-dis.	7 785
Wakerley	Northampton	Parish	223	**Wallingford** {	„ „	P. Bor.	7 794
Wakes-Colne	Essex	Parish	535		Berks	M. Bor.	2 793
Walberswick	Suffolk	Parish	315	Wallingford Cas. Prec.	„	Parish	30
Walberton	Sussex	Parish	588	Wallington	Herts	Parish	238
Walburn	York	Tnship.	28	Wallington, &c.	Norfolk	Parish	69
Walby	Cumberland	Tnship.	40	Wallington Demesne	Nrthumb.	Tnship.	210
Walcot	Lincoln	Parish	201	Wallington	Surrey	Hund.	46 686
Walcot	Somerset	Sub-dis.	11 268	Wallington	„	Hamlet	983
Walcot	„	Parish	26 281	Wallingwells	Notts	Parish	25
Walcot w. Membris	Worcester	Hamlet	442	Wallisea	Essex	Island	124
Walcott	Lincoln	Hamlet	605	Wallop, Nether	Hants	Parish	946
Walcott	Norfolk	Parish	141	Wallop, Over	„	Parish	508
Walcott	Oxon	Hamlet	8	Wallsend	Northumberland	Sub-dis.	6 715
Walden	Essex	L. Sub.	24 766	Wallsend	„	Parish	6 715
Walden, Kings	Herts	Parish	1 183	Wallsend	„	Tnship.	2 371
Walden, St. Paul	„	Parish	1 123	Wall Town	„	Tnship.	68
Walden Stubbs	York	Tnship.	159	Walmer	Kent	Parish	3 275
Waldershare	Kent	Parish	104	Walmersley	Lancaster	Sub-dis.	5 062
Waldingfield, Great	Suffolk	Parish	622	Walmersley, Christch.	„	Ecl. Dis.	3 269
Waldingfield, Little	„	Parish	412	Walmersley, &c.	„	Tnship.	5 298
Walditch	Dorset	Parish	175	Walmgate	York	Sub-dis.	22 632
Waldridge	Durham	Tnship.	945	Walmley, St. John	Warwick	Ecl. Dis.	621
Waldridge	Northumberland	Tnship.	4	Walmsgate	Lincoln	Parish	77
Waldringfield	Suffolk	Parish	205	Walmsley, Christch.	Lancaster	Ecl. Dis.	3 415
Waldron	Sussex	Parish	1 132	Walney Isle	„	Island	294
Wales	York	Parish	305	Walpole, St. Peter	Norfolk	Sub-dis.	2 925
Walesby	Lincoln	Parish	351	Walpole, St. Andrew	„	Parish	709
Walesby	Notts	Parish	327	Walpole, St. Peter	„	Parish	1 252
Walford	Hereford	Parish	1 204	Walpole	Suffolk	Parish	540
Walford, &c.	„	Tnship.	206	Walsall	Stafford	L. Sub.	109 691
Walgherton	Cheshire	Tnship.	194	Walsall	„	District	59 908
Walgrave	Northampton	Parish	650	Walsall	„	Sub-dis.	30 415
Walham Green	Middlesex	Ecl. Dis.	6 931	Walsall	„	Parish	39 690
Walker	Northumberland	Tnship.	6 473	Walsall Borough	„	Tnship.	8 166
Walker	„	Ecl. Dis.	5 843	Walsall Foreign	„	Tnship.	31 524
Walkeringham	Notts	Parish	683	Walsall, St. Peter	„	Ecl. Dis.	10 418
Walkerith	Lincoln	Tnship.	83	Walsall Wood, St. Jno.	„	Ecl. Dis.	1 701
Walkern	Herts	Parish	823	**Walsall**	„	Borough	37 760
Walkhampton	Devon	Parish	831	Walsden	Lancaster	Ecl. Dis.	3 934
Walkingham Hill, &c.	York	Parish	28	Walsham	Norfolk	Hund.	5 241
Walkington	„	Parish	618	Walsham, North	„	Sub-dis.	6 942
Walkmill	Northumberland	Tnship.	7	Walsham, North	„	Parish	2 896
Wall	„	Tnship.	484	**Walsham, North**	„	Town	2 896
Wall	Salop	Sub-dis.	2 361	Walsham, South:—			
Wall	Stafford	Tnship.	87	St. Lawrence	Norfolk	Parish	220
Wall, St. John	„	Ecl. Dis.	243	St. Mary	„	Parish	336
Wallasey	Cheshire	Sub-dis.	10 723	Walsham-le-Willows	Suffolk	Sub-dis.	5 99?

Name of Place.	County.	Description.	Population.	Name of Place.	County.	Description.	Population.
Walsham-le-Willows	Suffolk	Parish	1 290	Walton, East	Pembroke	Parish	223
Walshcroft	Lincoln	Wapen.	10 134	Walton, West	„	Parish	397
Walsingham	Norfolk	District	21 118	Walton & Womaston	Radnor	Tnship.	219
Walsingham	„	Sub-dis.	6 492	Walton	Somerset	Parish	731
Walsingham, Gt.	„	Parish	512	Walton in Gordano	„	Parish	191
Walsingham, Lit.	„	Parish	1 069	Walton	Stafford	Tnship.	114
Walsoken	Norf. & Cambs	Sub-dis.	5 435	Walton	Suffolk	Parish	988
Walsoken	Norfolk	Parish	2 683	Walton on Hill	Surrey	Parish	475
Walterstone	Hereford	Parish	173	Walton	„	Sub-dis.	5 613
Waltham	Berks	Parish	848	Walton on Thames	„	Parish	4 010
Waltham, White	„	Parish	917	Walton	York	Parish	221
Waltham	Essex	Hund.	9 428	Walton	„	Tnship.	471
Waltham Abbey	„	Sub-dis.	5 044	Walwins Castle	Pembroke	Parish	350
Waltham Abbey	„	Parish	5 044	Walworth	Durham	Tnship.	180
Waltham Abbey	„	Tnship.	2 933	Walworth	Surrey	Sub-dis.	44 463
Waltham Abbey	„	Town	2 873	Walworth, St. John	„	Ecl. Dis.	7 426
Waltham, St. Paul	„	Ecl. Dis.	531	Walworth, St. Paul	„	Ecl. Dis.	11 770
Waltham, Great	„	Parish	2 380	Walworth, St. Peter	„	Ecl. Dis.	32 011
Waltham, Little	„	Parish	684	Wambrook	Dorset	Parish	286
Waltham Bishops	Hants	Parish	2 267	Wampool	Cumberland	Tnship.	99
Waltham, North	„	Parish	484	Wanborough	Surrey	Parish	192
Waltham Cross	Herts	Ecl. Dis.	2 029	Wanborough	Wilts	Parish	960
Waltham	Kent	Parish	608	Wandsworth	Surrey	L. Sub.	52 963
Waltham	Leicester	Sub-dis.	4 367	Wandsworth	„	District	70 403
Waltham on Wolds	„	Parish	672	Wandsworth	„	Sub-dis.	13 346
Waltham	Lincoln	Parish	856	Wandsworth	„	Parish	13 346
Waltham, Cold	Sussex	Parish	447	Wandsworth, St. Anne	„	Ecl. Dis.	7 613
Waltham, Up	„	Parish	71	Wangford	Suffolk	Hund.	9 626
Walthamstow	Essex	Sub-dis.	10 594	Wangford	„	District	13 619
Walthamstow	„	Parish	7 137	Wangford, Blything	„	Parish	862
Walthamstow, St. Jas.	„	Ecl. Dis.	2 179	Wangford	„	—	701
Walthamstow, St. John	„	Ecl. Dis.	1 052	Wangford, Mildenhall	„	Parish	50
Walthamstow, St. Peter	„	Ecl. Dis.	784	Wanlip	Leicester	Parish	117
Walton	Bucks	Parish	95	Wansford	Northampton	Parish	180
Walton Inferior	Cheshire	Tnship.	395	Wansford	York	Tnship.	224
Walton Superior	„	Tnship.	160	Wanstead	Essex	Parish	2 742
Walton	Cumberland	Sub-dis.	2 782	Wanstrow	Somerset	Parish	454
Walton	„	Parish	407	Wantage	Berks	Hund.	9 537
Walton, High	„	Tnship.	144	Wantage	„	L. Sub.	13 113
Walton, Low	„	Tnship.	263	Wantage	„	District	17 308
Walton	Derby	Tnship.	1 082	Wantage	„	Sub-dis.	7 304
Walton upon Trent	„	Parish	430	Wantage	„	Parish	3 925
Walton-le-Soken	Essex	Parish	697	Wantage	„	Tnship.	3 064
Walton Cardiff	Gloucester	Parish	70	**Wantage**	„	Town	3 064
Walton-le-Dale	Lancaster	Sub-dis.	8 654	Wantisden	Suffolk	Parish	106
Walton-le-Dale	„	Tnship.	7 383	Wapley & Codrington	Glouc.	Parish	358
Walton	„	Sub-dis.	11 834	Waplington	York	Tnship.	58
Walton on Hill	„	Parish	85 058	Wappenbury	Warwick	Parish	251
Walton on Hill	„	Tnship.	3 598	Wappenbury	„	Tnship.	98
Walton (Knaptoft P.)	Leicester	Hamlet	240	Wappenham	Northampton	Parish	650
Walton on Wolds	„	Parish	221	Wappenham	„	—	567
Walton, East	Norfolk	Parish	175	Wapping, St. John	Middlesex	Parish	4 038
Walton, West	„	Parish	950	Warbleton	Sussex	Parish	1 431
Walton	Northampton	Hamlet	209	Warblington	Hants	Parish	2 196

Name of Place.	County.	Description.	Population.
arborough	Oxon	Parish	764
arboys	Hunts	Sub-dis.	3 355
arboys	,,	Parish	1 911
arbstow	Cornwall	Parish	419
arburton	Cheshire	Parish	484
arcop..	Westmoreland	Parish	806
arden..	Beds	Parish	597
arden..	Kent	Parish	47
arden..	Northumberland	Parish	716
arden-Law	Durham	Tnship.	73
ardington	Oxon	Chap.	732
ardle ..	Cheshire	Tnship.	154
ardle St. James	Lancaster	Ecl. Dis.	2 176
ardleworth	,,	Sub-dis.	17 840
ardleworth	,,	Tnship.	17 840
ardleworth St. Jas.	,,	Ecl. Dis.	7 130
ardleworth St. Mary	,,	Ecl. Dis.	10 610
ardley	Rutland	Parish	68
ardlow	Derby	Tnship.	181
ardour	Wilts	Parish	710
are ..	Herts	L. Sub.	13 662
are ..	,,	District	16 515
are ..	,,	Sub-dis.	5 886
are ..	,,	Parish	5 397
are ..	,,	Town	5 002
are, Christchurch	,,	Ecl. Dis.	1 690
areham	Dorset	Division	10 846
areham	,,	L. Sub.	18 216
areham	,,	District	17 072
areham	,,	Sub-dis.	6 230
areham	,,	P. Bor.	6 694
arehorne	Kent	Parish	412
arenford	Northumberland	Tnship.	20
arenton	,,	Tnship.	114
areside, Trinity	Herts	Ecl. Dis.	696
aresley	Hunts	Parish	292
arfield	Berks	Parish	1 497
arford, Great	Cheshire	Tnship.	380
argrave	Berks	Hund.	4 940
argrave	,,	Sub-dis.	6 658
argrave	,,	Parish	1 806
arham All Saints	Norfolk	Parish	318
arham St. Mary	,,	Parish	74
ark	Northumberland	Parish	899
ark ..	,,	Tnship.	546
arkleigh	Devon	Parish	330
arksburn	Northumberland	Tnship.	199
arkton	Northampton	Parish	315
arkworth	,,	Parish	1 111
arkworth	,,	—	35
arkworth	Northumberland	Sub-dis.	7 631
arkworth	,,	Parish	5 087
arkworth	,,	Tnship.	730
arlaby	York	Tnship.	81
Warleggon	Cornwall	Parish	295
Warley ..	York	Tnship.	6 482
Warley, Great	Essex	Parish	1 220
Warley, Gt., Christch.	,,	Ecl. Dis.	1 734
Warley, Little	,,	Parish	485
Warley-Salop	Worcester	Tnship.	372
Warley-Wigorn	,,	Hamlet	1 183
Warlingham	Surrey	Parish	602
Warmfield	York	Parish	1 045
Warmfield w. Heath	,,	Tnship.	783
Warmingham	Cheshire	Parish	1 205
Warmingham	,,	Tnship.	358
Warminghurst	Sussex	Parish	106
Warmington	Northampton	Parish	724
Warmington	Warwick	Parish	452
Warminster	Wilts	Hund.	10 098
Warminster	,,	L. Sub.	15 670
Warminster	,,	District	15 942
Warminster	,,	Sub-dis.	7 643
Warminster	,,	Parish	5 995
Warminster	,,	Town	3 675
Warminster, Christch.	,,	Ecl. Dis.	2 166
Warmley, St. Barnabas	Glouc..	Ecl. Dis.	2 016
Warmsworth	York	Parish	361
Warmwell	Dorset	Parish	148
Warnborough, South	Hants	Parish	369
Warndon	Worcester	Parish	164
Warnford	Hants	Parish	460
Warnham	Sussex	Parish	1 006
Warningcamp	,,	Tithing	107
Warpsgrove	Oxon	Parish	20
Warren ..	Pembroke	Parish	121
Warren Houses	Suffolk	Parish	26
Warrington	Bucks	Hamlet	74
Warrington	Lancaster	L. Sub.	84 087
Warrington	Lanc. & Chesh.	District	43 875
Warrington	Lancaster	Sub-dis.	24 050
Warrington	,,	Parish	26 960
Warrington	,,	Tnship.	24 050
Warrington	Lanc. & Chesh. {	M. Bor.	26 431
		P. Bor.	26 947
Warrington, St. Paul	Lancaster	Ecl. Dis.	9 266
Warsill ..	York	Parish	82
Warsop ..	Notts	Sub-dis.	3 689
Warsop ..	,,	Parish	1 426
Warsop ..	,,	Tnship.	1 374
Warter ..	York	Parish	539
Warthill	,,	Parish	217
Warthill Copyhold	,,	Tnship.	190
Warthill Freehold	,,	Tnship.	27
Wartling	Sussex	Parish	914
Wartnaby	Leicester	Chap.	116
Warton..	Lancaster	Sub-dis.	3 562
Warton..	,,	Parish	2 161

Name of Place.	County.	Description.	Population.	Name of Place.	County.	Description.	Population.
Warton w. Lindeth	*Lancaster* ..	Tnship.	581	Watermillock ..	*Cumberland*	Chap.	576
Warton.. ..	,, ..	Tnship.	446	Water Newton..	*Hunts* ..	Parish	149
Warton.. ..	,, ..	Ecl. Dis.	1 325	Water Orton ..	*Warwick* ..	Hamlet	218
Warton..	*Northumberland*	Tnship.	55	Waterperry ..	*Oxon* ..	Parish	231
Warton, Trinity	*Warwick* ..	Ecl. Dis.	582	Waterperry ..	,, ..	—	200
Warwick ..	*Cumberland*	Parish	324	Waterstock ..	,, ..	Parish	147
Warwick ..	,, ..	Tnship.	205	Water Stratford .	*Bucks* ..	Parish	179
Warwick Bridge	,, ..	Tnship.	994	Waters Upton ..	*Salop* ..	Parish	206
Warwickshire ..	.. ..	County	561 855	Watford ..	*Herts* ..	L. Sub.	20 355
Northern Division ..	..	N. Div.	460 347	Watford ..	,, ..	District	20 355
Southern Division ..	..	S. Div.	101 508	Watford ..	,, ..	Sub-dis.	7 418
Warwick ..	*Warwick* ..	L. Sub.	56 131	Watford ..	,, ..	Parish	7 418
Warwick ..	,, ..	District	44 047	Watford ..	,, ..	—	4 347
Warwick ..	,, ..	Sub-dis.	10 589	Watford ..	,, ..	Town	4 385
Warwick ..	,, ..	Borough	10 570	Watford, St. Andrew	,, ..	Ecl. Dis.	946
Warwick, St. Paul	,, ..	Ecl. Dis.	2 545	Watford ..	*Northampton*	Parish	450
Wasdale Head ..	*Cumberland*	Tnship.	49	Wath ..	*York* ..	Sub-dis.	1 700
Wasdale, Nether	,, ..	Chap.	192	Wath	,, ..	Parish	718
Washbourne, Great	*Gloucester*	Parish	83	Wath	,, ..	Tnship.	207
Washbourne, Little	,, ..	Hamlet	28	Wath	,, ..	Sub-dis.	8 468
Washbrook ..	*Suffolk* ..	Parish	451	Wath upon Dearne	,, ..	Parish	13 820
Washfield ..	*Devon* ..	Sub-dis.	2 731	Wath upon Dearne	,, ..	Tnship.	1 690
Washfield ..	,, ..	Parish	471	Wath ..	,, ..	Tnship.	18
Washford Pyne .	,, ..	Parish	182	Watlington ..	*Norfolk* ..	Parish	588
Washingborough	*Lincoln* ..	Parish	1 213	Watlington ..	*Oxon* ..	L. Sub.	15 468
Washingborough	,, ..	Tnship.	589	Watlington ..	,, ..	Sub-dis.	4 409
Washingley ..	*Hunts* ..	Parish	75	Watlington ..	,, ..	Parish	1 938
Washington ..	*Durham* ..	Parish	5 981	Wattisfield ..	*Suffolk* ..	Parish	615
Washington ..	,, ..	Tnship.	1 829	Wattisham ..	,, ..	Parish	220
Washington ..	*Sussex* ..	Sub-dis.	4 189	Watton ..	*Herts* ..	Sub-dis.	4 138
Washington ..	,, ..	Parish	908	Watton	,, ..	Parish	864
Washton ..	*York* ..	Tnship.	148	Watton ..	*Norfolk* ..	Sub-dis.	6 056
Wasing ..	*Berks* ..	Parish	76	Watton	,, ..	Parish	1 365
Wasperton ..	*Warwick* ..	Parish	269	Watton ..	*York* ..	Parish	343
Wass ..	*York* ..	Tnship.	129	Wauldby ..	,, ..	Tnship.	47
Watchfield ..	*Berks* ..	Tnship.	431	Wavendon ..	*Bucks* ..	Parish	879
Waterbeach ..	*Cambs* ..	Parish	1 485	Waver Holme, East	*Cumberld.*..	Tnship.	526
Watercombe ..	*Dorset* ..	Parish	37	Waverley ..	*Surrey* ..	Ville	52
Waterden ..	*Norfolk* ..	Parish	44	Waverton ..	*Cheshire* ..	Parish	736
Water Eaton ..	*Bucks* ..	Hamlet	242	Waverton ..	,, ..	Tnship.	337
Water Eaton ..	*Oxon* ..	Hamlet	115	Waverton ..	*Cumberland*	Tnship.	574
Water Eaton ..	*Wilts* ..	Tithing	85	Wavertree ..	*Lancaster* ..	Sub-dis.	10 845
Waterfall ..	*Stafford* ..	Parish	533	Wavertree ..	,, ..	Tnship.	5 392
Waterfall ..	,, ..	Tnship.	468	Wavertree, Trinity	,, ..	Ecl. Dis.	3 065
Water Fulford ..	*York* ..	Tnship.	35	Wavertree, St. Mary	,, ..	Ecl. Dis.	1 897
Watergall ..	*Warwick* ..	—	14	Wawne ..	*York* ..	Parish	408
Waterhead ..	*Cumberland*	Tnship.	410	Wawne	,, ..	Tnship.	322
Waterhead ..	*Lancaster* ..	Ecl. Dis.	3 941	Waxham ..	*Norfolk* ..	Parish	75
Wateringbury ..	*Kent* ..	Parish	1 370	Waxholme ..	*York* ..	Tnship.	84
Waterloo ..	*Hants* ..	Parish	243	Wayford ..	*Somerset* ..	Parish	191
Waterloo, Christch.	*Lancaster*	Ecl. Dis.	2 046	Wayland ..	*Norfolk* ..	Hund.	7 783
Waterloo Road 1st	*Surrey* ..	Sub-dis.	15 269	Wayland	,, ..	L. Sub.	7 783
Waterloo Road 2nd	,, ..	Sub-dis.	18 640	Wayland	,, ..	District	11 562
Waterloo, St. John	,, ..	Ecl. Dis.	10 262	Weald, North ..	*Essex* ..	Parish	842

Name of Place.	County.	Description.	Population.	Name of Place.	County.	Description.	Population.
Veald, South ..	Essex ..	Parish	5 209	Welborne ..	Norfolk ..	Parish	200
Veald, South ..	„ ..	—	2 116	Welbourn ..	Lincoln ..	Parish	664
Veald ..	Kent ..	Liberty	824	Welburn ..	York ..	Tnship.	121
Veald ..	Oxon ..	Hamlet	848	Welburn (Bulmer P.) „	„	Tnship.	575
Veardale ..	Durham ..	District	16 418	Welbury ..	„ ..	Parish	258
Veardley ..	York ..	Tnship.	171	Welby ..	Leicester ..	Chap.	64
Veare ..	Somerset ..	Parish	677	Welby ..	Lincoln ..	Parish	499
Vear-Gifford ..	Devon ..	Parish	494	Welches Dam ..	Cambridge..	Parish	132
Veasenham All Saints	Norfolk	Parish	360	Welcombe ..	Devon ..	Parish	209
Veasenham St. Peter	„ ..	Parish	320	Weldon..	Northampton	Sub-dis.	2 543
Veaver ..	Cheshire ..	Tnship.	148	Weldon, Great ..	„ ..	Parish	816
Veaverham ..	„ ..	Sub-dis.	6 449	Weldon, Great ..	„ ..	Hamlet	302
Veaverham ..	„ ..	Parish	2 782	Weldon, Little ..	„ ..	Hamlet	514
Veaverham ..	„ ..	Tnship.	1 530	Welford ..	Berks ..	Parish	1 030
Veaverthorpe ..	York ..	Parish	1 033	Welford ..	Glouc. & War.	Parish	677
Veaverthorpe ..	„ ..	Tnship.	601	Welford ..	Northampton	Parish	1 099
Vebheath ..	Worcester ..	Tnship.	823	Welham ..	Leicester ..	Parish	65
Vebtree ..	Hereford ..	Hund.	8 944	Well ..	Lincoln ..	Wapen.	3 727
Veddiker ..	Cumberland	Tnship.	70	Well ..	..	Parish	99
Veddington ..	Warwick ..	Parish	74	Well ..	York ..	Parish	963
Vedgwood ..	Stafford ..	Tnship.	783	Well ..	„ ..	Tnship.	371
Vedhampton ..	Wilts ..	Tithing	231	Welland ..	Worcester ..	Parish	802
Vedmore ..	Somerset ..	Sub-dis.	6 265	Wellesborough, &c.	Leicester ..	Hamlet	93
Vedmore ..	„ ..	Parish	3 653	Wellesbourne ..	Warwick	Sub-dis.	3 026
Vednesbury ..	Stafford ..	Sub-dis.	21 968	Wellesbourne Hastings	„ ..	Parish	800
Vednesbury ..	„ ..	Parish	21 968	Wellesbourne Mountford	„ ..	Parish	742
Vednesbury ..	„ ..	Town	15 298	Wellhaugh	Northumberland	Tnship.	522
Vednesbury, St. Jas. „		Ecl. Dis.	6 631	Wellingborough	Northampton	L. Sub.	25 591
Vednesbury, St. John „		Ecl. Dis.	3 437	Wellingborough	Nptn. & Beds	District	24 224
Vednesfield ..	„ ..	Tnship.	8 553	Wellingborough	Northampton	Sub-dis.	10 885
Vednesfield Heath „	..	Ecl. Dis.	5 049	Wellingborough	„ ..	Parish	6 382
Veedon ..	Bucks ..	Hamlet	425	**Wellingborough**	„ ..	Town	6 067
Veedon ..	Northampton	Sub-dis.	5 926	Wellingham ..	Norfolk ..	Parish	145
Veedon Beck ..	„ ..	Parish	2 189	Wellingore ..	Lincoln ..	Parish	943
Veedon Loys ..	„ ..	Parish	555	Wellington ..	Hereford ..	Parish	626
Veeford ..	Stafford ..	Parish	399	Wellington ..	Salop ..	District	23 873
Veeford ..	„ ..	Tnship.	290	Wellington ..	„ ..	Sub-dis.	14 046
Veeke ..	Hants ..	Parish	529	Wellington ..	„ ..	Parish	12 998
Weekley ..	Northampton	Parish	268	**Wellington** ..	„ ..	Town	5 576
Week St. Mary..	Cornwall ..	Sub-dis.	2 570	Wellington Christch. „	..	Ecl. Dis.	3 654
Week St. Mary..	„ ..	Parish	611	Wellington ..	Somerset ..	L. Sub.	16 045
Week St. Germans	Devon ..	Parish	325	Wellington ..	Som. & Devon	District	20 480
Weel ..	York ..	Tnship.	126	Wellington ..	Somerset ..	Sub-dis.	8 305
Weeley ..	Essex ..	Parish	630	Wellington ..	„ ..	Parish	6 006
Weethley ..	Warwick ..	Parish	33	**Wellington** ..	„ ..	Town	3 689
Weeting All Saints	Norfolk ..	Parish	365	Wellington ..	Stafford ..	Ecl. Dis.	5 555
Weeton ..	Lancaster ..	Ecl. Dis.	1 017	Wellow, East ..	Hants ..	Parish	332
Weeton w. Preese	„ ..	Tnship.	465	Wellow..	Notts ..	Parish	468
Weeton ..	York ..	Tnship.	317	Wellow ..	Somerset ..	Hund.	9 783
Weeton St. Barnabas „	..	Ecl. Dis.	317	Wellow..	„ ..	Parish	1 087
Weetslade	Northumberland	Tnship.	2 828	Wellow, West ..	Wilts ..	Parish	408
Weighton, Market	York ..	Parish	2 589	Wells ..	Norfolk ..	Sub-dis.	7 301
Weirs ..	Hants ..	Parish	4	Wells next the Sea „	..	Parish	3 464
Welbeck ..	Notts ..	Parish	12	**Wells next the Sea** „	..	Town	3 098

Name of Place.	County.	Description.	Population.	Name of Place.	County.	Description.	Population.
Wells	Somerset	L. Sub.	21 889	Wenlock	Salop	M. Bor.	19 699
Wells Forum	,,	Hund.	7 314			P. Bor.	21 590
Wells	,,	District	21 889	Wennington	Essex	Parish	130
Wells	,,	Sub-dis.	11 254	Wennington	Lancaster	Tnship.	180
Wells	,,	City	4 648	Wensley	York	Parish	2 337
Wells, East, St. Thos.	,,	Ecl. Dis.	973	Wensley	,,	Tnship.	318
Welney	Norf. & Cambs	Chap.	1 101	Wensley & Snitterton	Derby	Tnship.	582
Welsh Bicknor	Hereford	Parish	80	Wentllooge	Monmouth	Hund.	51 442
Welsh Hampton	Salop	Parish	516	Wentnor	Salop	Parish	664
Welsh Newton	Hereford	Parish	226	Wentworth	Cambs	Parish	180
Welshpool	Montgomery	L. Sub.	6 652	Wentworth	York	Tnship.	1 650
Welshpool	,,	Hund.	2 895	Wenvoe	Glamorgan	Parish	504
Welshpool	,,	Parish	4 814	Weobly	Hereford	District	9 018
				Weobly	,,	Sub-dis.	5 317
Welshpool	,,	M. Bor.	7 304	Weobly	,,	Parish	849
		P. Bor.	5 004	Wepre	Flint	Tnship.	709
Welsh St. Donats	Glamorgan	Parish	275	Wereham	Norfolk	Parish	597
Welsh Whittle	Lancaster	Tnship.	148	Werneth	Cheshire	Tnship.	3 464
Welton	Lincoln	Parish	692	Werneth	,,	Ecl. Dis.	3 464
Welton in Marsh	,,	Parish	468	Wernith, St. Thos.	Lancaster	Ecl. Dis.	5 888
Welton-le-Wold	,,	Parish	335	Werrington	Devon	Parish	664
Welton	Northampton	Parish	592	Werrington	Northampton	Hamlet	697
Welton	Northumberland	Tnship.	93	Wervin	Cheshire	Tnship.	78
Welton	York	Parish	863	Wesham & Medlar	Lancaster	Tnship.	563
Welton	,,	Tnship.	688	Wessington	Derby	Tnship.	519
Welwick	,,	Parish	472	Wessington Christch.	,,	Ecl. Dis.	519
Welwyn	Herts	L. Sub.	3 438	West	Cornwall	Hund.	19 678
Welwyn	,,	Sub-dis.	2 211	West	,,	L. Sub.	24 367
Welwyn	,,	Union	2 211	West	Westmoreland	Ward	8 072
Welwyn	,,	Parish	1 612	West Acklam	York	Parish	108
Wem	Salop	District	10 644	West Acomb	Northumberland	Tnship.	800
Wem	,,	Sub-dis.	7 282	Westacre	Norfolk	Parish	415
Wem	,,	Parish	3 802	West Adderbury	Oxon	Tnship.	346
Wembdon	Somerset	Parish	934	West Allington	Lincoln	Parish	135
Wembley, St. John	Middlesex	Ecl. Dis.	896	West Alvington	Devon	Sub-dis.	4 835
Wembury	Devon	Parish	561	West Alvington	,,	Parish	925
Wembworthy	,,	Parish	453	West Anstey	,,	Parish	299
Wendens Ambo	Essex	Parish	419	West Appleton, &c.	York	Tnship.	115
Wendlebury	Oxon	Parish	257	West Ardsley	,,	Parish	1 646
Wendling	Norfolk	Parish	371	West Ashby	Lincoln	Parish	526
Wendon-Lofts	Essex	Parish	61	West Ashford	Kent	District	15 137
Wendover	Bucks	Sub-dis.	5 042	West Ashton	Wilts	Tithing	314
Wendover	,,	Parish	1 932	West Ashton, St. John	,,	Ecl. Dis.	314
Wendron	Cornwall	Sub-dis.	9 314	West Auckland	Durham	Tnship.	2 581
Wendron	,,	Parish	9 851	West Ayton	York	Tnship.	385
Wendy	Cambs	Parish	128	West Bagborough	Somerset	Parish	495
Wenham, Great	Suffolk	Parish	260	West Barkwith	Lincoln	Parish	150
Wenham, Little	,,	Parish	95	West Barming	Kent	Parish	24
Wenhaston	,,	Sub-dis.	8 791	West Barsham	Norfolk	Parish	92
Wenhaston	,,	Parish	948	West Beckham	,,	Parish	329
Wenlock	Salop	Hund.	1 774	Westbere	Kent	Parish	220
Wenlock	,,	L. Sub.	19 690	West Bergholt	Essex	Parish	906
Wenlock, Little	,,	Parish	988	West Bilney	Norfolk	Parish	253
Wenlock, Much	,,	Parish	2 494	West Blatchington	Sussex	Parish	59

Name of Place.	County.	Description.	Population.	Name of Place.	County.	Description.	Population.
Westborough	Lincoln	Parish	245	West Chinnock	Somerset	Parish	553
Westbourne	Sussex	District	6 957	West Cholderton	Wilts	Parish	191
Westbourne	,,	Sub-dis.	3 726	West Clandon	Surrey	Parish	329
Westbourne	,,	Parish	2 165	West Clayton	York	Tnship.	1 532
Westbourne Park	Middlesex	Ecl. Dis.	8 488	West Cliffe	Kent	Parish	122
West Bradenham	Norfolk	Parish	387	West Coker	Somerset	Parish	1 012
West Bradford	York	Tnship.	289	Westcote	Gloucester	Parish	245
West Bradley	Somerset	Parish	136	Westcott	Bucks	Hamlet	278
West Bretton	York	Tnship.	504	Westcott Trinity	Surrey	Ecl. Dis.	1 060
West Bridgford	Notts	Parish	390	**West Cowes**	Hants, I. W.	Town	5 482
West Bridgford	,,	Tnship.	280	West Cowes	,,	,,	Ecl. Dis.	4 591
W. Brompton, St. Mary	Mddlx.	Ecl. Dis.	4 236	West Cranmore	Somerset	Parish	292
West Bromwich	Stafford	L. Sub.	71 325	West Dean	Gloucester	Tnship.	8 254
West Bromwich	Staff. & Worc.	District	92 480	West Dean	Sussex	Parish	681
W. Bromwich, N. E.	Stafford	Sub-dis.	20 207	Westdean	,,	Parish	153
W. Bromwich, S.W.	,,	Sub-dis.	21 588	West Dean	Wilts & Hants	Parish	446
West Bromwich	,,	Parish	41 795	West Dean	,, ,,	—	310
West Bromwich	,,	Town	17 024	West Deeping	Lincoln	Parish	349
West Bromwich Chrch.	,,	Ecl. Dis.	22 246	West Denton	Northumberland	Tnship.	466
West Bromwich Trinity	,,	Ecl. Dis.	4 593	West Derby	Lancaster	Hund.	263 716
West Broughton	Lancaster	Sub-dis.	3 169	West Derby	,,	District	225 845
West Broughton	,,	Tnship.	1 183	West Derby	,,	Union	156 561
West Brunton	Northumberland	Tnship.	128	West Derby	,,	Sub-dis.	52 740
West Buckland	Devon	Parish	321	West Derby	,,	Parish	52 694
West Buckland	Somerset	Parish	901	West Dereham	Norfolk	Parish	679
West Budleigh	Devon	Hund.	2 981	West Dowlish	Somerset	Parish	52
West Bulmer	York	L. Sub.	10 501	West Down	Devon	Parish	554
West Burton	Notts	Parish	67	West Drayton	Middlesex	Parish	951
Westbury	Bucks	Parish	379	West Drayton	Notts	Parish	96
Westbury	Gloucester	Hund.	7 681	West Ella	York	Tnship.	154
Westbury	,,	Sub-dis.	10 409	West End, Mortimer	Hants	Tithing	442
Westbury on Severn	,,	District	20 189	West End, St. James	,,	Ecl. Dis.	2 141
Westbury on Severn	,,	Parish	2 501	Westerdale	York	Parish	279
Westbury on Trym	,,	Parish	8 329	Westerfield	Suffolk	Parish	325
Westbury on Trym	,,	—	1 975	Westerham	Kent	Parish	2 196
Westbury	Salop	Sub-dis.	2 545	Westerleigh	Gloucester	Parish	1 582
Westbury	,,	Parish	2 545	Westerton	Durham	Tnship.	196
Westbury	,,	Tnship.	1 655	West Exe, St. Paul	Devon	Ecl. Dis.	2 622
Westbury	Somerset	Parish	664	Westfa	Carmarthen	Hamlet	1 511
Westbury	Wilts	Hund.	6 495	West Farlam	Cumberland	Tnship.	498
Westbury	,,	District	11 751	West Farleigh	Kent	Parish	399
Westbury	,,	Sub-dis.	5 751	West Felton	Salop	Parish	1 067
Westbury	,,	Parish	6 495	Westfield	Norfolk	Parish	124
Westbury, &c.	,,	Tnship.	5 751	Westfield	Sussex	Parish	883
Westbury	,,	P. Bor.	6 495	Westfirle	,,	Sub-dis.	2 379
West Butterwick, &c.	Lincoln	Tnship.	907	West Firle	,,	Union	2 379
West Butterwick	,,	Ecl. Dis.	907	Westfirle	,,	Parish	631
Westby w. Plumpton	Lancaster	Tnship.	601	West Firsby	Lincoln	Tnship.	61
West Camel	Somerset	Parish	338	West Flegg	Norfolk	Sub-dis.	4 571
West Challow	Berks	Tnship.	192	West Fordington	Dorset	Ecl. Dis.	1 059
West Chelborough	Dorset	Parish	73	Westgate	Northumberland	Sub-dis.	37 477
West Chevington	Nrthumberld.	Tnship.	161	Westgate	,,	Tnship.	21 272
West Chickerell	Dorset	Parish	660	West Gilling	York	Wapen.	16 115
West Chiltington	Sussex	Parish	668	West Gilling	,,	L. Sub.	21 078

Name of Place.	County.	Description.	Population.	Name of Place.	County.	Description.	Population.
West Grimstead	*Wilts* ..	Parish	251	West Knighton	*Dorset* ..	Parish	26:
West Grinstead	*Sussex*	Parish	1 403	West Knoyle ..	*Wilts* ..	Parish	18:
West Hackney ..	*Middlesex* ..	Sub-dis.	24 265	West Langdon ..	*Kent* ..	Parish	10(
West Hackney ..	,, ..	Ecl. Dis.	24 265	West Langton ..	*Leicester* ..	Tnship.	8:
West Haddlesey	*York* ..	Tnship.	213	W. Lavington, St. Mary *Sussex*		Ecl. Dis.	17:
West Haddon ..	*Northampton*	Parish	963	West Lavington .	*Wilts* ..	Parish	1 58:
West Hagbourne	*Berks* ..	Liberty	164	West Lavington .	,, ..	—	97
West Haggerstone	*Middlesex* ..	Sub-dis.	23 260	West Layton ..	*York* ..	Tnship.	8:
Westhall	*Suffolk* ..	Parish	468	West Leake ..	*Notts* ..	Parish	17
West Hallam ..	*Derby* ..	Parish	559	West Leeds ..	*York* ..	Sub-dis.	47 23
West Halton ..	*Lincoln* ..	Parish	422	West Leicester ..	*Leicester* ..	Sub-dis.	26 99(
West Halton ..	,, ..	Tnship.	315	West Leicester Forest ,,		Parish	5
West Halton ..	*York* ..	Tnship.	131	Westleigh ..	*Devon* ..	Parish	49
West Ham ..	*Essex* ..	District	59 319	West Leigh ..	*Lancaster* ..	Sub-dis.	9 44:
West Ham ..	,, ..	Sub-dis.	25 195	West Leigh ..	,, ..	Tnship.	4 43
West Ham ..	,, ..	Parish	38 331	Westleton ..	*Suffolk* ..	Sub-dis.	10 07
Westham ..	*Sussex* ..	Sub-dis.	2 594	Westleton ..	,, ..	Parish	94(
Westham ..	,, ..	Parish	833	West Lexham ..	*Norfolk* ..	Parish	15:
Westhampnett ..	,, ..	District	14 811	Westley ..	*Suffolk* ..	Parish	14(
Westhampnett ..	,, ..	Parish	502	Westley-Waterless *Cambs* ..		Parish	21:
West Hang	*York* ..	Wapen.	14 788	West Lilburn *Northumberland*		Tnship.	24:
West Hanney ..	*Berks* ..	Tnship.	384	West Linton ..	*Cumberland*	Tnship.	56:
West Hanningfield	*Essex* ..	Parish	527	West Littleton ..	*Gloucester* ..	Parish	12(
West Hardwick .	*York* ..	Tnship.	86	West Lockinge ..	*Berks* ..	Hamlet	6(
West Harle	*Northumberland*	Tnship.	17	West London ..	*Middlesex* ..	District	27 14:
West Harling ..	*Norfolk* ..	Parish	124	West London ..	,, ..	Union	26 99:
West Harlsey ..	*York* ..	Tnship.	61	West London North ,, ..		Sub-dis.	11 75(
West Harnham .	*Wilts* ..	Parish	285	West London South ,, ..		Sub-dis.	15 39:
West Harptree ..	*Somerset* ..	Parish	539	West Looe	*Cornwall* ..	Town	77(
West Harroldston	*Pembroke* ..	Parish	149	West Lulworth ..	*Dorset* ..	Parish	44(
West Hartford	*Northumberland*	Tnship.	62	West Lydford ..	*Somerset* ..	Parish	32(
West Hatch ..	*Somerset* ..	Parish	432	West Lynn, St. Peter *Norfolk* .		Parish	46:
W. Hartlepool, Ch.Ch. *Durham*		Ecl. Dis.	9 708	West Macclesfield *Cheshire* ..		Sub-dis.	16 57:
West Haukswell *York* ..		Tnship.	58	West Maidstone .	*Kent* ..	Sub-dis.	10 90:
West Heddon *Northumberland*		Tnship.	36	West Malling ..	,, ..	Parish	2 08(
West Hendred ..	*Berks* ..	Parish	351	West Markham .	*Notts* ..	Parish	19:
West Herrington *Durham* ..		Tnship.	752	West Marsh, Trinity *Kent* ..		Ecl. Dis.	45:
West Heslerton .	*York* ..	Tnship.	341	West Matfen *Northumberland*		Tnship.	35:
Westhide ..	*Hereford* ..	Chap.	174	West Meon ..	*Hants* ..	Sub-dis.	2 17:
West Hoathly ..	*Sussex* ..	Parish	1 120	West Meon ..	,, ..	Parish	84:
West Horndon ..	*Essex* ..	Parish	94	West Mersea ..	*Essex* ..	Parish	94:
Westhorpe ..	*Suffolk* ..	Parish	227	Westmeston ..	*Sussex* ..	Parish	56:
West Horsley ..	*Surrey* ..	Parish	706	Westmeston ..	,, ..	—	288
Westhoughton ..	*Lancaster* ..	Sub-dis.	5 156	Westmill ..	*Herts* ..	Parish	35:
Westhoughton ..		Tnship.	5 156	Westminster ..	*Gloucester* ..	Hund.	2 924
,, St. Bartholomew ,, ..		Ecl. Dis.	8 879	Westminster ..	*Middlesex* ..	District	68 213
West Hyde, St. Thos. *Herts* ..		Ecl. Dis.	466	Westminster ..	,, ..	Division	250 74:
West Hythe ..	*Kent* ..	Parish	130	Westminster ..	,, ..	P. City	254 62:
West Ilsley ..	*Berks* ..	Parish	432	All Saints ..	,, ..	Ecl. Dis.	7 04:
West Itchenor ..	*Sussex* ..	Parish	167	Christchurch ..	,, ..	Ecl. Dis.	6 874
West Keal ..	*Lincoln* ..	Parish	511	St. Andrew ..	,, ..	Ecl. Dis.	4 028
West Kington ..	*Wilts* ..	Parish	405	St. Luke ..	,, ..	Ecl. Dis.	9 219
West Kirby ..	*Cheshire* ..	Parish	2 059	St. Mary ..	,, ..	Ecl. Dis.	9 76:
West Kirby ..	,, ..	Tnship.	413	St. Matthew ..	,, ..	Ecl. Dis.	7 536

Name of Place.	County.	Description.	Population.	Name of Place.	County.	Description.	Population.
St. Stephen	Middlesex	Ecl. Dis.	7 127	Weston-Lullingfield	Salop	Ecl. Dis.	319
Trinity	,,	Ecl. Dis.	6 365	Weston Rhyn	,,	Tnship.	1 081
Westminster St. Margt.	,,	Parish	30 730	Weston & Whixhill	,,	Chap.	265
Ward No. 1	,,	Ward	7 558	Weston	Somerset	Parish	3 127
Ward No. 2	,,	Ward	13 737	Weston-Bamfylde	,,	Parish	146
Ward No. 3	,,	Ward	9 435	Weston in Gordano	,,	Parish	175
Westminster St. John	,,	Parish	37 483	Weston super Mare	,,	Parish	8 038
Ward No. 1	,,	Ward	11 049	Christchurch	,,	Ecl. Dis.	1 597
Ward No. 2	,,	Ward	15 513	Emmanuel	,,	Ecl. Dis.	2 434
Ward No. 3	,,	Ward	10 921	Weston Zoyland	,,	Parish	894
West Monkton	Somerset	Parish	1 153	Weston Jones	Stafford	Tnship.	97
West Moor	,,	—	31	Weston un. Lizard	,,	Parish	275
Westmoreland		County	60 817	Weston upon Trent	,,	Parish	502
West Moulsey	Surrey	Parish	459	Weston	Suffolk	Parish	261
West Ness	York	Tnship.	57	Weston Coney	,,	Parish	254
West Newton, &c.	Cumberland	Tnship.	649	Weston & Ember	Surrey	Hamlet	1 718
W. Newton St. Mathw.	,,	Ecl. Dis.	422	Weston un. Weatherley	Warw.	Parish	274
West Newton	Norfolk	Parish	268	Weston	York	Parish	450
West Newton	Northumberland	Tnship.	95	Weston	,,	Tnship.	112
West Newton	York	Tnship.	220	Westoning	Beds	Parish	784
Westoe	Durham	Sub-dis.	29 382	West Orchard	Dorset	Parish	103
Westoe	,,	Tnship.	26 266	West Overton	Wilts	Tnship.	429
Westoe, St. Hilda	,,	Ecl. Dis.	12 133	Westow	York	Sub-dis.	2 952
West Ogwell	Devon	Parish	51	Westow	,,	Parish	635
Weston Turville	Bucks	Parish	724	Westow	,,	Tnship.	409
Weston Underwood	,,	Parish	398	West Park	Wilts	Tithing	6
Weston-Colville	Cambs	Parish	537	West Parley	Dorset	Parish	268
Weston	Cheshire	Tnship.	965	West Peckham	Kent	Parish	446
Weston (Wybunbury P.)	,,	Tnship.	500	West Pennard	Somerset	Parish	836
Weston All Saints	,,	Ecl. Dis.	673	West Pickering Lythe	York	L. Sub.	10 353
Weston Underwood	Derby	Tnship.	227	West Pinchbeck	Lincoln	Ecl. Dis.	1 415
Weston upon Trent	,,	Parish	321	West Poringland	Norfolk	Parish	46
Weston-Peverell	Devon	Chap.	315	Westport St. Mary	Wilts	Parish	1 615
Weston Birt	Gloucester	Parish	190	West Putford	Devon	Parish	362
Weston, Kings	,,	Tithing	216	West Quantoxhead	Somerset	Parish	223
Weston, Lawrence	,,	Tithing	884	West Quarter	Northumberland	Tnship.	257
Weston sub Edge	,,	Parish	369	West Rainham	Norfolk	Parish	369
Weston upon Avon	Gloucester & Warwick	Parish	137	West Rainton	Durham	Tnship.	1 447
				West Rainton	,,	Ecl. Dis.	4 096
Weston upon Avon	Gloucester	—	80	West Rasen	Lincoln	Parish	245
Weston Corbet	Hants	Parish	13	West Ravendale	,,	Chap.	50
Weston Patrick	,,	Parish	165	West Retford	Notts	Parish	637
Weston-Beggard	Hereford	Parish	372	Westrill & Starmore	Leicester	—	3
Weston un. Penyard	,,	Parish	828	West Robeston	Pembroke	Parish	152
Weston	Herts	Parish	1 196	Westrop	Wilts	Tithing	714
Weston, Old	Hunts	Parish	426	West Rounton	York	Parish	222
Weston	Lincoln	Parish	750	West Row	Suffolk	Watch	1 294
Weston-Longville	Norfolk	Parish	471	West Rudham	Norfolk	Parish	487
Weston by Welland	Nrthamptn.	Parish	204	West Scaleby	Cumberland	Tnship.	342
Weston-Favell	,,	Parish	470	West Scrafton	York	Tnship.	112
Weston	Notts	Parish	380	West Sculcoates	,,	Sub-dis.	15 007
Weston on Green	Oxon	Parish	459	West Sedgemore	Somerset	—	6
Weston, South	,,	Parish	92	West Shaftoe	Northumberland	Tnship.	31
Weston	Salop	Tnship.	44	West Sheffield	York	Sub-dis.	17 307

Name of Place.	County.	Description.	Population.	Name of Place.	County.	Description.	Population.
West Shefford ..	Berks ..	Parish	538	West Worlington	Devon ..	Parish	193
West Sherborne .	Hants ..	Parish	649	West Wratting..	Cambs ..	Parish	777
West Shutford ..	Oxon ..	Tnship.	360	West Wretham .	Norfolk ..	Parish	207
W. Smethwick, St. Paul	Staff. ..	Ecl. Dis.	2 817	West Wycombe .	Bucks & Oxon	Sub-dis.	7 156
West Somerton..	Norfolk ..	Parish	244	West Wycombe .	Bucks ..	Parish	2 161
West Stafford ..	Dorset ..	Parish	220	West Wymer ..	Norfolk ..	Sub-dis.	20 159
West Stockwith .	Notts ..	Tnship.	538	Wetheral ..	Cumberland	Sub-dis.	3 886
West Stoke ..	Sussex ..	Parish	94	Wetheral ..	,, ..	Parish	3 377
West Stow ..	Suffolk ..	Parish	238	Wetheral ..	,, ..	Tnship.	666
West Stower ..	Dorset ..	Parish	215	Wetherby ..	York ..	District	6 668
West Sunderland	Durham ..	Sub-dis.	8 517	Wetherby ..	,, ..	Sub-dis.	6 668
West Tadcaster .	York ..	Tnship.	1 646	Wetherby ..	,, ..	Tnship.	1 682
West Tanfield ..	,, ..	Parish	623	Wetherden ..	Suffolk ..	Parish	479
West Tarring ..	Sussex ..	Parish	606	Wetheringsett ..	,, ..	Parish	1 072
West Tarset	Northumberland	Tnship.	112	Wetherley ..	Cambs ..	Hund.	5 212
West Teignmouth	Devon ..	Parish	3 963	Wethersfield ..	Essex ..	Parish	1 727
West Thorney ..	Sussex ..	Parish	93	Wettenhall ..	Cheshire ..	Tnship.	263
West Thornton..	Nthumbland.	Tnship.	62	Wetton ..	Stafford ..	Parish	452
West Thorpe ..	Lincoln ..	Parish	54	Wetwang ..	York ..	Parish	827
West Thurrock..	Essex ..	Parish	1 039	Wetwang ..	,, ..	Tnship.	623
West Tilbury ..	,, ..	Parish	385	Wexham ..	Bucks ..	Parish	196
West Tisbury ..	Wilts ..	Parish	653	Weybourn ..	Norfolk ..	Parish	285
West Tisted ..	Hants ..	Parish	282	Weybread ..	Suffolk ..	Parish	713
West Tofts ..	Norfolk ..	Parish	193	Weybridge ..	Surrey ..	Parish	1 603
West Torrington	Lincoln ..	Parish	165	Weyhill.. ..	Hants ..	Parish	444
West Town St. Matthew	York	Ecl. Dis.	3 431	Weymouth ..	Dorset ..	District	27 328
West Tytherley .	Hants ..	Parish	469	Weymouth ..	,, ..	Sub-dis.	12 858
West Ville ..	Lincoln ..	Parish	150	Weymouth ..	,, ..	Parish	3 515
West Walton ..	Norfolk ..	Parish	950	**Weymouth** ..	,, ..	Borough	11 383
West Walton ..	Pembroke ..	Parish	397	Weymouth, St. John	,, ..	Ecl. Dis.	1 062
Westward ..	Cumberland	Parish	1 136	Whaddon ..	Bucks ..	Parish	955
West Ward ..	Westmoreland	L. Sub.	8 072	Whaddon ..	,, ..	Tnship.	493
West Ward ..	,, ..	District	8 072	Whaddon ..	Cambs ..	Parish	319
West Ward (Leeds P.)	York ..	Ward	25 361	Whaddon ..	Gloucester ..	Parish	125
Westwell ..	Kent ..	Parish	999	Whaddon ..	Wilts ..	Parish	40
Westwell ..	Oxon ..	Parish	169	Whaley w. Yeardsley	Cheshire..	Tnship.	1 052
West Wellow ..	Wilts ..	Parish	408	Whalley ..	Lanc. & York	Sub-dis.	2 963
West Whelpington	Nrthumbld.	Tnship.	66	Whalley ..	,, ,,	Parish	167 456
Westwick ..	Cambs ..	Hamlet	78	Whalley ..	Lancaster ..	Tnship.	806
Westwick ..	Durham ..	Tnship.	76	Whalley Range..	,, ..	Ecl. Dis.	3 980
Westwick ..	Norfolk ..	Parish	207	Whalton	Northumberland	Parish	495
Westwick ..	York ..	Tnship.	26	Whalton ..	,, ..	Tnship.	314
West Wickham .	Cambs ..	Parish	550	Whaplode ..	Lincoln ..	Parish	2 462
West Wickham .	Kent ..	Parish	737	Whaplode Drove	,,	Hamlet	844
West Winch ..	Norfolk ..	Parish	470	Wharfedale ..	York ..	District	15 453
West Wittering .	Sussex ..	Parish	616	Wharram le Street	,,	Parish	140
West Witton ..	York ..	Parish	659	Wharram Percy .	,,	Parish	484
Westwood ..	Warwick ..	Ecl. Dis.	620	Wharram Percy .	,,	Tnship.	56
Westwood w. Iford	Wilts ..	Parish	469	Wharton ..	Cheshire ..	Tnship.	2 234
Westwood Park .	Worcester ..	Parish	22	Wharton, Christch.	,, ..	Ecl. Dis.	2 395
West Woodhay .	Berks ..	Parish	130	Wharton ..	Westmoreland	Tnship.	51
West Woodyates	Dorset ..	Parish	20	Whatborough ..	Leicester ..	Tnship.	13
West Worcester .	Worcester ..	Sub-dis.	8 593	Whatcote ..	Warwick ..	Parish	180
West Worldham	Hants ..	Parish	89	Whatcroft ..	Cheshire ..	Tnship.	72

Name of Place.	County.	Description.	Population.	Name of Place.	County.	Description.	Population.
Whatfield	Suffolk	Parish	340	Whissendine	Rutland	Parish	693
Whatley	Somerset	Parish	423	Whissonsett	Norfolk	Parish	692
Whatlington	Sussex	Parish	343	Whistley in Hurst	Berks	Liberty	1 178
Whatmore	Salop	Tnship.	59	Whiston	Lancaster	Tnship.	1 727
Whatton, Long	Leicester	Parish	779	Whiston	Northampton	Parish	69
Whatton	Notts	Parish	763	Whiston	Stafford	Tnship.	708
Whatton	,,	Tnship.	353	Whiston	York	Parish	1 185
Wheatacre, All Saints	Norfolk	Parish	160	Whistones	Worcester	Tithing	3 191
Wheatacre Burgh	,,	Parish	298	Whitacre, Nether	Warwick	Parish	479
Wheatenhurst	Gloucester	District	7 813	Whitacre, Over	,,	Parish	285
Wheatenhurst	,,	Parish	411	Whitbeck	Cumberland	Parish	213
Wheatfield	Oxon	Parish	89	Whitbourne	Hereford	Parish	891
Wheathampstead	Herts	Parish	1 960	Whitburn	Durham	Parish	1 215
Wheathill	Salop	Parish	123	Whitby	Cheshire	Tnship.	792
Wheathill	Somerset	Parish	38	Whitby Strand	York	Liberty	16 331
Wheatley-Carr-Booth	Lanc.	Tnship.	46	Whitby Strand	,,	L. Sub.	23 633
Wheatley, North	Notts	Parish	461	Whitby	,,	District	23 633
Wheatley, South	,,	Parish	32	Whitby	,,	Sub-dis.	14 484
Wheatley	Oxon	Sub-dis.	3 679	Whitby	,,	Parish	14 014
Wheatley	,,	Hamlet	1 031	Whitby	,,	Tnship.	8 142
Wheatley	,,	Ecl. Dis.	1 031	**Whitby**	,,	P. Bor.	12 051
Wheatley	York	Parish	137	Whitchester	Northumberland	Tnship.	46
Wheelock	Cheshire	Tnship.	588	Whitchurch	Bucks	Parish	884
Wheelock, Christch.	,,	Ecl. Dis.	1 869	Whitchurch	Devon	Parish	1 340
Wheelton	Lancaster	Tnship.	1 260	Whitchurch Canonico	Dorset	Sub-dis.	4 095
Wheldrake	York	Parish	678	Whitch. Canonicorum	,,	Parish	1 533
Wheldrake	,,	Tnship.	631	Whitchurch	Glamorgan	Parish	2 274
Whelnetham, Great	Suffolk	Parish	504	Whitchurch	Hants	District	5 522
Whelnetham, Little	,,	Parish	194	Whitchurch	,,	Sub-dis.	5 522
Whelpington, Kirk	Nrthumbld.	Tnship.	190	Whitchurch	,,	Parish	1 962
Whelpington, West	,,	Tnship.	66	Whitchurch	Hereford	Parish	857
Whenby	York	Parish	109	Whitchurch	Oxon & Berks	Parish	857
Whepstead	Suffolk	Parish	677	Whitchurch, St. Davids	Pemb.	Parish	1 085
Wherstead	,,	Parish	245	Whitchurch, Newport	,,	Parish	318
Wherwell	Hants	Parish	626	Whitchurch	Salop, &c.	District	11 272
Whessoe	Durham	Tnship.	153	Whitchurch	,,	Sub-dis.	7 651
Wheston	Derby	Hamlet	63	Whitchurch	Salop & Chesh.	Parish	6 093
Whetstone	Leicester	Parish	1 077	Whitchurch	Salop	Tnship.	5 986
Whetstone, St. John	Middlesex	Ecl. Dis.	1 801	**Whitchurch**	,,	Town	3 704
Whicham	Cumberland	Parish	327	Whitchurch	Somerset	Parish	394
Whichford	Warwick	Parish	698	Whitchurch	Warwick	Parish	234
Whichford w. Ascott	,,	—	496	Whitcliffe w. Thorpe	York	Tnship.	224
Whickham	Durham	Sub-dis.	5 921	Whitcombe	Dorset	Parish	71
Whickham	,,	Parish	5 921	Whitcomb Magna	Gloucester	Parish	165
Whickham	,,	Tnship.	1 277	Whitechapel	Lancaster	Ecl. Dis.	646
Whilton	Northampton	Parish	350	Whitechapel	Middlesex	District	78 970
Whimple	Devon	Parish	736	Whitechapel Church.	,,	Sub-dis.	8 062
Whinbergh	Norfolk	Parish	220	Whitechapel North	,,	Sub-dis.	12 122
Whinfell	Cumberland	Tnship.	86	Whitechapel	,,	Parish	37 454
Whinfell	Westmoreland	Tnship.	179	1 East Ward	,,	Ward	12 322
Whippingham	Hants, I. W.	Parish	3 915	2 Middle Ward	,,	Ward	10 032
Whipsnade	Beds	Parish	195	3 South Ward	,,	Ward	15 100
Whisby	Lincoln	Tnship.	90	Whitechapel, St. Jude	,,	Ecl. Dis.	6 652
Whishaw	Warwick	Parish	216	Whitechapel, St. Mark	,,	Ecl. Dis.	15 326

Name of Place.	County.	Description.	Population.	Name of Place	County.	Description.	Population.
Whitechapel ..	York ..	Ecl. Dis.	1 755	Whitridge	Northumberland	Tnship.	5
White Colne ..	Essex ..	Parish	400	Whitsbury ..	Wilts & Hants	Parish	204
Whitecross Street	Middlesex ..	Sub-dis.	14 778	Whitson ..	Monmouth ..	Parish	85
Whitefriars ..	Kent ..	Parish	10	Whitstable ..	Kent ..	Sub-dis.	5 221
Whitefriars ..	Leicester ..	Parish	119	Whitstable ..	„ ..	Parish	3 675
Whitefriars ..	Middlesex ..	Precinct	1 155	**Whitstable** ..	„ ..	Town	4 183
Whitefriars ..	York ..	Ward	1 807	Whitstone ..	Cornwall ..	Parish	391
Whitegate ..	Cheshire ..	Parish	1 535	Whitstone ..	Gloucester ..	Hund.	13 786
Whitehaven ..	Cumberland	District	39 950	Whitstone ..	Somerset ..	Hund.	12 030
Whitehaven ..	„ ..	Sub-dis.	14 064	Whittingham ..	Lancaster ..	Tnship.	583
Whitehaven ..	„ ..	Tnship.	14 064	Whittingham	Northumberland	Parish	1 923
Whitehaven ..	„ ..	P. Boro.	18 842	Whittingham ..	„ ..	Tnship.	703
Whitehaven Christch.	„ ..	Ecl. Dis.	4 131	Whittington ..	Derby ..	Parish	2 864
Holy Trinity..	„ ..	Ecl. Dis.	5 088	Whittington ..	Gloucester ..	Parish	217
St. James ..	„ ..	Ecl. Dis.	5 916	Whittington ..	Lancaster ..	Parish	421
St. Nicholas ..	„ ..	Ecl. Dis.	3 815	Whittington, Great	Nrthumbld.	Tnship.	224
White Lackington	Somerset ..	Parish	260	Whittington, Little	„ ..	Tnship.	19
White Ladies Aston	Worcester ..	Parish	353	Whittington ..	Salop ..	Parish	1 895
White Notley ..	Essex ..	Parish	508	Whittington ..	Stafford ..	Parish	819
Whiteparish ..	Wilts ..	Parish	1 225	Whittington ..	Worcester ..	Chap.	309
White Roothing	Essex ..	Parish	466	Whittle ..	Northumberland	Tnship.	32
Whiteshill, St. Paul	Gloucester ..	Ecl. Dis.	1 516	Whittle (Shilbottle P.)	„ ..	Tnship.	40
Whitestaunton ..	Somerset ..	Parish	250	Whittlebury ..	Northampton	Parish	487
Whitestone ..	Devon ..	Parish	571	Whittle le Woods	Lancaster ..	Tnship.	2 151
White Waltham	Berks ..	Parish	917	Whittle le Woods	Lincoln ..	Ecl. Dis.	2 856
Whitfield ..	Derby ..	Tnship.	5 679	Whittlesey ..	Cambs ..	District	6 966
Whitfield ..	„ ..	Ecl. Dis.	13 040	Whittlesey ..	„ ..	Parish	6 966
Whitfield ..	Kent ..	Parish	264	**Whittlesey** ..	„ ..	Town	4 496
Whitfield ..	Northampton	Parish	265	Whittlesford ..	„ ..	Hund.	4 121
Whitfield	Northumberland	Parish	381	Whittlesford ..	„ ..	Parish	800
Whitford ..	Flint ..	Sub-dis.	8 043	Whitton ..	Durham ..	Tnship.	40
Whitford ..	„ ..	Parish	3 666	Whitton & Trippleton	Hereford	Tnship.	109
Whitgift ..	York ..	Parish	2 298	Whitton ..	Lincoln ..	Parish	215
Whitgift ..	„ ..	Tnship.	315	Whitton	Northumberland	Tnship.	59
Whitgreave ..	Stafford ..	Tnship.	182	Whitton ..	Radnor ..	Parish	115
Whitgreave ..	„ ..	Ecl. Dis.	182	Whitton ..	Salop ..	Tnship.	82
Whitkirk ..	York ..	Sub-dis.	3 978	Whitton w. Thurlston	Suffolk .	Parish	565
Whitkirk ..	„ ..	Parish	3 032	Whittonditch ..	Wilts ..	Tithing	138
Whitley.. ..	Berks ..	Hamlet	744	Whittonstall	Northumberland	Tnship.	219
Whitley, Lower .	Cheshire ..	Tnship.	211	Whitwell ..	Derby ..	Parish	1 487
Whitley Over ..	„ ..	Tnship.	367	Whitwell House	Durham ..	Parish	180
Whitley Lower..	„ ..	Ecl. Dis.	578	Whitwell ..	Hants, I. W.	Parish	570
Whitley..	Northumberland	Tnship.	419	Whitwell ..	Norfolk ..	Parish	487
Whitley.. ..	Somerset ..	Hund.	14 174	Whitwell ..	Rutland ..	Parish	104
Whitley.. ..	York ..	Sub-dis.	2 009	Whitwell ..	York ..	Tnship.	56
Whitley.. ..	„ ..	Tnship.	356	Whitwell on Hill	„ ..	Tnship.	201
Whitley Lower..	„ ..	Ecl. Dis.	1 042	Whitwick ..	Leic. & Derby	Sub-dis.	9 874
Whitley Lower..	„ ..	Tnship.	1 042	Whitwick ..	Leicester ..	Parish	6 439
Whitley Upper..	„ ..	Tnship.	947	Whitwick ..	„ ..	Tnship.	3 759
Whitlingham ..	Norfolk ..	Parish	25	Whitwood ..	York ..	Tnship.	1 723
Whitmore ..	Stafford ..	Sub-dis.	1 302	Whitworth ..	Durham ..	Parish	3 629
Whitmore ..	„ ..	Parish	345	Whitworth ..	Lancaster ..	Sub-dis.	14 006
Whitnash ..	Warwick ..	Parish	393	Whitworth, &c. ..	„ ..	Hamlets	14 006
Whitney ..	Hereford ..	Parish	260	Whitworth ..	„ ..	Ecl. Dis.	8 324

Name of Place.	County.	Description.	Population.	Name of Place.	County.	Description.	Population.
Whixley	York ..	Sub-dis.	3 731	**Widnes** ..	Lancaster ..	Town	4 803
Whixley ..	,, ..	Parish	954	Widnes St. Mary	,, ..	Ecl. Dis.	3 872
Whixley ..	,, ..	Tnship.	605	Widworthy ..	Devon ..	Parish	188
Whixoe	Suffolk ..	Parish	145	Wield	Hants ..	Parish	304
Whorlton ..	Durham ..	Tnship.	292	Wigan	Lancaster ..	L. Sub.	73 900
Whorlton East & W.	Nrthmbld.	Tnship.	62	Wigan	,, ..	District	94 561
Whorlton ..	York ..	Parish	1 008	Wigan	,, ..	Sub-dis.	37 658
Whorlton ..	,, ..	Tnship.	650	Wigan	,, ..	Parish	78 190
Whorwelsdown..	Wilts ..	Hund.	5 505	Wigan	,, ..	Tnship.	37 658
Wibtoft	Warwick ..	Tnship.	79	**Wigan**	,, ..	Borough	37 658
Wichaugh ..	Cheshire ..	Tnship.	24	Wigan, St. Catherine	,, ..	Ecl. Dis.	15 909
Wichenford ..	Worcester ..	Parish	366	Wigan, St. George	,, ..	Ecl. Dis.	10 732
Wichnor ..	Stafford ..	Tnship.	152	Wigan, St. John	,, ..	Ecl. Dis.	1 544
Wick	Glamorgan .	Parish	423	Wigan, St. Thomas	,, ..	Ecl. Dis.	8 788
Wick & Abson ..	Gloucester ..	Parish	833	Wigborough, Great	Essex ..	Parish	428
Wick-Rissington	,,	Parish	206	Wigborough, Little	,, ..	Parish	92
Wick St. Lawrence	Somerset ..	Parish	270	Wilbraham, Great	Cambs ..	Parish	596
Wick	Worcester ..	Chap.	318	Wilbraham, Little	,, ..	Parish	353
Wicken	Cambs ..	Parish	995	Wiggenhall ..	Norfolk ..	Sub-dis.	6 171
Wicken-Bonant .	Essex ..	Parish	173	St. Germans ..	,, ..	Parish	633
Wicken ..	Northampton	Parish	529	St. Mary Magdalen	,,	Parish	825
Wickenby ..	Lincoln ..	Parish	288	St. Mary the Virgin,	,,	Parish	307
Wicker	York ..	Ecl. Dis.	10 796	St. Peter ..	,, ..	Parish	153
Wickersley ..	,, ..	Parish	709	Wigginton ..	Herts ..	Parish	641
Wickford ..	Essex ..	Sub-dis.	2 061	Wigginton ..	Oxon ..	Parish	338
Wickford ..	,, ..	Parish	462	Wigginton ..	Stafford..	Tnship.	670
Wickham Bishops	,,	Parish	616	Wigginton, St. Leonard	,, ..	Ecl. Dis.	466
Wickham, St. Paul	,,	Parish	409	Wigginton ..	York ..	Parish	349
Wickham ..	Hants ..	Parish	1 019	Wigglesworth ..	,, ..	Tnship.	267
Wickham Forest	,,	—	15	Wiggonby ..	Cumberland	Tnship.	218
Wickhambreux..	Kent ..	Parish	461	Wiggonholt ..	Sussex ..	Parish	34
Wickham, East .	,,	Parish	836	Wighill	York ..	Parish	280
Wickham, West .	,,	Parish	737	Wight, Isle of ..	Hants ..	Division	47 428
Wickhambrook..	Suffolk ..	Sub-dis.	4 825	Wight, Isle of ..	,, ..	L. Sub.	55 362
Wickhambrook..	,, ..	Parish	1 452	Wighton ..	Norfolk ..	Parish	612
Wickham Market	,,	Sub-dis.	4 322	Wigland ..	Cheshire ..	Tnship.	193
Wickham Market	,,	Parish	1 571	Wigmore ..	Hereford ..	Hund.	6 309
Wickham Skeith	,,	Parish	564	Wigmore ..	,, ..	Parish	499
Wickhamford ..	Worcester ..	Parish	124	Wigsley.. ..	Notts ..	Tnship.	105
Wickhampton ..	Norfolk ..	Parish	119	Wigston.. ..	Leicester ..	Sub-dis.	7 314
Wicklewood ..	,, ..	Parish	806	Wigston Magna .	,, ..	Parish	2 521
Wickmere ..	,, ..	Parish	268	Wigston Parva..	,, ..	Hamlet	75
Wickwar ..	Gloucester ..	Parish	949	Wigtoft ..	Lincoln ..	Parish	732
Widcombe, North	Somerset ..	Tithing	101	Wigton	Cumberland	District	23 273
Widdington ..	Essex ..	Parish	409	Wigton	,, ..	Sub-dis.	10 052
Widdington ..	York ..	Tnship.	33	Wigton	,, ..	Parish	6 023
Widdrington	Northumberland	Parish	502	Wigton	,, ..	Tnship.	4 357
Widecombe in Moor	Devon ..	Parish	854	**Wigton**	,, ..	Town	4 011
Widford ..	Essex ..	Parish	257	Wigton	York ..	Tnship.	130
Widford ..	Herts ..	Parish	456	Wike (Burstall P.)	,, ..	Tnship.	3 016
Widford ..	Oxon ..	Parish	33	Wike (Harewood P.)	,, ..	Tnship.	126
Widley	Hants ..	Parish	725	Wilbarston ..	Northampton	Parish	721
Widmerpool ..	Notts ..	Parish	151	Wilberfoss ..	York ..	Parish	632
Widnes	Lancaster ..	Tnship.	6 905	Wilberfoss ..	,, ..	Tnship.	386

Name of Place.	County.	Description.	Population.	Name of Place.	County.	Description.	Population.
Wilburton	Cambs	Parish	560	Willington	Durham	Tnship.	2 39
Wilby	Norfolk	Parish	98	Willington, St. Stephen „		Ecl. Dis.	3 78
Wilby	Northampton	Parish	456	Willington	Flint	Tnship.	33
Wilby	Suffolk	Parish	560	Willington	Northumberland	Tnship.	3 03
Wilcot	Oxon	Parish	12	Willington	„	Ecl. Dis.	79
Wilcot	Wilts	Parish	651	Willisham	Suffolk	Parish	18
Wilcrick	Monmouth	Parish	28	Willitoft	York	Tnship.	6
Wildboarclough	Cheshire	Tnship.	293	Williton	Somerset	L. Sub.	25 96
Wilden	Beds	Parish	501	Williton & Freemanners „		Hund.	17 34
Wildon-Grange	York	Tnship.	27	Williton	„	District	19 91
Wildsworth	Lincoln	Hamlet	150	Williton	„	Sub-dis.	5 67
Wilford	Notts	Sub-dis.	5 048	Willoughby Waterless	Leicester	Parish	37
Wilford	„	Parish	604	Willoughby	Lincoln	Parish	78
Wilford	Suffolk	Hund.	8 087	Willoughby, Scot	„	Parish	1
Wilfred	York	Tnship.	172	Willoughby, Silk	„	Parish	23
Wilksby	Lincoln	Parish	57	Willoughby on Wolds	Notts	Parish	57
Willand	Devon	Parish	382	Willoughby	Warwick	Parish	37
Willaston (Neston P.)	Cheshire	Tnship.	340	Willoughton	Lincoln	Parish	62
Willaston	„	Tnship.	767	Willybrook	Northampton	Hund.	6 99
Willen	Bucks	Parish	80	Wilmington	Kent	Parish	1 05
Willenhall	Stafford	Sub-dis.	25 809	Wilmington	Sussex	Parish	25
Willenhall	„	Tnship.	17 256	Wilmslow	Cheshire	Sub-dis.	7 53
Willenhall, St. Anne	„	Ecl. Dis.	3 923	Wilmslow	„	Parish	6 61
Willenhall, St. Stephen	„	Ecl. Dis.	6 168	Wilne	Derby	Parish	2 09
Willenhall, Trinity	„	Ecl. Dis.	1 936	Wilnecote	Warwick	Tnship.	1 35
Willenhall	Warwick	Hamlet	109	Wilnecote, Trinity	„	Ecl. Dis.	1 65
Willerby	York	Parish	468	Wilpshire	Lancaster	Tnship.	22
Willerby (Kirk Ella P.)	„	Tnship.	251	Wilsden	York	Sub-dis.	4 90
Willerby (Willerby P.)	„	Tnship.	71	Wilsden	„	Tnship.	2 88
Willersey	Gloucester	Parish	373	Wilsden w. Allerton	„	Ecl. Dis.	4 42
Willersley	Hereford	Parish	13	Wilsford	Lincoln	Parish	64
Willesborough	Kent	Parish	1 780	Wilsford, Amesbury	Wilts	Parish	14
Willesden	Middlesex	Sub-dis.	3 897	Wilsford, Pewsey	„	Parish	52
Willesden	„	Parish	3 879	Wilsford	„	—	26
Willesley	Derby	Parish	45	Wilshampstead	Beds	Parish	1 03
Willey	Beds	Hund.	9 639	Wilsthorpe	Lincoln	Tnship.	6
Willey	Hereford	Tnship.	158	Wilsthorpe	York	Tnship.	1
Willey	Salop	Parish	149	Wilstrop	„	Tnship.	9
Willey	Warwick	Parish	141	Wilton	Somerset	Parish	1 03
Williamston	Pembroke	Chap.	535	Wilton	Wilts	District	10 67
Willian	Herts	Parish	281	Wilton	„	Sub-dis.	5 77
Willingale Doe	Essex	Parish	438	Wilton	„	Parish	1 93
Willingale Spain	„	Parish	207	Wilton	„	P. Bor.	8 65
Willingdon	Sussex	Parish	709	Wilton Beacon	York	L. Sub.	8 92
Willingham	Cambs	Sub-dis.	9 633	Wilton	„	Chap.	18
Willingham	„	Parish	1 630	Wilton	„	Tnship.	92
Willingham	Lincoln	Sub-dis.	4 037	Wiltshire		County	249 31
Willingham	„	Parish	520	Northern Division		N. Div.	146 46
Willingham, North	„	Parish	203	Southern Division		S. Div.	102 84
Willingham, South	„	Parish	340	Wilverley Walk	Hants	—	3
Willingham	Suffolk	Parish	142	Wily	Wilts	Parish	48
Willington	Beds	Parish	290	Wimbish	Essex	Parish	93
Willington	Cheshire	Parish	106	Wimbledon	Surrey	Sub-dis.	4 64
Willington	Derby	Parish	477	Wimbledon	„	Parish	4 64

Name of Place.	County.	Description.	Population.	Name of Place.	County.	Description.	Population.
Wimblington	Cambs	Hamlet	1 114	**Windsor**	Berks	Borough	9 520
Wimboldsley	Cheshire	Tnship.	99	Windsor, New, Trinity	,,	Ecl. Dis.	3 055
Wimbolds-Trafford	,,	Tnship.	113	Windynook	Durham	Ecl. Dis.	2 635
Wimborne	Dorset	Division	20 890	Winestead	York	Parish	173
Wimborne	,,	L. Sub.	30 649	Winfarthing	Norfolk	Parish	615
Wimborne	Dorset & Hants	District	17 253	Winford	Somerset	Parish	934
Wimborne	Dorset	Sub-dis.	5 433	Winforton	Hereford	Parish	162
Wimborne	,,	Town	2 271	Winfrith, Newburgh	Dorset	Parish	1 020
Wimborne Minster	,,	Parish	4 807	Wing	Bucks	Sub-dis.	2 492
Wimborne Minster	,,	—	3 413	Wing	,,	Parish	1 504
Wimborne St. Giles	,,	Parish	436	Wing	Rutland	Parish	342
Wimbotsham	Norfolk	Parish	508	Wingate	Durham	Tnship.	2 143
Wimeswould	Leicester	Parish	1 209	Wingate Grange	,,	Ecl. Dis.	1 995
Wimpole	Cambs	Parish	406	Wingates, St. John	Lancaster	Ecl. Dis.	1 857
Wincanton	Somerset	L. Sub.	22 213	Wingates	Northumberland	Tnship.	162
Wincanton	Som. & Dorset	District	21 500	Wingerworth	Derby	Parish	433
Wincanton	,, ,,	Sub-dis.	6 007	Wingfield, North	,,	Parish	7 339
Wincanton	Somerset	Parish	2 450	Wingfield, North	,,	Tnship.	785
Winceby	Lincoln	Parish	67	Wingfield, South	,,	Parish	1 241
Wincham	Cheshire	Tnship.	642	Wingfield	Suffolk	Parish	593
Winchcomb	Glouc. & Worc.	District	10 082	Wingham	Kent	L. Sub.	27 582
Winchcomb	Gloucester	Parish	2 937	Wingham	,,	Sub-dis.	2 878
Winch, East	Norfolk	Parish	434	Wingham	,,	Parish	1 060
Winch, West	,,	Parish	470	Winglund—			
Winchelsea	Sussex	Parish	719	,, nr. Sutton St. Mary	Lincoln	—	98
Winchendon, Nether	Bucks	Parish	316	,, nr. Tydd St. Mary	,,	—	14
Winchendon, Upper	,,	Parish	220	,, nr. Walpole St. Peter	Norf.	—	14
Winchester	..	Diocese	1267794	Wingrave	Bucks	Parish	863
Winchester	Hants	Division	18 946	Winkbourne	Notts	Parish	172
Winchester	,,	L. Sub.	18 946	Winkfield w. Ascot	Berks	Parish	2 508
Winchester	,,	District	26 607	Winkfield w. Rowley	Wilts	Parish	362
Winchester, New	,,	Union	23 785	Winkleigh	Devon	Sub-dis.	2 472
Winchester	,,	Sub-dis.	14 930	Winkleigh	,,	Parish	1 425
Winchester	,,	City	14 776	Winksley	York	Tnship.	223
Winchester City	,,	L. Sub.	14 776	Winlaton	Durham	Sub-dis.	10 424
Winchester College, &c.		Parish	41	Winlaton	,,	Parish	7 372
Winchester, Trinity	,,	Ecl. Dis.	1 872	Winlaton	,,	Tnship.	6 809
Winchfield	,,	Parish	329	Winlaton St. Paul	,,	Ecl. Dis.	4 163
Winchmore Hill	Middlesex	Ecl. Dis.	1 674	Winmarleigh	Lancaster	Tnship.	246
Wincle	Cheshire	Tnship.	343	Winnall	Hants	Parish	120
Winder, Low	Westmoreland	Tnship.	12	Winnersh	Berks	Liberty	582
Windermere	,,	Parish	4 223	Winnibriggs & Threo	Lincoln	Wapen.	10 793
Windle	Lancaster	Tnship.	12 229	Winnington	Cheshire	Tnship.	460
Windlesham	Surrey	Parish	2 090	Winnington	Stafford	Tnship.	191
Windlestone	Durham	Tnship.	134	Winscales	Cumberland	Tnship.	98
Windley	Derby	Tnship.	217	Winscombe	Somerset	Parish	1 326
Windrush	Gloucester	Parish	290	Winsford	,,	Parish	574
Windsor	Berks	L. Sub.	15 885	Winsham	,,	Parish	1 033
Windsor	Berks & Sur.	District	21 301	Winshill	Derby	Tnship.	880
Windsor	,, ,,	Sub-dis.	13 621	Winslade	Hants	Parish	183
Windsor Castle	Berks	—	308	Winsley	Wilts	Ecl. Dis.	985
Windsor, New	,,	Parish	6 728	Winslow	Bucks	L. Sub.	7 671
Windsor, New	,,	—	6 533	Winslow	,,	District	9 265
Windsor, Old	,,	Parish	1 835	Winslow	,,	Sub-dis.	9 265

Name of Place.	County.	Description.	Population.	Name of Place.	County.	Description.	Population.
Winslow	*Bucks*	Parish	1 890	Wirksworth	*Derby*	L. Sub.	23 901
Winslow	*Hereford*	Tnship.	440	Wirksworth	,,	Sub-dis.	6 072
Winson	*Gloucester*	Chap.	181	Wirksworth	,,	Parish	7 098
Winstanley	*Lancaster*	Tnship.	633	Wirksworth	,,	Tnship.	3 717
Winster	*Derby*	Tnship.	971	**Wirksworth**	,,	Town	2 592
Winston	*Durham*	Parish	342	Wirral	*Cheshire*	Hund.	69 448
Winston	*Suffolk*	Parish	352	Wirral, Higher	,,	L. Sub.	10 228
Winstone	*Gloucester*	Parish	230	Wirral, Lower	,,	L. Sub.	71 564
Winstree	*Essex*	Hund.	5 014	Wirral	,,	District	18 420
Winterborne—				Wirswall	,,	Tnship.	107
,, Abbas	*Dorset*	Parish	205	Wisbech	*Cambs*	Hund.	11 624
,, Came	,,	Parish	125	Wisbech	,,	L. Sub.	18 681
,, Came	,,	—	116	Wisbech	*Cambs & Norf.*	District	33 323
,, Clenstone	,,	Parish	106	Wisbech	*Cambs*	Sub-dis.	9 276
,, Herringstone	,,	Parish	52	Wisbech St. Mary	,,	Parish	1 887
,, Houghton	,,	Parish	284	Wisbech St. Peter	,,	Parish	9 276
,, Kingstone	,,	Parish	589	**Wisbech**	,,	M. Bor.	9 276
,, Monkton	,,	Parish	86	Wisborough Green	*Sussex*	Parish	1 682
,, St. Martin	,,	Parish	458	Wiseton	*Notts*	Tnship.	124
,, Steepleton	,,	Parish	191	Wishaw	*Warwick*	Parish	216
,, Stickland	,,	Parish	444	Wishford, Great	*Wilts*	Parish	381
,, Thomson	,,	Parish	39	Wisley	*Surrey*	Parish	166
,, Whitechurch	,,	Parish	554	Wispington	*Lincoln*	Parish	85
,, Zelstone	,,	Parish	199	Wissett	*Suffolk*	Parish	427
Winterbourn	*Berks*	Tithing	377	Wissington	,,	Parish	254
Winterbourne	*Gloucester*	Parish	3 067	Wistanstow	*Salop*	Parish	1 121
Winterbourne	,,	Tnship.	1 446	Wistanswick	,,	Tnship.	240
Winterbourne	*Wilts*	Sub-dis.	1 917	Wistaston	*Cheshire*	Parish	331
Winterbourne—				Wiston	*Pembroke*	Parish	713
,, Basset	,,	Parish	249	**Wiston**	,,	P. Bor.	713
,, Dantsey	,,	Parish	171	Wiston	*Suffolk*	Parish	254
,, Earls	,,	Parish	276	Wiston	*Sussex*	Parish	311
,, Gunner	,,	Parish	150	Wistow	*Hunts*	Parish	532
,, Monkton	,,	Parish	214	Wistow	*Leicester*	Parish	247
,, Stoke	,,	Parish	383	Wistow	,,	Tnship.	40
Winteringham	*Lincoln*	Parish	858	Wistow	*York*	Parish	849
Wintersett	*York*	Tnship.	141	Wiswall	*Lancaster*	Tnship.	465
Winterslow	*Wilts*	Parish	904	Witcham	*Cambs*	Parish	495
Winterstoke	*Somerset*	Hund.	25 792	Witcham Gravel		Hamlet	23
Winterton	*Lincoln*	Sub-dis.	9 806	Witchampton	*Dorset & Hants*	Sub-dis.	4 196
Winterton	,,	Parish	1 780	Witchampton	*Dorset*	Parish	588
Winterton	*Norfolk*	Parish	682	Witchford	*Cambs*	Hund.	29 287
Winthorpe	*Lincoln*	Parish	305	Witchford	,,	Parish	559
Winthorpe	*Notts*	Parish	269	Witchingham, Great	*Norfolk*	Parish	642
Winton	*Westmoreland*	Tnship.	301	Witchingham, Little	,,	Parish	33
Winton	*York*	Tnship.	97	Witchling	*Kent*	Parish	147
Wintringham	,,	Parish	602	Withall	*Worc. & War.*	Ecl. Dis.	1 093
Wintringham	,,	Tnship.	331	Witham	*Essex*	Hund.	12 211
Winwick	*Lancaster*	Sub-dis.	1 798	Witham	,,	L. Sub.	24 185
Winwick	,,	Parish	704	Witham	,,	District	16 324
Winwick w. Hulme	,,	Tnship.	451	Witham	,,	Sub-dis.	6 947
Winwick	*Northampton*	Parish	122	Witham	,,	Parish	3 455
Winwick	*Nptn. & Hunts*	Parish	380	Witham on Hill	*Lincoln*	Parish	548
Wirksworth	*Derby*	Hund.	23 901	Witham on Hill	,,	Tnship.	236

Name of Place.	County.	Description.	Population.	Name of Place.	County.	Description.	Population.
Witham, North .	Lincoln ..	Parish	278	Wittering, West .	Sussex ..	Parish	616
Witham, North .	,, ..	Tnship.	216	Wittersham ..	Kent ..	Parish	877
Witham, South..	,, ..	Parish	531	Witton w. Twambrooks	Chesh.	Chap.	3 677
Witham Friary .	Somerset ..	Parish	576	Witton-Gilbert..	Durham ..	Parish	2 098
Withcall ..	Lincoln ..	Parish	121	Witton-le-Wear .	,, ..	Parish	1 366
Withcote ..	Leicester ..	Parish	45	Witton ..	Hunts ..	Parish	311
Witheridge ..	Devon ..	Hund.	10 144	Witton ..	Lancaster ..	Sub-dis.	8 115
Witheridge ..	,, ..	Sub-dis.	5 449	Witton ..	,, ..	Tnship.	3 292
Witheridge ..	,, ..	Parish	1 237	Witton, St. Mark	,, ..	Ecl. Dis.	5 297
Witherley .	Leicester ..	Parish	528	Witton, Blofield .	Norfolk ..	Parish	144
Witherley ..	,, ..	Tnship.	450	Witton, Tunstead	,, ..	Parish	269
Withern ..	Lincoln ..	Sub-dis.	4 643	Witton, Long	Northumberld.	Tnship.	152
Withern ..	,, ..	Parish	528	Witton, Nether .	,, ..	Parish	486
Withernsea ..	York ..	Tnship.	202	Witton, Nether..	,, ..	Tnship.	301
Withernwick ..	,, ..	Parish	499	Witton Shields ..	,, ..	Tnship.	19
Withersdale ..	Suffolk ..	Parish	225	Witton ..	Warwick ..	Hamlet	126
Withersfield ..	,, ..	Parish	624	Witton, East ..	York ..	Parish	621
Witherslack ..	Westmoreland	Tnship.	489	Witton, E. Within	,, ..	Tnship.	326
Withiel	Cornwall ..	Parish	367	Witton, E. Without	,, ..	Tnship.	295
Withiel Florey..	Somerset ..	Parish	164	Witton, West ..	,, ..	Parish	659
Withington, Lower	Cheshire ..	Tnship.	578	Wiveliscombe ..	Somerset ..	Sub-dis.	3 526
Withington, Old	,, ..	Tnship.	169	Wivesliscombe ..	,, ..	Parish	2 735
Withington ..	Gloucester ..	Parish	783	Wivelsfield ..	Sussex ..	Parish	1 162
Withington ..	Hereford ..	Parish	970	Wivenhoe ..	Essex ..	Sub-dis.	4 428
Withington ..	,, ..	Tnship.	788	Wivenhoe ..	,, ..	Parish	1 843
Withington ..	Lancaster ..	Tnship.	2 712	Wiverton Hall ..	Notts ..	Parish	11
Withington, St. Paul	,, ..	Ecl. Dis.	2 775	Wiveton ..	Norfolk ..	Parish	232
Withington ..	Salop ..	Parish	232	Wix ..	Essex ..	Parish	752
Withnell ..	Lancaster ..	Tnship.	2 059	Wixamtree ..	Beds ..	Hund.	7 142
Withnell ..	,, ..	Ecl. Dis.	2 160	Wixford ..	Warwick ..	Parish	123
Withybrook ..	Warwick ..	Parish	337	Woburn ..	Beds ..	L. Sub.	11 684
Withycombe ..	Somerset ..	Parish	349	Woburn ..	,, ..	District	11 684
Withycombe Rawleigh	Devon..	Parish	2 145	Woburn ..	,, ..	Sub-dis.	6 771
Withycombe Rawleigh	,, ..	—	578	Woburn ..	,, ..	Parish	1 764
Withyham ..	Sussex ..	Sub-dis.	3 048	Wokefield ..	Berks ..	Tithing	133
Withyham ..	,, ..	Parish	1 597	Woking..	Surrey ..	Hund.	15 113
Withypoole ..	Somerset ..	Parish	307	Woking..	,, ..	Sub-dis.	6 171
Witley ..	Surrey ..	Sub-dis.	6 354	Woking..	,, ..	Parish	3 819
Witley ..	,, ..	Parish	1 555	Wokingham ..	Berks ..	District	14 465
Witley ..	Worcester ..	Sub-dis.	3 480	Wokingham ..	,, ..	Sub-dis.	7 807
Witley, Great ..	,, ..	Parish	445	Wokingham ..	,, ..	Parish	4 144
Witley, Little ..	,, ..	Chap.	208	**Wokingham** ..	,, ..	Town	2 404
Witnesham ..	Suffolk ..	Parish	634	Wolborough ..	Devon ..	Parish	4 427
Witney ..	Oxon ..	L. Sub.	20 146	Wold ..	Northampton	Parish	472
Witney ..	Oxon & Glouc.	District	23 238	Woldingham ..	Surrey ..	Parish	67
Witney ..	Oxon ..	Sub-dis.	7 556	Wold Newton ..	Lincoln ..	Parish	189
Witney ..	,, ..	Parish	5 180	Wold Newton ..	York ..	Parish	351
Witney ..	,, ..	Tnship.	2 989	Wolferlow ..	Hereford ..	Parish	112
Witney ..	,, ..	Town	3 458	Wolfhampcote ..	Warwick ..	Parish	444
Witson ..	Monmouth ..	Parish	85	Wolford, Great..	,, ..	Parish	534
Wittenham, Little	Berks ..	Parish	134	Wolford, Great..	,, ..	Tnship.	292
Wittenham, Long	,, ..	Parish	583	Wolford, Little..	,, ..	Hamlet	242
Wittering ..	Northampton	Parish	235	Wollaston ..	Northampton	Parish	1 443
Wittering, East .	Sussex ..	Parish	223	Wollaston ..	Salop ..	Chap.	367

Name of Place.	County.	Description.	Population.	Name of Place.	County.	Description.	Population.
Wollaston	Worcester	Tnship.	2 041	Wonford	Devon	Hund.	29 24
Wollaston	„	Ecl. Dis.	2 041	Wonford	„	L. Sub.	28 39
Wollaton	Notts	Parish	555	Wonston	Hants	Parish	70
Wollescote	Worcester	Tnship.	1 517	Wooburn	Bucks	Parish	2 24
Wolphy	Hereford	Hund.	7 962	Wood	Kent	Parish	26
Wolsingham	Durham	Sub-dis.	5 531	Woodall, &c.	York E.	Tnship.	10
Wolsingham	„	Parish	5 531	Woodall, &c.	York W.	Tnship.	67
Wolstanton	Stafford	District	54 356	Woodbank	Cheshire	Tnship.	6
Wolstanton	„	Sub-dis.	9 563	Woodbastwick	Norfolk	Parish	29
Wolstanton	„	Parish	32 029	Woodborough	Notts	Parish	89
Wolstanton	„	Tnship.	1 842	Woodborough	Wilts	Parish	40
Wolston	Warwick	Parish	1 263	Woodbridge	Suffolk	L. Sub.	43 47
Wolston	„	Tnship.	814	Woodbridge	„	District	22 75
Wolterton	Norfolk	Parish	48	Woodbridge & Wilford	„	Sub-dis.	7 78
Wolverhampton	Stafford	L. Sub.	156 583	Woodbridge Out	„	Sub-dis.	3 73
Wolverhampton	Staff. & Salop	District	126 902	Woodbridge	„	Parish	4 51
Wolverhampton	Stafford	Union	111 033	**Woodbridge**	„	Town	4 51
Wolverhampton, Eastern	„	Sub-dis.	36 346	Woodbridge St. John	„	Ecl. Dis.	2 418
Wolverhampton, Western	„	Sub-dis.	24 514	Woodbury	Devon	L. Sub.	15 374
Wolverhampton	„	Parish	113 832	Woodbury	„	Sub-dis.	3 91
Wolverhampton	„	Tnship.	60 860	Woodbury	„	Parish	1 966
		M. Bor.	60 860	Woodbury-Salterton	„	Ecl. Dis.	498
Wolverhampton „ {		P. Bor.	147 670	Woodchester	Gloucester	Parish	816
St. George	„	Ecl. Dis.	6 759	Woodchurch	Cheshire	Sub-dis.	4 030
St. James	„	Ecl. Dis.	4 700	Woodchurch	„	Parish	3 922
St. John	„	Ecl. Dis.	10 788	Woodchurch	„	Tnship.	94
St. Mark	„	Ecl. Dis.	6 282	Woodchurch	Kent	Parish	1 262
St. Mary	„	Ecl. Dis.	8 413	Woodcote	Salop	Chap.	150
St. Matthew	„	Ecl. Dis.	6 451	Woodcott	Cheshire	Tnship.	33
St. Paul	„	Ecl. Dis.	6 029	Woodcott	Hants	Parish	80
Wolverley	Worcester	Sub-dis.	3 204	Wood-Dalling	Norfolk	Parish	508
Wolverley	„	Parish	2 905	Wood-Ditton	Cambs	Parish	1 375
Wolverton	Bucks	Parish	2 370	Wood-Eaton	Oxon	Parish	83
Wolverton, St. Geo. „		Ecl. Dis.	1 793	Woodend	Northampton	Hamlet	254
Wolverton	Hants	Parish	146	Wood Enderby	Lincoln	Parish	244
Wolverton	Norfolk	Parish	179	Woodford	Cheshire	Tnship.	392
Wolverton	Warwick	Parish	159	Woodford	Essex	Parish	3 457
Wolvesley	Hants	Parish	12	Woodford, St. Paul „		Ecl. Dis.	844
Wolves-Newton	Monmouth	Parish	193	Woodford, Daventry	Nrthmptn.	Parish	735
Wolvey	Warwick	Parish	958	Woodford, Thrapston	„	Parish	912
Wolviston	Durham	Tnship.	653	Woodford Grange	Stafford	Parish	13
Wolviston St. Peter	„	Ecl. Dis.	787	Woodford	Wilts	Parish	500
Womaston & Walton	Radnor	Tnship.	219	Woodgreen	Hants	Parish	345
Wombleton	York	Tnship.	340	Wood Green	Middlesex	Ward	3 154
Wombourn	Stafford	Sub-dis.	4 991	Woodhall	Lincoln	Parish	276
Wombourn	„	Parish	2 236	Woodham	Bucks	Hamlet	38
Wombridge	Salop	Sub-dis.	6 597	Woodham	Durham	Tnship.	218
Wombridge	„	Parish	2 601	Woodham Ferris	Essex	Parish	947
Wombwell	York	Tnship.	3 738	Woodham Mortimer	„	Parish	324
Womenswould	Kent	Parish	276	Woodham Walter	„	Parish	598
Womersley	York	Parish	996	Woodhay, East	Hants	Parish	1 533
Womersley	„	Tnship.	445	Wooday, West	Berks	Parish	130
Womastow	Monmouth	Parish	150	Woodhorn	Northumberland	Parish	2 962
Wonersh	Surrey	Parish	1 438	Woodhorn	„	Tnship.	171

Name of Place.	County.	Description.	Population.	Name of Place.	County.	Description.	Population.
oodhorne Demesne	Nthmb.	Tnship.	15	Woolbeding	Sussex	Parish	338
oodhouse	Leicester	Chap.	1 205	Wooldale	York	Tnship.	5 322
oodhouse Eaves	„	Ecl. Dis.	1 163	Wooler	Northumberland	Sub-dis.	6 378
oodhouse	Northumberland	Tnship.	33	Wooler	„	Parish	1 697
oodhouse Hall	Notts	Parish	62	Woolfardisworthy, Crediton	Dn.	Parish	175
oodhouse	Salop	Parish	9	Woolfardisworthy, Hartland	„	Parish	776
oodhouse	York	Hamlet	55	Woolhampton	Berks	Parish	559
oodhouse, Christch.	„	Ecl. Dis.	3 324	Woolhope	Hereford	Parish	803
oodhouse, St. Mark	„	Ecl. Dis.	6 072	Woolland	Dorset	Parish	132
oodhouses	Stafford	Tnship.	26	Woollaston	Gloucester	Parish	971
odhurst	Hunts	Parish	554	Woolley	Hunts	Parish	114
oodland	Devon	Chap.	169	Woolley	Somerset	Parish	71
oodland	Durham	Tnship.	252	Woolley	York	Chap.	531
oodland-Eyam	Derby	Tnship.	258	Woolpit	Suffolk	Parish	1 008
oodlands, St. Mary	Berks	Ecl. Dis.	348	Woolsington	Northumberland	Tnship.	64
oodlands	Dorset	Parish	495	Woolstanwood	Cheshire	Tnship.	65
oodlands, St. Mary	Kent	Ecl. Dis.	157	Woolstaston	Salop	Parish	64
oodlands, St. Paul	Hants	Ecl. Dis.	1 175	Woolsthorpe	Lincoln	Parish	615
oodlands	Wilts	Tithing	1 139	Woolston	Gloucester	Parish	81
oodleigh	Devon	Parish	213	Woolston, &c.	Lancaster	Tnship.	496
oodley & Sandford	Berks	Liberty	917	Woolstone	Berks	Tnship.	256
oodmancote	Gloucester	Hamlet	431	Woolstone, Great	Bucks	Parish	71
oodmancote	Sussex	Parish	331	Woolstone, Little	„	Parish	125
oodmancott	Hants	Parish	87	Woolstrop	Gloucester	Hamlet	55
oodmansey	York	Hamlet	231	Woolton Hill	Hants	Ecl. Dis.	821
oodmansterne	Surrey	Parish	271	Woolton, Much	Lancaster	Sub-dis.	4 608
oodnesborough	Kent	Parish	889	Woolton, Little	„	Tnship.	1 062
ood Newton	Northampton	Parish	529	Woolton, Much	„	Tnship.	3 546
ood-Norton	Norfolk	Parish	250	**Woolton, Much**	„	Town	3 296
ood Plumpton	Lancaster	Chap.	1 462	Woolton, Much	„	Ecl. Dis.	3 538
ood Rising	Norfolk	Parish	97	Woolvercott	Oxon	Parish	617
oodsetts	York	Tnship.	164	Woolverstone	Suffolk	Parish	239
oodsford	Dorset	Parish	193	Woolverton	Somerset	Parish	171
oodside	Cumberland	Tnship.	387	Woolwich	Kent	Parish	41 695
oodside Quarter	„	Tnship.	676	Woolwich Arsenal	Kent	Sub-dis.	18 776
oodside Ward	Nrthumberld.	Tnship.	121	Woolwich Dockyard	„	Sub-dis.	22 919
oodside	York	Ecl. Dis.	2 815	Woolwich, St. Thos.	„	Ecl. Dis.	8 263
oodstock	Oxon	L. Sub.	11 958	Wooperton	Northumberland	Tnship.	67
oodstock	„	District	14 236	Woore	Salop	Tnship.	783
oodstock	„	Sub-dis.	7 778	Woore St. Leon.	Salop & Staff.	Ecl. Dis.	839
oodstock	„	Parish	1 201	Wootton	Beds	Parish	1 349
oodstock	„	P. Bor.	7 827	Wootton	Berks	Parish	384
oodstone	Hunts	Parish	347	Wootton Underwood	Bucks	Parish	266
oodthorpe	Derby	Tnship.	302	Wootton-Fitzpaine	Dorset	Parish	307
oodthorpe	Leicester	Hamlet	67	Wootton-Glanville	„	Parish	300
oodton	Norfolk	Sub-dis.	4 216	Wootton, North	„	Parish	76
oodton	„	Parish	531	Wootton	Hants, I.W.	Parish	79
oodville	Derby & Leic.	Ecl. Dis.	1 408	Wootton St. Lawrence	„	Parish	917
oodwalton	Hunts	Parish	388	Wootton	Kent	Parish	163
oodyates, West	Dorset	Parish	20	Wootton	Lincoln	Parish	591
ookey	Somerset	Parish	1 129	Wootton, North	Norfolk	Parish	247
ool	Dorset	Parish	590	Wootton, South	„	Parish	150
oolavington	Somerset	Parish	415	Wootton	Northampton	Parish	837
oolavington	Sussex	Parish	488	Wootton	Oxon	Hund.	23 011

Name of Place.	County.	Description.	Population.	Name of Place.	County.	Description.	Populat
Wootton	Oxon	Parish	1 238	Wormley	Herts	Parish	5
Wootton-Courtney	Somerset	Parish	378	Wormshill	Kent	Parish	2
Wootton, North .	,,	Parish	322	Wormsley	Hereford	Parish	1
Wootton	Stafford	Tnship.	185	Worplesdon	Surrey	Parish	17
Wootton (Eccleshall P.)	,,	Tnship.	202	Worsall, High	York	Chap.	1
Wootton-Wawen	Warwick	Sub-dis.	3 797	Worsall, Low	,,	Tnship.	2
Wootton-Wawen	,,	Parish	2 253	Worsbrough	,,	Sub-dis.	5 8
Wootton-Wawen	,,	Tnship.	676	Worsbrough	,,	Tnship.	5 3
Wootton-Bassett	Wilts	Sub-dis.	5 675	Worsley..	Lancaster	Sub-dis.	14 0
Wootton-Bassett	,,	Parish	2 191	Worsley..	,,	Tnship.	11 8
Wootton-Rivers .	,,	Parish	444	Worstead	Norfolk	Parish	7
Worcester		Diocese	857 775	Worsthorne, &c..	Lancaster	Tnship.	8
Worcestershire..		County	307 397	Worsthorne, St. John	,,	Ecl. Dis.	1 0
Eastern Division		E. Div.	186 431	Worston	,,	Tnship.	
Western Division		W. Div.	120 966	Worston	Stafford	Parish	
Worcester	Worcester	L. Sub.	50 967	Worth ..	Cheshire	Tnship.	7
Worcester	,,	District	30 969	Worth-Matravers	Dorset	Parish	3
Worcester, North	,,	Sub-dis.	10 725	Worth ..	Kent	Parish	4
Worcester, South	,,	Sub-dis.	11 651	Worth ..	Sussex	Sub-dis.	4 5
Worcester	,,	City	31 227	Worth ..	,,	Parish	2 9
Worcester, St. Paul	,,	Ecl. Dis.	2 668	Wortham	Suffolk	Parish	9
Wordwell	Suffolk	Parish	65	Worthenbury	Flint	Parish	5
Worfield	Salop	Sub-dis.	4 955	Worthin	Salop & Mont.	Parish	3 7
Worfield	,,	Parish	1 785	Worthin	Salop	Tnship.	3 1
Workington	Cumberland	Sub-dis.	10 765	Worthing	Norfolk	Parish	1
Workington	,,	Parish	7 834	Worthing	Sussex	L. Sub.	8 3
Workington	,,	Tnship.	6 467	Worthing	,,	District	18 9
Workington	,,	Town	6 467	Worthing	,,	Town	5 8
Workington, St. John	,,	Ecl. Dis.	2 610	Worthing, Christch.	,,	Ecl. Dis.	3 2
Worksop	Notts	L. Sub.	15 198	Worthington	Lancaster	Tnship.	1
Worksop	Notts, &c.	District	20 704	Worthington, &c.	Leicester	Tnship.	1 1
Worksop	Notts	Sub-dis.	8 373	Worthys, The	Hants	Sub-dis.	2 5
Worksop	,,	Parish	8 361	Worthy, Headbourn	,,	Parish	1
Worksop	,,	Town	7 112	Worthy, Kings..	,,	Parish	3
Worlaby	Lincoln	Parish	526	Worthy, Martyr.	,,	Parish	2
Worlaby by Alford	,,	Parish	37	Worting	,,	Parish	1
Worldham, East	Hants	Parish	235	Wortley	York	District	38 5
Worldham, West	,,	Parish	89	Wortley	,,	Sub-dis.	2 5
Worle ..	Somerset	Parish	980	Wortley	,,	Union	24 0
Worleston	Cheshire	Tnship.	368	Wortley	,,	Tnship.	1 1
Worlingham	Suffolk	Parish	192	Wortley	,,	Sub-dis.	24 5
Worlington, East	Devon	Parish	284	Wortley (Leeds P.)	,,	Tnship.	12 0
Worlington, West	,,	Parish	193	Wortley, New, St. John	,,	Ecl. Dis.	7 3
Worlington	Suffolk	Sub-dis.	3 705	Worton ..	Oxon	Hamlet	
Worlington	,,	Parish	349	Worton, Nether .	,,	Parish	
Worlingworth ..	,,	Parish	740	Worton, Over ..	,,	Parish	
Wormbridge	Hereford	Parish	91	Worton..	Wilts	Tithing	4
Wormegay	Norfolk	Parish	423	Worton, Christch	,,	Ecl. Dis.	5
Wormelow	Hereford	Hund.	11 667	Wortwell	Norfolk	Parish	4
Wormhill	Derby	Tnship.	418	Wothersome	York	Tnship.	
Wormingford	Essex	Parish	503	Wothorpe	Northampton	Hamlet	
Worminghall	Bucks	Parish	354	Wotton under Edge	Gloucester	Sub-dis.	5 7
Wormington	Gloucester	Parish	79	Wotton under Edge	,,	Parish	3 6
Wormleighton	Warwick	Parish	203	Wotton under Edge	,,	Town	2 7

Name of Place.	County.	Description.	Population.	Name of Place.	County.	Description.	Population.
Wotton, St. Mary	Gloucester	Hamlet	1 562	Wrockwardine-Wood	Salop	Tnship.	3 317
Wotton Ville	,,	Parish	91	Wrockwardine-Wood	,,	Ecl. Dis.	3 637
Wotton	Surrey	Hund.	10 483	Wroot	Lincoln	Parish	392
Wotton	,,	Parish	823	Wrotham	Kent	Sub-dis.	5 857
Woughton on Green	Bucks	Parish	314	Wrotham	,,	Parish	3 336
Wouldham	Kent	Parish	433	Wroughton	Wilts	Parish	1 721
Wrabness	Essex	Parish	226	Wroxeter	Salop	Parish	616
Wragby	Lincoln	Sub-dis.	4 537	Wroxhall	Warwick	Parish	144
Wragby	,,	Parish	619	Wroxham	Norfolk	Parish	409
Wragby	York	Parish	594	Wroxton	Oxon	Parish	751
Wraggoe	Lincoln	Wapen.	8 363	Wroxton	,,	Tnship.	540
Wramplingham	Norfolk	Parish	194	Wuerdle	Lancaster	Sub-dis.	8 201
Wrangdike	Rutland	Hund.	4 199	Wuerdle w. Wardle	,,	Tnship.	8 201
Wrangle	Lincoln	Parish	1 198	Wyberton	Lincoln	Parish	608
Wratting, West	Cambs	Parish	777	Wybunbury	Cheshire	Sub-dis.	16 901
Wratting, Great	Suffolk	Parish	423	Wybunbury	,,	Parish	4 985
Wratting, Little	,,	Parish	193	Wybunbury	,,	Tnship.	567
Wrawby	Lincoln	Parish	2 961	Wychwood	Oxon	Parish	106
Wrawby	,,	Tnship.	1 257	Wycliffe	York	Parish	162
Wraxall	Dorset	Parish	83	Wycomb & Chadwell	Leicester	Chap.	139
Wraxall	Somerset	Parish	912	Wycombe	Bucks & Oxon	District	35 138
Wraxhall, North	Wilts	Parish	466	Wycombe, High	Bucks	Sub-dis.	11 589
Wray	Lancaster	Sub-dis.	2 270	Wycombe, West	Bucks & Oxon	Sub-dis.	7 156
Wray, Trinity	,,	Ecl. Dis.	878	Wycombe, Chipping	Bucks	Parish	8 373
Wraysbury	Bucks	Parish	735	Wycombe, Chipping	,,	Tnship.	4 152
Wray w. Botton	Lancaster	Tnship.	797	Wycombe, Chipping ,, {		M. Boro.	4 221
Wreay	Cumberland	Chap.	166			P. Boro.	8 373
Wrecclesham	Surrey	Ecl. Dis.	1 271	Wycombe, West	,,	Parish	2 161
Wreighill	Northumberland	Tnship.	13	Wyddiall	Herts	Parish	213
Wrelton	York	Tnship.	222	Wye	Kent	Sub-dis.	5 767
Wrenbury	Cheshire	Sub-dis.	6 033	Wye	,,	Parish	1 594
Wrenbury	,,	Parish	2 505	Wyeston	Notts	Tnship.	124
Wrenbury w. Frith	,,	Tnship.	531	Wyfordby	Leicester	Parish	144
Wreningham	Norfolk	Parish	437	Wygfair	Denbigh	Tnship.	278
Wrentham	Suffolk	Parish	1 051	Wyham w. Cadeby	Lincoln	Parish	135
Wressell	York	Parish	423	Wyke Regis	Dorset	Parish	2 025
Wrestlingworth	Beds	Parish	657	Wyke Regis, Trinity	,,	Ecl. Dis.	4 438
Wretham, East	Norfolk	Parish	257	Wyke Champflower	Somerset	Chap.	99
Wretham, West	,,	Parish	207	Wyke, St. Mark	Surrey	Ecl. Dis.	521
Wretton	,,	Parish	490	Wyke	Sussex	Sub-dis.	2 909
Wrexham	Denbigh	L. Sub.	26 476	Wyke	York	Ecl. Dis.	3 016
Wrexham	Denbigh, &c.	District	47 975	Wykeham, East	Lincoln	Parish	35
Wrexham	Denb. & Flint	Sub-dis.	17 546	Wykeham	York	Parish	521
Wrexham	,,	Parish	19 780	Wyken	Warwick	Parish	148
Wrexham	Denbigh	Borough	7 562	Wykin	Leicester	Hamlet	76
Wrexham Abbott	,,	Tnship.	2 557	Wylam	Northumberland	Tnship.	1 040
Wrexham Regis	,,	Tnship.	4 959	Wyldecourt	Dorset	Tithing	216
Wribbenhall	Worcester	Ecl. Dis.	1 057	Wylye	Wilts	Parish	489
Wrightington	Lancaster	Tnship.	1 618	Wymering	Hants	Parish	1 071
Wrington	Somerset	Parish	1 617	Wymersley	Northampton	Hund.	10 896
Writhlington	,,	Parish	367	Wymington	Beds	Parish	349
Writtle	Essex	Sub-dis.	5 076	Wymondham	Leicester	Parish	851
Writtle	,,	Parish	2 374	Wymondham	Norfolk	Sub-dis.	8 702
Wrockwardine	Salop	Parish	4 365	Wymondham	,,	Parish	4 952

Name of Place.	County.	Description.	Population.	Name of Place.	County.	Description.	Population.
Wymondham ..	*Norfolk* ..	Town	2 152	Yarpole.. ..	*Hereford* ..	Parish	63
Wymondley, Great	*Herts* ..	Parish	314	Yarwell.. ..	*Northampton*	Parish	40
Wymondley, Little	,, ..	Parish	318	Yate	*Gloucester* ..	Parish	1 13
Wynford Eagle .	*Dorset* ..	Parish	137	Yate & Pick-up Bank	*Lanc.* ..	Tnship.	1 11
Wyrardisbury ..	*Bucks* ..	Parish	735	Yateley	*Hants* ..	Parish	2 80
Wyre Piddle ..	*Worcester* ..	Chap.	229	Yateley	,, ..	Tithing	1 01
Wyresdale, Nether	*Lancaster*..	Tnship.	667	Yatesbury ..	*Wilts* ..	Parish	23
Wyresdale, Over	,, ..	Tnship.	524	Yattendon ..	*Berks* ..	Parish	26
Wyrley, Great ..	*Stafford* ..	Tnship.	890	Yatton	*Hereford* ..	Tnship.	22
Wyrley, Gt., St. Mark	,, ..	Ecl. Dis.	2 067	Yatton	*Somerset* ..	Sub-dis.	8 23
Wysall	*Notts* ..	Parish	274	Yatton	,, ..	Parish	1 85
Wytham ..	*Berks* ..	Parish	176	Yatton Keynell..	*Wilts* ..	Parish	55
Wythop.. ..	*Cumberland*	Tnship.	87	Yaverland ..	*Hants, I. W.*	Parish	6
Wythop Mill ..	,, ..	—	12	Yaxham ..	*Norfolk* ..	Parish	47
Wyton	*York* ..	Tnship	76	Yaxley	*Hunts* ..	Parish	1 41
Wyverstone ..	*Suffolk* ..	Parish	302	Yaxley	*Suffolk* ..	Parish	51
Wyville w. Hungerton	*Lincoln*	Parish	155	Yazor	*Hereford* ..	Parish	28
				Yeadon	*York* ..	Sub-dis.	7 19
Yaddlethorpe .	*Lincoln* ..	Tnship.	124	Yeadon.. ..	,, ..	Tnship.	4 25
Yafforth ..	*York* ..	Chap.	204	**Yeadon**	,, ..	Town	4 10
Yalding.. ..	*Kent* ..	Sub-dis.	4 882	Yeadon, St. John	,, ..	Ecl. Dis.	4 25
Yalding.. ..	,, ..	Parish	2 706	Yealand Conyers	*Lancaster* ..	Tnship.	272
Yalding, St. Margaret	,, ..	Ecl. Dis.	801	Yealand Redmayne	,, ..	Tnship.	209
Yale	*Denbigh* ..	Hund.	5 384	Yealmpton ..	*Devon* ..	Sub-dis.	9 209
Yanwath, &c. ..	*Westmoreland*	Tnship.	381	Yealmpton ..	,, ..	Parish	1 035
Yanworth ..	*Gloucester* ..	Chap.	123	Yearsley ..	*York* ..	Tnship.	180
Yapham ..	*York* ..	Tnship.	169	Yeaveley ..	*Derby* ..	Tnship.	263
Yapton	*Sussex* ..	Sub-dis.	3 006	Yeaveley, Trinity	,, ..	Ecl. Dis.	295
Yapton	,, ..	Parish	589	Yeavering	*Northumberland*	Tnship.	51
Yarborough ..	*Lincoln* ..	Wapen.	26 168	Yeddingham ..	*York* ..	Parish	108
Yarborough ..	,, ..	Parish	279	Yeldersley ..	*Derby* ..	Tnship.	194
Yarcombe ..	*Devon* ..	Parish	815	Yeldham, Great .	*Essex* ..	Parish	696
Yardley.. ..	*Herts* ..	Parish	574	Yeldham, Little.	,, ..	Parish	307
Yardley Gobion .	*Northampton*	Hamlet	650	Yeldon	*Beds* ..	Parish	286
Yardley Hastings	,, ..	Parish	1 152	Yelford	*Oxon* ..	Parish	14
Yardley.. ..	*Worcester* ..	Parish	3 848	Yelling	*Hunts* ..	Parish	414
Yardley Wood..	,, ..	Ecl. Dis.	687	Yelvertoft ..	*Northampton*	Parish	631
Yarkhill ..	*Hereford* ..	Sub-dis.	4 585	Yelverton ..	*Norfolk* ..	Parish	59
Yarkhill ..	,, ..	Parish	568	Yeovil	*Somerset* ..	District	28 189
Yarlett	*Stafford* ..	Parish	21	Yeovil	,, ..	Sub-dis.	9 535
Yarlington ..	*Somerset* ..	Parish	246	Yeovil	,, ..	Parish	8 486
Yarm	*York & Durh.*	Sub-dis.	25 079	**Yeovil**	,, ..	M. Bor.	7 957
Yarm	*York* ..	Parish	1 401	Yeovilton ..	,, ..	Parish	342
Yarmouth ..	*Hants, I. W.*	Parish	726	Yeovilton ..		—	230
Yarmouth, Great	*Norfolk* ..	L. Sub.	30 338	Yerbeston ..	*Pembroke* ..	Parish	118
Yarmouth ..	,, ..	District	30 338	Yetminster ..	*Dorset* ..	Sub-dis.	4 298
Yarmouth Northern	,, ..	Sub-dis.	17 265	Yetminster ..	,, ..	Parish	1 430
Yarmouth Southern	,, ..	Sub-dis.	13 073	Yetminster ..	,, ..	—	696
Yarmouth, Great	,, ..	Parish	30 338	Ynisymond ..	*Glamorgan* .	Hamlet	372
Yarmouth ..	*Norf. & Suff.*	Borough	34 810	Ynysawdre ..	,, ..	Hamlet	345
Yarmouth, Little	*Suffolk* ..	Hamlet	1 714	Ynyscynhaiarn..	*Carnarvon*..	Parish	3 138
Yarnfield ..	*Somerset* ..	Hamlet	61	Yokefleet ..	*York* ..	Tnship.	190
Yarnscombe ..	*Devon* ..	Parish	423	York	.. ..	Province	6138507
Yarnton ..	*Oxon* ..	Parish	294	Diocese of Carlisle ..	..	Diocese	266 591

Name of Place.	County.	Description.	Population.	Name of Place.	County.	Description.	Population.
Diocese of Chester ..	..	Diocese	1248416	Yscirvechan ..	*Brecon* ..	Hamlet	228
„ Durham..	..	Diocese	858 095	Ysclydach ..	„ ..	Hamlet	305
„ Manchester	..	Diocese	1679326	Ysgwyddgwyn ..	*Glamorgan* .	Hamlet	537
„ Ripon ..	..	Diocese	1167288	Yspytty..	*Denb. & Carnv.*	Sub-dis.	2 935
„ Sodor and Man..		Diocese	52 469	Yspytty.. ..	„ „	Parish	869
„ York ..	..	Diocese	866 322	Yspyttyystradmeiric *Cardigan* .		Parish	160
orkshire ..	.. ..	County	2033610	Yspyttyystwyth .	„ ..	Parish	843
East Riding ..	..	E. R.	240 227	Ystrad ..	*Carmarthen*	Hamlet	160
North Riding	..	N. R.	295 483	Ystradgunlais ..	*Brecon* ..	L. Sub.	4 444
West Riding..	..	W. R.	1497900	Ystradgunlais ..	*Brec. & Glam.*	Sub-dis.	12 328
Northern Division, W. R.	..	N. Div.	781 943	Ystradgunlais ..	*Brecon* ..	Parish	4 345
Southern Division, W. R.	..	S. Div.	715 957	Ystradgunlais, Lower „	..	Hamlet	3 801
ork .. .. *York*	..	District	59 909	Ystradgunlais,Upper „	..	Hamlet	544
ork .. .. „	..	Union	59 158	Ystradowen ..	*Glamorgan* .	Parish	248
ork .. .. „	{	M. City	40 433	Ystradvelltey ..	*Brec. & Glam.*	Sub-dis.	3 303
		P. City	45 385	Ystradvelltey ..	*Brecon* ..	Parish	668
ork Castle .. „	..	—	267	Ystradvelltey, Lower „	..	Hamlet	299
ork, St. Thomas „	..	Ecl. Dis.	3 669	Ystradvelltey, Upper „	..	Hamlet	369
ork Town .. *Surrey*	..	Ecl.Dis.	1 407	Ystradyfodwg ..	*Glamorgan* .	Parish	3 857
oulgreave .. *Derby*	..	Tnship.	3 738	Ystradyfodwg,Home „	..	Hamlet	1 011
oulthorpe, &c.. *York*	..	Tnship.	125	Ystradyfodwg, Middle „	..	Hamlet	1 203
oulton.. .. „	..	Tnship.	73	**Zeal-Monachorum** *Devon* ..		Parish	549
oxall .. .. *Stafford*	..	Sub-dis.	4 765	Zeals	*Wilts* ..	Tithing	559
oxall .. .. „	..	Parish	1 443	Zeals, St. Martin „		Ecl. Dis.	559
oxford.. .. *Suffolk*	..	Parish	1 111	Zennor	*Cornwall* ..	Parish	933
sccifiog .. *Flint*	..	Parish	1 475				
scirvawr .. *Brecon*	..	Hamlet	189				

EXPLANATION for REFERENCE.

Union.—The "**District**" of the same Name shows the Population of the "**Union**," when not otherwise expressed, as under the supervision of the Superintendent Registrar of the District. Appointed Pursuant to the Statute 6 and 7 William IV. cap. 86.

District—"**Superintendent Registrar's Districts**—are generally co-extensive with the 'Poor Law Unions' of the same name, but in some instances two or more **Unions** are combined to form one **Registration District**. In cases where the *Union* differs from the *District*, the Name and Population of the former is also inserted.

"For **Parishes** (in Cities and Boroughs) known only by the name of a *Saint*, search should be made under the letter S, where the abbreviation *St.* is classed as though written *Saint* in full.

"The **Ecclesiastical Districts** are usually inserted under the name of the Parish or Place out of which they have been formed, unless they have a clearly defined Name.

Spelling.—"Should any Place not be found on a first reference, it should be searched for under some probable variation of spelling. In some few cases the words in the Column headed 'Name of Place' have been abbreviated to reserve space.

Counties.—"When the same word occurs as the principal Names of Places in different *Counties*, the *Alphabetical Order of the County* settles the priority of insertion, and in all such cases a departure from a strictly Alphabetical arrangement has been deemed allowable.

Boundaries.—"Before quitting the subject of our 'Territorial Divisions,' it may be useful to point out how necessary it is, when citing the **Population** of a **Place**, to state explicitly what limits are referred to. For example, the term 'Manchester' may mean the 'Parish,' the 'Township,' the 'Parliamentary Borough,' the 'Municipal Borough,' the 'Registration or Poor Law District,' or the 'City,' in a popular sense, including Suburban Places. A want of precision in speaking of Places which give Name to several *local sub-divisions* not unfrequently leads to mistakes, and when such Places are compared with others, without proper care being taken to apply the comparison to corresponding boundaries, *erroneous inferences are drawn*, and thus the **Parish** may be taken for the **Town** of the same *Name*, and *vice versâ* the 'Town' for the 'Parish,' *etc.*, unless care is taken to define the 'Territorial Limit,' or **Area.**"

ISLANDS IN THE BRITISH SEAS.

Name of Place.	Description.	Population.	Name of Place.	Description.	Populat.
Alderney, Isle	Island	4 932	St. Saviour .. *Isle of Jrsy.*	Parish	3 7
			Trinity[h] .. ,,	Parish	2 2
Guernsey, Isle	Island	29 804			
			Jethou, Isle	Island	
Câtel .. .. *Isle of Gnsy.*	Parish	2 071			
Forest .. .. ,,	Parish	612	Man, Isle of	Island	52 4
St. Andrew .. ,,	Parish	1 049			
St. Martin .. ,,	Parish	2 000	Andreas .. *Isle of Man.*	Parish	1 9
St. Mary-de-Castro ,,	Parish	2 071	Arbory .. ,,	Parish	1 4
St. Peter-du-Bois ,,	Parish	1 141	Ballaugh .. ,,	Parish	1 2
St. Peter-Port ,,	Tn.& Pr.	16 388	Braddan[i] .. ,,	Parish	2 7
St. Sampson .. ,,	Parish	2 781	Bride .. .. ,,	Parish	9
St. Saviour .. ,,	Parish	942	Castletown .. ,,	Town	2 3
Torteval .. ,,	Parish	365	Conchan[k] .. ,,	Parish	14 1
Vale .. .. ,,	Parish	2 455	Douglas .. ,,	Town	12 5
			German[l] .. ,,	Parish	4 7
Herm, Isle	Island	41	Jurby .. .. ,,	Parish	9
			Lezayre .. .. ,,	Parish	2 5
Jersey, Isle	Island	55 613	Lonan .. .. ,,	Parish	2 9
			Malew[m] .. ,,	Parish	5 0
Grouville[a] .. *Isle of Jrsy.*	Parish	2 628	Marown .. ,,	Parish	1 1
St. Brelade[b] .. ,,	Parish	2 354	Maughold[n] .. ,,	Parish	4 5
St. Clement[c] .. ,,	Parish	1 448	Michael .. ,,	Parish	1 3
St. Helier[d] .. ,,	Tn.& Pr.	29 528	Patrick .. ,,	Parish	2 7
St. John .. ,,	Parish	1 815	Peel .. .. ,,	Town	2 8
St. Laurence[e] .. ,,	Parish	2 255	Ramsey .. ,,	Town	2 8
St. Martin .. ,,	Parish	3 558	Rushen .. ,,	Parish	3 30
St. Mary .. ,,	Parish	1 040	St. Ann .. ,,	Parish	6
St. Ouen .. ,,	Parish	2 320	Sark (Great and Little)	Isles.	5
St. Peter[f] .. ,,	Parish	2 671	Scilly Isles .. ,,	Isles.	2 4

[a] *Grouville* includes the ancient village of Gorey, but a considerable and populous portion of the modern Gorey extends into the adjoining parish of St. Martin. This latter portion embraces Gorey Harbour, and includes the crews of the oyster fishing vessels (205 persons) who were afloat on the night of the 7th April, 1861, also 71 persons on board of Her Majesty's Ship "Dasher," stationed there for the protection of the fishery.

[b] *St. Brelade's* includes the town of St. Aubin and village of La Cônueire.

[c] *St. Clement's* includes the village of Le Bourg.

[d] The parish of *St. Helier* includes the village of Ville-es-Nouaux.

[e] *St. Laurence* includes the village of Millbrook.

[f] *St. Peter's* includes the village of Beaumont.

[g] *St. Saviour's* parish includes George Town, a suburb of St. Helier, and the villages of Five-Oaks and Longueville. "St. Saviour" continues to [a] favourite parish with native families remov out of town and families coming to reside in Island, from the beauty of the country and proximity to the town of "St. Helier," hence increase of its population.

[h] *Trinity* includes the village of La Croiserie

[i] *Braddan* parish contains the other portion the Town of Douglas (493 inhabitants).

[k] *Conchan* parish contains the greater part the Town of Douglas (12 018 inhabitants).

[l] *German* Parish contains the Town of Pe (2 848 inhabitants).

[m] *Malew* Parish contains the Town of Cast town (2 373 inhabitants). Census, 1861.

[n] *Maughold* Parish contains the Town Ramsey (2 891 inhabitants).

Peel.—The increase may be attributed to the general improvement of trade, and especiall the increase of ship-building.

Lezayre.—Increase from contiguity to the increasing town of Ramsey.

Ramsey.—Many English residents have recently settled in this town.

Douglas is rapidly rising as a watering-place and as a place of trad

ISLANDS off the MAINLAND.

POPULATION of the several **Islands**, around the Coast of **England** and **Wales**, including the **Channel Islands**. Census of **1851** and **1861**, with the **Increase** or **Decrease**, in the 10 years.

Population.* (Official Census.)		Islands in the British Seas. *Topographically arranged.*	Increase or Decrease between 1851 and 1861.	
1851.	**1861.**		**Increase.**	**Decrease.**
268 465	276 007	Total Islands off the Mainland (including the Channel Islands) .. .. .. }	7 542	—
		West Coast.		
52 344	52 444	Isle of Man	100	—
43	25	Calf of Man	—	18
306	294	Walney .. .. .. *Lancaster* ..	—	12
17	4	Peel .. .. .. ,, ..	—	13
3	5	Chapel .. .. .. ,, ..	2	—
8	3	Holme .. .. .. ,, ..	—	5
10	7	Hilbre .. .. .. *Cheshire* ..	—	3
57 318	54 603	Anglesey.. .. .. *Anglesey* ..	—	2 715
9	6	Skerries .. .. .. ,, ..	—	3
92	81	Bardsey .. .. .. *Carnarvon* ..	—	11
12	15	Ramsey .. .. .. *Pembroke* ..	3	—
6	2	Skoholm .. .. .. ,, ..	—	4
86	73	Caldy .. .. .. ,, ..	—	13
4	21	Barry .. .. .. *Glamorgan* ..	17	—
34	48	Lundy .. .. .. *Devon* ..	14	—
		Scilly Islands.		
1 668	1 532	St. Mary .. .. .. *Cornwall* ..	—	136
416	399	Trescoe .. .. .. ,, ..	—	17
211	185	St. Martin .. .. .. ,, ..	—	26
204	200	St. Agnes.. .. .. ,, ..	—	4
118	115	Bryher .. .. .. ,, ..	—	3
10	—	Sampson .. .. .. ,, ..	—	10
		South Coast.		
147	132	St. Michael's Mount .. *Cornwall* ..	—	15
7	8	Looe .. .. .. ,, ..	1	—
29 757	29 804	Guernsey.. .. .. *Channel Isle*..	47	—
57 020	55 613	Jersey .. .. .. ,, ..	—	1 407
580	583	Sark .. .. .. ,, ..	3	—
46	41	Herm .. .. .. ,, ..	—	5
3 333	4 932	Alderney.. .. .. ,, ..	1 599	—
3	5	Jethou .. .. .. ,, ..	2	—
50 324	55 362	Isle of Wight .. .. *Hants* ..	5 038	—
		East Coast.		
13 385	18 494	Sheppey .. .. .. *Kent*	5 109	—
16	13	Coquet .. .. .. *Northumberland*	—	3
20	23	Fern .. .. .. ,, ..	12	—
908	935	Holy Island .. .. ,, ..	27	—

* Official Census of England and Wales, 1861. General Report, Vol. 3, p. 106.

𝕷𝖔𝖓𝖉𝖔𝖓—within the Police District—Area—Inhabited Houses and Population.*

Area.—The *Metropolitan Police District* extends over the whole of Middlesex (exclusive of the City or *Municipal* London) and the surrounding Parishes in the Counties of *Surrey, Kent, Essex, and Hertford*, of which any part is within **12** miles from "Charing Cross," and those also of which any part is not more than **15** miles in a straight line from Charing Cross.

The **Area** of the **Metropolitan** Police District is **439,770** statute acres, equal to **687** square miles. The **City** or Municipal Police District is **725** statute acres, equal to **1·13** square miles, and including this the *Metropolitan and City Police Area* is represented by a square of **26·24** miles to the side.

LONDON within the Police District.*	Inhabited Houses, 1861.	Population, 1861.
Metropolitan POLICE DISTRICT	421 231	3 110 654
City of London POLICE DISTRICT	13 298	112 063
Total ..	434 529	3 222 717
The "Metropolitan Police District" includes :— All the Parishes and Places within the limits of "LONDON" (exclusive of the City of London) and the	346 123	2 691 926

Additional Parishes :—

In Middlesex.—

				Inhabited Houses	Population
Acton	Great Stanmore	Hornsey	Ruislip		
Ashford	Hampton	Ickenham	Shepperton		
Chiswick	Hampton Wick	Isleworth	South Mimms		
Cowley	Hanwell	Kingsbury	Staines		
Cranford	Hanworth	Laleham	Stanwell		
Ealing	Harefield	Little Stanmore	Sunbury		
East Bedfont	Harlington	Littleton	Teddington	31 853	175 671
Edgware	Harmondsworth	Monken-Hadley	Tottenham		
Edmonton	Harrow - on - the -	New Brentford	Twickenham		
Enfield	Hill	Northolt	Twyford Abbey		
Feltham	Hayes	Norwood	West Drayton		
Finchley	Hendon	Perrivale	Willesden and		
Fryern Barnet	Heston	Pinner	Uxbridge		
Great Greenford	Hillingdon				

In Surrey.—

				Inhabited Houses	Population
Addington	Cuddington	Long Ditton	Sanderstead		
Banstead	East Moulsey	Malden	Sutton		
Barnes	Epsom	Merton	Thames Ditton		
Beddington	Ewell	Mitcham	Wallington		
Carshalton	Farley	Morden	Warlingham	19 222	109 981
Cheam	Ham-with-Hatch	Mortlake	West Moulsey		
Chessington	Hook	Penge	Wimbledon and		
Coulsdon	Kew	Petersham	Woodmansterne.		
Croydon	Kingston - upon - Thames	Richmond			

* *Official Census of England and Wales, 1861. Vol. I, p. 224.*

Additional Parishes (*Continued*).				Inhabited Houses, 1861.	Population, 1861.
Kent.— ckenham, xley, mley, islehurst, ayford	Down, East Wickham, Erith, Farnborough	Foots Cray, Hayes, Keston, North Cray	Orpington, St. Mary Cray, St Paul Cray and West Wickham	5 837	31 005
Essex.— rking, igwell, ingford, genham	East Ham, Little Ilford, Loughton	Low Leighton, Waltham Abbey, Walthamstow	Wanstead, West Ham and Woodford.	14 521	83 444
Herts.— denham, ashey, aeshunt	Chipping Barnet, East Barnet	Elstree, Northam	Ridge, Shenley and Totteridge.	3 675	18 627

PULATION of **72 Cities, Boroughs,** and **Towns** in **England** and **Wales,** of more than 20,000 Inhabitants at the Census of 1861, for the last Seven Decennial Censuses, within the same, or nearly the same, limits or boundaries.

City, Borough, or Town. (*Alphabetical.*)	POPULATION.* (*Official Census.*)						
	1801	1811	1821	1831	1841	1851	1861
ndon[a]	958 863	1 138 815	1 378 947	1 654 994	1 948 417	3 362 236	2 803 989
hton-under-Lyne[b] P.	6 391	7 959	9 222	14 035	22 678	29 791	33 917
th .. .. M. & P.	33 196	38 408	46 700	50 800	53 196	54 240	52 528
rkenhead[c] .. P.	667	795	1 313	4 195	11 563	34 469	51 649
rmingham .. M. & P.	70 670	82 753	101 722	143 986	182 922	232 841	296 076

Within the limits adopted by the Registrar-General for the "*Weekly Table of Births and Deaths in London.*" The boundaries are uniform for the whole period.
Present Parliamentary limits of "Ashton-under-Lyne," 1841-61; and nearly the corresponding area, 1801-31.

[c] "Birkenhead" Parliamentary Borough, 1851 and 1861; for previous years the population of the four Townships of Birkenhead, Claughton, Oxton, and Tranmere is inserted; in 1851 their population amounted to 33,525, and in 1861 to 50,384 persons.

Note.—When not otherwise distinguished, the boundaries or *superficial areas* are the same as the present limits for all the periods for the 60 years.

(M.) Municipal Borough; (P.) Parliamentary Borough; and (M. P.) Municipal and Parliamentary limits co-extensive, or the same.

* *Official Census of England and Wales,* 1861. *General Report, Vol.* 3. *p.* 102.

Population of 72 Cities, &c. *(continued)*.

City, Borough, or Town. *(Alphabetical).*			POPULATION.* *(Official Census).*						
			1801	1811	1821	1831	1841	1851	1861
Blackburn	..	M. & P.	11 980	15 083	21 940	27 091	36 629	46 536	63 126
Bolton..	..	M. & P.	17 966	24 799	32 045	42 245	51 029	61 171	70 395
Bradford	..	M. & P.	13 264	16 012	26 307	43 527	66 715	103 778	106 218
Brighton	..	P.	7 440	12 205	24 741	41 994	49 170	69 673	87 317
Bristol[d]	..	M. & P.	61 153	71 433	85 108	104 408	125 146	137 328	154 093
Burnley[e]	..	M.	3 918	5 405	8 242	10 026	14 224	20 828	28 700
Bury[f] ..	..	P.	9 152	11 302	13 480	19 140	24 846	31 262	37 563
Cambridge	..	M. & P.	10 087	11 108	14 142	20 917	24 453	27 815	26 361
Canterbury[g]	..	M. & P.	9 000	10 200	12 779	13 679	17 904	18 398	21 324
Cardiff..	..	M. & P.	1 870	2 457	3 521	6 187	10 077	18 351	32 954
Carlisle[h]	..	M. & P.	9 415	11 476	14 416	18 865	21 550	26 310	29 417
Chatham[i]	..	P.	12 940	15 787	19 177	21 124	24 269	28 424	36 177
Cheltenham	..	P.	3 076	8 325	13 396	22 942	31 411	35 051	39 693
Chester[j]	..	M. & P.	15 174	16 140	19 949	21 344	23 866	27 766	31 110
Colchester	..	M. & P.	11 520	12 544	14 016	16 167	17 790	19 443	23 809
Coventry	..	P.	16 034	17 923	21 448	27 298	31 032	36 812	41 647
Croydon[k]	..	—	Not ascertainable 1801–1841.					10 260	20 325
Derby ..	..	M. & P.	10 832	13 043	17 423	23 627	32 741	40 609	43 091
Devonport	..	P.	27 154	35 257	39 621	44 454	43 532	50 159	64 783
Dover[l] ..	..	M. & P.	8 028	11 230	12 664	15 645	19 189	22 244	25 325
Dudley	..	P.	10 107	13 925	18 211	23 430	31 232	37 962	44 975
Exeter[m]	..	M. & P.	17 412	18 896	23 479	28 242	37 231	40 688	41 749
Halifax[n]	..	M. & P.	12 010	12 766	17 056	21 552	27 520	33 582	37 014

[d] Present limits of "Bristol," 1841-61; nearly the same limits are taken for the previous years.

[e] Municipal Borough in 1861; Town of "Burnley," 1851; nearly the same limits, 1801-41.

[f] "Bury" Parliamentary Borough, 1841-61; for 1801-31 the population of the Townships of Bury and Elton is inserted; in 1841 their population was 25,912; in 1851, 32,262; and in 1861, 38,569.

[g] "Canterbury" City, present limits, 1841-61. Ancient limits, 1801-31; the population within the same limits was 15,003 in 1841; 14,100 in 1851: and 16,643 in 1861.

[h] City of "Carlisle," 1841-61; and the present limits, as nearly as possible, for the previous years.

[i] Parliamentary Borough of "Chatham," 1841-61; nearly the corresponding limits for 1801-31.

[j] Old limits of the City of "Chester," 1801-31; present limits, 1841-61. Population within the old City was 23,115 in 1841; 26,800 in 1851; and 30,136 in 1861.

[k] For 1851 and 1861 the population of "Croydon" Town is entered. The entire parish contained 5,743 persons in 1801; 7,801 in 1811; 9,254 in 1821; 12,447 in 1831; 16,712 in 1841; 20,343 in 1851; and 30,240 persons in 1861.

[l] Borough of "Dover," 1841-61; nearly the same limits, 1801-31.

[m] Old limits of "Exeter," 1801-31; present Parliamentary limits, 1841-61. Population within the old limits was 31,305 in 1841; 32,818 in 1851; and 33,738 in 1861.

[n] Present limits of "Halifax" Borough, 1841-61; the corresponding area, as nearly as possible, 1801-31.

Note.—When not otherwise distinguished, the boundaries or *superficial areas* are the same as the present limits for all the periods for the 60 years.

(M.) Municipal Borough; (P.) Parliamentary Borough; and (M. P.) Municipal and Parliamentary limits co-extensive, or the same.

* *Official Census of England and Wales*, 1861. *General Report, Vol. 3. p. 102.*

Population of 72 Cities, &c. *(continued)*.

City, Borough, or Town. *(Alphabetical.)*		POPULATION.* *(Official Census.)*						
		1801	1811	1821	1831	1841	1851	1861
..stings°	P.	2 982	3 848	6 111	10 097	11 617	17 011	22 910
..ddersfield	P.	7 268	9 671	13 284	19 035	25 068	30 880	31 877
..ll?	M. & P.	29 580	37 005	44 520	51 911	67 308	84 690	97 661
..wich	M. & P.	11 277	13 670	17 186	20 201	25 384	32 914	37 950
..eds	M. & P.	53 162	62 534	83 796	123 393	152 074	172 270	207 165
..icester	M. & P.	17 005	23 453	31 036	40 639	50 806	60 584	68 056
..ncoln	M. & P.	7 197	8 599	9 995	11 217	13 896	17 533	20 999
..verpool?	M. & P.	82 295	104 104	138 354	201 751	286 487	375 955	443 938
..cclesfield?	M. & P.	8 743	12 299	17 746	23 129	32 629	39 048	36 101
..idstone	P.	8 027	9 443	12 508	15 790	18 086	20 801	23 058
..anchester	P.	76 788	91 130	129 035	187 022	242 983	316 213	357 979
..erthyr Tydfil?	P.	10 127	14 945	20 959	27 281	43 031	63 080	83 875
..wcastle-upon-Tyne	M. & P.	33 048	32 573	41 794	53 613	70 337	87 784	109 108
..wport (Mon.)?	M. & P.	1 423	3 025	4 951	7 062	10 815	19 323	23 249
..rthampton	M. & P.	7 020	8 427	10 793	15 351	21 242	26 657	32 813
..rwich	M. & P.	36 854	36 256	50 288	61 116	62 344	68 713	74 891
..ttingham	M. & P.	28 801	34 030	40 190	50 220	52 164	57 407	74 693
..dham	P.	21 677	29 497	38 201	50 513	60 451	72 357	94 344
..xford?	M. & P.	11 694	12 931	16 364	20 649	24 258	27 843	27 560
..ymouth	M. & P.	16 040	20 803	21 591	31 080	36 520	52 221	62 599
..rtsmouth	M. & P.	33 226	41 587	46 743	50 389	53 032	72 096	94 799
..reston	M. & P.	12 174	17 360	24 859	33 871	50 887	69 542	82 985
..eading	M. & P.	9 742	10 788	12 867	15 595	18 937	21 456	25 045
..ochdale?	P.	8 542	10 753	14 017	19 041	24 272	29 195	38 184

? "Hastings" Parliamentary Borough, 1841-61. For 1801-31 the population within the old Borough is entered. In 1841 there were 22,797 persons; in 1851, 17,076; and in 1861, 11,570 within the ancient limits.
? Borough of "Kingston-upon-Hull," 1841-61; nearly the corresponding limits, 1801-31.
? "Liverpool" Borough for 1841-61; nearly the corresponding area is taken for 1801-31.
? "Macclesfield" Borough, 1841-61. Macclesfield Township (containing 24,137 in 1841; 29,648 in 1851; and 27,475 in 1861) is entered for previous years.
? "Merthyr-Tydfil" Parliamentary Borough, 1841-61; the corresponding limits, as nearly as possible, 1801-31.

? "Newport" Borough, present limits, 1841-61; St. Woollos Parish, 1801-31; a portion of the Parish, containing in 1851, 1,149, and in 1861, 1,780 persons, is not within the present limits of the Borough.
? "Oxford," as returned in the Population Abstracts, 1801-31; present extended limits, 1841-61; the population within the ancient limits in 1841 was 23,855; in 1851, 25,249; and in 1861, 25,249. Resident members of the University are included.
? "Rochdale" Parliamentary Borough, 1841-61; nearly the corresponding limits, 1801-31.

Note.—When not otherwise distinguished, the boundaries or *superficial areas* are the same as the present limits for all the periods for the 60 years.

(M.) Municipal Borough; (P.) Parliamentary Borough; and (M. P.) Municipal and Parliamentary limits co-extensive or the same.

* *Official Census of England and Wales*, 1861. *General Report*, Vol. 3, *p.* 102.

Population of 72 Cities, &c. *(continued)*.

City, Borough, or Town. (*Alphabetical.*)		POPULATION.* (*Official Census.*)						
		1801	1811	1821	1831	1841	1851	1861
Salford[w]	M. & P.	18 088	24 744	32 600	50 810	68 386	85 108	102 44?
Sheffield	M. & P.	45 755	53 231	65 275	91 692	111 091	135 310	185 17?
Shrewsbury[x]	M. & P.	14 739	16 825	19 854	21 297	18 217	19 681	22 16?
Southampton	M. & P.	7 913	9 617	13 353	19 324	27 744	35 305	46 96?
South Shields	M. & P.	11 011	15 165	16 503	18 756	23 072	28 974	35 23?
Stalybridge[y]	M.	Not ascertainable 1801–41.					20 760	24 92?
Stockport[z]	M. & P.	14 830	17 545	21 726	25 469	50 154	53 835	54 68?
Stoke-upon-Trent[1]	P.	23 278	31 557	40 237	51 589	68 444	84 027	101 20?
Sunderland	P.	24 998	25 821	31 891	40 735	53 335	67 394	85 79?
Swansea[2]	M. & P.	10 117	11 963	14 896	19 672	24 604	31 461	41 60?
Tynemouth	M. & P.	13 171	17 548	23 173	23 206	25 416	29 170	34 02?
Wakefield[3]	P.	10 581	11 393	14 164	15 932	18 842	22 057	23 15?
Walsall[4]	M. & P.	10 399	11 189	11 914	15 066	19 857	25 680	37 76?
Warrington[5]	P.	11 321	12 682	14 822	18 184	21 346	23 363	26 94?
Wigan	M. & P.	10 989	14 060	17 716	20 774	25 517	31 941	37 65?
Wolverhampton	P.	30 584	43 190	53 011	67 514	93 245	119 748	147 67?
Worcester[6]	M. & P.	11 460	13 814	17 023	18 610	27 004	27 528	31 22?
Yarmouth	M. & P.	16 573	20 448	21 007	24 535	27 865	30 879	34 81?
York	M.	16 846	19 099	21 711	26 260	28 842	36 303	40 43?

[w] The population within the present limits of "Salford" Borough is given for 1841-61; and for previous years that of the three Townships of Salford, Broughton, and Pendleton; their population in 1841 was 68,026; in 1851, 84,773; and in 1861, 101,787.

[x] "Shrewsbury" Poor Law Incorporation for 1801-31. The present Borough for 1841-61. The population of that part of the Incorporation not included in the present Borough in 1841 was 3,301; in 1851, 3,423; and in 1861, 3,621 persons.

[y] Municipal Borough of "Staleybridge" is situate partly in Townships of Dukinfield and Staley in *Cheshire*, and partly in Ashton-under-Lyne Parish in *Lancashire*; the population in 1861 within the limits adopted for the Town in 1851 was 21,720 persons.

[z] "Stockport" Borough for 1841-61; the population within the present limits is given; for the other years that of Stockport old Borough or Town-ship, which contained 28,431 inhabitants 1841; 30,589 in 1851: and 30,746 in 1861.

[1] Parliamentary Borough of "Stoke-upon-Tren? (including Hanley Municipal Borough) co? prises an important part of the Staffordshi? Pottery District; present limits throughout.

[2] "Swansea" Borough, 1841-61; limits for 1801-? as nearly as possible.

[3] "Wakefield" Parliamentary Borough, 1841-6? nearly the corresponding limits, 1801-31.

[4] "Walsall" Parish, 1801-31; the Borough, 1841-6? Part of the Parish not included in the Borou? contained 995 persons in 1841; 1,142 in 185? and 1,930 in 1861.

[5] Parliamentary limits of "Warrington," 1841-6? the corresponding area, as nearly as possib? 1801-31.

[6] The City of "Worcester," as returned in the Pop? lation Abstracts, 1801-31; extended limits (co? sisting of parts of parishes of which the Pop? lation, prior to 1841, cannot be ascertaine? 1841-61.

Note.—When not otherwise distinguished, the boundaries or *superficial areas* are the same as t? present limits for all the periods for the 60 years.

(M.) Municipal Borough; (P.) Parliamentary Borough; and (M. P.) Municipal and Parl? mentary limits co-extensive or the same.

* *Official Census of England and Wales*, 1861. *General Report, Vol. 3, p. 102.*

Glossary

Of the *Prefixes* and *Affixes* to the **Names** of **Cities, Towns,** and **Places.**

⁎⁎ The present **Glossary** is an extension of that printed in the Enumeration Abstracts of 1831
1841. Most of the Welsh appellatives (distinguished as **Br.,** *British*) are given on the authority
e late *Mr. Rickman;* for the signification of the others the following works have been consulted :—
orth's *Anglo-Saxon Dictionary,* Jamieson's *Gaelic Dictionary,* Kemble's *Saxons in England,* and
ale's and *Lewis's Topographical Dictionaries.*
The following abbreviations are used:—**A.S.,** Anglo-Saxon; **Br.,** British; **Cel.,** Celtic;
French; **Gael.,** Gaelic; **Lat.,** Latin; **Scan.,** Scandinavian; **Sax.,** Saxon; but as many of the
es are common to several dialects, **it is not intended to convey that they are all of the
ise origin suggested.**

APPELLATIVES.

r (*Br.*) *The confluence of waters, the mouth
    of a river, a port.*
aird, ard (*Cel.*) *an eminence, a promontory,
    high, lofty.*
(*Br.*) .. .. *by, about*
(*Br.*) .. .. .. *many, numerous*
Br.) .. .. *upon*
aird (*Cel.*) .. *high, lofty (Arduus, Lat.)*
in (*Cel.*) .. .. *a field*
ater (*Cel.*) .. .. *a height, high, lofty*
n, aven (*Br.*) .. .. *a river, a stream*

h, bychan, fechan (*Br.*) .. .. *little, small*
(*Cel.*) .. .. *a village*
(*Br.*) .. .. .. *high, lofty, tall*
(*Fr.*) .. .. *fine, pleasant, beautiful*
w (*Br.*) .. .. *birch trees*
(*Scan.*) *a beacon-stone, a tower on which
    the beacon fire was set*
e, Bel (*Br.*) .. .. .. *a town*
dd, bardd (*Br.*) .. .. .. *a bard*
, bein, pen (*Cel.*) .. .. *a hill or mountain*
ws (*Br.*) *a place of moderate temperature
    between hill and vale*
r, blar (*Cel.*) *a field or plain clear of woods,
    frequently abounding in heather*
e, bôd (*Br.*) .. .. .. *abode, home*
tel, bothel (*A. S.*) .. .. *a dwelling place*
rne, bourn (*A. S.*) *a stream, brook, river,
    fountain, well*
e (*Cel.*) .. .. *a hill, an open field*
g, bridge (*Sax.*) *a bridge, a passage of wood
    or stone over a river*
h (*Br.*) .. .. .. *of divers colours*

Bro, fro (*Br.*) .. .. *a plain*
Bron, bryn, bre (*Br.*) *a slope, a hill-side, a peak*
Burg, burgh, borough, bury (*A. S.*) *a town, city,
    castle, or fort*
By (*Scan.*) *a dwelling, originally a single farm,
    afterwards a town in general* ⁎

Cae (*Br.*) .. .. .. *a hedge, a field*
Car, caer, gaer (*Br.*) *a fort or fortress, a town*
Cairn, carn (*Cel.*) *a memorial heap of stones*
Cambus (*Cel.*) *a promontory, the curve or bend
    of a river*
Canol (*Br.*) .. .. *middle*
Carse (*Cel.*) .. *low or fertile land, a valley*
Capel (*Br.*) .. .. *a chapel*
Carog (*Br.*) .. .. *a brook*
Carrig, graig, craig (*Br.*) *a rock, a large stone*
Caster, cester, chester, *an encampment, a fortified
    town, a city, fort, castle;
    ceaster (Sax.), castrum
    (Lat.)*
Cefn (*Br.*) .. *the back or ridge of a mountain*
Cell, celli (*Br.*) .. .. *a cell, a grove*
Cemmin, cennin (*Br.*) .. *a leek, a plant*
Cen (*Br.*) .. .. .. *the skin*
Church (*A. S.*) .. .. .. *(See Kirk)*
Ci (*Br.*) .. .. *a dog*
Cil (*Br.*) .. *a small church, a retreat*
Claws, clâs (*Br.*) .. .. .. *a cloister*
Clawdd (*Br.*) .. .. *a ditch, a fence*
Clack, clachan (*Cel.*) .. *a small village*
Clegyrog, -rawg (*Br.*) .. *rocky, rugged*
Cliffe (*A. S.*) *The cut off (cleft) or broken moun-
    tains on the sea sides; a rock*

⁎ The places in England with names terminating in *-by* are, with few exceptions, found in the
lities selected by the Danes for conquest or colonization.

GLOSSARY (*continued*).

Clydog, -dawg (*Br.*)	*a shelter*
Coch, goch (*Br.*)	*red*
Coed, goed (*Br.*)	*a wood*
Col, cul (*Cel.*) ..	*the back or hinder part*
Combe (*A. S.*)	*a low place enclosed with hills, a valley*
Côr, gor (*Br.*)	*a choir*
Cors (*Br.*)	*a marsh, a bog*
Cott, cote (*A. S.*) ..	*a cot, cottage, bed, den, a covering, shelter for men or animals*
Croes, crwys (*Br.*)	*a cross*
Crug (*Br.*)	*a mount*
Cwm (*Br.*)	*a dale, a valley*
Cyd (*Br.*)	*with*
Cylch (*Br.*)	*a circle*
Cymmer (*Br.*)	*the confluence of rivers*
Dale, dahl (*Sax.*)	*A dale, a meadow or valley (generally conjoined with the name of a river flowing through the dale.)*
Dau (*Br.*)	*two*
De (*Br.*)	*the south*
Dee, die (*Cel.*)	*a dark stream*
Den (*A. S.*)	*forest, outlying pasture in the woods*
Den (*Cel.*) ..	*a small valley, a dingle*
Dewi (*Br.*)	*Davy, David*
Dinas (*Br.*)	*a fortified mount*
Dir (*Br.*)	*certain, sure*
Discoed (Is coed) (*Br.*) ..	*beneath the wood*
Diserth (*Br.*)	*a desert*
Dol (*Cel.*)	*a flat field, a meadow*
Dôl (*Br.*)	*a dale, a valley*
Don (*A. S.*)	*(sometimes synonymous with* den, *and sometimes with* ton, *which see)*
Du (*Br.*)	*black, dark*
Dun, dum (*Cel.*)	*the ridge of a hill, a hill or fort on a hill;* dunum (*Lat.*) druim (*Gael*)
Drum, drom (*Cel.*) ..	*a knoll, a ridge*
Dyffryn, *i. e.* dyft-hynt (*Br.*)	*the course of waters' a wide valley*
Eccles, eglis, eglyws	*A church or place of worship;* ecclesia (*Lat.*), eglise (Fr.), *eaglais* (Gael)
Eden, eddain	*A gliding stream* [deduced from *eddain* (Cel.) and traced to *ea* (A. S.) water, and *den* (Cel.) a vale]
End (*A. S.*)	*end, extremity, point*
Erch (*Br.*) ..	*dun or dark colour, horrible*
Escob, esgob (*Br.*)	*a bishop*
Esk (*Cel.*)	*water, a stream*
Ey, ay, ea (*A. S.*)	*an isle (*Ig*, an island, Heb,* ai *habited land, island)*
Fâ, fan, man (*Br.*)	*a place*
Fab (*Br.*)	*father*
Fair, mair (*Br.*)	*the Virgin Mary; a town or church dedicated to the Virgin Mary*
Fechan (*Br.*)	*little, small*
Fell (*A. S.*) ..	*a hill, a mountain, a ridge*
Fetter (*Cel.*)	*a pass, a ravine*
Ffin (*Br.*)	*a boundary*
Fford (*Br.*)	*a way, a passage*
Ffraid (*Br.*)	*St. Bride*
Ffynnon (*Br.*)	*a well*
Field, feld (*A. S.*)	*a piece of land, a field, a plain, tilled or uncultivated land*
Figen, fign, *i. e.* migen, or mign (*Br.*)	*mire, a bog*
Fold, fald (*A. S.*) ..	*an inclosure for sheep*
Force, foss (*Scan.*)	*a waterfall*
Ford (*Scan.*)	*a ford, the shallow part of a river where a passage may be effected,* (furt, *Ger.*)
Forth, porth (*Cel.*) ..	*a haven, a harbour*
Galt (*Br.*)	*the side of a hill, a cliff*
Garth (*Scan.*)	*a large farm*
Garth (*Cel.*)	*a hill, a promontory*
Gate, gat, gap (*Scan.*)	*an entrance into a city; a large door; a way, or road, a path, a passage*
Gelli, celli (*Br.*) ..	*hazel, hazel-coppice*
Genau (*Br.*)	*a mouth, a pass of a mountain*
Glann (*Br.*)	*the bank of a river*
Glâs (glase) (*Br.*)	*blue, verdant*
Glen (*Cel.*)	*a small valley, a vale, generally taking its name from a river flowing through it (*gleann, *Gael.*)*
Glynn, glyn (*Br.*)	*a glen, a valley*
Gof (*Br.*)	*a smith*
Gogo, *i. e.* gweddio (*Br.*)	*to pray*
Gusse (*Br.*)	*furrows*
Gwald (*Br.*)	*a hem, skirt, or border*
Gwartheg (*Br.*)	*cattle*
Gwastadedd (*Br.*)	*a plain*
Gwrth (*Br.*)	*against, opposite, by*
Gwy (*Br.*) ..	*a stream, the river Wye*

GLOSSARY (continued).

wyn, wynn, wen, cain (Br.) .. *white, fair*
wydd (Br.) .. .. *underwood*
yll, *i. e.* cyll (Br.) .. .. *a hazel tree*

Hall (A. S.) .. .. *a hall*
Ham (A. S.) *a home, farm, property, habitation village, hamlet, or town*
Hampstead (A. S.) *a homestead; see* ham *and* stead
Hampton (A. S.) *ham,* and *ton,* or *tun,* which see
Haugh, or how (Scan.) .. .. *a hill*
Haven (Scan.) .. .. *a harbour, a haven*
Havod, hafod (Br.) *a summer hut, a shealing*
Helygen (Br.) .. .. *a willow, or sallow tree*
Heli (Br.) .. .. *salt*
Hên (Br.) .. .. .. *old, ancient*
Hill (A. S.) .. .. .. *a hill, a mountain*
Hithe, hythe (A. S.) .. *a little haven, or port*
Hir (Br.) .. .. *long*
Holm (A. S.) *a river island; a green plot of ground surrounded by water; lying along a river; also, ocean, abyss*
Horn (A. S.) *a dwelling, a residence (aern,* Sax.)
Holt (A. S.) *a rising ground or knoll, covered with trees*
Hurst (A. S.) *a wood or thicket; a grove; a place ornmented with trees (hyrst,* Sax.)
Hynt (Br.) .. *a journey, a way, a course*

Ing (A. S.) *nouns terminating in* ing, *denote (1) an action, (2) originating from, son of, descendant of, thus forming patronymic nouns. It often occurs in the accusative plural, denoting descendants, or sons of, inhabitants of, race of* *
Ingdon (A. S.) .. *a ton, held* .. *see* ing *and* don
Ingham (A. S.) *the house, or town of the race of, ex. gr., Rockingham, the home of the family of the Rock*
Ington (A. S.) .. .. *the town of the* ings
Ilar (Br.) .. .. *St. Hilary*
Illtyd (Br.) .. *a preacher of Christianity*
Inch, inish (Cel.) .. .. .. *an island*
Inver (Cel.) .. .. *the mouth of a river*
Inver is compounded of *Ion,* deserving of, and *Ar,* to till (*arare,* Lat.), *i. e.* Ion-ar, worthy of

tillage; hence, it is probable, agriculture was first attempted on such fertile spots as the plots of ground situated at the mouth of a river generally are
Is, ys, isa, dis (Br.) .. .. *lower, inferior*
Isâf (Br.) .. .. *lowest*

Ken (Br.) .. .. .. *a head or top*
Ken (Cel.) .. .. .. *white, clear*
Kil, cil, cell (Gael.) .. *a churchyard, a burying ground, a chapel [Kil, in Scotland, is the usual appellative of a church village.]*
Kin, can (Cel.) *a cape or headland (ceann* Gael.)
Kirk (A. S.) *church [kirche (Teut.), kirke (Dan.), kyrka (Swed.), kerche (Dutch)]*
Knoll (Cel.) .. *a rising ground, a little hill*
Kyle (Cel.) .. *an arm of the sea, a frith*

Law (A. S.) *a detached hill or mount, generally of a conical shape (loe,* Sax.)
Le, or lle (Br.) .. .. *a place*
Ley, ly, lea (A. S.) .. *a pasture, a meadow, a common, a field laid down (leag,* Sax.)
Lin, linn, (Cel.), llyn, lynn (Br.) *a deep pool, a lake, any water*
Lith, leith, lid (Cel.) .. *a flood, gushing, rapid*
Llan, lan (Br.) *a spot cleared for public meetings or conference, an inclosure, a church, or town with a church*
Llan-badrig (Br.) .. *Church of St. Patrick*
Llan-bedr (Br.) .. *Church of St. Peter*
Llan-dewi (Br.) .. .. *Church of David*
Llan-fihangel (Br.) .. *Church of St. Michael*
Llan-stephan (Br.) .. *Church of St. Stephen*
Llan-dau-saint (Br.) .. *Church of two Saints*
Llan-tris-saint (Br.) .. *Church of three Saints*
Llan-faur-saint (Br.) .. *Church of four Saints*
Llan-pum-saint (Br.) .. *Church of five Saints*
Llanerch (Br.) .. .. .. *a glade*
Llawr (Br.) *the ground, the floor of a building*
Llech (Br.) .. *a slate, any broad flat stone*
Llechwedd (Br.) *the side of a hill, a steep ascent*
Llethyr (Br.) *a steep ascent or descent, a cliff*
Llwyd (Br.) .. .. *grey, hoary, brown*
Llwydog, -dawg (Br.) .. .. *of a grey colour*
Llwyn (Br.) .. .. .. *a wood, a grove*
Llyn (Br.) .. .. *a lake, a pool, a pond*

* Mr. Kemble endeavours to show that the places terminating in -ing have been ancient "Marks."—*See* Saxons in England, vol. ii., p. 58.

GLOSSARY (*continued*).

Llŷr (*Br.*) .. .. .. *the sea shore*
Llys (*Br.*) .. *a palace, a hall, or court-house*
Loch, lough (*Cel.*) .. *a lake, inland water*
Logie, logan (*Cel.*) *a hollow place, a plain or meadow within rising ground*

Mab, mac .. .. *a child, a boy, a son*
Madog, madoc (*Br.*) .. .. *good, righteous*
Maen, main (*Br.*) .. .. .. *a stone*
Maenor (*Br.*) .. .. *a manor*
Maes (*Br.*) .. .. .. *a field, a heath*
Mair, fair (*Br.*) .. .. .. *Mary*
Manachlog (*Br.*) .. *a monastery or abbey*
Mawr (*Br.*) .. ..*great, large*
Mel (*Br.*) .. .. *honey*
Melin (*Br.*) .. .. *a mill*
Mere .. .. .. *a lake, water, the sea*
Merthyr (*Br.*) .. .. *a martyr*
Mih-Angel (*Br.*) .. *Michael the Archangel*
Minster (*A. S.*) *a conventional church or abbey, a monastery*
Moch (*Br.*) .. .. *a hog*
Moel (*Br.*) .. .. .. *bald, crop-eared*
Monde (*Cel.*) .. *the mouth* (*mund,* Germ.)
Mont, monte (*Fr.*) .. *a mount, or mountain*
Moor, muir, mor .. .. *heathy ground*
Mouth (*A. S.*) .. .. *entrance of a river*
Mynach, monach (*Br.*) .. .. *a monk*
Mynydd (*Br.*) .. .. .. *a mountain*
Mynys (*Br.*) .. .. .. *the rising ground*

Nant (*Br.*) .. .. *a brook, a river, a ravine*
Nawdd (*Br.*) .. .. .. *refuge, sanctuary*
Ness (*Scan.*) *a headland, a promontory or cape* (*nese,* Sax., *nasus,* Lat.)
Neth, nethy (*Cel.*) .. .. *a whirling stream*

Od (*Br.*) .. .. *snow*
Ochill (*Cel.*) .. .. .. *high, lofty*
Onnen (*Br.*) .. .. .. *an ash tree*
Or (*Br.*) .. *a border, the edge, the coast*

Pant (*Br.*) .. *a hollow or sinking ground*
Pawl (*Br.*) .. *a pole, a pale, a stake*
Pebyll (*Br.*) .. .. *tents, pavilions*
Pen, pan, ben (*Br.*) *a hill, a head, a summit, a promontory*
Pentre (*Br,*) .. .. .. *a village*
Pistill (*Br.*) .. .. .. *a waterfall*
Plwyf (*Br.*) .. .. *the people, a parish*
Pont, bont (*Br.*) *a bridge* (*pont,* Fr., *pons,* Lat.)

Pool (*A. S.*) *properly a detached or enclosed piece of water; a haven, a harbour* (*pul,* Sax.)
Port, porth *a gate* (*porte,* Fr., *porta,* Lat.)*, a haven or port for ships* (*port,* Fr., *portus,* Lat.)
Pum (*Br.*) .. .. *five*
Pwll (*Br.*) .. .. *a pool, a ditch, a pit*

Rhayadr (*Br.*) .. .. .. *a cataract*
Rhiain (*Br.*) .. .. .. *a maiden, a virgin*
Rhiw (*Br.*) .. *an ascent, the side of a hill*
Rhodwydd (*Br.*) .. .. *an open course*
Rhos, cors (*Br.*) .. .. *a marsh, a bog*
Rhudd (*Br.*) .. .. .. *ruddy*
Rhyd (*Br.*) .. .. .. *a ford*
Rhydd (*Br.*) .. .. *free*
Rhyn (*Br.*) .. *a mountain, hill, or promontory*
Ridge, rig (*A. S.*) .. .. *the back*
Rigg (*Scan.*) .. .. *a mountain ridge*

Rhôs, rose (*Cel.*), ros, ross (*Gael.*) *a promontory, a peninsula*
Roy, rue (*Cel.*) .. .. .. *red*

Sarn (*Br.*) .. *a causeway, a pavement*
Scybor (*Br.*) .. .. .. *a barn*
Ship (*A. S.*) .. *form, condition, state, dignity*
Side (*A. S.*) *ample, broad, vast, various, diverse*
Staple (*A. S.*) .. *an established market, a staple*
Stead (*A. S.*) .. *a place, station* (*steda,* Sax.)
Stock, stoke (*A. S.*) .. *a place* (*stok,* Sax.)
Stone, stan (*A. S.*) .. .. *a stone, a rock*
Stow (*A. S.*) .. .. *a place, a residence*
Stir, stadir (*Cel.*) .. *an habitation, an estate*
Stitchel (*Cel.*) .. .. *an eminence*
Strath, or ystrad (*Cel.*) *a valley near the confluence of two rivers*
Strom (*Cel.*) .. .. *impetuous, rapid*
Spyddyd, *i. e.* ysbyddad (*Br.*) *hospitality, an hospital*
Swydd (*Br.*) .. .. *a lordship, an office*

Tal (*Br.*) .. .. .. *the head, the front*
Tar, tarbat (*Cel.*) .. .. *a promontory*
Tarn (*Norw.*) .. .. *from tjorn, a small lake*
Teviot (*Cel.*) *tranquil, quiet, that which expands*
Thorne (*A. S.*) .. .. .. *thorn*
Thwaite (*Scan.*) .. *an isolated piece of land*
Thorpe (*Scan.*) *a collection of houses separated from the principal estate; a village*

Ir (*Br.*) .. .. *the earth, land, territory*

oft (*Scan.*) .. .. *a field*

on, town (*A. S.*) *a close, a house, a village, a town; an inclosure of houses or territory lying within the boundary of a town (tun, Sax.)*

'or (*Br.*) .. .. *a detached eminence*

'owyn (*Br.*) .. .. .. *a sandy marsh*

'rueth (draeth) (*Br.*) .. .. *an estuary*

'raws (*Br.*) .. .. *a cross, crosswise*

'ref, tre, try .. *a house, a home, a village, a township, a town*

'roed (*Br.*) .. *the foot, the foot of a hill*

'ron, troon (*Cel.*) .. *a point, a promontory*

'y (*Br.*) .. .. *a house*

'yr (*Br.*) .. .. .. *a tower, a castle*

Tyne, tain (*Cel.*) .. *a flood, running water*

Uch, uwch (*Br.*) .. *upper, higher, above*

Uchâf, uwchaf (*Br.*) .. .. *highest*

Uchel (*Br.*) .. .. *lofty*

Uise, or ise (*Cel.*), usk, uisk, or Esk (*Br.*) *water, a river*

Ville (*Fr.*) *a small collection of houses, a village, a town (villa, Lat.)*

Wald (*A. S.*) .. .. *a wood, a forest, a grove*

Ware (*A. S.*) *inhabitants, dwellings (waras, Sax.)*

Wark (*Dan.*) *fortified works (werigan, Sax.)*

Wald, weald (*A. S.*) *a woody district, a forest (walda, or wealt, Sax.)*

Wath (*Cel.*) .. .. *a ford*

Waun, i. e. gwaun (*Br.*) .. *a meadow, downs*

Weald .. .. *a wood*

Wedd, i. e. gwedd (*Br.*) .. .. *an aspect*

Weem (*Cel.*) .. .. *a cove, or cave; a bay*

Well (*A. S.*) .. .. .. *a spring of water*

Wen, i. e. gwen. (*Br.*) .. .. *white, fair, clear*

Wern, i. e. gwern (*Br.*) .. *alder trees*

Weth, i. e. gwrth (*Br.*).. .. *by, or near to*

Wic .. .. *a village*

Wick, wich (*A. S.*) *the bend of a river, or of the sea-coast; a bay, a dwelling, a station, a castle (vig, Norw.)*

With (*Scan.*) .. .. .. *a forest*

Wold, would (*Scan*) .. .. *a hill, a forest*

Wood (*A. S.*) .. .. *a wood, a forest, a tree*

Worth (*A. S.*) *a farm-court; a country habitation, a village or town; a farm, a manor, an estate*

Wych, i, e. gwych (*Br.*) *cheerful; neat, brave*

Wyl (*Br.*) .. .. *a flow, or gushing out*

Wyllt, i. e. gwyllt (*Br.*) *wild, untamed, savage*

Y (*Br.*) .. .. *..of, on the*

Ych (*Br.*) .. .. *an ox*

Ych, uwch (*Br.*).. .. .. *upper, above*

Yfed (*Br.*) .. .. *to drink, moist, damp*

Yewen, ywen (*Br.*) .. .. *a yew tree*

Ym (*Br.*).. .. .. .. *in, or by*

Yn (*Br.*) .. .. .. *in, at*

Ynys (*Br.*) .. .. .. *an island*

Yr (*Br.*) .. .. *the*

Ys (*Br.*) .. .. *below*

Ysceifiog (*Br.*) .. .. *hunting ground*

Ysgwyd (*Br.*) .. .. *a shield, a buckler*

Ysgwdd (*Br.*) .. .. .. *a shoulder*

Yspytty (*Br.*) .. .. *an hospital*

Ystrad (*Br.*) .. *a vale, a street, or paved way*

Ystum, ystym (*Br.*) *a situation, figure, or bending*

Ywen (*Br.*) .. .. .. *a yew tree*

The term *County* was given to these divisions because they were governed by *Counts*, that is *Earls*. They were also called *Shires*, which means *Divisions*, from (*A. S.*) *sciran*, to cut or divide. The County Town is that in which the general business of the County is transacted, and the assizes held. Before the passing of the Reform Bill, it was the only place for polling at County Elections.

Bedfordshire—formerly Bedicanfordshire. Bedicanford is from (*A. S.*) *bedician*, to fortify; and *ford*. It means *the ford near the fortress.*

Berkshire—a contraction of *bare-oak shire*, so called because meetings were held at a bare or polled oak in Windsor Forest.

Buckingham—(*A. S.*) *boc*, a beech tree; and *ham*, a dwelling.

Cambridgeshire—from the *bridge* over the *Cam*, on which river the town stands.

Carlisle—from *caer*, a fortified place, and *Luil*, a contraction of *Luguvallum*, the Roman name of the town.

Chelmsford—the ford of the Chelmer, the river it stands on.

Cheshire—formerly Chestershire. Chester is only the altered form of *ceaster, a fortified place.* It received the name from its strong fortifications, and the city now contains the ruins of more Roman defences than any other town in England.

Cornwall—from Brit. *cernyw* (*pr. kernoo*), a horn; and (*A. S.*) *walli, foreign.* The first part of the name was given by the Britons, from its jutting out into the sea in the shape of a horn; the latter by the Saxons, because it continued to be inhabited by the Britons, who were *foreigners* to them.

Cumberland—from *Comb,* a valley. This county abounds in hills, and consequently in valleys. It was a part of the old British kingdom of Cumbria, which extended from the mouth of the Clyde to the *S.* of Yorkshire, on the *W.* side of the Island.

Devon—land of the *Damnonia.*

Derbyshire—from *deor, a wild animal,* and *by, a dwelling.* Or it may be a contraction of *Derwentby,* the town being on the Derwent.

Dorsetshire—a contraction of Dorchestershire—the land of the *Dornsætan,* from *Sætan* settlers.

Durham—from (*A. S.*) *deor, a wild animal,* and *ham,* abode. It was also called *Dunholm,* from *Dun,* a hill, and *holm,* an island; the city being on a hill, and almost surrounded by the river Wear. The Bishop now signs himself *Dunelm.*

Essex—from *East,* and *Seaxe, Saxons.*

Exeter—formerly Exchester, from *Ex,* the river on which it stands, and *ceaster,* a fortified place.

Gloucester—perhaps from British *glow, splendid,* or strong; or Welsh *gleaw, strong,* and *ceaster.*

Hampshire—a contraction of Hamptonshire, i.e., the shire of Hampton, the old name for Southampton.

Herefordshire—from (*A. S.*) *here,* an army; and *ford,* i. e., *where the army went over.*

Hertford—(*A. S.*) *heart, a stag;* and ford. The arms of the town are a stag in the water.

Huntingdonshire—means the hunter's hill, from *hunt,* and (*A. S.*) *dun,* a hill.

Ipswich—formerly *Gyppenswich,* from *Gipping,* a tributary of the Orwell, on which it stands, and *wic,* a dwelling.

Kent—from a Celtic word meaning *projection,* on account of its jutting out so far into the sea.

Lancashire—formerly Lancastershire. Lancaster is from the *Lune* (the river the town stands on), and *castra* or (*A. S.*) *ceaster, a fortified place.*

Leicestershire—from *Leir,* the old name of the *R. Soar,* on which it stands, and *ceaster,* a fortified place.

Lewes—from (*A. S.*) *leswes, pastures.*

Lincolnshire—from (*Brit.*) *llyn, a lake or pool,* and (*Lat.*) *colonia, a colony.* It was formerly called *Lindum,* from *llyn,* and (*Brit.*) *dinas,* a hill. The full name, Lindum Colonia, means *the colony on the hill near the water.* The old part of Lincoln is high, and in the event of a flood the neighbourhood is even now covered with water.

Maidstone—a contraction of Medway's town; it being on that river.

Middlesex—the Middle Saxons, so called as being between the E. Saxons and W. Saxons.

Newcastle—from a castle built by Robert, the son of William the Conqueror. It was formerly called *Monkchester,* on account of its numerous monastic institutions.

Norfolk—*North,* and (*A. S.*) *folc,* people.

Northamptonshire—from (*A. S.*) *ham,* an *abode,* and *ton, town.* It was formerly called Hamtun or Hampton, as many places in England are still. Such places were originally named merely *ham,* but as they increased in size the term *ton* was affixed to them. This town was called *North*ampton, to distinguish it from another flourishing *hampton,* which was called *South*ampton.

Northumberland—*land North of the Humber.* This county retains very nearly the name of the (*A. S.*) kingdom, which extended from the Humber to the Forth.

Norwich—from *Nord, North,* and *wic, a dwelling,* probably so named to distinguish it from *Sudbury,* i. e. the *South bury* or town.

Nottinghamshire—formerly *Snotenga-ham,* from *ham,* a home, and possibly *Snotenga caves,* which are numerous under and near the town, excavations having been made by the people for various purposes. It may be remembered, that the murderers of Mortimer, Isabella's paramour, entered the castle by a subterranean passage.

Oxford—the ford of oxen.

Rutlandshire—from (*A. S.*) *rude, red,* and *land.* The soil is in many parts of a reddish colour.

Shropshire—*Scrobbesbyrigscir,* also *Scrobsætan* (from Sætan, settlers). Shrewsbury is from (*A. S.*) *scrobb,* a shrub, and *bury,* a town, i. e., *the town amongst shrubs.*

Somerset—the land of the *Sumorsœtan.*

Staffordshire—from (*A. S.*) *staef, a staff* or *pole,* and *ford,* from *faran, to go.* It may mean the ─t of the river which could be gone over by means of stilts. This mode of going over a river was ─e not uncommon.

Suffolk—(*A. S.*) *Suth,* South, and *folc,* people.

Sussex—from *Suth,* South ; and *Seaxa,* Saxons.

Surrey—from *Suth,* South, and *ea, land near water ;* so called from being south of the Thames. ─ne think the last part of the word is from *rica,* a kingdom, in which case it would mean the southern ─gdom.

Taunton—from *Tone,* the river it is upon, and *ton, a town.*

Warwickshire—Warwick is an abbreviation of *Waeringwic,* which means a fortified place ; *vering* ─ng a bulwark, and *wic,* a dwelling.

Westmorland—from (*A. S.*) *mor, a moor* or heath. The *West moor land,* i. e., the land in the ─est abounding in moors.

Worcestershire—the etymology is very uncertain. It was formerly called *Wigraceaster,* which ─y be connected with (*A. S.*) *wig, war ;* if so, it would mean *war city,* but this is very doubtful, for ─ reason can be assigned for such a name.

Wiltshire—a contraction of *Wiltonshire.* Wilton is a town on the *Wily,* from which it is ─med the land of the *Wilsœtan* (from *Sœtan settlers*).

Yorkshire—York is probably from *Ure,* (a part of the river now called the *Ouse,* seems to have ─en once called the Ure and *Wic,* a village.) It is called in (*A. S.*) *Eurewic.* The old Roman name ─as *Eboracum.* The Archbishop still signs himself *Ebor.*

Somerset House, London, 1864.

THE END.

PRINTED BY HARRISON AND SONS. 81. MARTIN'S LANE

(1865)   1864   1870

	(1865)	1864	1870
London	3,015,494		3,251,884.
Liverpool	476,368	500,676	493,846.
Manchester	354,970	366,855	355,665.
Salford	110,830	117,162	124,805.
Birmingham	327,842	352,296	343,696.
Leeds	224,075	236,746	259,281.
Bristol	161,800	167,457	182,524.
Edinbourg	174,150	177,089	
Glaskow	423,725	449,868	
Dublin	317,666	319,985	
Sheffield			239,947.
Bradford			145,827.
Stoke-Upon-Trent			130,507.
Newcastle-Up-Lyne			128,160.
Hull			121,598.
Portsmouth			112,954.

1870.
England   21,494,931
Wales   1,217,135.
Scotland   3,360,018.
Ireland   5,411,416.

CPSIA information can be obtained at www.ICGtesting.com
Printed in the USA
LVOW03s1951201014

409623LV00018B/693/P